INSIDERS' GUIDE® TO
BEND & CENTRAL OREGON

Help Us Keep This Guide Up to Date

Every effort has been made by the authors and editors to make this guide as accurate and useful as possible. However, many things can change after a guide is published—establishments close, phone numbers change, hiking trails are rerouted, facilities come under new management, etc.

We would love to hear from you concerning your experiences with this guide and how you feel it could be improved and be kept up to date. While we may not be able to respond to all comments and suggestions, we'll take them to heart and we'll also make certain to share them with the authors. Please send your comments and suggestions to the following address:

The Globe Pequot Press
Reader Response/Editorial Department
P.O. Box 480
Guilford, CT 06437

Or you may e-mail us at:

editorial@globe-pequot.com

Thanks for your input, and happy travels!

INSIDERS' GUIDE® SERIES

Insiders' Guide®
to Bend &
Central Oregon

SECOND EDITION

Leslie Cole and Jim Yuskavitch

Guilford, Connecticut
An imprint of The Globe Pequot Press

Insiders' Guide is a registered trademark of The Globe Pequot Press.

Back cover and spine photos by Jim Yuskavitch
Maps by Brandon Ray, © The Globe Pequot Press
ISBN: 0-7627-1057-8

Manufactured in the United States of America
Second Edition/First Printing

Contents

Directory of Maps

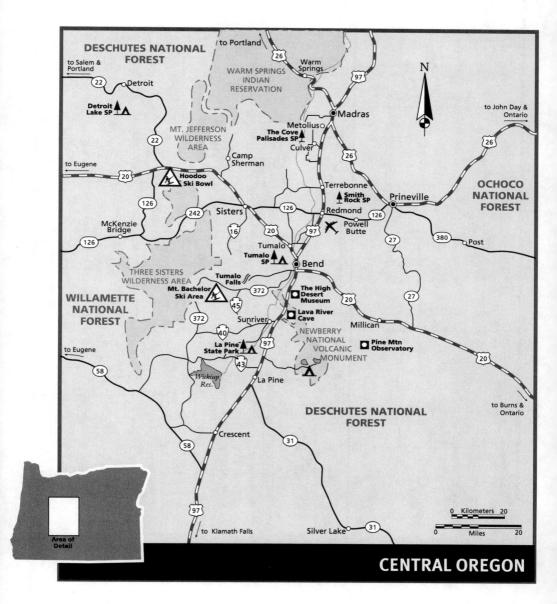

DESCHUTES NATIONAL FOREST

to Portland

to Salem & Portland

22 Detroit

Detroit Lake SP

MT. JEFFERSON WILDERNESS AREA

22

to Eugene

20

126

242

Sisters

McKenzie Bridge

126

16

20

Hoodoo Ski Bowl

Camp Sherman

WARM SPRINGS INDIAN RESERVATION

26

Warm Springs

97

Madras

Metolius

The Cove Palisades SP

Culver

26

Terrebonne

Smith Rock SP

Redmond

126

Prineville

126

27

380

Post

OCHOCO NATIONAL FOREST

26

to John Day & Ontario

N

97

Powell Butte

Tumalo

Tumalo SP

Bend

The High Desert Museum

20

27

WILLAMETTE NATIONAL FOREST

THREE SISTERS WILDERNESS AREA

Tumalo Falls

Mt. Bachelor Ski Area

45

372

372

40

Sunriver

La Pine State Park

43

Wickiup Res.

Lava River Cave

NEWBERRY NATIONAL VOLCANIC MONUMENT

Millican

Pine Mtn Observatory

20

97

La Pine

to Eugene

58

58

Crescent

31

DESCHUTES NATIONAL FOREST

to Burns & Ontario

97

to Klamath Falls

Silver Lake

31

0   Kilometers   20

0   Miles   20

Area of Detail

CENTRAL OREGON

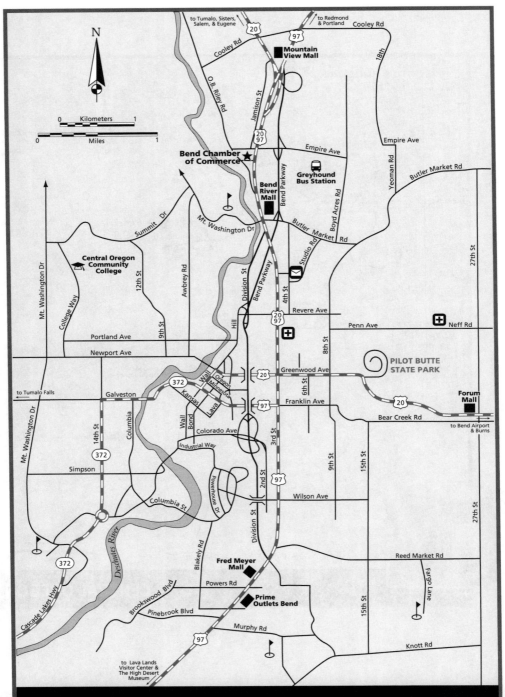

BEND

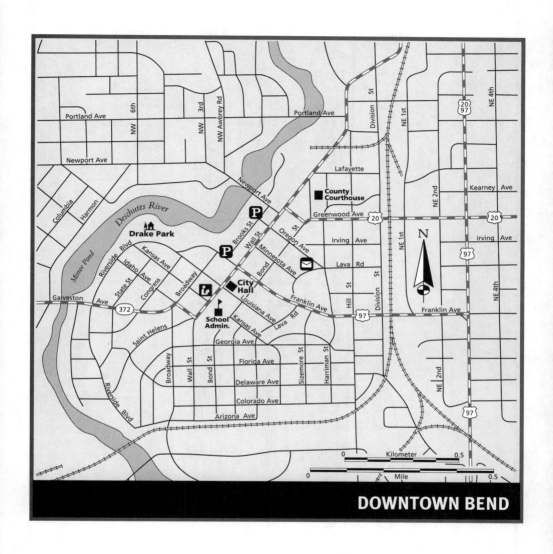

DOWNTOWN BEND

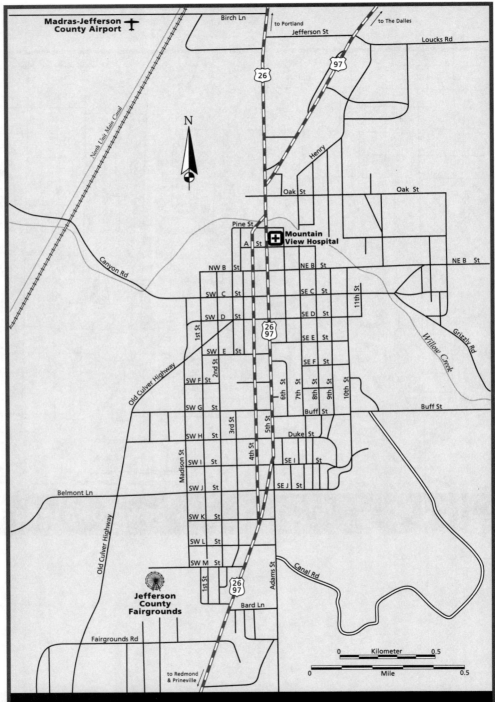

MADRAS

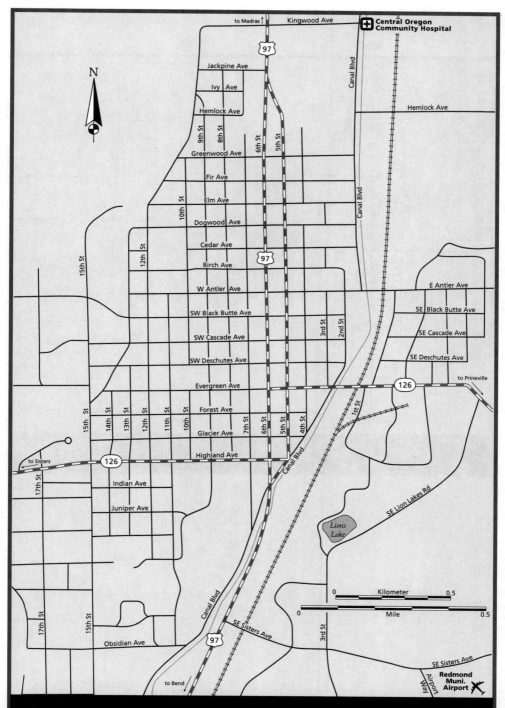

REDMOND

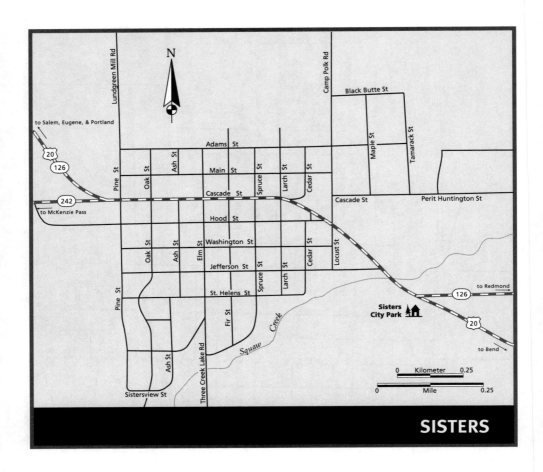

SISTERS

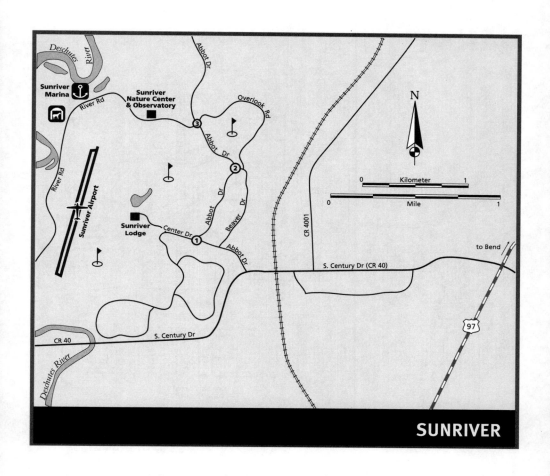

SUNRIVER

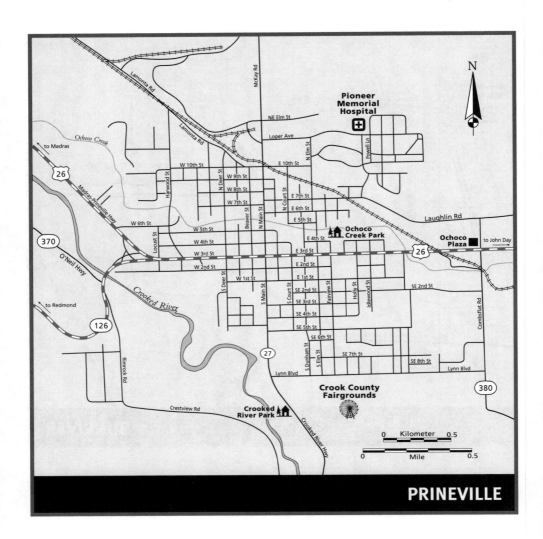

PRINEVILLE

Acknowledgments

It is in the nature of Central Oregonians to be good neighbors. And all it takes is the smile of a stranger to bring out the best in us. This was proven to me over and over in the course of researching this book. Most of the folks I met and interviewed were strangers to me, and most of them were not getting paid to promote their community, yet they couldn't have been more helpful.

Did you ever hear the story of Stone Soup, where a soup that was started with a stone in a pot of water got better and better as each member of the community added a carrot, an onion, etc.? This happened to me with this book, and here are a few of the ingredients. Tom Lohmann at the Deschutes Brewery in Bend gave me the brewery's secret recipe for its fabulous marionberry cobbler, and the Department of Horticulture at Oregon State University in Corvallis gave me information about the history of Oregon's favorite berry. I learned about the historic patterns of Pendleton blankets from the sales staff at Leavitts Western Wear in Sisters and The Oregon Store in Bend. The Richardson family at Richardson's Recreational Ranch in Madras kindly allowed me to reprint their write-up on thundereggs, our state rock, for one of our Close-ups.

Our bed-and-breakfast innkeepers were especially informative when it came to providing insight into the best places to eat, shop, and visit in their neighborhoods. I can certainly recommend the bed-and-breakfast style of traveling because of this extra benefit. I don't need to list the owners and operators all by name here—just look in our chapter devoted to bed-and-breakfast inns.

Central Oregon's chambers of commerce were very helpful, trying their best to answer my questions, even when the business in question was not a member. The fine people who staff the desk at the Bend Welcome Center got used to seeing me come in every couple of weeks with a new topic of inquiry, and Joyce Janecka, the U.S. Forest Service representative at the Bend Welcome Center, even proofed our early Web site posting. David Wilkins at the Sunriver Chamber of Commerce spent quite a bit of time talking to me about his community. The chambers of commerce in Sisters, Redmond, La Pine, Prineville, and Madras all pitched in at my requests. The public affairs staff and biologists of the Deschutes National Forest and the Ochoco National Forest, and the rangers at the Newberry National Volcanic Monument Lava Lands Visitor Center were all helpful with my inquiries.

The real estate chapter took a lot of support from the community. In particular, Barbara Nicholson of Tumalo Real Estate in Bend spent hours with me going over an outline of neighborhoods and price ranges that she had prepared, as well as sharing insights on buying ranch properties. Realtors at John L. Scott in Bend, La Pine Realty and Cascade Realty in La Pine, Sunriver Realty, and Coldwell Banker First Resort Realty in Sunriver all spent time with me going into detail about their towns, neighborhood by neighborhood.

Golf was another topic that required technical assistance, which I received in volumes from Norma Ploen at Golf City in Bend. Besides giving me the inside scoop on every golf course in Central Oregon, Norma went so far as to lend me a study she'd compiled on golf that contained copies of golf magazine articles and statistics.

When I went to a new restaurant, I'd try to take as many people as possible with me. I'd find out about specialties or signature dishes, then have the other people in my party order them. I got one dining partner—Kev Arends, who happens to be a former marketing manager for Insiders' Publishing in our area—to order fish 'n' chips with a side of Irish mashed potatoes at a new Irish pub in Bend. Then we shared our plates around the table—he only got to eat part of his meal. Kev, by the way, was incredibly helpful and a source of constant feedback from the community, expanding my understanding of the book's audience and my duties as a writer.

Thank goodness for co-authors. I am glad that Jim was just a phone call away when I needed to come up for a breath of fresh air. While he researched his own chapters, Jim also kept an eye out for material that could be of use to me. It sure helps to have another pair of eyes and ears in a region where there is so much going on. As we reach presstime, I have to give a heartfelt "thank you" to the editor of our first edition, Dave McCarter, for his seemingly endless patience.

More than anyone else, my husband, Ben Lindner, made my contribution to this book possible. He proofread every chapter, offering loud exclamations about any little exaggerations, obtuse phrasings, or lapses in my memory. "How come you didn't tell them about Llast Camp Llama's pack trips?" he yelled at me as I did the dishes. Other times, he did all the dishes, walked our border collie puppy, Liv (not an easy job), and fed our sheep while I typed away at the computer, all in the hopes his efforts would help me get to bed earlier. He visited restaurants he never would have gone to, ate dishes he never would have eaten (after I did the ordering for both of us), and consumed more courses than were good for his waistline, just so I could test as many specialties of the house as possible. I most appreciated Ben's putting up with my absentmindedness and inattention as I concentrated on the thousands of little details and bits of information that went into the making of this book. And now Ben gets to go on a diet.

I am looking forward to the next update. Who knows what new and fascinating aspects of this great area I'll discover and who I'll meet? Meanwhile, I hope you enjoy reading this guide and those that follow. Have fun in Central Oregon!

—Leslie D. Cole

Any book project of this depth and breadth requires the help of many people. In the course of researching the material that fills the pages of *The Insiders' Guide to Bend & Central Oregon,* I relied, like Blanche Dubois, on the kindness of strangers. I didn't count the number of times I dropped in on a business to find out what they were all about, or called a chamber of commerce or government agency for an obscure statistic, but it was in the hundreds. The people I met and talked with during my research were, without fail, ready to help me in whatever way they could. They answered the "dumb" questions that are a writer's stock in trade or suggested someone else who might have the information I sought. And you know, having lived in Oregon for more than 20 years, I wasn't a bit surprised. Busy people agreed to meet with me for an interview or fax me critical information on short notice. Even the at-a-loss employees of area businesses, who picked up the phone when I called to double-check facts, cheerfully answered my strange questions about whether the business name was spelled with or without a hyphen or if their address was on a street or an avenue.

In short, too many people helped with this book in one way or another to list them all. But there are a few I would like to single out. The staff at all the Central Oregon chambers of commerce provided me with considerable help and information in the writing of this book, in particular Jackie French of the Bend Chamber Visitors and Convention Bureau and Denissia Withers Costello of the Redmond Chamber of Commerce. I'm especially grateful to local Realtors Rob Trout, Dave Goodwin, Kathy Overall, and Dick "Rhino" Reinertson, who took time from their busy schedules to explain to me the history and intricacies of the Central Oregon real estate market. Carrie Gilmore of the Bend/La Pine School District provided me with lots of information on Central Oregon education and schools and put me in touch with many additional sources as well. And thanks to Cate O'Hagan, executive director of the Central Oregon Arts Association, who gave me a thorough overview of our local arts scene.

One person I worked extremely closely with throughout this project was co-author Leslie Cole, who gave me advice and support whenever it was needed. Another was editor Heather Carreiro, who shepherded this revised edition to completion. Thanks to you both. And last but not least, I want to express my deep thanks and appreciation to my wife, Nikki, who gave me valuable input and suggestions, suffered through my late-night bouts of writing, and graciously accepted the last-minute cancellation of a long-planned outing or two when deadlines arrived sooner than I had expected. To all of you, named and unnamed, my heartfelt thanks. I could not have done it alone.

—Jim Yuskavitch

How to Use This Book

Hello there, and hold it a moment! Before you jump to a more exciting chapter—maybe one on our fabulous fishing, glorious golf courses, or the bounty of fine restaurants in our area—we suggest you skim this section and also the chapter called Getting Here, Getting Around. The information you will discover, particularly here in How to Use This Book, will arm you with what you need to get the most out of our guide and Oregon's beautiful, thrilling, and vast High Desert region.

When you walk into a huge variety store, like a Wal-Mart for example, the sheer number of items can be overwhelming at first. After a minute or two, sometimes with the assistance of a store employee, you get your bearings and locate the department that contains the items you are looking for. If the store wasn't so well-organized, shopping there would be a frustrating experience, and you probably wouldn't want to visit there again.

What you don't see when you walk into one of these superstores is the tremendous effort that is invested to enable you to find what you are looking for. We have made a similar commitment to make *The Insiders' Guide to Bend & Central Oregon,* a book loaded with all sorts of information, easy and enjoyable for you to use.

Every new team of authors hired to write an Insiders' Guide is faced with the same monumental task: how to take thousands of features and facts and structure it all in a way that makes sense to everyone reading the book.

First, we started with a list of chapters that highlight the unique aspects of Central Oregon. For example, Golf, Fishing, Camping, and Snowplay (our term for winter recreation) are so important in our area that we gave each an individual chapter. Other chapters detailing the area's Restaurants, Hotels and Motels, and Bed-and-Breakfasts will help make your visit comfortable and enjoyable, while Attractions, Kidstuff, The Arts, and Daytrips will keep you busy while you're here.

Other chapters, such as Retirement, Neighborhoods and Real Estate, Education and Child Care, Media, and Healthcare, provide information to assist newcomers or folks interested in relocating. Chapters on History; Area Overview; and Forests, High Desert, and Volcanoes are included to empower our readers with insights into the landscape and local cultures.

Please feel free to read the chapters in any order, but we do hope you will eventually get around to them all. Each is written so that it can stand independently. Read the chapters you need right away, then later, let the rest of the book pique your interest. After all, you might at some point want to know the name of some of those lumpy black rocks. That's when the real process of discovery kicks in.

Organizing the Information

Many of our chapters are organized geographically. We have divided Central Oregon into six areas: Bend, Sisters/Camp Sherman, Redmond, Sunriver/La Pine, Prineville, and Madras. Take a look at our Central Oregon maps, and this division should make some sense to you.

We did take some liberties in dividing the southern section of Central Oregon between Bend and Sunriver/La Pine. This general area includes the Cascades Lakes Highway, Brothers and Pine Mountain, Sunriver, and La Pine. The Cascades Lakes were included with Bend because access to this area most commonly originates in Bend via Century Drive. Millican and Pine Mountain were also included with Bend, again because of access—this time via U.S.

Highway 20 east of Bend. The High Desert Museum, 7 miles south of the city on U.S. Highway 97, is the last attraction covered in the Bend area.

The Sunriver/La Pine region, for our purposes, is the area along U.S. 97 south of the High Desert Museum. The Lava Lands Visitor Center, 15 miles south of Bend, is included in the Sunriver/La Pine region. Lava Lands Visitor Center has a Bend postal address, but we included it in the Sunriver/La Pine region because it is part of the Newberry National Volcanic Monument, which lies mainly between Sunriver and La Pine. (Such is the stuff of a travel guide editor's nightmares.)

When we felt proximity would be an important deciding factor for our readers, we divided chapter content into these six regions. Some of these geographically organized chapters include Restaurants, Hotels and Motels, Bed-and-Breakfasts, and Nightlife. Within each geographic area, establishments are usually itemized alphabetically. In the case of the Shopping chapter, the regions themselves are again categorized, using handy headers such as Antiques, Malls, and Bookstores to help you find exactly what you're looking for.

A variation on the geographical organization occurs when a chapter covers a number of topics, such as the Education and Child Care chapter. There, the topical headers, such as "Public Schools" or "Colleges and Universities," come first, and then schools or agencies are arranged by town, with Bend coming first. Camping has two key topical sections as well—one for camping options that have hookups, the other for "Really Roughing It"—which are then split into regions. Media and The Arts are chapters where topics are followed by alphabetized listings.

We abandon both the regional and topical organizational structure when the "when" is most important. Our Annual Events chapter is arranged chronologically so you can look up the month of your planned visit and see what's going on. History and Worship are narrative chapters arranged chronologically.

A Few More Details

Insiders' stays away from any kind of rating system for dining and lodging. We have selected as many establishments as

Spectacular vistas are only one of the rewards awaiting visitors to Central Oregon. PHOTO: JIM YUSKAVITCH

we felt we could wholeheartedly recommend—so any business that's in our book should be a safe bet. Each place is described in as much detail as possible to help you decide which is best for you. A price code is included for lodging and restaurant options because we know cost is an important decision factor. Please note that many of the restaurants did not know we were researching them, and no freebies of any kind were accepted from any establishment covered in this book.

Within a few chapters you will notice gray boxes that contain important factual reference information. Every chapter also includes a number of Insiders' Tips—little tidbits of information on a variety of chapter-specific issues. The index at the back of this book can zoom you to a specific place or topic. Several chapters also include Close-ups, our term for sidebar stories that cover related, human-interest topics that are worth delving into in detail.

Central Oregon is growing faster than ever. In 2000, Bend was voted by a major publication to be Best Place to Retire, and the news was picked up and passed along by Jay Leno, among others. Also in 2000,

Deschutes County was the third-fastest-growing county in the United States. We had a difficult time keeping certain chapters, such as Restaurants, Hotels and Motels, Bed-and-Breakfasts, Nightlife, Real Estate, and Shopping totally up-to-date, even as we wrote the book. Judging from this, we can be pretty certain that exciting new places will continue to be added and old places will change names and appearances between now and the third edition. Hey, surprises are part of what makes life interesting!

We also encourage you to check out Insiders' Guide Online at www.insiders.com. It's a great way to preview books covering all corners of the country that are available for purchase at your local bookstore or from the Web site. If you have comments about this book, we'd love to hear from you. Write to us at:

The Insiders' Guide to Bend & Central Oregon
c/o The Globe Pequot Press
P.O. Box 480
Guilford, CT 06437
www.globe-pequot.com

Area Overview

Fire and Ice Will Suffice

Life in Central Oregon is a volcanic blast—literally. In fact, geologists paint a rather hellish early picture of the place. Ten million years ago Central Oregon was dotted with nearly perpetually erupting volcanoes spewing cinders and ash into the ancient sky and blasting craters in the earth, forming volcanic peaks, buttes, cinder cones, and lava caves. Rivers of slow-moving molten rock oozed from cracks in the ground and flowed across the then-level land, creating a vast bedrock of basalt and extensive fields of lava. Thirty million years earlier, a chain of volcanoes along the edge of the sea that then covered western Oregon roared to life, pouring enormous amounts of lava onto the surrounding countryside, giving birth to the Cascade Mountain Range. Central Oregon was on fire.

Plates within the earth moved, fault lines buckled and tilted, bursting the surface at its seams, creating ridges and raising the newly formed mountains even higher. The land cooled, and a subtropical climate embraced Central Oregon. Then, 2 million years ago, a series of Ice Ages descended and massive ice floes gouged the land.

The climate changed yet again, about 10,000 or 12,000 years ago, becoming warmer. And drier too, the result of the massive wall created by the Cascade Mountains, which block the flow of moist air masses from the Pacific Ocean. The ice slowly retreated, revealing a newly remade landscape. In the wink of an eye, geologically speaking, Central Oregon was transformed from fire and brimstone to green trees and cool breezes.

High Desert Paradise

Stand atop one of our more modest summits—say, 4,139-foot Pilot Butte, right at Bend's eastern city limits—and take in what our fiery history has wrought. To the east lies the High Desert, a lonely and often unappreciated land of rimrock, vast sagebrush expanses, scattered settlements, isolated ranches, and the West's largest juniper forest. Those who take the time to know this place find sublime beauty in quiet canyons, the cry of a soaring hawk, or the sight of pronghorn antelope in the distance.

Now, turn 180 degrees and feast your eyes on the Cascade Mountains, one of the West's major ranges, sprawling from British Columbia to California. Eight major peaks, varying from 7,802 to 10,495 feet in elevation, punctuate the Central Oregon skyline—Mount Jefferson; Three Fingered Jack; Mount Washington; North, Middle, and South Sister (collectively known as the Three Sisters); Broken Top; and Mount Bachelor. They are sky-piercing islands in a sea of trees.

If you were to don your climbing boots at the base of the mountains and begin trekking upwards, you would first pass through a bright, open forest of ponderosa pines that eventually gives way to firs, cedars, and spruces in the cooler, moister, higher elevations. By the time you reached 7,000 feet in elevation, alpine meadows would be beneath your feet as you wandered through glorious open land.

Persevere onward, up to the summit of one of the high peaks, and you would find yourself scrambling over a steepening terrain of rock and snow. The view from the roof of the Cascades would reveal a seemingly endless mountain forest of ridges and high-country lakes, ice-blue and clear. In summer, the Cascades invite you to relax in a grassy meadow by a rushing stream. In winter, they're a frozen fortress whose secrets can be unlocked with a pair of skis or snowshoes.

Bend is a city where a river runs through it—the Deschutes River, that is. PHOTO: THE RIVERHOUSE

To the north, the Deschutes River, a world-class trout fishery, cuts its way through deep canyons as it flows to the Columbia River from its birthplace in the mountains. Anglers wade its waters, delicately floating flies (with such names as Adams Parachute, Elk Hair Caddis, and Crazy Eddie) through riffles and pools, hoping to entice a Deschutes River redsides (otherwise known as a rainbow trout) from its liquid lair. To the south, a nearly unbroken blanket of pines unfolds to the horizon.

Central Oregon weather is as near to perfect as anyone can reasonably expect. Humidity levels are low. We average 130 days of sunshine per year (the highest in the state) with an additional 90 days of mostly sunny weather. Average January temperatures range from a high of 44 degrees to a low of 19. Average high and low July temperatures run from 86 to 41 degrees. Average yearly precipitation ranges from a bit more than 9 inches to nearly 20 inches—a far cry from the wet, western side of the Cascades, where some coastal areas may get up to 100 inches of rain annually. Generally, 55 to 65 percent of our yearly precipitation falls as snow, with communities closer to the mountains receiving the lion's share. Average annual snowfall in Deschutes County, which takes in much of the east side of the Central Oregon Cascades, is about 34 inches.

This is Big Country, and there's plenty to explore. Within the three-county area that our book covers, we have two national forests, six wilderness areas, a national grassland, a national monument, an internationally renowned rock-climbing area, and seven wild and scenic rivers. And those are just the better-known places. For those who love clean air, spectacular views, nature, wildlife, hiking, backpacking, fishing, hunting, camping, skiing, or any one of a long list of outdoor recreational activities—the reason most people come here to visit or to live—there is only one word to describe Central Oregon: Paradise.

Old West, New West

But in every paradise, there is bound to be a devil skulking about with the potential to cause trouble. Here, that troublemaker is growth—rapid growth. Central Oregon is in the throes of transforming itself from its traditional rural, natural resources–based economy that pivoted on agriculture, ranching, and timber, to a more urban and diversified economy including tourism, high technology, and manufacturing. Refugees from more crowded parts of the country, particularly southern California, have been flocking here in a big way for the past decade or so, seeking a better lifestyle, less crime, and a healthy environment to retire to or raise a family in. Newcomers, rejoicing in their new home of wide-open spaces and plenty of elbow room, are often perplexed to meet old-timers who are feeling a bit hemmed in.

Deschutes County, the largest in Central Oregon, saw a 30 percent population increase between 1990 and 1996. With a current population of 122,050 it was the fastest-growing county in the state during the decade of the 90s. The other two Central Oregon counties, Crook and Jefferson, have also seen population increases of 36 and 39 percent, respectively. Some 153,558 people live in the three-county area that makes up Central Oregon.

The effects of these recent changes are particularly evident in Bend, Central Oregon's economic hub and the epicenter of this region's growing pains. Bend's population has grown by 170 percent, from 20,447 to 55,080 between 1990 and 2002. Subdivisions and shopping centers have sprouted on what were, just a short time ago, bare patches of sagebrush and juniper lands on the fringes of the city limits. Major national retail chains are staking out territories here—unheard of a few years ago—and highway engineers hope the $102 million Bend Parkway (a limited-access bypass for through traffic), completed in 2001, will alleviate some of the city's traffic congestion troubles. Some predict that Bend will eventually become one of Oregon's largest metropolitan areas.

Outlying areas are feeling the pressures of growth as well. Farmers, discovering that the properties owned by their families for generations now have substantial development value, are tempted to sell out. Oregon's model land-use planning laws, enacted by the Oregon Legislature in 1973 to lessen urban sprawl and protect valuable farm and forestlands from development, are being tested as civic boosters, seeking to forge a strong local economy, face off against environmentalists and residents who fear the impacts of unrestrained growth on the Central Oregon lifestyle and environment. The battles can be quite heated.

There are cultural clashes as well, as urbanites move into this still essentially rural area, bringing their city sensibilities along with them. As the forests, rivers, and other natural resources of Central Oregon become valued more for their aesthetic, biological, and recreational attributes instead of their commodity worth, pressure is being put on the region's traditional industries—livestock, agriculture, and logging—to change the way they do business.

The U.S. Forest Service is allowing fewer logging operations on its lands as it looks to outdoor recreation as the major public use of forests in the future. Ranchers and farmers are being prodded to take less water from streams and rivers to irrigate their crops, leaving more for fish and wildlife. The economic pain these changes are causing some people is only made worse by the knowledge that the rural traditions that once defined Central Oregon, and most Central Oregonians, may be moving into the past.

But that's not to say all is doom and gloom by any stretch of the imagination. You'll find the people here to be dynamic, friendly, caring, and generous—and working together to make Central Oregon a better place tomorrow than it was yesterday. If change has been difficult for us, it's been mostly for the better. Central Oregon is more diverse and vibrant than it ever has been. New people are coming here, with new and better ideas. New businesses are taking root and growing. There is more to do and see here than ever before—more art, more culture, and big plans for the future.

The people who are moving here are really little different from the old-timers whose ancestors arrived by covered wagon. Westerners have always sought out new territories and landscapes to call home, reinventing themselves and their new homes to meet their needs and their dreams. The history of the West is one of movement and change. Central Oregon is just having another go at it.

Central Oregon Regions

To make your explorations a bit easier, we've divided Central Oregon into six regions. As you travel around the area, you'll be surprised by the diversity of landscapes, sights, things to do and see, and the old and the new existing side by side.

In the northern parts of Central Oregon, you'll find ranch lands and farmlands with herds of cattle grazing in one pasture and flocks of llamas and other exotic animals in the next. Generations-old ranches sit alongside new subdivisions. Closer to the mountains, luxury summer and winter resorts are just a short drive from trailheads leading into rugged wilderness.

In our cities—still small towns by most measures—you'll find fine restaurants, art galleries, lovely parks, and shopping galore. And from just about everywhere you might walk or drive in Central Oregon, you can see the peaks of the High Cascades, scraping the cobalt-blue sky of the western horizon.

Bend

Central Oregon's economic hub and its most populous city, Bend is located along a double-curve on the Deschutes River (hence the city's name) where 19th-century pioneers forded the stream on their way to points west. Although the city has attracted a variety of businesses in recent years, including some high-tech and light manufacturing enterprises, tourism is an important component of Bend's economy. And the continued presence of wood products–related industries within the city and numerous small ranches on its outskirts reveals that the place has not completely severed its traditional roots in farming, ranching, and logging. In fact, along with tourism, agriculture and lumber are the primary industries in Deschutes County, where Bend lies.

Most people who visit Central Oregon begin in Bend, and with good reason. The city offers a generous helping of amenities and things to do. A good way to introduce yourself to Bend is by exploring its downtown core—small enough to easily cover on foot, with plenty of shops, art galleries, and sidewalk cafes to provide a pleasant afternoon's diversion.

Immediately west of downtown, you'll find lovely Drake Park, right along the Deschutes River. It's a favorite location for locals seeking a quiet spot in the sun to eat their lunch and watch the river go by. Drake Park is also a focal point for many of

Insiders' Tip

When traveling through the rural back roads of Central Oregon, you may notice that a lot of people who you don't know wave as you go by. Folks are just plain friendly out here. Wave back.

The first settlers began moving to Central Oregon in 1863. PHOTO: JIM YUSKAVITCH

the city's annual events—from marathons to music festivals (see our Annual Events chapter). Nightlife and the number and variety of restaurants have improved greatly in recent years as the town has grown and new people with different tastes and interests have come to live or visit (see our Restaurants and Nightlife chapters).

From Bend, you are within easy striking distance of many of the things that make the Central Oregon experience so special. Within the immediate area you'll find 27 city parks, two state parks, and five golf courses. (Golf is a trademark activity in Central Oregon—the area boasts a total of 24 courses. For more information, see our Golf chapter.)

A virtually mandatory stop for visitors is The High Desert Museum, 3.5 miles south of Bend off South U.S. Highway 97. Born from an idea tossed around the evening campfires of a few "desert rats" a little more than 20 years ago, The High Desert Museum has blossomed from a small, local natural history museum into a world-class educational center. Tucked away on 150 acres of ponderosa pine forest, the museum focuses on interpreting the natural and cultural history of the Intermountain West—a vast, arid region between the Rocky, Cascade, and Sierra Mountains that encompasses eight states and a portion of Canada and includes Central Oregon. (See our Attractions, Kidstuff, Retirement, and Education and Child Care chapters for more on The High Desert Museum.)

Another Bend-area "must-do" is a drive on the Cascade Lakes Highway, an 87-mile loop south and west of the city that takes you into the Cascade Mountains, past Mt. Bachelor Ski Area (one of the West Coast's top ski areas) and to more than a dozen high-country lakes and awesome mountain views (see our Daytrips chapter). Once you've seen all that, you'll be more than ready to set about discovering what else Central Oregon has to offer.

Sisters/Camp Sherman Area

With a population of 911, the tiny hamlet of Sisters ranks as one of Central Oregon's smaller communities. Nestled against the eastern slope of the Cascade Mountains, Sisters has remade itself from a typical, small Western town into a popular tourist destination featuring downtown buildings constructed with an 1880s Western theme and a variety of unique and interesting specialty shops. Some of the region's largest and most popular annual events, including the Sisters Outdoor Quilt Show and Sisters Rodeo, are held here (see our Annual Events chapter).

Sisters is also a gateway to some of the most gorgeous mountain country in the state. Camp Sherman and the Metolius River Recreation Area, located a dozen miles west of town off U.S. Highway 20, are favorite getaways for campers and trout anglers. A federally designated Wild and Scenic River, the Metolius arises full-size from underground springs originating in the nearby Three Sisters Wilderness Area and flows ice-cold and crystal clear beneath a canopy of ponderosa pine trees in the Deschutes National Forest, the summits of Three Fingered Jack and Mount Jefferson towering above. A cluster of small resorts in the tiny community of Camp Sherman are popular destinations during the summer months as are the numerous campgrounds that line the river.

Continuing west on U.S. 20 eventually leads you to the 4,817-foot-high summit of Santiam Pass, in the heart of the Cascade Mountains. Here, backpackers and hikers gain access to a variety of trails leading deep into mountain wilderness. Cross-country skiers flock here during winter as well. On the summit of the pass you'll find Hoodoo Ski Bowl, long popular with local downhill skiers seeking reasonably priced lift tickets and relief from the crowded slopes of more popular ski areas.

A second major access to the mountains from Sisters is up Oregon Highway 242, passing stunning views of the Three Sisters across a green expanse of pasture before plunging into the forest and up the steep, narrow McKenzie Highway to its 5,325-foot-high summit. At this point you'll find yourself in the middle of an ancient and immense lava flow with unobstructed views of most of the Central Oregon Cascade peaks. Designated a state Scenic Byway, the McKenzie Highway is a favorite summer and fall drive over the mountains, although it is closed by snow during the winter and spring (see our Daytrips chapter).

If you're thinking that all this beauty existing in an area of only 911 people is too good to be true, you're right. Actually there are small private communities scattered throughout the area, surrounded by the Deschutes National Forest and largely out of sight of passersby. It's estimated that about 10,000 people live in this western corner of Deschutes County.

Insiders' Tip

When driving around Central Oregon, watch for deer crossing the road. Many are killed each year in collisions with motor vehicles, which can cause significant damage to the vehicles involved as well as potential injury to their occupants. Most likely to be on the roads during their mid-May to mid-June and November and December migration periods, deer may be encountered at any time of the year, particularly in the early morning and evening hours.

Redmond

Hard-working Redmond has been growing in prominence in Central Oregon in recent years as people discover choice homesites nestled in the juniper and sagebrush along the Deschutes River canyon just a bit west of the city limits. Situated in northeastern Deschutes County, you're in ranch country when you're in the Redmond area. Small family ranches and farms are the norm in the immediate countryside and you'll see lots of livestock grazing in irrigated pastures. You'll also notice that you've left the mountains behind and crossed into the high plains—a land of wide-open spaces, rimrock canyons, and buttes.

Since 1990, Redmond's population has increased from 7,165 to 13,705. Nevertheless, the city has maintained its ranching and farming roots and feel with potatoes, lumber, and livestock being some of the primary commodities produced around these parts. The Deschutes County Fairgrounds is also in Redmond, making it the home of many Central Oregon events. Most notable of these are the area's two largest annual get-togethers, the Deschutes County Fair and the Central Oregon Home and Garden Show (see our Annual Events chapter). However, other smaller events are held here as well, including many horse and livestock-oriented shows and competitions, reflecting the whole area's ranching tradition.

Visitors who come to Central Oregon by air see Redmond first, since our commercial airport is here. Also at the Redmond Municipal Airport is the Redmond Air Center, from which the U.S. Forest Service deploys aircraft and smoke jumpers to fight forest fires throughout the United States. Redmond has two local golf courses along with two state parks within the immediate area, including the world-famous rock-climbing area, Smith Rock State Park.

Sunriver/La Pine Area

About 15 miles south of Bend, off U.S. Highway 97, is Sunriver, a planned residential community and full-service resort that opened to the public in 1969 and now has about 1,800 full-time residents. Many visitors to Central Oregon opt to make this upscale resort their base of operations. During summer Sunriver offers golf, tennis, mountain biking, horseback riding, and fishing on the nearby Deschutes, Little Deschutes, and Fall Rivers as well as a host of other indoor and outdoor activities. Sunriver is just 18 miles from Mt. Bachelor Ski Area, making it a popular winter destination as well. Another 9 miles down the road will bring you into La Pine, an unincorporated city of about 16,000 people and a popular area for retirees looking for an out-of-the-way place to settle.

The primary attractions in this part of Central Oregon are Newberry National Volcanic Monument to the north and east and the High Cascade lakes to the west. Created by Congress in 1990 and administered by the U.S. Forest Service, Newberry National Volcanic Monument encompasses more than 50,000 acres of lakes, forest, lava flows, caves, mountain peaks, a wealth of spectacular geological formations, and more than 150 miles of hiking trails. Five-hundred-square-mile Newberry Volcano is the monument's centerpiece; it contains two trout- and salmon-filled lakes and draws scads of campers and anglers each summer. The caldera is also believed to be one of the best archaeological areas in the Pacific Northwest, and archaeologists are continually making new discoveries about early Native Americans there. (For more on the national monument, see our chapters on Daytrips; Other Outdoor Recreation; Fishing; and Forests, High Desert, and Volcanoes.)

La Pine also provides a jumping-off point for anglers heading for Davis Lake and Crane Prairie and Wickiup Reservoirs to the west, three of the southernmost and largest bodies of water on the Cascade Lakes Highway and all known for their trophy-size trout.

Prineville Area

Livestock, lumber, and outdoor recreation make up the primary industries of Crook County. When Prineville refers to itself as the "Cowboy Capitol of Oregon," they aren't exaggerating by much. With Prineville's population at 8,205 and a total countywide population of 18,150, the whole area still retains its Western traditions and small-town atmosphere.

Tucked into the fertile valley of the Crooked River, Prineville has always relied on the timber cut from the nearby Ochoco National Forest to help sustain its economy. But the many thousands of hunters, anglers, hikers, rock hounds, and campers who flock to the Ochoco Mountains and Prineville and Ochoco Reservoirs provide an important addition to the local economic mix. In fact, the Ochoco National Forest, long favored by elk hunters for its large herds of this sought-after game animal, also offers outstanding summer hiking and camping solitude in its three wilderness areas at a time when trails in the Cascade Mountains are becoming a bit busy.

The Crooked River just below Bowman Dam, 12 miles south of Prineville, is starting to receive wider recognition for its outstanding rainbow trout fishing within a beautiful and easy-to-get-to desert canyon environment. Ochoco Reservoir, 7 miles east of Prineville, is a popular destination for trout fishing while 12-mile-long Prineville Reservoir, created by 1,100-foot-high Bowman Dam, is famous, at least locally, for its bass fishing. (For more on these reservoirs, see our Parks and Fishing chapters.)

Prineville is the only incorporated town within 2,991-square-mile Crook County. Small rangeland settlements such as Post and Paulina, the working ranches spread over thousands of acres, and the sight of cowboys along the road, mending barbed-wire fence, give testimony to life in the Old West—how it was and how it still is.

Madras Area

On the northern fringe of Central Oregon, the Madras area is serious agricultural country where farmers raise sugar beets, carrots, mint, flower seeds, bluegrass, garlic, radishes, wheat, and potatoes on about 60,000 acres of irrigated croplands and ship it out to domestic and international markets. It's the most culturally diverse part of Central Oregon as well, where the grand-children of early settlers live alongside Native Americans from the nearby Warm Springs Indian Reservation. There is also a growing population of Hispanic residents, many of whom work at area farms.

Although many travelers view Madras and its environs as a place to pass through on their way to the mountains, this breadbasket of Central Oregon also offers much of the beauty and recreational opportunities for which this area is famed. The dog days of summer attract hordes of anglers, boaters, water-skiers, and other watersports enthusiasts to Lake Billy Chinook at The Cove Palisades State Park and to Lake Simtustus, southwest of Madras in the deep canyon where the Deschutes, Crooked, and Metolius Rivers meet. Haystack Reservoir, on the nearby Crooked River National Grassland, is a hot spot for bass fishing. Just a short, 20-minute drive north of downtown Madras will put you on the lower Deschutes River with its famed rainbow trout and steelhead fishery (see our Parks and Fishing chapters).

The surrounding farmland has its own charms as well. This open country stretching from horizon to horizon offers the best unobstructed panoramic view of the Cascade Mountains in Central Oregon, while the lush green fields conjure up images of idyllic childhoods spent chewing on a piece of grass beneath a big, friendly tree and watching hawks soar lazily in the sky above.

Insiders' Tip

If you are out photographing the mountains of the High Cascades, put a polarizing filter on your lens. It will render the sky a deeper, more pleasing blue while cutting the glare from the peaks' snowy slopes.

"What Mountain Is That?"

Since the high peaks of the Cascade Mountains are prominently visible from just about anywhere you go in Central Oregon, most people end up having a question or two about the range that they'd like answered. Here's a bit of information about our major peaks that will answer some of your queries and perhaps pique your interest in finding out more about our mountains. You'll also find additional information about Central Oregon's mountains and the areas surrounding them in our Daytrips; Other Outdoor Recreation; Camping; Snowplay; and Forest, High Desert, and Volcanoes chapters.

Mount Jefferson

Oregon's second-highest mountain was first spotted by the Lewis and Clark expedition on March 30, 1806, and the group promptly named the peak after the president who had sent them on their great exploration. Mount Jefferson's elevation is 10,495 feet, and it sports snow throughout the year, largely due to the five glaciers that cling to its slopes. The largest, Whitewater Glacier, covers the mountain's east and northeast slopes and is clearly visible from Central Oregon. Sprawling from about the 7,000-foot area to the 10,000-foot level, Whitewater Glacier is the largest chunk of ice in the state. Other glaciers on the mountain include Waldo Glacier, Milk Creek Glacier, Russell Glacier, and Jefferson Park Glacier.

Mount Jefferson, located within the 117,354-acre Mount Jefferson Wilderness, was first climbed in 1888 and has been a favorite destination for Oregon mountaineers ever since. Mount Jefferson is large enough to be seen from much of Central Oregon. A good place for an unobstructed view of this major mountain peak is at the turnoff along U.S. Highway 20, about 9 miles west of Bend.

Three Fingered Jack

Historians don't quite know how this peak, located within the Mount Jefferson Wilderness, got its rather unusual name. At 7,848 feet in elevation, it is one of the smaller Cascade peaks. But its jagged skyline gives it a spectacular appearance, especially during winter when it is clad in snow and ice.

Three Fingered Jack was first climbed by a party of six mountaineers from Bend on September 3, 1923. An outstanding close-up view of this dramatic peak may be had right off U.S. Highway 20, about 3 miles west of Santiam Pass.

Mount Washington

The centerpiece of the 52,516-acre Mount Washington Wilderness, 7,802-foot Mount Washington was, obviously, named for our first president, but by whom remains a mystery. Its summit spire is actually a volcanic plug—a chunk of lava that had hardened within the mountain's crater vent, then slowly was revealed after thousands of years of erosion wore away the mountain's outer shell of softer rock.

The summit of Mount Washington was first reached by a group of climbers from Bend on August 26, 1923, some of whom would be among the first to ascend Three Fingered Jack less than a month later. A great view of Mount Washington can be seen from the turnout along the south side of U.S. Highway 20, about 16 miles west of Sisters.

North, Middle, and South Sister

These three major Central Oregon peaks that dominate the landscape of the 283,402-acre Three Sisters Wilderness include North Sister (10,094 feet), Middle Sister (10,053 feet), and South Sister (10,358 feet). Often collectively referred to as the Three Sisters, they were originally called Faith, Hope, and Charity—the order of the names running from north to south—by early pioneers.

All together, these three peaks have a total of 15 glaciers. Their massive sizes and year-round snow and ice make the Three Sisters easily the most spectacular set of mountains in Central Oregon. Terrific views of these peaks are available from two spots on Oregon Highway 242—just west of Sisters by the Patterson Ranch and at the summit of the McKenzie Pass—as well as along the Cascade Lakes Highway a couple of miles west of Mount Bachelor.

Oregon mountaineers have been climbing all of the Sisters since the late 1800s. North Sister may have been climbed as early as 1857, but it is not known for certain.

Broken Top

With its sawtooth summit, it's obvious how 9,165-foot Broken Top got its name. Located in the Three Sisters Wilderness, it has two glaciers along its slopes, Bend Glacier and Crook Glacier. The best views of Broken Top are from the Cascade Lakes Highway, just west of Mount Bachelor.

Mount Bachelor

Mount Bachelor got its name due to the fact that it rises at a distance so far from the Three Sisters, though earlier in the century it was also often called Brother John. In January 1956, a new ski area was dedicated on the mountain's slopes. Today, Mt. Bachelor Ski Area is one of the West Coast's top skiing destinations. You can treat yourself to a couple of classic views of this 9,065-foot mountain from Sparks and Hosmer Lakes, both along the Cascade Lakes Highway west of Bend.

The second-highest mountain in Oregon, 10,495-foot Mount Jefferson looms against the western horizon. PHOTO: JIM YUSKAVITCH

Getting Here, Getting Around

The Big Picture
By Auto
By Air
By Bus
By Train
By Taxi
Other Transportation

No matter how you get here or from what direction, as long as it's light out you're in for a scenic adventure with many tempting attractions along the way. (We'll point out a few handy, short stops in our description of each route later in this chapter.) If you are driving and plan, based on mileage figures, to arrive in Central Oregon in time for lunch, don't be surprised if it's time for dinner when you finally get here. Access to our beautiful part of the world isn't exactly easy or as the crow flies, as we explain shortly. If you're flying in, you can start making plans during your aerial preview.

The Big Picture

The state of Oregon has two interstates. Interstate 5 runs north-south along the wet, western quarter of the state, forming our main lifeline with Washington and California. Interstate 84 starts at Portland and follows the Columbia River east along our northern border until it intersects with Interstate 82 from Washington. It then heads southeast, cutting across northeastern Oregon's wheat lands until it reaches Boise, Idaho.

The Cascade Range forms a 10,000-foot-high barrier between I-5 and Central Oregon. The range is crossed by four small highways that follow the canyons cut by some of Oregon's famous fly-fishing rivers up the west side of the Cascades. There the northernmost route, U.S. 26, crosses the range at Blue Box Summit, elevation 4,025 feet. The three southern routes converge and cross over at Santiam Pass, elevation 4,617 feet.

The majority of travel to and from Central Oregon is via automobile between the cities on I-5 and those on U.S. Highway 97. In good-to-fair weather, the average driving time for the 165- to 215-mile trip (depending on your route) between Portland and Bend is approximately three-and-a-half to four hours. The 125-mile drive over the winding mountain roads from Eugene or Salem to Bend takes about two-and-a-half hours.

Our Central Oregon towns form a cross, with U.S. 97, the main north-south route, stringing together the towns of Madras, Terrebonne, Redmond, Bend, Sunriver, and La Pine. The western arm of the cross is anchored by U.S. 20 at Sisters, and the eastern arm, U.S. 26, leads to Prineville. From top to bottom, our imaginary cross is 75 miles long; from west to east, it's 39 miles wide. The Bend Parkway, U.S. 97, was completed in 2001 and provides an alternate route through the commercial section of Bend. Also in 2001, the former route of U.S. 97 through the commercial area of Bend, primarily via Third Street, was changed, at least in its official title, to U.S. 97 Business. U.S. 20 was tied into the parkway in only one location: If you are heading northbound on the Bend Parkway, U.S. 97, at the northern end of Bend you can exit directly onto U.S. 20 westbound toward Sisters. For all other transitions between U.S. 20 and U.S. 97, you will have to use U.S. 97 Business. If we Benders (locals) occasionally slip up and tell you a place is "right on 97," when we really intended to say 97 Business, please forgive us and read between our lines!

U.S. 97 Business in Bend and in Redmond are the region's primary commercial strips. Bend, the region's economic hub and a major tourist destination, offers the most motels, restaurants, and retail outlets. Traffic along the 6-mile stretch of U.S. 97 Business through Bend can get congested on weekday afternoons, and on weekends during the tourist seasons. Allow 20 to 30 minutes to travel from one end of Bend to the other during peak times. Major commercial development also has spread east of Bend along U.S. 20. U.S. 20 converges with U.S. 97 Business at the north end of Bend just south of the Mountain View Mall, until it turns east at the intersection of Third Street and Greenwood Avenue.

Although all the towns have small, general aviation airports, Redmond is the site of Central Oregon's commercial airport, offering scheduled flights to and from Seattle and Portland, where many incoming visitors to Central Oregon connect. For convenience to the airport, you might choose to spend the night in Redmond. For the most extensive range of amenities, choose Bend as your base of operations. Sisters, Redmond, Sunriver, La Pine, Prineville, and Madras make ideal destinations for specific outdoor recreation-oriented vacations.

By Auto

Most roadways within Central Oregon are two-lane highways (other than short portions of U.S. 97 south of Bend, and between Redmond and Bend, which are four-lane). Speed limits max out at 55 mph. Mountain roads are frequently rainy or snowy, so plan on taking your time. For recorded road condition information, call (800) 977-6368 in Oregon, or (541) 889-3999 from out of state.

If you are a Web crawler, you can find some excellent information at the Oregon Department of Transportation's Web site, including video pictures of Santiam Pass on U.S. Highway 20, Government Camp on U.S. Highway 26, and Willamette Pass on Oregon Highway 58. More video camcorders are being added in other locations. These videos are updated every five minutes, and some have current temperatures and wind conditions. From this Web site, you can get to other pages that have road and current weather conditions. The address is www.tripcheck.com.

Central Oregon has a very healthy population of deer, so it is important to maintain constant vigilance while driving. Many rural highways pass through open range, so there may be livestock on the roads as well.

U.S. Highway 97

Again, the area's main north-south route is U.S. 97, which bisects the state. It is patrolled by state police, sometimes in white, four-wheel-drive SUVs, so watch your speed in those rural areas.

Approaching Central Oregon from the north, you will leave the great Columbia River behind as you head south through rolling ranch lands and open range. Along this route you may be tempted to stop at several photogenic ghost towns, or perhaps at an antiques store. If you look to the west as you make your way along, you will see the landmark peaks of the famous volcanoes that make up the Cascades. Don't count on finding gas along the 100-mile stretch between I-84 and Madras.

This route is sometimes a good choice for getting to Portland and western Washington when snow closes the passes in the Cascades. The highest elevation on U.S. 97 north of Madras is 3,360 feet. U.S. 97 and its western fork, U.S. Highway 197, connect with I-84, which will get you to I-5 along the Columbia River Corridor—a 210-mile, four-plus-hour trip. The corridor can develop its own unique weather systems and seems to be closed at different times than the mountain passes. Occasionally, there are severe winds, fog, or heavy snow, so always check road conditions.

> ### Insiders' Tip
> The Bend Parkway's speed limit, at 45 mph, is lower than you might expect.

South of Bend the gentle landscape benefits from some additional moisture, yielding lodgepole pine forests with trout-filled rivers and hundreds of lakes, including the state's prize gem—stunning Crater Lake. Some parts of these southern forests have been afflicted by beetle infestations; the solution has been a topic of ongoing controversy in the West.

U.S. 97 is dotted every 30 to 50 miles or so with tiny lumber towns, so gas and convenience-store food are usually readily available. Elevations start at about 3,000 feet at Bend and reach 4,900 feet near Chemult, so occasional heavy snows can be expected in the winter. Klamath Falls, at Oregon's southern border, is a good-size city with all the expected amenities.

U.S. 97 is an enjoyable alternative to I-5 when traveling between California and Central Oregon, and it avoids many of the more extreme mountain passes, including I-5's snow-laden Siskiyou Summit at the Oregon-California border, as well as the passes in the Cascade Mountains.

Crossing the Cascade Mountains

The shortest route between two points is a straight line, and there are a number of small highways that create just that between Central Oregon and the major cities along I-5.

Approaching Bend from I-5 and the verdant Willamette Valley, you will travel through a temperate rain forest as you cross the Cascade Mountains. Leaving behind the vine maples of the western foothills, the highway becomes a deep corridor lined with sometimes snowy (but always magnificent) fir trees, with ferns crowding at their feet. Suddenly the rich dampness gives way to sunshine as you reach the pass and scenic overlooks, then descend into hemlocks, scented ponderosa pine, and, finally, open lands of sagebrush and juniper trees that signal your arrival in the High Desert.

U.S. Highway 26 from Portland

This scenic, two-lane highway crosses the Mount Hood National Forest and the Warm Springs Indian Reservation before it reaches Madras. The road gets up to 4,025 feet in elevation at the base of Timberline Ski Area. Nearby is the Mount Hood Meadows Ski Area. Skiers returning home to Portland can create slow, bumper-to-bumper westbound traffic on Saturday and Sunday evenings. The Mount Hood Information Center can be reached at (503) 622-4822 for information on road conditions and amenities. During summer there are plenty of beautiful spots to stop for a picnic or short hike in the national forest, and several small towns that have food and gas outlets. The next amenities on U.S. 26 will be 46 miles from Government Camp at Warm Springs, site of Kah-Nee-Ta Resort and the excellent Museum at Warm Springs (see our chapters on Other Communities; Attractions; and Resorts, Ranches, and Vacation Rentals).

Oregon Highway 22 from Salem to U.S. Highway 20

This is an alternative to U.S. 26 from Portland, as Oregon 22 does not get all the winter ski traffic. The road closely follows the beautiful North Santiam River for almost its entire length. Small logging towns with limited gas and food options

> ## Insiders' Tip
> We recommend that visitors passing north or south on U.S. 97 through Bend use the Bend Parkway as a bypass of Bend's commercial strip. There are several local exits on the parkway, but we'd consider utilizing the parkway for local travel to be on the intermediate-to-advanced navigation level.

are 20 to 30 miles apart. Oregon 22 connects with U.S. 20 just west of the Santiam Pass.

U.S. Highway 20 from Albany over the Santiam Pass

This twin sister to Oregon 22 follows the South Santiam River part of the way, then heads up into the mountains where it joins with Oregon Highways 126 and 22 just west of the Santiam Pass. The small town of Sweet Home at the halfway point offers gas and food. U.S. 20 continues over Santiam Pass, elevation 4,617 feet, into Sisters and on to Bend. Although on the map it looks like a straight continuation of U.S. 20 east of the U.S. 22 intersection, in actuality it is U.S. 22 that makes a straight continuation. U.S. 20/Oregon 126 west is a turn to the southwest.

Oregon Highway 126 from Eugene to U.S. Highway 20

The McKenzie River carved the path for this small mountain highway. Tiny logging towns along the way sell limited gas and food every 20 or 30 miles. Several spectacular waterfalls provide excellent places to stop, stretch your legs, and shoot a few photos along the stretch of Oregon 126 between Belknap Springs and the intersection of U.S. 20.

Oregon Highway 138 from Roseburg

Although technically Oregon 138 does not connect Central Oregon with I–5, we add it here for those travelers from southern Oregon, or those coming from California via I–5, who wish to do a little sight-seeing on their way to our region, or for those who wish to wet a line in the North Umpqua River. The North Umpqua is one of Oregon's most famous steelhead fisheries. Oregon 138 is just a few feet away from the water, and as one might expect it is dotted with tiny towns that cater to fly-fishing folk. The upscale Steamboat Inn, (541) 496–3495, offers a superb gourmet lunch, or you can reserve a deluxe package with an overnight stay and elegant dinner. This is one of the least-traveled routes into Central Oregon, and we suggest you avoid it during winter

storms. In good weather it's a wonderful scenic drive, but make sure you have a full tank of gas. The highest elevation along Oregon 138 is 5,920 feet. The easternmost portion of the route is closed during winter; detour south along Oregon 62.

Oregon Highway 62 from Medford

Another scenic route across southern Oregon is Oregon 62. A great reason to take this small mountain highway is the fact that it goes by one of Oregon's most spectacular volcanic attractions, Crater Lake. It's a fairly efficient route to Bend in summer when the northern route, Oregon 138, is open. The elevation at Crater Lake is 6,225 feet.

The Eastern Approach

From the east you'll be coming across the wide-open desert of the Great Basin, with the tall wall of the Cascade Mountains in the distance. Side roads leading to fossil sites, sand dunes, or interesting volcanic attractions may end up adding an hour or more to your trip.

U.S. Highway 26 from Ontario

U.S. 26 passes through beautiful mountain terrain and lower ranch lands. It starts at Ontario on Oregon's eastern border and heads out through ranch lands before reaching the Malheur National Forest, where it tops out at 5,280 feet at Dixie Pass. Then it's back once again to rolling pastures, open range, and canyons

183,000-acre preserve that shelters more than 280 species of migrating birds. There is a visitors center as well as a self-guided drive through some remarkable volcanic formations. As you approach Bend, you will come to the two-building town of Millican and the turnoff for the Pine Mountain Observatory (see our Forests, High Desert, and Volcanoes chapter).

Oregon Highway 31 from Lakeview

Starting 23 miles north of Lakeview, where it intersects U.S. Highway 395, Oregon 31 traces the edge of the Fremont National Forest on a picturesque route through High Desert and vast ranch lands with herds of cattle and irrigation pivots that reach as far as the eye can see. Along the way is Summer Lake, a popular birding spot, and signs that point the way to the ghost town of Fort Rock, about 12 miles north of the lake (see our Daytrips chapter). Oregon 31 passes through the southeastern part of the Deschutes National Forest and ends at the town of La Pine, 32 miles south of Bend. This is an excellent route to choose if you are approaching from the Reno area on U.S. 395.

as it follows the John Day River. The Sheep Rock Unit and Painted Hill Unit of the John Day Fossil Beds National Monument (see our Daytrips chapter) offer two interesting detours. Small towns with limited services are about 30 miles apart. John Day is the largest town in the area; it's at the halfway point between Ontario and Prineville. The road then rises once more as it passes through the lovely Ochoco National Forest before entering Prineville.

U.S. Highway 20 from Ontario

It's almost a flip of the coin as to whether you should choose U.S. 20 or U.S. 26 as you leave Ontario for Central Oregon. U.S. 20 is more arid and rugged, and it lacks the two brief respites provided by the national forests along U.S. 26. However, the desert can be very interesting and photogenic. Certainly if there are winter storms about, U.S. 20 would be a better choice.

The city of Burns, about 125 miles west of Ontario with a population of about 3,000, has all the basic amenities and some gas stations and diners are open late to service the truck traffic. Just south of Burns is the Malheur National Wildlife Refuge, a

By Air

According to one taxi driver in Bend, it's kind of hard to say whether there are more business travelers or more tourists coming through the Redmond Airport. That's because so many business travelers bring their skis, tennis rackets, or fly rods with them.

Commercial Flights

Portland International Airport
7000 Northeast Airport Way, Portland
(503) 249–0700, (800) 819–9460
www.portofportland.com/FLIGHTS.HTM
Portland International Airport (PDX) is the closest major airport to Central Oregon. Located in northeast Portland next to the Columbia River, it is about 210 miles from Bend.

One of the top 35 airports in the United States, PDX saw almost 13 million air travelers in 2000. The airport has five concourses and 62 gates. Alaska, American, America West, Continental, Delta, Hawaiian, Northwest, Southwest, TWA, and United/United Express are national airlines servicing the airport. There are also six regional airlines including Horizon Air, which connects to Redmond. It adds up to an average of almost 30,000 total flight operations per month.

PDX is serviced by all major car rental companies. The ones with on-site airport locations include Avis Rent A Car, (503) 249–4953, (800) 831–2847; Budget Car and Truck Rental, (503) 249–4556, (800) 527–0700; Dollar Rent A Car, (503) 249–4792, (800) 800–4000; Hertz Rent A Car, (503) 249–8216, (800) 654–3131; and National Car Rental, (503) 249–4907, (800) 227–7368.

National car rental companies with off-site locations servicing the Portland International Airport are Alamo Rent A Car, (503) 252–7039, (800) 327–9633; Enterprise Rent-A-Car, (503) 252–1500, (800) 325–8007; and Thrifty Car Rental (503) 254–3392, (800) 367–2277.

When it's time to return to PDX to leave the area, you should plan on arriving at the airport an hour prior to departure, or two hours early during holidays.

Redmond Municipal Airport
2522 Southeast Jesse Butler Circle, Redmond
(541) 548–6059
www.flyrdm.com

The Redmond Municipal Airport offers about 15 scheduled flights daily to Portland, Seattle, and San Francisco via Horizon Air, (800) 547–9308, and United Express, (800) 241–6522.

This is one airport that is still actually a pleasure to use. It's so small that the waiting area for arrivals, departures, and baggage claim are all in one spot. Passengers deplane via a rolling staircase and walk to the terminal. Their baggage often rolls along beside them in an airport buggy. Bags are then placed on a moving belt on the opposite side of the terminal wall, and passengers standing a few feet away on the inside of the wall can pick up their bags as the belt comes through the door.

This said, like all of Central Oregon, our airport is experiencing some growing pains. A new parking area located across the entrance drive to the airport was added in 2001. A small addition to the terminal allowed space for an on-site restaurant, Honkers Hangar, a branch of the Honkers in the Old Mill District in Bend. Honkers serves breakfast, lunch, and dinner, and the full bar is open until 9:00 P.M. Royal Blend, a local espresso-shop chain, also has an outlet at the terminal.

When departing, travelers should arrive an hour prior to their scheduled flight out of Central Oregon. The Redmond terminal features a deli and gift shop, and the waiting area has a really cool table with Legos for the kids.

Today, as mentioned, most visitors to Central Oregon come by automobile, perhaps because most of their trips are recreational in nature. Also, rates between Portland or Seattle and Redmond are fairly expensive.

There are four car rental agencies at the airport terminal: Avis Rent A Car, (541) 923–3750, (800) 331–7423; Budget Car Rental, (541) 923–0699, (800) 255–5520; Hertz Rent A Car, (541) 923–1411, (800) 654–3131; and National Car Rental, (541) 548–0650, (800) 227–7368.

Insiders' Tip
Renting a car at the Portland International Airport will cost an extra 10 percent airport tax. At the Redmond Municipal Airport, the airport tax for on-site rentals is 11.1 percent. You will avoid the tax by using a company that has an off-site location.

A couple of Bend residents welcome visitors during a local celebration. PHOTO: BEND METRO PARK & RECREATION DISTRICT

Enterprise Rent-A-Car, (541) 383–1717, (800) 736–8222, is the only off-site agency that services the airport.

Shuttle Services

C A C Transportation/Central Oregon Breeze
(541) 389–7469, (800) 847–0157

C A C Transportation runs one scheduled bus per day each way between Portland International Airport and the Redmond Municipal Airport, then on to the Bend Riverhouse. The buses make stops at the Redmond Big O (a coffee shop), Madras Tiger Mart gas station, Gresham Max station (on Portland's light-rail network), and Portland Union Station (which offers Amtrak service).

The cost to shuttle from Bend to PDX is $38 one-way and $69 for the round-trip. You will need to make a reservation 24 hours in advance. Payment can be made by credit card over the phone, or you may pay the driver. In 1998 C A C bought a new shuttle that's the size of a small school bus but with more comfortable seats. (This note's for those of you who have ridden the old bus!) The bus is white, with CENTRAL

OREGON BREEZE on the side; it's wheelchair-accessible. C A C also charters buses. They will answer the phone, "Redmond Airport Shuttle."

Redmond Airport Shuttle
(541) 382–1687, (888) 664–8449

Owned by C A C Transportation, this is similar to a taxi service. It differs in that you must reserve 24 hours or more in advance, and the trip must start or end at the Redmond Municipal Airport. Cost to go from the airport to a motel in Bend is usually about $19.00 for the first person, plus $8.00 per additional person. To go from the airport to Sunriver is $38 for the first person and $15 for additional persons.

Smile Shuttle Service
(541) 389–0423, (888) 376–4533,
(800) 484–3980, code 8380
www.smileshuttle.com

Smile Shuttle Service can take you anywhere you want to go in Oregon, including to or from the Portland International Airport. Smile has all-wheel-drive minivans for use in winter, plus a 2001 Grand

Caravan, a maxi-van that holds 14, and a Chevy Caprice Classic for situations where it would inconvenience a passenger to climb up into a van.

Some flat rates include $20.00 for one person from Bend to Sunriver (plus $5.00 for each additional person) and $20.00–$22.50 from Bend to the Redmond Municipal Airport for the first person ($5.00 for each additional person). Children cost $2.50. They suggest you call at least two hours in advance, and Smile is open 24 hours a day, more or less.

By Private Aircraft

Bend

Bend Municipal Airport
63132 Powell Butte Road
(541) 388–0019, The Flight Shop
(800) 261–0019
www.flightshopinc.com

The Bend airport has one lighted but uncontrolled 5,005-foot runway, and space for helicopter landings. Air Life, the local air ambulance service, bases its Pilatus fixed-wing aircraft here. Elevation is 3,453 feet.

The Flight Shop offers avgas, jet fuel, repairs, instruction, and charter flights. Flight instruction costs $35 per hour for the instructor plus $53 per hour for a small Cessna. Charter rates depend on distance and weight, but they will travel up to a 300-mile radius. You can call ahead and ask these folks to pick up a Hertz rental car for you.

Redmond

Redmond Municipal Airport–Roberts Field
2522 South Jesse Butler Circle
(541) 548–6059
www.flyrdm.com

Roberts Field at the Redmond Municipal Airport is a controlled airfield with two 7,000-foot runways situated at an elevation of 3,077 feet. Jet fuel, avgas, and repairs are offered by Butler Aviation, (541) 548–8166, as well as Redmond Air, (541) 923–1355. Redmond Air also offers lessons at $35.00 for instruction and $38.65 per hour for a small Cessna. Sightseeing flights are $100 per hour for three people. There's a 24-hour attendant.

Sunriver/La Pine Area

Sunriver Airport, Sunriver
(541) 593–4603

This airport features one lighted, 5,500-foot runway, and it is at an elevation of 4,159 feet. SunAir, (541) 593–1860 or (800) 793–1860, provides avgas, jet fuel, repairs, flight training, and scenic charter flights over Central Oregon, Mount St. Helens, and the Columbia River Gorge. Flight instruction costs $35 per hour, plus $80 per hour for a Cessna 172. Charter flights are available to points all over the West Coast. Local scenic flights cost $165 per hour for up to three persons. Sunair can arrange for a Hertz rental car for you. The Sunriver Airport is owned by Sunriver Resort.

Insiders' Tip

From mid-fall through mid-spring, many Central Oregon residents drive to Portland the night before their flight at the Portland International Airport, just in case they experience a longer travel time due to bad weather. During good weather, travelers should plan on leaving Bend no less than six hours before their flight.

Prineville Area

Prineville Airport
716500 Airport Road, Prineville
(541) 447-1118

This is an uncontrolled field with two runways—one 5,000 feet, the other 4,000 feet. It is situated at an elevation of 3,246 feet. In addition to traditional general aviation, the airport is popular with hobbyists who fly ultra-lites, gyro-copters, and other experimental aircraft. Prineville Aviation offers avgas, jet fuel, and service. They also offer flight instruction, and scenic flights, for $95 per hour.

Madras Area

Madras Jefferson County Airport
2028 Northwest Airport Way, Madras
(541) 475-6947

Madras, at an elevation of 2,234 feet, has two lighted, uncontrolled runways—one 5,000 feet, one 2,200 feet. Mobley Aviation provides avgas, jet fuel, and maintenance and can be reached at the main airport number. Instruction costs $32 per hour on the ground, or $44 air time, plus plane rental at $70 per hour for a Cessna 172. Alternatively, if you'd like to hire Don, their pilot/instructor, to take you up for a tour, the charge will be $114 per hour.

By Bus

Greyhound Bus Lines
2045 U.S. Highway 20, Bend
(541) 382-2151, (800) 231-2222
www.greyhound.com
McDonalds
2456 U.S. Highway 97, Redmond
(541) 504-1263
Lapine Mini Mart
52539 Highway 97 (3 miles north of LaPine center), La Pine
(541) 536-3288
McDonalds
498 Northwest Third Street, Prineville
(541) 447-2571
McDonalds
28 North Oak Street, Madras
(541) 475-3580

Greyhound operates three buses per day out of Central Oregon; one terminates in Portland, one in Seattle, and one eventually ends up in Los Angeles, stopping in Redding and Sacramento, California. The Bend address is the main office; call that office for the most reliable information (you won't always reach someone at the other locations). The Bend terminal location is open Monday through Friday from 8:00 A.M. to 5:00 P.M. (it's closed for lunch from about 1:30 to 2:30 P.M.), with evening hours from 8:30 to 9:45 P.M.; Saturday from 8:30 A.M. to 3:00 P.M., and Sunday from 8:30 A.M. to 2:00 P.M. Tickets may be purchased from the Bend terminal or at the McDonalds and the Lapine Mini Mart listed above. The one-way fare between Bend and Portland is $22 on weekdays, or $24 on weekends. From here to Seattle is $48 or $51, respectively.

By Train

Amtrak
(800) 872-7245
www.amtrak.com

Boy, are we on the map! Amtrak's Coast Starlight winds between Seattle and Los Angeles, with daily stops at Chemult in both directions. Chemult is a small town on U.S. 97 about 55 miles south of Bend.

There is no station at Chemult, just an unstaffed shelter near the tracks on Second Street at U.S. 97. You have to carry on your baggage.

The northbound train arrives in Chemult at 9:13 A.M. Travel time to Portland is 6 hours and 10 minutes, and the cost ranges from $28 to $33. The return train stops in Chemult at 8:15 P.M. C A C Transportation and Smile Shuttle Service (see Shuttle Services in the By Air section) each run a shuttle between the Amtrak stop in Chemult and Redmond and Bend.

Amtrak's Web site is user-friendly and very informative. Their Web page describing the Coast Starlight highlights the scenic and tour-worthy aspects of the route.

By Taxi

Bend is where the majority of the taxi service is in Central Oregon, with just one company based in Redmond.

Adventure Shuttle
P.O. Box 1789, Bend
(541) 385–7002
www.CogWild.com
"A Taxi for You and Your Gear" is their motto, and, as you might expect, they cater to folks who travel to remote areas with lots of gear. They offer a spacious 15-passenger van, and 1987-vintage seven-passenger AWD Volkswagon van. With a special-use permit for the Deschutes,

Willamette, and Ochoco National Forests, Adventure Shuttle can drop you off at a trailhead for a backpacking trip, or at a put-in on a river with your boat and gear, and pick you up at your take-out. They also have a mountain bike tour company called Cog Wild, where they will arrange trips. And, Adventure Shuttle does have a local taxi license, so if you just need to get you and your gear from one point in town to another, they can do that, too. Not surprisingly, a canine passenger doesn't phase them.

Bend Cab Co.
(541) 389–8090
Bend Cab will show up 24 hours a day with a metered sedan or wagon. The company services Central Oregon. They'll also come and give your battery a jump start if you get stuck somewhere.

City Cab
(541) 385–3304, Bend exchange
(541) 548–0919, Redmond exchange
There's some debate about which local taxi service has been around longest. The answer, apparently, lies in the longtime Redmond phone number, which makes City Cab the oldest even though it's had more than one owner and name. City Cab services Central Oregon from Bend with nonsmoking Chrysler Caravans and sedans, and skis can be accommodated. Trips can be flat rate ($30–$35 from Bend to Sunriver) or metered.

Insiders' Tip

Mileage markers on Oregon's state highways are numbered from north to south, and west to east, with the exception of I-5, which is an interstate. The exit numbers are numbered according to their mileage marker location. This makes it easy to judge how far you need to travel to get to your exit, or to the state border. For example, on the Bend Parkway, U.S. 97, exit 138 is 138 miles south of the Oregon/Washington state line.

Errands on Call
(541) 382–0441; (541) 312–0242, pager

Errands On Call will take people and/or stuff from one part of Bend to another in nonsmoking vehicles. The best time to reach someone is during regular business hours.

Executive Limousine
(541) 383–2787

When they say limousine, they mean it—complete with the red-carpet service. Weddings, proms, anniversaries, and VIPs make up the main market for Executive. Limos have a two-hour minimum. The big Lincoln Continental rents for $75 per hour; a smaller version rents for $65 per hour. The Buick LeSabre 4-passenger short-stretch goes for only $50 per hour. Executive also has a seven-passenger van that's good for a few people with lots of gear, at $45 per hour with a one-hour minimum. The cost to go from the Redmond Airport to Sunriver is usually about $45 for the van, or $250 to go from Bend to the Portland International Airport. Executive offers a dinner special, which includes at least three hours use of a limo (at the hourly rate) with a $30 coupon toward dinner at a restaurant of your choice. You can grab a quick bite and then cruise for the rest of the three hours or longer, or you may wish to have your limo parked in front of a fancy restaurant while you leisurely sip a glass of fine wine at a linen-decked table.

Owl Taxi Service
(541) 382–3311

This is a classic taxi service that operates 24 hours a day. Based in Bend, Owl covers Central Oregon with metered sedans.

Redmond Taxi Service
(541) 548–1182

In a class by itself is Redmond Taxi Service, founded by Jim Hamilton, who passed away in 1999. Jim ran his service more like a Robin Hood than a taxi driver, along with his younger partner Kelly O. Kelly has taken over for Jim, and he carries on the tradition of serving many senior citizens, including picking up their groceries and occasionally taking a small dog to the vet (with a sheet spread on the seat, of course). Kelly also takes normal taxi customers, and he operates mostly within the city limits of Redmond, usually by himself, but occasionally he has an assistant driver in a second car.

Other Transportation

Bike Paths

Bike paths in Bend are more for the recreational rider than for people actually peddling as a form of serious transportation. Most highways and roads do not have real bike paths. A map on bike paths in Bend, including the beautiful 3-mile Deschutes River Run Trail, can be obtained at the Central Oregon Welcome Center, or call the Parks and Recreation Department at (541) 389–7275.

Ski Shuttle

Mt. Bachelor Ski Area provides shuttle service between the mountain and a parking lot at Simpson and Colorado Streets in Bend. The cost for the 22-mile trip is $2.00 each way. For information, call (541) 382–2442 or (800) 829–2442.

RideShare

Central Oregon RideShare
16 Northwest Kansas Avenue
(800) 576–7665

This is a nonprofit service that helps match people for carpooling, according to locations and preferences. Serving Deschutes, Jefferson, and Crook Counties, RideShare is a joint project of the Oregon Department of Transportation, the City of Bend, Deschutes County, the Oregon Department of Energy, Oregon State University Extension Service, and Commute Options for Central Oregon.

History

Introduction

The history of Central Oregon is the history of the West. First and foremost, it was a wild land, known only to scattered tribes of indigenous people, then explored by fur trappers who unwittingly paved the way for the waves of settlers who would come later. Central Oregon has seen its share of famous frontier figures, explorers, generals, and railroad builders.

The color and violence of the West is here, too. Indian raiders attacked white settlements in defense of their homelands, striking fear in the hearts of early homesteaders. Range wars left the high plains awash in blood. But the history of Central Oregon is also about the road builders and entrepreneurs, the dryland farmers and the immigrants, the loggers and the stockmen who fashioned, through the course of decades, a home and a civilization. Here is a small slice of their story.

First People

Human occupation of Central Oregon began at least 10,000 years ago, when nomadic hunters, whose tribal names are forever lost to history, wandered the region. They were in all likelihood direct—and not-too-distant—relatives of the prehistoric peoples who had been migrating across the Bering Strait beginning just a few thousand years or so earlier. During this period, around 11,000 B.C., the ocean was about 300 feet lower than it is today, creating a land bridge between Asia and North America that was relatively easy to cross. In an ongoing migration, wandering groups of prehistoric hunters and their families followed vast herds of game across the Bering land bridge from Asia to a new world that, collectively, they would spend the next 8 or 10 millennia colonizing.

Having crossed the strait into what is now Alaska, the wanderers fanned out into different migration routes that, over time, took them and their descendants to different parts of the continent as well as to Central and South America. One of those migration routes, up the Yukon Valley, down the east side of the Rocky Mountains, then west toward the Pacific Coast, brought some of these Stone Age pioneers to the Oregon High Desert.

In 1938, University of Oregon anthropologist Dr. L. S. Cressman made an astonishing discovery while excavating a cave in the Fort Rock Valley 50 miles southeast of Bend. What he and his crew found in Fort Rock Cave, along with stone arrowheads, scrapers, drills, and some basketry fragments, were nearly 100 sandals made of sagebrush bark. When carbon-dated, they were found to be about 9,000 years old, the most ancient evidence of human occupation in Oregon. Later, Cressman carbon-dated charcoal from some of the earliest campfires set in the cave and found them to be more than 13,000 years old.

What happened to these very first Central Oregonians is anybody's guess. Died off? Moved on? Evolved or assimilated into other tribes? When the first white people came to Central Oregon in the early 19th century, they were greeted by a very different cast of characters. Most numerous were Northern Paiutes and Shoshones, heirs of the desert culture begun so many thousands of years earlier.

Other local tribes included Tenino, Umatilla, Cayuse, and Nez Perce.

These indigenous peoples were semi-nomadic, depending on fish and game and a variety of plants, roots, herbs, and berries for sustenance. They typically lived in traditional villages during winter then dispersed in small groups into the mountains and forests for the summer.

By the time the first white explorers began poking about Central Oregon in the early 1800s, local tribes had acquired new technologies that revolutionized their cultures—the horse, the tepee, and the rifle. Acquired by trade with tribes to the east, horses (which were initially acquired by Indian traders via raiding parties on Spanish settlements in Mexico) suddenly gave the Native Americans of Central Oregon the power to travel long distances in search of game. Acquisition of guns, also through trade, exponentially increased the effectiveness of these formerly foot-bound people in their pursuit of game. Adoption of the tepee, the perfect portable shelter, made the Native Americans all the more mobile. By the 1820s, the Shoshones were making regular forays into Idaho to hunt bison, which had been extirpated from Eastern Oregon—some say the result of the increased effectiveness of Indian hunters brought about by the horse and the gun.

In Search of Beavers

The first white people to see Central Oregon were nomads of another sort—men in search of the beaver, an innocuous, water-dwelling rodent whose luxurious fur was pressed into a high-grade felt that made up the hats worn by the world's most fashionable gentlemen of the early 1800s. A cutthroat business with a high mortality rate, American and British entrepreneurs formed fur-trading companies and fielded parties of trappers who roamed the wilderness, catching beaver—whose pelts would be shipped to the fur dealers back east—and fighting Indians while exploring and charting the West in the process.

Although the proof is not definitive, the first white people to see Central Oregon

were probably a group of "mountain men" under the employ of the 19th-century tycoon John Jacob Astor, who had established a fur-trading post at the mouth of the Columbia River on the Oregon coast in 1811, calling it Fort Astoria. In the autumn of 1812, the fort's food stores were getting low, and a party of hunters was dispatched to the Oregon interior in search of game. They returned to Astoria in March 1813, reporting that their travels had taken them through some 500 miles of uncharted territory. It's believed that, in the course of their wanderings, the party reached the Bend area. The letters S and R (the initials of the group's leaders), along with the date 1813 found carved into the face of a bluff along the Deschutes River, offer the only tantalizing physical evidence of a visit.

The first documented exploration of Central Oregon by whites was by a brigade of Hudson Bay Company beaver trappers under the command of Peter Skene Ogden, who arrived in December 1825. Traveling with 40 or 50 men, accompanied by their wives and children, Ogden traveled up the Deschutes River from their trading post in Walla Walla, Washington. They then cut cross-country to the Crooked River near Prineville, trapping beavers as they went, before heading east and out of the area. Apparently finding the beaver trapping good, Ogden and his men returned to Central Oregon the following year, this time under orders from their superiors to trap the area clean so that none of the valuable animals would be left behind for competing fur companies.

Grand Exploration

By 1840, Oregon's interior was slowly becoming known, largely due to the incidental explorations conducted by the mountain men in their quest for furs. But if the West was ever going to be settled by civilized people, it would have to be explored and mapped in a more orderly and scientific manner. And the United States Army had just the man for the job— 2nd Lt. John Charles Frémont.

A controversial historical figure, Frémont was an explorer and surveyor. The latter years of his career were marked by misfortune and a failed bid for the country's highest office in 1856 as the Republican party's first presidential candidate.

Politically well-connected as the son-in-law of Thomas Hart Benton, a powerful Democratic senator from Missouri, Frémont was chosen to command two exploratory trips along the Oregon Trail in 1842 and 1843–44.

In December 1843, on his second expedition, Frémont and his party—which included legendary mountain men Thomas Fitzpatrick and Kit Carson—passed through Central Oregon, moving up the west side of the Deschutes River, crossing the Metolius River, and continuing south past present-day Bend at Tumalo Creek. The group then moved up the Little Deschutes River near Sunriver and La Pine, eventually turning southeast into the Great Basin Desert.

Frémont was as taken with the scenic grandeur of Central Oregon as those who came after him, recording in his journal for December 2, 1843: "In the first rays of the sun, the mountain peaks [Mount Jefferson and the Three Sisters] this morning presented a beautiful appearance, the snow being entirely covered with a hue of rosy gold."

While some historians regard Frémont as less an explorer than a follower of already-discovered trails, and as a shameless self-promoter, the detailed accounts and maps resulting from his Western explorations played a substantial role in fueling public interest in establishing new settlements in Oregon and California.

Wagons West, Wagons Lost

In the late 1830s, economic depression and widespread disease including malaria, tuberculosis, cholera, dysentery, typhoid and scarlet fever, diphtheria, and a host of other maladies were sweeping the American Midwest. A spate of severe flooding had damaged farmlands and precipitated

crop failures in the upper Mississippi Valley. By 1837, crop prices and land values had crashed. Farmers were losing their homes and their lands to foreclosure.

Meanwhile, word was getting out about the Oregon Country and the fertile Willamette Valley, just west of the Cascade Mountains. It was a place to begin a new life of health and prosperity—with free land to boot. The U.S. government was giving 640 acres of land in western Oregon's lush valleys to each family who would settle there.

The Great Migration west began as a trickle. Then the floodgates opened. Between 1840 and 1860, 53,000 immigrants braved the 2,000-plus-mile journey across the continent by oxen-drawn wagon to settle in Western Oregon. The trip typically began in Independence, Missouri, and paralleled, to a great extent, much of the route of today's Interstates 80 and 84, before intersecting with the Snake River on the Oregon-Idaho border at what is now Ontario, Oregon. From there, the wagon trains forded the Snake River into Oregon, pushing ahead through the Blue Mountains, then connecting with the Columbia River and following that great waterway down to Fort Vancouver (now Vancouver, Washington), which served as the immigrants' final staging area for settlement in the Willamette Valley.

The westering wagons bypassed Central Oregon, following instead the long and arduous, but well-established, Oregon Trail. That was the route, that is, until

1845, when the survivors of Meek's Lost Wagon Train came creaking through Central Oregon on a hellish journey across the Oregon desert. They were in search of a shortcut to the promised land. Instead, they found misery and death and gave birth to a legend.

With three grueling months of travel across the Great Plains behind them, the members of a 480-wagon immigrant party were encamped at Fort Boise, a way station along the Oregon Trail in what is now the state of Idaho, and were preparing to launch the last leg of their journey to a new life.

As fate would have it, the Reverend Elijah White was at the fort, passing through on his way back east on church business. Chatting with the bone-weary wagoneers around their bright and cheerful campfires, he told them how they could shave many weeks off the final leg of their journey by striking out directly west, across the Oregon High Desert, instead of the longer, albeit safer, traditional route. The possibility of a quick conclusion to their journey was music to the immigrants' ears. No matter that White personally knew nothing about such a wagon route, or that there was, in fact, no such wagon road. In fact, no wagon train had ever before tried to make the crossing.

The immigrants discussed the idea among themselves and made a decision. About 800 people in 200 wagons would give it a try. Former mountain man Stephen Hall

Meek, who was traveling with the party, volunteered to lead the group for $5.00 per wagon (though he, too, knew nothing about such a wagon route and had never been through that area).

On August 24, 1845, the wagon train left the Snake River on the Idaho border and struck out across the desert of Eastern Oregon. All went fairly well until they reached Wagontire Mountain, southwest of present-day Burns. Water supplies were low, and springs and streams were scarce commodities on the dry, sagebrush flats. People sickened and died. The wagon masters began to doubt the pathfinding abilities of their guide.

While the company was camped at a place called the Sinks of Lost Creek, Meek was interrogated. It quickly became apparent he had no idea where they were and was completely unfamiliar with the area. A small group of wagons had set out ahead of the main party, but returned, terrified by the unending bleakness of the country before them. One hundred men were sent to search for water. They scoured the desert for seven days, returning empty-handed.

Anger toward Meek ran high, and a group of the immigrants planned to hang him early one morning (fashioning a hanging tree from wagon tongues, since there were no trees readily available). But Meek and his wife were saved when some sympathetic immigrants hid them in one of the wagons.

After bitter arguments and prayer, the party recognized that it was foolhardy to continue across the desert with no guide and little prospect of finding water. The decision was made to head northwest, back to the Columbia River and the Oregon Trail. The wagon train split into two groups, with one heading toward the Crooked River—camping one night on the site that would eventually become Prineville—the other going west to the Deschutes River. Both parties then turned north, reaching The Dalles on the Columbia River in early October, having left at least 70 of their number buried along the trail in the Central Oregon wilderness. The "shortcut" had taken 46 days for them to travel from Fort Boise to The Dalles—at least twice as long as it took by the established route.

The story doesn't end there. Somewhere along the way, in the vast Central Oregon wilderness, a few of the immigrant children discovered some pretty yellow rocks and brought them back to camp in a blue bucket. Later, upon closer examination, they were found to be gold nuggets. The only problem was that nobody could quite remember where they were found. When the survivors of Meek's Lost Wagon Train finally reached the Willamette Valley and told their story, the legend of the Lost Blue Bucket Mine was born. Throughout the past 150 years, many have retraced the wagon ruts of that ill-fated company, searching in vain for the fabled gold mine. The only evidence of its existence is the story of the pioneer immigrants, desperately lost and dying of thirst in a vast wilderness, who found a bucket of gold that they would gladly have traded, if they could have, for a bucket of water.

Staking a Claim

The Willamette Valley was beginning to get a little crowded by the early 1860s, especially for owners of large herds of cattle, who were having difficulty finding grazing lands that weren't already occupied by other settlers. So these pioneers, who had rushed past Central Oregon on their way to settle the valley, now cast their eyes on the area's rich grasslands—an ideal place to fatten their cattle during the summer months.

Central Oregon had not been completely ignored during the previous decade. In 1853 another lost wagon train, under the leadership of Elijah Elliott, had passed through. They, too, had taken what had become known as the "Meek Cutoff" at Ontario, eventually reaching the Deschutes River and crossing the Cascade Mountains near Willamette Pass, southwest of La Pine. Although they deviated from the route Meek's original party took, they suffered the same hardships and deprivations.

Two years later an expedition, which included Lieutenants George Crook and Phil Sheridan (both of whom would later become famous in the Western Indian wars), surveyed Central Oregon in search of a potential railroad route from the Willamette Valley to Sacramento, California.

In 1861 gold was discovered in northeastern Oregon, and would-be miners flocked from Western Oregon towns over the Cascade Mountain passes to the goldfields. Gold had also been discovered in Idaho during this same period, which only increased the eastward stream of miners.

Felix Scott Jr., a businessman from the Willamette Valley city of Eugene, decided there was money to be made hauling goods by wagon to the goldfields of Idaho, then selling these needed supplies to the miners for a good price. But to do that efficiently, he needed a direct route over the Cascades. So in 1862, with 9 wagons filled with supplies and 900 head of cattle trailing along, Scott and his partners hacked and picked their way over the lava-covered McKenzie Pass, arriving in Central Oregon in the fall. Because winter was closing in, and not wishing to be caught by bad weather on the high plains that lay between them and the Idaho goldfields, the party hunkered down along Trout Creek, a tributary of the Deschutes River, and became the first white people to spend the winter in Central Oregon.

But it was in 1864 that the Willamette Valley cattlemen finally found their opportunity to exploit the lush grazing land that lay just over the mountains. On March 12, 1864, the Willamette Valley and Cascade Mountain Wagon Road Company was incorporated by a group of stockmen and farmers, who would build a road to bring their horses, sheep, and cattle to Central Oregon's summer rangeland.

Construction began in 1865, taking the McKenzie Pass route. It was opened as a toll road in 1872. The toll for using the road was $2.00 for a wagon drawn by two horses, $2.50 for one drawn by four horses, $1.00 for a man on a horse, 10 cents per head for cattle and horses, and 5 cents for each sheep.

The first settlers began moving to Central Oregon in 1863. As new roads were built over the mountain passes, making travel easier, growing numbers of people began viewing Central Oregon as a desirable place to settle. A series of laws passed by the federal government, which were designed to encourage the settlement and economic growth of the West, further spurred people to the region in search of homes. The Homestead Act of 1862 allowed a U.S. citizen to purchase 160 acres of Western lands for about $16 after having lived on and cultivated that land for five years. He could purchase it for $1.25 per acre after 14 months.

Other laws that allowed settlers to gain title to public domain lands in Central Oregon and throughout the West included the Mineral Land Act of 1866, the Timber Culture Act of 1873, the Desert Land Act of 1877, and the Timber and Stone Act of 1878. Although there were strict rules and procedures by which individuals were to obtain land, fraud was rampant. Unscrupulous individuals and businesses used these laws to illegally transfer vast amounts of public lands into private ownership.

Businessmen who set up small mercantiles on the plains to sell goods to passing miners were among the first permanent settlers in Central Oregon, along with stockmen who laid claim to the best grazing lands along stream and river bottoms. The homesteaders, who would form the bedrock of Central Oregon's permanent white population, soon followed.

Indian Wars

But these early settlers were not moving into an empty land. The Indian tribes who called Central Oregon home for thousands of years watched with growing alarm as increasing numbers of white settlers came into their country.

The Warm Springs and Wasco tribes of Central Oregon had a history of friendliness toward whites. In 1855 they signed a treaty with the U.S. government that officially recognized them as the Confederated Tribes of Warm Springs, established the Warm Springs Indian Reservation, and granted them extensive hunting, fishing, and water rights throughout their historic homelands. The U.S. Army had even issued an order in 1856 forbidding white settlements east of the Cascades in order to keep the two races separated and to minimize conflicts. But that order was rescinded in 1858, as Willamette Valley settlers began to take an interest in Central Oregon.

While the Warm Springs tribes retained their cooperative and friendly relations with whites, the Paiutes were a different story. Ranging throughout Central and Southeastern Oregon, the Paiutes resented the encroachment on their lands by miners and settlers. Paiute Chief Paulina led his band of 50 or 60 warriors against miners, homesteaders, and the U.S. Army through much of the 1860s, burning cabins and killing their occupants, stealing livestock, and plundering supply trains on the way to the goldfields. Between 1860 and 1867, Chief Paulina made life in Central Oregon exceedingly unsafe; he attacked residents of the Warm Springs Indian Reservation as readily as he did white settlers.

By 1865, Indian attacks on settlers and miners had become so serious that the army was forced to set up military outposts throughout Central and Eastern Oregon. Soldiers guarded the growing number of immigrant roads that were being built east of the Cascades as well as the local white population, which by then lived under a virtual state of siege.

Despite almost constant pursuit by the army, Warm Springs Indian scouts, and local ranchers, Chief Paulina always managed to elude his pursuers, vanishing into the wilderness after each attack. Then, on April 25, 1867, Paulina's luck ran out. A group of ranchers found him and his warriors along Trout Creek, near the present-day town of Ashwood, eating a butchered cow they had rustled from a local stockman. The ranchers opened fire and the Indians scattered, leaving one of their number lying still on the ground—Chief Paulina.

With Paulina's death, Indian attacks in Central Oregon ceased, though other bands of Paiutes continued their war against the white invaders in Eastern and Southern Oregon as well as in parts of Idaho, Nevada, and Northern California. It wasn't until 1878 that Indian uprisings in Oregon were finally extinguished.

Izee Sheep Shooters and Other Civic Organizations

It's a coincidence of history that gold was discovered in northeastern Oregon in 1861, at about the same time that good grazing lands were growing scarce in the Willamette Valley. Western Oregon ranchers were moving herds of cattle over the McKenzie and Santiam Passes to feed the mining camps and to exploit the untouched grazing lands east of the mountains.

More than 100,000 head of cattle were brought over from the Willamette Valley during the 1860s; in the process, the great cattle empires of the High Desert were founded. By the late 1860s there were many cattle and sheep ranches in Central Oregon, leading to disputes over access to the best grazing lands. This eventually sparked a vicious Central Oregon range war that peaked between 1902 and 1906.

Cattle ranchers charged that grazing sheep destroyed the native range grasses, leaving the land barren in their wake. Central Oregon sheepmen and cattlemen also competed for the rich grazing to be had during the summer in the high country meadows, each racing to get their animals to these coveted pastures as soon as the weather permitted. Competition for forage became more intense and acrimonious as many thousands of animals crowded the public domain rangelands. The cattlemen wanted the sheep off "their" rangeland. It was only a matter of time before the situation exploded.

The first anti-sheep campaign was organized in Grant County in the mid-1890s by a group of cattlemen who called themselves the Izee Sheep Shooters. Their mission was to keep sheep off nearby summer rangeland; their strategy was straightforward and deadly. They would surprise a sheep camp, capture the herders and camp tenders, blindfold them, lash them to a tree, then shoot the entire herd of sheep.

The work of the Izee Sheep Shooters earned such a good reputation among Central Oregon cattle ranchers that in July 1896, a representative of the group was invited to help Crook County stockmen organize a similar endeavor. Thus, in a fashion, the Crook County Sheepshooters Association was incorporated.

Their charter was as simple as their sheep-control methods, and all members of the association had to agree to them. If a sheepherder was killed during a mission, he would be buried on the spot. If one of their own were killed, he would be brought home to be buried, with no mention of how he met his demise. And if any association member was captured by the law and brought to trial, he was duty-bound to lie on the witness stand about his involvement with the group. Only a few of the 30 or so stockmen who attended the association's first meeting declined to join.

Next they established "deadlines"—boundaries on the rangeland over which no sheep or sheepmen would be allowed to pass. They marked these lines of death with great blazes on trees. Any sheep caught on the wrong side of the deadlines would be shot, and the sheepherder would be at risk of execution as well.

Having worked out the rules and the boundaries, the Crook County Sheepshooters Association was ready to begin the slaughter. In July 1903, they killed more than 2,400 sheep at Benjamin Lake on the Crook-Lake County line. In January 1904, 500 sheep were killed on a ranch near the town of Paulina. In February 1904, under cover of darkness, six armed men shot, clubbed, and stabbed 3,000 sheep that had been placed in a corral for the night at Silver Lake, 65 miles southeast of Bend. Another 2,300 Silver Lake–area sheep were killed by 10 masked men who first captured and

The Bend Fire Station was built between 1908 and 1909 and remained in use until recently.

PHOTO: JIM YUSKAVITCH

bound the herders. In August 1905, more than 1,000 sheep on Big Summit Prairie in the Ochoco Mountains were killed.

The harassment of the sheepmen continued unabated. The sheep shooters would try to stampede the flocks at night, drive them over cliffs, destroy sheep camps, and snipe at passing herders and their flocks. At one point, in July 1904, a group of sheep owners from nearby Wasco County met with the Crook County cattlemen to try to work out their differences. But the meeting was a bust, and within a few days the Crook County Sheepshooters shot 64 sheep to death on Mill Creek, 15 miles east of Prineville.

Members of the Central Oregon Wool Grower's Association were incensed and offered rewards totalling $1,500 for information leading to the arrest and conviction of the sheep killers. But it was no

deterrent. Barely 6 months later another 500 sheep were executed by gunmen in Crook County. The last of the killings occurred in Lake County in April 1906, when masked men killed about 1,800 sheep, driving many of the doomed animals over the edge of a nearby cliff to fall to their deaths.

The Central Oregon range war that had claimed more than 10,000 sheep was finally ended. But not by the law or a negotiated truce between sheepmen and cattlemen. In 1893 the federal government had created the Cascade Forest Reserve, which encompassed much of what is now the Deschutes and Ochoco National Forests. In November 1906 the forest supervisor, whose headquarters was in Prineville, received orders to divide the public rangelands into grazing allotments, giving sheepmen and cattlemen with a history of grazing in the area legal rights to graze on specified sections of the forest. With both camps now guaranteed exclusive use of a certain amount of grazing land, the cattlemen were no longer threatened by encroaching herds of sheep, and they abandoned their ruthless and bloody campaign. The identities of those who participated in the sheep killings as members of the Crook County Sheepshooters Association were never discovered.

The Town Builders

By 1916 most of the land that had been made available by the government for homesteading in Central Oregon had been claimed. The best, well-watered lands had been claimed by the first settlers, decades before. Those that came late and took what was left were discovering that, in the High Desert, you couldn't grow much of value on land without water. Central Oregon was the home of many a novice farmer who was slowly going broke. By the 1920s, when a period of drought gripped the region and springs and watering holes dried up, most of these farmers would be gone, their land claims taken by the county for payment of taxes or reverting back to the federal government.

There were towns, too, in places that once were just a collection of small cabins. Bend was incorporated in 1904 and had a population of 500. Redmond, 15 miles to the north, was incorporated in 1905. La Pine was developed by a speculator who gambled that a railroad would eventually be built through the town—a gamble he lost. Sisters was platted in 1901, although there had been people living in the area since the 1860s, when the army established Camp Polk 3 miles away during the Indian wars. Prineville got its first post office in 1871 under the name Prine, after Barney Prine, the town's founder. In 1910 its population was 1,042.

The three counties that make up Central Oregon were in place as well. Deschutes County, named after the waterway early fur trappers called "The River of the Falls," was established in 1916. Crook County, named for Maj. Gen. George Crook, a veteran of the Civil War and the Indian wars in the West, was created in 1882. Jefferson County, named after Mount Jefferson, which had been named by explorers Lewis and Clark in honor of President Thomas Jefferson, was created in 1914.

The railroad, too, had finally come to Bend—vital for the city's growth and prosperity because it allowed the export of the natural timber and lumber resources that were so plentiful in Central Oregon. For years, Central Oregon communities had lobbied and schemed for the development of a railroad into the region.

In 1909 James J. Hill of Great Northern, Northern Pacific, and Burlington Railroads began construction of tracks down the west side of the Deschutes River from The Dalles, on the Columbia River. He intended to lay tracks through Bend, all the way down to San Francisco. On the east side of the river, Edward H. Harriman of the Union Pacific and Southern Pacific Railroads was doing the same thing.

Competition between the two companies and their work crews was fierce and included some gunplay. But Hill had the upper hand. He had secured the right-of-way for crossing the Crooked River, and Harriman was forced to negotiate a deal whereby both companies agreed to use a single track south from the community of Metolius in Jefferson County. The "golden spike" was driven by James J. Hill himself

Insiders' Tip

When driving around Central Oregon watch for the brown OREGON HISTORY signs posted at turnouts and scenic viewpoints. They'll give you an overview of important historic events that took place at various locations.

Long-abandoned homesteads scattered throughout Central Oregon are poignant reminders of early settlers who were driven out by the droughts and hard economic times of the 1920s and '30s.

PHOTO: JIM YUSKAVITCH

at the railroad track's end in Bend on October 1, 1911. It would be another 16 years before the rails would be extended farther south.

It was estimated that Central Oregon contained 26 billion board feet of lumber just waiting to be harvested from its vast ponderosa pine forests. Fully aware of the economic potential, private speculators had been buying up local timberlands since the mid-1890s. A significant amount of these lands were obtained fraudulently, through the abuse of federal laws that made public lands available for homesteaders at low prices. These programs were intended by the federal government to encourage and assist families in settling the West. But commercial interests often used them to obtain huge amounts of valuable land in Central Oregon and throughout the West.

One of the most notoriously abused of these federal programs was the Timber and Stone Act of 1878. This act permitted settlers to buy up to 160 acres of land for $2.50 per acre in order to obtain the timber and stone they required for the development of their farms and ranches. Initially, the act was used little by local settlers. But in 1902, when timberland speculation reached its peak in Central Oregon, many claims were filed by people who had no intention of settling in the area. Instead, they obtained ownership of their 160 acres and then sold the land to timber companies. Some of these scam artists were even in the employ of the timber companies.

Today it's difficult to tell how many acres of private forestland were obtained illegally. However, the problem became so acute that in July 1903 President Theodore

Roosevelt withdrew Central Oregon timberlands from the public domain; Roosevelt established the national forests program three years later to protect the forests from such unscrupulous dealings.

With the arrival of a railroad line in Bend, lumber, milled from locally cut trees, could now be economically shipped to outside markets. Although there had been a number of small mills in the Central Oregon area since the turn of the 20th century, they were primarily used to supply local lumber needs. The railroad provided the economic incentive for the big operators to move into the area. A railroad was so economically important that the city of Prineville actually financed its own railroad trunk line in order to ship locally milled lumber to Oregon's major transcontinental railroad lines along the Columbia River and then to market.

The two largest lumber mills in Bend were the Shevlin-Hixon mill and the Brooks-Scanlon mill. Both began operations in 1916 and quickly expanded. By 1923, Brooks-Scanlon had two mills in operation; directly across the Deschutes River, Shevlin-Hixon had three. During the 1920s, both companies combined were cutting up to 500 million board feet each year.

The establishment of these large mills (as well as many smaller ones) in Central Oregon communities had a significant economic impact, providing employment for hundreds as well as supporting numerous local businesses that provided related goods and services. With the opening of the Shevlin-Hixon and Brooks-Scanlon mills, Bend's population swelled to 5,414 by 1920. Prineville was actually seeing its population shrink before the big lumber mills began moving in during the late 1920s.

But the most valuable natural resource in Central Oregon was water. This fact was recognized by the earliest settlers, who staked their claims along rivers and streams whenever possible since there wasn't enough rainfall in the region to support crops, and underground water was often hundreds of feet beneath the surface. The rivers could be tapped for water to irrigate crops.

In the 1870s, ranchers and farmers irrigated their fields by digging ditches to divert water from nearby streams. But as the century came to a close, water development in Central Oregon became more organized—irrigation companies and water districts formed to more efficiently collect and distribute water throughout the region.

This rush to irrigate the High Desert was bolstered by passage of the Carey Act in 1894, which allowed families to receive ownership of 160 acres of desert land if they improved at least one-eighth of it by irrigation. In other words, settlers would be given a substantial piece of arid land and the right to use river water to irrigate it. All the beneficiaries of the Carey Act had to do was pay to get the water to their properties.

That's where the irrigation companies entered the picture. Using money raised by the sale of stocks, they built the canals that delivered water to ranchers and farmers throughout Central Oregon—although it took half a century to complete the job. Finally, Central Oregon bloomed and prospered, as land that was once dry and brown now glistened green with crops of alfalfa, hay, wheat, and potatoes.

Times They Were A-changin'

With its basic infrastructure and core population in place, Central Oregon set about harvesting its bounty. Cutting and milling timber was a primary economic activity as was producing livestock and raising such crops as potatoes, peppermint, alfalfa, hay, and wheat. Central Oregonians were comfortable and satisfied with the lifestyle they and their pioneering descendants had carved from this splendid piece of real estate. But big changes were on the horizon.

The first ones were economic. By the 1950s, years of intensive logging had taken their toll on Central Oregon's timber supply. It was becoming clear that there were not enough trees left in the forest to sustain all the area's mills—at least not at the rate they were being cut. One of the first mills to close was Shevlin-Hixon, which sold

A Walk on the Historic Side

In spite of Bend's rapid recent growth, the influx of new residents and booming construction of new residential and commercial buildings during the past decade or so, you'll still find reminders of the city's rough-and-tumble pioneer days in the form of the nearly 40 historic buildings that are scattered throughout the downtown area.

Dating anywhere from 1908 to 1938, these old homes and business establishments were built in a variety of architectural styles including Craftsman, Mediterranean, progressive American, Colonial Revival, American Foursquare, Brick Vernacular, Mission, and many more. Nine are listed on the National Register of Historic Places. Each has a story to tell that speaks not only of Bend's history and early development, but also of the lives, joys, and hardships of the people who once lived here.

Take, for example, the Bend Amateur Athletic Club building on Northwest Wall and Northwest Idaho Streets. Built in 1918 in an eclectic architectural style, it boasted a bowling alley, auditorium, lounge, and library, and was intended to be a cultural and recreational center for local residents. But an influenza epidemic hit the city the same year the building was completed, forcing it to be used first as an infirmary, where volunteers tended to the sick with camphorated oil, quinine, and moonshine whiskey.

Members of the Trinity Episcopal Church met in the Old Liberty Theater, which was built in 1917 on Northwest Wall Street, until they raised the money to build a church 4 blocks down the street in 1929. But even with their own house of worship, everything wasn't a bed of roses. The large cross on the steeple was a frequent target of lightning, and members of the congregation were constantly rushing to douse the

The Pine Tavern, a popular downtown Bend eatery, was built in 1936 in English tavern style.

PHOTO: JIM YUSKAVITCH

blazes that inevitably broke out at their church after a big storm. They finally erected a lighting rod, and the church caught fire no more.

Fire was always a serious threat to early Western towns, as buildings were usually made of wood. Around 1919 and 1920, local builders began to construct buildings of brick to reduce the city's overall vulnerability to fires. The Bean Building, also on Northwest Wall Street, is an example of the structures built during this phase.

Of course, it's no small irony that buildings in Bend were beginning to be constructed of brick during the very time that the local timber industry was fueling the town's economic boom. That heyday is long gone, but you can see some of its former glory at the Shevlin-Hixon House on Northwest Congress Street. Built in 1920 by the Shevlin-Hixon Company as housing for its managers, it's a grand example of the American Foursquare architectural style. Another house that hails from the heady times when timber was king is the J. P. Keyes house. Built in 1912, it was the home of John Pease Keyes, vice president and general manager of another Bend-area timber giant, Brooks-Scanlon Company. Keyes was a pioneer of the Western timber industry and among the first to recognize, in the late 1880s, the economic potential of Central Oregon's pine forests.

The Deschutes Historical Society and the Bend Chamber of Commerce have teamed up to produce *Heritage Walk*—a great self-guided historical walking-tour booklet covering the downtown Bend area. It's divided into two loop walks that begin and end at Drake Park. Each route covers about 10 blocks and will take you to a total of 45 historic buildings or the locations of former structures important to Bend's past. In addition to providing a photograph and historical vignette with each building, the booklet is filled with fascinating short articles about Bend's history and the people who helped make Central Oregon what it is today. You can pick one up at the Central Oregon Welcome Center, 63085 North U.S. Highway 97, Bend. It's well worth the $3.00 purchase price.

And if you are a patron of history, you may want to sponsor a Heritage Walk historical site. Sponsorships are $1,000 for individuals and families and $1,500 for businesses. The money is dedicated to preserving Bend's historical heritage. For more information on becoming a sponsor, contact the Bend Chamber of Commerce at (541) 382–3221.

its Central Oregon holdings to Brooks-Scanlon in 1950. More than 800 mill workers lost their jobs in that shake-up. But the industry rebounded by developing ways to make new wood products out of scraps that in the past would have been regarded as waste. Plants that made particle board, veneer, plywood, and molding were established in Bend, Prineville, Madras, and Redmond in the 1950s and 1960s.

Public opinion regarding the industry shifted during the 1980s and 1990s, with many people and groups starting to view forests as more than sources of wood products. There has been a growing appreciation of the role forests play in providing habitat for fish and wildlife as well as recreational opportunities and aesthetics, and this has put immense pressure on the timber industry to scale back its logging activities and adopt less environmentally destructive techniques.

Lawsuits brought by environmental groups to protect these newly recognized forest values have resulted in a decrease in the amount of timber cut from national forestlands. Nevertheless, the timber industry continues to be an important economic force and is regarded as a primary industry in all three Central Oregon counties. More than 3,000 people are employed in the wood products industry in Deschutes, Jefferson, and Crook Counties. Wood product–related businesses are

The Old Post Office, built in Bend in 1932, also housed the headquarters of the Deschutes National Forest. PHOTO: JIM YUSKAVITCH

currently among Central Oregon's 50 largest employers.

Things have changed on the agricultural front as well. Although recently completed dams on the Deschutes and Crooked Rivers were bringing water to irrigate lands that were previously not farmable, advances in the technology used for harvesting and processing crops were eliminating many farm jobs. Farmers without access to adequate amounts of water found it necessary to take part-time jobs in town to make ends meet.

There were social changes, too. In the early 1970s, outsiders started to discover Central Oregon's natural beauty and quality of life. And they were moving here. Some were retirees; some were professionals, who found work as doctors, lawyers, and engineers. But many were young people, willing to work any job they could find if it meant they could afford to stay. In 1960 the population of Deschutes County was 23,100. The following 10 years added another 7,300 people. By 1980 the county population was 62,142.

Recession in the early 1980s slowed the influx into Central Oregon. But as the national economy improved during the latter part of the decade, new waves of people arrived. Houses and land were still relatively cheap, and the construction industry boomed. By 1990 Deschutes County's population was 74,958.

The most recent U.S. Census Bureau figures show all three Central Oregon counties among the 10 fastest-growing in Oregon over the past decade, with Deschutes at number one. Deschutes County's population is 109,600; Jefferson County's population is 18,600; and 18,150 people live in Crook County. In terms of growth, these figures peg population increases for Deschutes, Jefferson, and Crook Counties at 46.2, 36, and 28.6 percent, respectively, since 1990. Central Oregon's population is expected to reach nearly 200,000 by the year 2010.

Outdoor recreation and other leisure activities had always been an important part of the Central Oregon experience. For decades, local residents had hunted, fished, camped, and climbed the mountains here. People from other parts of Oregon had been vacationing here for decades as well, first coming by wagon and later by automobile. But the newcomers were more often than not enticed to move to Central Oregon specifically for the recreational opportunities and the beautiful environment.

Resorts and resort communities such as Black Butte Ranch, Sunriver, Inn of the Seventh Mountain, Kah-Nee-Ta, and Mt. Bachelor Ski Area were developed to meet the demand for the leisure activities and high-quality lifestyles new residents and visitors were seeking.

Mt. Bachelor Ski Area was among the first of these recreation-oriented developments built in Central Oregon. Its dedication ceremony was held on January 8, 1956. By the early 1970s, the major resort communities of Sunriver and Black Butte Ranch had been developed as well as the Inn of the Seventh Mountain, which was constructed on Century Drive at the edge of the Deschutes National Forest to serve the skiers who flocked to Mount Bachelor during the winter and the growing number of summer visitors.

Over the next 25 years, tourism blossomed in Central Oregon as more and more people discovered its natural beauty and recreational opportunities, pursuing such activities as camping, fishing, mountaineering, river rafting, horseback riding, cross-country skiing, and mountain biking. As golf has grown in popularity in recent years, Central Oregon has responded with the development of new golf courses and new resort communities that offer prospective residents the opportunity to live within a few dozen steps from the fairway of their choice. Central Oregon has no less than 24 golf courses, with more on the drawing board. (See our various chapters on recreation in Central Oregon, including individual chapters on Snowplay, Golf, Parks, and Fishing, for more information.)

Today tourism is as important to the Central Oregon economy as the area's traditional, natural resource–based industries. Spending by tourists visiting Deschutes County each year regularly exceeds $300 million, while Crook and Jefferson Coun-

> ## Insiders' Tip
> The Three Sisters Mountains that dominate the Central Oregon skyline were originally called Faith, Hope, and Charity by early pioneers. Today they are known as North, Middle, and South Sister.

ties come in at $20 million and $53 million, respectively.

As the 21sth century unfolds, Central Oregon has seen many changes. Once an area that westering pioneers hurried past, it is now a focus for a new migration of people seeking a better place to live, work, and play. The challenge for the future will be to build a strong, sustainable economy without destroying the things that make Central Oregon the place that it is.

What tomorrow will bring we don't know. That chapter of Central Oregon history is still being written.

If you feel like delving a little deeper into Central Oregon history, our historical societies are the places to start. They maintain collections and displays of artifacts, books, manuscripts, and photographs. Perhaps most importantly, they have knowledgeable historians who can help you better understand the past and its impact on the present and the future.

Contact the Oregon Historical Society, 1200 Southwest Park Avenue, Portland, (503) 222-1741, www.ohs.org; Deschutes County Historical Center, 129 Northwest Idaho Avenue, Bend, (541) 389-1813; or Crook County Historical Society, 246 North Main Street, Prineville, (541) 447-3715, www.bowmanmuseum.org.

Hotels and Motels

Amenities and Policies

Hotel and Motel Listings

In the late 1990s Central Oregon saw a tremendous boom in motel construction, caused mainly by the expansion of national chains into our area. The demand has not quite caught up to availability, which for most of the year makes lodging a very low-stress issue for visitors. These days visitors will find an excellent selection of high-quality lodging throughout Central Oregon and typically a few days advance notice for reservations will suffice. If you are a bit flexible, you can often show up in the afternoon and find a comfortable place to stay that night, with the exception of major holidays and a few major-event weekends in summer. We've come a long way since the Oregon Trail days when you were lucky if you pitched your tent next to an entrepreneur who sold hot meals and hot baths.

Tourist volume has a tremendous impact on prices and, obviously, on availability. Our tourist trade is seasonal—summer is our high season and winter our second-highest. Spring and fall are usually very quiet. It sounds like a simple formula, but tourist volume isn't quite as predictable as this might suggest. Weather and annual events also play an important role in determining how busy our towns are, as they affect motel rates and availability. For example, motel rates can go up as much as double for the Sisters Quilt Show on the second Saturday in July. Rooms for that weekend are booked a year in advance. One proprietor told us that on quilt show weekend you aren't paying for the room, you are paying for the date. Two other special events that can have a major impact on lodging are the Sisters Rodeo on the second weekend in June and the Deschutes County Fair the first weekend in August. (See our Annual Events chapter for more on all these happenings.) Holidays are also extremely busy times for area hotels and motels. In spring and fall, our slow seasons, it's possible to find some real deals, especially if you speak directly with our local establishments instead of going through a centralized reservation system. Our price codes reflect average summer weekend rates.

Oregon, Washington, Idaho, California, and British Columbia in Canada all work together to stagger school spring breaks through March and April so that all the families don't hit the tourist areas simultaneously. Spring break does cause some rates to go up.

The national chains publish prices for each season. They offer the best values during the peak season, but they don't lower prices much in the off-season periods. They sometimes raise their rates by 10 to 20 percent for special events. Because of the consistency in rates and general high standards for comfort, these motels make up the bulk of our listings.

Prices at the mom-and-pop motels can fluctuate on the spur of the moment. Proprietors watch the vacancy signs up and down the street; when they see a few NO signs light up, they may raise their rates a bit. On special-event weekends, when many motels may be fully booked a year in advance, some smaller places might raise their rates significantly. When business is slow they will cut prices drastically. Although the room decor is usually bare bones, we include at least one or two small motels for each geographic area because most of the time they offer the lowest rates.

Amenities and Policies

Unless otherwise noted, expect our listed hotels and motels to have smoking and nonsmoking rooms, cable TV with remote control, phones, air-conditioning, a bathtub with shower, in-room coffee, free continental breakfast, and barrier-free rooms. Many places allow small pets in the rooms (some for an extra charge as noted), but none of the units we checked out seemed to be the worse for the experience.

The term "suites" is used very liberally by our local establishments. It sometimes refers to a single room that may have a sitting area and/or a small refrigerator and microwave to distinguish it from a "room." Be sure to ask for specifics. Regarding credit cards, this is probably the only type of business in Oregon where most everyone (unless noted) accepts Visa, MasterCard, American Express, Discover, and even Diners Club.

For lodging options with on-site recreation, please see our Resorts, Ranches, and Vacation Rentals chapter. Our Bed-and-Breakfasts chapter offers even more possibilities.

Price Code

Our pricing key reflects the average summer weekend rate. Special annual events and holidays might push prices higher than what is noted here. If you intend to visit Central Oregon for these special occasions, we strongly advise you to make your arrangements well ahead of time.

Room rates are for two people in one room with a queen- or king-size bed. The room tax is included in our code. Some motels have suites or fancier accommodations that cost much more than a basic room. These were not taken into consideration in the pricing key. Ask for details if you're looking for something larger or fancier. For all of our listed hotels and motels, parking and continental breakfast are provided free, and most places do not charge for local calls. If small pets are accepted, it is at the manager's discretion, and there is usually an extra fee as noted. Here's the price breakdown.

$	$35 to $65
$$	$66 to $100
$$$	$101 to $175
$$$$	$176 and higher

Hotel and Motel Listings

Bend

You can't go wrong basing your visit to Central Oregon in Bend. The city has more services and amenities than all the other towns in our area combined. U.S. Highway 97, the main north-south route through town, has 6 miles of commercial development. Add to that a lovely downtown area and at least another 4 miles of development along U.S. 20. There are fast-food restaurants and fine eateries, a regional hospital, national variety store chains, cinemas, and dozens of local shops. Between Awbrey Glen Golf Club, Lost Tracks Golf Club, Orion Greens Golf Course, and River's Edge, golfers can swing away at a combined 63 holes of golf right in town.

Bend also has an array of motels. We have chosen the best lodgings available in a variety of price ranges.

Bend Cascade Hostel $
19 Southwest Century Drive
(541) 389-3813, (800) 299-3813, direct

It's amazing that lodging rates as low as these can even allow for a toll-free number! Granted, you will sleep in a bunk bed in an austere, single-sex dormitory and share a common bathroom (very clean, and one for each gender). And they'll charge you an extra dollar for a small bundle of mismatched sheets and a towel if you didn't bring your own.

Regardless, $14 a night year-round is pretty incredible. People of all ages and walks of life visit our local hostel—some for the price and others for the communal experience. Kids under age 18 are half-price. There are 43 beds, including one room for a family with a double-size lower bunk. When the situation calls for it, another 10 people can sack out on the futons in the living room.

A couple of coin-operated laundry machines, one common-area telephone, and kitchen privileges (which include cleaning privileges) are the main conveniences. A key draw is the big living-room area complete with books and games. It's a place where visitors from all over can get to know one another. Don't even think about bringing your pet.

They require at least 24-hour advance reservations with a credit card, or two weeks by mail with a check. The best way to get in touch with Mike, the manager, is

In Central Oregon there's always plenty of time to stop and smell the roses. PHOTO: JIM YUSKAVITCH

the old-fashioned way—by phone. Master-Card, Visa, and Discover are the accepted credit cards.

Best Inn and Suites (Formerly Comfort Inn) $$
61200 South U.S. Highway 97 Business
(541) 388–2227, (800) 228–5150, centralized reservations

A very cozy woodstove surrounded by chairs and couches in the lobby provides a warm welcome on cold dark nights, and a side table with cookies and coffee are a nice touch. Rooms are decorated in burgundy Indian prints, and furnishings include a table and chairs. Overall the accommodations here were comfortable. Pets are accepted at no extra charge, and if you actually bring the pet in with you to the front desk, Rover or Fluffy will get a complimentary biscuit. Bargain hunters will be glad to know that this motel is on the south end of town close to the Bend Factory Outlets, as well as some fast-food places.

This motel used to be affiliated with Comfort Inn; the management and owners have not changed. Partly due to the fact that Best Inn and Suites has the only 24-hour pool and spa in town (and we'd add partly because they're nice folks) their summer weekends book well in advance.

Best Western Entrada Lodge $$
19221 Century Drive
(541) 382–4080, (800) 528–1234, centralized reservations
www.bestwestern.com

Nestled in ponderosa pines 4 miles west of Bend, on the road to Mt. Bachelor Ski Area (which is another 18 miles), this motel offers a lovely summer or winter retreat. In the main lobby, with its 1970s decor, is a large fireplace pit, a breakfast area with wood tables for the free continental breakfast, and coffee, tea, and cookies in the afternoon.

Several tan buildings with shake roofs house the rooms, which are good-sized, comfortably furnished, and look out onto a park-like setting. A coin laundry, fax, and photocopying are available, and the rooms have dataports. The pool is open during warm weather; the outdoor hot tub is open all year. Pets are accepted for a $5.00 charge.

Best Western Inn and Suites of Bend $$
721 Northeast Third Street
(541) 382–1515, (800) 528–1234, centralized reservations
www.bestwestern.com

Conveniently located on U.S. 97 Business, which runs through the middle of town, this motel is popular with recreational visitors as well as business travelers. The contemporary furnishings are done in pleasant muted colors, and there's plenty of space to spread out your luggage. A suite is actually a single oversized room with a queen-size bed and pull-out couch, small refrigerator, and microwave. Pets are welcome for a $5.00 daily surcharge. Rates temporarily go up about 30 percent on the second weekend in July for the Sisters Quilt Show.

Hampton Inn $$
15 Northeast Butler Market Road at North U.S. 97 Business
(541) 388–4114, (800) 426–7866, centralized reservations
www.hamptoninns.com

This modern facility is conveniently located on U.S. 97 at the north end of town near shopping and restaurants. The well-insulated rooms are clean and decorated in contemporary pink and teal green, and they come complete with iron and ironing board and HBO. About 75 percent of the units are nonsmoking rooms. Fruit and coffee are available in the lobby all day, in addition to a free continental breakfast in the morning. Copy and fax service, dataports for the phones, and a hospitality suite are amenities that are appreciated by business travelers. The outdoor pool and spa are nice for a dip, but the traffic noise nearby can be a bit bothersome. Pets are allowed free of charge. They are so confident you'll be happy with your experience that they offer a 100 percent money-back guarantee.

Hawthorn Suites Ltd. $$
755 Southwest 13th Place
(541) 382–5006, (888) 388–5006, direct
www.hawthorn.com

Built in the summer of 1998, this attractive motel is just a stone's throw from the corner of Colorado Avenue and Century Drive. It's right behind one of Bend's best breakfast places, The Original Pancake House (see our Close-up on "Best Breakfasts in Central Oregon" in the Restaurants chapter).

This property offers good-size motel rooms in addition to suites. The very modestly priced rooms (just higher than our $ price-code range) each have a work desk with a two-line phone and dataport, and a queen-size bed. For an extra $30, the suites are almost twice the size of the standard rooms and have a kitchenette and a couch in a sitting area. One-bedroom suites are available—a combination of a motel room and a basic suite. Rooms have HBO, and pets are not allowed. Breakfast features hot dishes including eggs, sausage, and bacon. Hawthorne Suites has a small conference center, meeting room, coin laundry, outdoor pool and spa, fax and copy service, and a fitness center.

Holiday Inn Express Hotel & Suites $$
20615 Grandview Drive
(541) 317–8500, (888) 919–7666, direct
www.rogueweb.com/holidaybend

The lobby's two-story river-rock fireplace, rose floor tiles, floral-patterned couches, and elegant appointments distinguish this brand-new hotel (built in 1998) as a corporate, as well as a tourist, stopover. Just off the lobby is a separate breakfast room for the free continental service.

The Holiday Inn Express has two configurations of the standard room, and both are comfortably sized and tastefully decorated. The first is popular with business travelers. It has one king-size bed, a work desk and chair, and an easy chair. The second standard room comes with two queen-size beds and a small table with chairs. For about $25 more you get into the suite price range. One interesting variation on the suite here is the Kids' Suite: It has a queen-size bed back toward the room windows, and in the center of the room is a walled-off alcove with bunk beds and the kids' own TV/VCR/Nintendo unit.

The west-side rooms on the third floor are the quietest, and they have awesome views of the Cascades. All rooms have dataports and HBO. The smoking rooms have been relegated to one floor of one wing. Pets are allowed in certain rooms for a $5.00 charge. The hotel has an indoor pool with spa, an outdoor sunbathing patio, a coin laundry, meeting rooms, a fitness room, and fax and copy service. This 99-room hotel overlooks U.S. 97 Business, less than a mile north of the Mountain View Mall. The toll-free number and Web site are direct to the hotel.

Phoenix Inn $$
300 Northwest Franklin Avenue
(541) 317-9292, (888) 291-4764, direct
www.phoenixinnsuites.com

Perched on a small hill overlooking downtown Bend, the rooms on the west side of the Phoenix's third floor not only have the best Cascade views, but they also offer nice views of Bend's lights at night. These rooms don't cost any more than the eastside rooms. The lobby is elegantly furnished with leather couches, a gas fireplace, and an enormous arrangement of fresh flowers.

The urbane, leather-couch theme is carried into the sitting areas of the mini-suites. Each unit has a work desk with a two-line phone and dataport (another two-line phone is next to the bed) and a kitchenette with refrigerator and coffeemaker. Deluxe suites have Jacuzzis. The hotel also has an indoor pool, spa, fitness center, coin laundry, and two meeting rooms, plus fax and copy service. Pets are not allowed. The toll-free number reaches the front desk. Built in 1998, the Phoenix Inn is about 3 blocks from downtown Bend, making it the most convenient choice for those who'd like to stroll around our historic downtown.

The Pine Ridge Inn $$$–$$$$
1200 Southwest Century Drive
(541) 389-6137, (800) 600-4095
www.pineridgeinn.com

Perched on a canyon wall above the Deschutes River, this unique country inn falls somewhere between a small hotel and a bed-and-breakfast. The 20 suites, each with a spacious sitting area, are decorated to the nines. The eclectic assortment of furniture, much of it custom-made, can best be described as a mixture of antiques and country cottage reproductions. Each room features a high bed, afghan-draped couches, table and chairs, private porch, fireplace, live plants, and two telephones with dataports. Decor features a fly-fishing, golfing, or country-casual theme with coordinating artwork and unique printed fabrics. Hidden in an armoire in the sitting area is a TV with VCR; videos are complimentary. There is a larger suite with separate bedroom, Jacuzzi tub and two sinks, and three telephones.

Grown-ups are served tea and cookies when the friendly and accommodating staff turns down the bed; kids get hot chocolate, cookies, and popcorn. An extra $6.50 will buy you a one-day pass for the upscale Athletic Club of Bend (see our Indoor Recreation chapter), which is a 15-minute walk away. A hearty breakfast featuring locally roasted Royal Blend coffee is served in a breakfast room that doubles as a meeting room. Wine and microbrew tastings are offered by the management in the afternoons. You may schedule a massage or facial for an extra charge. A romance package, which includes roses, champagne, bathrobes, and breakfast in bed, is available, as is a golf package. If you want to pamper yourself without getting fancy or putting on your shoes, they offer a free movie library.

The building is entirely nonsmoking, and pets are not allowed. The rates are constant throughout the year. Even the least-expensive downstairs room facing away from the river would be a lovely experience and a good value. The Pine Ridge Inn is approximately 2 miles west of downtown Bend and on the road to Mt. Bachelor Ski Area, which is 25 miles farther west. Their toll-free number and Web site are direct to the inn.

Red Lion Inn North $$
1415 Northeast Third Street
(541) 382–7011, (800) 733–5466, centralized reservations
Red Lion Inn South
849 Northeast Third Street
(541) 382–8384, (800) 733–5466, centralized reservations
www.redlion.com

These two motels are on U.S. Highway 97 Business in the heart of Bend, only 5 blocks apart. Both feature 75 large, well-appointed rooms recently redecorated with brightly colored fabrics. An iron and ironing board, HBO, and Showtime are a few of the standard luxuries. An outdoor pool and spa can be found at both locations. The North location has two saunas; the South location has a barbecue pit and picnic area. Guests from one Red Lion Inn can use the other location's facilities.

The Red Lion Inn is pet-friendly, and does not charge extra if you want to bring your pooch. They do raise rates when business is especially brisk, and you can also expect to pay an extra 10 percent or more for the Sisters Quilt Show weekend.

The Riverhouse Resort $$
3075 North U.S. Highway 97 Business
(541) 389–3111, (800) 547–3928, direct
www.riverhouse.com

A great location at the north end of Bend next to the Deschutes River, nicely appointed rooms, deluxe facilities, and reasonable prices have made this one of our most popular motels. With all of its recreational amenities, including golf, tennis, swimming, spa, sauna, and Nautilus room,

we would technically classify this as a resort. However, The Riverhouse gets a lot of one-night tourist and business travelers, and we would be shortchanging these readers if we left it out of this section.

When you arrive you are greeted by courteous desk clerks dressed in business attire. The various wings and separate buildings housing 220 guest rooms have brown siding and shake roofs and are intertwined with paved parking areas. The buildings almost stretch to the edge of the river, where you'll still find natural vegetation. Across the river are the River's Edge Golf Course and tennis courts, all owned by The Riverhouse. Golf and ski packages are available. The complex offers a nicely landscaped outdoor pool and spa and an indoor pool and spa.

The Poolside Cafe and Lounge serves deli-style food and cocktails to sunbathers. The Crossings at the Riverhouse Steakhouse has a dining room overlooking the river, and the resort's Fireside Nightclub is a very popular nightspot, with entertainment on the weekends (see our Nightlife chapter).

Basic guest rooms have kelly green or brown carpeting with subdued tones in the fabrics. Appointments are above-average and include homey touches like decorator tissue boxes, a soap dispenser, hair dryer, and VCR. Higher-end deluxe rooms offer fireplaces and private spas, and real suites accommodate up to 10 people. For an extra $10 you can upgrade a basic room to one with a river view—it's well worth the extra money. The living-room suite, with its separate bedroom, is also a very good deal.

Pets are allowed for no extra charge. Video rentals and room service are available at extra cost. Room rates are published and remain stable throughout the season. The toll-free number is a direct line to the property.

Shilo Inn Suites Hotel $$$
3105 O. B. Riley Road at U.S. 97 Business
(541) 389–9600, (800) 222–2244, centralized reservations
www.shiloinns.com

The Shilo Inn's 151 rooms in multiple, separate buildings are spread out over a quiet, seven-acre campus with a beautifully

The Metolius River runs clear and cold through a fragrant forest of ponderosa pines. PHOTO: JIM YUSKAVITCH

landscaped pool and spa at its center. The rear of the property fronts the Deschutes River, granting the best rooms a wonderful view and the sound of rushing water. The exterior has a trademark blue tile roof with log-like columns supporting second-story walkways along the olive brown facades.

This motel caters to conventions, banquets, and skiers, and you are paying extra for some deluxe amenities. The rooms are standard and functional—smallish and typically furnished with dark-colored fabrics and carpeting. Nice touches include real shower doors on the tub/shower units and two bathroom sinks, an iron, hair dryer, small refrigerator, microwave, and premium cable TV channels.

The most economical rooms don't offer much in the way of a view, but for an extra $15 you can get a sensational view of the river—we say it's worth it. Shilo Inn refers to its standard rooms as mini-suites; the more deluxe ones have a sitting area, Jacuzzi tub and/or fireplace. The property has one true, multiroom suite—the Shilo Suite—with a living room. A full buffet breakfast at the adjacent restaurant is included in the rate, and you can work off

the bacon and eggs in the two pools (one indoor), two spas, sauna, steam room, and fitness center. The restaurant is a full-service dining facility with a lounge with a full bar and entertainment on the weekends (see our Nightlife chapter). Room service is available at an extra cost, but the shuttles to the Redmond Airport and the Mt. Bachelor shuttle bus parking lot in Bend are complimentary.

The Shilo Inn usually has four rate levels each year. July and August have the highest rates, but the prices remain constant from weekend to weekend within those two months. Pets are allowed in certain buildings for a $7.00 per day surcharge. The O. B. Riley Road address is a bit misleading; the inn is actually a stone's throw away from U.S. Highway 97 Business at the north end of Bend.

Sleep Inn of Bend $
600 Northeast Bellevue Drive at U.S. 20
(541) 330–0050, (800) 627–5337, centralized reservations
www.sleepinn.com

Built in 1996, this motel is an excellent choice for budget accommodations. The spotless, modern rooms are not that large but are well designed and decorated in cool pastel tones. Also lending to the coolness of the room are recessed fluorescent lights that fill the air with a soft brightness. Walking into a Sleep Inn room is a refreshing change from some other dark motel rooms where you have to strain your eyes to read. Amenities include an outdoor pool and spa, copy and fax services, and telephones with dataports. The pet surcharge is $8.00 per day.

The motel is adjacent to a quiet shopping center at the corner of U.S. Highway 20 and 27th Street at what is currently (and probably temporarily) the eastern edge of Bend. In the same shopping center are a couple of fast-food restaurants and a Royal Blend Coffee House, a good place for bagels (see our Restaurants chapter). Rates go up about 10 percent for the Sisters Quilt Show, pushing them just past the line into the next price range; for that weekend, the price is still relatively low.

Sisters/Camp Sherman Area

Sisters is a picturesque little town with a Western theme. Ponderosa pine trees surrounding the town frame beautiful views of the Three Sisters. U.S. Highway 20 forms the main route through town. Sisters has a half-dozen restaurants, one supermarket and one small market, gas stations, video rentals, an excellent fly-fishing shop, a great bookstore, and quite a number of boutiques and gift shops.

Just outside the town limits is the Deschutes National Forest with its virtually unlimited year-round recreational opportunities. Here you will find skiing and snowmobiling, fly-fishing, mountain biking, horseback riding, and white-water rafting. Great views can also be enjoyed from Aspen Lakes, a 27-hole championship golf course 3 miles east of Sisters on Oregon Highway 126.

Thirteen miles west of Sisters, in the Deschutes National Forest at the headwaters of the Metolius River, is the resort area of Camp Sherman. Most of the accommodations in Camp Sherman would be classi-

fied as resort lodging; look for more information on these properties in our chapter on Resorts, Ranches, and Vacation Rentals. Please refer to our Shopping, Snowplay, Restaurants, Golf, Fishing, Neighborhoods and Real Estate, and Recreation chapters for more area information.

Best Western Ponderosa Lodge $$
505 U.S. Highway 20, Sisters
(541) 549–1200, (800) 849–0686, direct
www.bestwesternponderosalodge.sisters.com

This 49-room motel has an exceptionally nice setting, back from the highway and nestled in a ponderosa pine forest. The comfortable rooms have unique, custom-designed Western-style furniture that uses rawhide strips. Each room also has a hair dryer, iron, and ironing board. Outside is a beautiful pool and spa surrounded by pine trees. A meeting room and fax service are available. Rooms where pets are allowed are limited in number; if you are traveling with Fido, there is a $10 per day surcharge, and you will need to make an advance reservation. At the close of the Sisters Quilt Show (held the second Saturday in July), reservations are accepted for the following year, with preference given to current Quilt Show patrons. As you might imagine, the motel is booked within minutes for the following year's show.

Comfort Inn of Sisters $$
540 U.S. Highway 20, Sisters
(541) 549–7829, (800) 228–5150, centralized reservations
www.comfortinn.com

Built in 1994, this motel has retained a fresh, new appearance. The rooms have burgundy carpets with either navy or dark green fabrics, and all come with a small table and two chairs. For a higher rate you can get a kitchenette. Outside is a sparkling, heated swimming pool and spa that have recently been enclosed in glass. Pets are allowed at the manager's discretion. There is no extra charge, but the inn will bill you for any required extra cleaning. A coin laundry and meeting room are available, as well as fax service. Rates stay stable throughout the season, but the chances of getting a reservation for the

Quilt Show are remote. Next door and part of the Comfort Inn complex is the nice Mountain Shadow RV Park (see our Camping chapter), which would work out well if you want to get together with some RVing friends.

Sisters Motor Lodge **$**
511 West Cascade Avenue, Sisters
(541) 549-2551
The owners have completed the long process of renovating this older motel, and the results are wonderful. Rooms are now decorated in the manner of a bed-and-breakfast inn, and they even have cute names like Picket Fences (with quaint, country furnishings) and Kah-Nee-Ta (with a Native American motif). Most of the regular motel rooms are fairly modest in size and have stall showers; a few rooms have kitchenettes. Hostess and manager, Barbara Page, loves to bake and offers fresh-baked goodies in the office every morning.

The upstairs lodge suite 10 is in a quiet location toward the back of the property, overlooking pastoral pastures and the Three Sisters. It has a kitchenette and sitting area, plus a larger bathroom with a tub and shower. The lodge suite costs about $20 more than a regular room, and we recommend it. Downstairs is the Paws Awhile studio suite 11 with a kitchenette, dining area, and bath with stall shower, also $20 more than a regular room. Pets are allowed for $5.00 a day (no puppies), and the entire motel is nonsmoking. Sisters Motor Lodge takes only Visa, Master-Card, and Discover.

Redmond

Redmond is a rapidly growing Western city. Espresso shops have recently been added to the utilitarian mix of feed stores and tractor repair places, and the residential makeup is changing from predominantly ranchers to suburban families.

The town is at the intersection of U.S. Highway 97, Oregon Highway 126, and U.S. Highway 26, making it a central location for travel to and from Bend (16 miles away), Sisters, Prineville, and Madras. North of town is Smith Rock State Park, a favorite spot for rock climbers and photographers. Nearby, the Crooked River and Deschutes River are excellent fisheries. Eagle Crest Resort offers two championship golf courses and an 18-hole putting course for golf enthusiasts.

U.S. 97 is the main commercial route through town. Within the downtown area it splits into one-way streets, with northbound traffic on Fifth Street and southbound traffic on Sixth Street. Fast-food restaurants can be found along U.S. 97 on the south end of town, along with gas stations, a Wal-Mart, cinemas, supermarkets, and other commercial amenities. The community hospital is on the north end of town.

The Redmond Municipal Airport, Central Oregon's only commercial airport with connections to Portland and Seattle, is important to business and recreational visitors (see our Getting Here, Getting Around chapter). Redmond is also home to the Deschutes County Fairgrounds, where weekend events draw large numbers of people. The largest annual event is the Deschutes County Fair, a five-day affair ending on the first Sunday in August (see our Annual Events chapter). Motel rooms book far in advance for the fair, as well as for the Sisters Quilt Show, which takes place about 18 miles west of Redmond, in July. Our chapters on Attractions, Restaurants, Golf, Fishing, and recreation have more information about this area.

Best Western Rama Inn $$
2630 Southwest 17th Place at U.S. 97
(541) 548–8080; (800) 528–1234, centralized reservations; or (800) 821–0543, direct
www.bestwestern.com

Subdued colors lend a calmness to the tasteful decor in this well-maintained motel. Serious travelers who pack a 100-watt light bulb in their toilet article bag will feel vindicated—the lighting in our test room was a bit too dim for easy reading. Suites with living rooms are available. Conveniently located on U.S. Highway 97 about 2 miles from the Redmond Airport, a free airport shuttle service is one of this motel's amenities. Business folks will also appreciate the conference rooms and copy and fax services. Free HBO, an indoor pool and spa, and a sauna help make your stay a pleasant one. Pets are not allowed. Rates jump about 30 percent for the Sisters Quilt Show in July. This motel is owned by the same franchisee that owns the Best Western Rama Inn in Madras and the New Redmond Hotel/Travelodge (see subsequent listing).

New Redmond Hotel/Travelodge $–$$
521 South Sixth Street
(541) 923–7378, (800) 578–7878, centralized reservations
www.travelodge.com

The New Redmond Hotel was built in 1927. It was extensively remodeled in 1993 and is affiliated with Travelodge and the group that owns the Best Western Rama Inns. The grand lobby is warmly furnished with a mixture of antiques and modern pieces and carpeting patterned after an Oriental rug. Contemporary couches form a cozy seating area in front of a large stone fireplace. When we visited, the coffee table beckoned with a half-finished jigsaw puzzle.

A reliable old elevator will get you to the upper floors, where you will find spacious and comfortably appointed rooms. The furniture is contemporary, and the bathrooms have been redone with the most basic of modern aesthetics. However, with the high ceilings, tall windows, and original woodwork, you never forget you are in a historical building.

Standard rooms, living room/bedroom suites, and a conference room are available. The hotel's downtown location means you can conveniently walk around the city after dinner. There is an exercise room and a hot tub to relax in after working out. The hotel is on the southbound side of U.S. 97. Pets are not accepted. There is an Italian restaurant, Sully's, in the building. Room rates are reasonable, even when they go up 20 percent for the Sisters Quilt Show in July.

Sunview Motel & Resort $
Southwest 5010 Clubhouse Road, Crooked River Ranch
(541) 923–0944, (800) 282–0944, direct

Located in the Crooked River Ranch subdivision about 13 miles northwest of Redmond (see our Other Communities chapter), the "resort" aspect of this private motel means that Sunview guests are allowed to use CRR's beautiful swimming pool. Also, the motel is only about a mile from the Crooked River Ranch Golf Course (see our Golf chapter).

This unique motel consists of 16 modern octagonal buildings, divided into two units each. These standard units have a queen-size bed, a small kitchenette, and a connecting door. Two of the octagons offer deluxe amenities with one large suite with a queen-size bed, sleeper sofa in the sitting area, and kitchenette with wet bar. The rooms are well maintained and comfortably appointed with contemporary furniture. Free cable TV with HBO and Cinemax is included. The kitchenettes have microwaves. If you are into world-class golfing but aren't interested in spending lots of money on other amenities, this is a very good value and a pleasant lodging experience. Temperatures in Crooked River Ranch are often warm enough even in winter to golf, so if the weather report looks favorable you might want to check on their discounted winter rates.

Super 8 Motel–Redmond Airport $
3629 Southwest 21st Place
(541) 548–8881, (800) 800–8000, centralized reservations

The two things we liked best about this national chain motel is the fact that it is fairly new (built in 1997) and it's just a half-mile from the Redmond Airport and even closer to the Deschutes County Fairgrounds and Expo Center. There are an indoor pool and spa, meeting room, and fax service; pets are allowed with a refundable $25 deposit. The rooms are small and minimally furnished, but they are clean and new. This motel is adjacent to and visible from U.S. 97. On the south end of town, take the Yew Avenue exit off U.S. 97 and turn east toward the airport. Super 8 does not offer an airport shuttle, but they do accept pets.

Sunriver/La Pine Area

Sunriver and La Pine are the two main Central Oregon communities south of Bend on U.S. 97. Sunriver is a large resort area; its lodgings are covered in our Resorts, Ranches, and Vacation Rentals chapter. La Pine is a small logging town to the south with very basic amenities along its short commercial strip.

The area surrounding La Pine is very interesting for its volcanic history as well as its excellent recreational opportunities in the Deschutes National Forest, LaPine State Park, and the newly expanded, 18-hole Quail Run Golf Course. Please refer to our Snowplay, Restaurants, Neighborhoods and Real Estate, Golf, Fishing, and recreation chapters for more information.

Best Western Newberry Station Resort Motel $$
16515 Reed Road at U.S. 97, La Pine
(541) 536–5130, (800) 210–8616, direct
www.bestwestern.com

Built in 1996, this handsome motel's 40 rooms each has a unique decor. The standard room we checked out was spacious and featured a big plaid couch in a sitting area. Wing-back chairs and Victorian-style furniture add a comfortable touch to the grand lobby with its fireplace, sweeping staircase, and adjacent breakfast room. Suites, a conference room, and fax and copy services are available, and the telephones have dataports for your laptop computer. Small dogs are allowed with a refundable $25 deposit. The motel, located at the north end of town, is visible

Insiders' Tip

In Oregon the only tax you will run into is the transient room tax. In Bend, Redmond, La Pine, and Prineville the rate is 7 percent. In Sisters it's 8 percent; in Madras it's only 6 percent. Oregonians are not accustomed to getting a bill for more than the price of the service or product. When in Oregon, do as the Oregonians do. To that end, we have based our price key on the gross (tax-included) prices. If the person giving you information on room rates neglects to specify if tax is included, you might want to ask.

from U.S. 97. The toll-free number is a direct line to the motel.

Prineville Area

This old logging and ranching town of 5,000 inhabitants is the county seat for Crook County, the geographical center of Oregon, and the home of the regionally famous Les Schwab Tires. Driving through town on U.S. Highway 26, you'd think you were on Main Street U.S.A. There's nothing fancy about the storefronts, supermarket, community hospital, feed stores, or gas stations—but they're plenty good enough for ranching folks, loggers, and the locals who work in some branch of the tourist industry. Talk to just about any resident, and you'll find that they love their little town.

There are plenty of recreational opportunities surrounding Prineville. To the south and west is fly-fishing in the Crooked River. All around are hiking, rock hounding, fossil beds, and camping. The nearby Ochoco National Forest has lakes and streams for exploring. Winters in Prineville are mild, and the hot, dry summers are perfect for enjoying watersports at the Prineville Reservoir State Park. You can play 18 holes of golf year-round at Prineville's Meadow Lakes. Our chapters on restaurants, golf, fishing, and recreation have more information about this area.

Best Western Prineville Inn $$
1475 East Third Street (U.S. 26), Prineville
(541) 447-8080, (800) 528-1234, centralized reservations
www.bestwestern.com
Pastels in a Southwestern motif grace this handsome motel. The lobby has a brick floor, comfortable couches, and a fireplace. The rooms are good-sized and furnished in a contemporary, Southwestern style and come complete with hair dryers, irons, and ironing boards. Folks who don't light up will be happy to know there is a whole nonsmoking wing, and pets are not allowed in the rooms. The indoor pool and spa were upgraded in 2001 and are even more beautiful than before, and are open year-round, and there is a coin laundry. A conference room, fax, and copy services are available to business guests. Next door is a coffee shop.

Rustler's Roost Motel $
960 West Third Street, Prineville
(541) 447-4185
On the flip side of the coin, here is an older motel that has its own brand of Western charm. Outside it resembles a hotel from the Gold Rush era, with its two-story balcony, white Victorian trim, and gray facade. Inside, the avocado-colored bathroom fixtures, Formica vanity, and old-style television and telephone give away the secret of the motel's 1960s origin.

However, the huge and simple bedrooms with their treasured antique furnishings put this motel in its own unique category. Some of the rooms have kitchenettes, they all have cable TV, and pets are welcome (at the manager's discretion) with a $5.00 per day surcharge. You will find complimentary coffee in the front office every morning (not really breakfast). The Ranchero Mexican Restaurant is next door.

The motel is owned by a couple of missionaries who are currently in China. The resident manager takes care of the motel and its customers as if she owned the place. The room rates are low all year to keep the working customers coming back. If there is no answer when you call, call again later.

Madras Area

Madras remains an agricultural community surrounded by large ranches. In town you will find the basic commercial services including two supermarkets, several restaurants, a community hospital, gas, and the expected tractor sales and seed supplier. If you look hard, you can find a good cup of espresso at Petals 'n' Poseys on Fourth Street (see our Restaurants chapter).

Nearby Lake Billy Chinook is popular for boating, windsurfing, and swimming, and there are excellent golfing opportunities within 45 minutes of Madras at Kah-Nee-Ta Resort. U.S. 97 is the main route through town. It splits into two one-way streets in the downtown area: southbound is Fourth Street; northbound is Fifth

Street. Please refer to our Restaurants, Golf, Fishing, Neighborhoods and Real Estate, and recreation chapters for more information.

Best Western Rama Inn $$
12 Southwest Fourth Street, Madras
(541) 475–6141, (888) 528–1234, centralized reservations
www.bestwestern.com

This completely remodeled motel is really lovely. The carpets are a lush green, with accompanying fabrics done in light pink and green prints or plaids. A pool is a welcome amenity during Madras' hot summers. The sauna, outdoor spa, and exercise room will warm you up when the weather turns cool. Or relax in your room with free HBO. Fax and copy services are available.

The summer rate is steady throughout the season. The inn charges $10 per day extra for small pets, which is not too surprising since they have spanking-new carpets. Mexico City, a good Mexican restaurant, is close by (see our Restaurants chapter). This independently owned franchise is in downtown Madras on Fourth Street (which is actually southbound U.S. 97) at the corner of B Street. There is another Best Western Rama Inn owned by the same company in Redmond.

Sonny's Motel and Restaurant $
1539 Southwest U.S. Highway 97, Madras
(541) 475–7217, (800) 624–6137, direct
www.sonnysmotel.com

Sonny's is something of a landmark in Madras. It has been around for decades, and its location right on the main highway on the south end of town is very visible. The rooms are pleasant, having been refurbished not too long ago with gray or green carpets and mauve fabrics. Suites and Jacuzzi rooms are available if you are looking for more deluxe accommodations. There is a very nice outdoor pool and spa, and recent improvements include a barbecue and picnic area, basketball hoop, and horseshoes for the kids. A coffee shop–type restaurant is on the premises. A nice feature is that the summer room rate is published and stable. The one-time pet fee is $10. A free continental breakfast is available Monday through Saturday.

Bed-and-Breakfasts

A Home Away from Home
Bend
Sisters/Camp Sherman
    Area
Redmond
Sunriver/La Pine Area
Prineville Area

Central Oregon is blessed with an impressive array of bed-and-breakfasts, each one unique. We have included places where you feel you ought to take your shoes off before entering, and places that would laugh at the suggestion. Whether you'd like an urban experience or a more rural experience among ranches or forests, you will find it within Central Oregon. We take our bed-and-breakfast traditions seriously; for the most part our innkeepers hold themselves to very high standards of perfection.

Bend and Prineville take pride in their century-old historic houses. These homes have been passionately restored to their original splendor and decorated to the nth degree. Guests who enjoy an old-fashioned romantic experience will fall in love with the Lara House (1910) and The Sather House (1911) in Bend, and the Elliott House (1908) in Prineville. Turn-of-the-20th-century-era afficionados will especially enjoy The Sather House and the Elliott House for their exceptional architecture, furnishings, china, and glass work. Antiques lovers of 19th-and early-20th-century artwork and furniture could spend hours listening to the stories behind the elaborate furnishings of the Australian Outback Country Lodge Bed and Breakfast, the contemporary home of a pair of avid collectors in Sisters. Or, take a shorter step back in time, only 40 years or so, and visit The Country Inn The City, in Bend, where you just might find homemade jams simmering on the stove.

Some folks like to fashion their leisure-time experience around a favorite activity or hobby theme, and several of our inns fall into various recreational categories. Horse lovers might enjoy Rags to Walkers Guest Ranch or the Lazy Rockin' B'nC Ranch. Fly fishers will feel at home at the Deschutes River Lodge in Redmond; western art lovers would enjoy the fine commercial gallery that is integrated into the DiamondStone Guest Lodge and Gallery in La Pine. If strolling through an old downtown district and stopping at boutiques, antiques shops, and art galleries is your thing, the Blue Spruce Bed & Breakfast in Sisters, or the Lara House and The Sather House in Bend will fit the bill. For diehard hikers who are ready for the luxury of not having to carry their own gear, Llast Camp Llamas Bed and Breakfast in Redmond can outfit you with a pack llama or two to do the heavy work as you traipse your way through our national forests.

A popular new trend in B&Bs is to build a large-scale home from scratch and feature three or four master suites and spacious common areas. These rather grand lodges fulfill the aspiring innkeepers' dreams of creating the perfect bed-and-breakfast inn. These innkeepers pride themselves at creating perfectly orchestrated getaways for their guests. Juniper Acres Bed & Breakfast and Cricketwood Country Bed and Breakfast, both in Bend, the Blue Spruce Bed & Breakfast and the Lazy Rockin' B'nC Ranch in Sisters, the Deschutes River Lodge and Rags to Walkers Guest Ranch in Redmond, and La Pine's DiamondStone Guest Lodge would all fit into this category. Martha Stewart could learn a thing or two from some of these innkeepers!

If Ms. Stewart's level of performance is a bit much for you, then you might prefer the pre-Martha-era character of The Country Inn The City, or the Gazebo Bed and Breakfast. Or, treat yourself to a dip in a heated pool and then relax in a deep easy chair with a good book at Conklin's Guest House in Sisters. Amateur aviators who want to tell their friends they flew their little Cessna to a bed-and-breakfast will be happy to know that Conklin's is right next to the small Sisters general aviation airport.

The listings for each town are prefaced with a brief introduction that touches on some of the area's highlights. For more information on things to do, refer to our Restaurants, Shopping, Attractions, Nightlife, Snowplay, Fishing, Other Outdoor Recreation, History, The Arts, and Parks chapters.

A Home Away from Home

When you stay in a bed-and-breakfast or guest house, you are entering someone's home. Bed-and-breakfast owners often are in it for the enjoyment, and not for profit.

You may be interviewed on the phone when you call for a reservation, as some innkeepers prefer to screen their guests. You shouldn't expect to bring your pet, although the Cricketwood Country Bed and Breakfast in Bend and the Diamond-Stone Guest Lodge in La Pine accept some canines. None of the homes allows smoking. DiamondStone Guest Lodge, Rags to Walkers Guest Ranch, and the Lazy Rockin' B'nC Ranch can board your horses on-site for an extra charge.

A few inns prefer not to accept young children. Most of these innkeepers feel their other guests have come to get away from the stressful influences of racing feet and kids yelling for Mom. For your maximum enjoyment and relaxation when traveling with your children, we suggest that you stay at the inns that enjoy having young guests. These sometimes include Gazebo Bed and Breakfast, DiamondStone Guest Lodge, Llast Camp Llamas, and Rags to Walkers Guest Ranch. Juniper Acres welcomes babies, toddlers, or older kids when their second guest room is unoccupied. The Elliott House, The Sather House, and Conklin's Guest House accept children age 12 and older. Inns sometimes welcome children only when there are no other guests that might be bothered by noise. Inns that have family pets usually do not allow them to enter the guest rooms. However, if you are very allergic to cats or dogs, you should always ask about animals on the premises. Only the DiamondStone in La Pine has phones in the rooms; the others allow guests to use the family phone. By popular demand, many inns have added TVs and VCRs to the guest rooms.

Breakfast time is often flexible but is usually between 8:00 and 9:00 A.M. Some innkeepers will accommodate more than one serving time for different guests, and this might vary depending on how busy they are. If you want to leave very early for your day's outing, ask in advance if your hosts will prepare you a cold breakfast or pack you one to go. Breakfasts are included in your room rate, and you don't get credit if you skip your morning meal. Our innkeepers will accommodate special dietary needs, which should be discussed when you make reservations.

Speaking of reservations, they are usually required, as it takes a fair amount of preparation to ready a private home for overnight guests. Bed-and-breakfast travel is quite popular these days and B&Bs tend to get booked. Central Oregon bed-and-breakfast inns are consistently full during summer weekends. Some weeks are booked solid, so make your summer reservations as soon as possible. Christmas, Valentine's Day, and Sisters Quilt Show weekend are three very popular bed-and-breakfast holidays/events that you should book early—even as much as 12 months in advance. Traditionally, innkeepers will expect you to mail a deposit when you make your reservation, then pay the balance with a check when you arrive (personal checks are usually okay). When you make your reservation, ask about the refund policy for cancellations—some deposits may not be refundable. More and more inns accept credit cards these days; we have noted the ones that do. Another sign of the times are Web sites for bed-and-breakfasts, which are included with each listing. Most of the inns have sites with very good graphic content, and are worth visiting.

Price Code

Our price key rates are based on two persons in a single bedroom, and breakfast is included. Innkeepers usually quote prices without tax, which will tack on an additional 6 to 8 percent. However, we are following the Oregon tradition of thinking of costs in bottom-line terms (no surprises for us!), and therefore our price code includes tax. In winter, most places discount their rooms between 10 and 20 percent. More than two people in one room costs extra.

$ .... $50 to $80
$$ .... $81 to $110
$$$ .... $111 to $160

Bend

When you stay in Bend you are at the heart of Central Oregon with many resources at your fingertips. Spend a day window-shopping for antiques, fine apparel, books, and gift items along Bond Street and Wall Street in old downtown Bend (see our Shopping chapter). Have a picnic at Drake Park. Pick up a heritage-walk map from the Central Oregon Welcome Center or the inn where you are staying and stroll the streets of Bend, admiring the century-old houses and city buildings. Follow the pleasant walking path along the Deschutes River near Drake Park, or hike up Pilot Butte cinder cone for a 360-degree view of Bend and the mountains.

Visitors from states that have a sales tax love to fill up their shopping carts with computer software, electronics, and small appliances at Costco. Good deals on a wide range of merchandise can be found at the Prime Outlets Mall, on the southern end of Bend's main drag, U.S. 97 Business. Bend also has two historic districts, both with excellent shopping opportunities. One is the Old Downtown District, and the second is our restored Old Mill District that had its grand re-opening in 2001.

Both fine and casual dining options abound throughout the city (see Restaurants), and you can have your pick of cinemas in the evening or drop in at one of the many nightspots for some music. When you've done the town, head for the hills. Cool forests, snowy mountains, warm painted deserts, and hundreds of holes of golf are all close by.

The Country Inn The City $, no credit cards
1776 Northeast Eighth Street
(541) 385-7639

This inn is a 1920 homestead on an acre of lawns with fruit trees. After you park in the rear parking lot, you will be gaily welcomed at the back door by Lois Wolcott or her daughter, Sherry Glover. It's a perfectly fitting introduction to this very casual bed-and-breakfast. First you enter a tidy, open kitchen decorated in 1970's colors. Barking dogs outside are scolded and a little dog inside gets shooed aside as the two women divide their attention between their guests and their canine companions.

As Lois and Sherry lead you to your room, you realize that you are traveling through a living patchwork of an abode. Rooms have various carpets of differing vintages. A happy cacophony of knick-knacks, tchotchkes, and memorabilia is neatly lined up on shelf after shelf. "Everything works!" chirps Lois, as she picks up a little musical statuette and winds it up. The china lady twirls to the sound of tinkling music. On the way to the bedrooms is an inviting library with its walls lined with bookshelves and more memorabilia; it almost makes you wish it would rain so you could spend time exploring. Upstairs is an odd collection of beds, chairs tucked into niches, and dressers divided between three bedrooms that share a bath. The beds look like the type that could take being flopped into. There's a half-bath at the foot of the stairs. Lois and Sherry have rooms off the kitchen with their own bath.

Imagine how this house smells while the two hostesses are making up a batch of sauce from apples or pears picked from their fruit trees, or cooking marionberry syrup! The baked French toast stuffed with cream cheese and blueberries sure sounds delicious. Breakfast is served in the kitchen.

On summer days the expansive, red-painted front porch beckons. While there, take a look at the bottom concrete step to see a small handprint and footprint made by one of Judge Foley's children. The Foley

Breakfast with a view at Conklin's Guest House is an experience you'll never forget.

PHOTO: CONKLIN'S GUEST HOUSE

family lived in the house at the time the concrete for the front steps was poured: 1947.

Lois and Sherry prefer to devote their hospitality to adult guests only. If comfy and lively, not fancy or serene, is your preference, and you enjoy experiencing life the way it used to be before color TV was invented, then this might be your cup of tea. The Country Inn is conveniently located 8 blocks east of Third Street (which is U.S. Highway 97 Business) at Revere, about a mile east of the Revere exit off the Bend Parkway. The two ladies welcome guests all year except perhaps when the house is filled with their grandchildren and great-grandchildren, and they maintain the same, reasonably modest rates all year.

Cricketwood Country Bed and Breakfast $$
63520 Cricketwood Road
(541) 330–0747, (877) 330–0747
www.cricketwood.com

Jim and Tracy Duncan welcome guests into their lovely country home on the east side of Bend, just eight minutes from downtown. Peace and quiet reign supreme in this area of mini-ranches. The couple

purchased this pre-existing inn in 1999 and gave the place quite a remodeling to fit their idea of the perfect bed-and-breakfast. Sumptuous is the one word that describes the Duncan's Cricketwood experience.

Outdoors, the expanses of manicured green lawns, artfully framed by mature trees and a winding seasonal brook, offer a respite of peace and tranquility from the hustle and bustle of life in the 21st century. In the distance are hay fields and pastures, and the tops of mountains peeking over the trees. The west-facing veranda on the front of the cedar house and the east-facing decks with their umbrellaed tables offer the first inklings of the pampered life that awaits. To the side of the house at the end of the driveway are two signs over the garage that read: GUEST PARKING, another clue to the character of this inn.

The guests' welcome is perfectly orchestrated, right down to the soft background music that bathes the spacious dining room and living areas. On the dining-room table are clipboards with the breakfast menus. The initial tour takes you past their library of sights and attractions in Bend and Central Oregon, past the fountain in the Roman Garden–styled sitting room with its demure statue named Rebecca, and on to your guest room.

On the ground floor is a spacious guest room called The Secret Garden that they like to call the honeymoon suite because of its king-size bed, fountain, two-person spa tub, and huge walk-in shower. Garden murals decorate the walls above the bed and around the spa.

Upstairs is a very large suite called the Exotic Garden Suite, and exotic it is with leopard-print pillows and throws. A king-size bed occupies the central alcove behind some very sultry sheer curtains. Double beds fill two alcoves, one on each side of the center alcove. The pair of La-Z-Boy recliners parked in front of a TV that rests on a bamboo chest reminds you that you are still in the United States. The 6-foot claw-foot tub, surrounded by a mural of a jungle scene, has been cast in infamy by a photo of Jim using the tub that you can see in their brochure and on their Web site.

Also upstairs is a smaller room called The Country Garden, with a very picturesque mural of the view from the back of their house and a picket-fence headboard.

All three rooms have a TV/VCR and CD player, robes and slippers, mini-refrigerators, candles, and private baths stocked with bubble bath.

In the morning you can take a stroll through the countryside before breakfast. Serious walkers should ask the Duncans to tell them about the 2-mile loop through their rural neighborhood of small ranches and two-lane country roads. There are two acres of parklike lawns surrounding the house—perfect for croquet and badminton. In summer the tiny bridge over the brook is a great spot to pose for a snapshot.

Jim and Tracy are co-chefs, and they cook up a storm for their guests. On arrival you will be provided with a mouthwatering checklist of breakfast items that's longer than most restaurant menus, including gourmet items such as Crème Brûlée Baked French Toast or a hearty Breakfast Potato Casserole with smoked or fresh salmon, cheeses, and sour cream. You may have your breakfast on the oak table in the din-

ing room or outside on the deck, or even delivered on a tray to your room. If you have a special request, go ahead and ask.

With advance reservations, and at no extra charge, you will be invited to join the family at 6:00 P.M. for what they call Light Hors D'oeuvres. Available nightly except on Saturday, this repast could more appropriately be called a light supper. In the evening, relax in the guest living room with its La-Z-Boy recliners, TV, VCR, beverage-filled refrigerator, and big fireplace. Or, go and take a peek in the closet of your bedroom. There, among the labeled shelves ("extra blankets," "extra pillow," "guest robes," "guest toilet articles," etc.), will be a box labeled "Games" and inside it are cute little games a couple on their first—or second—honeymoon might want to indulge in. On the more mundane side of things, the downstairs hall closet has a large collection of videos as well as the games, toys, and puzzles that you might expect to find at a bed-and-breakfast.

Since the Duncans have gone to a great extent to make their inn a wonderfully romantic getaway, it's probably not the best choice for families traveling with small children. However, their little guest cottage out back next to their hay field would serve nicely for a family with kids. Although the cottage is usually considered a vacation rental (lacking food service), it wouldn't surprise us if the Duncans just might be able to come up with some special arrangements for a modified bed-and-breakfast experience. Pets are allowed in the cottage.

Summer weekends are usually all booked by February, and for an impromptu visit during the rest of the year you may have to call a month or so ahead for a weekend reservation. By prior arrangement, Cricketwood may be able to board your dog for $10 per night. In keeping with their policy of saying "yes!" the Duncans accept Visa, MasterCard, and American Express. Although the new owners of Cricketwood have only been in full swing since 2000, they have earned a faithful and enthusiastic following. About 40 percent of their visitors are repeat guests, and they'll try their best to make a repeat visitor out of you, too.

Gazebo Bed and Breakfast $, no credit cards
21679 Obsidian Avenue
(541) 389–7202
www.moriah.com/gazebo

This cedar shake house is nestled among warm-scented sagebrush and juniper trees in a neighborhood that is about 10 minutes southeast of downtown Bend. A gazebo sits in a rock garden that offers a beautiful view of the Cascade Mountains from Mount Hood to Mount Bachelor. Hosts Gale and Helen Estergreen welcome guests to their empty nest.

As you enter you will notice vaulted ceilings in the living room of this roomy country home. Helen has collected the antique and older oak furniture that gives the living room a warm, friendly feel. Guests are welcome to use the family TV and phone.

The two ground-floor bedrooms share a full bath. A single couple can have the place to themselves, or two sets of friends or a family can take over both bedrooms. (There is a cheaper rate for two couples.) The rooms are pleasantly decorated with beige carpeting, peach and green spreads on the iron beds, and quilted wall hangings.

Morning smells great with apple puff pancakes, huckleberry waffles, or peach blintzes. If you're lucky, Helen may make a breakfast casserole—a variation of the traditional breakfast, with eggs, sausage, and green pepper baked in the oven.

Children are welcome at this very simple, pre-Martha-Stewart-style inn, and there are no pets on-site.

Juniper Acres Bed & Breakfast $$, no credit cards
65220 Smokey Ridge Drive
(541) 389–2193
www.juniperacres.com

Two-story windows that rise to a sharp peak like the prow of a ship command a panoramic, seven-peak view of the Cascade Mountains. Situated on nine quiet, forested acres, this spectacular log home was built by Vern and Della Bjerk, who have a business selling log homes. Having a bed-and-breakfast was a dream for Della and Vern for many years, and after the struggle to build their home, they can now relax and

have fun. Juniper Acres is just off U.S. Highway 20 about 6 miles west of Bend.

As you step inside you experience a feeling of airy spaciousness and the warm effect of the log walls. Della's small handmade quilts deck the walls, and her homemade rag dolls and carousel horses add a youthful, lively ambiance. Some guests have picked up quilting supplies in town and stayed a few extra days to share Della's hobby with her. After a day of activities or sewing, guests often join their hosts for a quiet evening on the big comfortable couches in front of the fire.

On arrival you'll find a plate of freshbaked cookies awaiting you in your room. The two guest rooms are on the main level, and the hosts live upstairs in the loft. The rooms are air conditioned, and each has its own full bath and TV/VCR. The beds are covered in rich garnet and teal green colors, and the rooms are wonderfully comfortable. One has a pretty floral motif, and the other one Della considers to be in a more masculine style. Handcrafted artworks grace the walls.

In the morning, guests are served a delicious breakfast on the oak table in the dining room. Baked pears and French toast stuffed with cream cheese and ricotta, or a summery, cold fruit soup and frittata, will greet you when you are ready to eat. You can go for a walk along dirt roads through the forest, and there is a deck with a barbecue grill that guests are welcome to use.

The Bjerks have very young grandchildren who visit them, so the house is equipped to handle a baby or toddler guest. They also enjoy having older children visit. Kids are accepted by special arrangement when there are no other guests. There are no pets on the premises.

Lara House Bed and Breakfast $$–$$$
640 Northwest Congress Street
(541) 388–4064, (800) 766–4064
www.larahouse.com

We have long admired the handsome facade and graceful lawns of this 1910 Craftsman-style house across from Drake Park and Mirror Pond, so this was a wonderful opportunity to invite ourselves inside for a tour. This is a bed-and-breakfast that follows the traditions of an old inn. It is owned and hosted by Doug and Bobbye Boger.

The spacious living room, with its original mantel and large brick fireplace, is beautiful. When we visited, home-baked cookies and a Crockpot with simmering hot cider gave the room a wonderful smell. Flanking the living room and dining room is a long, cheerful sunroom.

You may choose to have your breakfast at the oak dining room table or, on a nice day, in the sunroom. The breakfast menu might include Belgian waffles with a yogurt parfait, French toast stuffed with sour cream and fresh fruits, a chili egg puff, croissant a la orange, or spinach quiche with pumpkin muffins.

You can spend a summer evening sitting on the large veranda and watching the world go by, or relax in the hot tub on a cold winter night. Indoors, during our visit, guests indulged in conversation or played games in front of the fireplace, while delicate music played in the background. In defiance of its historical setting, Lara House has a TV with VCR and a collection of videos tucked away in the corner of the sunroom they call the den.

A modern staircase tucked behind the fireplace takes you to the second floor, where you find the Drake Room, which is decorated with a duck motif. It has a sitting area and claw-foot tub with shower. Wicker furniture creates a garden theme in the Deschutes Room, which has a queen-size bed and a bath with double vanity and a shower. Iron furniture and earth tones compliment the Shevlin Room, with its big bathroom and Jacuzzi tub and shower. The 1940s era is explored in the Cascade Room with its big, two-person loveseat, black-striped wallpaper, and shower bath.

On the third floor is a charming attic suite known as the Summit Room. The Summit Room takes up the entire, 700-square-foot attic. Its living-room area includes a mini-refrigerator, microwave, and TV/VCR. There is a king-size bed and a big bathroom with a large tub and shower. We thought the freestanding pedestal sink with floating mirror was an

interesting solution to the low eaves and sloping ceiling. The toilet is in a tiny closet.

The Lara House is a short walk from downtown Bend. The inn accepts Visa, MasterCard, American Express, and Discover. If you are traveling with children, you might inquire if innkeepers Doug and Bobbye can accommodate you.

The Sather House Bed and Breakfast
$$–$$$
7 Northwest Tumalo Avenue
(541) 388–1065, (888) 388–1065
www.satherhouse.com

Five years ago Robbie Giamboi, a widow with a mission, purchased the old Sather House. Fortunately, the window coverings made the rooms so dark she couldn't see how bad the interior was, or else we might not be where we are today. After seven months of working 12 hours a day, hiring and firing two general contractors, and finally doing the contracting herself, the house has been returned to its original splendor. To quote Robbie, "I was taken over! I was in my element!" The result is an artful restoration of a Craftsman-style house built in 1911 that is now on the National Register of Historic Places and featured on the front cover of the local heritage walk tour guide. It is right in

The largest guest room is the Garden Room with its beige carpeting and green striped wallpaper, lace curtains, and private bath. On the bed is an ivory Battenburg spread. The Victorian Room is done in frosty blues with pale pink accents. It has a private bath with a claw-foot tub and is a favorite with women.

Men are often drawn to the English Room with its deep navy wallpaper, gold curtains, and faux painted walls. The ceiling is currently a deep green (Robbie may experiment with another color), and on the wall is an old photo of American World War I soldiers that Robbie found in the old barn—just one of many treasures that she has discovered and brought to light. The English Room has a private bath with a shower/tub. At night in the lamplight this is a very warm and cozy room. The small Country Room, with its soft mauve, blue, and green tones, has its own brightly lit bath with a tub. It's a hit with single persons and young couples.

Take into consideration the fact that there are a lot of antiques and a somewhat formal atmosphere when deciding whether The Sather House would be a comfortable choice for your children age 12 and older. The entire house is pet- and dander-free. Visa, MasterCard, American Express, and Discover are accepted.

Sisters/Camp Sherman Area

The Cascade Mountains seem to sparkle more when viewed from Sisters than from anywhere else we know. Maybe it's the contrast between the cold snowy peaks, the lush green meadows, and the soft ponderosa pine trees. Add to that one of the most charming little downtowns in Oregon and you get a truly wonderful setting for a bed-and-breakfast.

Strolling along the sidewalks until a window display of pottery, artwork, or gift wares lures you in is a very popular pastime in this tourist town. Most innkeepers we interviewed said they usually don't serve breakfast until 9:00 A.M. because the shops don't open until 10:00 A.M. Lunches are generally terrific at the small eateries scattered between the shops. If you just

town just a few blocks from Drake Park and about 6 blocks from downtown Bend.

What impressed us most was Robbie's powerful use of color. The living room is elegantly restrained. The wallpaper is in rich creams, there are deep red silk roses on the mantelpiece, and lace curtains at the windows. The furniture is antique with a modern piece or two slipped in unobtrusively. The dining room is equally elegant. Robbie serves a formal breakfast on real china, and brings out the silver when she does her cold-weather late-afternoon teas next to the fire. From the sparkling white-and-chintz-blue-kitchen come Dutch babies (puffy German pancakes) with peaches and raspberries, potato pancakes with applesauce, French toast with yogurt and marionberries, or cheese strada—a baked cheese, egg, and bread dish. A sweet orange bread is another favorite.

When you ascend the beautiful staircase (note the original, Craftsman-style banister), you will enter a large hallway done completely in a rich berry color, ceiling included. A telephone and two chairs are arranged for the guests' use as well as a small refrigerator stocked with beverages.

want a pick-me-up, there are several places where you can get an ice cream or frozen yogurt, or stop in at the Sisters Coffee Company (see our Shopping chapter) for a latte made with coffee beans roasted daily.

On rainy days head for the Paulina Springs Book Store (again, see Shopping), where you can relax on a couch after perusing the beautifully arranged shelves. Start your day at The Fly Fisher's Place if you came here to wet a line (see our Fishing chapter). On summer weekends, consider making a reservation at Bronco Billy's Ranch Grill & Saloon for a pleasant dinner in a historic setting (see Restaurants).

Sisters gets more snow and keeps it longer than the other towns in Central Oregon. During winter there's a good chance you'll be able to Nordic ski or snowshoe from your door. Just outside town is the pristine Deschutes National Forest, where you can hike to the top of Black Butte cinder cone. Two fabulous daytrips are within 20 minutes of Sisters. First, drive west on U.S. Highway 20 to Camp Sherman and hike through a pine forest along the incredibly beautiful Metolius River. For another great summer outing, head up Oregon Highway 242 to McKenzie Pass for some beautiful vistas and an interesting interpretive walk through lava fields. Along the way to the pass you will drive by an elk farm. (See our chapters on Snowplay and Other Outdoor Recreation for more information.)

If you are interested in staying in Camp Sherman, see the lodging options listed in our Resorts, Ranches, and Vacation Rentals chapter.

The Australian Outback Country Lodge Bed & Breakfast $$$
68733 Junipine Lane, Sisters,
(541) 549-4312, (800) 930-0055
www.sisterslodging.com

Five minutes is all it takes to go from the bustle of downtown Sisters to the serene quiet of the Australian Outback Country Lodge B&B, a two-story, 1970s country home nestled among pines and aspens on nine wooded acres. Sometimes it takes a moment or two, and a deep breath of fresh air, to become aware of the bustle of nature in this woodland setting. What at first seems to be a deep hush surrounding the home reveals itself to actually be the whisper of breezes through the pine needles, the chirps of birds and squirrels, and the almost imperceptible crunching of grazing deer.

Richard and Margaret Mason purchased what was known as the Squaw Creek Inn, an existing bed-and-breakfast, in 2001. Since there was some legislation brewing to change the potentially politically incorrect name of Squaw Creek, which runs behind the property, to a new name, Richard and Margaret decided to make a clean break with the past and come up with a new name for the inn to reflect the change in ownership. After having run a bed-and-breakfast for 15 years in Amish country Lampeter, Pennsylvania, called The Australian Walkabout Inn Bed & Breakfast, it seemed appropriate to call the new inn The Australian Outback Country Lodge. Richard is a native of Australia, and the Masons enjoy adding a touch of his homeland to their inn, including having a "dingo" dog named Wiskers (actual parentage unknown).

The actual move from Pennsylvania to Sisters must have been something to see. Their new inn, a contemporary house with a high gabled roofline and cathedral ceiling in the great room, is decorated with countless pieces of antique furniture, paintings, Oriental rugs, and memorabilia that they brought with them.

The cozy great room is where breakfast is served, and the round, claw-foot oak tables will be dressed in all their finery when guests check in, ready for the next morning's repast. For real antiques buffs, listening to Margaret's stories behind her collection could take the better part of the day, but for the rest of us average folks her welcome tour includes only a brief story about a special piece or two—such as her 18th-century American pine séance table.

The guest rooms all have appropriately Aussie names, such as The Snowy River Room, or The Walkabout. Each one is unique, but all have been extensively decorated in styles ranging from Victorian to pioneer Americana/Aussie. The rooms look out onto decks, or, on the lower level, onto a patio, so they can all be accessed directly from the outside. Each room has its own private bath, TV/VCR, a tea/coffeemaker, mini-fridge, and robes.

The decks are a wonderful place to relax and observe the wildlife close at hand, which in summer includes the Masons' collection of pet doves. Not far from the house is a hot tub. A short stroll through the woods to the back of the property brings you to Squaw Creek. A pair of RV parking spaces are available, which would provide the perfect opportunity for RVing and non-RVing friends to rendezvous in style.

Breakfast is a romantic affair with candles and fine china, Australian teas, homemade breads, fresh fruits, and a main course.

The Masons have done a great deal to the property in the short time they have owned it, but what we saw when we visited was just the beginning. More renovations and additions are in the plans, including adding a few tepees to the local landscape and a heated aviary for Margaret's pampered feathered friends. Despite their passion in their roles as innkeepers, this is also a real family home, with the Masons' two children, dog, and pet birds. Antiques-wary, older children are welcomed as guests, and a pet might be accommodated by prior arrangement. Visa and Master-Card are accepted.

Blue Spruce Bed & Breakfast $$$
444 South Spruce Street, Sisters
(541) 549–9644, (888) 328–9644
www.bluesprucebandb.com

Before Vaunell and Bob Temple could start building their dream bed-and-breakfast inn, they had to spend six months tearing down old ramshackle buildings and hauling almost a century's worth of debris away from the one-acre lot with it's fabulous location just 3 blocks south of downtown. Nowadays, looking at the beautiful two-story farmhouse and manicured grounds, you'd never guess what preceded this stately sight. As their guests would agree, it was worth the effort.

Inside is an inn designed for perfection. The grand entry is two stories high, with a staircase that rises to an open, banistered walkway from which the four guest rooms are accessed. A large great room opens off the entryway, with its round dining table and huge seating area and fireplace. Beyond is a wide wraparound porch overlooking a peaceful backyard with an expanse of lawn edged in pine trees where you can watch the deer come and graze.

Vaunell's dream kitchen is off-limits to guests, especially while she prepares a luscious breakfast starting with fresh-squeezed OJ and fresh-ground coffee, with perhaps some lemon soufflé & blueberry pancakes, or orange pecan-stuffed French toast. Breakfast is served family-style at the big round dining table with its huge custom-made lazy Susan, or in nice weather out on the deck. After a hard day of skiing or fishing, or after strolling the quaint streets of downtown Sisters with its beautiful shops, guests return to the inn, where a cookie jar with fresh-baked delights and a refrigerator stocked with ice cream await. Or take some fresh microwave popcorn and a video to your room. Here's an Insiders' tip for you: Guests who visit over the Thanksgiving holiday are invited to join the Temples for their holiday dinner.

It would be difficult to say if guests feel more pampered before they head for bed or after they have retired for the day. The spacious guest rooms are decorated to the nines in hunting, fishing, cowboy, or forest themes. You'll smile when you see your room! Each one has a king-size bed, TV/VCR, gas log fireplace, mini-fridge with beverages, and bathrobes to make sure you are absolutely comfortable. The private bathrooms are to die for, with a heated towel rack next to the spa tub, and a separate shower. You might decide to spend your holiday in your room!

Visa, MasterCard, American Express, and Discover are accepted. Pets need to stay at a nearby pet resort in Sisters.

Conklin's Guest House $$–$$$, no credit cards
69013 Camp Polk Road, Sisters
(541) 549–0123, (800) 549–4262
www.conklinsguesthouse.com

Having been in operation since 1986, you might say innkeepers Frank and Marie Conklin are experts at making you feel right at home. And when you walk

Peace and quiet and a country ambiance are just a few of the attractions of a bed-and-breakfast.
PHOTO: CONKLIN'S GUEST HOUSE

through the front door, that's exactly how you feel—like you're home.

This is a more old-fashioned style of bed-and-breakfast, and we don't say this because of the antiques and cozy ambiance. Conklin's guests tend to use their guest rooms more like bedrooms—for sleeping. On a sunny morning guests may find it difficult to get started on a day of fun in Central Oregon because it's so pleasant after breakfast to relax around the patio and chat with other guests. In the evening, folks who aren't spending the night on the town tend to gravitate to the comfortable couches and deep armchairs in the living room for a good read, or perhaps to share their travel stories with fellow travelers.

The rambling, century-old ranch house has been renovated to perfection. The house is entered through a foyer filled with shelves of touring information and guidebooks. It takes a few minutes to absorb the richness of the large living area, which is done in deep burgundy and filled with old chairs and comfortable couches, fringed lamp shades, a baby grand piano, books, and artwork everywhere. It sounds chaotic, but it's actually well-ordered. On closer

examination you'll find plenty of choices for a spot to call your own. The far wall opens with white French doors; beyond is a lovely solarium with terra-cotta tiles and hanging plants. In the distance are views of the Three Sisters mountains.

Breakfast is served in the solarium on white lawn tables. As you eat, you'll have a view of the heated pool, lawns, and ponds. During summer, breakfast moves out to the covered seating area surrounding the pool. Breakfast might be a beautifully arranged plate with frittata, sausage, and fresh fruit accompanied by a nice espresso. Speaking of the pool, it's a heated pool and a very inviting one at that! If you like, you can catch your own trout for breakfast and Marie will cook it up splendidly—it's the only time you can keep what you catch in the trout pond.

All the uniquely decorated standard rooms have claw-foot tubs with separate showers. The barrier-free Lattice Room, which was occupied when we visited, is on the ground floor. Down the hall is the Forget-Me-Not Room, with its deep green carpet and wallpaper, white wicker furniture, and four-poster bed with fireplace.

Upstairs is a family-size room called Heather Room. This large room, formerly called the dormitory, is newly renovated in pastels with a seating area of wicker furniture, a queen-size bed, plus two twin beds tucked away in an alcove. A huge bathroom for this room is connected to the bedroom. Also upstairs are the cherry-colored Columbine Room and the gracious Morning Glory Suite, which offers a mountain view from the claw-foot tub.

The lawns surrounding the pond and gazebo make a beautiful spot for weddings. Off-street parking is available for up to 200 people. In fact, Conklin's has become so popular with brides-to-be that most of their summer weekends are booked with weddings. Summer travelers will probably be steered toward weekday visits. Weekends are usually available to singles, couples, and families during fall, winter, and spring. The Conklins are within walking distance of a small, general aviation airport; they will be happy to pick you up there or at the Redmond Airport. Because of the unfenced pool, the Conklins welcome children age 12 and older.

Insiders' Tip

If you want to express your appreciation to your host and hostess and are looking for something to buy them, note whether they have any collections. Most collect something, whether it's dolls, coffee-table books, whatever. A guest at the Elliott House bought the owners a piece of Depression glass for their collection, and they cherish the memory.

Lazy Rockin' B'nC Ranch $$–$$$, no credit cards
69707 Holmes Road, Sisters,
(541) 548–0178, (888) 488–0178
www.sistersbedandbreakfast.com

For Burt and Cindy Murray, a chance to live on 40 acres on the outskirts of Sisters in a fabulous new inn they built from scratch is a dream come true. Cindy, with her background in interior design, and having raised six children, found the job of being an inn designer and innkeeper came very naturally. Burt, formerly a financial advisor, is now proud to call himself head ranch hand and assistant innkeeper. The single-story inn they designed sits in the middle of a meadow that reaches out into miles of sagebrush and juniper forest. Seven peaks of the Cascade Range are held perfectly by the rough fingers of the evergreen trees, and are reflected in the lovely pond next to the house. A small decorative waterfall element at the edge of the pond adds its voice to the sounds of the breeze in the junipers.

Two big black labs, Ace and Valentine, loll and lounge on the front veranda, gently offering arriving guests their first welcome. Inside, the great room beckons with its comfy leather couches on either side of a river rock fireplace and windows framing views of the Cascades. Cindy describes her inn's design style as "farmhouse with a touch of hunting lodge." The decor throughout the house is tastefully understated. The simple country motifs stenciled around the walls are the handiwork of Cindy, who not only did the stenciling work but also designed many of the stencils.

The great room, with the exception of the kitchen, is for the use of the guests. Breakfast is served at 9:00 A.M. (give or take an hour at the request of the guests) at the big table in the dining area. A lovely gourmet breakfast—coffee or tea and cakes followed by a hot main entree—is served in the main inn dining room. In the evening you'll find refreshments await you at the dining-room table. A 1924 Steinway grand piano sits regally to the side of the dining area. Guests with expertise on the ivory keys are welcome to play it, calmly supervised by a pair of caribou-head trophies mounted on the wall above.

Two separate master suites, beautifully decorated with hand-sewn quilts, lie past the dining area. These rooms open onto a small hallway with its own entrance to the front of the house. The Summer Room, a third master suite done in yellow and blue, is located off the living room. As its name implies, it is usually used for guests in the summer, and in the winter reverts back to being Cindy's sewing room. All three main-floor rooms have TV/VCRs and private baths with jetted tubs.

A fourth guest suite is upstairs in what might have originally been intended to be a triple-car garage. It has its own entrance from the side of the house where Cindy has hand-stenciled picket fences along the stairwell walls. There's plenty of room to spread out in front of the gas stove in the sitting area, which also has a TV/VCR, and there are two double beds. Below this room, opening right off the main entry-way, are the innkeepers' quarters.

A few hundred yards away is a separate building called the Bunkhouse that serves as a vacation rental or as extra B&B rooms when the main inn is full. Its common area and three bedrooms (one a master suite, two that share a bath) are also beautifully decorated in the farmhouse/hunting-lodge style. On a cold day, the plaid living-room couches in front of the gas fireplace/stove would be the perfect spot to snuggle up with a book picked from the collection on the bookshelves that line the living-room wall. The living room also has a small TV and VCR.

Besides the two labs and a cat or two, the family members in situ include three horses, one specifically designated for a guest rider. Guest horses can be boarded at the ranch for an extra charge. The ranch is bordered on two sides by Bureau of Land Management lands, so there's plenty of riding available right from the ranch. Other outdoor activities at the ranch include horseshoes and just lazing about on the verandas. Sisters is a 10-minute drive to the west, and there are five championship golf courses within 25 minutes from the ranch. The pond next to the house is unfenced, making the ranch unsuitable for younger guests. Payment may be made by check or cash, and please, no pets other than of the equine species.

Rags to Walkers Guest Ranch $$$
17045 Farthing Lane, Sisters
(541) 548–7000, (800) 422–5622, in Oregon
www.ragstowalkers.com

Accommodations are first-class at this magnificent, 100-acre Tennessee walking horse ranch. Hosts Bonnie Jacobs-Halousek and Neal Halousek built the big, early-20th-century-style farmhouse in 1994 and included four extra master bedrooms for their grown children and grandchildren to use when visiting. Since the rooms were empty much of the time, they decided to open their doors to bed-and-breakfast guests.

The name of the inn, Rags to Walkers, is a pun on the ol' rags-to-riches story and accurately traces Bonnie's success from her days in the clothing business to where she and Neal are today—raising horses on a beautiful ranch in Sisters. Neal was a P.E. teacher before joining Bonnie in their retail business. These extremely gracious and energetic hosts have taken Central Oregon hospitality to new heights.

The house is extraordinary, with an expansive living room that opens onto a wraparound porch with incredible views of the Cascade Mountains. Around the house stretch acres and acres of green fields outlined with almost 4 miles of white rail fencing. Artistically placed near the buildings are four ponds stocked with trout, each with its own waterfall, and meandering, artificial brooks.

The five guest rooms (one is a two-bedroom suite) are very spacious and nicely decorated in an uncluttered, country style with antiques and reproductions. The cream-colored walls with off-white or oatmeal carpets lend an elegant air, and you automatically take off your shoes on entering. Every room has a king-size bed, TV with VCR tastefully hidden away, a fireplace, and a luxurious private bath. Wreaths of dried flowers and old-time pictures grace the walls. The largest quarters—the master suite—features a huge walk-in shower and a two-person Jacuzzi tub with views.

rooms decorated with antiques and wood floors. Every room has a private bath with a claw-foot tub and a showerhead shaped like a giant sunflower. Even the pearl, push-button light switches look authentically antique. Occasionally when the main house is full, bed-and-breakfast guests may be invited to sleep in the vacation house.

You might want to consider chartering a plane to fly into the Sisters Airport just for the pleasure of being picked up in the white Rags to Walkers limousine. They also offer the royal treatment for commercial fliers arriving at Redmond Airport (see our Getting Here, Getting Around chapter). It's a toss-up as to whether to visit Bonnie and Neal when the weather is cold so you can snuggle in bed and gaze at the fire, or when the weather is warm and all the fields are green and the wildflowers are blooming. Rags to Walkers Guest Ranch accepts Visa and MasterCard.

Despite its elegance, this is a house that yearns for the bustle of children. On the main floor is an enormous playroom with exercise equipment, a pool table, a wet bar, and closets full of games and toys. A couple of other closets open into double beds for extra people. Bonnie and Neal say kids love sleeping in the closet beds! Well-mannered children of all ages are welcome but must be supervised by their parents.

Outside, guests may enjoy 2½ miles of paved paths. Bring your bikes or borrow one of the nine bikes at the ranch (one is a tandem!). Kids love to fly along the paths on their in-line skates. Fly-fish in the ponds, ride the horses, or bring your own horses. Horse boarding is $15 per day.

A gourmet breakfast of a frittata or quiche, fresh fruit, and homemade bread with fresh-squeezed orange juice is served in the dining room or on the porch. Bonnie and Neal are armed with an outdoor kitchen to cook up a barbecue dinner on the porch; if you're interested, call ahead to make arrangements. Golf carts are available to whisk you to their 27,000-square-foot riding arena, where you may schedule an English or Western riding lesson for an extra charge.

Next to the arena is a new, Victorian-style vacation house with seven guest

Redmond

The small town of Redmond has its origins in ranching, and it is still surrounded by fields of alfalfa and pastures with cattle, sheep, llamas, and emu—the exotic, ostrichlike bird that many people thought would make them rich. Once the birds became plentiful, however, prices plummeted. You'll know an emu ranch when you see one—it will have a tan, igloo-shaped house for each bird.

Just north of Redmond is Smith Rock State Park, with its beautiful cliffs and rock formations that are so popular with rock climbers. It's an excellent spot for a picnic. Also nearby are the Crooked River and Deschutes River, both loved by fly fishers, and of course there is unlimited hiking. Kevin Costner thought this landscape was so striking he filmed his post-apocalyptic epic *The Postman* near Smith Rock along the Crooked River.

Downtown Redmond has some interesting antiques shops, a few restaurants, an older cinema, and several supermarkets. Redmond is also home to our spectacular Deschutes County Fairgrounds and Expo Center, which is located right next to our county's commercial airport.

Deschutes River Lodge $$$
5087 Northwest Woody Court
(541) 923–4701
www.deschutesriverlodge.com

Fly fisher–folk and nature lovers in general will be at home in this lodge, tucked away in a wooded enclave north of Redmond, set back just enough from the edge of the Deschutes River Canyon. Expansive layers of decks provide the ideal spot for watching the birds and deer, or taking that perfect photo of the Cascade peaks in the morning light. On a quiet night of a new moon, lie back on a chaise longue while gazing up at a sky lit only by the vast Milky Way.

The lodge was the vision of Jeanene Stentz, a woman with a mission. Jeanene started preparing for the role of innkeeper long before the lodge opened. For years she had been tying flies professionally, but, being a mother of six, she lacked the time and, frankly, the encouragement to get into fishing herself. It happened that she met her future partner, avid fly fisherman Dick Stentz at a fly-tying class that she was teaching. To make a long story short, Jeanene became Mrs. Stentz and the couple settled into a beautiful cedar house with cedar-lined cathedral ceilings and a huge view of the Cascades. The next step for Jeanene was to graduate from the Western Culinary Institute, where she focused on cooking for the hospitality industry. Finally, a guest house was made out of their three-bay garage, with three guest rooms and private baths. Lots more decking was added to connect the guest house with the main lodge, and the Deschutes River Lodge opened for business in 1998.

The guest house has a motel-type layout with each room opening onto a lovely covered boardwalk. Early risers can leave for a day of fishing without disturbing the rest of the guests. The boardwalk leads to the kitchen in the main lodge. Guest rooms are beautifully decorated in hunter green and earth tones with natural wooden wainscoting and custom plaid bedding. The Cascade Room has one queen-size bed. The Redside (named after our local subspecies of rainbow trout) and Steelhead Rooms, both designed with fly-fishing friends in mind, each have a pair of extra-long twin beds that can be converted into a king-size bed.

Inside the lodge is a very comfortable common area with a fully stocked fly-tying bench and library for the use of guests. Jeanene can help with tips on tying flies, and Dick will give you directions to some great fishing spots, including historic Tetherow Crossing, just a few minutes' drive away. Guide services can be arranged with one of their many contacts at the local fly shops. For the nonfishing guests, a telescope and comfy chairs will provide for a relaxing evening. Or you may want to discuss the area's geology with Dick, another of his passions. As you might imagine, breakfasts cooked by Jeanene in her professionally-equipped kitchen can be quite a gourmet affair, and add to that the option of an equally incredible dinner (for an extra charge and with advance notice). You have your choice of dining on the deck or being seated at the dining table under the light of a large Currier and Ives hanging lamp with fishing and hunting vignettes on the glass shade.

Jeanene and Dick welcome Visa and MasterCard, but please leave pets at home. There is a two-night minimum on weekends and holidays. Winter rates are discounted by 30 percent.

Llast Camp Llama Bed and Breakfast $,
no credit cards
4555 Northwest Pershall Way
(541) 548–6828

Central Oregon is one of the largest llama ranching areas in the country, and here you have an opportunity to be a guest at a working ranch, courtesy of Buck and Aileen Adams.

Perched on a hilltop overlooking pastoral green fields is a small bed-and-breakfast that has delighted travelers and adventurers alike since 1985. While some folks visit Llast Camp Llamas simply for the peaceful, rural experience and country-style hospitality, others come because they are interested in llamas, or in packing with llamas. Call for directions to this marvelous country home in an agricultural area about 10 minutes north of Redmond

The guest accommodations consist of a suite of two rooms and a full bath. The sitting room, done in comfortable Americana with blues and beiges, has a couch and cable TV. The couch opens out to sleep a second couple or children in the same party. The bedroom is done in Panama style with yellow and white, and it has a queen-size bed. Both rooms are air-conditioned. The privilege of being the ranch's only guests comes at no extra charge, and children are welcome.

Aileen likes to create a different homemade breakfast every morning. Some of her dishes might include waffles or hotcakes, and there's always fresh fruit. Guests are welcome to help Buck with chores around the ranch, feed the 12 llamas, or just tag along to say howdy. It's pretty tempting to simply kick back and hang out on the deck. When evening comes, the outdoor hot tub has privacy fencing so you may relax in comfort while gazing at the stars.

For more adventurous guests, Buck and Aileen will arrange a pack trip for two nights or more in the beautiful wilderness of the Cascade Mountains, complete with transportation, llama gear and food, and a couple of well-trained pack llamas to do the hard work. Bring your own sleeping bags, tent, and dried food. That hot tub will feel great when you return. Reserve these trips ahead of time.

Insiders' Tip

Every establishment has those days in the late fall, winter, or early spring when business is at its slowest. Some bed-and-breakfast owners will offer a two-night stay for the price of one, especially Sunday through Thursday. Feel like you need a little pampering? Call around for deals.

Sunriver/La Pine Area

This southern part of Central Oregon features some very exciting recreational opportunities. Explore obsidian flows and lava tube caves at the Newberry National Volcanic Monument. Fly-fish in the nearby Fall River or Deschutes River, golf at the 18-hole Quail Run Golf Course, hike, or Nordic ski the many acres of forest in the Deschutes National Forest.

The small town of La Pine has a few restaurants and conveniences. Sunriver, a complete resort community, has a broader selection of eateries as well as shopping, a fly-fishing store, and other sports-equipment rentals. There is one bed-and-breakfast in this area.

DiamondStone Guest Lodge and Gallery
$$–$$$
16693 Sprague Loop, La Pine
(541) 536–6263, (800) 600–6263
www.diamondstone.com

Tucked away in the sunny lodgepole pine forest with Mount Bachelor peaking over the treetops is DiamondStone, a modest two-story bed-and-breakfast lodge.

Innkeepers Doug and Gloria Watt are entrepreneurs, and the telephones in each guest room reflect their business orientation. They do not live at the house, allowing their guests to have the house more or less to themselves.

The house is very tastefully decorated in a Western theme (no cowboy-boot lamps!) with beautiful paintings and sculptures by a carefully selected array of Northwest artists. Their home doubles as a commercial art gallery, and the artworks that you see are for sale. In the vaulted living room you'll find a warm fireplace, cable TV, VCR, and a CD player, plus an extensive collection of music and videos, and books. In a hallway are guidebooks and brochures for guests' perusal or purchase. Outside the adjoining dining area is a pleasant deck with table and chairs; these often provide views of deer and other wildlife as well as the Cascade Mountains.

On the main level, the beds in the two-bedroom suite are covered with quilts, and the custom-made yellow pine furniture has carved silhouettes of mountains or geometric patterns. Each bedroom has a private bath and cable TV with HBO and VCR. Upstairs is a two-room suite with a living room and bedroom. It has a TV, a lovely bath, and beautiful views. There is also a huge upstairs deck that is a relaxing spot to spend a summer evening.

Outside is a hot tub for the enjoyment of the guests. In another part of the lodge is a small exercise room. DiamondStone is adjacent to Quail Run Golf Course (see our Golf chapter), and the Watts adds golf package rates to their long list of amenities. There are a lot of small roads that you can explore while riding complimentary bikes. Nearby is the gentle Little Deschutes River, great for canoeing or a little fishing (see our recreation chapters).

Typical of the Watts' concern for their guests' comfort, they prepare breakfast in a separate kitchen so as to not disturb anyone sleeping late. Only fresh-baked breads or muffins are done in the main kitchen because they love having guests wake up to the smell of baking. A weekend specialty of the house is "abelskievers"— puffy round delicacies made with pancake batter in a special pan. Freshly squeezed juice, coffee, fresh fruit, cereal, and yogurt round out the meal.

Doug and Gloria have a pet corgi whose job title is "Official Greeter." She likes to play catch with children, who are also welcome. Guest dogs are welcomed for an extra charge of $20 per night. There's a fenced acre that could accommodate a guest horse or two. Visa, MasterCard, Discover, and American Express cards are accepted.

Prineville Area

The home of ranchers, loggers, and employees of Les Schwab Tires, Prineville has a lot of small-town character and just enough amenities to make everyone happy. There is one very good dinner house, one very good sandwich eatery, and an espresso place for visiting urbanites who miss home.

Surrounding Prineville are Bureau of Land Management desert lands with fossil beds, interesting birds and wildflowers, minerals for rock hounds, and the Crooked River for trout fishing (see our Fishing and various recreation chapters). Bring your camera for some great photo opportunities; sunrise and sunset are the best times to catch knock-your-socks-off pictures in the desert. To the east are the Ochoco National Forest and Prineville Reservoir, two places where you can go in the summer to cool off. Folks golf year-round at Meadow Lakes Golf Course (see Golf).

The Historical Elliott House $, no credit cards
305 West First Street
(541) 416–0423
www.empnet.com/elliotthouse/

Andy and Betty Wiechert, refugees from the big city of San Francisco, absolutely love life in a small town. They feel that even visiting Bend, which they do on occasion for a change of scenery or some serious shopping, is too urban an experience for them. They can't wait to get back to their beautiful 1908 Queen Anne Victorian-style house on a quiet side street in the center of Prineville, which they describe as "gracious and magical."

The house has been on the National Register of Historic Places since 1989, when the prior owners were also operating a bed-and-breakfast. Andy and Betty were primarily interested in the house's historical aspect when they bought it, but have since decided to carry on the tradition of having house guests—purely for the enjoyment of it. They just love being innkeepers, and feel that people who frequent B&Bs are a special kind of folk. Betty says when she opens the door to first-time guests she already feels like they're family. They like to tell the story about the time they spoke for a while with a guest named Bill—they were shocked to discover the man was actually William Hurt, the actor.

The Wiecherts are antiques collectors, and the Elliott House is hardly large enough to hold their entire collection. Antiques are displayed in every nook, cranny, and niche. Their Depression glass collection is very extensive and fills many cabinets. Andy loves to demonstrate the 1916 Wurlitzer Player Piano or the 1906 Edison phonograph.

Upstairs are the two guest rooms. Since these share a Victorian bath down the hall, only one room is rented at a time unless there is a family or friends who want both rooms. The Weicherts would prefer that their guests be completely comfortable and happy, than to try to fill both bedrooms with strangers. On the weekday we visited, one room was occupied by a couple visiting from Italy who were building a new house in Prineville. The Elliott House had been their American headquarters off and on during the four-year process of looking for real estate and then during the construction of their house. We didn't see their room, but it has a king-size bed. The other second-floor room is smallish, with lovely floral wallpa-per and a high double bed with an iron bedstead. On the third floor, the attic is in the process of being fashioned into a guest sitting area. It has comfortable couches and a big-screen TV with VCR.

Betty goes all out at breakfast. It is an elegant affair with candles and antique china. You may choose between such delicacies as strawberry-filled crepes, Swedish waffles, traditional eggs and bacon, and fresh scones. Everything is homemade fresh to order.

After breakfast your hosts will be happy to lend you bicycles or golf clubs. The residents here include two dogs and two cats, one of whom, a Persian, has exclusive use of the third bedroom on the second floor. Children age 12 and older are welcome, but no more pets, please! Being the only bed-and-breakfast in Prineville, at least for the time being, they tend to have a full house, so you might want to reserve ahead.

Resorts, Ranches, and Vacation Rentals

Bend Area

Sisters/Camp
   Sherman Area

Redmond

Sunriver/La Pine
   Area

Madras Area

This chapter features a diverse collection of destinations that have two things in common: They would all be excellent places to spend a week or two, and for the most part, you won't need your sleeping bag. Beyond that, these lodging options offer very different experiences—from rustic lakeside cabins with no indoor running water to posh resorts where all you'll need to bring are a toothbrush and some dude duds. Whether you like to spend your vacations being a cowpoke, on the golf course, fishing on a glassy lake, or pretending that you live here, you can find your dream in Central Oregon.

Most of our resorts are in the Bend area (which includes the Cascade Lakes Highway), the Sisters/Camp Sherman area, and the Sunriver/La Pine area. Redmond has one resort, Eagle Crest, and the Madras area has one, Kah-Nee-Ta, which is at Warm Springs Indian Reservation. Within each geographical region, we have broken these accommodations down into the following four categories.

Destination resorts are comfortable, often luxurious properties that usually offer restaurants and a smorgasbord of recreational opportunities such as golf, swimming, skating, Nordic skiing, biking, tennis, and/or horseback riding. These options offer enough attractions and activities that guests might not need to leave the resort, unless they are interested in a night on the town. For this category, we have included property-management companies that represent vacation rentals within resort settings.

A few vacation rentals within destination resorts are handled by the owners, but most are managed by property management companies that take care of everything from collecting your money to arranging for linens and cleaning services. In Sunriver, rentals are usually handled by these management companies.

Ranches are destination resorts with the added attraction of being part of a working ranch. Generally, guests are welcome to help out with chores, or they can at least observe the routines of the ranch hands. On-site activities are expanded to include trail rides and recreational opportunities such as acres of hiking trails.

Rustic resorts are either near Bend on the Cascade Lakes Highway, in the Camp Sherman area west of Sisters, or in the Newberry National Volcanic Monument between Sunriver and La Pine. These are cabins (ranging from really rustic to the posh side of rustic) located within the Deschutes National Forest, alongside either a lake or a river. These accommodations offer a variety of recreational opportunities including boating, fishing, waterskiing, hiking, sailing, Nordic skiing, and snowmobiling.

Vacation rentals are located outside of a resort area. As in most other parts of the country, these come in all shapes and sizes—from Spartan to very upscale—and at various prices. Vacation rentals offer a feeling of independence that some travelers really appreciate. You can shop for and cook your own food, create your own vacation routine, and be your own person in total privacy.

We have provided names of people and companies that handle more than 700 rentals, but you may also contact local chambers of commerce for more listings (see below).

Obviously, when talking about such a wide range of lodging options, to create a standardized pricing key, like you'll find in our other accommodations chapters, is impossible. Some of these resorts and rentals rent on a nightly basis, some weekly; many of them offer a variety of package deals that may or may not include meals. We've tried to provide basic pricing information that the average traveler would find useful in making a decision. Unless otherwise stated, all of our listings accept major credit cards. As always, call to find out more about costs.

You might also want to contact the local visitors centers and chambers of commerce, always good places to get listings of vacation rentals and more information about area resorts and ranches.

Bend Visitor & Convention Bureau
63085 North U.S. Highway 97, Bend
(541) 382–8048, (800) 949–6086
www.visitbend.org

La Pine Chamber of Commerce
51425 South U.S. Highway 97, Suite A, La Pine
(541) 536–9771
www.lapine.org

Madras/Jefferson County Chamber of Commerce
274 Southwest Fourth Street, Madras
(541) 475–2350, (800) 967–3564
www.madras.net

Prineville/Crook County Chamber of Commerce
390 Northeast Fairview Street, Prineville
(541) 447–6304

Redmond Chamber of Commerce
446 Southwest Seventh Street, Redmond
(541) 923–5191
www.redmondcofc.com

Sisters Area Chamber of Commerce
164 North Elm Street, Sisters
(541) 549–0251
www.sisterschamber.com

Sunriver Area Chamber of Commerce
Sunriver Village Mall, Building O, Sunriver
(541) 593–8149
www.sunriver-direct.com

Bend Area

Destination Resorts

Courtyards at Broken Top
61999 Broken Top Drive
(541) 385–9492, (800) 410–0592
www.bendvacationrentals.com

This lovely gated golf community offers upscale lodging facilities for guests in beautifully appointed townhomes. All of the units are equipped with a kitchen, washer, and dryer, and include daily maid service. Some have views, gas fireplaces, barbecues, hot tubs, and decks, and all are nonsmoking and do not allow pets. Summer rates range from $240 to $290 a night. There is a two-night minimum for summer weekends and a three-night minimum for holidays. Passes to the Athletic Club of Bend are complimentary, and guests may also take advantage of Broken Top's tennis courts and bike paths. Members of another private golf club only are welcome to use the private Broken Top Club golf course

Insiders' Tip

Web sites and vacation rental properties seem to be made for each other, like ham and eggs. The property-management companies, and a few individual owners, have extensive Web sites with lots of photos and detailed descriptions of each rental home, making the task of choosing a vacation spot much easier than it used to be.

and other club facilities. The fabulous Broken Top Club restaurant is open to the public. Bend Vacation Rentals is the exclusive rental agent for the Courtyards.

Elkai Woods at Widgi Creek
18707 Century Drive
(541) 317–5000; (800) 327–5102, Widgi Creek Realty; (541) 382–4449, Widgi Creek Golf Club
www.widgi.com

A golfer's dream, Elkai Woods at Widgi Creek, adjacent to the Widgi Creek Golf Course back nine (see our Golf chapter), is part of a development that is tucked up against the Deschutes National Forest. Guests who can tear themselves away from the greens may take advantage of the miles of national forest trails that lead along the beautiful Deschutes River, or just relax in the Olympic-size pool, hot tubs, and exercise room.

The posh accommodations range from a 500-square-foot motel room–like studio with full bath for $75 per night, up to the 2,400-square-foot, three-bedroom townhome for $250 per night. All the townhomes are completely outfitted with contemporary, country-style furnishings, gas fireplace, gas barbecue, washer/dryer, fully equipped kitchen, and two-car garage. Linens and towels are included. Some of the townhomes have golf course views. All units are nonsmoking, and pets are usually not allowed (so, if you travel with a small pet you might want to ask).

Inn of the Seventh Mountain
18575 Southwest Century Drive
(541) 382–8711, (800) 452–6810
www.7thmtn.com

This family- and group-oriented resort was built in the 1970s. Surrounded by the Deschutes National Forest, the fully self-contained resort is the closest lodging to Mt. Bachelor Ski Area. Guests may enjoy two swimming pools, a miniature golf course, a recreation building with sauna, two restaurants, tennis courts, and a volleyball court. These recreational amenities make up the core of the complex, with condo units forming a large semicircle around the central area.

Each condo looks out onto the Deschutes National Forest, and some have views of Mount Bachelor. A standard room (like a motel room) with one bed is $75. The same room with two beds that sleeps four is $108. The Fireside rooms, which offer a kitchen and fireplace, go for $135. A one-bedroom condo with a kitchen is $160, and condo prices go up to $310 for a three-bedroom, three-bath unit that sleeps eight.

This resort offers supervised youth programs for kids of all ages, golf at Widgi Creek next door (see our Golf chapter), and miles of trails for hiking and fishing in the Deschutes River along the back of the property. Named after Mount Bachelor, the seventh-largest mountain in the Cascades, the Inn of the Seventh Mountain is only 10 minutes from Bend and 20 minutes from skiing at Mt. Bachelor Ski Area. Other activities for both kids and adults involving modest fees include roller-skating and ice-skating (skate rentals available), in-line skate and bike rentals, horseback riding, sleigh rides, white-water rafting, and canoeing (including a quiet dinner raft trip). Ski, golf, and other packages are available.

Mount Bachelor Village Resort & Conference Center
19717 Mt. Bachelor Drive
(541) 389–5900, (800) 452–9846
www.mtbachelorvillage.com

A luxury condominium complex overlooking the Deschutes River, Mount Bachelor Village offers more tranquility and fewer activities than other destination resorts. On-site are an upscale health club and Scanlon's gourmet restaurant, plus a heated pool, tennis courts, and a small conference facility. The Ski House condos, built in the 1980s, offer basic lodging starting at $105 for a one-bedroom unit and going up to $194 for a two-bedroom unit. The River Ridge section of townhomes is newer and much more luxurious, with designer furnishings and a hot tub for each unit on an outside deck overlooking the Deschutes River. These run around $190 per night for a one-bedroom townhome, up to $340 per night for the

A plethora of high mountain lakes greet visitors to the rustic resorts that dot the Cascades Lakes Highway. PHOTO: JIM YUSKAVITCH

three-bedroom unit. The River Ridge Executive accommodations are single rooms, more like a motel, and range from $85 to $115 per night.

If peace and quiet in a beautiful setting is what you need, it's all here. Located on Century Drive about a mile east of the Inn of the Seventh Mountain, the drive to Mt. Bachelor Ski Area is just a few minutes farther from Mount Bachelor Village Resort, but skiers desiring a more tranquil experience think it's worth it.

Ranches

Deschutes River Ranch
20210 Swalley Road
(541) 382–7240, (888) 377–4242
www.drrresort.com

This 410-acre ranch is just 10 minutes north of Bend, but you wouldn't know it. The Ranch looks more like cattle country, with wide-open spaces and 1¾ miles of the Deschutes River running through the property. Guests can fly-fish this private stretch of these famous waters year-round or splash in the waterfalls on a warm day. Trail riding with horses rented at the Deschutes River Ranch stables is a very popular pastime. Other recreational opportunities include tennis courts, a heated swimming pool, spa and exercise room, softball, volleyball, and a children's playground. A corral and several trails for horseback riding are also available.

Nightly accommodations consist of 22 private homes or timeshares, built in the 1970s, located in groves of juniper and poplar trees. A fully furnished three-bedroom, two-bath ranch-style house with fireplace, garage, washer/dryer, full kitchen, phone, and cable TV/VCR rents for $150 per weeknight for up to four persons, or $175 per weekend night. The fifth and sixth guests cost an additional $5.00 each per night. Linens, towels, and tableware are included. Weekly rates are available.

Rock Springs Guest Ranch
64201 Tyler Road
(541) 382–1957, (800) 225–3833
www.rocksprings.com

This dude ranch offers unique and luxurious experiences. Designed in 1969 from the ground up to be a full-service guest ranch, Rock Springs has been extremely successful in sharing this vision with its guests. The ranch is open to vacationing guests, which are primarily well-to-do families, from late June through August and over the Thanksgiving holiday.

The one-week rate includes pick-up at the Redmond Airport, all gourmet meals prepared in the lodge's dining room, a rustic cabin with modern amenities, and any activities you wish to partake in. These include use of your own personal horse (cantering allowed), plus games, youth programs (basically summer camp–type activities for kids), tennis, swimming, a spa, and more. The main lodge is decorated with knotty-pine paneling and leather furniture. The lodge and spa overlook a huge, rock-walled reflecting pond that is actually Rock Springs itself. The scenery surrounding the guest ranch, tucked away in its own private valley adjacent to the Deschutes National Forest, is so Western in flavor that every September Rock Springs stages a photo opportunity with horse wranglers and running horses that attracts famous photographers from around the world.

Such deluxe accommodations, facilities, and soup-to-nuts services don't come cheap. The weekly rate for one adult, based on double-occupancy, is $1,900 and the single-occupancy rate is $2,300. Children ages 6 through 16 are $1,425 per week, and ages 3 through 5 are $1,135 per week. These rates include absolutely everything except the 7 percent county room tax and the 8 percent gratuity, both of which will be automatically tacked on to your bill.

The rest of the year, when it's not accepting vacationers, Rock Springs caters to small conference groups of 20 to 50 people at a time. When we say "caters to," we mean bends over backwards to accommodate each group's needs. The ranch has its own group facilitator on staff to assist with all logistical planning, a new 4,500-square-foot conference center, and outdoor challenge courses.

Located just 9 miles north of Bend, trips to area golf courses, museums, or shopping areas can be arranged. By the end of their vacation week, however, most guests don't want to leave this magical place. In fact, some have returned to work here during the summer months. Those who return the following summer as guests can get their "own" horse again if they wish!

Rustic Resorts

Crane Prairie Resort
Forest Service Road 4270, Crane Prairie Reservoir, Deschutes National Forest
(541) 383-3939
www.crane-prairie-resort-guides.com

Crane Prairie Resort is about 40 miles from Bend at an elevation of 4,400 feet. From the Cascade Lakes Highway, head east on Forest Service Road 42 for about 3 miles; then, just after you cross the Deschutes River, turn north on Forest Service Road 4270. The resort is about 4 miles from there. Crane Prairie Resort is open during fishing season, late April through the first of November, snow permitting. It attracts a mostly fishing-oriented clientele. It has a store that's well stocked with fishing tackle, and there are boat rentals, a boat ramp, gas, and moorage. The store sells propane and has coin showers but no phones, and no cell phone service. The resort also has some RV camping and is adjacent to a Forest Service campground that has tent camping (see our Camping chapter).

The handful of cabins are very rustic. They have just enough electric wiring to provide electric lights, but don't plan on running your blow dryer. All the cabins are heated with woodstoves and come with linens, but you can still bring along your sleeping bags if you like. The small cabins with two double beds and no running water cost $40 per night for up to four people. The larger cabins have a downstairs with one double bed and an upstairs with three double beds; these are $50 per night for four people. The larger units also have a quasi-kitchen consisting of one small faucet with cold water and a small propane cookstove—that's it. Additional people are $5.00 per night. Pets and smoking are okay if guests clean up. Bring warm clothing to wear at night for the trek to the bathroom facilities.

Crane Prairie starts accepting reservations on January 3. To make reservations you will need to contact the resort directly by phone. The resort's Web site is minimalist, and they don't have online reservations.

Cultus Lake Resort
Cultus Lake, Forest Service Road 4635,
2 miles west of the Cascade Lakes Highway,
Deschutes National Forest
(541) 408–1560, summer
(541) 389–3230, winter (voice mail)
(800) 616–3230, reservations and additional information
www.cultuslakeresort.com

Imagine a mountain lake at an elevation of 4,700 feet, surrounded by pine forest. The pristine body of water is 4.5 miles long, 2 miles wide, 230 feet deep, and so crystal-clear you can see much of the bottom. Then fill the lake with mackinaw and rainbow trout, add a sandy beach and a resort with cabins and all the trimmings, and you've got yourself a very nice vacation destination.

Boating is very popular at Cultus Lake. It's one of only two lakes in the Cascade Lakes area where waterskiing is allowed. The resort rents fishing boats, Jet Skis, kayaks, canoes, pontoon boat, buoys, and paddleboats, and it offers groceries, gas, and oil. The beach offers swimming and sunbathing.

Small lakeside cabins (numbers 11 through 15) with two beds and a shower/bath cost $74 per night for two people, or $490 per week for two, and hold a maximum of four people. Cabins 16 through 23 also sleep four, but these offer electric kitchens refurbished in 2001 and equipped with utensils and dishes, a fireplace, and a shower/bath. For two persons the rates run from $82 per night up to $610 per week.

The larger cabins that sleep up to six go from $105 per night for four up to $500 per week. These all have a kitchen, shower/bath, and fireplace. Cabin 24, the largest unit, sleeps as many as eight at $105 per night for four, or $700 by the week. For all the cabins, additional guests cost $5.00 each per night, or $35.00 each by the week. Pets, on the other hand, cost $7.00 per night.

All cabins have knotty-pine walls, cement floors, heat, linens, and towels. The resort grounds are very pretty, planted with annuals and surrounded by tall pines,

fir trees, and hiking trails. A small restaurant serves a full breakfast and lunch daily, and burger-fare in the evening. All-you-can-eat homemade alder-smoked rib dinners are the extra-special specials on Friday and Saturday nights (June 14–August 31) for $12.95 per adult, first come first served. The restaurant is open from late May through early September, with additional limited hours in the off-season.

Cultus Lake Resort is open from May 15th through mid-October. From July 4th week through Labor Day, cabins are available by the week only, from Sunday to Sunday. All other times there is a two-night minimum. Smoking and pets are allowed in all cabins.

Elk Lake Resort
Elk Lake, Cascade Lakes Highway, Deschutes National Forest
(541) 480–7228
www.elklakeresort.com

This circa 1923 resort is 33 miles west of Bend on the Cascade Lakes Highway. In summer and winter, this place really hums with activity. The lake provides swimming, great sailing, and sailboarding in the summer. Fishing is good in the early summer and fall. The resort rents kayaks, canoes, rowboats, pedal boats, and motorboats, and offers moorage. Mountain bike trails leave from the resort. It is only 1.5 miles to the Pacific Crest Trail, making Elk Lake Resort a popular rest stop for backpackers. Supply packages can be sent to the resort via UPS, and the staff will hold them for backpackers for a $5.00 charge.

In winter, Elk Lake Resort, at an elevation of 4,893 feet, is a popular ski and snowmobile lodge. The road between Dutchman Flat Sno-Park and the resort is closed during winter. Guests may choose to Nordic ski from Dutchman Sno-Park or snowmobile from Wanoga or Edison Sno-Parks. (Read about Sno-Park parking permits in our Snowplay chapter.) The resort is downhill from the northern road closure, but on the return trip you will have about 1,000 feet of elevation gain. The resort sometimes offers winter shuttle service, depending on available equipment, so if making the high elevation trek isn't your idea of a good time, give them a call. Skiers go backcountry skiing on groomed trails from the lodge; snowmobilers travel on the road and on trails to the south and east that are maintained by the Moon Country Snowmobile Club. Dogsled tours are available to the lake. Call the resort for more information. Nordic skiing usually continues through April. May is the winter-to-summer transition month, and offers spring skiing and/or hiking.

The lodge is the central building, and it houses the restaurant, general store, and office. The resort sells gas and oil for snowmobiles and boats. Fourteen cabins are open almost year-round, with a four-tier rate structure: summer/holidays, winter/active, shoulder, and quiet. Summer/holidays are the highest rates. The camping cabins are log cabins that sleep four, with no kitchen and a heated vault toilet outside; they cost $15 to $45. Bring your own bedding. The eight housekeeping cabins sleep four to 16 and cost between $60 and $200 in high season, and $40 to $100 in the quiet season. These all have complete kitchens with dishes and utensils. Bedding, linens, and towels are included in these rates. A laundromat and public shower facility were added in 2001. Tent camping sites are available at the resort, so check them out in our Camping chapter.

The restaurant serves breakfast, lunch, and dinner except during the quiet season. Homemade fries and burgers are popular, or for a hearty warm-up go for the soups or stews. In summer, don't miss the hand-packed ice cream milkshakes. Wine and microbrewery beers are also offered. If you are making your own meals, their well-stocked store has camping supplies as well as the necessary tourist memorabilia.

Elk Lake Resort is open year-round except for a short break in spring and usually a six-week break in fall. You may make reservations up to two months ahead of your arrival date. There is a two-night minimum on weekends, and a three-night minimum for holiday weekends. With the exception of the Memorial Day weekend, April and May are the least expensive quiet season rates. For stays of seven nights or more, a 10 percent discount is available.

Pets are accepted for certain cabins during spring, summer, and fall at $7.00 per day per pet. Smoking is not allowed in the cabins or the lodge.

Twin Lakes Resort
Twin Lakes, Forest Service Road 4260 at South Twin Lake, Cascades Lakes area, Deschutes National Forest
(541) 593–6526
www.twinlakesresort.com

Twin Lakes Resort is tucked next to South Twin Lake near the Deschutes Channel at an elevation of 4,300 feet, within walking distance of North Twin Lake and Wickiup Reservoir. The location makes this a very popular spot for fishing folk who are after kokanee salmon and trophy rainbow and brown trout. The resort sells fishing tackle and daily fishing licenses, propane and gas, and rents canoes, kayaks, paddleboats, and motorboats. This family-oriented resort also offers swimming, hiking, and picnicking. Nearby Wickiup Reservoir is one of only two Cascade Lakes that offers waterskiing.

Accommodations include a small guest cabin with a modern bath and two twin beds that rents for $55 per night. The lakeside fourplex units have electric kitchenettes, two queen-size beds, modern baths, and fireplaces. These units rent for $90 per night for two people. There are also rustic log cabins with lofts and separate bedrooms, decks, full kitchens, and modern baths (no fireplaces). These sleep up to 12 and rent for $135 per night for two. Extra guests and pets cost $5.00 per day each, and smoking is allowed in all of the cabins. All housekeeping cabins have electric heat, and linens are provided. The resort also has a convenience store, an RV park (see our Camping chapter), laundry facilities, and public showers. Their restaurant, Steaks on the Lakes, burned down in February 2001. Owners Shawn and Kathy Peterson are in the process of rebuilding.

To reach Twin Lakes Resort from the Cascade Lakes Highway, head east about 4.5 miles on Forest Service Road 42. One mile after you pass the Deschutes River, turn south on Forest Service Road 4260. The resort is about 1 mile on your right.

Vacation Rentals

Arline McDonald's Vacation Homes
1530 Northwest Jacksonville
(541) 382–4534
www.bendvacationhomes.com

Arline manages five rental houses in west Bend that are privately owned by other individuals. All are fully furnished, have linens and towels, and are nonsmoking.

The secluded Three Pines Lodge, near Shevlin Park, is a grand, four-bedroom house that sleeps eight adults, plus children on the floor. Its grandness is in part attributed to a sweeping panorama of seven Cascades peaks. The Lodge rents for $300 per night, and pets are not allowed.

The Cascade View Chalet has five bedrooms and sleeps up to 10 adults. The entire house rents for $250 to $275 a night. The Grandview Chalet has three bedrooms and comfortably sleeps six adults for $200 per night. These two homes are in a subdivision off Century Drive about 20 minutes from Mt. Bachelor Ski Area.

A fourth home is called the Westside Pines Vacation Home. It's a cozy, three-bedroom house a mile from downtown Bend, which rents for $150 per night.

Spruce Cottage is located 1.5 blocks from Drake Park, walking distance from downtown Bend. This was an old mill cottage that was gutted by fire. The entire interior was replaced in 2000 with a very pretty and homey decor. This charming little dollhouse rents for $110 per night. The single bedroom and bath are perfect for a couple; in a pinch a close friend or child could sleep on the couch.

Pets are negotiable for the Cascade View, Grandview, and Westside Pines houses and Spruce Cottage. (Arline says she likes to meet the pet so she knows they see eye-to-eye on certain topics!) There is a charge of $20 per pet, per visit. Special requests, such as champagne, flowers, or a welcome basket, can be accommodated. Prices are higher for the Christmas holidays.

Cascade View Ranch
60435 Tekampe Road
(541) 388–5658
www.cascadeviewranch.com

Peace, quiet, simplicity, and views of the Cascades—that's what you get at this 60-acre ranch in southeast Bend just five minutes from town. The grounds are manicured to perfection. Up until recently, owners Don and Joann Jacobs had a herd of Icelandic horses and miniature donkeys, but these days the Jacobs have simplified their lives by finding their livestock new homes.

Their 2,500-square-foot ranch-style guest house was gutted in 1995 and completely remodeled to provide understated comfort with its fine, old furnishings, beautiful towels and linens, washer/dryer, TV with VCR, and phone. This nonsmoking, three-bedroom house rents for a very reasonable $125 per night for two people, plus $25 for each additional person up to nine persons total. The weekly rate for two is $700; monthly rate for two is $2,200.

Golf enthusiasts will be happy to hear that one of Bend's premier public golf courses, Lost Tracks Golf Club (see our Golf chapter), is just five minutes away.

If you are a bit flexible with your dates, six months' advance notice during fall, winter, or spring will get you a reservation. Summers are largely booked by repeat guests, but openings sometimes occur, so give it a shot. Gracious hosts Joann and Don love animals, and travel-wise pets are welcomed.

Sisters/Camp Sherman Area

Resorts in this area are found in the beautiful Deschutes National Forest west of Sisters at Black Butte Ranch, Camp Sherman, and Suttle Lake.

Destination Resorts

Black Butte Ranch
U.S. Highway 20, 8 miles west of Sisters
(541) 595–6211, (800) 452–7455
(800) 399–2322, golf reservations
www.blackbutteranch.com

There is no more spectacular setting than Black Butte Ranch. You enter through ponderosa pine trees and aspens into a vast opening with drop-dead, close-up views of the white-capped Three Sisters. Golf and tennis are king and queen at Black Butte. The two award-winning, 18-hole golf courses are beautifully landscaped and manicured (see our Golf chapter). The 1,830 acres of forested grounds offer 16 miles of biking and jogging trails, a trout pond for fly-fishing, and an equestrian center. Fly fisherpersons can also take the short drive to a world-class fishery, the Metolius River. Fly rods, canoes, and paddleboats are available for rent at the lodge pool or recreation center. Horseback-riding lessons, guided trail rides, pony rides, and even meal rides are offered, and boarding is offered if you'd like to bring your own faithful steed. You can play a game of tennis at one of the 23 courts or simply relax in one of the heated swimming pools. A conference facility and gourmet restaurant top the list of amenities.

Accommodations include hotel-style rooms, suites, luxury condos, and resort homes. This is an upscale resort, and you may expect the accommodations to be well-appointed and tastefully decorated. Clusters of taupe or gray homes with sloped roofs stand among the ponderosa trees. Homes on the fairways cost much more to rent than homes in the woods, and the houses on the golf courses (Big Meadow and Glaze Meadow) are more spacious and grander. Pets are not allowed.

There is a two-night minimum for all homes, which jumps to a six-night requirement in July and August. Many homes are nonsmoking. High season rates, quoted here, run from May 1st through October 1st, plus major holidays. Lodge rooms run $90 to $125 for a standard room or a deluxe unit with a larger bathroom. There is no minimum-stay requirement at the lodge. A one-bedroom condo suite goes for $142. Private homes rent from $150 to $350 per night for four to fourteen persons. Golf and ski packages are available.

Lake Creek Lodge
13375 Southwest Forest Service Road 1419, Camp Sherman
(541) 595–6331, (800) 797–6331
www.lakecreeklodge.com

Deep in the cool forest surrounded by smooth carpets of manicured green lawns, we fell in love with this spot at first sight. It was so tidy and peaceful we could hardly believe that this was a family resort! We debated whether Lake Creek should be considered a destination resort or a rustic resort, but with its dedication to kids' activities and the evening meal in the lodge dining room being such an important component of the Lake Creek Lodge experience, we felt it was better suited to the destination resorts category.

Delicious country buffet dinners are served in the pine-paneled dining room in the homey main lodge; kids get to eat together in their own dining room. Children have other special privileges, including being first in line for dinner. Outside you'll find a heated pool and tennis court, plus swimming, jogging, and hiking. Kids can fish only in the Lake Creek pond. Nearby is the Metolius River, a famous catch-and-release, fly-only fishery. In winter Lake Creek Lodge makes for a perfect retreat, with Nordic skiing from the front door. The lodge is also available for conferences.

The 16 housekeeping cabins look like small homes with knotty-pine paneling and comfy furniture, and some have screened porches. One has a fireplace. Accommodations include linens and towels, and three units are nonsmoking. Housekeeping cabins with a living room, kitchen, bath, and two or three bedrooms that sleep six to nine people in the high season (July 1st to Labor Day weekend) start at $185 for two persons, plus $60 for each additional person.

There is no minimum stay in summer, but there is a two-night minimum from November 1 to May 1. Open all year, their cheapest rates are in winter, when cabins range from $95 to $180 per night. The summer rates include dinner but not breakfast. You can get your morning meal in the dining room a la carte, or you may order the Wrangler breakfast for $8.00. Food service is available only during the summer. Rates do not include room tax or gratuity. Lake Creek Lodge does not accept credit cards. They welcome well-mannered pets.

Rustic Resorts

Metolius River Resort
25551 Southwest Forest Service Road 1419, Camp Sherman
(541) 595–6281, (800) 818–7688
(or 81–TROUT as they like to say)
www.metolius-river-resort.com

Rustic is more a state of mind than the reality at these very attractive, wood-shake cabins built in 1992. This is a beautiful little resort consisting of 11 rustic beauties in a ponderosa forest. It's next to the Metolius River and behind an excellent summer dinner place, the Kokanee Cafe (see our Restaurants chapter).

Inside, each cabin is tastefully decorated with knotty pine, contemporary "camp" furniture done in plaids, a lovely river-rock fireplace with firewood, TV with satellite dish, phone, fully equipped kitchen, and linens. Units have one downstairs bedroom with a queen-size bed, and an upstairs loft with a queen-size bed or two twins, allowing a maximum of four adults per cabin, not including children. Some have sleeper sofas. The cabins rent for $180 per night for two people with a two-night minimum. The third and fourth person cost an additional $10 each per night. All the units are nonsmoking, and pets are not allowed.

At an elevation of 3,000 feet, Metolius River Resort is open year-round, offering outstanding recreational opportunities including fly-fishing, hiking and mountain biking, Nordic skiing from your

doorstep, alpine skiing at Hoodoo Ski Bowl (about 15 miles to the west), and shopping in Sisters, 14 miles to the southeast. The Camp Sherman store sells fly-fishing supplies.

Suttle Lake Resort
13300 U.S. Highway 20, 14 miles west of Sisters
(541) 595–6662

Suttle Lake sparkles under the blue sky, surrounded by the deep green of majestic pine trees, rimmed with the tips of snowy peaks. Families return every year to play in the sunshine and water, or to romp in the storybook winter snow. Located in the Deschutes National Forest, there are lots and lots of trails. Take your choice of a short trip around the lake, a daytrip to another local lake or mountain peak, or tackle part or all of the nearby Pacific Crest Trail. For downhill skiers and boarders, Hoodoo Ski Area is just 4 miles to the west.

Under new ownership since 1999, Suttle Lake Resort has undergone a major facelift. A dozen charming, log-style sleeping cabins have been built, and what used to be two very rustic, older cabins were remodeled and are now offered as full-service lodging. These old cabins, named Historic Falls and Guard Station, sleep up to six persons and rent for $125 per night. They are fully furnished one-bedroom, one-bath units, and come complete with linens. The new, rustic sleeping cabins have a queen-size bed, bunk beds, and a sofa bed, and rent for $50 per night. You will need to bring all your standard camping gear except for tent and mattresses. Campsites without hookups are available for $20.00 per night for a family of up to five; additional persons are $3.00 each. Both the rustic cabin guests and campground guests have free use of the public toilets and showers that are available in the boathouse.

The old boathouse has been renovated and now houses a full-service eatery, The Boathouse Restaurant, serving lunch and dinner Wednesday through Saturday, and brunch and dinner on Sunday during summer. The wood-fired brick-oven pizzas are tempting, and can be enjoyed along with a glass of wine or a Pacific Northwest microbrew. Dinner fare ranges from light meals such as sandwiches, to entrees as elegant as rack of lamb or cioppino. A new store and gift shop, also located in the boathouse, provide many of the necessities of vacation life. The marina rents out motorized fishing boats, paddleboats, canoes, and rowboats.

To get to Suttle Lake, travel 13 miles west of Sisters on U.S. 20.

Vacation Rentals

Grammer Roundhouse
Located in Tollgate, Sisters
Contact: Kathy Tremper, 9601 Northwest
25th Avenue, Vancouver, WA
(360) 696–8169

Yes, this house is round. Built by John M. Grammer as a family vacation home, the house is now owned by his son, John E., who rents it to visitors for their own family reunions. Located in the Tollgate neighborhood of Sisters, 2 miles west of the town, the house is surrounded by towering pines and has a peak of the Cascades that can be seen from the second story. With two bedrooms plus a loft, there's room for 10 guests, and it rents for $75 per night. A garage was added with an additional guest room furnished with a pair of bunk beds. The garage room rents for an additional $25 per night. Tollgate is about 16 miles from Hoodoo Ski Area. No credit cards are accepted.

Lazy Rockin' B'nC Ranch
69797 Holmes Road, Sisters
(541) 548–0178, (888) 488–0178
www.sistersbedandbreakfast.com

Located on 40 acres, 10 minutes east of Sisters, is the Rockin' Lazy B'nC Ranch, a bed-and-breakfast inn with a lovely guest house that Burt and Cindy Murray call their Bunkhouse. The view from the Bunkhouse is of miles of sagebrush ringed with juniper forest, topped with seven white-capped peaks of the Cascade Mountains.

Cindy, formerly an interior designer, has beautifully decorated the bunkhouse in a style she calls "farmhouse with a touch of hunting lodge." The cozy and cheerful living room features plaid couches, bookshelves packed with books,

a gas stove, and a TV/VCR. The kitchen is fully equipped. One bedroom is a master bedroom with its own bathroom; two smaller bedrooms share a bath. The picture-perfect Bunkhouse rents for $200 per night, and can sleep up to eight guests.

The Murrays keep three horses of their own. Guests are invited to bring their own horses for an extra charge. With Bureau of Land Management lands adjacent to the property, there are miles and miles of public lands for riding. Another option available to bunkhouse guests for an extra charge is to partake of the gourmet breakfast Cindy serves to her B&B guests who are staying at the main house.

The ranch is located just north of Oregon Highway 26, on the edge of the triangle formed by Sisters, Redmond, and Bend, making it convenient to golf, restaurants, the Redmond airport, and other attractions. The Murrays accept checks or cash, and do not allow smoking. A discounted rate may be available in the off-seasons.

Pine Cone Cottage
642 South Ash, Sisters
(541) 549–9419

This picturesque log cabin is nestled among tall pine trees, just 6 blocks from downtown Sisters. Charmingly appointed with log furniture, a river-rock fireplace, and private deck, the one bedroom plus loft sleep up to six guests. It's all very

> ## Insiders' Tip
> Most of the resorts have Web sites, which are usually good for a preview of the place if you have never been there before. At the time of publication only a few offer online reservations, so expect to make a call or two.

clean and tidy, and smoking is not permitted. A well-behaved pet is allowed.

Many of owner Susan Metke's guests are repeat customers who will often book a year in advance, especially for popular weekends and holidays such as during the Sisters Quilt Show in July. Summer rates are $110 per night or $550 per week. In winter, except holidays, the house rents for $90 per night or $250 per week. There is a two-night minimum stay. No credit cards are accepted.

Rags to Walkers Guest Ranch
17045 Farthing Lane, Sisters
(541) 548–7000, (800) 422–5622, in Oregon
www.ragstowalkers.com

Looking for a big, beautiful house to bring a whole crew of people to Central Oregon? Well, this might be your spot. With the addition of two renovated farmhouse rentals to the existing farmhouse rental, this would be the perfect vacation spot for a large family, a family reunion, corporate retreat, or a big bunch of friends.

Hosts/owners Bonnie Jacobs-Halousek and Neal Halousek built a big, turn-of-the-20th-century-style farmhouse and included four extra bedrooms for their grown children and grandchildren to use when visiting. Since the rooms were empty much of the time, they decided to open their doors to other guests. They chose the name, Rags to Walkers, a pun on the rags to riches story, which traces Bonnie's success in the clothing business that led to where they are today, raising Tennessee walking horses on a gorgeous ranch in Sisters.

The bed-and-breakfast inn was so successful, Bonnie and Neal felt they needed more space. So they built a brand-new, country-Victorian-style vacation house called the White House, with seven guest rooms decorated with antiques and wood floors throughout. Every room has a private bath with a claw-foot tub and a showerhead shaped like a giant sunflower. Even the pearl, push-button light switches look authentically antique. The house has a huge kitchen and an enormous dining room, the likes of which you'd really like to have around Thanksgiving. The dining room is furnished with a huge Victorian table and lots of chairs. All around the house are lush green pastures, white fences, and Cascade views. The White House rents for $750 per day in high season and sleeps up to 16 guests.

Bonnie and Neil have expanded again, adding the three-bedroom Farm House which rents from $175 to $375 and sleeps two to six, and the four-bedroom Andrus House, which sleeps ten and costs $175 to $450. Prices vary according to the number of guests and season. Adjacent to their main property, the two houses are fully equipped as vacation rentals. Both are decorated in the picturesque country style with comfy quilts, feather pillows, and period decor for which Bonnie has become locally renowned. For those of you who have enjoyed a stay at the White House, you will be delighted to find the claw-foot tubs and an occasional sunflower showerhead that are vintage Bonnie.

Guests may enjoy 2.5 miles of paved paths. Bring your bicycles or enjoy yourself on one that is provided with each house (including a tandem!). Kids love to fly along the paths on their in-line skates. Catch-and-release fly-fish in three ponds, ride Bonnie and Neal's Tennessee Walker horses, or bring your own mounts. Horse boarding is $15 per day. Guests who cherish a little scenic peace and quiet are welcome to find a longue chair under a tree and read, or watch the horses frolic. After an active day relax in the hot tub that comes with each of the houses.

By prior arrangement, Bonnie and Neal are armed with an outdoor kitchen to cook up a barbecue dinner on the porch. Golf carts are available to whisk you to the 27,000-square-foot riding arena, where you can schedule an English or Western riding lesson for an extra charge. (For more on Rags to Walkers, see the listing in our Bed-and-Breakfasts chapter.) The accommodations at Rags to Walkers are all nonsmoking, and pets are not allowed.

Squaw Creek Ranch Historic Homestead
P.O. Box 1784, Sisters
(541) 549–4072
www.squawcrkranch.com

Built in 1900, this homestead on 316 acres is now on the National Historic Registry. Hosts Kathy and Frank Deggendorfer lived in this house for two years while they built another new home nearby, and in 2001 they turned the old homestead into a unique vacation rental. In this very private setting within the walls of Squaw Creek Canyon, it's easy to imagine yourself a Central Oregon pioneer in the early 20th century, but difficult to imagine that you are only 3 miles east of Sisters!

The house is a beautifully restored, two-story home with a wraparound veranda. The interior has been completely modernized, including telephones (local calls are free), TV/VCR and satellite service, laundry, and gas barbecue. With three bedrooms and 1.5 baths, the house is comfortably furnished, complete with handmade quilts on the beds, and sleeps as many as nine guests.

Surrounded by meadows of wild flowers with grazing deer, guests are welcome to explore hundreds of miles of walking trails or take advantage of the nearby golfing, skiing, and fishing.

Rates start at $100 per night for two persons plus $10 for each additional person, and there is a two-night minimum. There is an 8 percent county tax. Smoking and pets are not permitted, but local boarding can be arranged. Holidays are getting booked quickly, but being a new player in the community means that getting reservations is relatively easy. This will no doubt change as word spreads!

Tollgate Vacation Rentals
P.O. Box 1181, Sisters
(541) 549–0792
www.tollgatevacationrentals.com

Since 1993, Tollgate Vacation rentals has been managing and renting second homes in the Sisters area. They offer seven homes in Sisters, plus two in nearby Eagle Crest Resort. Most of the homes are a modest ranchstyle with comfortable, if unremarkable, furnishings. The Eagle Crest homes are a pair of chalets that are slightly more upscale. All their homes are fully furnished and equipped, and none allow smoking or pets. Access to amenities such as hot tubs, swimming pools, or tennis vary with each location. Rates range from $80 to $150 per night.

Redmond

Destination Resorts

Eagle Crest Resort
1522 Cline Falls Road
(541) 923–2453, (800) 682–4786
www.eagle-crest.com

Two championship 18-hole golf courses, a Mid Iron course built in 1999, and an 18-hole putting course are star attractions at this High Desert resort. The rolling meadows and fairways, enjoyed by golfers year-round, offer an intensely lush green contrast to the stunning views of the Cascade peaks. If the golf doesn't hook you, the sparkling heated outdoor pool, the indoor pool at the Ridge Sports Center, the spa, or the hot tubs will.

One hundred luxury lodge rooms and suites at the Inn at Eagle Crest, plus upscale townhome rentals, are available to guests. The clustered homes have gray vertical siding and sloped roofs. The interiors are bright and furnished mostly with contemporary decor, and the units are air-conditioned. Free HBO, phones, and radios are standard. Townhomes come with a fireplace, fully equipped kitchen, gas barbecue, Jacuzzi tub, two decks, and views of either the Deschutes River or the golf courses. Lodge rooms with one queen-size bed start at $97, or $109 with a golf view and a small deck. A one-bedroom suite is $132 or $145 per night and includes a sleeper sofa and a small kitchenette. Townhomes, with two or three bedrooms, range from $220 to $309 per night. These rates are for high season: June through September. During low season, late fall and January through March, you may expect to pay about 25 percent less. Golf packages are available.

Other amenities include tennis, several pools to choose from, a restaurant and poolside snack bar, nature and bike trails, programs for kids and families, a shuttle to Mt. Bachelor Ski Area, and the Deschutes River at your back door. Central Oregon is ideal for horseback riding, so call the resort and ask about arrangements for trail rides or lessons. The new

6,000-square-foot convention center can host groups as large as 350 people and offers the latest in technology. And, of course, we can't leave out the sunny, glorious High Desert weather. Eagle Crest is less than 10 minutes from the Redmond Airport and offers free shuttle service to registered guests.

Sunriver/La Pine Area

Just 15 miles south of Bend off U.S. Highway 97 and surrounded by the Deschutes National Forest, Sunriver is Central Oregon's largest destination resort. A true resort in every sense of the term, Sunriver is a town unto itself, with its own schools, fire protection, dining, a general store, and lots of boutique-type shops in the village, a general aviation airport (see our Getting Here, Getting Around chapter), and lots of on-site recreation. Unlike most towns, however, Sunriver is a designed community. Master planners and an architectural review board ensure a pleasant homogeneity in its buildings and landscaping, while out-of-town guests enjoy Sunriver's user-friendly layout. Sunriver is a very popular vacation destination that never closes.

Located between Sunriver and the town of La Pine, about 30 miles east of Highway 97, are two rustic resorts in the Newberry National Volcanic Monument at Paulina and East Lakes. Both have enough amenities (stores, restaurants, etc.) to help you enjoy this rugged, outdoor vacation experience. These resorts are also only about 15 minutes away from a wide range of amenities—to the south in La Pine or to the north at Sunriver.

Destination Resorts

Sunriver Resort

This is a beautifully manicured resort with forested areas of lodgepole and ponderosa pine nestled along the banks of the Deschutes River. Its three championship golf courses (see our Golf chapter), a dozen or so restaurants, swimming pools and tennis courts, 30 miles of bike paths, a nature center and observatory (see our Attractions chapter), a marina with boat rentals, and stables offering trail rides will keep every member of the family happily entertained. Sunriver Village also offers just about everything you could ask for in the way of groceries, video rentals, and lots of fun shopping. The only reason to leave the resort is to enjoy the nearby natural wonders, or to catch a movie in Bend.

The Deschutes River runs through the 3,500-acre property, where guests can land big rainbow trout on a fly, rent a canoe or raft, or sign up for a white-water trip. The bike paths wind through ponderosa forests and along the river, offering incomparable family biking in summer and Nordic skiing in the winter. Kids can enjoy a variety of scheduled activities.

Sunriver, the community, is comprised mainly of private property homeowners. Some land is still owned by Sunriver Resort, the corporation that owns the 211-room Sunriver Lodge, marina, pools, tennis courts, golf courses, and the Village—a retail

Insiders' Tip

If staying connected with the outside world is important to you, ask if telephones are available in the rooms or on-site when you make your reservations. Some destination resorts and vacation rentals consider phones to be inappropriate for a vacation experience and intentionally don't provide them in the rooms. Rustic resorts don't have phones in the cabins, and many have only cell-phone service.

mall (see our Shopping chapter). The lodge, which provides accommodations much like a hotel, is covered in this section. Sunriver Resort is also a large property manager, renting out and managing hundreds of private homes on behalf of the individual homeowners, and there are other property-management companies that also represent private homeowners at Sunriver. Between the five management companies we list below, there are more than 700 homes available for rent at Sunriver. Sunriver Resort and the other property-management companies all have online reservation services, and are listed in the Vacation Rentals section that follow this section.

Whether you are renting a private home or you have reservations for a guest room at Sunriver Lodge, all guests follow the signs to the lodge for 24-hour check-in.

Sunriver Lodge
One Centre Drive, P.O. Box 3609, Sunriver
(541) 593–1000, Sunriver Lodge front desk,
(800) 547–3922, toll-free reservations at the
lodge, as well as Sunriver Resort vacation
rental reservations
www.sunriver-resort.com

Guest rooms in the spectacularly refurbished Sunriver Lodge feature a stone fireplace and private deck. They go for $179 in summer, then drop down to $119 in winter, for one or two people. Lodge Village Suites sleep up to six people and offer a continental kitchen, dining and living area, stone fireplace, loft, and two baths for $269 from June through September; they drop to $169 in January. Chalets have the same suites with an additional adjoining guest room. The rates range from $449 down to $339, and they can sleep up to 12 people.

During summer there is a five-night minimum stay. Rates are highest in summer, moderate in spring and fall, and lowest in winter after New Year's Day. Special rates and minimum-stay requirements are in effect for holidays. All lodge guests have access to the members/guests-only Crosswater golf course and restaurant, plus discounts on greens fees to Sunriver's other two championship golf courses. Resort amenities such as the pools, spas, tennis courts, bike paths, exercise room, and intra-resort transportation are free.

Vacation Rentals

Vacation rental guests have access to the Meadows and Woodland Golf Courses, free swimming in two pools, spas, free use of the 29 tennis courts, bike paths, exercise room, and intra-resort transportation. For rentals by property owners directly, contact the Sunriver Chamber of Commerce, Tuesday through Saturday, or check out the For Rent by Owner link on the chamber's Web site. Rates quoted do not include taxes.

Sunriver Chamber of Commerce
Sunriver Village Mall, Building Number 0
(downstairs next to miniature golf/ice rink),
P.O. Box 3246, Sunriver
(541) 593–8149
www.sunriver-resort.com

Bennington Properties
P.O. Box 3367, Sunriver
(541) 593–6300, (888) 610–9700
www.benningtonproperties.com

Bennington Properties offers almost 50 homes in Sunriver that run the gamut from simply comfortable and conveniently located, to grand homes in a premier location such as right next to the Deschutes River or the fairway.

Rates are set in a three-tier structure, with summer being the most expensive season and the rest of the year considered low season except for holidays, which are priced in the mid-range. In summer a modest but nice home that sleeps up to six costs from $100 to $125 per night. If you prefer a home in a premier location that sleeps up to eight, you can expect to pay from $200 to $240 per night. Even larger homes that sleep 10 to 14 persons range from $175 to $400 per night.

All their properties are nonsmoking, and a few accept pets for a $50 per visit fee plus a damage deposit. Their Web site offers a very straightforward listing of their properties with good photos, but to make reservations you must call their toll-free number.

Discover Sunriver Vacation Rentals
Sunriver Village Mall, Building Number 9,
P.O. Box 3247, Sunriver
(541) 593–2482, (800) 544–0300
www.discoversunriver.com

Discover Sunriver Vacation Rentals manages more than 100 quality three- and four-bedroom homes, as well as condos and cabins in Sunriver. All homes are contemporary in architecture, and generally are also contemporary in decor and furnishings. Most homes have a hot tub, garage, and gas barbecue, and some have bikes. A typical three-bedroom home that sleeps eight rents for $100 to $235 per night. In a category they call Big Homes, houses that sleep 10 to 12 range from $242 to $423 per night.

The cabins and condos vary more in furnishings, ranging from contemporary to older, cabin-style interiors. Condos sleep six to eight people on the average for $112 to $206 per night. The smallest ones sleep two for $56 to $101 per night. Cabins, or one- and two-bedroom homes as they are called, sleep four to six and range from $77 to $182.

Many properties are nonsmoking, and pets are not allowed. A minimum two-night stay is required, and may be longer depending on the season and holiday.

The Rental Connection
Contact: Brenda Matwich
60970 Alpine Lane, P.O. Box 9088, Bend
(541) 383–1780, (888) 702–0761
www.rentconnect.com

The Rental Connection has more than 600 vacation rentals listed in Central Oregon, mostly in Sunriver, but with three homes in the Sisters area. All are nicely appointed homes in a country setting, and range from log construction to contemporary styling. One has a barn and paddocks so you may bring your own horses. Rates range from $165 to $275 per night for six to ten guests. Smoking and pets are not allowed. Photos of the houses may be viewed on their Web site.

StoneRidge Townhomes
Peppermill Circle, Clubhouse (off East Meadow Road), Sunriver
(541) 593–1502, (800) 255–2506
www.stoneridgetownhomes.com

StoneRidge is a development of 36 luxury townhomes in Sunriver within walking distance of the village. Each one has multiple timeshare owners. When the owners are not using their townhomes, the StoneRidge property-management arm rents the units out and maintains them.

The homes are exquisitely designed and furnished with designer furniture, Cuisinarts and gourmet cookware in the kitchens, original artwork, fireplaces, surround-sound entertainment systems, washer/dryers, plus a walk-in shower/bath and a TV with VCR in every bedroom. All the units are nonsmoking, and pets are not allowed.

A two-bedroom unit that sleeps four costs $210 to $240 per night. The three-bedroom units for six people go for $250 to $285. There are minimum stays of three to seven nights depending on the season. Use of an outdoor pool, spa, exercise room, tennis courts, and bike paths are included in the room rate. All you have to bring is food and personal items. Call their toll-free number to make reservations.

Sunray Vacation Rentals Inc.
56890 Venture Lane, P.O. Box 4518, Sunriver
(541) 593–3225, (800) 531–1130
www.sunrayinc.com

Sunray manages more than 200 unique condos, cabins, and homes, many in Sunriver, and divides them into four categories: Exceptional (large, elegant, and the most expensive), Premier (modern and very nice), Quality (with "mature" furnishings), and Standard (rustic or very basic). The most expensive option is a four-bedroom, two-level house with two gas fireplaces, sound system, barbecue, bikes, two Jacuzzi bathtubs, an outdoor hot tub, and high-end furnishings for $520. The least-expensive is a rustic one-bedroom cabin with a loft and a woodstove, TV with VCR, and washer for $100 per night. Between these two are many options in the $180 to $320 range with two bedrooms plus a loft, or three bedrooms. Some appear to have very Spartan furnishings, some are homier, but all look well-maintained and comfortable. Most are nonsmoking and a few allow pets. Their helpful Web site has a link that pulls up all the homes that allow pets.

Sunriver Resort
One Centre Drive, P.O. Box 3609, Sunriver
(800) 801–8765, (541) 593–1000
www.sunriver-resort.com

The 275-plus private rental houses and condos managed by Sunriver Resort have all the comforts of home—pillows on the couch, can openers, artwork, oven mitts, and bicycles. Upscale amenities often include high-end sound systems, rock fireplaces, pine ceilings, and hot tubs. Although every one is unique, they all meet the high standards of Sunriver Resort.

A two-bedroom Sunriver condo typically rents for $239 to $249 during summer, or $149 to $165 in January. A three-bedroom house would cost $299 to $399 per night during high season, or $165 to $185 in winter. Pricing is affected by house or condo location and views.

During summer there is a five-night minimum stay. All resort guests have access to the members/guests-only Crosswater golf course and restaurant, plus discounts on greens fees to Sunriver's other two championship golf courses. Resort amenities such as the pools, spas, tennis courts, bike paths, exercise room, and intra-resort transportation are free. Only a few of the properties allow smoking inside, and homeowners generally prohibit pet guests.

Sunset Realty
One Venture Lane, P.O. Box 3515, Sunriver
(541) 593–5018, (800) 541–1756
www.sr-sunset.com

Sunset Realty claims to be the second-largest property management company in Sunriver, with over 225 homes and condos under their management. From rustic cabins to posh homes, they have a vacation rental to fit your needs. Small units that sleep up to four range from $75 to $100 per night, and their largest homes that can sleep up to 16 guests top out at $450 per night. Their Web site provides an excellent source of descriptive information, or, if you aren't a cyber-surfer, their very nice team of reservationists can help you find what you are looking for in a Sunriver vacation rental.

Village Properties
Two Country Mall, P.O. Box 3310, Sunriver
(800) 786–7483
www.village-properties.com

The 145 condos and homes represented by this company cover quite a range of styles and prices, from upscale homes to the basic ski condo; lodging dates from the 1970s to the 1990s. A typical three-bedroom home that sleeps six to eight costs in the neighborhood of $135 for a smaller 1,400-square-foot home up to $300 per night for a spacious 2,400-square-foot home. Condos that sleep six rent for $120 to $140 per night. Special deals (such as four nights for the price of two) may be available in the fall.

Most of the units are nonsmoking; just a few accept pets. Amenities and furnishings vary greatly, so ask Village Properties to send a color brochure with photos of each property. They also have more detailed information in their office, so ask for more details.

Rustic Resorts

East Lake Resort and RV Park
East Lake, Oregon Highway 21, Newberry
National Volcanic Monument, La Pine
(541) 536–2230
www.EastLakeResort.com

High in the thinning pine forests at 6,400 feet, the air is crisp and the nights can get quite chilly. Fortunately, the rustic cabins in the trees near the lake have electric heat. Simple camping rooms in a four-plex cabin, with a sink and toilet but no shower, a double bed, and a single bed rent for $45 a night. Pay showers are available in the RV area. A one-room Lake Front housekeeping cabin with a living room/bedroom and two double beds costs $90 and sleeps up to four. Two-bedroom housekeeping cabins with full kitchens are $105 a night, and cabins top out with three bedrooms and four double beds at $125 a night. The snug, quite basic, Honeymooners cabin with a queen-size bed and two-burner kitchenette, that sleeps—you guessed it— two, is only $65 per night.

The resort was started in 1915, and decor (what decor?) is authentically "camp" in style. Cabins are fully equipped with linens, and smoking is allowed. Pets in the cabins are an extra $5.00. Public coin-op showers and laundry facilities are available, plus a cafe for breakfast and lunch, and a general store with gas and propane. East Lake Resort also has boat rentals, moorage, a beach, RV camping (see our Camping chapter), and a playground. This is a very popular area for fishing and hiking. It's open from mid-May through September.

East Lake Resort's Web site is one of the best we have encountered locally. It has well-organized details on just about everything, from cabin or RV camping rates, nearby attractions, local geology, species of fish—you name it. It does everything except take reservations, for which you will have to make an old-fashioned phone call.

Paulina Lake Resort
Paulina Lake, Oregon Highway 21, Newberry National Volcanic Monument, La Pine
(541) 536–2240
www.paulinalakeresort.evisionsite.com

Open in summer and winter, Paulina Lake Resort offers a variety of recreational opportunities, with loafing listed as one of their important activities. In summer, you'll find great fishing for rainbow and brown trout and kokanee salmon (with free advice). The record German Brown trout in five western states, at 27 lbs. 12 oz., was caught at Paulina Lake in 1993. Fishing boats are available for rent on this 10-mph lake. The resort's location within the Deschutes National Forest and inside Newberry Crater ensure unlimited opportunities for hiking, as well as sight-seeing at the local waterfalls and volcanic wonders (see our Forests, High Desert, and Volcanoes chapter). In winter, Paulina Lake is smack-dab in the middle of some of Central Oregon's best Nordic skiing and snowmobile trails.

The general store has groceries, fishing licenses, tackle, and bait. Rental boats, moorage, gas, and oil are available. A restaurant, housed in a log lodge that was built in 1929, serves breakfast and lunch seven days a week, and dinner from Thursday through Saturday during summer, with seasonal hours the rest of the year. Their specialty: Saturday Night BBQ Ribs.

Thirteen rustic cabins, named after birds, flock near the lake. All have knotty-pine interiors, woodstoves with firewood, bathrooms, linens, and kitchens with dishes, utensils, and a microwave. The cabins rent for different rates based on location and view. One-bedroom cabins that sleep two, three, or four range from $72 to $89 per night. Two-bedroom cabins that sleep up to eight are $89 to $108 per night, based on four people. Two large, three-bedroom cabins that sleep up to 10 go for $155 a night, based on six people. Extra people are charged $5.00 per day. A small, upstairs sleeping unit with two twin beds, kitchenette, and bath is $55 per night. One pet per cabin is allowed (during summer only) at $7.00 per day. Winter rates are 15 percent higher.

The summer season covers fishing season, from late April through the end of October. The winter season starts in approximately mid-December and goes through early March. In winter the resort is snowbound, and it's a 3-mile ski or snowmobile trip to get to the cabins. It's B.Y.O.S.—Bring Your Own Skis. Park your car at the Ten-Mile Sno-Park (permit required; see our Snowplay chapter). Since Karen and Todd Brown purchased the resort in 2000, they have gradually been adding new amenities, including snowmobile rentals and a Snocat shuttle service. MasterCard and Visa are accepted. Call the resort for availability and reservations.

Madras Area

Destination Resorts

Kah-Nee-Ta Resort
North of U.S. Highway 26, P.O. Box K, Warm Springs
(541) 553–1112, (800) 554–4786
www.kah-nee-taresort.com

Kah-Nee-Ta Resort is on the 640,000-acre Warm Springs Indian Reservation (see our Other Communities chapter) about 25 miles northwest of Madras. From U.S. Highway 26 at Warm Springs, turn north at the sign and keep following signs for 14 miles. Kah-Nee-Ta's desert climate offers year-round fun with an average of 300 sunny days per year. Summer highs are generally in the 90s; winter days are usually in the 40s. The main attractions at Kah-Nee-Ta include golf at the fabulous Kah-Nee-Ta Golf Course (see our Golf chapter), the Indian Head Casino, a stable with trail rides, guided kayak rides, fishing (special license needed), and lots of family fun in the sun.

Kah-Nee-Ta (pronounced kuh-NEE-tuh) consists of a village area (elevation 1,200 feet) along the Warm Springs River that contains the hot springs, and the lodge, which is past the village and up on a bluff. The hot springs were sold by the Native Americans many years ago to a doctor in Portland, but they were repurchased by the Confederated Tribes in the 1950s with funds from the sale of the tribes' fishing rights at Celilo Falls on the Columbia River. The initial village was completed in 1962. It was immediately flooded in 1963, rebuilt in 1964 (the year of its official grand opening), and destroyed again by flooding in 1995.

The new village, which reopened in February 1996, is quite spectacular. In its center is one of the most incredible Olympic-size swimming pools we've ever seen, with a 140-foot water slide and children's wading pool. The water slide is 21 feet high. The pool is heated with water from the hot springs and is maintained at 92 degrees in winter and 86 degrees in summer. If you visit just to swim, the charge is $6.00 for the pool (no pool charge for guests) plus $2.00 extra for the water slide, which is an absolute must for kids. This is a very busy place during summer—3,000 guests and visitors have been known to visit the pool on Saturdays in July. The pool has a bathhouse with a huge locker and shower facility.

Near the pool is Spa Wannapine, a gorgeous spa with hot tubs, massage, herbal wraps, and facials. The Wannapine building also houses a small deli and market/gift shop. Just outside the Wannapine building are vendor booths where the people of the local Indian tribes sell their crafts. Also nearby are an 18-hole miniature golf course and a place to rent bikes, fishing poles, basketball and volleyball equipment, and tennis rackets. Kah-Nee-Ta also offers Kids' Camp, with fun summer activities for kids.

Nearby are 20 colorful tepees—accurate, full-size reproductions that sleep up to 10 people for $69.95 per night for three. Additional people are an extra $6.00 per night. A shower/laundry facility is shared with the nearby RV park, which has 48 spaces with full hookups. Spaces cost $38 a night for three people, $29.95 for two people.

The lodge, built in 1972, has in its central sitting area the second-largest concrete and stone fireplace in Oregon. During winter, huge 24- to 30-inch diameter logs are burned in it. The lodge's floors and walls are made from beautiful woods, and high above is a tepee-like structure that holds up the ceiling. Pinecone light fixtures, wood carvings under the reception desk (depicting the legend of Coyote the trickster and protector), and yellow pine benches with carved fish continue the Native American theme.

Also at the lodge is the Juniper Dining Room, which offers a fine-dining experience, and the Pinto Grill and Deli for casual eats. You'll also find a gift shop, an exercise room with a hot tub on the balcony with an incredible view, and a pool with a poolside lounge that serves cocktails and hosts live music on summer nights at 10:00 P.M. The east wing of the lodge is farthest from the music and quieter. The lodge rooms are done in tasteful pastels with light wood furniture. The village offers a motel-style guest facility with 30 rooms, some with kitchenettes and fireplaces.

Rooms, for either the lodge or the village, cost $130 to $135 per night for two people. Different configurations of suites (one or two bedrooms, with or without kitchens, some with Jacuzzi tubs or fireplaces), called Executive Suites, range upwards of $210 per night.

Camping

For visitors and residents, families, and sporting types, camping is one of our most popular summer activities. Whether it's the fishing, hiking, boating, bird-watching, photography, or simply the love of waking up in the Great Outdoors that has brought you to our forests and deserts, camping is a big deal in Central Oregon. This chapter covers road-accessible camping and RVing. For off-road camping, including horse camps, please see our chapter on Other Outdoor Recreation.

Go ahead, name your favorite type of camping—we've got it. Like to "rough it" with full hookups near town? Or would you rather pitch your tent next to a lake or stream in a Forest Service campground? Perhaps you're the kind of outdoors person who enjoys packing your four-wheel-drive vehicle with a three-day supply of water, food, and gear and heading for a remote spot on Bureau of Land Management (BLM) land, where you have jackrabbits and hawks for neighbors? Whatever your choice, we've got you covered.

Central Oregon camping resources can be divided into two basic sections. Our first section covers camping with all the comforts of home away from home, which requires hookups. After that we have "Really Roughing It," a section on camping closer to nature, be it in a tent, RV, or camper. Some campgrounds, such as those in our state parks, offer both full hookups and campsites without hookups. These are listed in the first section. Walk-in sites for hikers and bikers are mentioned only when they are part of a drive-in campground.

Yurts with bunk beds and futon couches, tepees with carpeting and mattresses, cabins, and houseboats—what is camping coming to? The Oregon State Parks folks have added some pretty classy digs to their network of campgrounds, offering campers some of our best scenery along with some novel camping alternatives at very good values.

Roughing It Gets Easier in Our State Parks

Tumalo State Park offers yurts and tepees at only $27 and $29 per night, respectively. (Reserve early because yurts and tepees have become an overnight sensation; some people now spend their Oregon vacations yurt-hopping.) The LaPine State Park has basic cabins for $35 and yurts for $27. At the Prineville Reservoir State Park you can reserve a deluxe, two-room log cabin for $55 a night. The same log cabin with boat moorage at The Cove Palisades State Park goes for $65.

Of course, our fabulous state parks also have nice RV and tent sites. RV sites are larger and have either full or electric/water hookups. Tent sites are 44 feet or less in length, have no hookups, and can also be used by smaller RVs. Tent sites are fairly expensive ($15 to $16) compared with tent camping in Forest Service or BLM campgrounds, but the state parks with tent sites (Tumalo, Prineville, and Cove Palisades) offer prime recreational locations within 15 miles of town. Roads within the state parks are paved, and lighted bathrooms have flush toilets.

For yurt, tepee, and cabin camping at our state parks, you will need to bring everything you usually take for tent camping except the tent and mattresses. Bring bedding. All three types of lodging have electricity.

Any day-use-area fees are included in your camping fee; keep your camping receipt. Pets are allowed on leashes, and cleanup is required. For more information on our area state parks, please see our Parks chapter. Yurts, tepees, and cabins can be reserved all year. Some RV and tent sites can be reserved only from May through September.

State Park Reservations

Reservations may be made for our four state parks by calling Reservations Northwest, (800) 452–5687. In the off-season, call Monday through Friday from 8:00 A.M. to 5:00 P.M.; starting May 1 the lines are open until 9:00 P.M. on weekdays, plus 8:00 A.M. to 5:00 P.M. on Saturday. You must call at least two days but not more than nine months in advance. Visa and MasterCard are accepted. For general information, call (800) 551–6949, Monday through Friday from 8:00 A.M. to 5:00 P.M. You can also get more information about state parks, including reservation information, on their Web site at www.prd.state.or.us.

A Few More Details

Central Oregon's counties all charge room tax on campsites (6 to 7 percent). If you call ahead, most private RV parks quote rates not including tax, while public campgrounds (Oregon State Parks, Forest Service, etc.) usually include taxes in their rates. Ask to be sure.

We might mention that when we use the term "RV" in this chapter, we are very loosely referring to anything with wheels and beds, including pickup trucks with campers and tent trailers.

"ADA" stands for the Americans with Disabilities Act. Campsites and rest rooms that used to be called handicap-accessible are now referred to as "ADA campsites" or "ADA rest room."

Since campgrounds are often in remote areas outside the physical boundaries of our core towns, we have enlarged our core towns to be "areas." In other words, a campground with Bend or Prineville in the address line, for example, might actually be outside the city limits. And remember, an "F.S." road designator refers to a Forest Service road.

Home Away from Home

The following campgrounds all offer full hookups, lighted bathrooms with flush toilets, and picnic tables, and all accept MasterCard and Visa except as noted. All allow pets as long as they don't make noise, dogs are leashed, and owners clean up after their charges. Only Mountain Shadow RV Park in Sisters offers daily telephone hookups; all other places have public pay phones. Crown Villa RV Park in Bend has modem hookups.

Bend Area

The Bend area encompasses the section of the Deschutes National Forest to the west and southwest of Bend, including the not-to-be-missed Cascade Lakes Highway.

It's pretty amazing to find RV camping with hookups at the Cascade Lakes, especially since this area is so remote it doesn't even have regular phone service. Because there are so many Forest Service campgrounds in this area with hundreds of tent sites, the RV parks at Crane Prairie Resort and Twin Lakes Resort do not offer tent camping.

Bend Kampground
63615 North U.S. Highway 97, Bend
(541) 382–7738
Conveniently located on the north end of Bend a quarter-mile past the Mountain View Mall at Cooley Road, Bend Kampground offers pull-through trailer sites with full hookups and cable TV, as well as tent sites. The landscaping is grassy and mostly open with occasional mature deciduous trees. The sites are close together and near the highway.

Other features include a heated pool (open May through September), convenience store with deli sandwich bar, game room, horseshoes, volleyball, and a fishing pond, plus a dump station, gas pumps, and propane. Open all year, the Kampground's full-hookup sites cost $28, and a tent site with a covered shelter is $18.

Crane Prairie Resort
Forest Service Road 4270, Crane Prairie Reservoir, Deschutes National Forest
(541) 383–3939

This is RV camping at its rugged best. Crane Prairie Reservoir on the Cascade Lakes Highway, southwest of Sunriver at Forest Service Road 40 is about 55 miles from Bend. At an elevation of 4,400 feet, Crane Prairie is open during fishing season, late April through November 1, snow permitting. The gravel campsites with full hookups next to the lake run $22 per night. A few rustic cabins are available for $40 to $50 a night, and they come equipped with beds and electric lights. The resort is adjacent to a Forest Service campground that has tent camping.

Most of the guests are here to fish, so the resort has a store that's well-stocked with fishing tackle. It also offers its fishing guests boat rentals, a boat ramp, gas, and moorage. The store sells propane; it has coin showers but no phones. Crane Prairie starts accepting reservations on January 3.

Crown Villa RV Park
60801 Brosterhous Road, Bend
(541) 388–1131

The 25 acres of lush, manicured lawns at this RV park, tastefully dotted and crisscrossed with trees and paved roads, resemble a beautiful golf course without the hills or bunkers. Crown Villa really is a first-class RV park, as they like to say, with 106 nicely spaced sites with full or partial hookups (no tents). Newer RVs, well-behaved small pets, and RVers of all ages are welcome. Clotheslines, shabby-looking RVs (the owners reserve the right to make this decision) and cars, noise (including barking dogs), and stuff left lying about are not welcome. There are two ADA sites next to ADA rest rooms. Site managers will even lend a hand with the parking of larger RVs.

Retirees appreciate the secure, lighted grounds and like to play cards in the recreation building. The recreation building caters to groups and reunions with its full kitchen and covered dining area. Folks using the park on a longer-term basis (such as families waiting for their house to be built or business people here on temporary assignments) enjoy the mail and message service, monthly private phone lines, and laundry facilities. Crown Villa RV Park now has two modem connections, giving new meaning to the term full hookups.

Other amenities include RV washing (self-serve or with paid help), horseshoes, volleyball, basketball, a sandbox, individual storage units at each site, picnic tables, and 50-amp electrical service. The rate for full hookups is $39; without sewer it's $33. Rates include cable TV.

Lava Lake Lodge
Lava Lake, Forest Service Road 46, Deschutes National Forest
(541) 382–9443

This tidy lakeside resort is decorated with flowers and offers campsites with lots of nice trees. Guests can take advantage of a laundry, coin-operated showers, a marina, boat rentals, and a boat ramp. The small store sells propane and gas, and there is a dump station. Lava Lake is open from mid-April to late October, and of the RV parks on the Cascade Lakes Highway, it's the closest to Bend, which is about 45 miles away. RV camping is $20.40 with full hookups; tent sites are available for only $10.00.

The radio telephone at Lava Lake Lodge doesn't always work very well, so if you are unable to get through, drop them a letter. The mailing address is P.O. Box 989, Bend, OR 97701.

Sisters/Bend KOA Kampground
67667 U.S. Highway 20, Bend
(541) 549–3021, (800) 562–0363

Although this campground is 3 miles east of Sisters and 15 miles west of Bend, the U.S. Postal Service has given it a Bend address.

This tidy RV park is next to the Sisters Rodeo Grounds and offers a lovely pool and spa, playground, large fishing lake, miniature golf, a dump station, and a convenience store. The KOA has almost 100 pull-through sites with full hookups (including cable TV) that go for $35. Tent sites cost $30 and are located on dirt or gravel (no tents on the grass). There are two Kamping Kabins that run $50 and $55 each per night for two people, plus $2.00 to $9.00 extra per additional person. The KOA also has a list of do's and don'ts (mostly don'ts) as long as your arm—things like no suntan oil in or near the pool, no pets on the grass, no garbage in fire pits—so if you like a controlled environment, this is for you. The campground is closed in January and February.

The Sisters Rodeo, held on the second weekend in June (see our Annual Events chapter), is a very big deal for the Kampground. Only self-contained RVs are allowed that weekend, with hundreds of RVs camped in the 15-acre overflow area. The KOA starts taking reservations for the year on March 15, so if you want to camp here during the rodeo, you'd best call on day one. They accept MasterCard and Visa.

Tumalo State Park
Off U.S. Highway 20, 5 miles northwest of Bend
(541) 382–3586, (800) 452–5687

Here's one of the best ways we can think of to have your cake and eat it too. Pitch your kids' tent next to the Deschutes River, then hook your RV up to electricity, running water, and sewer service. Or just plunk your sleeping bag on a real mattress in a tepee or a yurt!

The sunny, forested Tumalo State Park is more tent-oriented than the other three state parks in Central Oregon. Tent sites without hookups account for 65 of the 87 total sites available at this park, which hugs a bend in the Deschutes River. Tent sites range from $15 for a standard site to $17 for a premium site next to the river in

Yurts, like this one at Tumalo State Park, are available for rent in several camping areas.
PHOTO: JIM YUSKAVITCH

the A Loop. The premium sites are worth the extra $2.00, unless you mind the extra mosquitoes. RV sites with full hookups cost $19. The four yurts are $27 per night. The two tepees cost $29 a night and sleep five or more people, depending on the exact model. Hiker/biker sites cost $4.00, and the two group sites are $60.00 each.

Again, A Loop sites are closest to the river. ADA sites and rest rooms are available. Amenities include showers, flush toilets, and firewood for purchase. You can walk or drive to swimming and fishing spots. At least one loop at Tumalo State Park is open all year.

Twin Lakes Resort
Forest Service Road 4260, Deschutes National Forest
(541) 593–6526
Situated at the neck of Wickiup Reservoir near North and South Twin Lakes, this nice resort is nestled in pine trees at the edge of the water at an elevation of 4,300 feet. Central to the resort is a large, rustic log building housing a general store, full-service restaurant, and office. The 22 sites with full hookups go for $26 per night and can be reserved a year in advance. For an extra $15, RVers can also pitch a tent in their site.

There are a number of fully-equipped cabins that can be rented at rates ranging from $90 to $145 per night. More guests can stay for $5.00 a head. Pets are allowed in the RV park for free; in the cabins they'll cost you an extra $5.00 a night. The more expensive cabins have full kitchens, and all of them have bathrooms.

With boat rentals, a boat ramp, a tackle shop, and guide services (not included in camping fee), Twin Lakes really caters to fisher-folk. If you don't think this is home away from home yet, note that they also have a Java Hut espresso stand. Coin-operated showers and laundry machines are also available. The resort is open from late April through mid-October, and Discover is accepted in addition to MasterCard and Visa. (For more about the resort, see our Resorts, Ranches, and Vacation Rentals chapter.)

Sisters/Camp Sherman Area

Mountain Shadow RV Park
540 U.S. Highway 20, Sisters
(541) 549–7275
This is a nice, modern RV park on the western edge of town. A new addition is

Campers take an afternoon snooze at Tumalo State Park. PHOTO: JIM YUSKAVITCH

an enclosed pool and spa, with a wading pool. The mostly young trees are still on the small side, so there's not a lot of shade, and sites are fairly close together. But the ADA rest rooms with showers are very nice and new.

All of the 105 sites have full hookups with 30- or 50-amp service for $29.95, and the rate includes cable TV. Tents and sleeping bags are not allowed on the manicured grass. Mountain Shadow is open all year and accepts American Express and Discover, along with Visa and MasterCard.

Redmond Area

The best camping in this area is at the Crooked River Ranch, a residential subdivision/resort. To get there, travel 6 miles north of Redmond on U.S. Highway 97, then 7 miles west at the signed turnoff. In fact, starting on U.S. 97, the signs to the resort and to both of our listed RV parks are large, plentiful, and easy to follow. Camping-oriented amenities at Crooked River include a good convenience store with a deli, gas, and propane, along with a couple of restaurants, the 18-hole Crooked River Ranch Golf Course (see our Golf chapter), and a riding stable.

Crooked River Ranch RV Park
14875 Hays Lane, Crooked River Ranch
(541) 923–1441, (800) 841–0563
www.crookedriverranch.com

Owned by the ranch, this is a large RV park with nicely manicured lawns that blend in with the surrounding 18-hole champion golf course. About half of the 91 RV sites have full hookups with cable TV and have 30- and 50-amp service; the other half offer water and electricity only.

Use of the resort's Olympic-size pool and large kiddie pool, tennis courts, and barbecue pavilion is included in the camping fee. Other amenities include horseback riding, rock climbing, volleyball, basketball, horseshoes, a laundry, and coin-operated showers. The RV sites cost right at $24.38 per night; partial hookups are about $20.14. There are also 17 grassy tent sites that rent for $14.84 per night. The RV park is usually open March 15 through October,

but the operators may soon try staying open all year. Reservations may be made for the coming season after January 1.

River Rim RV Park
14285 Business Circle, Crooked River Ranch
(541) 923–7239

You won't find a stone out of place at this neat little RV park with its gravel driveway and 24 sites, all of which have full hookups with reception of four TV stations. River Rim is a rather basic little place—its main feature, besides being so tidy and quiet, is that it's on the back nine of the Crooked River Ranch Golf Course. Guests get free passes to use the ranch's beautiful pool and tennis courts. Propane is available, and a laundry facility is planned for the near future. The full-hookup sites go for $18 per day. Located at the bottom of a warm, sunny canyon, River Rim is open all year.

Sunriver/La Pine Area

We have defined this region as being from Sunriver to La Pine, adjacent to U.S. 97, as far west as the LaPine State Park and as far east as the Newberry Crater in the Newberry National Volcanic Monument. The part of the Deschutes National Forest west of here is included in the Bend section. Sunriver has no camping outlets.

Cascade Meadows RV Resort
53750 U.S. Highway 97, La Pine
(541) 536–2244

Under new ownership since 1995, this membership-type campground welcomes nonmember guests. It's conveniently located at the junction of U.S. 97 and Oregon Highway 21 (or Paulina Road), 18 miles west of Newberry Crater and its fantastic lakes, recreation, and sight-seeing.

This is a large RV park with 101 pull-through sites with full hookups (no TV). It might be a tad too crowded for some folks. Sites cost $25 per night for full hookup and $20 for partial. There is a tent area offering grass or sawdust sites for $15. Also available are a cabin that sleeps four ($42.40 a night) and a trailer that also sleeps four (for $35). The nonsmoking cabin and trailer have TV, full kitchens, and bathrooms, but you'll need to bring linens or sleeping bags. Pets are allowed in the campground but not in the trailer or cabin.

The lawns and gravel roads at Cascade Meadows have been upgraded and the grounds planted with young trees. Another improvement includes 30- and 50-amp electric service. Two bathhouses have free showers and laundry facilities. The clubhouse has satellite TV with a VCR, along with a pool table and video arcade. Outside are a swimming pool and hot tub, as well as horseshoes, volleyball, shuffleboard, tetherball, and a playground.

The extensive list of services includes fax capability, phones for computer updates, bingo, line dancing, dog runs, storage facilities (plus RV and boat storage), movie rentals, ice, and propane. You won't need a license to catch fish in the trout pond. There is also a convenience store and restaurant. Cascade Meadows is open from April through November, and Discover is accepted as well as MasterCard and Visa.

East Lake Resort
East Lake, Newberry National Volcanic Monument, La Pine
(541) 536–2230
www.EastLakeResort.com

The pine tree forests start to get sparse when the elevation is 6,400 feet, and that lets the sun shine through. Among the trees a short distance from the lake is this resort, offering 38 RV sites with water and electric hookups that cost $15 per night. Other camping facilities at East Lake range from simple camping cabins with a sink

and toilet for $45, up to three-bedroom cabins with full kitchens for $125 a night. Cabins are fully equipped with linens and have electric heat. Pets in the cabins are an extra $5.00.

Public, coin-operated showers and a laundry are available, plus a cafe and general store with gas and propane, boat rentals, a beach, and a playground. This is a very popular area for fishing and hiking. The resort is open from May to September. (Please see our Resorts, Ranches, and Vacation Rentals chapter.)

LaPine State Park
La Pine State Rec Road, La Pine
(541) 536–2071, (800) 452–5687

Fly and spin fishers, hikers, and snow enthusiasts love the LaPine State Park. Surrounded by the Deschutes National Forest in one of the snowier parts of Central Oregon, 27 miles southwest of Bend, the park's 145 campsites are at an elevation of 4,200 feet. The campground's three loops hug the east side of the Deschutes River, right in the middle of an area with an extensive list of recreational opportunities. (See our various recreation chapters and the Parks chapter for more information.)

All campsites have RV hookups. The E Loop has water and electricity only and no showers; these sites cost $13. The F and G Loops, at $15 per site, have full hookups and showers. Sites G15 through G21 are closest to the river. Also available at $27 per night are three yurts; five one-room log cabins can be rented for $35. LaPine State Park has a dump station and an ADA campsite but no ADA rest rooms as of yet (one is planned when funding is available). The park is open all year.

Prineville Area

Crook County RV Park
1040 South Main Street, Prineville
(541) 447–2599, (800) 609–2599

This RV park's location next to the Crook County Fairgrounds pretty well guaranties it a full house from mid-May through July, when the fairgrounds hosts its main events. If you plan to stay at this tidy, close-in park during this period, you will need to reserve well ahead. The park is open all year, offering winter campers a moderate climate for off-season camping.

The 81 full-hookup sites include cable TV and cost $20.00; nine tent sites go for $9.00 a night. Options also include two camping cabins that sleep five at $25 each; bring linens or sleeping bags. This county RV park opened in 1993 and has four ADA sites and ADA rest rooms with showers, plus a dump station and newly planted trees. (Note that an air-conditioned RV would be good to have in the summer.) Visa and MasterCard are accepted here.

Lakeshore RV Park
12333 Northeast Ochoco Highway, Prineville
(541) 447–6059

This park is across the highway from Ochoco Reservoir. Its proximity to the lake and its convenience store with fishing tackle, a coin-op laundry, showers, and propane make this a popular spot to stay for bait fishers and boaters (see our Fishing chapter). Lakeshore is open all year with 32 full-hookup sites that cost $20 per night and 12 tent sites for $12 per night. Each gravel or dirt site has a picnic table, and tent sites have fire pits. The campground, built in 1954, features some juniper and poplar trees. They take MasterCard, Visa, and Discover. A deposit will be required for your pet, depending on its size and type.

Prineville Reservoir State Park
Juniper Canyon Road, Prineville
(541) 447–4363, (800) 452–5687

Fifteen miles south of Prineville at the end of Juniper Canyon Road, this state park offers excellent fishing and boating. The land is arid and open. The 22 full-hookup sites go for $22; there are sites with electricity and water only for $18, and tent sites go for $16. A more remote section of the campground offers primitive camping. It costs $7.00 per night to leave a vehicle in the parking lot overnight (many people boat camp on the far side of the reservoir, leaving their vehicle behind in the lot). There are also three deluxe, three-room cabins that sleep up to six people for

$55 per night. When they say deluxe, they mean deluxe. These cabins have heat, air-conditioning, full baths, and kitchens with refrigerators and microwaves (but no stove). You'll need to bring linens or sleeping bags, towels, and cooking utensils. Plan to do your cooking on the gas barbecue, and plan on reserving one of these babies 11 months in advance. There are also two two-room cabins with outside cooking only for $5.00 per night.

Other park amenities include showers, an ADA campsite, ADA rest rooms, and a boat ramp. The park is open all year. (See our chapters on Parks and Fishing for more information.)

Sun Rocks RV Resort
14900 South Juniper Canyon Road, Prineville
(541) 447–6540

A quiet, well-run, family-oriented resort that opened in 1993, Sun Rocks is just 2 miles from Prineville Reservoir. It offers gravel, pull-through RV sites with full hookups and 50-amp electric service. Full RV hookup is $24 for two people, one RV, and one vehicle. The grassy tent sites are in a grove of old juniper trees and rent for $17. The four cabins rent for $35 each. There are also three A-frames for $35. Use of the pool and spa is included in overnight rates. Day visitors can use the facilities for $3.50 per person.

The landscaping at Sun Rocks is open and sunny with newly planted young trees. A clubhouse with a full kitchen is available for groups, and you'll find a laundry, coin-operated showers, and ADA sites and rest rooms. Volleyball, horseshoes, basketball, and an excellent playground are a few of the outdoor attractions. However, the main attraction is the reservoir, so Sun Rocks offers free boat parking, and boat and trailer storage. The campground sells propane, ice, and firewood, and across the highway is a convenience store that sells fishing tackle and gas. Open year-round, Sun Rocks accepts MasterCard and Visa.

Madras Area

Mild winter weather and incredible lake fishing and boating are big attractions here in the northern desert communities of the Madras area.

The Cove Palisades State Park (Crooked River Campground and Deschutes River Campground)
Lake Billy Chinook, Culver
(541) 546–3412, (800) 452–5687

From the Old Culver Highway that runs between Madras, Culver, and U.S. 97, take the signed turnoff west to Lake Billy Chinook. Warm sunshine, fishing, and boating are the main attractions at this desert reservoir area. The state park features two campgrounds (described below), a marina that rents fully furnished houseboats (starting at $740 for two nights for a boat that sleeps 10), a restaurant, swimming, and boat rentals. Three group tent areas are available at $60 per area. The park is open all year. (Please see our chapter on Parks for more general information on The Cove Palisades State Park.)

As you enter the park, Crooked River Campground will be on your left overlooking the reservoir. This campground has 91 RV sites with water and electricity, a dump station, and showers. Sites cost $20. Continue south on the road around the lake, and you will come to the Deschutes River Campground, which offers 87 RV campsites with full hookups at $20 a night, plus 94 tent sites with no hookups at $16 a night. RV Loop A has an ADA site and rest room. Two fish-cleaning houses are available, and you'll be happy to know there are showers.

Jefferson County Fairgrounds RV Park
430 Southwest Fairgrounds Road, Madras
(541) 475–4460
www.jcfc.ws

The main attraction at this campground, as you might expect, is its location next to the fairgrounds. Some fairground events can lead to this park being booked a year in advance, so call as far ahead of time as you can. The 65 sites with full hookups, including cable TV, run $15 per night. There is a large grassy overflow area where tenters can pitch tents for $7.00; it also accommodates RVs that couldn't get a regular site for $10.00 a night. Note that this campground does not accept credit

cards. At times you'll find almost 400 RVs here. Free showers and ADA rest rooms just round out the amenities. The park is open from April to November.

KOA Madras/Culver
2435 Southwest Jericho Lane, Madras
(541) 546–3046, (800) 562–1992

This campground offers one of the quieter, off-highway KOA settings that we've seen. Nine miles south of Madras, turn east on South Jericho Lane at the sign that says TO HAYSTACK RESERVOIR. The campground is just up that road. This KOA is 2 miles from Haystack and 7 miles from Lake Billy Chinook, so it's a popular camping spot for fisher-folk and boaters.

The KOA was built in 1974, so many of the trees have had a chance to grow up; they now provide shade for some of the 83 pull-through sites. With full hookups, a site will cost you $22 per night; tenters pay $17 for a grassy spot. A Kamping Kabin that sleeps four costs $32. The free showers and laundry room are kept very clean, and the well-stocked convenience store carries fishing supplies. Outside you'll find a pool, playground, volleyball court, and horseshoes. This KOA is open all year and accepts American Express, Discover, Visa, and MasterCard.

Lake Simtustus RV Park
2750 Northwest Pelton Dam Road, Madras
(541) 475–1085

This RV park boasts warm winter weather, great fishing, and 91 campsites with full hookups from $16.00 to $22.50. The campground is right on the lake, and some of the sites have large shade trees. You can rent paddleboats, pontoon boats, and motorboats for fishing. A small store sells some tackle (just what you'll need here), snacks, and ice. Showers are free, and a boat ramp, boat parking, and moorage are offered. They'll even help you launch your boat if you wish. The park is open all year.

Really Roughing It

No hookups here! These places are for the serious campers who want to forego life's civilized touches—TV, air-conditioning, and refrigeration—when they get away. Unless otherwise noted, you should assume that no credit cards are taken at these camping areas, and that you'll be dealing with vault toilets. Folks with tents should be sure to check out the previous "Home Away From Home" section, as some RV parks also have tent sites.

To go one step further, dispersed camping is allowed in the national forests and Bureau of Land Management lands. Dispersed means heading out into the wilds and camping in an undeveloped site. There is no charge to camp or park in an undeveloped area, and likewise, there are no amenities. Here's where "no trace camping" comes in. You should keep in mind the negative impact that you and your vehicle could have on the natural environment. Please drive on gravel or dirt roads, and park in existing turnouts where vehicles have driven before you. Use an existing fire ring (if there is one) for your campfire.

Another consideration when roughing it is the possibility of starting a wild fire. Campfires are allowed in public lands as long as you use a fire ring. If you are camping in an undeveloped area, you may need to make your own fire ring. If the fire danger is high, campfires may be banned in undeveloped camping areas, and vehicular travel restricted to main roads. Contact the nearest Forest Service Ranger Station or BLM Ranger Station for an update on fire conditions before heading out.

For more descriptive general information on these camping areas, please refer to our chapters on Other Outdoor Recreation; Fishing; and Forests, High Desert, and Volcanoes.

Bend Area

If you were to ask a local where to go camping, the Cascade Lakes Highway in the Deschutes National Forest is probably the first place that would come to his mind. The loop route starts with Century Drive, west of Bend, which turns into Forest Service Road 46 as you enter the Deschutes National Forest. Forest Service Road 46 takes you all the way past Davis Lake, and you eventually end up (87 miles later) at U.S. Highway 97 at Crescent. You can get back to U.S. 97 sooner by cutting across on Forest Service Road 40, which takes you to Sunriver, or on Forest Service Road 42 to Forest Service Road 43, where you will come out just north of La Pine. (For more specifics on the Cascade Lakes Scenic Highway, see our Daytrips chapter.)

The Bend Ranger District gives special programs at some of these campgrounds from July 4 through Labor Day. Please contact the Bend/Fort Rock Ranger District Office in Bend, (541) 383-4000, for a schedule.

We'll start by covering the Cascade Lakes campgrounds, arranged alphabetically by lake names. Then we'll touch on campgrounds on the Deschutes River, also near the Cascade Lakes Highway, followed by a jump about 40 miles to the east to catch Pine Mountain, off U.S. 20.

Cascade Lakes Camping Areas

The Cascade Lakes Highway is Forest Service Road 46. For information on the Cascade Lakes Highway campgrounds, please call the Deschutes National Forest office in Bend at (541) 383-5300.

Crane Prairie (Crane Prairie Campground, Cow Meadow Campground, Quinn River Campground, Rock Creek Campground)

Crane Prairie Campground is about 55 miles from Bend at an elevation of 4,450 feet. From the Cascade Lakes Highway, head east on Forest Service Road 42 for

Insiders' Tip
Gloriously warm summer days can turn into very chilly summer nights in the mountains. Pack for 40-degree-temperature swings, and don't be surprised if you get an afternoon thundershower.

about 3 miles, then just after you cross the Deschutes River turn north on Forest Service 4270. Continue north about 4 miles.

Crane Prairie is one of the larger reservoirs, and it offers excellent fishing. The outstanding Crane Prairie Campground, next to the Crane Prairie Resort on Forest Service 4270, has paved roads and sites in a beautiful, tree-filled setting right next to the lake. The 146 campsites are $10, or $12 for a premium site. Drinking water and fish-cleaning stations are available at the campground, and coin-operated showers can be found at the resort next door. (See Crane Prairie Resort in the "Home Away from Home" section of this chapter.)

Accessible from Forest Service Road 40 is Cow Meadow Campground, which has 21 sites at $5.00 a night. Quinn River Campground is right off Forest Service Road 46 and has 41 sites, plus drinking water you have to pump; the cost is $10. At the southern end of the lake off Forest Service Road 46 is Rock Creek Campground, which offers 31 campsites, a boat ramp, and hand-pumped drinking water for $10.

Cultus Lake (Cultus, West Cultus, Cultus North Shore Coves)

From Forest Service Road 46, head west on Forest Service Road 4635 about 2 miles to reach Cultus Lake. The lake, situated at 4,700 feet, is popular for waterskiing, boating, and fishing. At the east end of Cultus Lake is Cultus Campground, with 55 sites for $10 per night. You'll find drinking water and a boat launch. On the north and west shores are two boat-in or hike-in campgrounds, called West Cultus and Cultus North Shore Coves, that run $5.00 per night. Nearby at the Cultus Lake Resort is a store that sells gas.

Little Cultus Lake

On the way to Cultus Lake, take a left onto Forest Service Road 4630, travel about 1.7 miles onto Forest Service Road 4635, then take a right (west) on Forest Service Road 4636 for about a mile. This campground is high up at an elevation of 4,800 feet. There are 10 campsites with drinking water and a boat ramp for only $5.00 a night.

Davis Lake (East and West Davis Campgrounds, Lava Flow Campground)

At 4,400 feet, Davis Lake is one of our lower-elevation lakes. It's the southernmost lake on the Cascade Lakes Highway, and only fly-fishing is allowed here. At the south end of the lake are the East and West Davis Campgrounds, both costing $8.00 per night. East has 33 campsites and hand-pumped drinking water; West offers the same setup but with only 24 sites. Lava Flow Campground, on the east side of the lake, has 12 sites and no drinking water. It is under Wildlife Closure from January 1 through August 31, and there is no fee. East Davis and Lava Flow campgrounds are reached via Forest Service Road 850, just off Forest Service 46. To get to West Davis Lake Campground take Forest Service Road 4660 for 3 miles, then head north on Forest Service 4669 for 2 miles.

Elk Lake (Point Campground, Elk Lake Campground, Little Fawn Campground, Little Fawn Group Camp)

This lake, right off Forest Service Road 46 on Forest Service 4625, is popular with boaters, and it offers three campgrounds and a group camp. Point Campground has 10 campsites, with fishing, swimming, and a boat ramp, for $10 per night. Elk Lake Campground offers 23 sites, a boat launch, and drinking water for $10 nightly. Little Fawn Campground has 20 sites and hand-pumped drinking water, and sites cost $8.00 a night. Little Fawn Group Camp can handle up to 60 people for $70 a day. Call (877) 444-6777 for group reservations.

Hosmer Lake (Mallard Marsh Campground, South Campground)

Across from Elk Lake, Hosmer Lake is very popular with fly fishers in float tubes, so it fills up fast. To reach the lake, take Forest Service Road 4625 to Elk Lake and take a right at the sign to Hosmer. Mallard Marsh Campground has 15 tent sites at $5.00 per night. South Campground offers 23 sites and a boat ramp—it's the preferred location at Hosmer. It's also $5.00 per night.

Lava Lakes

At the southeast end of Lava Lake is the campground by the same name. For $10 per night, it offers 43 sites, drinking water, and a boat ramp. On the other side of the access road is Little Lava Lake, with its corresponding campground and 10 sites (at $5.00 a night), drinking water, and a boat ramp. At Lava Lakes you will be at an elevation of 4,750 feet. Lava Lakes are approximately 38 miles from Bend. From Forest Service Road 46, head east 1 mile on Forest Service 550 and follow the signs.

North Twin Lake

This peaceful little lake has a campground with 19 sites and a boat ramp for small, nonmotorized boats. The sites cost $5.00 per night. From Forest Service Road 46, head east about 6 miles, then south on Forest Service 4260. You will almost immediately come upon North Twin Lake Campground.

South Twin Lake

South Twin Campground's 24 sites go for $12 a night. This campground actually has flush toilets, drinking water, and a boat launch for small, nonmotorized boats. To get here, simply keep heading south from North Twin Lake Campground another 2 miles.

Sparks Lake

This shallow lake at the tip of the loop drive is home to Soda Creek Campground, a seven-site location with no water. It's free of charge.

Wickiup Reservoir (Gull Point Campground, Reservoir Campground, Sheep Bridge Campground, Wickiup Butte, West South Twin)

This large reservoir at an elevation of 4,350 feet is another popular fishing spot. Gull Point Campground is a big one—there are 81 sites, two of which are group sites that go for $50 per night for up to 25 people (call 541-382-9443 for group reservations). The regular sites cost $10 each, and Gull Point offers flush toilets, drinking water, and a boat ramp.

On the west side of the reservoir off Forest Service Road 44 is Reservoir Campground, with 28 sites that cost $5.00 per night. Sheep Bridge Campground can be accessed by Forest Service 4260 at the north end of the reservoir. It has 18 sites for $5.00 nightly, plus a boat ramp and drinking water. Wickiup Butte is a small campground with eight sites that cost $5.00 per night. West South Twin Campground is near Twin Lakes Resort and South Twin Lake Campground. It offers 24 forested sites, flush toilets, piped-in water, and a boat ramp, all for $10 a night.

Upper Deschutes River (Deschutes Bridge Group Camp, North Davis Creek Campground, Bull Bend, Pringle Falls, Big River Campground)

Deschutes Bridge Group Camp has access to great fishing in the river. The 12 sites are $5.00 a night. Drinking water is available. North Davis Creek Campground is near Forest Service Road 46. It has 15 campsites for $8.00 each and features hand-pumped water and a boat ramp.

Bull Bend, located below Wickiup, has 12 sites ($5.00 per night) but no water. A short ways down is Pringle Falls, with six sites and no drinking water, for $5.00 per night. Big River Campground is located where Forest Service 42 crosses the river, and its 11 sites go for $5.00 nightly. There's no drinking water.

Other Bend Area Campgrounds

Pine Mountain Campground
Forest Service Road 2017, 8 miles south of Millican off U.S. Highway 20

Located 24 miles east of Bend at the Pine Mountain Observatory, this fairly primitive campground often hosts dozens of voyeurs eager to gaze into the dark night sky and start rattling off names of stars. The campground is utilized by troops of Boy Scouts, families, and serious stargazers. The elevation here is 6,250 feet, and there is no charge for camping. (See our Daytrips and Attractions chapters for more on Pine Mountain Observatory.)

Sisters/Camp Sherman Area

There are three clusters of "really roughing it" campgrounds in this area. The Three Creek Lake area is to the south of Sisters. McKenzie Pass is a second area west of Sisters, and the Camp Sherman/Metolius River Recreation Area has a dense concentration of campgrounds that hug the Metolius River. All the campgrounds in the Sisters/Camp Sherman area close down in September or October and don't open again until April or May, depending on the snow.

The Sisters Ranger District gives interpretive programs on weekends from July 4 through Labor Day. Contact the district office at (541) 549-7700 for a schedule or stop by the Camp Sherman store. You may get more information on the following campgrounds by calling the Sisters Ranger District.

Three Creek Lake (Three Creek Meadow Campground, Three Creek Lake Campground, Driftwood Campground)

From downtown Sisters take Forest Service Road 16 south. As you go up the grade there will be great views of the Cascades. You will first arrive at Three Creek Meadow Campground, at an elevation of 6,600 feet. The nine sites cost $10 per night, and you should bring your own water. Three Creek Lake Campground is right on the lake, surrounded by sunny ponderosa pine forests. Unfortunately there are only 10 sites at this

pretty spot, and they run $10 per night. Bring water. Nearby is Driftwood Campground, with five sites that cost $10 nightly. Three Creek Lake has a small beach, and in summer the water actually warms up a few degrees for swimming.

McKenzie Pass (Cold Springs Campground, Lava Camp Lake)

Head west out of downtown Sisters on U.S. Highway 20 and take the left fork just before you leave town. This is Oregon Highway 242. Cold Springs Campground, 4 miles west of town at a relatively warm 3,400-foot elevation, is a lovely, peaceful campground in a ponderosa pine forest with a brook running through it. The fee is $12, and there are flush toilets and piped water.

From this point the road goes up steeply over the next 10 miles, climbing to an elevation of 5,300 feet. Here you will find Lava Camp Lake with 10 sites, no fee, and no drinking water. The high-elevation terrain is stark, with a few small, twisted trees and lots of barren volcanic rock. Even during summer months it can get quite cold at night here, so bring warm clothes (actually, it can get cold during some summer days, too). The views and scenery here are striking.

As you continue over McKenzie Pass and down the west side, you technically leave the Deschutes National Forest and the coverage area for our book, but there are several more small, primitive campgrounds before you reach U.S. Highway 126.

Metolius River Recreation Area (Camp Sherman, Allingham, Smiling River, Pine Rest, The Gorge, Allen Springs, Pioneer Ford, Lower Bridge, Abbot Creek Campground, Canyon Creek Campground)

A famous, wild trout stream, the Metolius River is a very popular camping area. Eight Forest Service campgrounds are lined up along the eastern shore of the river from Forest Service Road 14 to Forest Service Road 1419, almost elbow to elbow. They are all in the same forest setting, with vault toilets and piped-in water. When most folks arrive, they simply drive into one after another until they find a site that suits them, rather like Goldilocks and the three bears' beds.

Fly fishermen cast their offerings into the crystal clear waters of the Metolius River, one of the most scenic fishing spots in the state, and a popular camping area. PHOTO: JIM YUSKAVITCH

All of the following sites cost $12 per night. We'll list them in order from south to north and offer some details. Camp Sherman boasts 15 trailer/tent sites with picnic shelters. Allingham has 10 trailer/tent sites. Smiling River is a big area, with 38 trailer/tent sites. Pine Rest's eight tent sites have picnic shelters. The Gorge has 18 trailer/tent sites. Allen Springs has 13 trailer/tent sites and four tent-only sites. Pioneer Ford has 18 trailer/tent sites and two tent-only sites, including one ADA campsite and ADA rest rooms. Lower Bridge has 12 tent-only sites.

The quiet and secluded Abbot Creek Campground is a few miles northwest of the Metolius on Forest Service Road 12. This would be a good bet if the other riverside spots are full. There is no charge to camp here. Canyon Creek Campground's four sites are also free, and you can get to them by heading north 12.3 miles on Forest Service 12, then east 1.6 miles on Forest Service Road 1200.

The village of Camp Sherman offers a full-service restaurant, deli, convenience store, and fly and fishing tackle.

Sunriver/La Pine Area

Rough camping south of Bend is concentrated in the Newberry National Volcanic Monument area. This is a real gem of a recreation area with two alpine lakes, volcanic sights, and forests for hiking. At an elevation of 6,400 feet, the air is sparkling clean, and the nights can get chilly. Campgrounds here are open May through October, or when the snow clears, which might be later than May.

A portion of the campsites at the lakes can be reserved through the National Reservation System at (877) 444-6777. The Visitor Center at Newberry Crater is open Wednesday through Sunday from July 4 through Labor Day, and the rangers give free nature talks and walks on the weekends. Call the Lava Lands Visitor Center, (541) 593-2421, for other scheduled interpretive events.

Oregon Highway 21 (Ogden Group Camp, McKay Crossing Campground, Prairie Campground)

On the way up to Newberry Crater are two campgrounds, and a third one is just a sidetrip to the east. Ogden Group Camp has group sites for $60 that must be reserved in advance by calling (877) 444-6777. Prairie Campground, on Oregon Highway 21, offers 16 forested campsites. The fee is $10 per night. About 2.7 miles east of Oregon Highway 21 on Forest Service 2120 is the McKay Crossing Campground, with 10 sites at $5.00 per night.

Paulina Lake (Little Crater Campground, Paulina Lake Campground, Newberry Group Camp)

Little Crater Campground, on the east side of Paulina Lake, a half mile north of Oregon Highway 21, has beautiful sites next to the lake. The 50 campsites cost $14 per night, and the campground has drinking water. Paulina Lake Campground on Oregon Highway 21 is also lovely, with 69 sites, drinking water, and flush toilets. Rates are $10, or $12 for a site close to the water. The reservation-only Newberry Group Camp (also on Oregon Highway 21) has three group sites that run between $60 and $90 a night. It also has a dump site. Call (877) 444-6777 for reservations. The nearby Paulina Lake Resort has a store with gas, a telephone, and a restaurant.

East Lake (East Lake Campground, Cinder Hill Campground, Hot Springs Campground)

About 2 miles east of Paulina Lake on Oregon Highway 21, East Lake Campground offers 29 lakeside campsites with flush toilets and drinking water. Inland sites are $10; waterfront sites are $12 (go with the waterfront sites if available!). At the end of the highway on the far eastern edge of the lake is Cinder Hill Campground, the largest campground in the area, with 110 sites, flush toilets, and drinking water. Forested sites go for $12 a night, and beachfront sites are $14. Individual campsites at Cinder Hill may be reserved through the National Reservation System at (877) 444-6777. Hot Springs Campground has 52 sites. These rent for $9.00 a night. The East Lake Resort has a general store, laundry facilities, public showers, gas, pay phones, and a cafe (see our Resorts, Ranches, and Vacation Rentals chapter).

Fall River

Fall River in the Deschutes National Forest, a favorite fly-fishing spot, is easily accessed from Forest Service Road 42, 12 miles west of U.S. 97. The Fall River Campground charges $5.00 for each of its 10 sites.

Prineville Area

Lower Crooked Wild and Scenic River

This stretch of the Crooked River offers excellent fishing and beautiful, High Desert canyon scenery. A 43-mile paved road, Oregon Highway 27, runs along the river and is dotted with nine primitive Bureau of Land Management campgrounds. Bring drinking water, a hat, and sunscreen. The campsites all cost $8.00 per night, and they are all open year-round. Two group camps, accommodating 9 to 24 people are also available for $20 per night. Chimney Rock is the only one with drinking water. For more information, contact the BLM office in Prineville at (541) 416-6700.

Ochoco Lake County Campground
U.S. Highway 26, Prineville
(541) 447-1209 (Crook County Parks and Recreation Office)

This well-managed county campground is about 7 miles east of Prineville, on the south side of the highway at Ochoco Reservoir. The 22 paved sites are nicely shaded and cost $14 a night. Four hiker/biker sites are $4.00 per person. Short trails lead to the water's edge, and you'll find a boat ramp and boat parking. Lighted bathrooms with flush toilets, a new shower, and ADA facilities complete this campground's amenities. This campground was formerly an Oregon state park until 1996. About a half mile east is another RV park (Lakeshore RV Park; see previous listing) with a convenience store and propane.

Ochoco National Forest

The following campgrounds and cabin are in the Ochoco National Forest, east of Prineville.

Cold Springs Guard Station
Just off Forest Service Road 30, Big Summit Prairie, Ochoco National Forest

This is a bird- and wildlife-watchers dream cabin, located on the eastern edge of the Big Summit Prairie. From Prineville head 15 miles east on U.S. 26, turn right at the fork on Oregon Highway 23, and drive 9 miles; then keep right as the road forks onto Forest Service Road 42 and go 22 miles. After you cross the North Fork of the Crooked River, head north on Forest Service Road 30 and follow the signs. The cabin comes with a shower/bath, full kitchen, living room, and two bedrooms, and it sleeps six to eight. Electricity comes from a propane generator. Drinking water is available. The cabin rents for $50 per night, and you bring your own linens or sleeping bags and towels.

Ochoco Divide Campground
U.S. Highway 26, Ochoco National Forest

Thirty miles east of Prineville at the summit of Ochoco Pass, elevation 4,700 feet, the Ochoco Divide Campground is a beautiful spot within an old-growth ponderosa pine forest, with 28 campsites and drinking water. The fee is $8.00. There is also a $4.00 additional vehicle charge. The campground has an ADA campsite and vault toilet.

Ochoco Forest Camp
Forest Service Road 42, 25 miles east of Prineville via U.S. 26 to Oregon Highway 23, Ochoco National Forest

This small, forested campground along Ochoco Creek has a total of six sites with drinking water. It's just behind the Ochoco Ranger Station at an elevation of 4,000 feet. There are a few fish in the creek, at least enough to keep the kids busy.

Tent sites are $8.00 per night and RV sites are $10.00. There is a $4.00 additional vehicle charge.

Walton Lake
Forest Service Road 22, Ochoco National Forest

To access Walton Lake, take U.S. 26 and then Oregon Highway 23 east out of Prineville for 25 miles until you get to the Ochoco Ranger Station, then head 7 miles northeast on Forest Service Road 22. Unlike the other campgrounds in the Ochoco National Forest, this very popular campground is sure to be full on peak summer weekends.

The lake offers boating (electric motors or person-powered), a sandy beach for swimmers, fishing, and nearby hiking. At an elevation of 5,000 feet, it has 30 sites set among old-growth ponderosa pines; they go for $8.00 per night. The day-use area charges $3.00 per vehicle on weekends.

Madras Area

The Crooked River National Grassland, a very interesting bird and wildlife habitat with viewing areas south of Madras, is managed by the Bureau of Land Management.

Haystack Reservoir
Forest Service Road 1130, Crooked River National Grassland

From Madras, travel 8 miles south on U.S. 97, turn east at the sign for Haystack Reservoir, and go 2 miles on Jericho Lane. Formed in 1957 by the creation of Haystack Dam, the reservoir was intended to hold Deschutes River water for irrigation purposes. It is stocked annually with kokanee salmon, rainbow trout, largemouth bass, and bluegill. The campground has 24 sites, drinking water, and boat ramps. Besides fishing and bird-watching, there are waterskiing, swimming, and windsurfing. The overnight fee is $8.00, with a $3.00 additional vehicle charge.

Insiders' Tip
Your paid campsite receipt will serve as a day parking pass if you are in an area where a trail park permit is required. (See our Forest, High Desert, and Volcanoes chapter for more on permits.)

Restaurants

As you can tell from the size of this chapter, Central Oregonians like to dine out; we like good food and we like variety. So it's no surprise that there are a lot of great places to eat—Bend alone has more than 200 restaurants. With so much competition in Bend, we had to be fairly choosy about which restaurants to include. Our Bend listings reflect a cross-section of the best foods, most fun experiences, and solid family fare. But even our less-populated areas offer exceptional dining experiences. Places such as the Seasons Cafe and Wine Shop in Sisters, The Trout House in Sunriver, Hog Heaven in La Pine, the Pioneer Club in Prineville, Pepe's in Madras, and Pug's Mug in Culver would all be welcome additions to the dining scene in any city.

At some of our finer restaurants you may get a chance to sample what is referred to as "Northwest cuisine." It's a loosely defined culinary style that celebrates our fresh, local ingredients. Generally speaking, Northwest cuisine is a combination of California spa cuisine and foods indigenous to the Northwest, along with some Pacific Rim influence and a little bit of our local Native American tradition. Salmon, halibut, sturgeon, sea bass, steelhead, trout, bay shrimp, oysters, Dungeness crab, and clams represent some of the bounty from Northwest waters at different times during the year.

Says Greg Unruh, head chef at Scanlon's in Bend, "Northwest cuisine uses grilling or quick sautéing to seal in juices, together with fresh herbs, fruit chutneys, hazelnuts, and Asian seasonings to bring out the fresh flavors of the dishes, rather than overladening them with heavy sauces." Typical Northwest dishes would include the scallops served in a roasted tomato broth featured at Broken Top Club, chicken breast prepared with a hazelnut crust at the Pine Tavern, or seared ahi tuna with fruit chutney at Kayo's. All three restaurants are in Bend.

For many years the Native Americans of the plateau, including our local Warm Springs tribes, smoked salmon fillets on sticks over alder wood fires. (This tradition carries on today—you can enjoy what is called a salmon bake at Kah-Nee-Ta Resort.) They then pounded the fillets with ground huckleberries to make a delicious and nutritious preserved food to carry them through the winter. Today you will occasionally come across salmon prepared with a huckleberry sauce. Berries, apples, pears, sweet onions, and other vegetables make sweet and succulent accompaniments to our fish and seafood as well as lamb and poultry. Dried or fresh raspberries, huckleberries, blackberries, and blueberries are added to almost everything here, from French toast to salads to lamb dishes. Berry cobblers are among our favorite desserts. You will also notice the frequent mention of marionberries. A gourmet blackberry, marionberries are native to Oregon.

It's the Time of the Season

Summer is the high season in Central Oregon. Restaurants here are busy during this time, though it's not like the major urban areas, where popular eateries can be booked up weeks in advance. Usually, calling the same day or a day in advance will get you a reservation at the places where you'll need one. Three exceptions would be the Fourth of July weekend, the second weekend in July (which brings the extremely popular Sisters Quilt Show), and New Year's Eve. For those times, we recommend you reserve a week or so in advance.

Most restaurants, at least in Bend, are open every day except Thanksgiving and

Christmas. If you are planning on visiting during the holidays, we suggest you research restaurant availability before you arrive. Either that, or plan on creating a motel room buffet spread with fixings from a supermarket. The Newport Avenue Market in Bend has some fancy prepared salads, smoked meats, imported cheeses, and crusty breads, as well as wines. The restaurants at the Inn of the Seventh Mountain, Black Butte Ranch, Sunriver Resort, and Kah-Nee-Ta Resort are open every day of the year. You do not have to be a resort guest to enjoy these dining spots, but you should reserve well in advance for the holidays.

Oregon is an inherently laid-back place. Even our nicest restaurants welcome guests in clean, very casual clothing. Some of our most-elegant restaurants, with cotton tablecloths, candles, and fresh flowers at each table, dress their servers in shorts and sneakers. However, bathing suits, skimpy tops, bare feet, and jeans with holes in them won't be considered appropriate. So dress comfortably, or dress up for fun.

Many of our smaller, more casual restaurants do not take reservations, but if you have six or more in your party, you should give them a call so they can try to accommodate you. Still, on high-season weekends waiting times seldom exceed 30 minutes; it's usually more like 10 or 20 minutes at most. Restaurants that are most likely to have a waiting line are noted in our descriptions.

You can assume that every restaurant's dining room is accessible to disabled persons. Any that are not will be noted in the individual listings. Rest rooms are not usually wheelchair-accessible, so if this is a concern you should call ahead.

For ice-cream parlors, please see our Kidstuff chapter. If you are looking for a really good morning meal, definitely check out this chapter's Close-up called "Best Breakfasts in Central Oregon."

This chapter is organized using our six geographical sections, and each region's eateries are then divided by food categories that may include American, Ethnic, Pizza, and Coffeehouses and Specialty Eateries. Listings for Bend use two subsections—"Downtown Bend," which focuses on the downtown area for the convenience of pedestrian shoppers and art-gallery hoppers, and "Other Bend Area Restaurants," which visitors will most likely visit by car.

Pricing Key

Our price-code indicators are based on what two people might order for a complete meal, not including dessert, special appetizer, drinks, or gratuity. Since so many restaurants include soup or salad in the entree price, we have included a dinner salad in our definition of a complete meal. If a restaurant menu is entirely a la carte, we added the price of a basic dinner salad to the entree cost.

If a restaurant serves at more than one meal time, the price code refers to the most expensive meal, which is usually dinner. The menus at all of our restaurants that serve breakfast and lunch contain many entrees priced at less than $10.

For some restaurants, we use a price-code range. Such is the case in our brewpubs, which essentially have two distinct levels of food. They offer the expected pub food like burgers, chili, nachos, and sandwiches, usually in the $4.00 to $6.00 neighborhood. However, the chefs at many of our pubs get bored making burgers and like to spread their wings a bit. The Deschutes Brewery ($-$$) has served Moroccan seasoned lamb patties with cumin yogurt sauce, couscous, and pureed carrots for $14 a plate—a much higher price level.

As is standard here in Central Oregon, most establishments accept MasterCard and Visa, a few more take Discover, but many do not take American Express. If no credit cards are mentioned in the write-up, please assume they take the basic two. Here are our pricing parameters.

$	$20 and lower
$$	$21 to $30
$$$	$31 to $45
$$$$	$46 and higher

Bend

Bend's 50,000-plus population supports more than 200 restaurants—more restaurants per capita than any other city in Oregon. (Of course, this statistic does not take into consideration our million or so visitors per year!)

Not only do we have a lot of restaurants, but the more urbane tastes of Bend's restaurant-goers also support a wide variety of ethnic and upscale eateries. Along with the urban influence comes a host of fast-food places that you will find all along Bend's main commercial strip, U.S. Highway 97, and at the east end of town in Bend's newest and rapidly growing commercial area on U.S. Highway 20.

Bend's specialties include Northwest cuisine, pub food and microbrewed beer, and great coffee. The best of these categories are listed below.

Most Bend restaurants are completely nonsmoking. Even the town's three brewpubs and one Irish pub (see our Nightlife chapter) do not allow smoking. A recent trend is to make patio dining areas nonsmoking as well—a nice change for nonsmokers, who can now dine outdoors without having to sit between two smoking tables, but another drag (no pun intended) for smokers. Some larger restaurants have separate smoking sections or allow smoking in the lounge, and these are noted. Sisters, Redmond, Prineville, and Madras go a little easier on the smoking restrictions.

Downtown Bend

American

Alpenglow Cafe $
1040 Northwest Bond Street
(541) 383-7676

This restaurant, which opened in 1994, was taken over in 1997 by a former Alpenglow server, Kimberly Gregg, and her husband, Daniel. He is now the chef, and the couple is carrying on with Alpenglow's high standards. Posted outside the front door next to a menu is an old sign that reads, FRESHNESS PLEDGE: $1,000 REWARD TO ANYONE FINDING A CAN OPENER ON THESE PREMISES. On the menu they continue: "We have a tiny freezer just big enough for our Ben & Jerry's ice cream and nothing else!" And it's this emphasis on homemade freshness that makes Alpenglow absolutely top-notch for breakfast and lunch.

Lean bacon and fresh salmon smoked right on the premises keep faithful customers lined up at the door. Real maple syrup is shipped here from a farm in Vermont. The kids' menu is presented along with a handful of crayons. (Read more about Alpenglow's breakfasts in our "Best Breakfasts in Central Oregon" Close-up.)

The creative lunches are equally superb. The 1040 Bond Street Sandwich (one of the few dishes with a cutesy name) is tops, with chicken and fresh pesto sauce. The chicken enchiladas are also popular, as are the wonderful salads. Don't pass on the daily soup specials.

Alpenglow celebrates 3,500 birthdays a year by sending $5.00 gift certificates to everyone on its Frequent Diner Program list, a program that also earns customers volume discounts. If you give them your e-mail address, they'll send you "love notes" listing their weekly specials.

At the north end of Bend's old downtown, this is a come-as-you-are place, but you might want to come a little early. Service can be a tad slow, especially if you are waiting for a table. We're not sure if it seems slow because the place is always busy, or if it's just our impatience to dig into a sublime culinary experience. You can expect a wait on weekend mornings—drop off a member of your party at the door to write your name on the white board while the driver parks the car. Alpenglow is open for breakfast and lunch every day except Christmas. Parties of five or more should call ahead; otherwise, there are no reservations for up to four people.

Bend Brewing Company $
1019 Northwest Brooks Street
(541) 383-1599

This charming little brewpub is in a park-like setting on the banks of the Deschutes River, which can be seen and heard from the nonsmoking patio. The interior mimics the view, with deep green carpeting and wood wainscoting. An elk head watches over the dining room from the smoke-free bar.

Pub food is good here, including burgers, pizza, and fish 'n' chips. The menu tops out with the hazelnut-breaded chicken breast with Riesling blue cheese sauce, or the New York steak. There are pasta salads and regular salads for vegetarians, and the daily lasagna special, which might have shrimp, sun-dried tomatoes, or roasted veggies, is another good choice. Best of all, you can accompany your meal with an excellent house-brewed ale. The children's menu is available until 8:00 P.M. Lunch and dinner are served daily.

Cafe Rosemary $$$$
222 Northwest Irving Avenue
(541) 317-0276

Folding plastic lawn chairs and concrete floor aside, this is an elegant little gem of a restaurant tucked away on a side street. Students of formal Euro-style interior decor will ogle the glazed yellow walls and white woodwork details, large windows covered with lace, formal tree topiaries, prints of Venus, and huge flower arrangements that occupy a large share of the space in the tiny dining room. This is one of the most romantic dining spots in Bend.

The lunch and dinner menus, listed cryptically on a blackboard, are as sophisticated as the decor and change daily. A server dressed in a starched white chef's jacket will explain in detail how each dish is created. Preparations are never mundane and at first may sound incongruous—such as an artfully arranged Atlantic lobster with a grapefruit butter sauce—but you can trust Cafe Rosemary to provide you with an elevated culinary experience.

Previous entree selections have included a boneless rack of lamb, thinly sliced and served over polenta with a Merlot sauce and a pile of shoestring sweet potatoes; and Fish Elvira en Pappillot, a fresh halibut with lime, crème fraîche, cilantro, and a strawberry salsa served in its wrapping. Dinners include a large and fabulously delicious salad of mixed greens, nectarines, berries, crumbled blue cheese, hazelnuts, and pecans with a very light lemon poppyseed dressing.

And don't miss out on the divine, fresh-baked desserts, such as a killer flourless chocolate cake with a small scoop of homemade ice cream that is richly vanilla and a snowy dusting of powdered sugar. Also offered are raspberry crème brûlée, and a tall, delicate poppyseed layer cake with whipped cream and fresh peaches and raspberries.

Appetizers are rarely offered, but you don't really need more food. For holidays and other special events, Cafe Rosemary does a prix fixe evening with six or more courses that starts around $40 per person and goes up to about $80 if wines are included.

Reservations are suggested but can usually be made the day of or before your visit. The entire restaurant—all 11 tables—is nonsmoking, as is the patio dining area, which has a handful of tables. If you want a lighter dinner of salad and dessert, show up around 8:45 P.M., just before closing time—the folks here are reluctant to allow one of their precious tables to be filled with light-eaters during prime dinner time.

Lunch, of perhaps a salad, pizette (a small pizza) or an interesting sandwich creation, is equally sophisticated but on the light side. Cafe Rosemary has an excellent selection of lesser-known Oregon and Washington wines, and the Washington house Chardonnay by the glass is excellent. As you may have gathered, this haven for high-end palates may not be the best choice for families.

Deschutes Brewery & Public House $–$$
1044 Northwest Bond Street
(541) 382-9242

The quality of the dining experience and the fact that this pleasant eatery feels much more like a restaurant than a bar earns this brewpub a listing in both our Nightlife and Restaurant chapters. If you look around the dining rooms, you will see about half the tables occupied by 20- and 30-somethings, and the other half taken by still-cool 40-plus-somethings and families. The big wood captain's chairs and tables, dark walls with pub artwork, gas fireplace, and high ceiling with hanging plants give the two dining areas a warm, friendly feel. Music underlies the din of animated conversation, and the hum of a television in the bar is barely discernible.

A tall pint of Black Butte Porter or Mirror Pond Ale is often followed up by an excellent brewery burger cooked the way you like it. A side of fries is cooked fresh and comes in a large basket. Don't miss the blackboard specials near the front door and on the back wall. The custom-made sausages change almost every night and make a delicious sandwich on a house-baked roll. Top 'em off with some sweet brewery mustard. The homemade-tasting soup specials change every night and are consistently good.

Also on the blackboard are big-time entrees—creative meat, fish, or veggie dinners that rarely repeat and are terrific. If you are in the mood for a sandwich, the "Brewery Cured" Pastrami Reuben and the Smoked Salmon Salad Sandwich are good picks. Burgers and sandwiches come with seasoned house potato chips, but you may substitute raw veggies with a side of salad dressing for dipping. A veggie burger can be ordered in place of a regular burger, and vegetarian black-bean chili and salads are also available for non-meat eaters. The awesome fruit cobblers take about 20 minutes to make. (Check out the recipe for the very popular marionberry version in our Shopping chapter Close-up, "Unique to Oregon.")

Service is prompt and professional. Many of the servers have been with the brewery for years. The bar and dining rooms are completely nonsmoking. This family-friendly pub welcomes kids anywhere except the bar itself, and children get their own menu along with a mug of crayons and a coloring placemat. The Deschutes Brewery is open every day for lunch and dinner. Beer, burgers, and fries are discounted on Monday nights. Year-round on Friday, Saturday, and Monday nights, you can expect a wait for a table, even if you come as late as 10:00 P.M. (no reservations). The pub usually serves food until 10:30 P.M. or later, so you won't miss dinner. The back of this restaurant has been renovated with large, wheelchair-accessible rest rooms.

Hans $$
915 Northwest Wall Street
(541) 389-9700

We were glad to see that this delightful little restaurant has doubled the size of its dining room with no ill effects. In the original room the walls are hand-painted parchment, and along the top is a pale garland of painted flowers. The polished wood floors were extended into the space next door, and the parchment-like wall treatment was also carried over, with an added touch—a delicate design of flowers pressed into the plaster walls. The tables have cotton cloths and sprigs of flowers.

The dishes are as exquisite as the decor, but the prices are surprisingly moderate. For lunch you may choose from two homemade soups or six salads with or without various meats, and delicious, design-your-own sandwiches with a choice of meats, cheeses, and condiments. The daily specials are often the best choice and include quiche, lasagna, burritos, grilled sandwiches, or hot pasta. At lunch, orders are placed at the counter. For dinner, more formal full table service is offered.

In the evening, your table may share a grilled pizza appetizer of wild mushrooms and pancetta with marinara sauce, chèvre, provolone, and mozzarella cheeses; or garlic chicken and chèvre cheese pizza with olive oil, fresh herbs, mozzarella cheese, roasted tomatoes, green onions, and artichoke hearts. A pizza will fill up one person for a light dinner.

The pastas are excellent. Try the penne and Portobello mushroom, with sun-dried tomatoes and roasted vegetables in a lemon herb butter sauce topped with Asiago cheese. The linguine and sautéed prawns, with roma tomatoes, red onions, garlic, basil, and olive oil, all topped with Asiago cheese, is another great option. Meat entrees include a sautéed chicken breast in a roasted garlic and herb demiglaze with potatoes au gratin, and sautéed Atlantic salmon fillet served with marionberry honey-butter sauce and basmati rice. The nightly specials are always tempting, and a nice selection of domestic and imported wines is available.

Don't forget to leave room for dessert, as chef Hans was originally a pastry chef and this is his forte. The pastry case is always filled with a dazzling display of cakes, tortes, pies, and tarts, and we've never been disappointed. Children can be accommodated, but this restaurant is not particularly family-oriented. The service is quite good, and the nonsmoking outdoor patio area is pleasant in summer. Unfortunately for weekend visitors, Hans is closed on Sunday, but it is open for lunch and dinner Monday through Saturday.

High Tides $$
1045 Northwest Bond Street
(541) 389–5244

Seashells and cowboy boots painted on the walls impart a feeling of fun and a celebration of this little eatery's specialty—fish and seafood. We think you'll celebrate discovering High Tides and its menu. First off, our soup recommendation is a happy toss-up between the creamy oyster spinach bisque and the Thai halibut soup, with bits of fresh halibut floating in a broth lightly touched by coconut milk, Thai seasonings, and a hint of spiciness.

Lunch and dinner entrees continue with a light mix of Asian, Italian, Mexican, and Northwest styles. For lunch, the Bangkok noodle bowl with stir-fried rock shrimp, scallops, peanuts, and veggies in a yellow curry sauce is a favorite. A selection of what they call Specialty Breads (which are actually hot open-face sandwiches on baguettes) includes the Seahawk Bread, with smoked salmon, shrimp, onion, and melted Havarti cheese. For dinner, the sturgeon fillet is charbroiled and served with a smoked tomato–rock shrimp sauce over basmati rice. Surf clam steaks (or crab cakes), each griddled in panko (light batter), are popular, along with the cioppino. Try their specialty, Key lime pie, for dessert.

The servers are as friendly as the decor, ensuring that your experience at High Tides will be an enjoyable one. They accommodated our every wish, including a request for a change in the menu. Owners John and MaryLynne Hamlin also own Tidal Raves in Depoe Bay, Oregon. High Tides is open Monday through Friday for lunch and dinner, plus Saturday night for dinner.

Pine Tavern Restaurant $$$
967 Northwest Brooks Street
(541) 382–5581

Established in 1936, this is Bend's oldest restaurant and a local institution. It was built overlooking the Deschutes River, which can be viewed from the lovely patio surrounded by flowers and lawns; it's open weather permitting. The main dining room was built around a large tree that pierces the ceiling and lives on to this day.

The Pine Tavern offers traditional and Northwest fine dining. It's an excellent spot for a business lunch or a celebratory dinner, and it's a popular tourist destination as well. The chef here likes to feature locally raised Oregon Country Beef and local lamb when available. The prime rib and filet mignon are excellent. The Alder Smoked King Salmon Linguine with Sauvignon Blanc cream sauce is a nice departure from the traditional.

Lighter fare includes a grilled prawn and spring salad, a chicken caesar salad, or a hazelnut-crusted chicken breast. Kids can choose from a hot dog, grilled cheese, or chicken strips. The award-winning desserts include homemade fruit cobbler or mud pie.

Lunch is served Monday through Saturday and includes a wide assortment of dishes such as a standard Reuben, chicken enchilada, Pine Tavern burgers, and fresh salmon quiche. The lounge features a full bar, and an extensive wine list with California, Washington, and Oregon wines is available.

The lounge and patio are nonsmoking areas, as is the dining room. Dinner is served daily, and reservations are recommended. Pine Tavern takes American Express in addition to Visa and MasterCard.

Ethnic

Baja Norte $
801 Northwest Wall Street
(541) 385–0611

A trendy little chain restaurant, this eatery fills the need for fast and healthy Mexican. The salsa bar offers four varieties of fresh salsas and condiments like pickled onions. The tostadas are excellent, with a huge pile of sautéed, fajita-like meat, veggies, guacamole, and sour cream on top of a crisp corn tortilla; you can even use mahimahi as the meat!

Everything is a la carte at Baja Norte, including chips. Real margaritas and beer (served in plastic glasses) are available. The decor is wildly colorful, especially in the rest rooms, and there is cute seating like you might see in a fast-food place. Order and pay at the counter, help yourself to salsa, and take a seat. The tables outside offer good people-watching. Baja Norte is open daily from lunch through dinner. There is another location in Sunriver (541–593–9374).

Cafe Mosaica $, no credit cards
852 Northwest Brooks Street
(541) 388–2467

This little place, formerly called Reflections of Bend, faces the pedestrian-only section of Brooks Street, so you won't notice it from your car. However, two parking lots are close by, and there is a walk-through corridor from Wall Street.

Leaning towards healthy vegetarian-oriented dishes, Cafe Mosaica (referring to the mosaics adorning its walls) offers Indian cuisine, sandwiches, and soups. They're open Monday through Friday from 8:00 A.M. to 2:30 P.M. and Saturday from noon to 3:00 P.M. They are also open on Thursday and Friday evenings from

6:00 P.M. until "closing," which is usually around 8:00 or 8:30 P.M.

Super Burrito $, no credit cards
118 Northwest Minnesota Avenue
(541) 317–1384

This obscure little hole-in-the-wall has a large following. There are between 10 and 20 varieties of burritos, wet or dry, each one huge. The Super Quesadillas with chicken or beef, green chiles, guacamole, and oozing cheese, wrapped up with a dinner plate–size flour tortilla, are also terrific. The Carne Asada Soft Tacos are also favorites, but it takes about three to make a dinner, and that can get pricey.

The menu is a la carte except for the usual special of enchiladas, rice, and beans. Ambiance is nonexistent. The seven indoor tables are designated for nonsmokers, but smokers may sit outside, weather permitting. Soft drinks are selected from a cooler (ice may or may not be available), and if you bring your own beer (they don't serve it) you should also bring a bottle opener because they can't always find theirs. As long as you are wearing some kind of clothing, you're welcome. We love this place. Super Burrito is open Monday through Saturday for lunch through dinner; it closes at about 8:00 P.M. There is also a Super Burrito II in Redmond at 122 Southwest Fifth Street; (541) 504–8512.

Toomie's Thai Cuisine $
119 Northwest Minnesota Avenue
(541) 388–5590

The food here is excellent and authentic. Savory dishes are wonderfully and delicately seasoned, and the spicy dishes are very hot. (All attempts to get the chef to tone down the spicy dishes have failed, so if you have a tender tongue we suggest you stick with the non-spicy menu items.)

All dishes are wonderfully prepared, so we're hard-pressed to recommend any one or two items. You will not be disappointed. The dining room is lovely, with white tablecloths and attractive bentwood chairs. On some evenings Toomie's has live acoustic music, but this varies throughout the year. Lunches are great, especially the lunch special—they take one meat item from the menu and make a plate of it with a small salad and bowl of rice. The Thai iced tea with cream is a favorite beverage. Wine and American and Thai beers are also served. Toomie's is open for lunch Monday through Friday and dinner seven nights a week. Reservations are accepted only for parties of five or more, and the Discover card is accepted, along with MasterCard and Visa.

Pizza

Pizza Mondo $
811 Northwest Wall Street
(541) 330-9093

Huge eggplants, tomatoes, and garlic cloves are painted on the walls above the eight tables at this downtown pizza place. Ingredients are real and fresh, and pizzas are made with a thin crust. Even when you order only a slice, the crust is still crispy on the bottom. Pizza by the slice usually includes the Big Cheese with 100 percent mozzarella cheese, fresh tomato sauce, herbs, and spices. Little Italy is another type usually available by the slice—it's loaded with pepperoni. A third, more exotic sliced pizza changes daily.

On the menu for whole pizzas are interesting concoctions such as Run Little Piggy with lots of prosciutto, pepperoni, Italian sausage, mushrooms, and black olives; and Jean-Claude Chevre with roasted peppers, roasted eggplant, roasted onions, kalamata olives, light cream tomato sauce, and mozzarella and chèvre cheeses. Salads and calzones are also available, plus draft and bottled beers and a house wine by the glass. Pizza Mondo is open daily from lunch through early evening.

Coffeehouses and Specialty Eateries

The Bend and Central Oregon area have excellent coffeehouses. The ones in Bend with seating are listed below.

Comfort Zone Coffee, Tea and Crepes $
824 Northwest Wall Street
(541) 317-5717

People line up at this unusual little eatery for the freshly made crepes. You can choose your fillings, from savory feta and spinach to sweet berries. The espresso and teas are also very good, but the seating is scarce. You might want to check out the seating situation (or plan on hiking to the park) before you get in line. Comfort Zone is open from breakfast through the afternoon, Monday through Saturday.

Starbucks Coffee $
812 Northwest Wall Street
(541) 382-9438
61535 South U.S. Highway 97
(541) 330-1998

Bend has been successfully invaded by this Seattle-based chain, with its urbane interiors and good espresso drinks and pastries. The shop takes American Express in addition to MasterCard and Visa. Drop by from early morning into the evening seven days a week.

Other Bend Area Restaurants

American

Broken Top Club $$$$
62000 Broken Top Drive
(541) 383-8210

If you are accustomed to the best, or if it's your night for a fancy dinner, you've discovered the right place. Broken Top Club is a private resort and golf course, but the restaurant is open to the public. The large homes are spectacular, and the landscaping is impeccable. After going though security at the main entrance guard house, a smooth paved drive winds to a clubhouse set amid fluttering aspens and tall pines.

The beautiful, award-winning building designed by Seattle architects Wimberly, Allison, Tong & Goo is entered from a large portico through massive, carved-wood doors. Inside, the space is cavernous, with a huge stone fireplace and custom metal work. In the dining room, an elegant touch shows through the lodge-style use of wood and stone.

The menu will tempt you with sophisticated appetizers such as warm quail salad, field greens tossed with raspberry vinaigrette, and the popular house-smoked fish platter—a seasonal assortment of fresh, smoked fish that might include salmon, sturgeon, halibut, trout, or prawns. The well-balanced selection of fish, meat, and meatless dinner entrees prepared in the Northwest style will satisfy the most discriminating tastes. The full rack of lamb with a mint pesto crust and huckleberry sauce or the sumptuously large scallops in roasted tomato broth over angel-hair pasta with Provençal vegetables, are two favorites.

If the evening entrees are out of your price range, treat yourself to an equally delectable lunch. Two of our midday favorites are the salmon club sandwich—herbed salmon with bacon, lettuce, and tomato on house-baked wheat bread—and the delicious chicken or beef torta: grilled meat on a house-baked Mexican-style roll with guacamole, refried beans, Monterey Jack cheese, and salsa. A casual Fireside Menu, which includes pizza, is available starting in the late afternoon; seating is in front of the fireplace, where there is a full bar. Smoking is allowed at the tables outside on the deck.

The professional staff is friendly and competent without being stuffy, and dress ranges from casual to dressy. Broken Top is open for lunch and dinner Tuesday through Saturday, and they accept American Express in addition to Visa and MasterCard. Banquet rooms are available. Children are graciously accommodated with special dishes, but this wouldn't really be considered a family place.

Honkers Restaurant $$$
805 Southwest Industrial Way
(541) 389-4665

Here's a fun place if there ever was one. Located in Bend's historic Mill A District (off Colorado Avenue by the Deschutes River), Honkers occupies a beautifully renovated mill building. The ceiling and windows are two stories tall. Pine paneling and split-log steps are reminiscent of the lumber that was milled here.

The painted footprints of a pigeon-toed goose lead along the sidewalk and up the front steps—that should clue you in that something unusual is waiting inside. We must first say that the food here is terrific. The menu itself, however, reaches new heights in lightheartedness with its irreverent names and descriptions. Check out the lunch menu item called Get Offa My Quesadilla, with roasted chicken, pepper jack cheese, black-bean pesto, mango, and tomatilla salsa; or the Log Jam Salmon—a slab of grilled salmon with Dijon mayo on a jalapeño hoagie roll. The Crab & Shrimp Flapjacks sound interesting, served with sweet corn relish and lemon-pepper mayo.

Dinners include White Lightnin' Salmon grilled with whiskey-maple glaze, horseradish marmalade, and onion-chive potatoes. The Just A Big Ol' Filet—a 10-ounce filet wrapped in apple-smoked bacon and served with whole roasted garlic, red wine gravy, and onion-chive potatoes—ought to fill you up. For the working types there's the "Bandsaw" Rib Eye, which is garnished with gooey potatoes. If you're into battered beef, the Nacho Mama's Chicken Fried Steak—"beat up and breaded New York, smothered in our famous Red Eye gravy with chipotle mashed potatoes"—is better than any other chicken-fried steak around. We could go on and on all night about Honkers' crazy but delicious dishes.

Save room for a dessert. Try a Honker Sundae or Mr. Mann's Rum Cake with toasted pecans and a homemade rum-caramel sauce. Honkers is open for lunch Monday through Friday (plus Saturday in summer) and daily for dinner. The Kids Korner menu has junior-size dishes. A full bar and wine list are available, plus a more casual pub menu. Honkers accepts Discover, along with Visa and MasterCard.

Insiders' Tip

It doesn't take too many visits to the same restaurant in Central Oregon to become a regular. The perks range from getting better seating to tidbits of local gossip.

(See our Nightlife chapter for more on Honkers.)

J.J. North's Grand Buffet $
2050 Northeast Third Street
(541) 382–3688

If large quantities of food at reasonable prices are what you are looking for, this is for you. J.J.'s is set back from the highway just north of the Rite Aid. The food is hearty, resembling a collection of American Sunday dinners—beef, ham, whipped potatoes and gravy, vegetables—and the prices (which include nonalcoholic beverages and desserts) are right. The non-smoking dining room is family-friendly with large tables and stacking chairs. J.J.'s is open seven days a week for lunch and dinner, and you can use your Discover card along with MasterCard or Visa. They also serve a breakfast buffet on Saturday and Sunday.

Kayo's Dinner House $$$
61363 South U.S. Highway 97
(541) 389–1400

Don't be taken aback by the '60s dinner-house decor (dark wood paneling and lava rock walls) or the scents from the adjoining cocktail lounge that might greet you at the front door. After you choose to sit in a smoking or nonsmoking section and pass the host's desk, you are in for an exceptionally nice evening at Kayo's, starting with the excellent service.

It's a real surprise these days to find servers as competent, gracious, and eager to please as the Kayo's staff. If something on the menu sounds almost but not quite perfect, just state your wish and a change will gladly be made. Dirty a knife on the salad, and a clean one shows up before the entree does. And if a new server lends a hand during your meal, he or she has been briefed on your needs.

While you ponder the extensive menu, a slightly spicy smoked salmon pate, with a small baguette is brought to your table. The delicious New England clam chowder is a must, and you can upgrade your soup/salad to clam chowder for $1.00. The wine list is extensive and moderately priced—a surprising discovery is that Kayo features two wines (one red, one white) for only $10 a bottle, and both are quite enjoyable. If you didn't tell your friends, they'd probably never know they were drinking bargain wines.

We suggest taking the money saved on the wine and going wild on the entrees! Most guests pass over the perfectly lovely selection of chicken, pork, and beef entrees, and focus on the menu's center page (or should we say center stage), where you'll find the photocopied "Fresh Today" sheet. The 30 or so seafood and fresh fish dishes listed clue you in to Kayo's forte.

The ahi tuna is a favorite, broiled rare with a papaya/mango salsa or dusted with (optional) Cajun marinade, then served with wasabi and a soy sauce dip. The tuna absolutely melts in your mouth. Salmon is expertly prepared and served with a hollandaise sauce, and it may be stuffed with Brie and Dungeness crab if you like. If fish doesn't suit your palate, the Fresh Today list contains dishes such as Steak David—filet medallions with crab, asparagus, and béarnaise; or local emu (an ostrichlike bird) broiled with a Mandarin orange brandy sauce.

The standard menu dishes offer sophisticated choices for more moderate prices. Chicken Calvados, with apples, brandy, and crème fraîche; choice prime rib; and New York strip are big contenders. The quail stuffed with prosciutto, spinach, and Gruyère and topped with raspberry sauce is fabulous. Three special dishes are prepared for the 12-and-younger crowd—hamburgers, fish 'n' chips, and fried chicken.

Dessert is worth saving room for. Our favorite is the Chocolate Decadence, with a raspberry puree and a dob of vanilla ice cream. Also fantastic is the Oregon Three-Berry Cobbler, in season. Open daily, Kayo's takes all credit cards. During the busy summer months, you might want to call a day ahead for a reservation. Kayo's has an affiliated restaurant in Redmond called Kayo's Roadhouse.

McGrath's Fish House $$
3118 North U.S. Highway 97
(541) 388–4555

Part of a small Oregon chain, McGrath's is very popular for both business folks and families. Prices are affordable, the booth tables are fairly private, and the wide selection of food is reliably good.

McGrath's is one of the best places in town for a business lunch. It offers a really nice selection of dishes, including a sumptuous seafood salad panini with crab, baby shrimp, poached salmon and halibut, plus tomato and melted cheddar cheese on focaccia. Other panini sandwiches include almond chicken, smoked salmon, and Louisiana chicken. The list of sandwiches goes on, with Hot Seafood Newport (choose shrimp, crab, or both with hollandaise sauce, tomato, and bacon on an English muffin), or you can switch gears to a Baja chicken or teriyaki chicken sandwich. Sandwiches come with New England clam chowder (recommended!) or Fishermen's Stew. The soup and salad plate with sourdough is popular with light eaters. Burgers are mesquite-broiled and excellent. Service is fairly quick and courteous.

At night the restaurant fills with families and tourists. The dinner menu is done in a popular style with a vast selection of dishes. Oysters, shrimp or crab cocktail, calamari rings, and New England clam chowder or Fishermen's Stew are standard starters. Big dinner salads can be topped with seafood, mesquite-broiled chicken, or blackened salmon. The mesquite-broiled seafood entrees are popular, and you can choose from Pacific red snapper or a broiled platter of halibut, salmon, and prawns. Just about every type of seafood that is popular in America and can be deep-fried is available. Dinners come with fresh-baked sourdough bread and a choice of two side dishes.

McGrath's aims to make everyone happy, so if fish is not your thing try the Chicken Dijonaise, featuring two sautéed chicken breasts with mushrooms, artichokes, red peppers, white wine, Dijon mustard, and garlic cream sauce. The mesquite-broiled 10-ounce New York steak is a good choice as well. There are also pasta dishes and a kids' menu.

Sunday Brunch is a big deal here, with a variety of traditional breakfasts including omelets, French toast, or Belgian waffles. Everything comes with the juice and pastry buffet, and you may order champagne. (For more information, see our Close-up, "Best Breakfasts in Central Oregon.")

McGrath's is open all day, every day, for lunch and dinner. Smoking is allowed in the lounge and on the patio. The restaurant uses a procedure called phone-ahead seating, where you can call as you are leaving for the restaurant (up to two hours ahead of time) to put your name on a waiting list. Otherwise, at peak times the wait can be 15 to 30 minutes. The restaurant also sells fresh fish. American Express, Diner's Club, and Discover are accepted in addition to MasterCard and Visa.

Original Pancake House $
1025 Donovan Street Southwest
(541) 317-0380

This large, family-style restaurant specializes in fabulous breakfasts served from 6:00 A.M. to 2:00 P.M. daily. The whole story is told in our Close-up, "Best Breakfasts in Central Oregon." In fact, breakfast is the only meal they do.

Original Pantry $
62910 O. B. Riley Road
(541) 383-2697

Housed in one of Bend's oldest homes, a charmingly restored Craftsman-style bungalow that was constructed in 1916, the Original Pantry is one of our more elegant breakfast and lunch (or should we say "luncheon") experiences. Small wooden tables and Victorian-style chairs are tastefully arranged in what must have been parlors and a dining room in this old house. Walls are pale lilac, accented with white curtains.

With about 15 years of restaurant experience and a brief time off to rest up, owners Steve and Vicki Hanson opened this pleasant eatery in 1998. Breakfast and lunch are very competently done (see our Close-up, "Best Breakfasts in Central Oregon"). The lunch menu offers quite a variety of choices. Homemade soups, meal-size salads, various incarnations of the hamburger, and a nice selection of American sandwiches are the basics. For a more substantial meal, Original Pantry offers teriyaki chicken breast with a salad, fish 'n' chips, and barbecued chicken breast. This smoke-free restaurant is open from Wednesday through Sunday for breakfast and lunch.

Scanlon's $$$
61615 Mt. Bachelor Drive
(541) 382-8769

Situated in the upscale Athletic Club of Bend just off Century Drive, Scanlon's is an interesting hybrid of a tony club with a friendly, casual ambiance. Comfortable booths and white-clothed tables are surrounded by rich wood paneling and an expansive bank of windows overlooking the lawns and pool. Scanlon's is the only restaurant in Central Oregon to offer cherrywood-fired, oven-roasted, and grilled meat dishes.

Dinners begin with a choice of homemade soup or salad, a delightful affair of fresh greens sprinkled with dried cranberries and walnuts. Try a wood-fired pizza for an appetizer or light dinner, which may be a Margherita pizza with Fontina cheese and roasted garlic, or perhaps one with barbecued chicken. Baked Brie, calamari fritti, and clam cakes are three other popular starters.

Signature main courses include wood-oven-roasted rack of lamb with bourbon tart cherry demiglaze and shoestring potatoes, or the pappardelle pasta—ribbons of pasta with chicken, baby prawns, and tomatoes in a spicy orange cream sauce. The salmon piccata is another favorite, with fresh spinach and artichoke hearts, angel-hair pasta, a lemon glaze, garlic, and caper butter. The dinner menu is seasonal with two or three changes per year. Lunches are also excellent, with a menu that changes every three weeks. A typical lunch dish might be a roasted eggplant, red pepper, and kalamata olive sandwich served on the fabulous house focaccia bread.

If you are interested in taking your children along on a deluxe, adult-style luncheon or dinner, this would be our best recommendation. Kids' menus are offered for lunch and dinner, and Scanlon's also offers free child care at the adjacent athletic club facilities. A small lounge and banquet rooms are available, and the entire facility is nonsmoking. Scanlon's serves lunch Tuesday through Friday and dinner Tuesday through Sunday.

Tumalo Feed Company $$$
64619 West U.S. Highway 20
(541) 382-2202

This is the place for a good steak with an attitude! The attitude part starts in the lobby of this old yellow, Western-style building 3.5 miles west of Bend. You'll be greeted with a big "Howdy!" The lobby has saddles, deer heads, and an old stove; the walls and front doors have collected business cards by the thousands.

Inside you'll find pleasant Victorian Western decor with wood tables and comfortable chairs or booths. Patrons are a mixture of tourists and possibly some locals who are all duded up in their best Wranglers for a birthday or anniversary celebration.

If you are daring, you might start your meal with an order of Mountain Oysters, "truly the tenderest cut of all." Fowl, in the form of baked chicken or quail, and grilled fish are on the menu, but that's not what brings in the crowds. Folks come here for the beef.

The rib steak is a favorite—a 15-ounce portion cooked to perfection. For a little extra change you can get the 20-ounce portion, which includes sautéed mushroom caps and onions, and take home a doggie bag big enough for another dinner. If you are seriously celebrating, there's the steak and lobster dinner—an 8-ounce piece of top sirloin with an 8-ounce Australian lobster tail—which is as ritzy as this place gets.

Before, during, and after the main entree comes a parade of side dishes, starting with fried onion rings with salsa, an iceberg lettuce salad with your choice of dressings, and garlic bread. Ranch-house beans and a hot iron skillet of pan-fried potatoes show up with dinner. After it's all cleared away you can choose from a sarsaparilla (root beer) float, sherbet, or an after-dinner liquor, which is included in your entree price. We can guarantee you won't walk away hungry!

Service, provided by cowgirls and cowboys, is very friendly and competent. A modest selection of wine and beer is available, and there is a full bar. We suggest a carafe of the house red. Smoking is allowed in the old-time saloon, where they will serve full dinners on request. On Saturday and Sunday, an excellent prime rib is offered, and we like to visit on Sunday when it's less crowded. A kids' menu of ribs, chicken strips, steak, or hamburger is free for children younger than age five.

The parking lot starts to fill up around 5:00 P.M. on Friday and Saturday nights. We recommend calling earlier in the day for reservations on weekends if late afternoon dining is not your style. This old dinner house was built before anyone gave any thought to wheelchair access, but they can usually round up a strong arm or two to get a wheelchair into the dining room. The rest rooms are too small for wheelchairs. The Tumalo Feed Company serves dinner seven nights a week. (For more information, see our Nightlife chapter.)

Ethnic

Chan's $
1005 Southeast Third Street
(541) 389–1725

Locals and visitors alike fill Chan's large, contemporary dining room, lured in by the huge portions and tasty dishes. The menu is enormous, with familiar names like mu shu, sweet and sour, sizzling and kung po dishes. Although the names are traditional, the dishes have been slightly altered to suit American tastes, with American vegetables or slightly different sauces. The results are still good, and you're likely to take a doggie box home with you. Spicy dishes are spicy, but Chan's will tone them down if you like, and they don't use MSG. Beer and wine are available to wash it all down. There are smoking and nonsmoking sections in the dining room, and Chan's is open daily for lunch and dinner. Visa, MasterCard, and Discover are accepted.

Kyoto Japanese Cuisine $$
235 Southwest Century Drive
(541) 318–5270

Sushi, teriyaki, and tempura are done equally well here. There is a sushi bar for a close-up view of the chef, but ordering is done through a server, the same as if you were at a table. Our favorite time to come is on Monday nights when sushi is half price—show up at 5:30 P.M. Open daily, Kyoto takes American Express, along with Visa and MasterCard.

Mexicali Rose $$
301 Northeast Franklin Avenue at Third Street
(541) 389–0149

This is a Bend institution, but if you were to walk into the dining room today, the decor is so pleasant and contemporary you would think this was a fairly new place. Booths made with cherry-colored fir wood line the deep green, mustard, or brick-colored walls, and fir partitions are accented with glass blocks. Attractive tables with delicate wooden chairs are in the middle of the space.

Margaritas come in a dozen different varieties, with different tequilas and fruits. If you are in the mood for something light for dinner, try the Carnitas Tostada—a platter-size dish piled high with lettuce topped with guacamole, with big chunks of sweet-cooked pork and beans hidden underneath it all. It's served in a flour tortilla shell, but you can substitute a crisp corn tortilla if you prefer. The enchiladas with rancheras or verde sauce are both old favorites. The verde version is somewhat spicy. Giant burritos are another standby. The service is efficient and accommodating. The dining room is all nonsmoking, but guests can light up in the lounge. Reservations are accepted for parties of eight or more. Mexicali Rose is a dinner-only place. It is open daily, and American Express is accepted as well as Visa and MasterCard.

Ranchero Mexican Restaurant $
150 Northeast Bend River Mall
(541) 330–0685

This restaurant serves popular Mexican dishes for lunch and dinner. The menu is quite extensive, including a large mariscos (fish and seafood) menu, chicken mole, kid-size dishes, and deep-fried ice cream for dessert. Service is friendly and prompt. Beer, wine, and cocktails are available, and the whole place is nonsmoking. Ranchero is open daily, until not quite 11:00 P.M. on

Friday and Saturday nights, and American Express and Discover are accepted in addition to Visa and MasterCard. There's another Ranchero location in Prineville.

Yoko's Japanese Restaurant and Sushi Bar
$$–$$$
1028 Northwest Bond Street
(541) 382-2999

This is a popular lunch and dinner spot for locals and tourists alike. Its downtown location, pleasant decor, and popular teriyaki, tempura, noodle, and sushi dishes all seem to come together to make this a successful eatery. The chicken teriyaki and shrimp tempura combination is a favorite, as is the sushi, sashimi, and shrimp tempura combo. The cooked entrees keep you in the lower price range, but filling up on sushi will put your dinner in the higher price-code bracket. Beer, wine, and sake are available. If you order take-out food, Yoko's adds a 15 percent gratuity on to the bill. The eatery is completely nonsmoking. They take reservations during the week only (although there isn't usually a wait) and are open Tuesday through Saturday for lunch and dinner.

Pizza

John Dough's Pizza $
34 Southwest Century Drive
(541) 382-3645

John Dough's looks a lot like a college dorm room, with dog-eared posters plastered on every vertical (or almost vertical) surface. The pizzas are good, with a hand-tossed crust and homemade sauce. The usual assortment of pepperoni and other meats are offered. A couple of the more unusual pies include the Artitack, with pesto, cheese, fresh-baked tomatoes, black olives, lots of artichoke hearts, olive oil, and garlic; and the Galloping Garlic Gourmet Lite, using part–skim mozzarella, sun-dried tomatoes, freshly roasted garlic, basil, spinach, and Parmesan.

You can build your own pizza, and salads and calzones are also on the menu. A good selection of bottled beers is available, and you can play video games or table soccer while you wait. If your party is feeling

particularly athletic, you can duck out the back door for a game of volleyball, complete with a sand-filled court.

J.D.'s is open daily for lunch and dinner, late into the evening. They'll deliver for an extra dollar.

Coffeehouses and Specialty Eateries

A Cup of Magic $, no credit cards
1304 Northwest Galveston Street
(541) 330-5539

As soon as you set foot into this Craftsman-style bungalow, you start to wonder if you're in Kansas anymore. Rich colors have been daubed onto the walls—blue on one wall, yellow on another. The ceiling is strewn with stars. Poetic excerpts in large pale writing appear on the walls in unexpected places. A clutter of small tables clings together like flotsam and jetsam; the chairs are all different colors, the table tops light-colored wood, like the floor. The rest rooms (voted No. 1 in a survey by a local publication) are sublimely decorated to the nines. The feeling of dreamy relaxation pervades the veranda, where oversized, custom-made Adirondack chairs have arms large enough to hold a pot of tea and a plate of something delectable. Alice, if she ever gets back from Wonderland, would feel right at home in one of these chairs.

The magical day starts at 7:00 A.M. with an excellent espresso or pot of tea, together with some excellent home-baked pastries. A low-cal choice of bagels, the best in town, is surprisingly rewarding. Lunches consist of divine soups (if they have their corn chowder, get it), heavenly salads graced with cinnamon-sugared bits of nuts, and delicious home-baked focaccia bread filled with roasted veggies. Your order will be taken at the counter and appear magically at your table. The fun continues at A Cup of Magic until late

Insiders' Tip
There is no tax on restaurant food, eaten in or taken out.

Best Breakfasts in Central Oregon

Lucky are the folks who wake up hungry, because in Central Oregon we have some incredible breakfast spots. No matter where you are, from Madras to Sunriver, we have a breakfast for you.

Perhaps we have so many good breakfast places because on weekends, outdoorsy folks like to chow down on a hearty meal before they head out for the day's activities. A big breakfast can carry them all the way through until late afternoon. This fits in with the fact that people tend to eat dinner a bit earlier here than in the big city. You'll see restaurants with full parking lots by 6:00 P.M.—maybe their patrons' eggs Benedict breakfasts have finally burned off! Oh sure, lunch has its place too—but that's often on weekdays at noon, and many folks like nothing better than breakfast for lunch! Fortunately for them, most of the places we feature serve breakfast all day.

We have four signature breakfast foods here in Central Oregon. The first—biscuits and gravy—is for the very hardiest of eaters. It's a carry-over from pioneer times, when flour and dried sausage were common pantry (or covered wagon) stores. Soda biscuits smothered with thick gravy containing bits of sausage make either a full breakfast or a side dish.

Another morning staple represents our more delicate side. They are our berries—raspberries, blueberries, huckleberries, and the illustrious Oregon cultivar, the marion blackberry or marionberry. If you visit in summer, be sure to order a featured special made with some type of berries—stuffed French toast, pancakes topped with berries, marionberry bars . . . the list goes on.

Smoked Northwest salmon is our third local breakfast delicacy. Unlike East Coast lox, our salmon is smoky and flaky. And lastly, we mustn't forget coffee—locally roasted on the dark and rich side. We love our coffee, plain or fancy (and fancy we have in abundance these days). Espresso shops featuring Northwest roasts have sprung up absolutely everywhere, even at gas stations.

Although many restaurants serve breakfast, not every place has a line out the door on weekend mornings. What follows is a rundown of the food folks are willing to wait in line for. (Prineville and Madras eateries won't always have a line out the door, but we've listed the best breakfasts in those neighborhoods as well.) A couple can eat at any of these restaurants for less than $20 in entree costs. We'll start with Bend, then work our way through our list of regions. Please note that every eatery covered also has a listing in the appropriate section of the main Restaurants chapter.

Bend

Alpenglow Cafe, at the north end of downtown Bend, 1040 Northwest Bond Street, (541) 383–7676, is definitely one of those places where you'll want to get your name on the waiting list as soon as you arrive. This is one of our most popular spots on Saturday and Sunday mornings. Alpenglow breakfasts are awesome, due in large part to some pretty incredible ingredients. They smoke their own Deschutes County bacon and fresh Northwest king salmon. All baked goods are made on the premises. Juice is fresh-squeezed; whipped cream is freshly whipped. You get the picture. The only processed food here is the maple syrup, which they ship in from Vermont at a rate of about 10 gallons per month.

Breakfast favorites at Alpenglow include the smoked salmon eggs Benedict with the aforementioned salmon, poached eggs, fresh basil, and tomato on a homemade

Raspberry-stuffed french toast at Alpenglow Cafe is a summer favorite. PHOTO: LESLIE COLE

English muffin with fresh hollandaise sauce. During summer, the French toast stuffed with whole fresh raspberries in a compote (see accompanying photo) is fabulous. Not in the mood for a big breakfast? Try a melt-in-your-mouth cinnamon bun or a piece of the cinnamon-spice coffee cake, washed down with a soup bowl–sized latte.

The wait can be 20 or 30 minutes here, and the service slows down a bit at peak times, but Alpenglow is worth the wait. Show up planning on reading part of the *Bulletin's* Saturday or Sunday edition.

McGrath's Fish House does a really nice brunch on Sunday from 10:00 A.M. to 2:00 P.M. Entrees include the High Tide omelette, with Dungeness crab, Oregon shrimp meat, mushrooms, green onions, and cheddar cheese with hollandaise sauce. For a change of pace, there's the stuffed French toast—two slices of egg bread with cream cheese, bananas, and preserves sandwiched between them, all topped with strawberries.

All entrees come with the juice, fruit, and pastry buffet. Smoking is allowed on the patio. This family restaurant doesn't take reservations, but you can call (541) 388–4555 up to two hours before you arrive to put your name on the waiting list. McGrath's is on the outer edge of the Bend River Mall parking lot at 3118 North U.S. Highway 97.

The **Original Pancake House** is at 1025 Donovan Street Southwest, (541) 317–0380. Its address is taken from a very small street, but the eatery actually sits at the corner of two large Bend roadways—Colorado Avenue and Century Boulevard, on the way to Mt. Bachelor Ski Area. The original Original Pancake House was started in Portland in 1953; it's now a chain with 85 franchised locations nationwide. The Bend restaurant is owned by one of the founder's nephews, Tom Hueneke, and his wife, Paddy.

Breakfast is the specialty here. In fact, it's all they do, from 6:00 A.M. till closing time at 2:00 P.M. daily, and they are very good at it. Real butter, real whipping cream, real eggs, and an old-fashioned sourdough yeast made on the premises are key elements in some of the most delightful breakfast concoctions imaginable. The pancake menu is huge, with 20 different pancake dishes; an occasional special features seasonal fresh fruit.

One unique dish is the Dutch Baby, which take about 20 minutes to bake. Served on a huge plate, the Dutch Baby looks like a collapsed soufflé, still tall around the edges but sunken in the middle. It's eaten with powdered sugar and fresh lemon (no syrup!), and it's absolutely delightful. Crêpes come with strawberry preserves, sour cream with triple sec, Montmorency cherries, and/or bananas.

If there was a popularity contest among the dishes at the Bend location of the Original Pancake House, the omelettes would run neck and neck with the pancakes and might actually win by a nose. No single egg dish wins hands down, but some good ones include the mushroom omelette (stuffed with fresh mushrooms and topped with a rich mushroom sherry sauce) and the ham and cheese omelette with hickory-smoked ham.

Waffles, hot cereals (old-fashioned ones—none of this quick stuff), smoked meats, and American-style coffee round out the menu. Get your name on the waiting list at the front door—it's first-come, first-served, even for large parties on the weekends. On weekdays, large parties can sometimes make reservations. The dining room is nonsmoking, and the eatery is open daily. Bring the family.

The **Original Pantry** is off the beaten track, 1 long block north of the Shilo Inn, at 62910 O. B. Riley Road, (541) 383–2697. Breakfast is served all day in this charmingly restored Craftsman-style bungalow house.

Create Your Own Omelettes are among the favorites, giving you a choice of 21 stuffings and toppings. The eggs Benedict has a spicy, homemade hollandaise sauce, and it also comes in an optional Create Your Own Eggs Benedict version that allows you to add spinach, tomatoes, cheese, mushrooms, bacon, ham, sausage, or avocado for an extra charge. The breakfast burrito, stuffed with scrambled eggs, potatoes, bacon, cheddar cheese, and onions, is definitely one for the road. Pancakes with blueberries or strawberries, crêpes filled with fresh fruits in season, and French toast made with thick egg bread are a few more good choices. The Original Pantry is open Wednesday through Sunday from 7:00 A.M. to 3:00 P.M.

The **West Side Bakery & Cafe,** 1005 Northwest Galveston Avenue, (541) 382–3426, is an institution in Bend. Families and tourists line up on weekend mornings for some of the most whimsical breakfasts in Central Oregon. While you wait you can watch the model train as it chugs along, in and out of holes in the partitions and along walls, its tracks suspended high in the air. On the walls are a stuffed gorilla and other animals, and posters and pictures of Hollywood stars, all somewhat dusty and cobweb-laced. Nonetheless, it's always a surprise for first-time guests when the pancakes show up in the shape of... (We can't tell you.)

Eggs, bacon, hash browns, lattes—it's all fairly basic, and it's all very good. Breakfast is served from 6:30 A.M. to 3:00 P.M. in West Side's nonsmoking dining rooms. You can also pick up some traditional American baked goods like bear claws or decorated cakes at the bakery counter. There is an additional listing for West Side Bakery & Cafe in the Bend section of this chapter, but we think the real story is here.

Sisters/Camp Sherman Area

For those of us who aren't guests or residents at **Black Butte Ranch,** it's a treat just spending an hour or two at this upscale resort, 8 miles west of Sisters on U.S. Highway 20. The setting can't be beat. The dining room windows frame views of Mount Washington and the Three Sisters, deep pine forests, rolling golf greens, and lakes teeming with wildlife.

The breakfast menu is fairly predictable but satisfyingly well-prepared, right down to the old-fashioned Irish oatmeal. You may start off with a bowl of fresh strawberries with crème Anglais, or a half of a ruby-red grapefruit. The omelettes feature cheddar cheese from Tillamook, Oregon, as does the Cascade Scramble, which is filled with mushrooms, green onions, and peppers and served with rosemary hash browns. Breakfast is served until 11:30 A.M. in the nonsmoking dining room. For information or reservations, call (541) 595–6211 or (800) 452–7455.

Redmond

The Country Nook is a very simple, small-town cafe with a homey decor. Inside, the dozen or so tables (half are smoking, half nonsmoking) are usually filled with truck drivers, ranchers, business people, and families. As soon as you sit down, a cup of coffee shows up pronto and orders are jotted down and passed along to the owner/cook.

We recommend the three-egg Denver omelette with ham, bell pepper, onion, and cheese. Three tender hotcakes may be substituted for the potatoes and toast. If you want something to stick to your ribs, try the eggs with two large pork chops or the 8-ounce hamburger steak with beef gravy and eggs. Of course, there are the usual biscuits and gravy, corned-beef hash, chicken-fried steak, and just plain eggs and bacon. The Country Nook, at 514 Northwest Greenwood Avenue, (541) 923–2213, is open daily, and breakfast is served until closing time at 2:00 P.M.

Sunriver/La Pine Area

The tony, lodge-style dining room of the spectacular **Meadows at the Lodge,** at One Centre Drive, Sunriver Resort, (541) 593–3740, is both elegant and casual. The tablecloths and flowers seem to harmonize with the Indian print–patterned fabrics and guests in shorts and sandals.

The breakfast menu is quite upscale, with specialties like sautéed venison medallions with scrambled eggs and hash browns, and seared razor clams and eggs served with asparagus and toast. These are in addition to traditional favorites including omelettes, eggs Benedict with Canadian bacon and fresh hollandaise, pancakes, and French toast. On weekends the restaurant offers a Hang-Town Fry—breaded and fried oysters (sometimes from Oregon) with creamed spinach. Breakfast is served until 11:30 A.M. every day of the year.

On the banks of the Deschutes River with views of the Cascades, the **Trout House Restaurant** offers a pleasant breakfast experience. Tall windows let in the sunshine, which is partly captured by hanging plants. Light-colored tables and chairs almost cover a deep green carpet.

Older couples and families chat comfortably over omelettes made with lox, bay shrimp, Dungeness crab, mushrooms, or ham. The Two Egg Breakfasts are an orchestrate-your-own affair. Choose from fresh Oregon ruby-red trout or razor clams dug off our coast, among other candidates, to accompany your pair of eggs. The Hang-Town Fry features Oregon oysters and eggs scrambled with spinach, mushrooms, and onions. The eggs Benedict is faithfully traditional. Other traditions include waffles, pancakes, French toast, and granola. Call it a morning with a mimosa, bloody Mary, or glass of champagne. The smoke-free Trout House, at the marina in Sunriver, (541) 593–8880, serves breakfast daily until 11:00 A.M. or until noon on Sunday.

Prineville Area

We have to admit it: The breakfasts at the **Sandwich Factory** are as good as their sandwiches. Our pick would be Number Five—The Omelette Supreme, a two-egg omelette with ham, cheese, tomatoes, avocado, and mushrooms, plus toast. Also available are your basic sourdough pancakes and French toast, and biscuits and gravy.

Breakfast begins to sound a bit like lunch with breakfast sandwiches featuring cream cheese, avocado, meat, mayo, lettuce, tomato, and sprouts on your choice of a bagel, English muffin, or Factory sourdough biscuit. Whatever you choose, this place will do an excellent job with it. One word of caution: If you don't want margarine, ask for butter. Breakfast goes from 7:00 A.M. until about 10:00 A.M. when the lunch orders start to roll in fast and furious. The Sandwich Factory is at 277 North Court Street, (541) 447–4429.

Madras Area

Pepe, of **Pepe's Mexican Bakery and Restaurant** in downtown Madras at 225 Southeast Fifth Street, (541) 475–3286, serves up an authentic Mexican breakfast in his popular little eatery and bakery shop. For big appetites there's the huevos rancheros—two eggs over easy on a crisp corn tortilla topped with tomatoes, onions, and rancheros sauce. ("Real huevos rancheros must have a crisp corn tortilla!" he says.)

The breakfast torta is one of Pepe's specialties. A big Mexican roll is stuffed with eggs scrambled with pieces of chorizo sausage, then topped with tomatoes, onions, cheese, and lettuce. For burrito fans, many of the torta ingredients, plus refried beans, can be stuffed into a big flour tortilla. Lighter eaters can choose from two display cases filled with Mexican specialty baked goods. Our favorites are the flaky pastries stuffed with either creamy custard or red berry preserves, or both. American-style coffee is available. Breakfast is served from 10:00 to 11:00 A.M., Monday through Saturday.

afternoon Monday through Saturday, or just until noon on Sunday.

Desert High Espresso $, no credit cards
2205 Northeast Division Street
(541) 330–5987

On a street dotted with modern-looking paint stores, auto body places, and a couple of large restaurants, this tiny little stone house looks like an artifact from another era. Inside are a few tables, a counter, and a short menu with espresso drinks, healthy sandwiches, and pasta salad, plus a plate of pastries on the counter. You may take your latte and pastry out back onto the small deck under a shady tree, where you will be a world away from the hustle of Division Street. For lunch a thick sandwich with albacore and sprouts is a delicious choice. Service is friendly and helpful. Desert High is open

morning through afternoon, Monday through Saturday.

Di Lusso Baking $
1234 Northeast First Street
(541) 383–8155

Sophisticated desserts and espresso drinks earn this bakery a listing in both our Shopping and Restaurants chapters. We suggest the tarts with fresh berries or a piece of flourless chocolate-raspberry cake. They also serve wine. Di Lusso is open Monday through Saturday from 7:00 A.M. to 9:00 P.M.

Royal Blend Coffee House $
601 Northeast First Street
(541) 382–6349
Crossroads Shopping Plaza, 547 Northeast Bellevue Drive
(541) 330–1642

1075 Northwest Newport Avenue
(541) 383–0873
744 Northwest Bond Street
(541) 312–4036

Three Royal Blend Coffee Houses are stationed on Bend's eastside and westside and 2 blocks from U.S. 97's central core. A fourth is located downtown on Bond Street. The coffee and fresh-baked pastries are some of the best in town. A wide selection of Bend-roasted coffee beans are available for purchase, ground or whole. All locations are open from early morning through late afternoon, Monday through Saturday. The westside location on Newport Avenue is also open Sunday. There are also two more Royal Blends in Redmond—one at the airport and a second (kiosk) located at 732 Southwest Sixth Street, (541) 408–0152.

Sisters/Camp Sherman Area

Charming downtown Sisters has dozens of boutiques and galleries, and a number of little food places to support the tourists that flock to its streets.

Fast food is represented by a Subway on the east end of Cascade Avenue and at the old-time Sno-Cap Drive-In at the west end of Cascade. The Sno-Cap has good homemade ice cream, the most popular flavor being Cascade Blackberry.

Please note that Cascade Avenue is what U.S. Highway 20 is called as it cuts through the center of town. If you head west on U.S. 20, you'll come to the Black Butte Ranch resort and then to Camp Sherman, which is to the north. Both offer deluxe dining experiences (see our chapter on Resorts, Ranches, and Vacation Rentals).

American

Ali's Town Square Deli $
161 East Cascade Avenue, Sisters
(541) 549–2547

This is a spacious eatery with casual lawn-type furniture inside and a few picnic tables outside. Order a cold deli sandwich from the counter with your choice of meat, cheese, bread, and toppings. Our

favorites are the pita specialties, including the Turkey Apple, with smoked and regular breast of turkey, apple, celery, raisins, and almonds tossed in a fat-free Italian dressing, and the Lemon-Ginger Chicken, with chicken, grapes, celery, onion, light mayo, relish, lemon, ginger, and other mild spices. The soups are good and homemade, and you can pick up an espresso or frozen yogurt. Ali's is open daily from morning to late afternoon.

Black Butte Ranch Lodge Dining Room $$$$
U.S. Highway 20, Black Butte Ranch
(541) 595–1260, (800) 452–7455

The stunning views from this upscale dining room could make anything taste great, but the food is superb in its own right. Eight miles west of Sisters on U.S. 20, Black Butte Ranch is a private resort with golf courses and fancy homes, but the restaurant is open to the public.

As you might expect at a golf resort, the dining room has an elegant feel to it. The Cascade Mountain views from the large windows are drop-dead gorgeous. Tables are draped in cotton cloths, with candles at night. The wine list is extensive, primarily featuring California and Northwest labels, with smaller sections for imported reds and whites. The champagnes also are imported.

Breakfasts are great here. See our "Best Breakfasts in Central Oregon" Close-Up for more details.

For lunch the roasted garlic and grilled chicken fettuccine finished with an herb cream sauce and white wine is popular. Sandwiches and burgers range from a Reuben on rye to the BLT and BBR Patty Melt. There's a tempting selection of luncheon salads, and the homemade soups are excellent.

Dinner brings a more formal air. The menu changes seasonally, but you might start with Crab Cakes Winchester Bay—crab and salmon blended together and served with a blackberry orange sauce. Ranch specialties include a Breast of Chicken Astoria that melts in your mouth; it's a sautéed chicken breast garnished with Dungeness crab, chanterelle mushrooms, Marsala wine, Dijon mustard, and cream. A popular fish dish is the grilled salmon fillet with dill sauce. On Friday and Saturday we recommend the Slow Roasted Western Ranch Prime Rib au jus with creamy horseradish. Three separate children's menus are available—one for each meal.

From March through October the dining room is open daily. In the off-season it is closed on Monday and Tuesday. The dining room accepts American Express, Diner's Club, and Discover, as well as Visa and MasterCard.

Bronco Billy's Ranch Grill & Saloon $$$
190 East Cascade Avenue, Sisters
(541) 549-7427

Formerly called Hotel Sisters, the owners recently changed the name because too many people passed by without realizing it was really a restaurant.

Built in 1910, this former hotel offers a nice historical setting for a restaurant. The interior is authentically decorated in Western Victorian style. The charming dining room is designated nonsmoking, while smoking is allowed in the adjacent saloon. In summer the covered deck (also nonsmoking) just past the saloon is enjoyable.

The claim to culinary fame at Bronco Billy's Ranch Grill & Saloon is the local Corriente beef—a lean and unusual breed of steer. The burgers made with this beef really are superior, and the steaks are delicious. For lunch try the Caballero, an award-winning concoction of Corriente ground beef, with melted Monterey Jack cheese, whole green chile, guacamole, and salsa. It's served with potato salad. For dinner our choice would be the New York strip. Entrees come with soup or salad, veggies, and potato or rice.

The restaurant is open daily for lunch and dinner, and a children's menu is available.

Coyote Creek Cafe & Lounge $$
Three Winds Shopping Center, U.S. Highway 20, Sisters
(541) 549-9514

Coyote Creek, popular among locals and travelers alike, recently remodeled its interior in "western ranch and bunkhouse" style, complete with weathered wood and tin roofs over the booths. The result is a cozy, pleasant atmosphere in which to dine.

Their signature fare is steak broiled over a live mesquite fire, but they offer plenty of other selections as well. These include seafood, pasta, sandwiches, and burgers. They offer a petite menu for kids and light eaters.

For lunches, our favorites are the taco salad and the hot albacore tuna sandwich. At dinnertime, we like the halibut and chips or their homemade pizza, which you can eat there or take out, baked or unbaked. They offer daily lunch and dinner specials.

During the summer you can eat on the back deck at umbrella-sheltered tables or play a little horseshoes at their outdoor horseshoe pits while you wait for dinner to be served. Reservations are accepted, but generally not needed except on summer weekends when there are lots of people in town for an event, such as the Sisters Outdoor Quilt Show.

Coyote Creek is open Monday through Friday from 10:00 A.M. to closing and Saturday and Sunday 9:00 A.M. to closing. Winter hours are 11:00 A.M. to 9:30 P.M. daily. They are open for breakfasts on weekends only.

Coyote Creek also has a lounge. With a full bar and regular live entertainment, it's a popular Sisters nightspot (see our Nightlife chapter).

Depot Deli $
250 West Cascade Avenue, Sisters
(541) 549-2572

This eatery's picnic tables on the covered veranda next to the sidewalk lure tourists away from their downtown shopping. Inside, a counter divides the dining room from the very busy kitchen. Place your order and pay the cashier, then take a number and find a table. Smokers can grab an ashtray and head for one of the tables under the trees in the pleasant backyard.

The food at Depot Deli—a wide range of American sandwiches and salads, burgers and hot dogs—is well prepared and filling. Beer and wine are available, and Henry's root beer is on tap. This old place has added espresso drinks and milk shakes made with espresso or Italian soda flavorings or fresh fruit. And whoa, get this!—tofu may be added to your breakfast eggs for an extra six bits! Tofu in Sisters! But don't worry, Depot Deli still serves bacon. Get in line for breakfast, lunch, and dinner daily. (Dinner features the lunch menu, served until early evening.) American Express is accepted along with Visa and MasterCard.

The Gallery Restaurant $
171 West Cascade Avenue, Sisters
(541) 549-2631

Tourists line up at this old-time coffee shop, conveniently located smack-dab in the middle of Sisters' shopping district. The food is what you might expect for a coffee shop—burgers, BLTs, eggs and bacon, and the like—and service is good. The dining room, with its old booths and mounted deer head, is now nonsmoking; smokers can eat in the adjoining bar. The Gallery serves breakfast, lunch, and dinner daily, from 6:00 A.M. to 9:30 P.M. (they may close earlier in the off-season), and a kids' menu is available.

Kokanee Cafe $$$
25545 Southwest Forest Service Road 1419, Camp Sherman
(541) 595-6420

The wonderful experience starts as soon as you set foot outside your car and breathe in the cool, pine-filtered air. Despite the onslaught of summer vacationers, the dense Camp Sherman forest blankets the evening with a deep hush. In front of the shingled cabin, dusty four-wheel-drive Suburus and Ford Explorers are parked elbow-to-elbow with shiny Mercedes and Lexus sedans. This remote restaurant is packed for the evening.

During the pause before being escorted to a table, you take in the vaulted pine ceiling with its architectural trusses, soft white walls, and fishing-oriented artwork. You are, after all, only yards away from the famous catch-and-release trout fishery, the Metolius River, though it is not detectable from the restaurant.

The woodwork details are honey-colored clear fir, trimmed in a Craftsman style. The river-rock fireplace sits cold and empty on this warm summer evening. The Kokanee Cafe, named for a type of land-locked sockeye salmon that inhabits the Metolius River, resides on the site of an old fishermen's cafe that dates from 1927. It is actually a modern version of this older restaurant, with major renovations and expansion, and without any ghosts.

You may choose to dine at a cozy table in the small, busy dining room or at a quieter table with green plastic chairs out on the nonsmoking deck with its canopy of canvas umbrellas. Friendly and accommodating, the servers rush from table to table.

A comment overhead at a nearby table goes something like this: "Why go to Europe when you have a place like this within an hour of Bend?" They must have been eating the grilled duck breast with marionberry sauce, a divinely tender and succulent affair with a taste of charcoal smoke (although it is gas-chargrilled). Mashed potatoes with a hint of cheese and roasted garlic and two fresh, crisp white corn cobettes dusted with parsley accompany the duck breasts, along with a beautiful pansy perched on the plate's margin. A lovely dinner salad with fresh local greens, lightly drizzled with a vinaigrette dressing and topped with a deep purple violet flower, precedes the duck.

The fresh fish specials, such as a grilled ahi tuna topped with a creamy avocado wasabi sauce, are always popular. The wine selection, mostly from Oregon and Washington with a few California offerings thrown in, is as accommodating as the service. Entrees come with soup or salad and fresh-baked bread. Children can choose from chicken breast with french fries or buttered fettuccine made especially for them, and there are several meatless pasta dishes and a garden burger for vegetarians.

If you passed up an appetizer of baked Brie (with a spoonful of roasted garlic in its center to spread on crackers) or the Walla Walla Sweet Onion Rings, you'll probably still have room for dessert. For chocoholics there's a sinfully delicious Prlain's Chocolate-Raspberry Truffle Cake. Everyone will enjoy the Oregon hazelnut cheesecake or Northwest mixed berry pie.

Dress is vacation-casual, with or without a gold watch and diamond earrings. Sneakers and jeans will do you just fine. Unfortunately, the Kokanee Cafe is open only from late April until late October. In July and August you'll need reservations at least a few days in advance. The fall foliage season in September and October is a scenic and quiet time to visit, and you probably won't need reservations.

Seasons Cafe and Wine Shop $
411 East Hood Street, Sisters
(541) 549-8911
This is the locals' secret lunch spot. Its location at the far east end of Hood Street, a stone's throw off the beaten path, is just out of the way enough to pare the clientele down to the folks in the know. And they're the lucky ones, as this place is a real find.

Owners and hosts Don and Joyce specialize in lunches of big sandwiches filled with real roasted turkey or roast beef with no additives. The Smoked Butte sandwich on sourdough—with turkey, ham, smoked mozzarella, and the rest of the fixins—is one of the favorites. Another is the Bleu Cow, which features roast beef with bleu cheese dressing on a focaccia roll. Liverwurst with onions, cucumber, and Dijon on rye, and albacore with kalamata olives, celery, and green onions with a tarragon-mayo dressing on a wheat roll each piqued our interest. Green salads, artichoke or mesquite-chicken quiche, and, during cold weather, hot soup round out the lunch menu. Kids can choose between PB&J or toasted cheese. The dessert case looked tempting with its fresh-baked pies and carrot cake.

A nice selection of bottled wines is available for purchase. Don has been in the wine business for many years and will help with your selection. During the off-season months Don and Joyce hold wine tastings once a month. Chilled wines may be purchased by the glass or bottle and enjoyed with lunch. Or, if you prefer, make it a cold pint of Deschutes Brewery draft beer.

Guests munch sandwiches and sip wine at picnic tables in the shade of the pine trees or in a sunny, creekside spot. There are also tables and booths in the casual, nonsmoking dining room. Stop by Monday through Saturday. Discover is accepted in addition to Visa and MasterCard.

Ethnic
The Royal Thai Café $$
160 East Cascade Avenue, Sisters
(541) 549-3025
When Sineet and Mark Spofford opened The Royal Thai Cafe in 1999, Central Oregon aficionados of Thai cuisine noticed—and flocked here. The reviews were good back then, they're still good, and they still flock here.

They offer a complete menu of classic, traditional Thai food including curry, noodle, and seafood dishes, along with soups and salads.

Some of the spicier dishes on the menu include Three Kings with beef, chicken, or pork mixed with stir fried onions, mushrooms, basil and Thai chilies, and red curry featuring bamboo shoots, peas, carrots, and your choice of chicken, pork, or tofu all in a spicy curry mix. Some of our favorites here include the mixed seafood tempura, Royal Thai pork ribs, and Thai-style fried rice; they also serve up wine and beer, including Thai brews.

The Royal Thai Cafe is open Tuesday through Sunday 4:00 P.M. to closing.

Coffeehouses and Specialty Eateries
Sisters Bakery $, no credit cards
251 East Cascade Avenue, Sisters
(541) 549-0361
This old bakery continues to faithfully offer fresh doughnuts and giant bear claws along with coffee. Just to show that an old dog can learn new tricks, the bakery now sells espresso (very good) and scones. Check out the marionberry pies and bars in July—they're the best. Sisters Bakery also offers pizza by the slice. It is open daily from early morning to late afternoon.

Redmond Area

Redmond is a former cow town that is growing and evolving rapidly. What we offer in these listings is a snapshot in time—you can expect some new additions if you travel here in the near future. There is a compact downtown area along Sixth Street between Deschutes and Forest Avenues with a number of nice antiques and gift shops. Perhaps in response to the antiques shoppers, Redmond has some fine coffee- and teahouses.

American

The Country Nook $
514 Northwest Greenwood Avenue, Redmond
(541) 923–2213

This bright little cafe, with its simple decor, serves up good American fare for breakfast and lunch (see our Close-up, "Best Breakfasts in Central Oregon").

For lunch, owner/chef Paul Wiles recommends the Paul Boy—a big sandwich with grilled prime rib, Swiss cheese, sautéed onions, lettuce, tomato, and dressing on grilled sourdough. Burgers, more sandwiches, soup and chili, a few salads, fried chicken, and fish 'n' chips round out the lunch menu. Seniors and children have short menus of downsized meals for breakfast and lunch. Half of the small dining room is for smokers, and half is non-smoking (about six tables each), and there are a couple of tables outside. The Country Nook faces north in a very small strip center between Fifth and Sixth Streets in downtown Redmond. Watch for the sign on the left as you drive north on Fifth Street. It's open daily.

Kayo's Roadhouse $$
250 Northwest Sixth Street, Redmond
(541) 548–5675

Formerly the high-end Paul's Dinner House and Lounge, it's now Kayo's Roadhouse, a laid-back barbecue and burger restaurant probably more compatible with Redmond's hard-working character than its original incarnation.

As soon as you walk through the door, you'll be greeted by a friendly host or hostess who will show you to your table. Walk carefully, though, as you're escorted through the dining room, because the floor will likely be littered with peanut shells. That's because each party of diners is served a complimentary bowl of peanuts

to snack on. While it's not mandatory to throw your shells on the floor, it does give a certain sense of perverse satisfaction.

On the menu you'll find a good selection of down-home eats. We're partial to the barbecued chicken. They also have a full-service bar.

The Roadhouse is open weekdays from 11:00 A.M. to 9:00 P.M. and weekends from 10:00 A.M. to 9:00 P.M.

Ethnic

Sully's Italian Restaurant $$
521 Southwest Sixth Street, Redmond
(541) 548–5483

The Italian entrees, including veal picatta, cannelloni, and chicken marsala are well-prepared and include antipasto, soup or salad, and hot garlic bread. Chicago-style pizza is also offered. Lunches are good. You can choose from a list of more than 20 sandwiches, including American and Italian favorites, or try a calzone.

The nonsmoking dining room is pleasant with its tall ceiling and windows and tables with green vinyl covers. Next door is a lounge that allows smoking. Wine, beer, and cocktails are available for dinner when the bar opens. Sully's is open for lunch Monday through Friday and for dinner daily. Children are welcome.

Coffeehouses and Specialty Eateries

Local Grounds $, no credit cards
457 Southwest Sixth Street, Redmond
(541) 923–3977

This charming little coffeehouse offers a lunch menu that includes a fresh roasted-turkey sandwich with cranberries and cream cheese, or a white chunk tuna sandwich. A garden salad may be garnished with chicken. Wrap it all up together and you get the local special—a half-sandwich, soup or salad, drink, and dessert, all for a good price. Desserts include pies, cakes, ice cream, pastries, and gourmet chocolates. This is a coffeehouse, so you'll have a good selection of espresso drinks made with Bend's Royal Blend coffee beans, plus Italian sodas, granitas, and tea. Local Grounds is open daily from morning through late afternoon.

The Wild Rose Tea Room $
422 Southwest Sixth Street, Redmond
(541) 923-3385

The Wild Rose offers the lightest of light lunches. If you wish, you can just have a scone (they make some of the best and freshest scones on earth) accompanied by a real pot of tea, served on real china at a table with a lace tablecloth, any time of day. The soups are outstanding; we tried one with fresh greens in broth and it was wonderful. Wild Rose offers a luncheon plate with tea sandwiches, a scone, fruit, and a small pot of tea. For the cold season a hot casserole dish is offered with a scone and tea.

As you eat, your eyes will wander over all the teapots and other finery in the shop—it's all for sale. The tearoom is open from morning through late afternoon from Tuesday through Saturday and is tucked in a little antiques mall with Past and Presents at the front. The shop takes Discover as well as MasterCard and Visa.

Sunriver/La Pine Area

The large, upscale resort of Sunriver supports a number of good eateries, two of which are noteworthy. The small town of La Pine also has two noteworthy eateries.

American

Hog Heaven Cafe and Soup Kitchen $-$$
51450 U.S. Highway 97, La Pine
(541) 536-2317

This has to be one of the most unpretentious gourmet places in Central Oregon. As you enter the restaurant you find yourself in part of the kitchen. A friendly face asks you to pick a table in the adjoining dining room—a pleasant space with a high cathedral ceiling, plants, and a fish tank. The decor includes simple gray carpeting and stacking chairs, but the overall appearance is clean and new and welcoming. The collection of a dozen or more pig figurines and animals that you might expect to find in a restaurant with a name like Hog Heaven is relegated to the kitchen area.

Hog Heaven is a family affair. Mom and Dad—Jim and Gail Crouch—have a second home here in La Pine but were unhappy with their choices of places to eat. Their brilliant idea was to convince their son, Scott (at that time a chef at a restaurant in Bend), to come to La Pine and start his own place. Or, we should say, their own place. After a bumpy start, this has become the most popular eatery in La Pine.

The menu crosses the cultural gap between small town and big city. It goes to show that if something is well-prepared and reasonably priced, everyone will like it. For dinner, Hog Heaven does everything from chicken-fried steak and fish 'n' chips to rack of lamb and pasta with rock shrimp in a garlic sauce. The 10-ounce New York steak with mashed potatoes and herb butter is a great value. As Jim likes to say, "In the long run, quality ingredients pay off."

Many dinner menu items are casual foods such as charbroiled burgers and dinner salads. Lunches are also casual with the same burgers, sandwiches, soups, and salads. Beverages are nonalcoholic. The eatery is open Tuesday through Saturday for lunch and dinner. If you're in town, hit it!

Hook, Wine and Cheddar $
Sunriver Village Mall, Building 22, Sunriver
(541) 593-1633

If you keep walking toward the back of this store, past rows of wine bottles and fly-fishing gear, you'll come to a deli counter and a few tables where you can pick up excellent sandwiches and fresh salads. The list is extensive; popular choices include the gyros and the fajita pita. A gourmet picnic lunch for two contains a half-bottle of wine and a selection of gourmet meats, cheeses, and crackers, all accompanied by olives, pepperoncinis, fresh fruit, and a sweet treat. A simpler box lunch is available with a sandwich, fruit, cookies, and chips. In the mornings, espresso or coffee and bagels are served. This unusual fly shop/deli is open daily from morning until late afternoon.

The Meadows at the Lodge $$$$
One Centre Drive, Sunriver
(541) 593-3740

First of all, we must say that the complete renovation of the lodge, completed in June

1998, is spectacular. In front of the massive structure is a fabulous waterfall made with natural lava rock, with bronze sculptures of otters playing and fishing in the water. You enter through the hotel lobby, and the main restaurant is ahead of you. Inside, the towering mass of the rock fireplace is powerful. At its base are polished wood floors, couches, and armchairs with Craftsman styling and Native American–patterned fabrics. Seated at a baby grand, a pianist plays. The nearby lounge allows smoking, but the air smells fresh.

The dining room is lovely, with cream-colored tablecloths and small copper lamps. The padded chairs have webbed leather backs, adding to a rustically elegant lodge ambiance. Breakfast, lunch, and dinner are served here, and the restaurant is busy all summer. During the warm months, eating on the deck overlooking the golf course and enjoying the mountain views is pleasant.

The breakfast menu is unique, with specialties like sautéed venison medallions with scrambled eggs and hash browns. There's more on the great breakfasts in this chapter's Close-up on "Best Breakfasts in Central Oregon." The lunch menu is equally delightful. It offers a nice selection of salads, including the China Hat Oriental Chicken Salad. Sandwiches include a focaccia sandwich of the day that is usually very good, the Fremont Burger with fries or cole slaw, and the Chief Paulina barbecued rotisserie pork loin with grilled pippin apple and sage aioli.

The dinner menu is a la carte. A wonderful start would be the Pacific razor clams, pan-seared with a Northwest Provençal. For big eaters there's the Ranch Hand, a grilled New York strip steak with a green peppercorn brandy glaze, oven-fired baked potato or mashed potato of the day, and fresh veggies. Other entrees include duck, trout, pasta, and rotisserie specials.

Children have extensive menus for both breakfast and lunch/dinner. The Meadows takes American Express, Visa, and MasterCard, and it is open 365 days a year. This is truly a fine addition to Central Oregon's dining scene.

The Trout House Restaurant $$$
57235 River Road, Sunriver Marina, Sunriver
(541) 593–8880

The exceptionally beautiful setting next to the Deschutes River makes The Trout House a pleasant dining experience. The ambiance is appropriately upscale yet casual. We love to go for Sunday brunch when the sun streams through the windows.

The breakfasts are, in a word, excellent (see our Close-up, "Best Breakfasts in Central Oregon"). For lunch, you can try the fresh grilled Ruby Red Trout, served with fries and green salad or potato salad, or you can stick with a good burger. Sandwiches include grilled roast beef and a Clubhouse for $6.00. Celebrate summer with a Crab Louie Salad or a chef salad.

Oysters and clams are available as appetizers throughout the day. Our picks from a traditional Northwest dinner menu include filet mignon and the mixed grill with rack of lamb, prawn sauté, grilled razor clams, and venison. Dinners include soup or salad, rice or potato, veggies, and bread.

We suggest making reservations. The Trout House is open daily and accepts Diner's Club and Discover in addition to MasterCard and Visa.

Ethnic

Baja Norte $
One West Mall, Sunriver Village
(541) 593–9374

This Baja Norte is part of a chain of healthy Mexican restaurants. Check the Downtown Bend listings for the rundown on what these popular eateries offer.

Hunan Chinese Restaurant $
51546 U.S. Highway 97, La Pine
(541) 536–3998

This restaurant was opened in 1998 by a family from Canton, China. Hunan offers the best Chinese food in Central Oregon, succeeding in the small town of La Pine by offering dishes that appeal to small-town American tastes in addition to authentic dishes.

The dining room is pleasant and new with dark gray carpeting, white walls, and little red accents on the tables. When we spent some time at the front counter waiting for a couple of take-out orders, we were surprised at the number of people who ordered Combination Dinner No. 2—pork or chicken chow mein, pork fried rice, fried shrimp, and sweet-and-sour chicken. We're not sure if this was because it was really the best combo dinner, or if word had gotten around this small town saying, "I had the Number 2 dinner, and it was good."

We tried the kung po chicken, a huge entree with lots of chicken and an excellent sauce (and maybe a few too many American-style vegetables like zucchini, carrots, and celery). A pork dish from the Yu Xiang Style section was excellent and unique, with a lightly tangy brown sauce and perfectly sliced vegetables and pieces of meat. We had enough leftovers for more meals. The rice was cooked perfectly, and the service was friendly and quick. Hunan is open daily for lunch and dinner. There is also a Hunan Chinese Restaurant in Redmond, (541) 923–5115.

Coffeehouses and Specialty Eateries

Sunriver Coffee Company $
Sunriver Village, Building 1, Sunriver
(541) 593–5282
Have a seat in one of the bentwood chairs and check out the lively artwork on the walls as you sip a house-roasted espresso and enjoy a homemade muffin or scone. The shop is open daily (including Christmas) from morning until late afternoon.

Prineville Area

A few fast-food places can be found along U.S. Highway 126 in Prineville.

American

Pioneer Club $$
1851 East Third Street, Prineville
(541) 447–6177
The pickup trucks line up in front of this old-time dinner house at the east end of town. This is Prineville's place to go for birthdays, anniversaries, and weddings. Service is very courteous and competent.

The dining room is traditional and graciously furnished in deep reds with white tablecloths. The first dining area is non-smoking, but there is an equally large smoking area in the adjacent room.

The 16-ounce porterhouse steak and prime rib are the specialties. The garlic whipped potatoes with cream gravy or brown gravy are really good as well. Your meal includes a salad or soup; rice or whipped or baked potato; and a small piece of homemade pie (a favorite is the Key lime), cake, or ice cream for dessert. There's an adequate wine list (the house red wine offered by the carafe is very drinkable), and a full bar is available. The Pioneer Club is a terrific dining experience. It is open for dinner daily.

The Sandwich Factory $
277 Northeast Court Street, Prineville
(541) 447–4429
This is one of the best spots in Central Oregon for sandwiches. The house specialty among the deli-style offerings is The Assembly Line, a huge sandwich with every meat and cheese the place offers. Foot-long sandwiches are also available; you can order fractions for less. Sandwiches come with margarine on them, so if this isn't your style, request that they leave it off. The Sandwich Factory also does a good breakfast—see our Close-up, "Best Breakfasts in Central Oregon," for the details. The decor is simple, with Formica tables and white, soda fountain–type chairs. The Sandwich Factory opens in the early morning and closes in the early evening Monday through Saturday.

Ethnic

Ranchero Mexican Restaurant $
969 Northwest Third Street, Prineville
(541) 416–0103
This is Prineville's mainstay for Mexican food. The menu is quite extensive, including a fish and seafood menu, chicken mole, kids'-size dishes, and deep-fried ice cream for dessert. Service is very friendly and prompt. Beer, wine, and cocktails are available. The dining room is nonsmoking, but smokers 21 and older can eat in the bar. This Ranchero is open daily, until

11:00 P.M. on Friday and Saturday nights, and it accepts American Express, Discover, Visa, and MasterCard. There's another, newer Ranchero in Bend (see our "Other Bend Area Restaurants" section).

Coffeehouses and Specialty Eateries

The Robin's Nest $
395 North Main Street, Prineville
(541) 447–8665

This cute gift shop serves espresso, beverages, and homemade muffins and scones from early morning to late afternoon Monday through Saturday.

Madras Area

Madras is an agricultural town with a large percentage of Native American and non-English-speaking residents, primarily Hispanic. The restaurants here reflect this mix of cultures, and it's definitely to Central Oregon's advantage. Please note that Fifth Street is U.S. Highway 97 running north; Fourth Street is U.S. 97 running south. A couple of fast-food restaurants can be found along the highway in town.

American

The Original Burger Works $, no credit cards
84 Southwest Fourth Street, Madras
(541) 475–3390

This little fast-food place serves good burgers and milk shakes. The Works tried out one of those snazzy computerized ordering machines where folks could just

push the buttons for everything that they wanted—flavor of shake, toppings on their burger, etc. Everyone ignored it and just shouted their orders at the cook, so order-taking is still done the old-fashioned way at the OBW. The most popular burger here is the large burger with the works—mayo, mustard, pickles, onions, lettuce, and tomato. It's a clean, nonsmoking establishment that's open daily from 11:00 A.M. to 9:00 P.M.

Ethnic

Ding Ho Chinese Restaurant $
36 Southwest I Street, Madras
(541) 475–4610

This restaurant, straddling the block between Fourth and Fifth Streets, doesn't look like much on the outside. It may have been a drive-in burger place in a previous lifetime. The food, however, is very good—not too oily and lightly cooked. We like the house chow mein, a light meal of chicken, pork, beef, and a couple of shrimp, with pan-fried noodles and a few veggies. The lunch specials are good bargains. Cantonese and Szechuan dinner entrees include rice but don't include a soup or salad. There are a few American dishes, with child-size portions available. Ding Ho is open daily for lunch and dinner.

Mexico City $
48 Southwest Fourth Street, Madras
(541) 475–6078

This charming little restaurant with white stucco walls has very friendly and prompt service. Colorful rugs hang on the walls, and one corner has a big toy cactus in it. Embroidered Mexican blouses are displayed for sale. The studded red vinyl chairs are very comfortable, and the cloth napkins add a classy touch.

A bowl of spicy salsa and homemade chips arrives soon after you sit down. The entrees are familiar but well-prepared, and a crisp fried churrito with cinnamon and sugar is complimentary at the end of your meal. Beer and wine are available. The restaurant is family-run by Salvador and Paula Montano, and it is open daily for lunch and dinner.

**Pepe's Mexican Bakery and Restaurant $,
no credit cards
221 Southeast Fifth Street, Madras
(541) 475-3286**

Pepe himself will greet you with a big "Welcome!" as you enter his little restaurant. In front of you is a tempting array of Mexican pastries in a large case. The ones that look like turnovers with a red jam and white cream filling are our favorites. Be careful or Pepe will talk you into taking a dozen! (They don't freeze well.) If you get to the eatery between 10:00 and 11:00 A.M., you can get a breakfast of huevos rancheros or torta with eggs and chorizo (see this chapter's Close-up on breakfasts).

Our favorite meal is the carne asada torta, a huge homemade Mexican roll stuffed with grilled steak and oozing with avocado, onion, lettuce, mayo, tomato, and salsa. (It also comes with chicken, but we don't think it's as good as the beef.) The other entrees are solid, if unexceptional. Pepe's is open for breakfast, lunch, and early dinner from Monday through Saturday.

Coffeehouses and Specialty Eateries

**Petals 'n' Poseys $
546 Southwest Fourth Street, Madras
(541) 475-6266, (800) 568-6266**

An espresso bar is tucked into the back of this small gift, flower, and book shop. The espresso is good, but you are limited to biscotti and cookies to go with your coffee. (Pick up a Mexican pastry at Pepe's and bring it over here!) The shop is open Monday through Friday from morning through late afternoon, and on Saturday morning.

**Pug's Mug $, no credit cards
701 West First Avenue, Culver
(541) 546-6382**

The name for this espresso/sandwich/ice cream shop was simply the obvious choice, according to Karen and Macy's college-age son and his friends from school. And you might say their pug, Pugsly, left a mark on the place, or at least some pug prints, when the dog walked on the wet concrete that would become an outdoor dining patio prior to the eatery's opening in summer 1998.

Since that fateful moment, Pug's Mug, the cafe, has been a big hit in the community, with its giant sandwiches with 6 ounces of meat; the favorite seems to be the real roasted turkey breast. Customers can choose to sit on comfortable wooden chairs in the dining room, with its white walls and green tile floor, or out on the patio. If they're in a hurry, they can pick up an espresso at the drive-through window. Ice-cream cones have been big in the hot months; come winter Karen will be serving up big pots of hot soup or chili. Pug's Mug is open from early morning through early evening Monday through Saturday. Due to sanitation laws, Pugsly will be there in spirit only.

Nightlife

Nightclubs
Pubs
Nonsmoking Nightlife

Believe it or not, despite all of our skiing, fishing, and ranch work, we Central Oregonians still have the energy to get out and party. Almost every night of the week, there's a place where you can drop in for some entertainment; on weekends, there are usually several nightspots to choose from.

Most of the action starts after 8:00 P.M., and in some places things don't get going until as late as 9:30 P.M. Cover charges vary from place to place and from night to night, and they are noted in each entry. The minimum drinking age in Oregon is 21. Young people up to age 26 can expect to be carded. In Oregon, a blood-alcohol reading of .08 or higher will get you a DUI charge; that's not very many beers or cocktails, so be careful out there. If you plan on drinking on your night out, either arrange for one of your party to be a designated driver or contact a taxi company at least an hour in advance of when you want to be picked up. You won't find taxis cruising our streets waiting to be hailed. (See our Getting Here, Getting Around chapter for taxi listings.)

A good place to find out more specific information on what's happening when you're in the area is the Saturday issue of Bend's daily paper, the *Bulletin*. It contains the much-anticipated Scene, a television guide insert that also has a user-friendly Nightlife page. The *Bulletin*'s Community Life section features arts and entertainment articles daily and offers an events calendar column. The *Source*, a free independent weekly newspaper that comes out on Wednesdays, has an excellent listing of current events. (See our Media chapter for more on the *Bulletin* and the *Source*.) Boomtown, a CD store at 910 Northwest Harriman Street in Bend, (541) 388–1800, has upcoming music events posted on their bulletin board. This is where you'll buy tickets for most concerts held in the area.

In Bend you will find a dozen places that regularly have music and/or dancing on Friday and Saturday nights. The Riverhouse has dancing on weeknights, and several restaurants occasionally have musicians or other entertainers during the week, in hopes of bringing in locals to increase weeknight business.

Bend, being slightly more liberal in nature, is casual when it comes to dress codes. Jeans are considered pretty. Women occasionally dress up a bit, but you will almost never see a jacket and tie—not even at the classiest places.

Redmond has a nice brewpub. Sisters is pretty sleepy in the off-season, with infrequent Saturday night events (check the listing for Coyote Creek Cafe). A couple of bars in town have live music on weekends during the summer. Sunriver has a few bars that sometimes offer music.

The smaller town of Prineville has a loyal group of regulars that keep two adjacent nightclubs really rocking on Friday and Saturday nights. If you enjoy small cow-town revelry, Prineville's the place to go. The entertainment scene here represents heartland America—you will find ranchers and mill workers getting dolled up to go out on the town. Some of the men will wear their newest Wranglers (over scuffed boots), a pressed cowboy shirt, a belt with a big buckle, and a nice, clean hat—black felt in the winter, straw in the summer. Women of all ages get out their dancing shoes—some wear loose frocks, others break out the blue jeans with a fringed or ruffled blouse and a pair of Ropers (lace-up cowboy boots) that they save for special nights. Some working men and unmarried "kids" will come as they are.

On our strange political landscape, where environmentalism and bottle bills thrive amidst political conservatism, whether a place allows smoking or is smoke-free is a major factor in determining the clientele. Many Central Oregon restaurants are completely nonsmoking. As you might imagine, there are a lot of folks who hang out in bars so they can smoke, eat out, and have a good time, and they have been the driving force behind much of Central Oregon's nightlife. On the other hand, there are people who wouldn't go into a smoky bar unless their lives depended on it.

Fortunately, there is a growing segment of the nightlife scene that caters to non-smokers, including all of our brewpubs. In other words, no one needs to stay home with a rented movie. We specifically mention the smoke-free policy in listings for our fresh-air nightspots. For other nightlife such as theater, book or poetry readings, and concerts, please refer to our The Arts chapter.

Nightclubs

Smoking is allowed at the following nightspots. For smoke-free establishments, jump ahead to Pubs and Nonsmoking Nightlife.

Bend

The Riverhouse Fireside Lounge
The Riverhouse Resort, 3075 North U.S. Highway 97
(541) 389–8810

Twenty-somethings right on up to 50-somethings pack this nightclub on Friday and Saturday nights. It's less crowded Sunday through Thursday, when the lounge has mostly locals and some business people staying at The Riverhouse Resort (see our Hotels and Motels chapter). Cocktails and beer are popular, and so are the sandwiches, pizzas, and restaurant-size steak dinners that are served at small tables around the dance floor. There's no cover charge and no minimum drink order if all you want to do is dance to the live rock bands that play Monday through Saturday during the busy season (possibly only Thursday through Monday nights in the off-season).

Dress is super-casual, predominantly blue jeans with an occasional fancy Western vest, and the air doesn't seem quite as smoky as most nightclubs. On some Sundays we are treated to the sounds of live Big Band music; the average age of the folks on the dance floor goes up a bit! Big Band nights are offered on the second and fourth Sundays of the month. There is a $10.00 cover charge, which includes a $5.00 gift certificate for drinks and food.

The Shilo Lounge
The Shilo Inn, North U.S. Highway 97 and O. B. Riley Road
(541) 382–4082

This motel lounge has a DJ on Friday and Saturday nights with no cover charge. The clientele is a mix of locals and the out-of-town guests at this large motel (see our Hotels and Motels chapter). You can get restaurant food in the lounge area, and there's a full bar. If The Riverhouse next door gets too loud for conversation, drive over to the Shilo.

Tumalo Feed Company
64619 West U.S. Highway 20
(541) 382–2202

This big old yellow ranch house serves up live country-western guitar music in the saloon on Thursday through Saturday nights starting at 7:00 P.M. The saloon is worth visiting just to admire the beautiful antique bar where cocktails and beer are served. Owner Robert Holly doesn't know the date the bar was built, saying only "it came around the Cape quite a while back." In the dining room the big rib steaks with mushrooms are good for a detour, and cocktails or the house red wine followed by an after-dinner drink make this a special night out.

Good blue jeans or denim skirts with gingham blouses are the order of the day. However, we do get a lot of city folks coming in on weekends with sneakers and shorts; if you didn't bring your Western duds, don't give it a second thought. There's no cover charge. Mosey on in, say howdy to the greeter, and enjoy a genuine sagebrush evening. We ranchers are usually asleep in bed by midnight, so get there on the early side.

Finding nightlife and evening entertainment is not a problem in Bend. PHOTO: THE RIVERHOUSE

Sisters/Camp Sherman Area

Bronco Billy's Ranch Grill & Saloon
190 East Cascade Street, Sisters
(541) 549–7427

If you are interested in old buildings and are looking for a nice place to have a drink, you might enjoy stopping in the beautiful saloon of this c. 1912 hotel. The decor is Victorian, and there just might be music on a warm summer Saturday night. Even if there isn't, go for the ambiance.

Coyote Creek Cafe & Lounge
Three Winds Shopping Center, 425 West U.S. Highway 20, Sisters
(541) 549–9514

The lounge door is under the red awning around the side of the restaurant. Inside is a full-service bar with a small seating area and a spot for a live band on Saturday nights. Live music happens fairly regularly during summer but maybe once a month during the rest of the year. There is usually no cover charge, and dress is casual.

Sunriver/La Pine Area

Village Bar & Grill
Sunriver Village Mall, Building 6, Sunriver
(541) 593–1100

Located next to the post office, this casual little bar with its rustic wood decor is a comfortable place to sip a nice micro-brewed draft beer or a cocktail. They have a large screen TV for watching the game. Dress is strictly come as you are.

Prineville Area

Champion's Sports Bar
380 North Main Street, Prineville
(541) 447–8005

This Prineville bar really jumps on Friday and Saturday nights when there's a live classic rock band. Local ranchers get all duded up in their best Wranglers and dance frocks and head to Champion's. They just put in a new dance floor and stage, as well as adding a restaurant, which offers pasta, steaks, seafood, and other American fare.

The full bar serves cocktails and a lot of Budweiser to a cross-section of Prineville society—from working men in T-shirts and dirty jeans to flirting 20-somethings.

One thing at this club that we haven't seen elsewhere is a real table for black-jack, which qualifies as social gambling under Prineville's city ordinance. There's no cover charge, which makes it easy for the folks who like to flit back and forth between Champion's and Morgan's, which is around the corner.

Morgan's Bar and Grill
121 Northeast Third Street, Prineville
(541) 447-3880

When partying in Prineville, if you're not at Champion's, you're at Morgan's. Filled mostly with couples, with a few singles here and there, this popular nightclub is packed on Wednesday and Saturday to hear free karaoke hosted by a live announcer. The slower songs attract more dancers than the fast rock tunes, and the folks sitting around the dance floor quietly sing along, reading the words on the big screen. On Friday nights there is a live band with no cover charge. The large bar in the center of the tavern serves lots of cocktails and beer. For patrons not into singing, there are shuffleboard and video poker machines. Attire is come as you are, but most locals usually dress up just a notch or two.

Pubs

We are proud of the world-class microbrewed beer we have in Oregon. This is where the current trend toward microbrews got its start, or so we like to think. We are lucky to have three microbreweries right here in the area. If you're a beer drinker, try them all: Each beer is unique, with a signature ambiance. Soon you may be calling one of the brewpubs your home away from home. Microbrew aficionados are known as purists in their desire to have an unadulterated taste in their beer—perhaps that's why all of these establishments fall into the nonsmoking, clean-air category.

Keep in mind the alcohol content in a giant pint glass will likely be greater than what you are used to in those 12-ounce bottles of beer you might be used to drinking. If you are making a night of it, stick with a designated driver or call ahead for a taxi. Or why not try a microbrewed root beer?

Bend

Aviemore Arms Pub and Grille
1020 Northwest Wall Street
(541) 385-8898

Bend's first Irish pub opened in the summer of 1998, bringing us a stylish new approach to beer drinking. You may not have noticed Aviemore, as the words painted on the glass windows are fairly low and of an elegant script that takes a few seconds to decipher. Inside, the high ceilings add to the pub's European air. Folks sit at the comfortable tables at the front of the restaurant, eating Aviemore's excellent fish 'n' chips while sipping one of the eight draft beers. The upstairs loft lounge has a pool table. Downstairs, you'll find a dartboard and large-screen TV. Local bands play on Saturday nights (usually for a $3.00 cover charge), and sometimes Aviemore has Celtic music on Thursday evenings.

Bend Brewing Company
1019 Northwest Brooks Street
(541) 383-1599

This cheerful brewpub with a wood-paneled interior overlooks the Deschutes River, making for a very pleasant spot to sit and sip a fine India Pale Ale, one of their most popular beers. The brewery specializes in light, smooth ales and sodas. The pub food is good too, so you can spend a whole evening at this place. It can get quite crowded on weekend nights. If there is a

> **Insiders' Tip**
> Elk and deer crossing the roads at night are part of Central Oregon's nightlife. Be alert on your way home!

wait, just put your name on the list and take a lovely walk near the river or around this charming older neighborhood in downtown Bend. Brewery tours are available by prior arrangement. There is a parking lot 1 block to the south.

Deschutes Brewery & Public House
1044 Northwest Bond Street
(541) 382–9242

A longtime favorite of Bendites, the Deschutes Brewery makes some of the best beers in the United States. They specialize in smooth, full-flavored brews, with one or two ales on the lighter side. The Black Butte Porter is the No. 1 beer. Find out what is on the seasonal list and try any of the cask-conditioned offerings—they are really special. Oregon wines are also featured.

On Friday and Saturday nights, the people are sometimes four-deep at the bar. On Monday night, beer and some pub dishes are reduced in price, so Mondays are also very busy. The food is good (especially the homemade sausage on a brewery baguette), and better yet, food is served until 10:00 P.M. or later. This is a casual family restaurant and pub, very tastefully decorated and comfortably furnished. It attracts young and old; the underage folks get to try the homemade root beer.

This location used to be the brewing site, and through a picture window you can still see some of the huge stainless-steel tanks for the beer. However, a few

years ago the popular outfit outgrew this location, and they built a large new brewing facility at 901 Southwest Simpson Avenue in Bend. Tours and tastings are run from noon to 4:00 P.M. on Saturday. Call (541) 385–8606 for information.

Honkers Pub
Honkers Restaurant, 805 Southwest Industrial Way
(541) 389–4665

If you're from out of town, the first thing you should do before attempting to find this attractive restaurant and pub is call for directions. Otherwise, you might never find Bend's mill district. Inside the huge Mill A building, built in 1915 and formerly owned by the Brooks-Scanlon lumber company, is a lovely bar and expansive dining area with knotty-pine walls and sliced logs for tables and stairs. The pub menu is outstanding, and they have an extensive list of excellent microbrews on tap, along with a full bar. Grab a seat in front of the fireplace for a deliciously relaxing evening. Though you can't go wrong filling up on the pub food, we also recommend dining in their restaurant (see our Restaurants chapter).

Redmond

Seventh Street Brew House
855 Southwest Seventh Street
(541) 923–1795

A little cottage strewn with strings of lights serves as the public house for Cascade Lakes Brewing Company. The white floor tiles and walls lined with colorful pub memorabilia sent by traveling customers give this brew house a bright, cheerful air. Rooster Tail Ale and Angus McDoogle Scottish Ale are the two brews most popular with local mavens. There is a short wine list. Meat and veggie pub foods are served by a friendly staff, and the menu includes kids' meals. Try the crisp, beer-battered zucchini.

The atmosphere is relaxed and the conversation and CD music are loud, with groups of friends clustering around small tables. Outside there is a lovely big deck with picnic tables where smoking is allowed. The Seventh Street Brew House is tucked in a convenient corner of Redmond that is easy to find if you know where you are going; the uninitiated should call for directions.

Insiders' Tip

From September through June, nightclubs don't always stick to regular schedules for live music. Call ahead for the specific scoop.

Nonsmoking Nightlife

Bend

Toomie's Thai Cuisine
119 Northwest Minnesota Avenue
(541) 388–5590

The excellent Thai food and white tablecloth service are accompanied by light classical and jazz piano on Sunday and Tuesday nights. There is no cover charge, as the music is for diners only. Beer and wine are available. This would be a good choice for a romantic night out.

Redmond

Crooked River Dinner Train
4075 Northeast O'Neil Road
(541) 548–8630

Ever get the urge to dress up in 1800s pioneer garb and hop aboard an old train for a great evening of saloon-style theater and dinner? Families and couples alike enjoy this three-hour ride in a 1948 train decorated in 19th-century finery. Two dining cars each have a full bar, and there is a separate smoking car. Diners are entertained by rowdy actors playing out murder mysteries on Saturday evenings throughout the year, with the addition of train robberies on Friday evenings during the summer. Passengers in casual attire are also welcomed. The special evening costs $71 per adult; children ages 4 through 12 are $38, and younger children are $20 (which does not include an entree). They also offer Sunday Suppers. The cost is $59 for adults and $38 for children ages 4 through 12. Call for reservations.

Shopping

Bend

Sisters/Camp
    Sherman Area

Redmond

Sunriver/La Pine Area

Prineville Area

Madras Area

Oregon is a popular shopping Mecca for Northwest bargain hunters, and Central Oregon is no exception. Folks often come from neighboring states just to shop here, not only because of our quality shops and broad selection, but also because we have no sales tax.

Oregon has never had a sales tax. Most of us hope it stays that way, though every few election years a politician tries to pass new legislation with some kind of sales tax included. So far we have voted them down. For shoppers, no sales tax makes life so much simpler: You pay the amount on the price tag and that's it.

This leads to some shopping aberrations. Believe it or not, Costco, one of those big wholesale warehouse membership stores with large boxes of stuff and low prices, is one of our most popular tourist shopping destinations. Visitors love making big purchases at Costco because they can save so much on sales tax. Their only limit is how much space they have in their cars or suitcases.

You'll probably hear Oregonians use the term "spendy." Spendy refers to high-priced items where part of what you are paying for is the prestige of ownership. People in other states might buy spendy cars and clothing; "real" Oregonians do not, or at least that's our popular myth. Garrison Keillor, of PBS radio and Lake Wobegon fame, once recorded one of his *Prairie Home Companion* shows in Portland, where he joked that the Portland Airport has a polyester detector that all out-of-state visitors have to pass through before they can enter Oregon. It does seem to be true that many Oregonians favor natural fiber clothing, as if it represented true, old-fashioned values. Comfort is considered an inalienable right, and you will find this reflected by much of the merchandise in our shops. Fancy clothing boutiques are fairly few and far between, while casual clothing is plentiful, along with shops that sell comfortable shoes. Very few business people wear traditional business clothing.

Famous Oregon products include juniper log furniture and Western arts (both native to Central Oregon), anything made with marionberries, carved myrtle wood from the coast, and high-quality woolen goods manufactured by Pendleton Woolen Mills in northeastern Oregon. You'll find some or all of these products all over Central Oregon.

Many stores accept only the two most common credit cards: Visa and MasterCard. Some take all the majors, but don't plan on shopping with only an American Express card. Many shops are reluctant to accept out-of-state checks, so if your credit cards fall short, you'll need to stop at a bank for some cash.

With the exception of major stores and mall shops, it's pretty standard for retailers to close at 5:00 or 6:00 P.M., and often you'll find a store you want to visit closes on Sundays. Also note that many of our hardware stores and other practical-goods-type places usually have a limited stock of merchandise on hand and normally special-order items for customers. This can make buying stuff frustrating if you are used to immediate gratification. Aggressive retailing is not what we're known for here.

All the Central Oregon towns, except perhaps La Pine, have enough commercial development to keep their residents largely independent of Bend—except for major purchases like cars. Bend, Sisters, and Sunriver have downtown areas that offer superb recreational shopping on foot. Bend also has a couple of indoor malls that make for comfortable all-season shopping, a very popular factory outlet mall, and miles and miles of commercial development where you can find just about everything that a big city has to offer. Redmond is great for antiques shopping and outfitting our cowboys and cowgirls. Prineville seems to have more than its share of good Western wear as well, and Madras makes a fun stop for a taste of Hispanic culture while en route north.

Parking—a major problem in many tourist destinations—is generally plentiful and free throughout Central Oregon. We've yet to see a parking garage.

We break down our Shopping chapter into the following major categories: downtown shopping districts and malls, bookstores, antiques (and, in some areas, gift shops), Western and ranch outfitters, and specialty food shops. Each town is listed below with its specialties. Galleries that sell works by local and regional artists are covered in our The Arts chapter. Outdoor sports stores can be found in the recreational chapter that relates to each sport.

Bend

In all of Central Oregon, Bend has the most to offer in terms of shopping, be it for the tourist or the local resident. The downtown area has a dense concentration of boutiques and gift shops, and it is perfect for a day of recreational shopping. The two indoor malls, Bend River Mall and Mountain View Mall, offer year-round comfort while strolling from shop to shop. At the south end of town is Prime Outlets—Bend, with more than 25 outlet stores.

U.S. Highway 97, the main north-south route through town, has about 5 miles of commercial development, with everything from car dealers and RV supplies to antiques dealers. Development is spreading eastward along U.S. Highway 20, where Costco used to be the only destination. There are three Albertson's Food Centers, two Safeway Food & Drug Stores, and a somewhat upscale Fred Meyer with good fish, among many other things, at the south end of town. Wal-Mart, Target, and ShopKO on U.S. 97 have really changed the nature of retailing in Central Oregon by offering discount prices and long, consumer-friendly hours. We used to shop in mom-and-pop hardware, grocery, and clothing stores; now we all seem to head to the big all-in-one places.

Shopping Districts and Malls

Downtown Bend

Downtown Bend is comprised of two main north-south streets. Bond Street is to the east and is one-way heading north. Wall Street is to the west and is one-way heading south. You can remember which is which if you can remember that "Bond is before Wall, and Wall is West."

Between these main arteries are two cross streets named after states: Minnesota and Oregon Avenues. Bond and Wall are capped off at the north end by Greenwood Avenue (which becomes U.S. 20) and by Franklin Avenue at the south end.

Park anywhere you can find a spot on Bond, Wall, Minnesota, or Oregon—it's all free. Failing that, try the public parking lot at the southwest end of town off Franklin Avenue by Drake Park.

Since there is no right or wrong way to circumnavigate the downtown area, we'll take the shops street by street from one end to the other. Most of the shops are on Wall Street; Bond Street has a lot of restaurants. We'll start at the north end of Wall Street and follow the traffic south.

Wall Street

Bringing a bit of the Far East to Central Oregon is Byzantine, purveyors of hand-painted Oriental Rugs, including new and antique. Next in line is Azila Nora, chock-full of gifts and antiques. Sportsvisionbend caters to the "socially unusual" (young) crowd, with very trendy, active beachwear and sportswear. Hanging out at Sportsvisionbend is a girl-guy thing and fits in nicely when combined with frequent visits to Goody's soda fountain across the street.

Across the street is Ranch Records, selling new and used CDs, records, and tapes. Leapin' Lizards Toy Company is a popular destination for kids. We liked the stars on the ceiling as well as the toys. A few doors down from Leapin' is Roberts on Wall Street, a very traditional men's and women's apparel store that dates

Local shops peddle a variety of wares. PHOTO: JIM YUSKAVITCH

from the 1930s. "Definitely Bend" is the description used for the style of women's wear at the Blue Teal Clothing Company; that apparently means sort of artsy, with natural fibers and colors. They also have a small selection of yuppie-esque natural furniture and accessories. If you brought Fido along, don't miss Painted Pony Trading Post, where they'll treat your pooch to a complimentary dog biscuit while you check out the exciting and fashionable Western home decor.

Local Joe claims its very casual khaki and denim clothing is guaranteed to fit. Next door is the elegant Donner Flower Shop, which, besides flowers, offers gifts of crystal and wax and an interesting metalware from Santa Fe called Namb.

At the Outback Bookstore (see the Bookstores section of this chapter) and Sara Bella you can pick up custom outdoor wear as well as books.

Cachet is an upscale boutique specializing in designer ladies' shoes. Next door, Designers Fine Jewelry is more like a place you'd expect to find in San Francisco, with expensive and exclusive Baccarat and Lalique crystal as well as fine jewelry.

On the east side of Wall Street, Paper Jazz presents a plethora of unusual wrapping papers by the sheet, along with nice cards and small gifts. While you may not think of Bend as beachfront property, you can buy beachwear at At The Beach, which makes sense for Bendites who are planning on going to some tropical locale for a vacation. Soleil Riviere is an aesthetic sort of shop offering Oregon-style home decor such as juniper beds, fine gifts, and original artworks. Next door, you can buy fine children's clothes at Topolino.

We time-warp back a couple decades as we enter Birkenstock of Bend, with about 50 styles of Birks and other comfy, if not too stylish, footwear and robust-looking socks. Next door is Dotson's Photo Center, a traditional camera store that sells film and used cameras, and processes photos. Phoebe's Fine Jewelry, where you can find an unusual selection of custom jewelry made by local artisans, shares a space with Dotson's.

Cross Wall Street and you arrive at the shores of Christmas by the Pond, a place with lots of gifts, including Gund stuffed animals. Running shoes and apparel meet hiking boots at the Foot Zone. Nearby is MicroSphere Computers, where you can pick up a new computer and finally get with the Web thing. If you don't like what they have in stock, they'll custom-build a system for you.

Time for a break: Try an old-fashioned espresso drink at Tuffy's Coffee & Company, Bend's oldest coffeehouse. (Read more about TC&C in this chapter's "Specialty Food Stores" section.)

Nearing the end of Wall Street is Ponderfusion, which means "to think deep thoughts." You will find an interesting and eclectic selection of ethnic gifts designed to inspire contemplation. Cross Wall Street at the intersection of Franklin Avenue, and you'll come to Starbucks, right on the northeast corner.

Franklin Avenue

Unless you stop in at Starbucks for an espresso and pastry, you can walk around the corner and discover a shop that isn't often noticed from the car—Oztralia, a shop full of clothing, hats, gifts, and sundry memorabilia from Down Under.

Cross Franklin Avenue to arrive at Redpoint Climbers Supply, where you can purchase everything you'll need to scale the steepest cliffs, from ropes to harnesses.

Minnesota Avenue

On the 1-block section of Minnesota Avenue, you'll find Karen Bandy Design Jeweler; she makes unique jewelry with gold and precious stones. Drop in if you have something special in mind. Next door is The Book Barn, which is listed in our Bookstores section. A couple of doors down, pop culture comes alive at Pegasus Books, which is really more comic books and sports cards than book-books.

Across the street is Periwinkle, where you can pick up gifts, jewelry, and furniture to name just a sampling.

Oregon Avenue

Tucked into a tiny corner of Oregon Avenue is Romantique, the place in town for lacy dresses for prom night, dreamy lingerie, wedding gowns, and mother-of-the-bride dresses.

Bond Avenue

Starting at Franklin Avenue and heading north with the flow of the traffic, you'll first come to Pfundamentals, with colorful gifts for your home and garden. Just up the street is James Barnett Antiques Books & Collectibles and the Bend Bungalo with its offerings of Craftsman furnishings. On the other side of the street, you'll find ladies shoes and lingerie at Steppin' Up, and next door, clothes for women and teens at Finders-Keepers. You can also spend some quality time looking over the quality furniture at Mucho Gust. Next is Bend Mapping and Blueprint, which sells maps and offers aerial photographs.

The Old Mill District
15 Southwest Colorado Avenue, Suite A
(541) 330–5000

Opened in 2001, The Old Mill District is a sprawling complex of art galleries, retail shops, professional offices, and other business concerns located on the west side of town along the Deschutes River. It's called The Old Mill District because it has been built on the area formerly occupied by Bend's historic lumber mills that hark back to Central Oregon's days as one of the country's biggest timber producers (see the History chapter).

While businesses are still moving into the district, The Shops at The Old Mill District have opened. Built to mimic the downtown area of a small town, its anchor stores include such familiar names as The Gap, Eddie Bauer, and Banana Republic. Smaller shops offering women's clothing

> **Insiders' Tip**
> In Bend, try to do your shopping in the morning. Traffic is worse in the afternoon, and worst of all on Friday and Saturday.

include Chico's, Timbuktu Station, and Victoria's Secret. Sun Pac has clothing for both women and youth. At Bath & Body Works you'll find a wide selection of potions and lotions, while the Candle Shop will regale you with its wonderful collection of candles, accessories, and gifts.

If you're looking to spiff your home up a bit, or trying for a new look, The Hen's Tooth offers lots of possibilities for lovers of country style, while The Compleat Bed & Breakfast has a great assortment of elegant items from pillows to nightshirts, all designed to add the look and feel of the B&B experience to your own home.

For culture, you'll find the Deschutes Gallery with its fine collection of Northwest Indian art and the "primitive" paintings of Jennifer Lake Miller at the gallery of the same name.

You can also grab a bite to eat at the Red Robin restaurant as well as take in a hit movie at the adjacent Old Mill 10 theaters.

Prime Outlets—Bend
61336 South Highway 97
(541) 382-4512

At the south end of Bend, this was one of the first outlet malls in Oregon. Discounted merchandise together with no sales tax is a primo combination, and this has been a very popular tourist destination. The mall, which is configured more like an outdoor shopping center with contiguous shops, a covered walkway in front, and acres of free parking, is open Monday through Saturday from 9:30 A.M. to 8:00 P.M., and on Sunday from 11:00 A.M. to 6:00 P.M.

If you are looking for clothing, the funniest T-shirts around are at Big Dog Sportswear, along with a bunch of other Big Dog attire and accessories. (We buy cute baby gifts here.) The huge Levi's Outlet By Most offers casual clothing, more for men than women. The North Face, Norm Thompson, Eddie Bauer, Columbia Sportswear, and L. L. Bean reveal the mall's current trend toward active, outdoorsy lifestyles. Spiff up your image with tennis shirts and shorts with Izod's alligator logo, or go one more notch up the business dress ladder with Van Heusen dress shirts. The store also has some casual wear for men.

Tools & More! will keep home-fix-it types busy for a while. L'eggs/Hanes/Bali/Playtex will take care of ladies' unmentionables. The mail-order company, Coldwater Creek, brings its Colorado-casual women's clothes to Bend.

Look down now and think about your feet. Would hiking boots from Danner fill the bill? Or how about something comfortable from the Bass Factory Outlet, or a pair of athletic shoes from the Nike outlet? Factory Brand Shoes will probably have something you like if the other places do not.

Girls can pick up some cute hair doo-dads at Claire's Accessories, and you can get a wallet for Dad from Wallet Works. Sunglass Hut International will provide the shades, and Prestige Fragrance and Cosmetics can make you look and smell your best.

The Dansk Factory Outlet always seems to have some pretty kitchen item we can't live without. The Kitchen Collection and Corning/Revere Factory Stores have lots more housewares and home decor items to choose from. Welcome Home, a national chain, raises gifts for the home to new heights with lots of scented candles and potpourri, framed pictures, table linens, and cute teddy bears. Another great place for gifts is Harry & David, where you can treat someone special (including yourself) to jams, candies, nuts, and other tasty morsels.

And you can buy everything you need for your next bash at the Paper factory, a party-accessories store. When you need a baby gift, stop at Carter's, a children's-wear specialist. And, last but not least, take home a few chocolates from the Rocky Mountain Chocolate Factory.

Bend River Mall
3188 North U.S. Highway 97
(541) 388-3644

This is a pleasant indoor mall with about 40 shops and two department stores. It's open Monday through Friday from 10:00 A.M. to 9:00 P.M., Saturday from 10:00 A.M. to 7:00 P.M., and from 11:00 A.M. to 6:00 P.M. on Sunday. The mall consists of one large building with interior mall shops, and several separate buildings housing a range of restaurants—from pizza to steaks to a fine-dining fish house.

The Bon Marche, one of the main anchor stores, is probably Central Oregon's nicest department store. Besides carrying a full line of fine apparel and accessories for men, women, and children, the Bon also has shoes, housewares, crystal and china, bed and bath linens and towels, luggage, perfumes, and cosmetics. Down the hall from the main department store is a satellite store called The Cube, which has junior clothing sizes for girls (and appropriate Muzak) while a second, called "Women's World," offers coats, dresses, and intimate apparel. A third has a great selection of childrens' clothes.

The second anchor, Sears, is at the other end of the mall. This is a scaled-down version of a big-city Sears, with a little of most everything. If they don't have something you need at this store, they will order it for you from another. They have a pretty good selection in the Craftsman tool department—we know from experience!

Next to The Bon Marche is RJ Classics home furnishings.

Walking along you'll come to The Oregon Store, a very popular place for tourists looking for better-quality souvenirs. Most everything sold here is made in Oregon, except the T-shirts and mugs, which are made elsewhere but later embroidered or decorated in Oregon. You can choose from marionberry jams, myrtle-wood carvings, and a good selection of Pendleton blankets that range from $50 to $200.

Diversions offers a nice array of gifts while Willoughby's Salon and Cosmetics is a boutique devoted to beauty products, and it also has a hair salon.

Two fine jewelers cover the next two corner locations: Zales The Diamond Store and Kay Jewelers, both chains offering nice selections of rings, earrings, diamonds, necklaces, and watches in moderate price ranges. (Kay was formerly Weisfield Jewelers.) Close by is Saxon's Fine Jewelers & Designers, with more moderately priced jewelry.

Down the way is Luv's Hallmark Shop, with the usual nice collection of cards and gifts.

Fun N Games is the big hangout for video game aces, where they buy, rent, and sell video games and gaming systems. Next door is the Candy Shoppe 2, where they make their own fudge. (Candy Shoppe 1, in the Mountain View Mall, offers more sweet stuff.) Vista Optical fits people with glasses at very reasonable prices, and in an island booth a United States Cellular Wireless Communications dealer is ready to set you up with one of those popular cell phones.

Kits Cameras is a fairly traditional camera store with the addition of one-hour photo processing. Across the way, The Brass Oak offers a wide selection of moderately priced oak furniture and soft, oversized couches.

Image Express is a portrait studio. You will need an appointment, but once you get your foot in the door your prints are done in one hour for $35 (it's more for extras). The Area Rug Connection has a wide selection of rugs, from genuine Navajos to wool and silk imports from Persia and 12 other countries. This shop, with its sound-deadening textiles, offers a moment of utter quiet if you want a break. Check our Bookstore section for more information on the mall's Waldenbooks location.

Corral West Ranchwear offers moderately priced Western apparel, hats, and boots. Folks accustomed to the higher prices of other stores find this relaxed place to be a nice change of pace. Corral West carries the main brands in boots and hats, like Justin and Ariat, Stetson and Resistol, and they also custom-shape hats for free.

Insiders' Tip

Be sure to bring MasterCard or Visa, or load up on traveler's checks. Don't rely on an American Express card alone, as many places in Central Oregon don't accept it.

The Forum Shopping Center
U.S. Highway 20 at 27th Street

The Forum Shopping Center is a newer center that features a large Safeway Food and Drug and Costco Wholesale as its major anchors. Other national chains in the same center include Pier 1 Imports, which specializes in attractive, imported home decor, dishes, and glassware; Office Max, a big office-supply superstore; Linens 'N Things, a linens and towels superstore; and Barnes & Noble Booksellers (see our "Bookstores" section).

Facing U.S. 20 are several smaller shops. Scrap-A-Doodle has everything you need for your scrapbook project; if you want to bring your own stuff in, you can use their workshop for $1.00 per hour. Next door, Imagine That has lots of artsy rubber stamps, and the store hosts workshops on making cards with different imprints. The Bonaventure Travel Store is a travel agency that went retail. In addition to selling airline tickets, it has a nice selection of travel luggage and accessories, a travel video rental library, maps from all over, and a small selection of guidebooks. VOS computers is a computer and technology store, and Baby Phases has lots of baby items from clothing to cribs.

Mountain View Mall
U.S. Highway 20 and U.S. Highway 97
(541) 388–1495

This is an older indoor mall at the Y formed at the north end of Bend by the intersection of two of the area's major highways. It has recently undergone quite a bit of renovation and boasts a good selection of shops attracting considerable retail traffic.

Outside you can easily see the main anchor tenants: Ross Dress for Less; The Emporium, an old-fashioned department store with nice apparel for the whole family; JCPenney, which is a bit smaller than the average JCPenney store; and G.I. Joe's, a large department store specializing in auto accessories and sporting goods. To the north is a Target, part of the national discount variety chain.

Inside the mall is Maurices, a women's clothing store. Zimm's Hallmark Shop is like most Hallmark shops—a wide variety of greeting cards and gifts. In the center of an aisle is Shamrock Jewelry, with inexpensive jewelry for the whole family.

BJ's Shoes and Apparel has a great selection of sporty clothes and footwear for the younger, active set. The name of the next store, H20 Sportswear, says it all—it offers beachwear for men and women.

Harry Ritchies Jewelers has beautiful displays of gold and diamonds.

Another interesting store is the Indian Dreams Trading Post. At first glance you might think you were seeing a bunch of reproductions made in Taiwan, but go in and take a closer look. Most of the Native American art and jewelry here is made by American Indian tribes. They have rugs in all price ranges as well as beads that you can string yourself.

The Shutterbug sells film and does one-hour processing. There's another Willoughby's Salon and Cosmetics store at this mall. Next door to Willoughby's is Foot Locker, with an extensive line of athletic shoes including Nike and Reebok. The staff here dresses in those striped, referee shirts.

Sam Goody has popular CDs and audiotapes. If you are in the mood for good old-fashioned romance, pick up something feminine to wear or decorate your home with at The Hen's Tooth. The Candy Shoppe makes a half-dozen varieties of homemade fudge and sells other candies in bulk.

Next to a small food court with six fast-food vendors is The Oregon Store, another gift shop where most things are made in Oregon. Hazelnuts are a popular gift here, along with other food items and myrtle-wood products. Bare Elegance, as its name implies, sells lingerie. The General Nutrition Center, better known as GNC, is a resource for vitamins and medicinals. Next is another location for the Pegasus Books, which, like the store in downtown Bend, sells pop culture stuff, comic books, sports cards, etc. Nearby is the Space Balls Arcade.

Inexpensive shoe fashions can be found at Payless Shoe Source. In the center of the aisle is West Coast Wireless, a cell-phone dealer (they're going to get you signed up one of these days, if they haven't already). Radio Shack is the last shop next to G.I. Joe's.

Antiques and Gift Shops

There are three primary areas in Bend for antiques. The main location is downtown Bend, where you can walk to a half-dozen or so shops that actually sell antiques as well as crafts. At the southern end of the commercial development along U.S. 97 is a small cluster of four antiques places, and at the north end (near the Bend River Mall) are a couple more.

Although we are amateurs when it comes to prices, it appeared that the vendors were pretty savvy about what each item was worth. You'll really have to hunt for a bargain, but you won't have to look far to find a lot of nice things.

Azila Nora
1002 Northwest Wall Street
(541) 389-6552

This little shop is in a house that's rather by itself on Newport Avenue. It offers a refreshingly different selection of decorative and amusing artsy gifts. Brightly colored windsocks, pillows in the shape of a huge bunch of grapes, colorful African pottery, and twisted-glass vases are a small, random sampling of what you may find. They are open Monday through Saturday from 10:00 A.M. to 6:00 P.M. and Sunday noon to 4:00 P.M.

Enchantments Fine Antiques
1002 Northwest Bond Street
(541) 388-7324

An exceptionally elegant shop, Enchantments specializes in European and Victorian furniture, crystal, and chinoiserie. It is open Monday through Saturday.

The Farm Antiques
961 Brooks Street
(541) 385-6022

Tucked back from the street in downtown Bend, next to the Pine Tavern Restaurant, is a marvelous little c. 1923 cottage that sits next to the Deschutes River. Inside is an excellent collection of early 1900s furniture and memorabilia, and even a room

celebrating the 1950s and '60s. Look for this hideaway Monday through Saturday.

Garden Gate Antiques
24 Northwest Greenwood Avenue
(541) 317-5650

Here's a small shop with some pretty antique clothing and other eclectic collectibles. Garden Gate is open Monday through Saturday.

Glenroe Antiques
841 Northwest Bond Street
(541) 385-8858

This small dealer of curiosities and keepsakes shares a space with James Barnett (see subsequent listing in this section) and is open Monday through Saturday.

Iron Horse
210 Northwest Congress Street
(541) 382-5175

Housed in a 4,000-square-foot building that was once an old market, the Iron Horse specializes in old English furniture and household items including table linens, armoires, and lead-glass mirrors. They are open Monday through Saturday.

James Barnett Antiques
848 Northwest Bond Street
(541) 330-0770

"Everything from A to Z" is the answer we got when we asked for the specialty of the house here. We noticed old fly rods, books, and Victorian furniture—all part of a large assortment of antiques. The shop is open Monday through Saturday.

Trivia Antiques
106 Northwest Minnesota Avenue
(541) 389-4166, (800) 898-4166

Do the places with the toll-free phone numbers do more business because they have toll-free numbers, or do they have toll-free numbers because they are doing more business? Anyway, this is a very busy shop, crowded with glassware and other antique memorabilia. The two owners, Karen and Wendy, teach a class on appraising antiques at the Central Oregon Community College. The shop is open daily at the corner of Bond Street in downtown Bend.

Bookstores

In addition to having some excellent bookstores, Central Oregon has discount department stores (such as Wal-Mart and Target) that offer good selections of paperback books. For late-night shopping, try Barnes & Noble Booksellers.

Barnes & Noble Booksellers
2690 Northeast U.S. Highway 20
(541) 318-7242

The tiny listing in the Yellow Pages belies the mammoth size of this national chain outlet that opened in 1997. It has by far the most extensive selection of general-interest books in Central Oregon as well as a cafe, book readings, and other events. Barnes & Noble, near Costco at 27th Street, is open until 11:00 P.M. daily.

The Book Barn
135 Northwest Minnesota Avenue
(541) 389-4589

Established in 1973, The Book Barn is an institution in Bend and is still going strong. Book lovers tend to use it as a meeting place, and often as a place to drop off books to be picked up by a literary friend. The store sells new, general-interest books as well as CDs, books on tape, calendars, and cards. It's closed on Sunday. Check out the store's very informative newsletter, *Book Barn Splinters*.

The Open Book
155 Northeast Greenwood Avenue
(541) 388-3249

If you drive by too fast you'll miss this great little bookstore that sits back across from Miller Lumber. It's actually a lot bigger than it looks from the front. The Open Book has thousands of used paperbacks and hardcover books, all in nice condition, and the shop recently started selling used CDs. The staff will keep your name on a waiting list if you are collecting certain titles, and they'll give you store credit if you bring in your old books. Henry, the book dog, will welcome you Monday through Friday; if you stop by on Saturday or Sunday you can say hello to a couple of golden retrievers.

The Outback Children's Bookstore
916 Northwest Wall Street
(541) 318-8258

Besides having an excellent selection of children's books, The Outback offers fun

Book lovers can spend hours browsing in our bookstores. PHOTO: JIM YUSKAVITCH

events like Easter egg hunts; live music, storytelling; and visits by authors, illustrators, and magicians. Pick up a frequent buyer card, and bring your kids Monday through Saturday.

Paperback Exchange
167 Northwest Greenwood Avenue
(541) 382–7144

Choose from approximately 50,000 used books at the Exchange. Prices are about half the price they were when they were new, and the store will take in trades. It's open Monday through Saturday.

Waldenbooks
Bend River Mall, 3188 North U.S. Highway 97
(541) 388–4655

A small but well-stocked outlet of the national chain, this Waldenbooks offers 10 percent off to members of its Preferred Reader Club. It is open daily with the same hours as the rest of the mall stores (see previous listing for Bend River Mall).

Specialty Food Stores

Chelsea Lane Wine & Gifts
61300 South U.S. Highway 97
(541) 385–5648

Insiders' Tip

Frequent-buyer discount cards, where you get a hole punched or a rubber stamp toward a free item each time you visit a store, are very popular in Central Oregon at places that sell espresso, video rentals, photo processing, baked goods, etc. Be sure to ask about them.

Chelsea Lane offers the largest and finest selection of regional and imported wines in Central Oregon. On Saturday afternoons, the shop offers free tastings. Other times, there are several bottles uncorked, with wine for sale by the glass. Jim and Raissa are quite knowledgeable about their wines and can help you with your selections from Monday through Saturday.

Di Lusso Baking
1135 Northwest Gavelston Avenue
(541) 383–8155

Big city–quality breads have arrived in Bend at last! Di Lusso's crusty, chewy breads will make you think of the Italian countryside whether you've been there or not. The ciabatta loaf or rolls are divine, and so is the rosemary bread. The desserts are delightful, too (and a bit pricey), and Di Lusso serves espresso at its three small tables. Stop by Monday through Saturday, and don't forget your frequent buyer punch card.

Farmer John's Produce
64678 Cook Avenue, Bend (just north of the intersection of U.S. Highway 20 in downtown Tumalo)
(541) 389–2968

This charming produce shop opened in summer 1998, much to the joy of Renee and John's loyal customers in Tumalo (who recalled the days when they used to have summer produce stands). Farmer John's specializes in produce that's as fresh as possible. During summer they get produce from lots of local friends who have organic gardens, and they also travel to Oregon's Willamette Valley for the berries and veggies that can't grow in Central Oregon. The rest of the year you'll find good quality stuff (organic and non) from California. Along with veggies, Farmer John's sells annuals in the summer, plus jams, honeys, olive oils, and holiday items (Christmas wreathes and the like). The store is open Monday through Saturday. (See our Other Communities chapter for more on the Tumalo neighborhood.)

Great Harvest Bread Co.
835 Northwest Bond Street
(541) 389–2888

By 10:00 A.M. they've pretty much finished baking the morning's special breads at Great Harvest, and they have the daily tasting tray all ready to go. They say smart folks drop by at lunch time and taste their way through lunch. Favorite varieties include the nutty tasting white bread, a sweet whole-wheat bread, and big cinnamon rolls. The daily specials can be as exotic as Spinach Feta or Rye Bread. It's all made, for the most part, with organic flours, unrefined sugar, and no preservatives. Other specials include some hefty breakfast pastries and muffins, baked Monday through Saturday.

McGrath's Fish House
3118 North U.S. Highway 97
(541) 388-4555

You might not think of this seafood restaurant as a place to buy fresh fish, but they regularly offer raw fresh salmon, halibut, shrimp, clams, and mussels for folks to take home and cook themselves. McGrath's is open daily (see our Restaurants chapter).

Newport Avenue Market
1121 Northwest Newport Avenue
(541) 382-3940

This upscale market rates a special mention because of the unusual selection of high-end and healthy foods like fresh mozzarella, natural meats (including Oregon Country Beef), Di Cecco pasta, and an excellent produce section. If you are from the big city and miss home, visit Newport Avenue Market. It is open daily until 8:30 P.M.

Royal Blend Coffee House
1075 Northwest Newport Avenue
(541) 383-0873
601 Northeast First Street
(541) 382-6349
547 Northeast Bellvue Drive, Crossroads Plaza Shopping Center
(541) 330-1642

All three locations serve house-roasted coffees and fresh pastries, and all sell excellent loose coffee beans. The stores are open Monday through Saturday (the Newport Avenue shop is also open Sunday) and usually close by 5:00 P.M. or so.

Starbucks Coffee Co.
812 Northwest Wall Street
(541) 382-9438
61535 South U.S. Highway 97
(541) 330-1998

The giant coffee roaster from Seattle has arrived in Bend, bringing pastries, excellent coffee beans, and lots of small tables with them. Both locations have tables outside—excellent for people-watching—and they are open daily.

Tuffy's Coffee & Company
835 Northwest Wall Street
(541) 389-6464

This was Bend's first coffeehouse, offering fresh-roasted coffee since 1975. For years Tuffy's was the second-largest seller of coffee beans in the state of Oregon. When they got their first espresso machine in 1982, they used to pour the cold milk into the espresso and steam everything together, instead of doing it separately like it is normally prepared today. They still serve espresso this way; it's called an Old Fashioned. The new owner, Tami Stayner, was raised in Bend and can tell you lots of great stories. Tuffy's is open seven days a week.

The Village Baker
1470 Southwest Knoll Avenue
(541) 318-1054

Bend's newest bakery brings fabulous pastries, including the best rugulah in Central Oregon. The mild, San Francisco–style sourdough bread is also excellent, especially when paired with the small but superb selection of imported cheeses and olives. Aaah, we're really happy now! Visit The Village Baker any day except Sunday. Look for them 1 block west of Century Boulevard behind John Dough's Pizza.

Western Wear, Tack, and Ranch Supplies

Custom Equine
64657 Bruce Avenue
(541) 389-2079

Custom Equine's collection of mostly English (plus a few Western) saddles, tack,

Unique to Oregon

So what can you take home that really celebrates Central Oregon besides a T-shirt with Mount Bachelor on it?

Oregon really is a unique and complex state . . . Perhaps we should even call it a state of mind. It's a place where family values run deep and wide without a lot of talk about one religion or the other. We are a conservative logging-, fishing-, and ranching-based culture that spawned the first bottle bill and the first bill supporting an individual's right to die. We smile readily at strangers, but ostentatious spending raises a polite eyebrow. We are our trees, our mountains and waterways, our pioneer history, and the fruits of our labor. And we love living where we do.

What follows is a rundown of terrific products that are unique to our state. These items are available throughout Central Oregon, and all (in one form or another) make great gifts or keepsakes.

For starters, why not take home a piece of Oregon's history? In the late 1800s, sheep ranchers, who had originally settled in western Oregon because of the climate's similarity to that of Scotland, had moved east onto the rangelands of Central and Eastern Oregon. In Pendleton, a rail town on the Columbia River, a plant was established to process the wool from these flocks. It grew from a seasonal business to a year-round enterprise once the weaving of blankets was added, and it was named Pendleton Woolen Mills.

The blankets were at first very simple in design and brightly colored. Later, Jacquard technology was added, enabling zigzags and other patterns. The blankets appealed to the pioneers, who had very little color in their lives, but more significantly they appealed to the Native Americans, who bought the blankets to wear as clothing. They came to be called Indian blankets.

In 1910 the company was purchased by the Bishop family, originally from Salem, Oregon. They immediately hired a textile designer, an Englishman named Joe Rownsley, who came to Eastern Oregon and lived with the Nez Perce nation in order to understand their art. The designs he produced were not Indian designs, but rather his own interpretations of them. They did, however, adhere to Native American rules of design, which included making the pattern extend to the very edge of the blanket so that the owner's spirit would not get trapped in his blanket. It must have been quite a unique (and a Western) phenomenon in the United States to have a business like Pendleton that showed so much respect for its Native American market to make such a serious investment in understanding it and accommodating it. That's especially true in light of the fact that this part of the market involved a minority group who were often looked down on and treated disrespectfully by whites.

Blankets were made for babies and small children, there were saddle blankets and bed blankets, and still others for women to wear as shawls. They became a standard of value for trading among the Indians and were used for ceremonial purposes. Pendleton designed blankets to commemorate famous people—one of the first was named after Chief Joseph. Pendleton went on to create special designs to commemorate other tribes and Western landmarks, as well as the national parks. Northwest blankets, besides the Chief Joseph (which is so popular they still make the pattern in 21 different colors), include the Beaver State (Oregon's nickname), the Harding (which was presented by the Indians to Mrs. Harding during President Warren G. Harding's visit to the area in 1923), Crater Lake, the Yakama, and the Chief Eagle, dedicated in 1976 to the memory of Chief Seelatse of the Yakama Nation.

In 1929 the love of bright colors inspired the production of a line of wool shirts, and this led to the design and production of other apparel, including a women's line that started in 1949. Today Pendleton is under its fifth generation of family management. Pendleton blankets are the only blankets authorized to be called "authentic Indian blankets."

Another raw material that gave inspiration to Oregon artisans is juniper wood. Juniper is indigenous to the High Desert and has long been considered by the timber industry to be junk wood. The Bureau of Land Management systematically allows the cutting of juniper trees for firewood because, like a weed, the juniper uses too much water and inhibits the growth of wild grasses that are needed for grazing purposes.

Local artisans have discovered that the slow-growing juniper produces a very hard wood, and its knots and gnarly shapes have a unique beauty. It is made into log furniture with a strong, pioneer flavor. Juniper-wood furniture is a grassroots phenomenon that is gaining in popularity; you will find it displayed for sale along U.S. Highway 97 between Bend and Redmond as well as in Sisters.

Of a more established nature is the myrtle-wood industry. American myrtle wood is unique in the world and is found along the coast in a 90-square-mile area that mostly lies in southwestern Oregon. Myrtle wood is also a very hard wood—20 percent harder than rock maple. The trees must be at least 150 years old to be big enough in diameter to be commercially useful. Much of the available wood comes to factories from areas that are being cleared for houses or rescued from mudslides, and some is harvested from forests. Once a myrtle tree is cut, it reproduces itself from its stump.

The myrtle is a tree with twists and gnarls, making it very appropriate for decorative products with its beautiful burls, tiger-stripe, fiddleback, quilt, and inkline grain patterns. Carbide-steel blades are used to turn the wood, special seasoning techniques are used to prevent it from cracking in the drying process, and the finish is

A Pendleton blanket's design extends all the way to the edge so that the owner's spirit does not get trapped in the blanket. PHOTO: LESLIE COLE

hand-rubbed oil. The results are a wide range of gift items, from inexpensive souvenirs to substantial art pieces. Items include beautiful bowls, candlestick holders, boxes, napkin rings, keychains, trays, clocks, and sometimes even tables.

No celebration of Oregon could be made without the inclusion of our favorite berry: the marionberry. The marionberry, or marion blackberry as it was originally named, was developed in 1956 in a joint effort between the United States Department of Agriculture and the Oregon Agricultural Experiment Station in Corvallis. It was named after Marion County, the western Oregon locale where it was tested.

A cultivar of the native Oregon blackberry plus other blackberry strains, the marionberry is a delicate, juicy blackberry that melts in your mouth with a rich, sweet blackberry flavor. Marionberries are so popular that you will find them sold as jams, jellies, and sauces all over Central Oregon. Summer is not truly summer until July, when the marionberries are in season. If you are here during midsummer, be sure to try some of our restaurants' specialties using fresh marionberries.

Here's a recipe for a marionberry creation that keeps hungry patrons returning again and again to a certain local brewpub and restaurant.

Deschutes Brewery Marionberry Cobbler

For berry filling:
4 pints fresh marionberries
1½ cups sugar
1 tbsp. fresh lemon juice
½ cup corn starch (mix with ¼ cup cold water)

For cobbler topping:
1 cup sugar
3 tbsp. butter
1 cup flour
1 tsp. baking powder
½ tsp. salt
½ cup milk

Cook the berries with the sugar and lemon juice. Add corn starch to thicken. Place in a 6-ounce ceramic baking dish and set aside.

Cream the butter and sugar for the topping in a small mixer until fluffy. Combine the dry ingredients, add milk, and combine butter mixture until smooth.

Apply the topping with a pastry bag. Bake at 350 degrees for 20 minutes or until golden brown. Garnish with a scoop of vanilla ice cream. Makes six servings.

(Recipe courtesy of the Deschutes Brewery & Public House in Bend. See our Restaurants chapter to find out more about this eatery.)

and horse-care products. Trailers and tack are both open for sales from Tuesday through Saturday.

The Feed Sack
The Stirrup Cup
926 Northeast Greenwood Avenue
(541) 389–1318 (Feed Sack)
(541) 388–1101 (Stirrup Cup)

These two companies are owned by the same folks and share one large space on Northeast Greenwood at 10th Street. The Feed Sack sells dog and cat food and supplies. The Stirrup Cup offers English saddles plus women's and children's English riding apparel. The shops are open Monday through Saturday.

J. & K. Urbach Custom Boots and Saddlery
2075 East U.S. Highway 20
(541) 385-4983

John, the dad, makes custom boots; Kevin, the son, makes saddles. In their shop, which is just west of Costco, are displayed silver spurs, hats, belt buckles and conchos, and other leather and silver gifts. Urbach is open Monday through Saturday. If you are interested in custom leather work, give them a call.

Mountain Country Farm and Garden
740 Northeast First Street
(541) 382-3511

Formerly Bend Farm & Garden Supply, this establishment has been providing Bend pet foods and supplies, livestock and horse supplies, animal health products, hay and straw, and garden supplies since 1948. Stop by Monday through Saturday until 5:30 P.M.

Spotted Mule Saddlery & Westernwear
2221 Northeast Third Street
(541) 389-9144, (800) 871-9144

The Spotted Mule's grand store is a popular tourist stop. Inside you'll find a huge selection of fancy Western apparel for men, women, and children, plus boots, cowboy hats, silver jewelry, and gifts. If you don't see a hat you like, they will shape one for you. The selection of Western and English saddles and tack is extensive; this is definitely a horse lover's dream come true. Prices do tend to run on the spendy side.

Sisters/Camp Sherman Area

The charming little town of Sisters draws a big crowd on summer days as well as on sunny weekends during the winter and spring holidays. The big attraction is strolling along the Old West–style boardwalks and admiring the storefronts while exploring the many small shops and boutiques that cater to the tourist crowd.

The town of Sisters arose in the 1880s when folks stopped here for a rest while traveling between Bend and the Willamette Valley along the Old Santiam Wagon Road, which went through what is now downtown. The town got its name from the beautiful view of the Three Sisters mountains that can be glimpsed between the ponderosa pine trees.

Although most of the town looks as though it has been around since 1800-and-something, Sisters' oldest building is the Hotel Sisters, which was built in 1917. Many of the other buildings date from the mid-to-late-1900s, but they were built or remodeled in the style of the late 19th century, per city-zoning ordinances. It might seem that allowing a local government to legislate a look of antiquity sounds like a recipe for disaster (or maybe a business plan for Disneyland), but the results have been quite successful. Sisters is a pleasant community and a wonderful destination for a day of strolling and shopping.

U.S. Highway 20 forms the main thoroughfare through town, where it's called Cascade Street. Watch the posted speed limits as you approach Sisters, as U.S. 20 at the east and west ends of town are kept under close scrutiny by the highway patrol.

Arts and crafts, gifts, and souvenirs make up the bulk of what is traded in Sisters, and most of it can be found in the 6 block section of downtown. Local residents and vacationers in RVs or condos get groceries at the small Sisters Market on Cascade Street and at Ray's Food Place, on U.S. 20 a half-mile west of downtown in the Three Winds Shopping Center. Throughout downtown plenty of small eateries do a good job of fortifying tourists with lunches, ice cream, and espresso. The Paulina Springs Book Company (see our listing in the "Bookstores" section) provides the weary with a perfect spot to snuggle up in an easy chair with a new book while the rest of their party handles the tough job of shopping.

The prime shopping area is in downtown Sisters along Cascade Street between Pine and Spruce Streets, encompassing 1 block south to Hood Street, which parallels Cascade. Pedestrian and vehicular traffic through town can be bumper-to-bumper on busy summer weekends. We suggest you head to Hood Street (where you'll find a number of nice shops as well) and leave your car in the first available spot. Except

Shopping is a popular pastime in Central Oregon. PHOTO: JIM YUSKAVITCH

for the first Saturday of the month from July through October, when there's a Saturday Market on Hood Street, traffic will be lighter here than on U.S. 20. Between Cascade and Hood, on cross streets Ash, Elm, Fir, and Spruce, are more parking slots and a few more shops.

Store hours fluctuate with the level of tourist traffic. Summer is the busiest season by far, with many shops staying open until 6:00 P.M. or later; most will be open on Sunday. (They roll up the sidewalks pretty early in Sisters....While you may not think 6:00 P.M. is particularly late, around here it is. Remember, tourists aren't the only ones who are supposed to be enjoying life in Central Oregon!) The rest of the year, expect the small shops to close around 4:00 or 5:00 P.M. and many to be closed on Sunday. If you are planning on going to Sisters for the specific purpose of visiting one shop, it would be wise to call ahead for hours. The grocery stores stay open until 11:00 P.M. year-round.

Downtown Sisters

Sisters is small enough for most folks to easily walk the whole downtown area, so don't worry too much about where you park. You will want to concentrate your explorations on Cascade Street (U.S. 20), Hood Street (which parallels Cascade one street to the south), and the short, 2-block side streets between the two. There are a few places of interest on Main Street, which is one street north of Cascade, including The Fly Fisher's Place (see our Fishing chapter). Count on shops being open from 10:00 A.M. to at least 4:00 or 5:00 P.M., Monday through Saturday.

Cascade Street

Start at the east end of Cascade Street with the Antler Arts and Chandeliers shop. The array of antler chandeliers, antler lamps and coat hooks, antler-handled Buck knives, and Native Americana is almost overwhelming. This would be the place to look if you wanted to take home a trophy-size souvenir. And it is not the place to be if you are a deer!

The Sisters Drug Company has a prescription counter in the back, but what catches most tourists' attention are the upscale gifts—the first you'll spot are the Godiva Chocolates right at the front entrance. Other big-name brands include Department 56 model villages, Fitz and

Floyd hand-painted ceramics, Boyd's Bears, and snowbabies. In the rear of the store is a section called the Cook's Nook, as well as a wine-tasting counter run by Marquam Vineyards from Molalla, Oregon. To the west of the drugstore is Common Threads, an aesthetic shop with brightly colored cotton clothing for men and women.

As you walk west, take a short detour in a sort of parking niche called The Town Square. Flanking the western row of parked cars will be three interesting shops. The Bedouin offers "ethnic and wearable art"—an eclectic assortment of exotic pieces of apparel and decor. Next door is Sundance Shoes, which sells comfortable and somewhat trendy footwear for men, women, and children. At the end of the niche is Hucklebeary's, with gifts, antiques, jams and jellies, and an outstanding collection of Boyd's Bears.

The Town Square Mall continues on the east side of the street behind Ali's. Go inside to find Scents and non-Scents, a small shop with a dozen open umbrellas (with whimsical designs like toads) hanging upside-down above your head. Back on earth you'll find scented soaps, cards, oils, and incense. Newport Kidsport has a small, upscale selection of kids' clothing in primary colors. The Sisters Gallery and Frame Shop has lots of western and religious art (see the listing in our The Arts chapter).

Back on Cascade Street, you'll come next to The Palace, a great spot for an ice-cream cone or an old-fashioned milk shake. You can peruse the collection of Hummels and other glass and china figurines while you lick your cone. At the corner of Cascade and Elm is the interesting combination of a souvenir shop and a state-licensed liquor store. It has an equally interesting name: The Gallimaufry. A bottle of Crater Lake Vodka or Cascade Mountain Gin, two premium liquors distilled by the Bendistillery in Bend, makes for a very unusual souvenir. When we say premium, we mean $19 for a fifth, but this is the sippin' stuff. Stick it in your freezer when you get home.

One door down is the Christmas Mountain Magic and Candy Bin, where Christmas happens year-round, whether your idea of Christmas is a wide selection of unusual tree ornaments or an eye-popping assortment of candies. They even have Pixy Stix, which we hadn't seen in years. Next is the $12 Store, where you will find an amazing selection of summery women's apparel and unisex T-shirts that say "Sisters" on them. None of them have price tags because everything in the store costs exactly $12.

Cross Ash Street to arrive at The Jewel, which, even if you are not in the market for some stunning custom jewelry, has an equally stunning collection of minerals that is worth a look-see. Proceeding west you'll find Ear Expressions, which has a vast selection of fashion earrings and some unique gift items best described as fun stuff. Cat lovers especially love the cat department with kitty-themed gifts including cat mousepads.

Next you will pass Lonesome Water Books and Kalamazoo's Antique Mall, both detailed in this chapter's "Antiques" section.

On the next block is the Stitchin Post, with armadas of bolts of fabric, quilting supplies, and some finished quilts. The staff is experienced and can help you with your sewing projects. One door down is the Wild Hare, a pretty, English garden–style shop with baskets, birdhouses, and other home and garden decor. Next, the Candle House specializes, not surprisingly, in candles and other gifts. After the candles comes Something Special, with a nice selection of gifts to decorate your home. Country Collections Antiques is at the end of the block.

A giant log chair beckons from the next block. Behind the chair and inside the Countree Cabin you'll find intriguing furniture made by local artisans from twisted juniper logs and pine. In summer they display beds, coat racks, and sculptures on the front lawn, and sometimes there will be a chainsaw artist hard at work on a sculpture. Countree Cabin is open daily in summer until 4:00 P.M. If you are coming to Sisters just for their log furniture during another time of year, you should call and ask about hours, which become more limited. The number is (541) 549–1573.

Now you can cross Cascade and head back. At Oak Street you will come to the Mountain Man Trading Post and Gallery, where you'll find a big selection of frontier souvenirs a la Davy Crockett. Choose from muskets, wrought-iron dinner triangles, Indian-type blankets, and other Native Americana. Down the block, Sisters Floral has feminine gifts as well as flowers, while the Garden of Eden has an eclectic mix of items from nice glassware to such joke items as "Billy Bob Teeth." Next door, The Tumbleweed Country Store features handcraft-type gifts and home decor.

Now, take a left down a narrow walkway to find The Toy Shoppe, a small, upscale children's apparel and toy retailer. At the end of the walkway is Silli Chili, which offers clothing, gifts, jewelry, and baskets, all with a Western flair, while next to them is Whimsical Arts, which offers just what the name says, including a good collection of brightly colored Mexican folk art statues.

Back on Cascade Street is Sisters Mercantile, which sells ladies' fine, casual apparel, and next to the Mercantile is the Sisters Cascade of Gifts, a small shop packed with gifts by Delft, plus Swarovski and Lenox crystal and Sandicast dog replicas. A shop selling leather handbags for $20 is next door (it's called the U.S. Leatherworks, but it doesn't have a sign), and then you come to the Sisters Market.

At the corner of Elm and Cascade is Leavitt's Western Wear, one of the best places in Central Oregon to shop for ranchwear and Western fashion apparel. See our listing in the Western Wear, Tack, and Ranch Supplies section below.

Down at the eastern end of Cascade Street is the Dusty Rose, a spacious, sweet-scented shop that sells dried flowers and other decorative items. And just when you think you are about to leave town, you'll arrive at Cliff Scharf, Silversmith and Gallery, with finely crafted art pieces, and gold and silver jewelry made by Cliff (see our The Arts chapter).

Hood Street

Now that we've covered Cascade Street, let's head south and do Hood Street, along with a couple of short detours to cover the cross-street blocks. As we mentioned earlier, Hood Street and the cross streets (they have tree names) are good places to find parking spaces. Shops in the area are concentrated between Oak Street to the west and Fir Street on the east side.

Across from the post office are Heritage USA Antiques and Crafters Mall, and Sisters Antiques and Sundries. Continuing west on Hood Street is a Radio Shack and Bailey & Company, purveyors of gifts and fine wines. You can drop off your vacation film just a bit farther up the road at Fotos in a Flash and it will be done by the time you're finished shopping for the day. Next to them is Out West Designs with handcrafted jewelry and trade beads and Buffalo Horn gallery, offering Western objects d'art.

One door north on our detour up Elm Street is The Dime Store, which has an extensive selection of toys and souvenirs, most of which, while inexpensive, do cost more than 10 cents.

Back on Hood Street, we continue west and come to The Paper Place, a small chain store with quite a collection of wrapping papers, cards, and gifts. Next is Signature Imports with folk art, clothing, and furnishings from around the world. After that is the Hen's Tooth, another small Oregon chain; its lace curtains hint at the romantic gifts inside.

Of interest to our shoppers will be Folk Arts & Company, which has a collection of arts and crafts created mostly by Oregon artists that is worth seeing. Many of the items are in an affordable price range. Next door is Pony Express Office & Art Supplies. Keep walking west and you'll find Paulina Springs Book Company, a general interest bookstore with a soothing atmosphere (see the listing in this chapter's "Bookstores" section). On the next block, at the northwest corner of Hood and Oak Streets, is Beacham's Clock Company, an internationally known manufacturer of fine clocks since 1965. They sell their own clocks as well as a good selection of antique clocks. The most popular time to drop by the store is at noon—as they put it, "the symphony at noon is simply striking." The store is closed on Wednesday and Sunday all year.

Main Street

In an old yellow building called The Place, which faces Elm Street, is Moments Remembered, a unique shop that does fine-art engraving on glass, rock, acrylic, metals, and wood. You can even give them a photo, of your baby, for example, and they can etch the image on a glass vase or other artistic medium. Walk west a bit more and there is the Habitat for Humanity Thrift Shop, with some of the classiest hand-me-downs this side of the Cascades. Just a hop, skip, and jump farther on is The Fly Fisher's Place, where you can pick up everything you need for your next fly-fishing adventure.

Antiques

Antiques, handcrafts, and mass-produced crafts seem to form one large continuum in Sisters as you pass from one shop to another. Many shops sell a few old things along with a lot of new stuff that looks old-fashioned. These are places where even a hard-core antique hound may be tempted to add a few modern pieces to round out his or her decor. The shops with primarily new "antiques" were covered in the "Downtown Sisters" section. However, there are four places in downtown that mainly sell goods that really are old.

Country Collections
351 West Cascade Street
(541) 549–7888

This is a classic antiques shop with windows full of Fostoria and other glassware. You'll also find Victorian furniture and other collectibles. The shop is open daily.

The Elder Sister
202 South Fir Street
(541) 549–1866

Just one door south from Hood Street, The Elder Sister has a nice collection of antiques (like old dolls and quilts in the front room), collectibles, and some used stuff in the back room. This old house doesn't have any heat, so it's open only from late May through mid-September, Wednesday through Sunday.

Kalamazoo's Antique Mall
221 West Cascade Street
(541) 549–1150

With between 20 and 30 dealers, this mall offers the largest selection of merchandise in Sisters, about half of which is modern, country home decor. The rest makes up an eclectic assortment of antiques and old things. The mall is open seven days a week.

Lonesome Water Books
221-C West Cascade Street
(541) 549–2203

If you have a special interest in an old book, map, or photograph, Tom and Maggie Hughes can probably direct you to the right spot in their extensive collection. The rows and rows of old volumes provide for some interesting browsing, and unlike some old bookstores, the atmosphere is light and airy due to many of the bookshelves being half-height. Lonesome Water Books is open daily.

Bookstores

Paulina Springs Book Company
252 West Hood Street
(541) 549–0866, (800) 397–0867

Book lovers take note! Paulina Springs is a general-interest bookstore with a very soothing atmosphere, enhanced by invitingly soft armchairs and complimentary coffee. You can pick up an equally soothing CD while you are here. The staff is service-oriented and will special-order any book they don't have on hand. During summer there are readings and discussion groups almost every week, and occasionally the

Insiders' Tip

In Sisters, parking spaces can get scarce by noon on summer days. Plan to arrive before noon and start your adventure with lunch.

store hosts musical performances by local artists. (For more on store events, see our The Arts chapter.)

Specialty Food Stores

Angeline's Bakery and Cafe
121 West Main Street
(541) 549-9112

Tucked away in a quiet spot 1 block north of U.S. 20 is this funky little bakery offering hearty breads, bagels, scones, muffins, cookies, and sandwiches. Angeline's is open seven days a week.

Sisters Bakery
251 East Cascade Street
(541) 549-0361

There's nothing like fresh doughnuts and hot coffee to take the chill off the morning. Breads, bear claws, and cinnamon rolls are some of the traditional offerings here. The shop has added hot soup to bring in more lunch customers, and espresso roasted by Sisters Coffee Company is available all day. The bakery is open seven days a week from 5:00 A.M. to 6:00 P.M.

Sisters Coffee Company
273 West Hood Street
(541) 549-0527, (800) 524-5282

No matter what time of year it is, walking into this tiny shop, with its rich smell of roasting coffee and creaky old plank flooring, is like stepping into a small corner of heaven on earth. The coffees are excellent, but there really isn't much seating, so the java is mostly sold as beans or in to-go cups. There is a small pastry selection. If you don't get enough of the beans while you're at Sisters Coffee, they will be happy to ship some to you via mail order. The shop is open daily.

Western Wear, Tack, and Ranch Supplies

Leavitt's Western Wear
100 East Cascade Street
(541) 549-6451

Leavitt's has a huge selection of ranchwear and Western fashion apparel. They also have an impressive cowboy boot department, including styles by Justin and Tony Lama. Your new cowboy hat will be custom-shaped exactly the way you like it at no extra charge. Proprietor John Leavitt is proud to make the claim that his store has the largest selection of Pendleton blankets under one roof (except maybe for the Pendleton factory itself). Leavitt's is open seven days a week.

Sisters Feed & Supply
102 East Main Street
(541) 549-4151

The somewhat more genteel population of Sisters tends to favor horses and pets, and that's what this feed store caters to. Stop by Monday through Saturday for vaccines, dog kennels, pet foods, halters, and horse feeds.

Redmond

Redmond has some of the best antiques shopping and ranch supply houses in Central Oregon. Being the second-largest city in the area, it also has a number of good supermarkets (including a Safeway and an Albertson's), a good variety of hardware and lumber stores, plus welding and other rural-community-oriented services.

Most of the commercial activity takes place on U.S. Highway 97, the north-south route through town. U.S. 97 splits into two one-way streets in downtown Redmond. Fifth Street runs north; Sixth Street runs south. There is also some commercial development along the east-west route through town, which is Oregon Highway 126 (called Highland and Evergreen Streets).

Antiques, Crafts, and Gifts

Country Pleasures Antique Mall
502 Southwest Evergreen Avenue
(541) 548-1021

At the corner of Evergreen and Fifth Streets, Country Pleasures has about 22 different vendors of mostly antiques and some used stuff. One interesting thing we saw was a collection of old marbles (spendy!). Since all goods are paid for at a central cash register without most of the vendors present, prices are nonnegotiable except on "Dicker Days"—the first Saturday in May and the Saturday after Thanksgiving. The mall is open daily.

The Memory Shoppe, and Past and Presents
422 Southwest Sixth Street
(541) 923-6748

At street level, Past and Presents sells hundreds of cute animals, figurines, and candles. Downstairs at the Memory Shoppe is the real antique stuff, with the specialty being furniture. The store is open seven days a week.

The Old Farmers Co-op
Antiques Mall
106 Southeast Evergreen Avenue
(541) 548-7975

Forty antiques dealers fill every nook of this 11,000-square-foot warehouse. The loading dock allows for additional displays of primitive farm and homestead implements. There's no negotiating since purchasing is centralized, but the prices are said to be good (however, if you compare nooks, some have better prices than others). The co-op mall is open seven days a week.

Terrebonne 2nd Hand
8329 U.S. Highway 97, Terrebonne
(541) 923-1197

Terrebonne is a small community at the north end of Redmond. It appears the folks at this little shop might have bought some old estates that included some nice old furniture as well as a lot of less valuable pieces. It's the type of place where you hope to find hidden treasure. The shop is open most days, but you should call ahead to be sure.

Tisket A Tasket Gifts
2498 South U.S. Highway 97, Suite D
(541) 548-3551, (800) 248-3551

The air is thick with the perfume of scented candles here, and everywhere you look are figurines. As they say, Tisket A Tasket has gifts for all occasions, and it is open seven days a week.

World of Treasures
403 Southwest Sixth Street
(541) 923-0226

World of Treasures specializes in Asian and other imported antiques, including carved wooden furniture and figurines. You will also find an incredible collection of old records. The store is open Monday through Saturday.

Western Wear, Tack, and Ranch Supplies

Big R Stores
3141 South U.S. Highway 97
(541) 548-4095

The Big R really is big, with about 50,000 square feet indoors and a couple of acres of livestock-handling equipment and fencing supplies stored outside. This Oregon chain has a wide selection of Western apparel and Carhartt ranchwear, livestock and horse supplies, tools, PVC and galvanized plumbing, some electrical supplies, dog kennels, pet food and supplies, vaccines, and just enough tack to act the part. The goods mostly come at list prices. The Big R usually has what you need, but hang on to your receipt—the return policies can be sticky. Big R is open seven days a week until 5:00 or 6:00 P.M.

Black Horse Saddlery and Keathley Country Leather
14908 Southwest Alfalfa Road, Powell Butte
(541) 548-0431

This is a pretty serious Western supply and repair shop for saddles, tack, and gun holsters. It also features spurs, bits, saddles, blankets, and hardware for making repairs. It is open Monday through Friday; you'll find the store at the north Y in Redmond, where the split U.S. 97 joins back together. Make sure you call ahead because they meet with customers by appointment only.

Central Oregon Ranch Supply
1726 South U.S. Highway 97
(541) 548-5195

This is where many locals go for livestock supplies. The business was started in 1976 by the Malotts, who still run it with the help of their two sons. Between the family members, one or another of the Malotts has firsthand experience with cattle and dairy cows, sheep, horses, and dogs, and you can get sound advice regarding almost anything on four legs. The store has one of the best selections of veterinary supplies you'll find outside a vet's office. Central Oregon Ranch is well-stocked in pet and livestock feed, hay and health products for horses, sheep, cattle, pigs, and pets. They also sell livestock-handling equipment made by Behlen and Ritchie, and they offer dog kennels at good prices. Central Oregon Ranch is open Monday through Saturday.

The Feed Barn
2215 North U.S. Highway 97
(541) 923-3333
These folks stock an extensive selection of feeds for every kind of livestock or pet imaginable, and sometimes you'll save a few cents buying it here. A smallish selection of supplies and vaccines for pets and livestock is offered. Non-livestock owners get big bags of birdseed here at good prices. We like to stop by regularly to check out the bulletin board to see who's selling what, and to buy the farm-fresh eggs (real farm, real fresh). In spring they sell chicks, just in case you want to try your hand at producing your own fresh eggs.

Sunriver/La Pine Area

These two communities are grouped together because of their proximity to each other and the fact that you can access both of them via U.S. Highway 97 south of Bend. That, however, is where the similarity ends.

Sunriver is a resort development that was started in the late 1960s. It has a planned, resort feel to it. Commercial development is primarily concentrated in Sunriver Village, with its pleasant pedestrian mall and perimeter parking. There is enough shopping in the village to make it worth a daytrip if recreational shopping is your thing. During the year special events, including live music performances, a quilt show, and food and wine galas, are held in the village (see our Annual Events chapter).

La Pine is a small, former logging town that has turned into a fishing, hunting, vacation, and retirement getaway. It is not a shopping mecca by any means, but it does have a little of everything to service residents and visitors. Most of the commercial development is right along U.S. Highway 97. At the south end of town is the La Pine Thriftway market, which is open seven days a week, unlike most other local businesses.

Sunriver Village

There are about 60 shops, service businesses, and restaurants within the village, catering to visitors and resort residents. Hours vary slightly from store to store, but generally speaking, village shops are open from 10:00 A.M. to 6:00 P.M. Monday through Saturday (or slightly later during summer), and from 10:00 A.M. to 5:00 P.M. on Sunday.

The Country Store is a full-service market with an on-premises liquor store and some take-out food. It is in Building 1, next to the first parking lot as you enter the village. Working counterclockwise from the Country Store, Building 2 houses Temptations Jewelry and Accessories, which offers casual, inexpensive, and colorful earrings and bracelets, along with other gifts such as clothes hangers with duck hooks and glass window ornaments.

On the boardwalk is Pacific Crest Clothing. The Hawaiian shirts and bikinis will warm you up just looking at them on a wintry afternoon. The store also sells Pendleton woolen goods and Patagonia pile outerwear. Dooney and Burke handbags and Segrid Olsen dresses are a couple more names that put this store in the spendy range. A few doors to the south of the ice-skating rink is Paper Station, where you can choose from a huge selection of high-quality shirts with "Sunriver" embroidered on them, napkins and party supplies, cards and wrapping papers, and pretty crockery—all while listening to Enya.

Across from the rink are Sunriver Sports—an outdoor outfitter—and Sunriver Snowboards, which rents boards as well as sells them.

Heading south toward the grocery store you'll find Signature Imports, with an eye-popping collection of artworks and curios imported from more than 40 countries. The walls are crowded with Indonesian furniture that looks like it came out of a Bogart movie, batik clothing, giant Mexican urns and handblown glassware, and jewelry and masks from Africa, Guatemala, and Indonesia. Oregon Gallery specializes in the landscape photography of Ron Keebler, who photographs Oregon's most beautiful places.

Next door is Buffalo Girls, which you don't want to miss. This Western-themed store has home furnishings made of bark-on tree branches and aged barnwood, antler chandeliers, beautiful Western dress-up clothing with intricate appliques and top-stitching, horseshoe toilet-paper holders, and salsa. It's worth a look-see, even if your home decor of choice is Ethan Allan Colonial. Besides, looking is free even if what you're looking at is on the spendy side.

Pass through a doorway, and you enter another shop run by the same owners—this time with less of a Western and more of a universal country theme. At Cate's Trading Company you'll want to cuddle up to something, whether it's the Boyd teddies and teddy-bear furniture, dolls, or your choice from among a floor-to-ceiling selection of cute gifts. Just down the way from Buffalo Girls is The Hook Fly Shop with everything you need to catch Central Oregon lunker trout. Next to them is the Village Mercantile & Outdoor, offering classy outdoorwear.

The T-Shirt Factory has a surprisingly aesthetic selection of quality shirts, sweatshirts, and summer dresses for grown-ups and kids; some part of Oregon is printed or embroidered on all of them. The store also sells Eagle Creek accessories.

The Zoo is a kids' toy store with oldies-but-goodies like plastic horses and robots, and lots of other neat stuff.

The Everything $12 Store does an amazing job of coming up with attractive women's dresses, shirts, and skirts that cost, you guessed it, $12 each. This is one store where you don't need to check the price tag, and since some of the clothing is one-size-fits-all, you may not even have to check the size tag.

Bookstores

La Pine Book Exchange Plus
16388 Third Street, La Pine
(541) 536–5580

This small store has thousands of general-interest books, including a large used-book section. The Exchange also offers UPS shipping and a fax service. The store is open Monday through Saturday.

Specialty Food Stores

Goody's Soda Fountain
Sunriver Village, Building 22, Sunriver
(541) 593–2155

Don't even think about calories when you step into this store. Homemade ice cream with homemade sundae sauces, chocolates, and old-fashioned candy such as Boston Baked Beans and candy necklaces are all very tempting. The soda fountain serves real sundaes in glass dishes along with shakes made in celery-green Hamilton Beach frappe machines. The question is not whether you want to splurge, but what to limit yourself to. Goody's is open daily during village hours.

Hook, Wine and Cheddar
Sunriver Village, Building 22, Sunriver
(541) 593–1633

A wine store/cheese store/sandwich shop, HW&C sells the makings for picnics and romantic evenings. When asked, they couldn't decide which sandwich was their most popular: Top votes went for the Reuben, Genoa salami, and gyros on pita bread. The folks here will pack a box lunch for you and bag up a bottle of wine from their excellent selection. The shop is open daily with village hours.

Hot Lava Baking Company
Sunriver Village, Building 17, Sunriver
(541) 593–3986

The aroma of huge cinnamon rolls, breads baked from scratch, along with bagels, cookies, pies, and cakes greets a visitor to Hot Lava Baking Company. They also serve deli sandwiches and espresso drinks, which you can take out or eat on the premises.

Sunriver Coffee Company
Sunriver Village, Building 1, Sunriver
(541) 593–5282

Sponged yellow walls, a deep blue ceiling, bentwood chairs, and energetic artwork on display are good signs that this is not your ordinary java stop. Some paintings are by owner Kim's sister; another is by one of the company's employees. At Sunriver they roast their own coffees, and they have quite a following. The shop is open daily.

Prineville Area

Prineville is primarily a ranching and logging town. You can expect to find all the things needed for these two occupations and not a lot more. There are a couple of supermarkets in town including an Ochoco Thriftway and an Erickson's Sentry (both supermarkets are open until 10:00 P.M.) You'll also find Rite-Aid, Madras Hardware & Home Center, Copeland Lumber Yard, and other suppliers of practical wares. While Prineville retailers may not be big on variety, they do what they do very well. What the town excels in are ranch-supply places catering to the hard-working folks, along with plenty of craft and gift shops.

Antiques, Crafts, and Gifts

The Robin's Nest
395 North Main Street, Prineville
(541) 447–8665

The interesting selection of gift and home-decor items here makes for pleasant browsing while sipping a cup of espresso available from the espresso counter. The Robin's Nest is open Monday through Saturday.

Silk & Sagebrush Antique Mall
341 North Main Street, Prineville
(541) 447–7731

About half of these vendors are antiques dealers; the other half are sellers of old-fashioned but modern crafts. The mall

environment is pleasant for strolling. Drop in and browse Monday through Saturday.

Western Wear, Tack, and Ranch Supplies

Fair Feed & Supply
105 Lynn Boulevard, Prineville
(541) 447–7106

Right on the corner of the Crooked River Highway as you head toward the fairgrounds, Fair Feed & Supply is pretty big in the pet and livestock supply category. They also sell livestock handling equipment like troughs and feeders, sacked feeds, and hay, as well as practical ranch apparel. The store is open Monday through Saturday.

Ochoco Feed & Farm Supply
West 10th Street, Prineville
(541) 447–6244

When we visited, no one in the store could remember when Ochoco Feed was opened, and no one knew the exact street address either! Still, everybody who's anybody knows where this institution is, including the mail carrier, so no one worries about details like an address. ("10th Street" isn't even on the business cards—it just says "Prineville.")

Ochoco carries just about everything you need for your ranch, including pet and livestock feeds and supplies, livestock handling equipment, Powder River panels, and vet supplies. Not only that, but you'll also find PVC and galvanized plumbing supplies, gardening stuff, small packets of flower seeds and 50-pound sacks of pasture grass seed, chainsaw chains, light bulbs, flashlights, and other tools and hardware. The store is open by 7:30 A.M., and it's even open on Sunday from 10:00 A.M. to 4:00 P.M., which just goes to show that an old dog can learn new tricks.

Prineville Men's Wear—The Store for Men and Women
231 North Main Street, Prineville
(541) 447–6580

This downtown shop is such a Prineville landmark that local VIP tire magnate Les Schwab buys his hats here. The store sold Wranglers back when the brand was called

Blue Bell. Started by Eddie Lane in 1950, son Jim carries on the tradition of providing old-fashioned service while selling an extensive, tidily merchandised array of Western apparel including men's dress clothing. You'll find everything from underwear to rows of cowboy boots and the aforementioned cowboy hats, which the staff will custom-shape for you just like they do for Les. Mosey on in Monday through Saturday.

W. W. Western Wear & Saddlery
720 North Madras Highway, Prineville
(541) 447–6890

Founded in 1973 by Tom and Georgia Fitzgerald with the working cowboy in mind, W. W. Western Wear still supplies quality ranch and dress apparel to today's modern cowboys and wanna-bes. The Fitzgeralds also sell McCall custom saddles from Colorado, Resistol and Stetson hats, Wranglers, handkerchiefs, and you name it. Georgia is an artist; her Western-life paintings are displayed for sale around the store. W.W. is open Monday through Saturday at the corner of U.S. Highway 26, the Madras-Prineville Highway, at the western edge of town.

Madras Area

In the heart of ranch country, Madras is a melange of cowboys, hay ranchers, Native Americans from the Confederated Tribes of Warm Springs, and Hispanic immigrants that mostly work agricultural jobs. U.S. Highway 97 forms the main artery through town, and the roadway splits into two one-way streets in the downtown section. Fifth Street runs north; Fourth Street runs south.

Erickson's Sentry is the older supermarket in town, and it straddles Fifth and Fourth Streets. Newcomer Safeway Food and Drug moved in at the north end of town, where U.S. Highway 26 and U.S. 97 fork. There is a Rite-Aid drugstore and a Coast to Coast Hardware that offers housewares in addition to traditional hardware. Copeland Lumber Yard bridges the gap from hardware to lumber.

Remember to dial 1 when calling Madras from the Central Oregon towns to the south.

Craft and Gift Shops

Old Hat Glassworks
1861 Southwest U.S. Highway 97, Madras
(541) 475–6414

Here is an amazing collection of blown-glass beads and pendants, vases, and other crafts made on-site by Walt Francis. Walt's wife, Pat, is the designer in the family and will point out a unique glass material called dichroic glass, a two-color iridescent material invented by NASA in the 1960s. Some of the vases are made with the unusual technique of cutting cold glass, which is somehow fused in an oven. The Glassworks is open Tuesday through Sunday.

Petals 'n' Poseys
546 Southwest Fourth Street, Madras
(541) 475–6266, (800) 568–6266

This charming little shop combines fresh flowers with pretty gifts, books, and an espresso bar. It is open Monday through Saturday.

Western Wear, Tack, and Ranch Supplies

The Feed Company
316 Southwest Madison Street, Madras
(541) 475–7556

This store used to be owned by the same folks that owned The Feed Company in Bend, but this location was sold to new owners. It supplies the Madras area with hay and livestock feed, pet food and supplies, and some tack. The Feed Company is open Monday through Saturday.

> ## Insiders' Tip
> Oregon has no sales tax and no food tax at restaurants. Your bill should be exactly the total cost of the items you purchased.

Attractions

The problem with Central Oregon's attractions lies in deciding which ones to squeeze into a weekend or week. We have been blessed with more than our share of awesome scenery and recreational opportunities, and fortunately we have some world-class museums and visitors centers to help travelers fully appreciate our natural resources.

We occasionally mention the need for a Northwest Forest Pass or Sno-Park permit. For more information on these, please see the Close-up in our Forests, High Desert, and Volcanoes chapter.

In this chapter you'll find places that appeal to a wide range of interests and age groups. Remember, there are dozens of other fun ideas in our chapters on Daytrips, Parks, Kidstuff, Indoor and Outdoor Recreation, Snowplay, Fishing, and Spectator Sports. Still, we couldn't help but cross-reference a few of our absolutely-not-to-be-missed natural attractions in this chapter.

Bend

Cascade Lakes Highway
Century Drive/Forest Service Road 46

If you were to tell anyone here that you only had one day to spend in Central Oregon and you wanted to know what you should do, there's a good chance you'd hear, "Take a drive on the Cascade Lakes Highway." This recreation-packed series of lakes and streams features knock-your-socks-off scenery with the High Cascades in the background. It's worth a visit of a half or whole day at least. Learn more in our Daytrips chapter.

Deschutes Historical Museum
129 Northwest Idaho Avenue
(541) 389–1813

Three blocks south of downtown in Bend's old Heritage Square next to the new Boys and Girls Club is our historical museum, appropriately packed full of memories. The building used to be the old Reid School, and you will probably overhear local visitors reminiscing about the days when they were students here.

Built in 1914 of pink volcanic tuff quarried nearby, the building was the last of its kind, because a new brick factory was completed in 1914 and supplied

builders from that point on. The volcanic tuff was said to be too soft to last (you could cut it with a handsaw), but the building has had the last laugh. Inside are old photographs of students with signs below like "Does anyone remember who this was . . . ?"

Within the three floors you'll find an accurate and comprehensive representation of Central Oregon's past from pioneer days to the mid-20th century. There's also an excellent little bookstore with historical books. Stop by Tuesday through Saturday from 10:00 A.M. to 4:30 P.M. Admission is $2.50 for adults and $1.00 for children ages 6 to 15.

The High Desert Museum
59800 South U.S. Highway 97
(541) 382–4754
www.highdesert.org

This would be right at the top of our list of must-see places in Central Oregon, but don't wait for a rainy day to come because much of the fun is outdoors. The museum features 20 acres filled with fascinating live exhibits including an otter pond with underwater viewing windows, a porcupine exhibit (with critters named Cactus, Spike, and Dart), and a birds-of-prey exhibit, all with hourly presentations by naturalists. Inside are exceptional dis-

A volunteer at The High Desert Museum shows off a golden eagle. PHOTO: JIM YUSKAVITCH

plays of natural and cultural history, including the history of early pioneers, and there is an excellent gift shop. Three major galleries feature permanent and changing exhibits in art and history.

Completed in 1999 was a 10,000-square-foot addition to the museum called the Hall of Plateau Indians followed by the 2001 opening of the much-awaited birds-of-prey exhibit, featuring a variety of live hawks, eagles, and owls with which to get acquainted.

Pioneer history is especially well-represented in the museum's annual events: the monthly weekends set aside to feature the operation of the authentic, turn-of-the-20th-century sawmill; Harvest Hoedown Celebration in October with a home-style setting, allowing visitors to help make and taste cider and ice cream, and enjoy draft horse rides and more; The High Desert Holidays Festival and Art Show at Thanksgiving; and Ruggers Rendezvous in July, when textile arts are displayed and demonstrated. (See our Annual Events chapter for more information.)

People are sometimes surprised at what a great experience they have at the museum; often, their only regret is that they didn't budget enough time. Plan on taking at least a half-day to tour the 40,000 square feet of museum space and 150 acres of outdoor area (including the 20 acres of exhibits). The Rimrock Cafe provides gourmet snacks, lunch, and coffee. The museum is open from 9:00 A.M. to 5:00 P.M. every day except Thanksgiving, Christmas, and New Year's Day, with extended summer hours June through Labor Day until 7:00 P.M. Admission is $8.50 for adults, $7.50 for teens ages 13 to 18 and seniors 65 and older, and $4.00 for kids ages 5 to 12. A typical July will feature upwards of 30 lectures, tours, classes, and programs, and one of the best ways to keep abreast of what's going on is to check out the museum's excellent Web site.

Pilot Butte
Oregon State Park
U.S. Highway 20
(541) 388–6211, (800) 452–5687
www.prd.state.or.us

There is probably no spot better known in Bend than this 4,139-foot landmark. We walk, jog, run, stroll, or drive its winding narrow road to the top at just about any excuse we can think of. Seems we're just hooked on the 360-degree views of the Cascades, High Desert, and Bend. In the morning before 11:00 A.M. you can get great, sunny photos of the Cascades. Or be there with your camera as the sun sets. After a nice dinner in town, drive to the top to watch the city lights. This butte is part of Pilot Butte State Park, which is listed in our Parks chapter.

Pine Mountain Observatory
9 miles south of Millican off U.S. Highway 20
(541) 382–8331
www.pmo-sun.uoregon.edu

After dark on Friday and Saturday evenings the rule here is: No camping lanterns, no headlights, and no white lights allowed—only small flashlights with red lenses that won't compete with the delicate light from the stars. At Pine Mountain Observatory, absolute darkness, a rarity these days, reigns supreme. In and around the observatory the darkness and the night sky tend to make visitors whisper in awe, while down the hill the primitive U.S. Forest Service campground is alive with the giggles of unseen kids.

The volunteer staff of Friends of the Pine Mountain Observatory welcome the public to view the planets and stars through three impressive telescopes with mirror diameters of 15, 24, and 32 inches. Just outside the observatory you'll usually find small groups of visitors from all over the Northwest; they bring their own telescopes and binoculars to enjoy the clear desert night with fellow stargazers.

From Bend, head 26 miles east on U.S. Highway 20 until you reach the town of Millican. Turn south just past the gas station (yes, there's only one) and take the gravel road 9 miles up the hill, keeping to the right. Pine Mountain has been described as an island in a sea of sagebrush. On your way up, notice how the sagebrush gives way to a ponderosa- and lodgepole-pine forest, hence the mountain's name. It's best to arrive in the late afternoon or early evening before dark. While you are waiting for the show to begin, take a short hike to the top of Pine Mountain, where you can watch the sun set.

The Observatory, operated by the University of Oregon, is open to the public on Fridays and Saturdays beginning at sunset from Memorial Day through Labor Day. Pine Mountain is at an elevation of 6,300 feet, where the hot summer days can turn into cold nights, so bring warm clothes. A $3.00 donation is appreciated. (For more information on Pine Mountain Observatory, see our Daytrips chapter.) Their Web site provides interesting insights into astrological lingo and happenings.

Tumalo Falls
Deschutes National Forest
Forest Service Road 4603, 14 miles west of Bend
(541) 383–5300
www.fs.fed.us/r6/centraloregon

Here's a beautiful spot to visit. You could make it an hour-long round-trip from Bend, or you could spend the whole day here. To get to Tumalo Falls from Bend, head west on Franklin Avenue, past Drake Park and across the river. Go straight at the stop sign and follow paved Skyliners Road 11 miles into the Deschutes National Forest. When the road turns to gravel, continue on Forest Service Road 4603 for another 3.5 miles and you're there.

The falls are 97 feet high and can be viewed from the parking lot; a short trail will get you closer. In winter the road is plowed as far as it is paved, and you can park (with a Sno-Park permit) and hike or ski to the falls. There are vault toilets, and the trail to the falls is partially wheelchair-accessible.

Sisters/Camp Sherman Area

Shopping and cultural events are the main things to do in Sisters. Natural wonders make up the balance of the area's attractions, especially at Camp Sherman.

Black Butte
U.S. Highway 20, 10 miles west of Sisters

Once a landmark used by the Native Americans and pioneers to guide their way, Black Butte is a 6,438-foot-high cinder cone that was formed over the top of what was then the riverbed of the Metolius

Take a journey to the stars at Pine Mountain Observatory, in the desert east of Bend.
PHOTO: JIM YUSKAVITCH

River (see our listing for the Headwaters of the Metolius River, below). You can drive part of the way up the base to the cinder cone, then hike the remaining 3 miles or so to the top for awesome views of Mount Jefferson, Three Fingered Jack, Mount Washington, and the Three Sisters from a moon-like perch. (For information on Black Butte Ranch, which is almost across the road from Black Butte, see our Resorts, Ranches, and Vacation Rentals chapter.)

Dee Wright Memorial Observatory
Oregon Highway 242, 14 miles west of Sisters

The Dee Wright Memorial Observatory, built in the 1930s by the Civilian Conservation Corps, sits atop windswept McKenzie Pass at an elevation of 5,324 feet. All around are 360-degree views of nearby lava flows, and in the distance are six peaks in the Cascades range—Mount Jefferson, Three Fingered Jack, Mount Washington, and the Three Sisters.

The observatory was severely damaged by lightning in 1989, but has recently been remodeled. You can walk into the observa-tory and view the scenery through some telescopes (your own binoculars would be better). Between the stark lava terrain and the observatory, you might expect to see Darth Vader come striding out from behind a rock.

A short, interpretive trail winds through lava fields, with descriptions of the formations and the flora that tries to survive in this harsh environment. Here and there you can still see the tracks of an old wagon trail that was built over the lava in 1872. (Imagine driving covered wagons and herds of cattle over this terrain, as they did in the 1860s!) The man who finally succeeded in building this wagon trail, John Craig, froze to his death nearby in 1877.

Oregon 242 is only open in summer and is not recommended for trailers. Because this is a trailhead for the Pacific Crest Trail, the USFS requires that you have a Northwest Forest Pass to park at the observatory. From downtown Sisters, head west on Cascade Avenue/U.S. Highway 20 and take the left fork onto Oregon Highway 242 before you leave town.

Headwaters of the Metolius and Camp Sherman Bridge
Oregon Highway 14, Camp Sherman

A visit to Camp Sherman to see the headwaters of this famous fly-fishing river is worth the trip. Cold water gushing out of the ground to give birth to a river is an amazing sight to behold. The water actually comes from under Black Butte, a cinder cone that grew itself right on top of the Metolius River's bed. The water now goes under the butte and springs up on the far side.

There's a pleasant trail along the river that leads from the springs to the Camp Sherman bridge about 2 miles to the north. Here you'll see people leaning over the bridge's railings, gawking at the huge trout (which are off-limits to anglers). The village store sells bags of food you can throw to the fish (the food, not the bag). The 40-degree water is too cold for feet. The trail continues another 8 miles along the river. A Northwest Forest Pass would give you the option of parking in an area on Forest Service lands without a hassle.

Patterson Ranch
Oregon Highway 242, west of Sisters

At the west end of town, take the Oregon Highway 242 fork west about a half-mile. On your left will be a large ranch with domestic Rocky Mountain elk and llamas. There are a couple of turnouts along

the fence—popular spots for visitors hoping to take a few snapshots of the grazing animals against the incredible backdrop of the Three Sisters and Mt. Washington.

Redmond

Redmond is the jumping-off point for a trip to Smith Rock State Park, a spot 10 miles northeast of town that attracts rock climbers from all over the world. The area is a beautiful spot for a picnic, hiking, or photographing the classic Western landscape. Kevin Costner shot much of his film *The Postman* near Smith Rock State Park. (See our chapter on Parks for a complete description of this area.) Redmond is also home to some of Santa's reindeer, a classic 1950s rock garden, and the Redmond Hotshot Crew, as well as the Deschutes County Fairgrounds and Expo Center, located next to the Redmond Municipal Airport.

Operation Santa Claus
4355 West U.S. Highway 26
(541) 548–8910
www.oscreindeer.com

The Christmas season and spring calving time are the highlights of the year for Operation Santa Claus. During the holidays, many of the reindeer that live here are on the job driving Santa's sleighs in Christmas parades all over the West, but they always keep some reindeer at home for local visitors to see. Call for a schedule of Christmas events. The small gift and souvenir shop (heavy on the Santa Claus theme) is open from Memorial Day through Christmas, but even if you happen to show up when no one is around, you can still see the reindeer and read the very interesting placard that tells their story. Admission is free daylight to dark. Their Web site is mainly geared to their commercial accounts, but you'll find a few photos of their reindeer.

Petersen Rock Gardens & Museum
7930 Southwest 77th Street
(541) 382–5574

Step back into the once-glittering universe of post–World War II as you enter this unique world of miniature bridges and ponds, towers, castles, churches, and even a replica of the Statue of Liberty—all studded with rocks and minerals collected within an 85-mile radius of the garden.

The artist was Rasmus Petersen, a Danish immigrant farmer who settled in Bend in 1906. Petersen collected the stones and built the gardens entirely by himself between 1935 and his death in 1952. He said the pursuit was less arduous than farming his 300 acres. The beauty and variety of the stones are quite amazing, as is Petersen's childlike sense of storytelling and patriotism. The rock sculptures are surrounded by four acres of green lawns, flowers, and trees, with peacocks and ducks wandering freely (watch where you step).

Inside the shop building is a museum filled with a vast number of polished rock specimens, petrified wood, thundereggs, and fossils. The old-fashioned gift shop offers polished stones, ashtrays, charms, stone necklaces, and postcards. Coca-Cola is available in the old glass bottles, and ice-cream bars are for sale. Don't overlook the room with the black lights; there's an extra admission charge of 25 cents to help defray the cost of replacing light bulbs that cost $2,200 each!

Taking in the dusty shelves and cobwebs, and the gaps where some of the stones have been stolen from the sculptures, it is a bit hard to imagine that this was once a major regional tourist attraction with more than 200,000 visitors a year. Among residents, frequent visitors, students, and rock hounds, Petersen's is a place everyone's been to at least once. The fact that it's open 365 days a year at 9:00 A.M. shows the ongoing devotion and stewardship of Mrs. Hegardt, Petersen's daughter. The museum closes at 5:30 P.M. in summer, an hour or so earlier the rest of the year. The grounds are open until dusk, or 7:00 P.M. in summer. A $3.00 admission is suggested for adults, $1.00 for teens ages 12 through 16, and 50 cents for kids ages 6 to 11. To get to the gardens on the southern end of Redmond, turn west off U.S. 97 onto 61st Avenue and follow the signs along residential streets.

Redmond Air Center
1740 Southeast Ochoco Way
(541) 504-7200
www.fs.fed.us/r6/centraloregon/rac

Here is an opportunity to get a fascinating look into the world of smoke jumping and Western wildfire fighting. This is the home of the Redmond Hotshot Crew, a team of 35 smoke jumpers who travel all over the lower 48 states and Alaska putting out fires in remote areas. In all, about 100 people are employed at the center during the fire season, including pilot and tanker crews, information services and central dispatch personnel. You may heft a complete set of gear that the jumpers carry to see how heavy it is, view where the jumpers sew their own gear, tour an airplane (if one is on the ground), and see the Dispatch Center, which serves the entire Deschutes National Forest and coordinates with other centers in the Northwest.

The folks at Redmond Air Center prefer that you call ahead and make a reservation for your visit, especially during the fire season from May through October. They want to have the staff and some handout materials available when you arrive. Tours are available with a reservation anytime Monday through Friday from 7:45 A.M. to 4:30 P.M.

Some tour highlights we recommend you see are the paraloft, where the crews store the parachutes; the air tanker base, where they fill the airplanes with retardant; and the Regional Fire Cache, where tools and equipment for 3,600 firefighters are stored and maintained. However, if center personnel are busy fighting fires, some areas might not be open for touring. The Redmond Air Center is on U.S. Highway 126 (Ochoco Way in this neck of the woods), 2 miles east of downtown Redmond.

Sunriver/La Pine Area

La Pine is surrounded by the Deschutes National Forest, where natural wonders make up the main attractions. The biggest draw is the southeastern section of the Newberry National Volcanic Monument;

the turnoff to the monument is just 5 miles north of La Pine. There is so much to explore and encounter here that you will find our main listing for the Newberry National Volcanic Monument in the Daytrips chapter. About a mile north of Oregon Highway 21 is La Pine State Rec Road, which leads west to the state park of that same name (only the park folks spell it "LaPine," with no space). This park offers year-round recreation and camping (see our Camping and Parks chapters).

Sunriver is a well-developed resort with lots of shopping and restaurants and the Sunriver Nature Center and Observatory.

**Newberry National Volcanic Monument
58201 South U.S. Highway 97, 4 miles north of Sunriver; Oregon Highway 21, 5 miles north of La Pine
(541) 593-2421, April through October
(541) 383-5300 (Bend office), November through March**

The Central Oregon landscape comes alive with meaning at the Lava Lands Visitor Center, which is the heart of the Newberry National Volcanic Monument. The center is probably the single most valuable source of knowledge of geology, archaeology, and wildlife available to our visitors.

Within the center are excellent exhibits on the volcanic history of the monument. A display showing the relative ages of the High Cascade mountains and local lava flows is particularly interesting. (And you thought Mount St. Helens was the only live volcano in the Northwest!) The Lava Lands Visitor Center is open from May through mid-October from 9:00 A.M. to 5:00 P.M. From May 1 to June 9, the center is open Wednesday through Sunday; June 12 through September 2 it's open daily; and from September 4 to October 19, it's back to Wednesday through Sunday.

The highlights outside the walls of the center are covered in our Daytrips chapter listing for the Newberry National Volcanic Monument. Just to tempt you, we'll mention a couple of things: You'll get the chance to take a short, interpretive walk through lava where NASA test-drove its lunar rover, and you can ride a shuttle to the top of Lava Butte, a 500-foot cinder cone. Both sites are right next to the visitors center.

The monument continues south and east of the visitors center. Right next to U.S. 97 is the 1-mile long Lava River Cave—the longest lava tube in Oregon. Opposite the road to Sunriver is Forest Service Road 9720, which leads to the Lava Cast Forest, where you can see what remains of a forest after a lava flow oozes through it. About 8 miles farther south is the eastern turnoff for Oregon Highway 21, which leads up to Newberry Caldera. At this site are a whole mountain of obsidian (part of a lava flow that's only 1,300 years old), two sparkling lakes, a waterfall, hot springs, two seasonal cafes, camping, and lots of recreation.

Five bucks will get you a one-day vehicle parking pass for the entire monument and $30 will buy you an annual pass. This is part of the Northwest Forest Pass program for 84 sites throughout the National Forest and Newberry National Volcanic Monuments, including Lava Lands visitors center. There will be a charge per person to enter Lava River Caves (the Northwest Forest Pass will admit one individual free).

**Sunriver Nature Center and Observatory
17620 River Road, Sunriver
(541) 593-4394, nature center; (541) 598-4406, observatory and telescope store; (541) 593-4442, administrative offices
www.sunrivernaturecenter.org**

"People are missing a great place if they don't come here!" That was the enthusiastic response from our naturalist guide when we visited the nature center. And she's right! This is a gem of an experience for folks of all ages. The facilities include a museum with live animals and hands-on exhibits, a box of bones found in the wilderness, plus a nature store, botanical garden, scenic lake, picnic area, and, of course, the observatory and its 12-inch reflecting telescope. Everything is small in scale, but what this place lacks in size it makes up in quality.

Take the self-guided trip along the bark-dust covered, quarter-mile Sam Osgood Nature Trail (visitors in wheelchairs will need a strong push) or attend spring and summer weekend walks and talks given by naturalists. The center rehabilitates and releases many rescued eagles,

Fee Demo Program

The USFS has published literature and posted signs referring to the Northwest Forest Pass, Adventure Pass, and Trail Pass. These are three names for the same permit, part of what is currently an experimental program called Fee Demo that requires the public to pay a fee to use public lands for any kind of recreation. This is a very controversial program, and many forest users oppose it as a form of double taxation. If you want to take a short dayhike, or stop your car and walk to an overlook to take a picture, you are supposed to have paid for a NW Forest Pass. If you cut firewood, pan for gold, have a grazing permit for your cattle, or use your public lands for a religious experience, you would not need to buy a Forest Pass. For more information on the Fee Demo program, check out these Web sites:

For the pros: www.fs.fed.us/r6/centraloregon/index. Click on Recreation, then click on NW Forest Pass.

For the cons: www.wildwilderness.org.

owls, and other birds, some of which should be available for viewing. A real highlight of the nature trail is viewing the two disabled bald eagles that live on an island in the center of the lake. General admission to the nature center is $3.00 for adults and teens and $2.00 for kids ages 12 and younger. This includes solar viewing at the observatory when it's open. (See our Kidstuff chapter for a description of scheduled classes at Sunriver Nature Center.)

The observatory offers viewing six nights a week from 9:00 to 11:00 P.M. during summer, with Thursday night being set off as Binocular Night. Visitors should bring warm clothes for nighttime viewing. Daytime astronomy sessions (included in the nature center admission fee) are offered, allowing visitors to view the sun from 10:00 A.M. to 2:00 P.M. Staff astronomers give in-depth talks at 9:00 P.M. on Saturday in summer; these discussions are $6.00 for adults and teens and $4.00 for children ages 12 and younger. The admission for evening observatory sessions is $3.00 for adults and teens and $2.00 for children ages 12 and younger, or free if you have already purchased admission to the nature center earlier that same day.

The Sunriver Nature Center and Observatory are open every day in summer, but you might want to call the observatory if clear weather is iffy. Operating times are cut back quite a bit during the rest of the year—call ahead for hours. Occasionally, special holiday or seasonal events—including a wildflower show in June, astronomy week in July, free Memorial Day and Thanksgiving weekend open houses, the autumn migration bird count in October, and Halloween festivities—are on tap (see our Annual Events chapter). To get to Sunriver Nature Center and Observatory, enter Sunriver at the main entrance and follow the signs through the One and Two traffic circles. When you get to traffic circle Three, keep going around until you spot the sign for River Road and the nature center.

Prineville Area

Prineville's warm sunshine and small-town atmosphere are two of its best-loved attractions. You are surrounded by a choice of lakes—the Ochoco Reservoir, Prineville Reservoir, and Haystack Reservoir are all nearby—for swimming, water-skiing, and bass fishing (see our Parks chapter). From Prineville, head east into the Ochoco National Forest for rivers and snowplay. And there's no end to the interesting rocks waiting for rock hounds and archaeology enthusiasts. (See our chapters on Snowplay; Other Outdoor Recreation;

and Forests, High Desert, and Volcanoes for more information.)

A. R. Bowman Memorial Museum
246 North Main Street, Prineville
(541) 447–3715
www.bowmanmuseum.org

In 1935 Arthur Ray Bowman bought this bank building, built in 1910, for his title insurance business. In 1971 his widow donated it to the city of Prineville for use as a museum. Since then it has been the home of Prineville's Hall of History, a chronological walk through Crook County's past.

Many of the items exhibited were donated by Prineville's pioneer families. On the second floor are life-size re-creations of a dining room, tack room, bedroom, the old Paulina store and post office, and a research library. The museum is open in summer Monday through Friday from 10:00 A.M. to 5:00 P.M., Saturday from 11:00 A.M. to 4:00 P.M., and Sunday from 11:00 A.M. to 5:00 P.M. In the off-season it's open Tuesday through Friday from 10:00 A.M. to 5:00 P.M., and Saturday from 11:00 A.M. to 4:00 P.M. The museum is closed in January. Admission is free, but donations are appreciated.

Madras Area

The Museum at Warm Springs
2189 U.S. Highway 26, Warm Springs
(541) 553–3331
www.warmsprings.com

The grounds and architecture of this new, 25,000-square-foot museum are quite striking. State-of-the-art exhibits reveal the tribal histories of the Wasco, Paiute, and Warm Springs tribes through their treasured personal artifacts, historical photographs and rare documents, graphics, music, and narratives. A tule mat lodge, wickiup, and plankhouse have been re-created to demonstrate what life was like for these Indians. There's even a re-creation of a Wasco wedding ceremony with a bride in a beautifully beaded dress. Demonstrations and performances take place in an outdoor amphitheater, and there's a picnic area along the lovely Shi-tike Creek. Inside is a unique gift shop.

The Museum at Warm Springs is worth a drive from any point in Central Oregon. It's open 9:00 A.M. to 5:00 P.M. daily except Thanksgiving, Christmas, and New Year's Day. Admission is $6.00 for adults and teens, $3.00 for kids ages 5 to 12. (See our chapter on Other Communities to learn more about the Warm Springs Indian Reservation.)

Richardson's Recreational Ranch
Old U.S. Highway 97, Madras
(541) 475–2680
www.orerockon.com/richards

This place is a rock hound's dream come true. Even if you are just a casual admirer of pretty rocks, Richardson's is worth a visit. The 17,000-acre ranch has been run by the Richardson family for some six generations. What started out as a cattle operation has, during the past 30 years, evolved into a tremendous, family-run rock operation. The business encompasses digging, finishing, importing, selling rock to customers around the world, and being host to thousands of visitors each year. Much of the acreage is currently leased out for cattle grazing, but there are still miles of rugged terrain for digging rocks.

You first arrive at the "office"—a large shop-style building that contains thousands of rock samples. Many of these rocks are from the ranch; the rest are brought in from other parts of the United States and the world. Both rocks for sale and an impressive museum collection are on display. Prices are reasonable—some downright cheap. The Richardson family would rather sell 10 rocks for $1.00 each than sell one rock for $10.00. A whole thunderegg (an agate-filled volcanic nodule) split in two and polished sells for about $4.00.

The center of the main room is filled with rows and rows of perfect spheres painstakingly ground down from boulders of all sizes. Spheres can take weeks to make, and that makes them some of Richardson's more expensive items. Prices start at about $1.006 per diameter inch. The largest sphere here, a magnificent specimen made of Arizona petrified wood, is about 13 inches in diameter, weighs in at around 200 pounds, and is priced at $2,500. Surrounding the office is about an acre of land covered with multicolored piles of rocks sold by the pound. Don't worry about packing them for home—the ranch ships hundreds of pounds of rocks all over the world every weekday.

While the office is a wonderland for the casual visitor, the real attraction lies about 20 minutes away at the thunderegg and agate beds. Thundereggs can be dug with a rock pick, which Richardson's will lend you for the day. Ledge agate must be chipped off with hard rock-mining tools that may be purchased at the office. Dig-your-own rocks costs 50 cents a pound, with extra charges for custom polishing or cutting. An added benefit is the ranch scenery, which has inspired many a 'hound to trade his pick for a camera. (It's also a plus for non-hound spouses without rocks in their heads.)

Richardsons provides free camping for customers (this is pasture camping without hookups), free showers, and rest rooms. Best of all, the ranch is open every day of the year from 7:00 A.M. to 5:00 P.M., weather permitting. The rock beds are open when the roads are passable. The ranch is busiest during summer, though it gets about 120 school group tours during the academic year. During summer dress for 90- to 100-degree weather—bring sunscreen, a hat, and food. From Madras, head 11 miles north on U.S. 97; just past milepost 81 watch for a sign leading to a turnoff to the east. We have to add another note about the Richardsons' hospitality here: Don't expect to enter a tourist attraction with the spit and polish of Disneyland. Facilities, and sometimes the local family personalities, can be on the rustic side.

Kidstuff

Bend

Sisters/Camp
   Sherman Area

Redmond

Sunriver/La Pine Area

Prineville Area

Madras Area

Boredom is not something that happens to folks in Central Oregon, not even the kids.

First of all, we have a virtually unlimited supply of three elements that are key to a kid's happy survival—snow, water, and open spaces. We guarantee that you can find a place where everyone can get wet and dirty, any day of the year. When you've had enough of being soaked and sloppy, you can always feed a pig, examine the skull of a coyote, or look at the stars with someone who actually knows their names. Bring lots of film: Your kids will look good in Central Oregon.

In this chapter we've compiled a sampling of things to do in good weather or bad. For another option during inclement weather, all the libraries in Central Oregon have storytelling hours. These include the Bend Library, (541) 388-6677; Sisters Library, (541) 549-2921; Redmond Library, (541) 548-3141; Sunriver Library, (541) 593-9285; La Pine Library, (541) 536-0515; Crook County Library (Prineville), (541) 447-7978; and the Jefferson County Library in Madras, (541) 475-3351. Local bookstores with story times include The Outback Children's Bookstore, on Wall Street in downtown Bend, (541) 318-8258, and Barnes & Noble Booksellers at The Forum Shopping Center on U.S. Highway 20, (541) 318-7242. Call for current schedules.

For even more possibilities, check out our chapter on Indoor Recreation.

Bend

Bend has a lot of everything, including fun stuff for kids. Take some stale bread to Drake Park and feed the ducks, grab a fishing pole and venture out to Shevlin Park, where the fishin' is easy, or just plain head for the hills, where you'll find no end of lakes and streams (or snow, as the season goes) for children to play in.

As for eats, there are plenty of fast-food places along U.S. Highway 97 through Bend, and east on U.S. Highway 20. A kid can lift up a tall frothy glass of home-brewed root beer at the Deschutes Brewery, 1044 Northwest Bond Street, Bend, (541) 382-9242, which welcomes kids anytime.

Outstanding picnic locations include Shevlin Park, Drake Park, Summit Park, Benham Falls, Tumalo Falls, Lava Lands Visitor Center, Tumalo State Park, and Cline Falls State Park. See more details on these sites in our chapter on Parks. And if you have your kids in tow on the Fourth of July, the Pet Parade in Bend is a must-see.

Here are some other suggestions.

Acrovision
63255 Jamison Road
(541) 388-5555

This busy place is home to the Super Mytes, Dino Mytes, and TKD Turtles—different exercise groups for specific age groups ranging from age 2 to adults. Acrovision even has rock climbing on an indoor climbing wall for older kids (from age 7 on up) available by advance appointment. The goal here is fun through gymnastics, and it's amazing to see these little kids doing flips and rolls. Acrovision is big—as in 17,000 square feet. It opened in 1998. If you want to be a member, there is an initiation fee of $43.50 in addition to a monthly rate depending on the types of activities you are interested in and the number of people in your family. The gym is open on Friday from 10:30 A.M. to noon for children of preschool age, and from 7:30 to 9:00 P.M. for children ages 6 to 12, and on Saturday from 6:30 to 8:00 P.M. for ages 6 and older. Acrovision is open Monday through Friday from 8:00 A.M. to 9:00 P.M. They offer birthday parties by advance arrangement on Saturday. (See our Indoor Recreation chapter for more on Acrovision.)

Baskin-Robbins 31 Flavors
1106 Northeast Third Street
(541) 388–2637
Fred Meyer Shopping Center,
(541) 385–1811

It's no secret that kids love ice cream. It's always comforting to know where you can get your 31 flavors. These locations are open until 10:00 P.M.

Bend Metro Park & Recreation District
200 Northwest Pacific Park Lane
(541) 389–7275

This agency runs an incredible number of recreational programs every year for all ages. There can be more than 50 classes running at any given time, focusing on everything from computer fun to magic to arts and crafts for kids.

Teens are offered kayaking, chess, and backpacking instruction. Summer camps for tots are geared for ages 18 months to 5 years and cost $15 to $28 per week for three two-hour sessions. Camp Cascade, for grades K through 4, has a myriad of themes with sessions of varying durations and prices. A full, five-day week from 9:00 A.M. to 4:00 P.M. costs about $130. Cougar Camps are held in Aspen Hall at Shevlin Park (see our Parks chapter) and have naturalist/environmental themes. A full week with seven-hour days runs about $155.

Kids can also join baseball, soccer, basketball, and softball teams. There are overnight trips to places like the Oregon Coast, and there's a latchkey program for students called Kids Inc. The Juniper Swim and Fitness Center, (541) 389–7665, offers aquatics programs for infants on up.

Pick up the 50-plus-page summer or winter guide around town at visitors centers or the Park and Recreation Program's main office. Residents get these in the mail. Prices listed are for out-of-district visitors. Folks living within Bend's urban boundaries have a pricing structure that sometimes saves about 20 percent. See our Parks chapter for more on the Bend Metro Park & Recreation District.

Benham Falls
4 miles from Lava Lands Visitor Center on Forest Service Road 9702

From the entrance to the Lava Lands Visitor Center, take the gravel road to the left and go 4 miles to the Benham Falls picnic and parking area. The Deschutes River is right there, although it's too deep and fast for swimming. Cold too. There's a three-quarter-mile trail that leads over a footbridge to Benham Falls, and it makes for an excellent outing for families of all sizes. These cataract-style falls tumble and roar as they try to cut their way through a lava flow that blocked the river's passage when Lava Butte erupted. Bring a camera, and binoculars if you are into bird-watching.

The Candy Shoppe
Mountain View Mall, U.S. Highway 97 and U.S. Highway 20
(541) 389–9566
Bend River Mall, 3188 U.S. Highway 97
(541) 382–6424

What kid out there doesn't have a serious sweet tooth? (A few parents we know have them, too.) The claim to fame here is six varieties of homemade fudge, but these shops have lots of other candies, too. The Mountain View Mall outlet is bigger. Both have mall hours.

Central Oregon Gymnastics Academy
63060 Northeast Layton Street
(541) 385–1163

"Outrageous" and "incredible" are two of the adjectives you'll hear when you call for information about this place. Kidnastics has a full program for all kids, from 18 months up to age 18. Playmanias are drop-in periods on Thursday, Friday, and Saturday from 11:00 A.M. to noon for newborns to kids age 5; cost is $4.00 per child and requires parental participation. There is open gym for kids ages 6 and up from 12:15 P.M. to 1:15 P.M. on Saturdays. The cost is $4.00. The academy also offers a variety of gymnastics classes for ages 18 months and older as well as half-day summer gymnastics camps. These run for four days with different programs and themes and are designed for ages 3 to 5. They cost around $80 for four half-day sessions. You can also schedule two-hour birthday parties here on Saturday or Sunday for 15 kids for $100. They feature an academic preschool program as well.

Funny Farm at Buffet Flat
64990 Deschutes Market Road between Bend and Redmond
(541) 389–6391

What looks like kitsch to a grown-up can be magic to a kid. Here's a place with unlimited magic.

Let's start our description as you drive into the parking lot at the Funny Farm. A juniper tree dressed in gold-colored glass grapes and a totem pole made of "found objects" might be the first two things you notice. Or perhaps it's the wooden cow cutouts ("to err is human, to love is bovine"). Or the big white dog named Bear, who lives on the roof and can be fed with a contraption of pulleys. Walk into the dark interior of the antiques store and a tiny version of Dorothy's voice wafts out of nowhere saying, "Toto, I don't think we're in Kansas anymore," a comment that seems very appropriate for the unusual world you have just entered.

The voice comes from a working 2-inch television that's inside an impressive dollhouse—just one item in a room packed with a mixture of antiques and collectibles (more of the latter), including many glass display cases of retro costume jewelry. An adult might take time to wander through the maze of rooms, where you'll see lots more including vintage clothing, life-size cardboard cutouts of Marilyn Monroe and John Wayne, hats and boas, and "atomic" art pieces from the '50s and '60s, and that's just scratching the surface. Nuggets of wisdom such as "it's the set of our sails, not the force of the gales, that determine the direction of our ship" (we're paraphrasing) are painted or pinned on doors and walls in locations that catch your eye with amazing accuracy. As you might imagine from the incredible scene before you, Halloween is high season at Buffet Flat.

Kids are invited to take the bag of animal crackers and a baby bottle of Kool-Aid and follow the gray carpeting through the maze of rooms and out a back door to the farm. Our first greeter was a goat named Babe, who normally hangs out in a tower made of planks and pipes but came down to earth when offered the bottle. A dozen goats, donkeys, and sheep live with Babe, and each one expects an animal cracker. The two potbellied pigs will come out for handouts (except when it's too cold), and chickens and roosters wander around.

Paint is peeling and faded, and the whole place has a slapped-together appearance, but you can't help but appreciate the rampant sense of humor. A gate to the goat pen is made of an old refrigerator door; pink flamingos are perched around their "nest"—a tire painted pink; there's the largest bowling ball garden in the West (seeds are available for purchase); an old ramshackle barn features a rainbow and clouds painted on its roof; and there's a "sound park," where junk makes noises in the wind. Junk and more junk is creatively arranged or just piled up all over. Pick up a free map so you won't miss any of the highlights that you might mistake for, well, junk.

In accordance with the brochure, which admits that unbridled greed is alive and well at Buffet Flat, everything you see is for sale or rent. Admission is free, but donations are appreciated. The Funny Farm at Buffet Flat is open 10:00 A.M. to 5:00 P.M. year-round. You'll find this place on the northeast corner of Tumalo Road and U.S. Highway 97, an intersection halfway between Bend and Redmond called Deschutes Junction. It's marked with a flashing yellow light, and that's the last time you will really know where you are. As the Funny Farm map says, "All is not lost, just those who try to use this map!" Bring your camera and come when the weather is fair.

Goody's Soda Fountain & Candy Store
957 Northwest Wall Street
(541) 389–5185

Eyes grow as big as pie plates when kids see all the delicious stuff made here. The homemade ice cream and hot fudge topping are really good. Goody's is open 10:00 A.M. to 9:00 P.M. Monday through Thursday, 10:00 A.M. to 10:00 P.M. Friday and Saturday, and noon to 8:00 P.M. on

Visitors to The High Desert Museum enjoy a wide variety of indoor and outdoor exhibits that interpret the natural and human history of the desert. PHOTO: JIM YUSKAVITCH

Sunday. This is a downtown Bend institution (see our Shopping chapter).

The High Desert Museum
59800 South U.S. Highway 97
(541) 382–4754
www.highdesert.org

Here's a wonderful stop for the whole family. It's covered thoroughly in our Attractions chapter, but the children's programs are worth a special mention here.

Every day at the museum—between 10:00 A.M. and 4:00 P.M. from May through September, and 10:30 A.M. to 3:00 P.M. October through April—hourly talks are presented at the outdoor Otter, Porcupine, and Birds of Prey exhibits. The otters provide endless entertainment in their pool, and you can go inside a building and see it all underwater through a window. Inside the museum the Hall of Exploration and Settlement, with its life-size exhibits of pioneers, is of special interest for kids. Don't miss the Desertarium, an indoor exhibit complex featuring live and rarely seen animals of the High Desert, including burrowing owls, bats, and lizards.

Throughout the year, special events for families are designed as much for fun as for education. In April the Family Science Festival has puppet shows, science and art activities, and explorations. One weekend each month from May through September, the kids can enjoy Sawmill-In-Action, when the authentic early-20th-century sawmill springs to life. Volunteers demonstrate the sawmill and its history.

October brings The Harvest Hoe Down Celebration at the Museum's Robbins Family Homestead. Kids can see the cider mill and other old homestead skills demonstrated; tastes of the fresh-made cider are included. The Saturday closest to Halloween is Bat Day—a batty event filled with activities, games, videos, puppet shows, and stories about bats. Kids come in costumes for a parade. The Holiday Festival and Art Show, held on the Friday and Saturday after Thanksgiving, features children's activities and pioneer music. Winter Wonderfest comes during winter break and lets kids discover the wonderfully mysterious world of winter. All these events are included in the admission price.

Kids are fascinated by the Birds of Prey exhibit at The High Desert Museum. PHOTO: JIM YUSKAVITCH

Special classes, workshops, and field trips for kids from kindergarten through junior high school ages are often scheduled at the museum. "Bubbleology—the Science of Bubbles" and "Kites on the Wing" (for grades kindergarten through 5); the five-day "Jaws and Claws"; and "Lifeways, Atlatls, Darts and Flintknapping: A Culture Camp" (for grades 6 and up) are just a few of the fascinating titles. Day classes cost $14 for nonmembers of the museum; weeklong day camps are $155.

The Silver Sage Trading store in the museum has some of the best gifts and souvenirs we've seen for kids. Outside is a picnic area. Admission for kids ages 5 to 12 is $4.00; it's $7.50 for youngsters ages 13 to 18. Check our Attractions chapter for more information on the High Desert Museum.

House of Rocks
67288 U.S. Highway 20

You've got to stop and see the 11,000-pound volcanic rock that rests on top of a Country Squire station wagon to poke fun at the way rock hounds like to schlep rocks all over. The rock that is perched on

top of the mobile home portico (where owners Leonard and Shirley live) weighs in around 8,000 pounds.

When Leonard and his wife bought this rock shop in 1993, Leonard wanted to get rid of the station wagon, but his wife talked him out of it. Instead he painted it orange (which the highway department didn't appreciate—too distracting to drivers on the highway), and now he's glad he kept it. Rock hounds from all over the country know just where his place is when he mentions the rock on the car. Two resident rock hounds of a different sort are Rocky and Stoney, Len and Shirley's Boston terriers.

Next to the mobile home is a very tidy rock store with more rocks than any one person or family could hope to find in one place. Behind the store, which you reach by following the Rock Garden Walk, is a big yellow trailer that is actually a museum. Inside are dozens of miniature houses made of tumbled beach agates, landscaped with tiny trees and scale-model dogs, horses, and people. The houses were created by a previous owner and took many years to make. Outside are a couple of swing sets and a dog-walking area, just in case you've brought along any kids or dogs who don't have rocks in their heads. House of Rocks is open daily from 9:00 A.M. to 6:00 P.M.

INCLIMB
550 Southwest Industrial Way
(541) 388–6764
www.inclimb.com

Everything's up at INCLIMB, where kids can enjoy 5,000 square feet of climbing terrain featuring an awesome bouldering cave, 20 top ropes, and the inspirational rock-and-roll machine, where the wall keeps rolling downward so you never get to the top.

The youth programs here include Hangtime, a Saturday belay session that runs from noon to 2:00 P.M. The fee is $10. INCLIMB also sponsors a Youth Climbing League for kids ages 9 and up. For $80 a month you get lessons, coaching, and the opportunity to compete in organized rock-climbing competitions.

For a $10 day pass, kids can drop in and climb the walls (without their parents on hand if they have previously taken a class or are age 12 or older). Kids age 11 and under are $7.00. Climbing shoes rent for $4.00. Advanced climbers can join INCLIMB's climbing league, which travels all over the world, and guided group sessions at Smith Rock are available for $65 per half day or $90 for a whole day.

Outdoor climbing at Smith Rock is $95 per half day or $175 for a whole day for one person. Groups of two to five people cost $80 per half day or $150 per whole day, and groups of six persons or more runs $75 per whole day, with half days available.

INCLIMB has a program for Scouts to earn merit badges, and it hosts birthday parties ($15 per person), where they'll add extra belayers in the birthday boy or girl's honor. Order in pizza and bring a cake. INCLIMB is open from noon to 9:00 P.M. Monday through Friday, noon to 8:00 P.M. on Saturday and noon to 5:00 P.M. on Sunday (but closed on Sunday during the summer). It's in Bend's Old Mill District.

Rocky Mountain Chocolate Factory
Factory Outlet Mall, U.S. Highway 97
(541) 383–1718

If the kids have to go shopping at the outlet stores with the parents, they will definitely need some chocolate fortification. Rocky Mountain Chocolate Factory is open during mall hours (see our Shopping chapter for more information).

Sun Mountain Fun Centre
300 Northeast Bend Rivermall Avenue
(541) 382–6161
www.sunmountainfun.com

This is not your ordinary bowling alley. Inside you'll find 24 kid-proof lanes with bumper guards plus billiards, video arcades, a full-service snack bar, and a lounge that serves beer and wine. The kid-friendly orientation means that lightweight bowling balls are provided. Outside are batting cages, an 18-hole miniature golf course, and go-carts.

Bowling is $2.75 per game except on Friday and Saturday nights, when it's $3.00. During slower times, discounts are available. Miniature golf costs $4.00 for kids 12 and under and $5.00 for adults. It is available all year (depending on the weather). If that's too sedentary, try racing around in the new go-carts for $5.00 a ride; the track is open daily during summer and Friday through Sunday at other times of the year. The center is open Monday through Thursday from 10:00 A.M. to 11:00 P.M., Friday and Saturday from 10:00 A.M. to 1:00 A.M. and Sunday from 10:00 A.M. to 11:00 P.M. This is a nonsmoking facility. Read more about Sun Mountain in our Indoor Recreation chapter.

Tumalo Falls
Forest Service Road 4603, 14 miles west of Bend
(541) 383–5300
www.fs.fed.us/r6/centraloregon

To get to Tumalo Falls, head west on Franklin Avenue past Drake Park and across the river. Go straight at the stop sign, and follow Skyliners Road 11 miles. When it turns to gravel, continue on Forest Service Road 4603 for another 3.5 miles. The falls are 97 feet high. You will need a Trail Park Pass to park here. (See our Close-up in the Forests, High Desert, and Volcanoes chapter for more on the passes; check our Attractions chapter for more on Tumalo Falls.)

Sisters/Camp Sherman Area

For kids, the best things about the Sisters area are out and about. Spend the day at Camp Sherman, where you can walk on a trail along the Metolius River. See the headwaters, where the entire river spews forth out of nowhere. At the Camp Sherman bridge you can throw stale bread to huge trout that are off-limits to anglers, but the frigid water is too cold for wading. If you brought your bike there are lots of dirt roads to explore. Nearby is the Wizard Falls Fish Hatchery, where kids can get an eyeful of large trout and maybe even throw some fish food into the water. The Metolius Recreation Area is an excellent spot for a picnic.

In downtown Sisters, kids will be happy to know there's actually a selection of ice-cream places. The Palace, at 158 West Cascade Avenue, (541) 549-0562, makes really good milk shakes; Ali's is 1 block east in the Town Square, serving healthy frozen yogurt desserts. The Rainbow Connection has ice cream as well as toys and stuff; it stays open to 5:00 or 6:00 P.M., depending on how busy they are. Sno Cap Ice Cream, a 60-year institution on the west side of Sisters at 380 West Cascade Avenue, (541) 549-6151, serves homemade ice cream. And if we haven't satisfied your sweet tooth yet, the Candy Bin at 121 West Cascade Avenue, (541) 549-1155, has a wide selection of what used to be penny candy.

At the west end of Sisters, about a half-mile down the road that leads to McKenzie Pass (Forest Service 242), is the Patterson Ranch, where kids can view Rocky Mountain elk and llamas from the turnouts along the fence.

Here are some other options in the area.

Sisters Organization for Activities and Recreation (SOAR)
P.O. Box 3099
(541) 549-2091

This community organization focuses on providing young people in the Sisters area with healthy, constructive activities including team sports, supervised games, art activities, and help with homework and after-school study. They focus on building social and intellectual skills, increasing physical health, and providing safe play and educational environments.

The program's special focus is "at-risk" children. A small fee is charged to participate in SOAR programs. Fees are based on a family's ability to pay, and no one is turned away.

Three Creek Lake
Forest Service Road 16

Begin your adventure in downtown Sisters by heading south on Elm Street, which turns into Forest Service Road 16. The beautiful, mostly paved road starts at 3,184 feet and climbs 12 miles through a sunny ponderosa forest to 5,700 feet. The lake is located in the Deschutes National Forest, at the base of a cliff known as Tam McArthur Rim along the border of the Three Sisters Wilderness. This picture-perfect alpine lake is fairly shallow, so it gets almost warm enough for swimming! There's even a small beach and several campgrounds nearby. On the way up are a couple of Sno-Parks good for some frosty snowplay.

Wizard Falls Fish Hatchery
Off Forest Service Road 14, 5 miles north of Camp Sherman
(541) 595–6611

Believe it or not, people visiting the Camp Sherman area make it a point to stop by the Wizard Falls Fish Hatchery for a half hour or so to see how the trout and salmon stocked in local streams are raised. In fact, about 40,000 people drop by this hatchery each year, where rainbow trout and brook trout, along with Atlantic and kokanee salmon, are cultured. You can wander around the grounds and observe the rearing pools and raceways full of the young fish that will eventually be released into lakes and rivers throughout Central Oregon. You'll see a display pond that holds 10- and 12-pound rainbow trout and a nearby settling pond where similar size trout may be seen swimming near shore.

Vending machines by the pond dispense 25-cent handfuls of fish feed that you can toss to the lunkers patrolling the pond's edges. The hatchery is also a great place for bird-watching, so bring your binoculars and field guide. The trout in the settling pond attract such fish-eating birds as bald eagles and ospreys, which you have a reasonable chance of spotting here. And there are usually plenty of ducks and geese around as well.

Wizard Falls Fish Hatchery is open all year, though the best time to come is in spring, when you are most likely to see wildlife. Hatchery operations are at their peak in March and May, when staff are busy preparing for the upcoming fishing season. This is a good time to visit if you are interested in seeing what hatchery workers do for a living. Staff members are happy to schedule tours for both large and small groups, but you'll need to call ahead to make arrangements. The hatchery is also a host site for Free Fishing Weekend events, held every year on the second Saturday in June. See our Fishing chapter for more information on this annual event.

Redmond

Redmond is a good area for scenic picnic spots such as Smith Rock State Park and the Peter Skene Ogden Wayside, which overlooks the Crooked River Canyon north of Redmond on U.S. 97 (see our Parks chapter). Kids can fish for free at Fireman's Pond, where everyone who grew up in Redmond used to fish when they were children. The pond is on Lake Road just off Sisters Avenue before you get to the Juniper Golf Course (see our Golf chapter).

For kid-friendly dining, you'll find a concentration of fast-food restaurants at the south end of Redmond along U.S. 97, and there's a Sno-Cap Drive-In outlet (see previous listing in this chapter) on the north end of town on U.S. 97 for some ice cream on the run.

Central Oregon Parks & Recreation
465 Southwest Rimrock Drive
(541) 548–6066
www.coprd.org

The COPR is an independent public agency that operates the Cascade Swim Center and offers other sports programs for kids. The swim center is open all year and costs $1.25 for kids 15 and younger, $2.50 for grown-ups. The schedule gets pretty complicated for the different age groups, so call for open swimming times.

In autumn kids ages 5 through 8th grade can join a soccer or basketball team for $35. During the summer, weeklong multi-sports camps are offered for ages 7 to 14. The cost is $48. A variety of other team sports are also offered.

> **Insiders' Tip**
> Kids younger than age 14 can fish without a license as long as they are accompanied by an adult who does have a fishing license.

Budding thespians can sign up for a weeklong program called the Missoula Children's Theater, where kids from kindergarten through 12th grade learn the art of drama and acting as well as the nuts and bolts of set staging and all the other skills that go into putting on great performances. The cost is $45.

For the more technical-minded, instructors from the Oregon Museum of Science and Industry in Portland come over regularly to run science-themed summer day camps for about $10 per class. Rates are slightly higher if you live out of the recreation district. Call for more information.

Deschutes County Fair
Deschutes County Fairgrounds
3800 Southwest Airport Way
(541) 548–2711
www.expo.deschutes.org
This July event is the biggest county fair in our coverage area. Kids will love the animal exhibits, where children from 4-H and Future Farmers of America and local ranchers display cattle, sheep, chickens, ducks, geese, rabbits, llamas, horses, and goats, along with critters you've probably never heard of. Youngsters will also get a

---

Insiders' Tip

Resident kids don't need to live on a ranch to join the 4-H club. The 4-H offers many neat pursuits for town-bound youngsters in fields such as dog training, rabbit raising, and home skills. For more information, contact the Oregon State University Extension Office in Redmond at (541) 548-6088.

---

kick out of the petting zoo, and there are the usual amusement park rides and sticky cotton candy. For more on the fair, including dates and admission prices, see the July section of our Annual Events chapter.

The Kid's Zone
3290 South U.S. Highway 97
(541) 548–0000
Billed as the largest soft-play zone in Central Oregon, this place has more padding than any place we've been on earth. The front of the facility is a pizza and fast-food restaurant with semicircular booths and private party rooms (the staff here is good at coordinating birthday parties, including the cake). It's all lit with bright fluorescent lights, and everything is clean and well maintained.

Beyond the restaurant is a dark, cavernous chamber—at first glance it might be a medieval torture chamber or maybe the machinery room of the Empire State Building. Soon you realize it's a two-story playground for kids.

When we visited, two boys repeatedly rolled down a padded, rounded staircase, perhaps honing their movie-stunt skills, while two small girls and a dad bobbed in a sea of small plastic balls. Moms sat in plastic chairs and chatted—with one eye on the speaker and the other on the kids—and occasionally whipped out a camera as their offspring popped out of the mouth of an enormous tubular slide. The romper room costs $4.95 for kids ages 4 to 12 and $2.95 for kids 3 and younger. Next door is a video arcade for the older siblings; that should take care of any problems you might have with lugging spare change around with you.

Outside Kid's Zone are batting cages for $1.00 and a small pool with seasonal bumper boats made of inner tubes fitted with a seat and a small motor. Boat rides are $3.00. You can give the go-carts a whirl for $4.00, but no bumping here. The outdoor activities are weather-dependent. The Kid's Zone is open Monday through Thursday from 10:30 A.M. to 9:30 P.M. and Friday through Sunday from 10:00 A.M. to 10:00 P.M. During the winter months, they are open from 3:00 P.M. to 9:00 P.M. Monday through Thursday, 11:00 A.M. to 10:00

P.M. on Friday and Saturday, and noon to 8:00 P.M. on Sunday.

This is not a place where you'd want to bring the latest book you're reading.

Operation Santa Claus
4355 West U.S. Highway 26
(541) 548–8910

Seeing the real reindeer is definitely worth a short visit, especially in April and May when the reindeer calves are little. The small gift and souvenir shop (heavy on the Santa Claus theme) is open from Memorial Day through Christmas, but even if you happen to show up when no one is there you can still see the reindeer and read the very interesting placard that tells their story. During the holidays some of the reindeer are loaned out to Santa Claus to drive his representatives' sleighs in Christmas parades all over the West, but they always keep some reindeer at home for visitors to see. Call for a schedule of Christmas events. Admission is free.

Petersen Rock Gardens & Museum
7930 Southwest 77th Street
(541) 382–5574

The gardens, with their intricate rock sculptures, pools, wandering peacocks, and picnic tables, make for a fun place to stop for a picnic. Kids especially love the museum room, with the black lights where the rocks really glow. For more information, see our Attractions chapter.

Sunriver/La Pine Area

Sunriver Resort, with its influx of visitors, has a lot to offer younger guests. In the village there's ice-skating in winter, and in summer the rink converts to a miniature golf course. Call (541) 593-5948 for details. The resort's Saddleback Stables, (541) 593-1221 extension 4420, offers Smallest Buckaroo pony rides for $6.00, along with hay wagon and Christmas carol rides. For teenagers the stables have special ice-cream socials as part of their Teen Only Rides, at $25 an hour.

The Village Bike Shop, (541) 593-2453, and Sunriver Sports, (541) 593-8369, both rent bicycles, trailers, and tagalongs so kids can explore the 30-plus miles of bike trails surrounding Sunriver. Village Bike Shop also rents sleds and tubes for snowplay. The public can rent canoes at the Sunriver Marina to paddle on the gentle Deschutes River.

Guests of the resort may take advantage of Fort Rock Park's playground; volleyball, basketball, and tennis courts; and softball and baseball fields. Other programs for resort guests include Sunriver Adventure Camps, five-day day camps for kids ages 5 through 11, which cost $100 per week and are also for resort guests/residents, as are the resort's two swimming pools and swim lessons. (For more on Sunriver, see our Resorts, Ranches, and Vacation Rental chapter.)

The LaPine State Park has water, forests, and plenty of sunshine—perfect for a picnic or a wet, cold romp. There's more on this park in our Parks chapter. Deschutes National Forest has an unlimited number of places where a kid could drown a worm (go fishing) or play in the snow (see our chapters on Other Outdoor Recreation and Snowplay).

Here are some other area places and pursuits your youngsters will love.

Goody's Soda Fountain & Candy Store
Sunriver Village Mall, Sunriver
(541) 593-2155

Just wait until you taste the homemade ice cream and hot fudge sauce here! You also can't go wrong sticking with the chocolates, or popcorn, or cotton candy, or...you get the idea. Goody's is open daily during summer from 10:00 A.M. to 10:00 P.M.; in winter it closes at 6:00 P.M. Sunday through Thursday.

La Pine Kid's Club
La Pine Elementary School, 51615 Coach Road, La Pine
(541) 536-7525

This is a wonderful latchkey program for school kids ages 5 through 12. Basically, the club is open when school is not, between the hours of 6:30 A.M. and 6:30 P.M. Activities include arts and crafts, daytrips for hiking, biking, fishing, and swimming, and whatever else the staff can come up with. In summer there are daily programs as well as sports camps. Funding comes from private and public sources, as well as through the user fee of $1.40 per hour per child, with a $1.25 fee for each additional child in the family.

Lava Lands Visitor Center and Lava Butte
Newberry National Volcanic Monument, U.S.
Highway 97, 4 miles north of Sunriver
(541) 593–2421, April through October,
(541) 383–5300, November through March

This is the visitors center for the Newberry National Volcanic Monument (see our Daytrips and Attractions chapters), a not-to-be-missed place for kids, especially on weekends when the nature talks are in full swing. Kids can learn about birds of the forest, volcanoes, and geology, and can even discover how to make arrowheads out of obsidian. Check out the rocks that can float, and admire (but don't feed) the ground squirrels that run up to your feet.

Getting restless? Head out the door to experience a bumpy lava flow with rough rocks—you'll have to touch it to believe it, and it extends as far as the eye can see. You can also ride the bus to the top of nearby Lava Butte, a cinder cone. On Saturday evenings atop Lava Butte, naturalists will help you name the constellations and catch sight of a bat. Just down the highway kids can experience walking in a mile-long lava-tube cave. If you pack a cooler, Lava Lands Visitor Center is a nice spot to have lunch.

Newberry National Volcanic Monument
Forest Service Road 21, just off U.S. Highway
97, 5 miles north of La Pine
(541) 593–2421, April through October,
(541) 383–5300, November through March

Although Newberry National Volcanic Monument is described in detail in the Daytrips chapter, we want to mention it here because kids would be fascinated by a visit. At this mountain of volcanic glass they can enjoy naturalist talks on flint-knapping, a short hike to 80-foot Paulina Falls, a cool drive to the top of Paulina Peak for views from its 7,985-foot elevation, and clear, mountain lakes with hot

springs. Families can rent rowboats, canoes, and paddleboats starting at $10 for two hours. During winter, rent snowshoes or tubes at the Village Bike Shop in Sunriver and come here to play—the Newberry caldera has snow later in the year than La Pine or Sunriver. And 10 miles north of Oregon Highway 21 is the Lava River Cave, an enormous, mile-long cave that's a guaranteed adventure.

Paulina Plunge Mountain Bike Tour
P.O. Box 8782, Bend
(541) 389–0562, (800) 296–0562
www.paulinaplunge.com

Thrills and chills are in store for ages 4 and older at the Paulina Plunge. High Cascade Descent Mountain Bike Tours will transport you about 20 miles from Sunriver to the rim of the Newberry Caldera, outfit you with a mountain bike, safety gear, and even a day pack, and it's all downhill from there. Fortunately, you won't descend the entire 2,500 feet all at once. Rather, your plunge will be broken up by visits to six waterfalls, including two water slides where you can have the splash of a lifetime. Let's hear it for the Moms and Dads who get to go swimming and biking and take pictures—all at once, while wearing squishy sneakers. All this for $50 per person. For an extra $5.00, they'll throw in lunch. It's advised that you make reservations two weeks in advance.

Sunriver Nature Center and Observatory
17620 River Road, Sunriver
(541) 593–4394, nature center
(541) 598–4406, observatory
www.sunrivercenter.org

Here's another great place for families that appears in our Attractions chapter, but we want to mention it here to focus on the options for children. Youngsters can explore a box of bones found in the wilderness, look at some resident bald eagles up close with a telescope, explore the center's eight acres of natural landscape, or attend spring and summer walks and talks given by naturalists daily when school is out (or weekends when school's in session).

The center rehabilitates and releases many rescued eagles, owls, and other birds, some of which will be available for viewing. During summer, the center regularly offers special classes geared for different age groups. Young Explorers is a two-hour session for kids ages 4 to 6; it meets on Tuesday and Thursday to explore nature through games and crafts. Cost is $12 per session. Older kids ages 7 through 10 can attend the Junior Naturalist programs that may focus on insects, pond life, or reptiles. These sessions are also held on Tuesday and Thursday for $12 per person. The Rocket Science class runs on Wednesday and Saturday and costs $15. Teens and adults can take a beginning bird-watching class on Sunday mornings for $3.00 per person.

The nature center is open Tuesday through Saturday from 10:00 A.M. to 4:00 P.M. Summer admission fees are $3.00 for adults and $2.00 for kids ages 12 and under. During the winter, they drop by a buck.

During summer the observatory offers viewing every night except Monday from 9:00 to 11:00 P.M. Visitors should bring warm clothes for nighttime viewing. Daytime astronomy sessions allow visitors to view the sun from 10:00 A.M. to 2:00 P.M. Staff astronomers give in-depth talks at 9:00 P.M. on Saturday in summer. Children age 12 and younger are $4.00 for the evening sessions. Adults are $6.00. Day sessions are included in the nature center admission fee.

Sunriver Nature Center and Observatory is open every day in summer, but you might want to call ahead to the observatory to check on the local weather. Hours are quite school-sensitive, with special hours set during spring break and holidays. To get to the nature center and observatory, enter Sunriver at the main entrance, follow the signs through the One and Two traffic circles, and when you get to circle Three keep going around until you spot the sign for the nature center. See our Attractions chapter for more general information.

Prineville Area

April brings the Crook County Rodeo, a terrific event with all the trappings, including the hilarious Mutton Busters—kids dressed up like cowboys who ride sheep bareback to see who can ride the longest. There's also a prize for best outfit.

Prineville's long hot summers provide great opportunities for fun in the sun and water at Ochoco Reservoir and the Prineville Reservoir State Park. There are still other options that kids would love—fishing, hiking, snowplay, and more—in the Ochoco National Forest, or you can take your fishing pole to the Crooked River Canyon south of Prineville. The Crook County Fair, small but complete and lots of country fun, is held in mid-July at the Prineville fairgrounds. For more information on these places and events, see our Parks, Annual Events, and recreation chapters.

For kid-type eats, Prineville has a few chain fast-food places along its main drag, including a McDonald's. For that all-important ice-cream cone, you can get the real stuff at the Tastee Treat, 493 East Third Street; the Dairy Queen Brazier at 600 West Third Street sells the usual soft-serve varieties and thick shakes.

Madras Area

Madras's proximity to lakes generates most of the excitement for kids during summer. Lake Billy Chinook has swimming, boat rentals, and camping. The Round Butte Overview, a park owned by Portland General Electric 12 miles southwest of Madras, is a great spot for a picnic with views of the lake.

There are a few fast-food places along the main drag in town. Here are a few other Madras-area options to keep the children happy.

Kah-Nee-Ta Resort
U.S. Highway 26, Warm Springs
(541) 553–1112, (800) 554–4786,
(800) 831–0100
www.kah-nee-taresort.com

What kid wouldn't want to sleep out in a tepee and listen to stories told by tribal members? It happens every Wednesday and Friday night, by appointment. The little ones can also go swimming in a naturally heated pool with a 140-foot water slide. Swimming is $7.00 for adults and youths, and $4.00 for kids ages 3 to 6; there is an extra $2.00 charge for the water slide, and it's worth every penny. For ages 7 and older there's an inflatable kayak trip on the Warm Springs River ($25 per person), and there is a one-hour horseback ride for kids ages 6 and older that costs around $20 per person. Also, there are volleyball and basketball courts.

Tepees are $69.99 per night in summer and sleep as many kids as you can line the floor with (10 people). You do not have to be an overnight guest to enjoy the pool and other facilities. Showers, fine dining (the Mongoliag Grill Buffet serves breakfast, lunch, and dinner), a world-class spa, a casino, an 18-hole golf course, and fast food are available. There's much more info on Kah-Nee-Ta in our Resorts, Ranches, and Vacation Rentals chapter, and you'll find background information on the Warm Springs Reservation in our chapter on Other Area Communities.

The Museum at Warm Springs
U.S. Highway 26, Warm Springs
(541) 553–3331
www.warmsprings.com

The beauty and vitality of Native American life come alive at the museum's state-of-the-art exhibits. Demonstrations and performances take place in an outdoor amphitheater, and there's a picnic area along the lovely Shitike Creek. There is much more information on The Museum at Warm Springs in our Attractions chapter. It is a must-see for visitors to Kah-Nee-Tah Resort.

Richardson's Rock Ranch
Old U.S. Highway 97, Madras
(541) 475–2680
www.orerockon.com/richards

If your kid has rocks in his head and lots of energy, this is the place to go. Let him (or her) dig thundereggs (volcanic nodules filled with agate; see the Close-up in our Forests, High Desert, and Volcanoes chapter) or chip away at some agate or jasper, all while camping under the stars. If you aren't up to such hard labor, there's a fabulous shop filled with pre-dug and polished stones and spheres that are amazing to behold. Again, see our Attractions chapter for more information on Richardson's Rock Ranch.

Annual Events

We're interested in just about everything here in Central Oregon, and that's reflected in the variety of events and festivals that take place every month of the year. We like animals and cars, rocks and snow, art and exercise. And you can count on an event built around those themes, and others, taking place sometime, somewhere around these parts. We like holidays, especially Christmas, when it seems as though the entire country is wrapped in festive lights, and everyone is on their way to a Christmas parade. We shine on the Fourth of July, when we fly the colors and settle down on blankets to watch fireworks pop and sizzle against the darkened sky.

We have our share of arts-and-crafts shows and Saturday markets, road runs and marathons. If you're a car buff, you're in luck: Central Oregon is a magnet for classic car shows and rallies. For a taste of the Old West, there are rodeos (this is, after all, cowboy country) and Native American powwows. And there are surprises, too. Who would guess that 20,000 people would come here to see a mammoth display of quilts from around the world? Or to play ancient Celtic games? And don't dismiss the small-town get-togethers in outlying rural areas, where you can experience the friendliness and spontaneity that only these homespun events can offer.

We've compiled this list of the most popular, most interesting, and most unusual area events to get you started. If you have specific interests that are not listed, local chambers of commerce can usually steer you in the right direction. Any admission fees are mentioned in the event description; otherwise they are free. Central Oregon also offers a full plate of annual music festivals and sporting events that are listed in our chapters on The Arts and Spectator Sports, respectively.

January

Winter Wonderfest
The High Desert Museum, 59800 South U.S. Highway 97, Bend
(541) 382–4754
For the full scoop on snow, bundle up and head for The High Desert Museum for Winter Wonderfest, held during the Christmas–New Year school vacation period. Museum volunteers will unlock the secrets of the winter wonderland for you. How do animals survive in the winter? Where do the insects go? Why is every snowflake unique? There are games, videos, storytelling, puppet shows, and lots of hands-on activities. The Winter Wonderfest is always held on a Saturday from 10:00 A.M. to 3:00 P.M. Admission to the museum is $7.75 for adults, $6.75 for seniors age 65 years and older, $6.75 for children ages 13 to 18, $3.74 for kids ages 5 to 12, and free for children age 4 and younger. (For more information on The High Desert Museum, see our Attractions chapter.)

February

Bend Winterfest
Mount Bachelor and Downtown Bend
(541) 385–6570
Snowy fun stretches from Mount Bachelor to downtown Bend on the first Friday, Saturday, and Sunday in February. You'll find a variety of events, including a Friday evening torchlight ceremony, fun and serious ski races at Mount Bachelor, professional ice-carving demonstrations, crowning of a "Snow Queen," dancing, and musical entertainment. Sponsored by Subaru, the company donates a car to be raffled each year. The $5.00 raffle ticket also serves as your entrance fee to all the events and activities. All proceeds

from the Bend Winterfest are dedicated to a different local charity each year.

Hoodoo Winter Carnival
Hoodoo Ski Bowl, off U.S. Highway 20 on Santiam Pass, Sisters
(541) 822–3799
www.hoodoo.com

Skiers and nonskiers alike flock to the summit of Santiam Pass, in the heart of the Cascade Mountains, during the second weekend of February to immerse themselves in the many pleasures of an Oregon winter. Sleigh rides, snow sculptures, a pie-eating contest, a children's treasure hunt through the bowels of a giant snow castle, and a Fly-A-Thon (combining cross-country skiing and fly-casting) make for a full plate of activities for kids and adults.

And speaking of full plates, there's a sumptuous chicken dinner at 5:00 P.M. At 7:30 P.M., torch-bearing skiers descend the mountain, and it's all punctuated by a display of fireworks at 8:30 P.M. There's skiing too, of course. Admission to all events is free. The dinner runs $7.50 per person. Lift tickets for adults and teens are $29; they're $22 for children ages 6 to 12. Night skiing tickets are $18 for adults and $14 for kids.

Eagle Watch
The Cove Palisades State Park, 7300 Jordan Road, Culver (off U.S. Highway 97, 15 miles southwest of Madras)
(541) 546–3412

Even if you're stuck with the turkeys all week long, you can still soar with the eagles at Lake Billy Chinook in The Cove

Palisades State Park. Sponsored by the Oregon Department of Parks and Recreation, Portland General Electric, and The Confederated Tribes of Warm Springs, Eagle Watch is held each year on a weekend in mid-February during the peak of the eagle migration. That's when as many as 200 bald eagles leave their summer homes in Washington state, Alaska, and Canada's Northwest Territories to take up winter residence at this Central Oregon state park. Once they arrive, they dine on the abundant trout and salmon to be found in Lake Billy Chinook.

Programs run from 9:30 A.M. to 4:30 P.M. each day and include eagle-viewing sessions from various points around the lake, natural-history talks by local biology experts, and Native American dances performed by members of The Confederated Tribes of Warm Springs. A light lunch and refreshments are provided on both days. On Saturday, volunteers from The High Desert Museum (see the Attractions chapter) give presentations on birds of prey—featuring an opportunity to meet some of the museum's feathered ambassadors, including eagles, hawks, and owls.

If you're a serious eagle watcher, you'll want to show up at 5:30 A.M. on both days for a guided trip to the lake's edge to watch these magnificent birds settle into their day roosts. There is no charge to participate in Eagle Watch. Programs are held at different locations and times throughout the park, so be sure to call ahead for a schedule of events.

Homestead Skills Showcase
The High Desert Museum, 59800 South U.S. Highway 97, Bend
(541) 382–4754

Pioneer skills are the focus of this annual event, as costumed museum volunteers demonstrate weaving, rug hooking, butter churning, wool spinning, rope splicing, saw sharpening, and tool making. You can give them a try as well. For the kids, there are pioneer games and toys.

Homestead Skills Showcase is held from 10:00 A.M. to 4:00 P.M. on a Saturday in February or March. Admission to the museum is $7.75 for adults, $6.75 for seniors age 65 and older, $6.75 for children ages 13 to 18, $3.74 for kids ages 5 to 12, and free for children age 4 and younger.

March

Spring Festival Flea Market and Auction
Crook County Fairgrounds, 1280 South Main Street, Prineville
(541) 447–6575
You can buy just about anything you want at the Crook County Fairgrounds from 9:00 A.M. to 4:00 P.M. on the first Saturday in March, when dozens of vendors lay out their wares. They've got gas stoves, used tires, pottery, power equipment, old tools, paintings, saddles, china, rifles, paint, mirrors, glasses, pots, pans, bowls, tables, chairs, cars, campers, knives, tablecloths, books . . . Did we leave anything out?

Spring Break Family Day
The High Desert Museum, 59800 South U.S. Highway 97, Bend
(541) 382–4754
It's a major yearly event at The High Desert Museum when throngs of families pack the museum grounds for a day of puppet making and shows, soap carving, crazy quilting, music, and demonstrations of pioneer crafts and skills. Family Day is always held from 10:00 A.M. to 3:30 P.M. on a Wednesday in late March, during spring break week for Central Oregon schools. It's a day of fun and learning for kids up to 13 years old. Admission to the museum is $7.75 for adults, $6.75 for seniors age 65 and older, $6.75 for children ages 13 to 18, $3.74 for kids ages 5 to 12, and free for children age 4 and younger.

Riverhouse Rendezvous
3075 North U.S. Highway 97, Bend
(541) 389–9178
Kayakers come from throughout the Pacific Northwest to compete in this slalom race held on the last weekend in March on the Deschutes River off Mount Washington Boulevard. Organized by the Oregon Kayak and Canoe Club and co-sponsored by The Riverhouse resort (the event is held on resort property), it is part of the Northwest Cup Series.

Saturday's action revolves around a swap meet, where boaters sell anything that has to do with floating rivers—kayaks, canoes, paddles, wet suits, and more—making it a great place to get good deals on gear. Twenty percent of sales go back to the club. The swap meet runs from 9:00 A.M. to 4:00 P.M. Saturday is also a free practice day, and boaters take to the water to run the course in preparation for Sunday's races, which include a variety of men's and women's classes. The entry fee is $20 to race in one event or $25 to race in more than one (or all). Races begin at 11:00 A.M. and usually finish up by 3:00 P.M. Each year, proceeds from this event are donated to a different charity or cause.

April

Bend Downtowners Art Hop
Downtown Bend
(541) 385–6570
Twice a year, on the first Friday of April and October, Bend merchants host an evening with local artists, who display their work in various stores in the central downtown area. Wander the streets and drop into the various shops between 5:00 and 9:00 P.M.; you'll find sculptors, potters, painters, performing artists, and more. The creativity will delight your eyes and ears while the tasty refreshments and treats served up by the merchants will please your palate. Many of the artists offer their works for sale.

Family Science Festival
The High Desert Museum, 59800 South U.S. Highway 97, Bend
(541) 382–4754
Held on a Saturday in April from 10:00 A.M. to 3:00 P.M. as part of The High Desert Museum's celebration of Earth Month, the Family Science Festival focuses on a different natural theme each year, utilizing puppet shows, live animals, videos, storytelling, nature explorations, and a variety of other hands-on activities to help museum visitors better understand the natural world. Admission to the museum is $7.75 for adults, $6.75 for seniors age 65

and older, $6.75 for children ages 13 to 18, $3.74 for kids ages 5 to 12, and free for children age 4 and younger.

The John Craig Memorial Race, Mail Carry and Tour
East snow gate, McKenzie Highway, Sisters
(541) 549–0251

This popular series of cross-country ski races commemorates the fatal 1871 attempt by John Templeton Craig to carry the Christmas mail from the community of McKenzie Bridge, on the west side of the Cascade Mountains, over the McKenzie Pass to Camp Polk at Sisters. A vicious snowstorm caught him in the mountains, and though he found shelter in a mountain cabin, he succumbed to the brutal cold and wet. His body was not recovered until two months later.

There are five races ranging from 3 kilometers to 20 kilometers, including events for both adults and kids as young as six. The sixth event, the 30 kilometer Mail Carry, is a commemorative long-distance ski over the pass to honor Craig's heroic, but ill-fated trek. The race is followed by a banquet at the Sisters High School. Awards and prizes are given out to race participants.

The race is generally held in mid-April, but is sometimes rescheduled depending on prevailing snow conditions. Event fees range from $5.00 for the Kids 3K Classic to $25.00 for the 10 kilometer and longer events.

Sports and Recreation Show
Jefferson County Fairgrounds, 430 Southwest Fairgrounds Road, Madras
(541) 475–4460

Central Oregon outdoor sports enthusiasts make a beeline for Madras on the first weekend of April to see the newest offerings at the Sports and Recreation Show. You'll find booths displaying all the latest in outdoor sporting gear—from hunting and fishing equipment to campers, off-road vehicles, and boats. Kids love the fishing pond, and you can even take home the fish you catch. For lovers of the great outdoors, the Sports and Recreation Show is the place to see that new model fishing rod or drift boat you just have to own. Admission is $2.00 per person.

The Salmon Run
Drake Park, Bend
(541) 385–6908

Sponsored by the Central Oregon Environmental Center, the Salmon Run is a great opportunity to help save the environment while burning off a few calories. Usually staged on a weekend in early May, runners gather at 9:00 A.M. at Drake Park, where the races begin (there is a 10-kilometer and 5-kilometer race). The route goes west to the Deschutes River before doubling back to conclude at the park. The entry fee is $12 for the 5-K race and $15 for the 10-K and includes a bike water bottle and automatic entry in a raffle featuring prizes donated by local merchants. All profits from the race are awarded as grants to conservation groups to restore fish habitat in area streams and rivers.

May

Central Oregon Home and Garden Show
Deschutes County Fairgrounds, 3800 Southwest Airport Way, Redmond
(541) 548–2711

Don't even think of building or remodeling a home or landscaping your yard until after the first weekend in May, when you can check out what has (for good reason) become the second-largest event in Central Oregon. More than 250 companies involved in the building, home decor, and landscaping industries show off their wares and services at the Home and Garden Show. The event takes place in three separate buildings, along with 20,000 square feet of outside exhibits. You'll find everything from an architect to design your home to a landscaper who can help keep your lawn in peak condition. The show runs from Friday through Sunday and is attended by some 25,000 people each year. Admission is free.

Migratory Bird Day
The High Desert Museum, 59800 South U.S. Highway 97, Bend
(541) 382–4754

Tourists aren't the only ones who flock to Central Oregon. Each spring the air is filled with the color and songs of a myriad of migratory bird species, which return thousands of miles from their wintering grounds in search of a place to build their nests. Fly on out to The High Desert Museum on the first Saturday in May to celebrate this nationally celebrated day. There are interpretive talks about birds, learning stations, and information on what you can do to help conserve our feathered friends for future generations. The event runs from 10:00 A.M. to 3:00 P.M. Admission to the museum is $7.75 for adults, $6.75 for seniors age 65 and older, $6.75 for children ages 13 to 18, $3.74 for kids ages 5 to 12, and free for children age 4 and younger. (For more information on The High Desert Museum, see our Attractions chapter.)

U.S. Bank Pole Pedal Paddle
Various locations, Bend
(541) 388-0002

Fit men and iron women from all over the country converge on Bend the second or third Saturday in May to compete (individually, in pairs, or in teams) in this six-event marathon. It begins with a downhill ski race at Mt. Bachelor Ski Area and ends, some 25 miles later, with a 200-yard sprint in Bend's Drake Park. In between, there is a cross-country skiing segment, 5-mile run, bicycle trek, and a frantic paddle down the Deschutes River. The race begins around 9:30 A.M. If you haven't crossed the finish line by 3:00 P.M., you probably don't need to concern yourself with the fact that that's when they start handing out the prizes.

If just reading about this race wears you out, never fear: The plethora of food booths and beer garden at Drake Park provide ample diversions for us slower-moving folk. The entry fee to compete in the race is $36 for individuals; for teams, it's $26 for each team member. The maximum number of team members is seven, one for each leg of the race and two for the canoeing part. On Sunday, the Kids' Mini Pole Pedal Paddle is held in Harmon Park, across the Deschutes River from Drake Park. It features bicycling, a guided raft

> **Insiders' Tip**
>
> It's virtually impossible to see the entire U.S. Bank Pole Pedal Paddle because so many roads are closed to traffic during the event. Most people prefer to station themselves along the footbridge at Drake Park, where they can watch the paddling portion of the race and the final 200-yard sprint.

trip, and an obstacle course. The entry fee is $50 per team, for six team members.

Collage of Culture
Friendship Park, Fourth and E Streets, Madras
(541) 475-2350

Cultures converge in the small agricultural community of Madras each year on the third weekend in May when a pastiche of music, dance, art, and foods from other lands mingle in Friendship Park. The mix is different every year—Native American, Japanese, Celtic, South American, Latino—but the results are always the same: a better understanding and appreciation of the richness and variety of the world's peoples. Sponsored by the Madras Chamber of Commerce, the event is free. People who donate money to help put on the event are treated to hot-air balloon rides. There is a concert on Saturday evening.

Sisters Art Stroll
Downtown Sisters
(541) 549-0251

Grab a map of participating shops from the Sisters Chamber of Commerce at 164 North Elm Street and spend the evening of the second Friday in May getting acquainted with Sisters-area artists. You'll

About 20,000 spectators show up to watch 'em. It kicks off with a 7:00 P.M. performance on Friday night, followed by Saturday shows at 1:00 and 7:00 P.M., and a final performance at 1:00 P.M. on Sunday. All your favorite events will take place—steer and calf roping, bareback riding, bull riding, wild horse racing, and barrel racing. In between shows, there's the Rodeo Parade at 9:30 A.M. on Saturday on West Cascade Street in downtown Sisters, featuring rodeo queens and their courts from all around the state. The Cowboy Dance is held Saturday evening at 9:00 P.M. at the Sisters Middle School, 15200 McKenzie Highway. Tickets run from $8.00 to $12.00. Kids ages 12 and younger are admitted free for the Friday evening show. Yahoo!

find them and samples of their work in various downtown stores, along with free snacks and refreshments provided by business owners. The art stroll begins at 4:00 P.M. and ends around 8:00 P.M.

Redmond Saturday Fair
Seventh Street and Evergreen Avenue, Redmond
(541) 923–5208
Strolling through the Redmond Saturday Fair is the perfect way to spend a lazy Saturday, shopping for a variety of food items and locally-made crafts including rugs, birdhouses, fine arts, homemade pillows, breads, organic garlic, soaps, and other items. The fair is held from 9:00 A.M. to 3:00 P.M. on the last Saturday of the month from May through September. You will find it on the green next to the Redmond Chamber of Commerce.

June

Sisters Rodeo
Sisters Rodeo Grounds, 4 miles east of Sisters off U.S. Hwy 20
(541) 549–0121
They don't call it "The Biggest Little Show in the World" for nothing. More than 400 professional rodeo cowboys plant their boots—and their butts—on the Sisters Rodeo Grounds during the second weekend in June for this big-time rodeo event.

Central Oregon Llama Show
Deschutes County Fairgrounds
3800 Southwest Airport Way, Redmond
(541) 548–2711
Central Oregon is the center of the world for llama ranching. That's what those wooly beasties are that seem to be grazing in every other pasture you drive by around these parts. The Central Oregon Llama Show, held the second weekend in June, is the perfect opportunity to get to know these South American transplants. You can watch them run obstacle courses, see them being sheared for their wool (which we're told is superior to sheep wool), or just mosey around and visit with the breeders and the animals. If you find yourself smitten with these gentle creatures, you can pick up a nice pet-quality llama at the show for less than 500 bucks.

Sunriver Area Chamber of Commerce Chili Cookoff
Sunriver Mall, Sunriver
(541) 593–8149
Sometime between mid-June and early July all the hot chili cooks gather at Sunriver for a showdown. Appropriately enough, the chili tasting begins at high noon. This chili cooking business is serious stuff, and the winners here will go on to bigger cookoffs. Just to make sure there's no cheating, all cooks have to whip up their custom-made chili in public, although we're con-

vinced they add their secret ingredients when nobody is looking. There is musical entertainment from 11:00 A.M. to 4:00 P.M. and plenty of food. Especially chili. A chili-tasting kit—consisting of a cup, spoon, and napkin—gives you five tastes for $5.00. Sunriver merchants put on their Red Hot Sale during the cook-off.

Sunfest Wine and Food Festival
Sunriver Village Courtyard, Sunriver
(541) 593–8704

Over the past couple of decades, Oregon has become a major producer of first-class wines. Each year on Father's Day weekend, representatives from 24 of Oregon's wineries set up booths at Sunriver and offer festivalgoers an opportunity to sample the fruits of their labor. Wine samples cost from 75 cents to $1.00. You're sure to find that perfect wine for your next dinner party, and the vintners will gladly sell you a bottle—or a case. There are plenty of food booths and Central Oregon's own hot country band, Countrified, serenades the crowd throughout the day.

Deschutes County Gem and Mineral Show
Deschutes County Fairgrounds
3800 Southwest Airport Way, Redmond
(541) 548–2711

Central Oregon is rock-hound country. For more than 15 years, people passionate about the inedible fruits of the earth have come together at the Deschutes County Fairgrounds from Thursday through Sunday during the third week in June to sell and to buy. Many of the 70-plus vendors who sell fossils, crystals, faceted stones, jewelry, rough rocks, and lapidary tools and equipment here have their own mining claims from which they wrest their treasures. The show runs from 10:00 A.M. to 5:00 P.M. all four days.

Pi-Ume-Sha Treaty Days
Warm Springs Indian Reservation, Warm Springs
(541) 553–1338

On June 25, 1855, the U.S. government signed a treaty with several bands of Central Oregon Indians granting them hunting, fishing, and water rights and consolidating them into the Confederated Tribes of Warm

Insiders' Tip

An important focus of the Deschutes County Gem and Mineral Show is to educate people about the hobby of lapidary. If you have any questions, don't be shy about asking. The vendors will happily tell you all about the joy of gems.

Springs. "Pi-Ume-Sha" means "let's celebrate," and celebrate they do.

Always held on the Friday, Saturday, and Sunday closest to June 25, Native Americans from all over the West arrive days before the event to set up their tepees for three days of dancing, trading, and games. Vendors sell a wide variety of Indian goods including beadwork, leather work, and silver and turquoise jewelry. A dress parade begins on Saturday at 10:00 A.M. with the Indian people and their horses dressed in all their finery. The powwow that follows is a dervish of color and motion as dancers move to the singing and the drums. There is also a fun run, a 14-mile endurance horse race, and an all-Indian rodeo. The powwow is held on the softball field behind the community center.

Crooked River Roundup
Crook County Fairgrounds, 590 Southeast Lynn Boulevard, Prineville
(541) 447–4479

If you don't believe Prineville is the "Cowboy Capitol of Oregon," then you haven't been to the Crooked River Roundup. For nearly 60 years the country's best buckaroos have made a beeline to this Professional Rodeo Cowboys Association–sanctioned rodeo held each year on the last weekend of June. Shows begin at 7:00 P.M. on Friday and Saturday and 1:00 P.M. on Sunday and include bareback riding, barrel racing, bull riding, calf roping, saddle-bronc riding, steer roping, and other events. General admission is $12 for adults and $10 for kids younger than age 12.

Mount Bachelor Dog Show
Deschutes County Fairgrounds
3800 Southwest Airport Way, Redmond
(541) 385-5537

An American Kennel Club–sanctioned event held each year on the last weekend of June or the first weekend of July, this show and obedience trial attracts as many as 1,200 dogs representing nearly 150 breeds.

Redmond Saturday Fair
Seventh Street and Evergreen Avenue, Redmond
(541) 923-5208

Shop for a variety of locally made crafts and food items including rugs, birdhouses, fine arts, homemade pillows, breads, organic garlic, soaps, and other items on the last Saturday of the month. The fair is also held in May, July, August, and September. See the listing among May's events for more information.

July

Village Green Craft Show
Village Green Park (at Washington Avenue and Fir Street), Sisters
(541) 549-0251

On the first Saturday of July, August, and September, well over 100 artisans and craftspeople gather at Village Green Park to sell their wares. You'll find custom-made fly-fishing rods, woodcrafts, jewelry, hand-tooled leather items, pottery, food, music, and much more. The market runs from 10:00 A.M. to 4:00 P.M.

Sisters Roundup of Gems
Sisters Elementary School, 610 East Cascade Street, Sisters
(541) 549-0251

Rock hounds may purchase fossils, crystals, faceted stones, jewelry, rough rocks, lapidary tools, and hand tools from more than 80 vendors at this four-day annual event. It's held on the week of the Fourth of July from Friday though Tuesday.

Old Fashioned July 4th Celebration
Downtown Bend
(541) 389-7275

Since 1932, Bend's Fourth of July celebration has kicked off with the Pet Parade for kids. Beginning at 10:00 A.M., it takes 50 minutes for all 1,200 costumed children on bikes, trikes, wagons, or on foot, accompanied by their favorite pet, to trek down Wall Street. In earlier times the parade's animal participants were predominantly horses, with even a few antelope and deer. Today you'll see mostly dogs and the occasional rabbit or hamster.

In the afternoon, the action shifts to nearby Drake Park, along the Deschutes River, where you will find booths jam-packed with crafts and food. Kids will find performing clowns, sack races, water-balloon tossing, a fishing pond, and a variety of old-fashioned games. The Deschutes County Public Library holds its annual fund-raising book sale on this day as well—a great opportunity to add to your library at bargain prices.

Fireworks get under way about 10:00 P.M., sponsored every year by the *Bulletin,* the local daily newspaper (see our Media chapter). Although they are launched from Pilot Butte on the east end of Bend, the show is readily seen from just about anywhere in town.

July Fourth Parade
Sixth Street, Redmond
(541) 923-5191

If your town wants to be a Flag City USA, all the residents have to do is buy

> ## Insiders' Tip
> Although you can see Bend's Fourth of July fireworks from just about anywhere in town, the best place to spread your blanket and watch the show is at the Pilot Butte Middle School football field.

Fourth of July celebrations bring out the patriot in all of us. PHOTO: BEND METRO PARK & RECREATION DISTRICT commemorative American flags honoring loved ones and send them off to Washington, D.C., where they are flown over the U.S. Capitol, then returned in time for the Fourth of July. Redmond is not only *a* Flag City USA; it's *the* Flag City USA. With more than 600 commemorative flags, it beats its nearest competitor by more than 400. On the Fourth of July (along with Veterans Day, Memorial Day, and the Deschutes County Fair Parade), all 600 flags are hung along both sides of Sixth Street, where they snap in the breeze as the parade passes by. The parade begins around midmorning and lasts about 30 minutes. If you want to participate in the Flag City USA program, a 4-by-6-foot flag with one name embroidered on it is $30 (two names are $35). Order forms are available at the Redmond Chamber of Commerce.

Old Fashioned July Fourth Community Celebration
Various locations, Prineville
(541) 447–6304
A full day of festivities awaits you at this Fourth of July celebration in the ranching community of Prineville. Start your day at

7:00 A.M. with a pancake breakfast sponsored by local merchants. It's just a few bucks per person. Then work off those calories at 8:00 A.M. by signing up for the Splash and Dash, an all-day race that combines swimming, bicycling, kayaking, and running. You can do it alone or talk a few friends into forming a team.

If you'd rather take it easy, make a stop around noon at Ochoco Creek Park, next to the Crook County Parks and Recreation building at 398 North Fairview Street. There you can visit the arts, crafts, and food booths and take in some real country music by Prineville's hometown band, Countrified. The fireworks commence at dusk and are set off at what the locals call "the viewpoint." The best views are from the grassy areas at the Y along U.S. Highway 26 on the west end of town.

Sisters Outdoor Quilt Show
Downtown Sisters
(541) 549–6061
When a couple of Sisters store owners displayed a dozen quilts in front of their shops two decades ago, they had no idea it would blossom into an international

Some 20,000 people come to Sisters each July to admire close to 1,000 quilts on display throughout the town during the Sisters Outdoor Quilt Show. PHOTO: JIM YUSKAVITCH

event. But it did, and today some 20,000 people come to this town of 911 residents on the second Saturday of July to admire the nearly 1,000 quilts on display, made by quilters from all over the world. The quilts are hung by community volunteers along the streets and storefronts throughout the downtown area and represent a wide variety of designs, from traditional styles to art quilts.

They're generally up and available for viewing by around 9:00 A.M., and the quilts are promptly taken down at 5:00 P.M. About one-third of the quilts are offered for sale, with the average price hovering around $600. Some go for much more. At 4:00 P.M. a special quilt, made earlier in the year by the East of the Cascades Quilters (the local group that sponsors the event), is raffled off. Tickets are $1.00 each.

The Sisters High School Booster Club usually puts on a barbecue, and a few other local nonprofit groups also sell food and drinks, but the day is primarily one of looking at and admiring the gorgeous works of art. For the five days prior to the event, a series of quilting workshops and lectures are offered, drawing students and instructors from around the country.

Bend Summer Festival
Wall, Oregon, and Minnesota Streets, Bend
(541) 385-6570

There's something for everyone at the Bend Summer Festival, whether it's fine food, fine arts, or fine music. Wall, Oregon, and Minnesota Streets, in the heart of downtown Bend, are closed off to traffic on the second Saturday and Sunday of July to make way for scads of booths featuring top-quality arts and crafts along with food served up by Bend's finest restaurants. There's a beer garden and two stages featuring national and local performing artists. For the kids, there are street chalk art, crafts, balloons, and folk music. It's Bend's summer bash, and everyone is invited to the day-long affair.

Ruggers Rendezvous
The High Desert Museum, 59800 South U.S. Highway 97, Bend
(541) 382-4754

Hidden away at The High Desert Museum are a group of museum volunteers who still practice the ancient art of rug making. There they laboriously create beautiful pieces from scraps of wool and natural dyes. You can watch their magic unfold from 10:00 A.M. to 4:00 P.M. at the Ruggers Rendezvous, held every year on a Saturday in mid-July. Admission to the museum is $7.75 for adults, $6.75 for seniors age 65 and older, $6.75 for children ages 13 to 18, $3.74 for kids ages 5 to 12, and free for children age 4 and younger.

Crook County Fair
Crook County Fairgrounds, 1280 South Main Street, Prineville
(541) 447-6575

This county fair, in the heart of cowboy country, won't disappoint you. It has livestock shows (from hogs and horses to bulls and bunnies), exhibits of country crafts and cooking, lots of food and drink, a carnival, and two evening concerts. Kids from the local 4-H and Future Farmers of America groups look forward to the fair all year, when they put the animals they've raised up for show, and maybe a blue ribbon. The fair is held Wednesday through Sunday during the third week of July. Admission is $4.00 for adults and $2.00 for children younger than age 12. The evening concerts run about $15 per ticket.

Walk the Art Beat
Downtown Redmond
(541) 923-5191

Art is where you find it. And on the third Friday in July, from 6:00 to 9:00 P.M. you'll find it all over downtown Redmond when local merchants invite area artists to display their work in their shops. Indoors, you'll see paintings, clay art, sculpture, and a variety of other media. But the art can't be contained, and it spills out into the streets where musicians, mimes, and dancers perform. Before you put on your walking shoes, stop by the Redmond Chamber of Commerce at 446 Southwest Seventh Street to pick up a map of participating shops.

Sagebrush Classic
901 Southwest Simpson Avenue, Bend
(541) 385-8606

Held on the third Friday and Saturday of July, this event was started in 1989 by the folks at Deschutes Brewery as a fundraiser to pay off the mortgage of the Rosie Bareis Community Campus, a nonprofit group that provides office space for a variety of Central Oregon social service organizations. On Friday, 50 amateur golf teams compete in a best-ball tournament, with tee times at 7:30 A.M. and 1:30 P.M.

But the big draw begins at 5:00 P.M. the following night, with gourmet meals prepared by more than a dozen chefs who literally come from all over the world. The list has included Max Burkhalter from the Grand Hyatt Jakarta in Jakarta, Indonesia; Peter Find of The Verandah in Hong Kong; and Ralph Frehner from the Grand Hyatt Erawan in Bangkok, Thailand. After dinner, guests may participate in a silent auction for airline tickets, vacation trips, mountain bikes, and a variety of other items donated by local and out-of-town businesses. The tournament, dinner, and auction are held at Broken Top Club, off U.S. 97 in Bend. The tournament fee for each four-person team is $1,500. Dinner tickets are $150 per person.

Annual Central Oregon Invitational Draft Horse Show
Eagle Crest Resort Equestrian Center
1522 Cline Falls Road, Redmond
(541) 923-2453

The second-largest draft horse show in the Pacific Northwest, this is the Muscle Beach party of horsedom. All the contenders are here—Belgians, Clydesdales, Percherons, and Shires. A variety of competitions take place from Friday evening through Sunday afternoon on the third weekend in July, many designed to simulate the workaday activities that once made these hardworking animals indispensable in the days before the internal combustion engine. You'll see them skid logs, pull plows, and back wagons up to a dock, recalling a time when Clydesdales really did deliver beer.

Part of the fun is the spectacle of seeing all the different teams gussied up for the show. Each horse team has its own color, all coordinated with the driver and wagon. Owners and trainers spend hours braiding manes and tails and weaving in sparkling streamers. The harnesses are shiny patent leather, hooves are polished, and the chrome on the wagons is buffed until it shines like mirrors. About 80 horses from throughout the United States and Canada compete in the event, along with the "Crazy Eights"—a 40-pony team that performs chariot races and other heart-pounding spectacles. Admission is $6.00 per person.

Flash Back Cruz
River Front Plaza, corner of Wall and Franklin Streets, Bend
(541) 382-3221

Visit Bend's River Front Plaza from 8:00 A.M. to 3:00 P.M. on the third Saturday in July for a display of classic autos sponsored by the Central Oregon Classic Chevy Club. All the cars on display were made in 1974 or earlier.

Jefferson County Fair
Jefferson County Fairgrounds, 430 Southwest Fairgrounds Road, Madras
(541) 475-4460

Held from Wednesday through Saturday on the last week in July, the Jefferson County Fair is a summer highlight for the folks who reside in the farm country on the northern edge of Central Oregon. Fairgoers are treated to a carnival, food booths, and scads of farm animals on exhibit, along with displays of locally created arts and crafts. Live music entertains the crowds throughout each day of the fair and a parade is staged in downtown Madras, beginning at 10:00 A.M. on Saturday. Fair tickets cost $5.00 for adults and $3.00 for children under age 12.

Redmond Saturday Fair
Seventh Street and Evergreen Avenue,
Redmond
(541) 923-5208
Locally made crafts and food items including rugs, birdhouses, fine arts, homemade pillows, breads, organic garlic, soaps, and other items may be purchased on the last Saturday of the month. The fair is also held in May, June, August, and September. See May's event listings for more information.

Oregon High Desert Classics Horse Show
J Bar J Boys Ranch, 62895 Hamby Road
(2 miles east of Bend off U.S. Highway 20)
(541) 389-1409
www.jbarj.org
Four-legged athletes gather in the ranch country just outside Bend for two five-day competitions over the last two weeks of July. One of the Pacific Northwest's largest horse shows, the Oregon High Desert Classics Horse Show is world-class. This is a hunter and jumper competition where horses are judged on their style, skill, and timing as they negotiate a series of high and low jumps. Some 500 thoroughbred horses, many valued in the hundreds of thousands of dollars, are entered in this event in preparation for future Olympic competitions. And yes, it's a free event.

High Desert Custom Car Classic
Mountain Shadow RV Park, 540 U.S.
Highway 20, Sisters
(541) 549-0251
Members of Customs Northwest, a regional custom car club, gather in Sisters during the last weekend of July to catch up on gossip, show off their cars, and have a good time. From 9:00 A.M. to 4:00 P.M. on Saturday, they display their impeccably cleaned and polished customized automobiles at the Mountain Shadow RV Park. Typically, the show—dubbed the

Insiders' Tip
Planning a Central Oregon vacation to coincide with an event of interest to you is a great way to add an extra dimension and more enjoyment to your visit.

"Show and Shine"—features around 160 cars. A small admission fee is charged. Later that evening, the action moves across the street and uptown, where the group, dressed in 1950s fashions, puts on a parade down West Hood Street accompanied by demonstrations of such beloved pastimes of that era as Chinese fire drills and wolf-whistling at girls. Be there or be square.

Central Oregon Tour of Homes
Various locations, Bend
(541) 389-1058
Whether you're seriously shopping or just curious, this self-guided tour of Bend-area homes, hosted by the Central Oregon Homebuilders Association, is the perfect opportunity to get your foot in the door. Open houses are held over a six-day period during either the last week of July or the first week of August. Information guides are inserted in the local paper, the *Bulletin,* which provides a map and feature story on each of the homes on the tour route. Featured homes represent the entire range of housing prices in the area, from under $100,000 into the millions.

Deschutes County Fair
Deschutes County Fairgrounds
3800 Southwest Airport Way, Redmond
(541) 548-2711
This is the big Central Oregon event of the year, beginning on the Wednesday before the first weekend in August and ending that Sunday. We head straight for the animal exhibits, where kids from 4-H

and Future Farmers of America and local ranchers display cattle, sheep, chickens, ducks, geese, rabbits, llamas, horses, and goats, along with critters you've probably never heard of. There are also exhibits on a variety of country crafts and skills including textiles, floral arrangements, weaving and spinning, fiber arts, ceramics, cake decorating, and gardening. In fact, there seems to be an exhibit category for every talent or hobby imaginable.

Kids love the petting zoo. More than 20 food vendors will keep your stomach from growling while you browse the many commercial exhibit booths. Free entertainment is provided on two stages throughout the course of the fair. The on-site carnival is where the action is in the evenings, with rides and games galore. There are two rodeo performances on Saturday and one on Sunday, along with two nights of big-name entertainment that, in the past, has featured the Nitty Gritty Dirt Band, the Marshall Tucker Band, BTO, Tanya Tucker, Kansas, and Joe Diffie. Fair hours are 9:00 A.M. to 10:00 P.M. on Wednesday and Thursday, 9:00 A.M. to 11:00 P.M. on Friday and Saturday, and 8:30 A.M. to 4:30 P.M. on Sunday. Admission is $6.00 for adults and $4.00 for children younger than age 12. Rodeo tickets cost around $5.00 per person, and the evening concerts run from $15.00 to $25.00 depending on the act.

August

Sunriver Quilt Show
Sunriver Village, Sunriver
(541) 593–8704

Quilters from around the Northwest hang their painstakingly crafted handmade quilts along the boardwalk in Sunriver Village on the first Saturday in August. There are generally about 100 to 150 quilts on display. In addition to admiring the skill and effort that goes into producing these quilts, you may also buy quilting supplies and materials from vendors who set up booths on the site. Some quilts are available for purchase. The show runs from 11:00 A.M. to 5:00 P.M.

Pioneer Picnic and Queen's Coronation
Pioneer Park (between South Court Street and South Elm Street), Prineville
(541) 447–3715

Hang on, pardner! Bull-riding is not for the faint of heart. PHOTO: DESCHUTES COUNTY RODEO

In pioneer days, community events were about the only time people living in far-flung settlements and homesteads had the opportunity to socialize with their neighbors and catch up on news. That rural tradition continues in Prinevelle on the first Saturday each August when local families gather at Pioneer Park for a picnic and crowning of the year's "Pioneer Queen," who is selected from a family whose roots in the area date back from at least 1916. Bring your own picnic lunch and lots of gossip. Ice cream and cake are free. The event begins at 12:30 P.M. and finishes by 3:00 P.M.

Village Green Craft Show
Village Green Park, Washington Avenue and Fir Street, Sisters
(541) 549–0251

Custom-made fly-fishing rods, woodcrafts, jewelry, hand-tooled leather items, pottery, food, and music can be found at this outdoor market on the first Saturday of the month. It is also held in July and September. For more information see our July event listings.

High Desert Celtic Festival
Crooked River Park, off Oregon Highway 27, Prineville
(541) 548–3139

A wee bit of the Scottish Highlands can be had in the High Desert on the second Saturday in August, when clans McPherson, McDuff, McCloud, and the rest unfurl their colors along the banks of the Crooked River. Bagpipes blare, minstrels sing of the days of yore, blacksmiths forge swords, and a good old-fashioned medieval battle may break out before the day is done. If you think you'd look good in a kilt (and we think you would), you can buy one from one of the many vendors selling Scottish wares. Then settle back to watch the Highland Games, where hardy Scotsmen and -women test their strength by hurling everything from sheafs of hay to 18-foot logs. And just when you think you've seen it all, the ceilidh, a proper Scottish Highlands party, begins, with singing, dancing, and enough corned beef and cabbage to satisfy all the laddies and lasses in attendance. Admission for the games is $8.00 for adults and $5.00 for seniors and students. There is no charge for children younger than age 6. The dinner costs an additional five or six bucks per person.

Sisters Antique Faire
Sisters Village Green Park (at Washington Avenue and Fir Street), Sisters
(541) 549–0251

If antiques are your interest, be in Sisters on the second weekend in August for a two-day extravaganza of the old and unusual. Dozens of antiques dealers lay out their treasures for you to pick through and purchase. A wide variety of great stuff is here to peruse, including Western and Native American paraphernalia along with some particularly fine old furniture. But take our advice, if you see something you like you'd better buy it on the spot—it probably won't be there tomorrow!

Harvest Run
Next to the Chamber of Commerce office
446 Southwest Seventh Street, Redmond
(541) 923–5191

The Harvest Run is primarily an event for the classic and vintage car buffs of the Drifter's Car Club. However, they hold a car show on Southwest Seventh Street on a Saturday in mid-August on the green next to the chamber office (446 Southwest Seventh Street). You can see a wide range of cherry cars, trucks, and motorcycles of 1974 vintage or older.

Bend Water Pageant
Drake Park, downtown Bend
(541) 385–6570

A traditional Bend event from the early part of the 20th-century, The Bend Water Pageant just faded away by the mid-1960s. But recently, this fun, neighborly community event has been revived and includes art displays, musical entertainment, an ice-cream social, youth dance, and historical lectures, all culminating with the launching of a three-story-high fiberglass swan into Mirror Pond. The Bend Water Pageant is held at Drake Park on the third weekend in August. There is no admission fee.

Redmond Saturday Fair
Seventh Street and Evergreen Avenue,
Redmond
(541) 923-5208

The last Saturday of the month brings vendors of locally made crafts and food items including rugs, birdhouses, fine arts, homemade pillows, and other items to the green next to the Redmond Chamber of Commerce. The fair is also held in May, June, July, and September. See May's event listings for more information.

Square Dance Festival
Deschutes County Fairgrounds
3800 Southwest Airport Way, Redmond
(541) 548-2711

For a country-style good time, the annual three-day Square Dance Festival, held during the last week of August, is the place to kick up your heels. In addition to dances every evening, there are workshops aplenty to help you brush up on your square- and round-dancing skills or to learn new dances. A $16 ticket buys you admission to all the dances. Another $6.00 will get you into the Saturday deep-pit barbecue. The festival is sponsored by Central Oregon's six square dancing clubs, but everyone's invited.

September

Village Green Craft Show
Village Green Park, Washington Avenue and Fir Street, Sisters
(541) 549-0251

Well over 100 artisans and craftsmen gather on the first Saturday of the month to sell custom-made fly-fishing rods, woodcrafts, hand-tooled leather items, and much more. The market is also held in July and August. For additional information, see the July listings.

Oregon High Desert Swap Meet
Deschutes County Fairgrounds
3800 Southwest Airport Way, Redmond
(541) 548-4467

Aficionados of classic automobiles and gearheads bent on speed and power can find just about any part they need for their latest project at this swap meet and car show. Nearly 15,000 car buffs converge here on the second Saturday of September to shop for hard-to-locate automotive parts and to talk shop with fellow enthusiasts. The meet is held in two buildings—one for car-related items, the other for antiques. Outside on the fairgrounds, you'll find cars for show and for sale ranging from classic rides and roadsters to hot rods and low riders.

Sisters Folk Festival
Paulina Springs Book Company, 252 West Hood Street, Sisters
(541) 549-0866

Workshops on songwriting, storytelling, guitar picking, and music as a profession, along with concerts by regional and national talent, are the hallmarks of this folksy get-together sponsored by the Paulina Springs Book Company. Held each year on the second weekend in September, the festival offers both good-time entertainment and the opportunity for serious folk musicians and other budding professionals to hone their skills. For more information, see our chapter on arts and culture.

Lake Billy Chinook Day
The Cove Palisades State Park, 7300 Jordan Road, Culver (off U.S. Highway 97, 15 miles southwest of Madras)
(541) 546-3412

A litter and trash clean-up by volunteers along the shores and rimrock of Lake Billy Chinook is the highlight of this event, held on a Saturday in mid-September. Activities also include natural-history lectures by local experts, storytelling performances by members of The Confederated Tribes of Warm Springs, and folk, Hispanic, and Native American dancing. There are also food booths, free kayak and canoe rides, and door prizes. The event is free, and you don't have to participate in the "litter patrol" to enjoy the various activities (but your help in keeping this spectacular state park clean sure would be appreciated).

Sunriver Fall Festival
Sunriver Village Courtyard, Sunriver
(541) 593–8704

By the third Saturday in September, there's a nip in the early morning air, but days are still gloriously warm and sunny. It's a sure sign of autumn in Central Oregon and a great time to venture down to Sunriver for the Sunriver Fall Festival. There are arts and crafts vendors, food booths, a beer garden, and live entertainment all designed to make a bright fall day even brighter. The festival runs from 11:00 A.M. to 5:00 P.M. and there is no admission charge.

Redmond Saturday Fair
Seventh Street and Evergreen Avenue, Redmond
(541) 923–5208

The Redmond Saturday Fair is held on the last Saturday of the month and features locally made crafts and food items including rugs, birdhouses, organic garlic, soaps, and other items. The fair is also held in May, June, July, and August. See the entry in our May listings for more information.

Harvest Hoedown
The High Desert Museum, 59800 South U.S. Highway 97, Bend
(541) 382–4754

Now you can finally see how Grandad cooked up that cider he was always sippin' on when Grandma wasn't looking. Mosey on over to the Homestead Cabin on the museum grounds and watch apples being pressed on an antique cider press. Museum staff will even let you help if you want to. Then dip your cup into the bucket and taste the freshest cider this side of the Cascade Mountains.

While you're there, the museum's very own Bitterbrush Band, armed with washboards, bottles, and ukuleles, will treat you to their special brand of music. The Harvest Hoedown holds forth from 10:00 A.M. to 3:00 P.M. on the last Saturday of September or the first Saturday of October. Admission to the museum is $7.75 for adults, $6.75 for seniors age 65 and older, $6.75 for children ages 13 to 18, $3.74 for kids ages 5 to 12, and free for children age 4 and younger.

Sisters in Sisters
various locations, Sisters
(541) 549–0251

On the last weekend of September, you'll find sisters from all over the country in the one town that seems like the obvious place for them to be—Sisters, of course. Intended to be a time for sisters to spend some time together along with other "sister-sister teams" there are luncheons, dinners, speakers, and a variety of outdoor activities and tours from fun hikes to character-building challenges. Registration fees are $160 for the entire weekend and $100 for Saturday events only. Advanced registration is required.

October

Bend Downtowners Art Hop
Downtown Bend
(541) 385–6570

On one evening in October, between 5:00 and 9:00 P.M., downtown Bend merchants host an evening with local artists, who display their work in various stores. This event is also held in April. For more information, see our April event listings.

High Desert Classic Sheep Dog Trials
3670 Southwest Obsidian, Redmond
(541) 548–7087

"Poetry in motion" might not be quite the right phrase, but these border collies sure can herd sheep. And their handlers aren't too shabby either. You can marvel at this impressive display of teamwork between human and dog on the first Friday, Saturday, and Sunday in October when border collies (the quintessential herding dog) and their owners arrive for this field trial. Using whistle and voice commands, the handler sends his or her dog out across the meadow to round up a handful of sheep, driving them back across the field and into a small pen. They make it look easy. Cash prizes and awards are given for the top performers, who come from throughout the West and Canada. The event is free to spectators.

The Bend Bigfoot Run
Inn of the Seventh Mountain, 18575 Southwest Century Drive, Bend
(541) 317-3568

On the first Sunday in October, several hundred runners line up at the Inn of the Seventh Mountain for the 10-kilometer run to Drake Park in downtown Bend. Started more than 20 years ago, it is the oldest road run event in the region. You can sign up in advance at the Foot Zone (845 Northwest Wall Street), a local shoe shop, or on race day at the Inn of the Seventh Mountain. Entry fees are $8.00 for advance registration, $12.00 on the day of the race.

Sisters Harvest Faire
West Hood Street, Sisters
(541) 549-0251

Nearly half of Hood Street, in downtown Sisters, is closed to traffic to make way for the 175-plus vendors who come from all over the Northwest to set up shop here on the second weekend in October. Because it's a juried event (crafters and artisans must qualify to participate), all the offerings are top-notch. You'll find pottery, handmade furniture, walking sticks, woodcrafts, metal work, leather items, and photographs, to give just a sampling. There is also live music by local bands and great food. The event runs from 10:00 A.M. to 5:00 P.M. on Saturday and 10:00 A.M. to 4:00 P.M. Sunday.

Fall Festival and Pumpkin Patch
Chase Ranch at Tillicum Park, Couch Market Road, 6 miles west of Bend
(541) 389-7275

Pumpkins don't grow in Central Oregon, so in late October the folks at the Bend Metro Park & Recreation District import a few thousand and spread them across a couple of acres of Tillicum Park for a day of Halloween fun. Take the kids, wander through the pumpkin patch, and pick one out to grace your front porch. Volunteers stand by with wheelbarrows to help you heft your prize back to the car. There are also hayrides, pony rides, crafts, a haunted house, fresh caramel apples, folk music, and storytellers. Admission to the festival is free. Tickets for rides and activities may be purchased for 50 cents each. Most activities will set you back one to three tickets. An $8.00 day pass will get you admission to all events and rides, and a pumpkin to boot.

Bat Day
The High Desert Museum, 59800 South U.S. Highway 97, Bend
(541) 382-4754

If you've always wanted to strap on a pair of human-size bat wings, your dream can come true during Bat Day at The High Desert Museum. Museum staff devote the entire day to educating visitors about bats and dispelling a few myths about them. There are videos, puppet shows, games, a costume parade for the kids, and, of course, bats. Bat Day is held on the Saturday closest to Halloween. Obviously. Admission to the museum is $7.75 for adults, $6.75 for seniors age 65 and older, $6.75 for children ages 13 to 18, $3.74 for kids ages 5 to 12, and free for children age 4 and younger.

November

Lord's Acre Auction and Barbecue
Powell Butte Christian Church, 13720 Southwest Oregon Highway 126, Powell Butte
(541) 548-3066

There was a time when farmers would set aside an acre of their field as the Lord's acre, and all the crops grown on that patch of ground would be donated to their church. Times have changed, but the spirit of giving hasn't. For the past half-century, residents of this small ranching community outside Redmond have donated harvest items to the Powell Butte Christian Church to help raise funds for its missionary work and construction needs. In the not-too-distant past, donations came in the form of sacks of potatoes, cords of wood, bales of hay, live chickens, steers, and pigs. Today, when the "country store" opens at 10:00 A.M. on the first Saturday of November, you're more likely to find locally produced meats, candies, breads, pastries, sauerkraut, and a Powell Butte

The Fall Festival and Pumpkin Patch at Chase Ranch at Tillicum Park is the highlight of many a local kid's October. PHOTO: BEND METRO PARK & RECREATION DISTRICT

specialty, sausage, offered at modest prices. There are morning and afternoon concerts, followed by an auction around 1:30 or 2:00 P.M. featuring handmade quilts, afghans, and comforters. Seven dollars will get you a pit-barbecued lunch of beef, ham, and lamb.

Tree Lighting Ceremony and Caroling
Sunriver Village Courtyard, Sunriver
(541) 593-8704

Christmas carols and a medley of holiday lights mark this annual event held on the Friday after Thanksgiving. At 5:00 P.M. a local choir group performs all-time-favorite Christmas carols. Then, in unison, the crowd counts down from 10 to 0, and the Christmas lights are turned on throughout the village and on three large, live trees. Santa is there in his sleigh, of course, talking with the children and handing out candy canes. It gets cold around here this time of year, so the 20 or so minutes it takes for the whole ceremony is just about right.

Starlight Parade
Sixth Street, Redmond
(541) 923-5191

Better stake out your spot along Sixth Street in downtown Redmond by 5:00 P.M. on the Saturday following Thanksgiving, because that's when the parade begins. In Redmond, you're either watching the Christmas parade, or you're in it. Holiday lights draped across parade floats twinkle on the street while the stars shimmer in the heavens above.

Sisters Holiday Celebration & Parade
West Hood Street, Sisters
(541) 549-0251

You'll usually find lots of animals in the Sisters Christmas Parade—horses, llamas, and (our favorite) the cart-pulling Welsh corgis. The high school band is there along with festive floats. The parade begins at 3:00 P.M. and proceeds down West Hood Street. At 5:00 P.M. the city Christmas tree, located on the corner of Hood and Ash Streets, is lit. Mr. and Mrs. Claus make an appearance to visit the kids. The Sisters community choir sings carols, and there are hot chocolate and hot apple cider to help take the chill off the night air. The Sisters Celebration is held every year on the Saturday after Thanksgiving.

High Desert Holidays
The High Desert Museum, 59800 South U.S. Highway 97, Bend
(541) 382-4754

This is The High Desert Museum's largest annual event, held from 9:00 A.M. to 5:00 P.M. on the Friday and Saturday after Thanksgiving. Regional artists display pottery, leather work, watercolors, and art created in other media, along with seasonal crafts made by museum volunteers from natural materials found in the desert. Our favorites are the wreaths made out of sagebrush. You can buy homemade breads, cakes, and cookies, and herbs grown the previous summer in the museum's pioneer garden, as well as many other unique High Desert gifts. Admission to the museum is $7.75 for adults, $6.75 for seniors age 65 and older, $6.75 for children ages 13 to 18, $3.74 for kids ages 5 to 12, and free for children age 4 and younger.

Tiny Lights Craft Show
Sisters Middle School, 115 North Locust Street, Sisters
(541) 549-0251

Handmade arts and crafts fill the Sisters Middle School from 9:00 A.M. to 5:00 P.M. on a Saturday in November. Because it's so close to the holidays, many of the crafts you will find here have a Christmas theme. More than 50 vendors participate. Food and music are available as well.

Starfest
Eagle Crest Resort, 1522 Cline Falls Road, Redmond
(541) 923-2453

Pile the gang in the car and head off to Eagle Crest Resort between November 23 and January 5 to view a spectacular display of holiday lighting. A 2-mile driving tour through the resort is a feast for the eyes. More than 70 lighting displays depict a variety of scenes—from Santa playing softball with one of his elves to a

42-foot-long dragon breathing flames. The tour is open to the public each night from 5:30 to 9:30 P.M. on weekdays and from 5:30 to 10:00 P.M. on weekends.

Admission to the driving tour is $5.00 per carload, $10.00 for a van with seven or more people, and $30.00 for buses. You may also tour the displays in a wagon drawn by draft horses for $11 per person. Wagon rides are offered on a regular schedule on Friday, Saturday, and Sunday evenings and at other times by reservation.

December

Free Ski and Ride Day
Mt. Bachelor Ski Area, off Cascade Lakes
Highway, 22 miles west of Bend
(541) 382–2442

Bring a donation of canned food or some warm clothing, and you can ski or snowboard for free from 9:00 A.M. to 4:00 P.M. on a Friday in December. Offered every year, this is an extremely popular event in Central Oregon. All donations are turned over to the Central Oregon Community Action Agency Network, a local social services agency, for distribution to the needy.

Community Tree Lighting
Mirror Pond Plaza, Downtown Bend
(541) 385–6570

While it's perfectly fine to take on a festive attitude earlier, the Christmas season in Bend officially begins at 6:30 P.M. on the first Friday of the month when the community Christmas tree is lit. The high school choir serenades the crowd, and the mayor gives a welcome speech. Llamas draped with holiday lights will dazzle you, and the kids love the cart rides drawn by miniature horses. Santa walks from Mirror Pond Plaza to Periwinkle's, at 953 Northwest Wall Street, where he stops to carefully consider the Christmas wishes of the children who have come to meet

him. Although the festivities end around 7:00 P.M., downtown stores stay open until 9:00 P.M. and serve up snacks, cider, and hot chocolate. Be sure to be back downtown the next day by noon for the Bend Christmas parade.

Christmas Parade and Tree Lighting
Downtown Prineville
(541) 447–6304

This parade begins at 2:00 P.M. on the first Saturday in December, and most people find the best vantage points along Third Street. Santa sets up shop on the county courthouse lawn at 300 East Third Street; kids can have their photographs taken with him for a small charge. The community Christmas tree, also on the courthouse lawn, is lit at 6:00 P.M. the previous evening. Local businesses stay open late for holiday revelers who want to do a little gift shopping after the public celebrations have concluded.

Trucker's Light Parade
Downtown La Pine
(541) 536–3572

For a holiday spectacle of a different sort, truck on down to La Pine and see how the big rigs celebrate Christmas. Area truckers put on quite a show when they wrap their rigs in lights and have themselves a convoy. The parade route begins at Memorial and Huntington Streets, then heads north to the La Pine Highway Center, ending at the La Pine Parks and Recreation Department office on Huntington and First Streets, where the trucks completely circle the building. The truckers give Santa a lift to the parks and recreation office, where he meets with the kids. A craft bazaar, including musical entertainment and food, is also held at the parks building from 10:00 A.M. to 8:00 P.M. The parade begins at 6:00 P.M. on either the first or second Saturday in December. As many as 35 trucks participate.

The Arts

If, before reading this chapter, you assumed there was little in the way of art and culture in our little corner of the desert, we're inclined to forgive you. Central Oregon is, in fact, brimming with creative minds and full of people who are enriching the lives of residents and visitors alike with music, dance, words, paintings, sculptures, and a myriad of other media. Some labor in obscurity, creating their art for the pure personal satisfaction it brings. Some hope to one day be known for their work. And some of our artists already are.

The scope and depth of Central Oregon's arts community is surprising. We have storytellers, costume makers, musicians, graphic artists, writers, glass workers, painters, photographers, poets, sculptors, songwriters, potters, actors, weavers, festivals, and galleries. And that's just the short list. Together, they are helping to create a vibrant Central Oregon that is a feast not only for the eyes, but for the mind and soul as well.

Art Associations and Support Groups

Art Station
313 Southwest Shevlin Hixon Drive, Bend
(541) 617–1317

Opened in 2001 in a historical 1911 railroad station, which was moved brick by brick from its original location on Division Street and reassembled along the Deschutes River, Art Station is a school for artists.

While there has been some renovation inside the building, most of the interior has been left in its original condition. Half the building is dedicated as a ceramics studio, while the other half is a multimedia studio. Here, students—both youths and adults—take classes that include ceramics, painting, tile making, wall hangings, and a host of others. Classes are typically a month long and range from about $40 for youths up to about $120 for adults. Art Station is affiliated with the Central Oregon Arts Association (see listing below).

Central Oregon Arts Association
Mirror Pond Gallery, 875 Northwest Brooks Street, Bend
(541) 317–9324

The Central Oregon Arts Association is one of about 150 regional arts associations working under the umbrella of the Oregon Arts Commission to serve and promote the arts in their respective areas. It provides support to local artists and groups involved in the visual, performing, and literary arts through networking, classes, lectures, and demonstrations. The group also offers technical assistance to art organizations in everything from fund-raising and marketing to bookkeeping and budgeting.

Based out of Mirror Pond Gallery (see the listing in the Art Galleries section of this chapter), the association is conducting a region-wide marketing effort to promote the idea of a cultural corridor that stretches from the Warm Springs Indian Reservation south to La Pine. They kicked off the promotion with the May 1998 arrival of ARTRAIN, an exhibit of art commissioned by The Smithsonian Associates and housed in five vintage railroad cars. The association has also recently published the first of an annual arts resources guide, which includes an extensive listing of local artists and their specialties.

In addition to helping members of the local arts community, the group also works to inform visitors and residents about the area's art and cultural resources.

"Central Oregon is a very visual place," says Cate O'Hagan, the association's executive director. "People who live here or come here to visit like to get out and see it. We want them to include the arts in their trips." Association memberships are $35 for individuals, $25 for seniors older than age 65 and for students, and $50 for families and businesses.

Farewell Bend Writers Roundtable
(541) 388–4495

There are about 60 members of this writers' support group, and they meet a few times each month to read their works-in-progress and discuss how to communicate their ideas and feelings more effectively. A diverse lot, the group's writers are engaged in a variety of literary projects including books, essays, magazine articles, poetry, fiction and nonfiction, fantasy, adventure, romance, and memoirs. The group meets at various members' homes four times each month from 7:00 to 10:00 P.M. (the days differ from month to month) and on two Thursday afternoons from 1:00 to 3:00 P.M. Yearly dues are $15, and membership includes a quarterly newsletter.

Jefferson County Arts Association
The Art Adventure Gallery, 185 Southeast Fifth Street, Madras
(541) 475–7701

Established in 1989, the Jefferson County Arts Association is affiliated with the Central Oregon Arts Association and works to promote the visual, performing, and literary arts in Jefferson County through the activities and programs of The Art Adventure Gallery, where it is based. See that listing in the Art Galleries section of this chapter for additional information. Individual memberships are $10.

Raku Artists of Central Oregon
1126 Northeast Burnside Avenue, Bend
(541) 382–7561

Raku is an ancient Japanese pottery-making art that brings out the natural colors found in the glazes that are used in the firing process. Raku Artists of Central Oregon was formed in 1992 and provides the dozen or so Bend-area practitioners of this technique a chance to network and share ideas. The group also provides an outdoor firing location—necessary for the fast-firing raku process—for members who don't have their own facilities. Members meet on the second Tuesday of the month. Membership is $25 per year.

Sagebrushers Art Society
117 Southwest Roosevelt Avenue, Bend
(541) 617–0900

With a current membership of around 80 members, the Sagebrushers Art Society has been around since the 1950s, and is dedicated to promoting the arts throughout Central Oregon. They offer art classes primarily in painting and drawing at their headquarters, which also serves as an art gallery (see listing under "Galleries") as well as a place for artists of all ability levels to confab, sharing ideas, techniques, and encouragement. Classes typically cost $10 to $15 per session. They also hold a "paint out" once each month, where members pick a Central Oregon location to spend the day painting. Membership in the Sagebrushers Art Society is $25 for the first year and $20 per year thereafter.

Museums

The High Desert Museum
59800 South U.S. Highway 97, Bend
(541) 382–4754

Changing exhibits at the High Desert Museum's Brooks Gallery interpret and

Insiders' Tip

Cascade Arts Review and the *Source* are the best publications in town for keeping up with the local art scene. For more information on these, see our Media chapter.

If you're thinking about finally attempting to get your art exhibited, try the Mirror Pond Gallery. The folks at the gallery review new work on a monthly basis for possible inclusion in their exhibits.

reveal many aspects of the West's desert country through the eyes and creative minds of artists working in photography, sculpture, painting, and a variety of other media. Exhibits run from six months to one year and have included such themes as birds in art, wildlife photography, and Indian tepee art. Admission to the museum is $7.75 for adults, $6.75 for seniors age 65 and older, $6.75 for children ages 13 to 18, $3.74 for kids ages 5 to 12, and free for children age 4 and younger. All activities are included in the price of admission. (See our Attractions chapter for more information on The High Desert Museum.)

The Museum at Warm Springs
2189 U.S. Highway 26, Warm Springs
(541) 553-3331

Located on the Warm Springs Indian Reservation, The Museum at Warm Springs is dedicated to educating the public about the history and culture of the native people who live in Central Oregon. Their Changing Exhibit Gallery features four three-month-long shows each year focusing on contemporary and traditional art created by Native Americans. Recent exhibits have included photographs from the museum's archives as well as contemporary portraits of tribal members, quilts, baskets, glass tapestry, beadwork, and traditional buckskin wed-

ding and jingle dresses that are festooned with bells and other noisemakers for "fancy dancing" ceremonies (exhibits curator Erania Palmer tells us that favorite traditional noisemakers include the tin lids from snuff cans). Museum admission fees are $6.00 for adults, $5.00 for seniors, and $3.00 for children ages 5 through 12. (See our Attractions and Other Communities chapters for more on The Museum at Warm Springs.)

Art Events

Bend Downtowners Art Hop
Downtown Bend
(541) 385-6570

Twice a year, in April and October, Bend merchants host an evening with local artists, who display their works in various stores in the main downtown area between 5:00 and 9:00 P.M. (For more information see our Annual Events chapter.)

Collage of Culture
Friendship Park, Fourth and E Streets, Madras
(541) 475-2350

A cultural smorgasbord is served up at Friendship Park in Madras on the third weekend in May with music, dance, art, and food from around the world. (For more details, see our Annual Events chapter.)

First Friday Gallery Walk
Downtown Bend
(541) 317-9324

On the first Friday of the month from April through December, the seven downtown art galleries stay open from 5:00 to 9:00 P.M. to give art lovers a little extra browsing time. Refreshments are served in the galleries. Participating shops include Avenida Art & Frame, Ballantyne & Douglass Fine Art Gallery, Cristina Acosta Art Studio, Deschutes Gallery, Frame Design and Sunbird Gallery, Mirror Pond Gallery, Mockingbird Gallery, Glass Chameleon Gallery and Framing, Smith Jones & Co. Fine Arts, and Charlotte's. For more information on individual galleries, see the listings in this chapter.

Madras First Thursday Art Walk

Held on the first Thursday of every month throughout the year, from 5:30 to 8:00 P.M., the Madras First Thursday Art Walk typically draws a couple of hundred people. Participating establishments include Inspirations Art Gallery, The Art Adventure Gallery (see the listings in this chapter), and Willow Creek Books & Tea Garden (154 Southwest Fifth Street).

Sisters Art Stroll
Downtown Sisters
(541) 549-0251

From 4:00 to 8:00 P.M. on the second Friday in May, you'll find shops in Sisters filled with the creations of local artists along with free snacks and refreshments provided by business owners. (See the May listings in our Annual Events chapter for more details.)

Walk the Art Beat
Downtown Redmond
(541) 923-5191

On the third Friday in July from 6:00 to 9:00 P.M., you'll find art all over downtown Redmond as local merchants invite area artists to display their work in their shops. (For all the information you'll need to walk the art beat, see the listing in our Annual Events chapter.)

Literary Arts

Barnes & Noble Booksellers
2690 Northeast U.S. Highway 20, Bend
(541) 318-7242
www.bn.com

Barnes & Noble Booksellers opened its huge Bend store in November 1997 and, along with an impressive selection of books, hosts readings by book authors a couple of times each month. Twice a week Weekly Story Time happens, where bookstore staff reads from a featured book. The store also sponsors a book discussion group that focuses primarily on fiction; they meet at various times each month. Store staff puts out a monthly schedule of events, which you may pick up at the store or procure off their Web site.

A Cup of Magic
1304 Northwest Galveston Avenue, Bend
(541) 330-5539

This coffee shop sponsors poetry readings every Saturday night beginning at 8:00 P.M. No need to make advance reservations, just drop in—to read or listen. Coffee shop staff tell us that the local poets appreciate donations from the audience to help fund their art.

High Desert Western Arts Gathering
Deschutes County Fairgrounds, 3800 Southwest Airport Way, Redmond
(541) 317-3747, (888) 224-3497

Cowboy poets, artists, and musicians from throughout the West have gathered since 1995 in Central Oregon on the first weekend in June to treat locals to the art, literature, and songs of the open range. Saturday and Sunday festivities are held at Deschutes County Fairgrounds, where you'll find music and poetry performances running all day long. Clinics on horsemanship and stock-herding dogs are offered, and demonstrations of horseshoeing, saddle-fitting, bootmaking, and other cowboy skills are featured.

The Western Art Show features cowboy creations in paintings, sculptures, bronzes, woodcarvings, and other media by such artists as Joelle Smith, R. E. Pierce, Larry Zabel, Shirley Bothum, and others. But the highlight of the gathering is the Saturday evening performance by such big-name cowboy poets and balladeers as Baxter Black and Don Edwards. Daily tickets for the fairground activities and events range from $5.00 to $10.00 per

Insiders' Tip

There are many privately organized book discussion groups in Central Oregon. Local bookstores can put you in touch with them.

person. Children younger than age 12 are admitted free. The evening performance runs around $20 per person.

Paulina Springs Book Company
252 West Hood Street, Sisters
(541) 549–0866

There's almost always something happening at this great little bookstore in downtown Sisters. During summer they have book readings and discussion groups going on just about every week as well as occasional acoustic music performances by local songwriters. Book authors who have given readings here include Whitney Otto (*How to Make an American Quilt*), Ivan Doig (*This House of Sky*), and Brent Walth (*Fire at Eden's Gate*). The store sends out a summer and winter newsletter to regular customers that lists the schedule of events.

Performing Arts

Music

Big Band Jazz
Music Department, Central Oregon
Community College, 2600 Northwest College
Way, Bend
(541) 383–7511

If the Big Band sounds of the '30s and '40s make you want to swirl your skirts, then do we have a band for you. Big Band Jazz grew out of a class at Central Oregon Community College in 1982 to become a community band dedicated to keeping the memory and music of Woody Herman, Glenn Miller, Stan Kenton, and the rest of the greats alive, though they play modern Big Band arrangements as well.

The 18 musicians who wield the basic instruments of the Big Band genre—saxes, trumpets, trombones, piano, bass, and drums—include a few professional band directors, a couple of bankers, a state policeman, a certified public accountant, several local business owners, and some high school and college students. The group gives two or three concerts each year at Central Oregon Community College's Pinckney Auditorium. Tickets are $5.00 for adults and $3.00 for seniors and students.

Cascade Chorale
Fine Arts Department, Central Oregon
Community College,
2600 Northwest College Way, Bend
(541) 383–7517

Formed in the early 1960s, the Cascade Chorale is part of the music program at Central Oregon Community College and is made up of about 100 singers including college students and community members. The chorale presents several performances each year at the college's Pinckney Auditorium; they also sing during the school year at various locations throughout Central Oregon. The group has also traveled abroad to perform. Tickets for concerts are $6.00 for adults and $4.00 for students. Information on concert schedules and purchasing tickets may be obtained by calling the college's box office at (541) 383-7575.

Cascade Festival of Music
842 Northwest Wall Street, #6, Bend
(541) 382–8381

This eight-day musical extravaganza has been staged in a big tent in Bend's downtown Drake Park since 1981 and is enjoyed by some 11,000 people each year. Performances are held over the week before Labor Day and include eight concerts, each beginning at 7:30 P.M., along with a children's concert usually scheduled for a weekend afternoon. Although most of the performances are of classical music, one Big Band and one pops concert also are presented as well as a bit of jazz and ethnic. Professional musicians and members of symphony orchestras come from throughout Oregon and the United States to perform at the Cascade Festival of Music. Advanced tickets range from $16 to $27.

Central Oregon Concert Band
Fine Arts Department, Central Oregon
Community College,
2600 Northwest College Way, Bend
(541) 383–7517

Like the Cascade Chorale, the Central Oregon Concert Band is also part of Central Oregon Community College's music program and has been in existence since about 1983. This 65-member band performs with a full complement of symphonic instruments and presents several concerts each year at COCC's Pinckney Auditorium. They also perform at various locations in Central Oregon during the summer. Concert tickets are $6.00 for adults and $4.00 for students. Call the college box office at (541) 383-7575 for up-to-date information on performance schedules and locations.

Central Oregon Symphony
P.O. Box 7953, Bend
(541) 317-3941

This volunteer group has been delighting Central Oregonians with the sounds of the symphony since 1967, but it has really experienced a renaissance over the past few years. Where once they performed for 300 people a year, they now play for more than 2,000—the group's talents have become more widely known throughout the community.

Made up of about 60 musicians, the Central Oregon Symphony performs three or four concerts each year. These are held between November and May at the Bend Senior High School, 230 Northeast Sixth Street, at 7:30 P.M. on Saturday, 3:00 P.M. on Sunday, and 7:30 P.M. on Monday. The concerts are free, and you can pick up tickets at Cliff Scharf Silversmith and Gallery, 431 East Cascade Avenue, Sisters; Central Oregon Music, 250 Northeast Greenwood Avenue, Bend; Mountain View Music, 1326 Northeast Third Street, Bend; The Book Barn, 124 Northwest Minnesota Avenue, Bend; Swing Shift Guitars, 528 Southwest Sixth Street, Redmond; and City Center Motel, 509 East Third Street, Prineville. You can also have two tickets mailed to you for a donation of $30 or more.

In addition to the symphonic performances, which are made up of strings, winds, woods, brass, and percussion, the group also brings in a variety of international artists. In recent years pianist Robert Thies, soprano Marie Landreth, and violinist Linda Wang have graced the high school stage.

Drake Park Munch & Music Concert series
Drake Park, Bend
(541) 389-0995

This free concert series offers a broad sampling of music played by Northwest musicians. Reggae, folk-pop, brass-band jazz, steel drums, and even disco revival are featured, and the event draws an eclectic crowd of locals. It's held at Drake Park in downtown Bend every Thursday from 5:00 to 8:30 P.M. from early July to mid-August.

Music in Public Places
Central Oregon Community College,
2600 Northwest College Way, Bend
(541) 383-7516

Chamber music is orchestra music played by 10 or fewer musicians. Music in Public Places provides small groups of local musicians from the Central Oregon Symphony Orchestra and Central Oregon Concert Band an opportunity to get together and play for the public in local stores, hospitals, churches, and other venues. They offer three or four performances between September and May that are typically free.

Music on the Green
Library Park, Seventh and Evergreen Streets, Redmond
(541) 923-5191

Since the first of these free concerts was organized back in 1992, they have been all about providing an eclectic mix of music. Scottish bagpipes, English dancers, cowboy blues, fiddlers, African music, and country rock are just a sampling of the sounds you'll find being performed from 5:30 to 6:30 P.M. every other Thursday from early July through early September at Redmond's Library Park. A Youth Night is also held during the course of the concert series, featuring the Redmond High School Jazz Band along with a couple of local rock and roll groups.

Obsidian Opera
P.O. Box 182, Bend
(541) 385-7055

Twice each year, in spring and fall, this professional company of 75 singers dazzles Bend opera-goers with performances of ensembles and scenes from Grand Opera. And to make sure that everyone enjoys the performance, they sing in English and are accompanied by a narrator, so

Where's the Art?

While we have galleries galore in Bend, you'll find quite a bit of our art outdoors. It's all due to the efforts of the four-woman committee that makes up the group Art in Public Places, along with the generous financial support of The Bend Foundation, a local philanthropic organization. The fruits of this dynamic duo's labors have resulted in some 20 pieces of specially commissioned art scattered in public areas throughout the city—and there's more in the works.

Beautiful examples include a two-dimensional bronze of Smith Rock State Park that adorns a wall at Lava Lands Visitor Center. At the Central Oregon Welcome Center, a school of bronze trout hangs frozen in midair, and five panels carved in brick at the Bend City Hall render the history of Deschutes County, utilizing themes including culture, farming, timber, recreation, and the Deschutes River.

Public art in Bend is found indoors as well. A batik depicting the Central Oregon landscape through fantastic shapes designed to take hold of a child's imagination graces a wall in the Deschutes County Library, and a weaving called "Dark Ombre" hangs in the county courthouse.

But public art—and Central Oregon's entire well-developed arts scene for that matter—has been a long time coming. The story really began in the late 1960s, when a group of about 15 local women formed an organization called Art Now to provide area residents opportunities to be exposed to art.

"At that time," says Jody Ward, who, along with Sue Hollern, Marlene Alexander, and Mary Ann Ebbs make up Art in Public Places, "there were no art galleries, art instruction, or theater groups in Bend." This group of Bend's earliest art patrons started holding fund-raisers ranging from bake sales and art sales to publishing a cookbook, and they used the money earned to put on art shows and bring art instructors to the area.

By the 1970s, all this work was starting to pay off as the Bend-area art scene began to grow and develop. New galleries arrived in town and various homegrown art-related groups were established. By the mid-1980s, Art Now also began to change, as founding members went off to directly participate as gallery owners or working artists within the art community they had helped to create. Out of this transformation, Art in Public Places was born.

Next, the Bend Foundation signed on as a long-term partner, agreeing to help fund the commissioning and placement of public art throughout the community. The foundation is the philanthropic arm of Brooks-Scanlon Inc. and Brooks Resources, local companies whose roots go back to Bend's early timber boom days (see our History chapter). It donates significant amounts of money to a great variety of community civic endeavors. Since the formation of Art in Public Places, The Bend Foundation has contributed well in excess of $500,000 to help finance public art in Bend.

But effective placement of public art throughout the community doesn't happen randomly. "We actually keep track of what's happening in the community, what public facilities are being built, and what's being planned for the future," explains Ward. Her group does this by talking to a variety of county, city, and parks officials. Once Art in Public Places has established what kinds of public parks, buildings, or other projects are on the drawing board, it selects one or more locations as sites for an art piece, all the while working closely with government officials.

Then a call goes out to Northwest artists, inviting them to submit samples of their work. The committee selects a few finalists, who then submit a proposal or a model of their artistic ideas for a final review. Other than the requirement that art destined for placement outdoors must be able to withstand the weather, the committee puts few constraints on the artists submitting concepts. "We tell them a little about what the place the art will be located is like and where it is, along with some information about Bend," says committee member Mary Ann Ebbs. "But we want to see their vision." The committee commissioned Seattle artist Maya Radoczy to create a cast glass-block window that graces the Deschutes County Library, which opened in the fall of 1998.

The group is also involved in smaller side projects. For example, it was instrumental in obtaining funding for the banners that hang in the foyer of the Mountain View High School auditorium as well as for the three whimsical sculptures at Bend's new Ronald McDonald House.

But the goal of Art in Public Places has really changed little since its origins so many years ago. "We want to expose people in Central Oregon to art that they might not otherwise see," says Ward. "We believe that art doesn't belong behind glass, it belongs outside. And someday, we'd like people to come to Bend not only for events like the Cascade Festival of Music, but for its outdoor art as well."

You can pick up a brochure showing the locations of Bend's public art and providing more information about Art in Public Places at the Mirror Pond Gallery (see listing in this chapter). Or contact Art in Public Places by writing to P.O. Box 6119, Bend, OR 97708.

Ann Bannard's bronze sculpture of an otter cavorts at Bend's Juniper Park. PHOTO: JIM YUSKAVITCH

you always know what's going on. Performances are held at a variety of venues. Admission ranges from $10 to $18.

Sisters Folk Festival
Paulina Springs Book Company, 252 West Hood Street, Sisters
(541) 549–0866
Workshops on songwriting, storytelling, guitar picking, and music as a profession, along with concerts by regional and national talent, are the hallmarks of this folksy get-together sponsored by the Paulina Springs Book Company. Held each year on the second weekend in September, the festival offers both good-time entertainment and the opportunity for serious folk musicians and other budding professionals to hone their skills.

Friday and Saturday evening concerts run from 7:00 to 10:00 P.M. Typically, eight to 10 acts perform during the course of the event. There are Saturday workshops as well. Recent workshop instructors have included renowned folk songwriters Guy Clark and Greg Barnhill. A songwriting contest, which draws entries from throughout the country, is also featured. Call to get the most recent concert and workshop prices.

Sunriver Music Festival
Sunriver Mall, Building 15, Sunriver
(541) 593–1084
www.sunrivermusic.org
The Sunriver Music Festival has been music to Central Oregonians' ears since its first performance in 1977. This year-round event, designed to bring classical music to the area, features five main concerts—four classical and one pops—during the last two weeks of August. The shows are held at the Great Hall in Sunriver, which was built during World War II to serve as the officers' club for a nearby military camp. A family concert, which presents excerpts from the main concert series, is held at the Pavilion, across from the Great Hall. The pops concert performance takes place at Mountain View High School in Bend.

During autumn, winter, and spring, the Fireside Concert series offers performances by a variety of artists from pianists

to gospel singers and includes champagne and dessert at the intermission receptions. Tickets for the main concerts run from $20 to $35 depending on seating. Students may purchase tickets for $7.00. The family concert costs $5.00 per adult, $3.00 for kids ages 12 and younger. Pops concerts tickets range from $30 to $35.

Theater

Community Theatre of the Cascades
148 Northwest Greenwood Avenue, Bend
(541) 389–0803
Except for a manager and part-time bookkeeper, the Community Theatre of the Cascades is an all-volunteer, nonprofit organization that has been providing talented community members the opportunity to become involved in stage play productions since the late 1970s. With so many skills needed to put on a play—actors, set designers, lighting technicians, costume designers, stagehands, box-office staff, and a host of others—there are plenty of jobs for just about anyone who is interested in volunteering.

Each year the group gives multiple performances of six stage plays from late August through June. The selections have included *Enemy of the People* by Arthur Miller, *The Mousetrap* by Agatha Christie, and Neil Simon's *Lost in Yonkers*. The company also puts on two dinner theaters each year at a local restaurant. Main per-

The Sunriver Music Festival has been bringing year-round musical performances to Central Oregon since 1977. PHOTO: SANDELL/SUNRIVER MUSIC FESTIVAL

Outstanding performances keep local theatergoers coming back again and again. PHOTO: COMMUNITY THEATER OF THE CASCADES

formances are presented at the group's intimate 130-seat Greenwood Street theater. Dinner theater locations vary from year to year.

Dinner theater tickets are $35. Main stage plays are $12.00 for adults and $6.00 for children ages 6 to 12.

Sisters Mad Hatter Children's Theater
473 East Hood Street, Unit 3A-STRS-59, Sisters
(541) 549–1153

This children's theater school was founded in 1997 and has about 35 kids from the Sisters area enrolled. For $25 per month, kids in kindergarten through 8th grade can learn the fine points of acting through weekly 90-minute classes that are offered June through September. Graduates put on three productions each year. These are held at the Sisters Middle School during winter, summer, and fall. Past productions have included children's versions of *Macbeth* (sans the violence), *The Phantom of the Opera, Cinderella,* and *Wind in the Willows.*

Visual Arts

Art Galleries

Bend
Art Impressions
369 Northeast Revere Avenue
(541) 382–2354
www.artimpressionsgallery.com

This small gallery and frame shop has an eclectic array of prints and posters including wildlife art, contemporary works, and photography. There is also some original framed art for sale as well. Reasonable prices make this a great place to dress up the walls of your home with good-looking work from well-known artists without breaking the bank.

Avenida Art & Frame
235 Southeast Wilson Avenue
(541) 389–7384

This small gallery and frame shop showcases the work of different artists on a revolving basis. When we visited, their walls were devoted to the works of Nancy Watterson Scharf, whose work combines transparent images laid over a base of stenciled or painted images. The underlying theme of her art is an exploration of women's roles and femininity, manifesting itself in pieces incorporating views of women, young girls, rolling landscapes, and flowers in hues of yellows, beiges, and greens.

Ballantyne & Douglass
900 Northwest Brooks Street
(541) 617-9516

A contemporary fine art gallery spread throughout a number of brightly-colored rooms, work displayed at Ballantyne & Douglass runs the gamut from original paintings and bronzes, to raku and glass art. Some artist's of note whose work you will find here include Maurice Harvey, Ron Hart, Lowrance McKee, and Gary Staten. We found the bronzes—from muses to eagles—especially striking.

Blue Sky Gallery
2600 Northeast Division Street
(541) 388-1877

In business since the late 1970s, Blue Sky Gallery is well-known by locals for its Western, wildlife, and landscape paintings. The front half of the gallery is devoted to the work of local artists, including wildlife art by Rod Frederick and Peter Mathios. Co-owner Gloria Gordon (husband Jim's oils of Mexico are on display here) reports that there has been an increasing interest in landscapes in recent years, so be sure to check out the Central Oregon scenes by High Desert artists Bill Hamilton and Jack Campbell. Other artists of note who exhibit their works here are Terry Boatman, Judy Larson, and Terry Isaac.

Blue Spruce Gallery & Studio
61021 South U.S. Highway 97
(541) 389-7745

The sign out front says, THE LARGEST SELECTION OF POTTERY IN THE NORTHWEST, and as you walk in the door, that claim is easy to believe. There is stoneware and pottery stacked on display tables on the gallery floor and on shelves lining the walls. Much of it is functional, including cups, plates, bowls, saucers, pitchers, and goblets (all oven- and microwave-safe), to name just a sampling. Owner and clay artist J. Robert Sant and his staff of potters work out of the studio in the back, producing the functional pieces and raku. Blue Spruce Gallery & Studio represents the work of about 140 artists. You'll find the pottery of Jim Robinson and Glen Burris here, as well as the landscape paintings of Susie Higdon.

Campbell Smith Gallery
550 Southwest Industrial Way, Studio 39
(541) 617-8803

When local artists Douglas Campbell Smith and Jenny Smith take off on their world travels, they bring along their paints, brushes, and other tools of their trade to depict the color and life they find while abroad. When they return home, they share their latest work at their studio located in the loft above the INCLIMB rock gym, where climbers have been known to take a break from their workout and amble upstairs for a bit of culture.

Jenny and Douglas work in both watercolors and acrylics. They host receptions every month or so to showcase new work from different places they have visited. Recent shows have included paintings of England, Cyprus, and Tuscany.

Charlotte's Fine Art & Collectibles
815 Northwest Wall Street
(541) 330-5907

Wildlife and High Desert watercolors of local artist Don Zylius grace the walls of

> ## Insiders' Tip
> Artists opening their own studios so they can meet and talk with people who admire their work is a growing trend in the Central Oregon art community.

The untitled sculpture by Richard Beyer of a man peering into an empty wallet seldom fails to turn heads in downtown Bend. PHOTO: JIM YUSKAVITCH

this gallery, along with Western landscapes in pastels of Joey Van Blokland and flamboyant and color abstract watercolors by Chris K. Williams. Another local artist, Franz Dutzler, has his masterful trout carvings displayed here as well. We especially liked the great lighting of Kathleen Kelhier's Central Oregon landscapes, which evoke the feeling of the area's wide-open spaces and expansive terrain.

Cristina Acosta Art Studio
550 Industrial Way, #28
(541) 388–5157
www.CristinaAcosta.com

Cristina Acosta's spacious gallery in the Old Mill District is covered with her brightly-colored work; upstairs is her studio where she produces what she calls "happy art" full of color and action. She works in acrylics and oils producing mats, paintings, and panels, all strewn (artfully) about her studio. And her subject matter is colorful and happy. Dancers swirl in a blur of color, there are flowers and cafe scenes, plates of food, small yellow ducks, and angels.

Tourists from distant places looking for a decorative piece made in the Northwest, but who don't have a Northwest decor theme at home, often find exactly what they are in search of at this studio.

Deschutes Gallery
520 Southwest Powerhouse Drive, #628
(541) 617–9472
www.deschutesgallery.com

Located at the Shops at the Old Mill District, Deschutes Gallery is the only gallery in town exclusively dedicated to Northwest Coast Native art, by Native American artists. Here you can marvel at hand-crafted masks with magical names like "wolf mask," "salmon woman," and "moon mask" by artists Carl Stromquist, Janice Morin, Brandon Farleigh, and others.

As you would expect this Native American art reflects the wild things valued by the Northwest Coast native culture—whales, eagles, bears, fish, and ravens, to name a few. You'll also find soapstone carvings of the Inuit people of the Arctic, depicting life on the polar ice, wooden bowls, jewelry, glass plates, and traditional decorative canoe paddles carved from cedar. The gallery also features a good selection of books about Northwest Coast art and Native cultures for aficionados and collectors who would like to learn more.

Frame Design and Sunbird Gallery
916 Northwest Wall Street
(541) 389–9196

Contemporary, ethnic, and traditional works of Pacific Northwest artists are the hallmark of this downtown Bend gallery where fine art pieces include desert landscapes by Tracy Leagjeld, Rick Bartow's dry point sketches, and ceramics by Dan Sprague. The gallery also features an extensive collection of the works of Central Oregon Native American artist Lillian Pitt.

Glass Chameleon Gallery
1024 Northwest Bond Street
(541) 385–0834

You'll find contemporary art (with an emphasis on Oregon and Central Oregon artists) as well as wildlife art at the Glass Chameleon Gallery. There are the bright and colorful abstract paintings of David McCaig, the careful, studied black-and-white landscape photography of Steve McBurnett, and the imaginative and wild and fanciful watercolors of Redmond artist Paul Allen Bennett. The earth-toned porcelain vases of Julie Reisner Forster and hand-blown glass by Michelle Kaptur are especially beautiful.

An adjoining room is filled with meticulous and studied wildlife art along with more contemporary pieces. Especially striking are the nature-theme steel sculpture wall hangings by Ken Scott, who lives just over the crest of the Cascade Mountains in Leaburg.

Mirror Pond Gallery
875 Northwest Brooks Street
(541) 317–9324

Mirror Pond Gallery is the flagship project and headquarters of the Central Oregon Arts Association (see previous listing in this chapter's Art Associations and Support Groups section). It is housed in a historic 1907 bungalow that was slated for demolition in 1992 until a group of citizens convinced the city to allow volunteers to renovate it for use as an art center. The city called off the wrecking ball, a dedicated group of volunteers raised the money to fix the place up, and Mirror Pond Gallery opened its doors in September 1994.

Today it provides a focal point for established and emerging artists to show their work and exchange ideas with other like-minded people. The gallery's monthly exhibits—featuring such themes as art created from paper, recycled material, or earth materials—challenge artists to create work specifically for particular shows. The front part of the gallery houses the changing exhibits; the sales gallery occupies the remainder of the building. Mirror Pond Gallery is a nonprofit gallery run by volunteers.

Mockingbird Gallery
869 Northwest Wall Street, Suite 102
(541) 388-2107

Mockingbird Gallery moved to Bend from Sisters around 1993, shifting from its original focus on Western art to impressionistic, realistic, and traditional original fine arts and limited-edition items. They represent well-known artists living and working in Washington, Oregon, Idaho, California, Utah, and Arizona, including many who have relocated to the West from other countries. Mockingbird's collection includes paintings, photography, bronzes, hand-blown glass, and raku pottery by such artists as Nnamdi Okonkwo, Ovanes Berberian, David Rudacille, Jacques and Mary Regat, Susan Glass, Lindsay Scott, and Bruce Jackson.

Sagebrushers Art Society Gallery
117 Southwest Roosevelt Avenue
(541) 617-0900

Home to the Sagebrushers Art Society, the front of this small gray building is dedicated as gallery showing the work of society members. The back area is a working studio where members work, attend classes, and network with other artists. For more information see their listing under "Art Associations and Support Groups" at the beginning of this chapter.

Smith, Jones & Co.
550 Southwest Industrial Way, #45
(541) 388-4245
www.sjfinecrafts.com

Clay art artists Sandy and Alex Anderson moved from Hawaii to Bend to open their gallery in the Old Mill District. In addition to their attached studio, where they produce a variety of dishes, bowls, and other pottery, they represent a number of Central Oregon artists, including photographer Carol Sternkopf, metal sculptors Danae Bennett Miller and Roger Fox, mixed media artists Laurie Fox and Pamela Kroll, and clothing designer Grace Grinnell.

Sisters/Camp Sherman Area
Buffalo Horn Gallery
103A East Hood Avenue, Sisters
(541) 549-9378

Western is the undeniable theme here, be it in the paintings of the quintessential Bev Doolittle, the atmospheric watercolor of elk and buffalo by M.S. Franco, or the mixed-media portraits of Native Americans under glass by the artist currently known as Alix. There are beautiful pen and inks of horses, wildlife and western prints, and huge, impressive steel sculptures of birds and landscapes by Ted Lettkeman.

The pieces here represent only a partial collection of Western and wildlife art from the Buffalo Horn Gallery. The most valuable pieces in this collection are available for the perusal of serious collectors by appointment only at their 3,000 square-foot warehouse.

Cliff Scharf Silversmith & Gallery of American Crafts
431 East Cascade Street, Sisters
(541) 549-0556

Jewelry designer Cliff Scharf came to Sisters in 1976, only to find that it was a bit too quiet and out of the way to make a living as a gallery owner. So he went on the road to market his creations in gold and silver at fairs and festivals, while also selling his lines to retail jewelry stores. Today, Sisters is a much busier place, and his gallery has been going strong since the early 1990s. Inside you'll find his jewelry on display (in addition to gold and silver, he also works in precious and semiprecious stones) as well as work in other media by a variety of artists including raku masks by Kathy Seymour, batiks by Gael Nagel, and acrylics on canvas by Nancy Watterson Scharf.

Folk Arts and Co.
222 West Hood Avenue, Sisters
(541) 549–9556

Tons of "earthy" art crowds every nook and corner of the Folk Arts and Co. gallery, with a virtual who's who of local artists and crafters represented in the displays. Being surrounded by vast forests, you'd expect area creative-types to be inspired by wood, and that's certainly the case here. There are bowls carved from ponderosa pine by Walter Rufer and bowls from juniper by Thomas Johasson. Charlie Young also carves bowls out of this ubiquitous High Desert tree. The work of Sisters potter Carol Kimball is here along with the lava rock and natural clay pottery fashioned by Bend's Annie Emond. There are photographic prints by Kris Falco and David Duck. In fact, there's far too much to list, so you'll just have to drop in and see it all for yourself.

Sisters Gallery & Frame Shop
161 East Cascade Avenue, #2, Sisters
(541) 549–9552

This small gallery has original paintings, prints, and posters of wildlife, landscapes, flowers, whimsical animals, religious scenes, and aviation art—including a number of rare, commemorative World War II pieces. The shop also does framing.

Soda Creek Gallery
183 East Hood Street, Sisters
(541) 549–0600

This gallery has one of the best collections of fine wildlife art in Central Oregon. The details of Carl Brenders' wildlife paintings are so finely rendered, it's easy to imagine his subjects might burst off the canvas and out the door. And Franz Dutzler's woodcarvings of trout, suspended in glass

cases, appear that they might at any moment swim off through the air. The carved wood bowls of Donald Wadsworth are beautiful in their simplicity.

Dan Rickards is another fine wildlife artist whose works you'll find here, along with clay-pot art by Lowell Hanna and Chris Haug. Representing the Western genre are Monte Langford (with his dignified portraits of Native Americans) and the horse watercolors paintings of Suzie Mather. Other top-notch wildlife artists represented here include scratchboard by Diane Versteeg, fish sculptures by William Bishop, and the mixed media whales by Don McMichael. The gallery is not entirely Western- and wildlife-oriented, however, and you will find a variety of other subject matter here as well.

Redmond
Theresa's Fine Framing & Gallery
515 Southwest Sixth Street
(541) 923–5208

Located in a downtown historic building that also houses the New Redmond Hotel, Theresa's Fine Framing & Gallery represents the talents of local and regional artists who work in pottery, art jewelry, blown glass, painting, and sculpture. "We have wildlife, landscapes, Western art, and a lot of fish," reports gallery owner Theresa. Of special interest are the coat hangers, dinner bells, and door knockers with horse, salmon, and other Western and nature motifs, created by artists at the nearby Dry Canyon Forge.

Sunriver/La Pine Area
Oregon Gallery
Sunriver Mall, Building 24, Sunriver
(541) 593–5011

Oregon Gallery represents the landscape photography of Ron Keebler, who specializes in depicting the scenic splendor of Central Oregon and the Oregon coast. The gallery also has some gift items and pottery, plus prints of the brightly colored, whimsical work of Oregon artists Mike Smith and Nancy Coffelt.

Madras Area

The Art Adventure Gallery
185 Southeast Fifth Street, Madras
(541) 475-7701

Home of the Jefferson County Arts Association, The Art Adventure Gallery features local and regional artists who work in a variety of media including painting, sculpture, pottery, blown glass, and woodwork. The gallery hosts a monthly show highlighting the work of an area artist, such as the abstract paintings of Crooked River Ranch artist Jimmy Ray Brown. Annual events include a Student Show, which presents the work of local students, and an All Jefferson County Show, with art created by county residents. The gallery also has a classroom and offers an art program for children.

Inspirations Art Galley
146 Southwest First Street, Madras
(541) 475-0136

Representing the work of 150 artists from Alaska to Arizona, Inspirations Art Galley is a fine art gallery offering work in a variety of styles and mediums. Some of that gallery's notable artists include sculptor Jeff Stuart, watercolorists Winnie Givot and Glenna Parker, and pastel artists Kathleen Keliher and Leslie Keller. And the raku pieces you'll find here are to die for.

Parks

Bend Area

Sisters/Camp
  Sherman Area

Redmond Area

Sunriver/La Pine Area

Prineville Area

Madras Area

Central Oregon has so much natural beauty that you would expect to find plenty of parks here. And you will. We have wilderness parks for camping and getting away from it all, and urban parks where you can take a break from your busy schedule to stretch out in the sun and read a book. Sports fans will be glad to find ball fields, soccer fields, and tennis courts galore. Nature lovers can hike and explore riverside trails and natural areas. And best of all, many of these parks are right in town—no matter which Central Oregon city you may happen to be in at the moment.

The city parks departments are a mixed bag. Bend, Redmond, and Prineville have formal parks and recreation departments that offer a variety of programs and classes. Other area communities do not, and their parks are administered and maintained by other branches of city government or by volunteers. We list the departments in various Central Oregon communities so you can contact them for more information.

Oregon's state parks are well-organized and developed. With 118 day-use areas and 49 camping areas throughout the state, Oregon has one of the best park systems in the country. Central Oregon is blessed with 10. Some parks have day-use fees, which currently run at $3.00 per vehicle. Annual permits, good for any state park, are $25. All have charges for camping, which vary depending on the type of campsite you choose and the amenities available. Our state park listings provide more information. Additional details on camping in Central Oregon state parks can be found in our chapter on Camping. You may also call (800) 551-6949 for up-to-the-minute information about Oregon state parks. Campsite reservations may be made at any state park by calling (800) 452-5687.

Bend Area

Bend Metro Park & Recreation District
200 Northwest Pacific Park Lane, Bend
(541) 389-7275

With more than 200 full- and part-time employees, the Bend Metro Park & Recreation District offers a complete range of year-round indoor and outdoor recreational activities to suit just about any interest and age. Programs include arts and crafts, team sports, day camps for kids, golf, bowling, tennis, and a variety of outdoor recreation classes and trips from birding to cross-country skiing (see our Other Outdoor Recreation chapter). The district also operates the Juniper Swim and Fitness Center (see our Indoor Recreation chapter). Bend Metro Park & Recreation District puts out a program of events and activities each summer, fall, winter, and spring. You may pick these programs up at the district office.

Bend City Parks

Bend's 27 parks offer something for everyone. Whether you're searching for a basketball court for a pickup game or planning a wedding reception and in need of classy digs, there is a park within the city limits that has what you're looking for. Softball and baseball fields, tennis courts, rollerskating facilities, jogging and fitness circuits, or a quiet trail along the Deschutes River for a little nature watching and peace and quiet are just some of the amenities available to Bend residents through its extensive park system.

All the parks are also available for special events such as conventions, weddings and receptions, corporate picnics, and other private affairs. For most parks, reservations are $35 to $100, depending on the size of your group. However, rates vary for others and are noted in the following park descriptions. Athletic fields may be reserved for $25 per day. A refundable deposit is generally required when you make your reservations. For more information on reserving parks and park facilities, contact the Bend Metro Park & Recreation District office.

Big Sky Park
Neff Road, east of Hamby Road, Bend
(541) 389–7275

In addition to some natural areas, Big Sky Park caters to team sports enthusiasts, providing both baseball and soccer fields along with a BMX track.

Brooks Park
Northwest Newport Avenue and Drake Road, Bend
(541) 389–7275

Brooks Park is a pleasant open-space park with a green lawn, perfect for enjoying the sunshine while catching up on your reading.

Canal Park
Butler Market Road and 27th Street, Bend
(541) 389–7275

Near an irrigation canal that flows along the north side of Bend, this park has baseball and soccer fields as well as natural areas and an open lawn.

Columbia Park
Northwest Columbia Street and Baltimore Avenue, Bend
(541) 389–7275

A perfect spot for family activities, Columbia Park is just west of the Deschutes River and boasts a playground and picnic area, a horseshoe pit, and open lawn space.

Drake Park
Northwest Riverside Boulevard and Brooks Street, Bend
(541) 389–7275

The location of numerous Bend events (see our Annual Events and The Arts chapters), 11-acre Drake Park is immediately west of the downtown area, along the Deschutes River at Mirror Pond. It has rest rooms, picnic areas, open space, big trees, and plenty of ducks, geese, and swans. It's a favorite spot for locals to have lunch or take in a warm, sunny Central Oregon afternoon. A paved bike path runs through the park.

Harmon Park
Northwest Harmon Boulevard and Nashville Avenue, Bend
(541) 389–7275

Just across the river from Drake Park, Harmon Park is a favorite starting point for kayakers and canoeists bound for a lazy river float trip. The park features a boat launch site, playground and picnic areas, softball and soccer fields, and rest rooms.

Hillside I Park
Northwest 12th Street and Trenton Avenue, Bend
(541) 389–7275

A jogging and fitness circuit is a highlight of Hillside I Park, which is well-used by locals looking to keep in tip-top shape. The park also has a playground, picnic area, and basketball court.

Hillside II Park
Northwest 10th Street and Trenton Avenue, Bend
(541) 389-7275

Immediately to the southeast of Hillside I Park, Hillside II Park is a laid-back place with a picnic area and open lawn—a great location to perfect your Frisbee game with your dog.

Hollinshead Park
1235 Northeast Jones Road, Bend
(541) 389-7275

In a residential area, Hollinshead Park's primary feature is the Hollinshead Barn, a two-story historic building available for group rentals of up to 75 people. The building has rest rooms, banquet tables, and a small kitchen with a refrigerator and freezer, gas oven, stove, and microwave oven. The park also features a paved bike path, a playground area, and a short hiking trail. Rental fees for the barn are $25 to $35 per hour Monday through Thursday, and $195 to $395 for 1 to 12 hours on weekends and holidays, depending on whether the event is private or commercial. A $250 refundable deposit is required when making your reservation application.

Juniper Park
Northeast Sixth Street and Franklin Avenue, Bend
(541) 389-7275

Full-featured 22-acre Juniper Park has a roller-hockey and roller-skating rink, playground and picnic areas, basketball and tennis courts, a softball field, a jogging and fitness circuit, and rest rooms. A group picnic area with a capacity of 200 people is available for rental for $50 to $75 per day, depending on the group size.

Kiwanis Park
Southeast Centennial Boulevard and Roosevelt Avenue, Bend
(541) 389-7275

A basketball court and softball field are some of the amenities found at Kiwanis Park, which is east of U.S. Highway 97. You'll also find a playground and picnic area. It is also a favorite location from which to watch the Fourth of July fireworks, which are set off from Pilot Butte, just to the north. The small group picnic area may be rented at a cost of $35 to $50, depending on group size.

McKay Park
Northwest Shevlin-Hixon Road and Colorado Street Bridge, Bend
(541) 389-7275

A popular Deschutes riverfront park, the grassy open spaces of McKay Park offers a pleasant place to read, nap, or even take a dip in the river.

Pacific Park
200 Northwest Pacific Park Lane, Bend
(541) 389-7275

Located at the office of the Bend Metro Park and Recreation District and along the Deschutes River, this park offers grassy, open space and flower beds. It's the sort of park in which to sit, relax, and watch the river go by.

Pageant Park
Northwest Drake Road and Nashville Avenue, Bend
(541) 389-7275

Adjacent to Harmon Park, along the Deschutes River, Pageant Park is an open-space park with a canoe and boat launch.

Pioneer Park
Northwest Hall and Portland Avenue, Bend
(541) 389-7275

Open grassy space and natural, unmanicured areas make Pioneer Park a great place to get away from it all without leaving the city. It has rest rooms, so you can stay all day. You can reserve this six-acre park for special events and activities for $75 to $100 per day, depending on the size of your group.

Ponderosa Park
Southeast 15th and Wilson Street, Bend
(541) 389-7275

Ponderosa Park sports a soccer and softball field for local sports, along with a roller-skating and roller-hockey rink, a fitness trail, and picnic and playground areas surrounded by open grassy lawns and natural areas. The park has rest rooms.

The Deschutes River offers canoers a pleasant and nearby float. PHOTO: BEND METRO PARK & RECREATION DISTRICT

Providence Park
Northeast Providence Drive, Bend
(541) 389-7275
A tennis court is the main feature of this park, but it also has a playground area in an open grassy setting.

Railroad Park
Southeast Railroad Avenue and Miller Avenue, Bend
(541) 389-7275
Railroad Park, in the southeast portion of town, has a basketball court and open lawn space.

Riverview Park
Northwest Yale Street and Division Street, Bend
(541) 389-7275
Riverview Park snakes along the natural landscape of the Deschutes River's west bank, offering hikers solitude accompanied by the sounds of birds and gently flowing water.

Robert Sawyer Park
North O.B. Riley Road, Bend
(541) 389-7275
A mix of open-space lawn and natural landscape, this 61½-acre park has a soft-ball field, picnic and playground areas, a hiking trail, and rest room. You can schedule a special group event here for $35 to $50 per day, based on the size of your event.

Shevlin Park
Northwest Shevlin Road, Bend
(541) 389-7275
A wonderful natural environment along crystal-clear aspen- and pine-lined Tumalo Creek on the western fringe of the city, 500-plus-acre Shevlin Park is a great place to get away from it all without having to go too far. You'll find picnic facilities as well as hiking trails. In winter, the park offers ice-skating and Nordic skiing (see our Snowplay chapter).

Aspen Hall, a day lodge available for group events, is here. The hall has 20 banquet tables, kitchen facilities, a large fireplace, rest rooms, and a deck that encircles the building and overlooks a pond. It's a favorite location for weddings and retreats. Rental fees for Aspen Hall are $35 to $45 per hour Monday through Thursday, and $245 to $700 for 1 to 12 hours on weekends and holidays, depending on whether the event is private or commercial. A $250 refundable deposit is required when making your reservation application.

Skyline Sports Complex
Mt. Washington Drive, Bend
(541) 389–7275

Skyline Sports Complex has four lighted soccer/softball fields, outdoor basketball courts, natural areas, rest rooms, a concession stand, and picnic and playground facilities.

Stover Park
Northeast Meadow Lane, Bend
(541) 389–7275

Along with a softball field and paved bikeway, this park has playground and picnic areas and rest rooms in a grassy, open-space setting surrounded by a hedge border.

Summit Park
Northwest Summit Drive and Promontory Drive, Bend
(541) 389–7275

Summit Park features tennis and basketball courts along with a picnic area and hiking trail surrounded by a mix of open lawn and natural vegetation.

Sunset View Park
Northwest Stannium Street, Bend
(541) 389–7275

A small park on the former site of the city dog pound, Sunset View Park offers a hiking trail and exercise stations in a quiet out-of-the-way location.

Sylvan Park
Northwest Three Sisters Drive, Bend
(541) 389–7275

The tennis court attracts many residents to this park. It also features a playground, picnic area, and hiking trail.

Woodriver Park
Southwest Woodriver Subdivision, Bend
(541) 389–7275

Just under an acre in size, a hiking trail leads through this park on Bend's southern outskirts. You'll also find a basketball court, a playground, and picnic tables here as well.

State Parks

Pilot Butte State Park
Just off U.S. Highway 20, on the eastern city limits of Bend
(800) 551–6949

This 4,139-foot butte has been a Bend landmark since the first pioneers used it as a reference point for navigating across the High Desert. Today, Pilot Butte is treasured by Bend residents for its stunning 360-degree views that take in the sweep of Central Oregon geography—from hot desert flats to cool mountain slopes. (The summit is reached by an appropriately narrow, winding road, of course.) And there's no better way to punctuate a warm summer Central Oregon day, than to watch the sun set behind the mountains from Pilot Butte. Pilot Butte is also a popular place for the keeping-in-shape crowd, and on weekends it often swarms with speed walkers, runners, and bicyclists. There is a hiking trail on the butte. No water is available, so be sure to bring some along with you. This is where the fireworks are launched for Bend's Fourth of July festivities (see our Annual Events chapter).

Tumalo State Park
Off U.S. Highway 20, 5 miles northwest of Bend
(541) 382–3586

On a prime chunk of real estate by the Deschutes River, Tumalo State Park is a cool, green haven surrounded by High Desert juniper and sagelands. Just a stone's throw from the Bend city limits, you'll find picnicking under the shade of ponderosa pines, willows, and alders (including a group picnicking area that may be reserved in advance), great trout fishing (see our Fishing chapter), and a riverside hiking trail. Throughout the summer the park staff gives interpretive talks and slide shows about the environment and wildlife of Central Oregon. The park has 64 tent camping sites, 21 RV camping sites with full hookups and a hiker/biker camping area, and a solar-heated shower and rest rooms. You may also arrange to stay in one of the park's tepees or yurts. RV campsites with full hookups are $16 per night. Tent camping sites are $13 per night. Nightly rates for tepees are $29. Yurts are $27. (See our Camping chapter for more information.) Tumalo State Park is open year-round.

Sisters/Camp Sherman Area

Sisters does not have a city parks and recreation department. Its two local parks are managed by the city's administrative offices. If you have specific questions about local parks, you may contact the City of Sisters, 150 North Fir Street, Sisters, (541) 549-6022.

City Parks

Sisters City Park
Jefferson Street, just off U.S. Highway 20, Sisters
(541) 549-6022

In a lovely stand of pines along Squaw Creek, which flows out of the Cascade Mountains and through town, Sisters City Park has both a day area and camping area. The day-use area is on the west side of the

creek and has picnic tables and barbecue pits. A foot bridge across the creek allows day users to get to the rest rooms, which are in the camping portion of the park. There are about 35 camping slots here, suitable for RV or tent camping (although there are no RV hookups available). There are picnic tables, fire rings, and barbecue pits along with potable water in the overnight area. Camping costs are $10.00 for RVs and $5.00 for tent campers. The 13-acre park is on the east end of town.

Village Green Park
Elm Street, between Washington and Jefferson Streets, Sisters
(541) 549-6022

This open, grassy, one-acre park in downtown Sisters is for day use only. It offers picnic tables and a barbecue pit, a playground for kids, and a small gazebo. There are also rest rooms with running water.

State Parks

E.R. Corbett State Wayside
Off U.S. Highway 20, 14 miles west of Sisters
(800) 551-6949

This park is primarily a staging area for cross-country ski trips into the adjacent Deschutes National Forest. Most people use it as a place to park their cars. You'll need a Sno-Park permit to leave your car here in the winter (see our Snowplay chapter).

Redmond Area

Central Oregon Park and Recreation District
465 Southwest Rimrock Drive, Redmond
(541) 548-7275

The Central Oregon Park and Recreation District was created primarily to manage the Cascade Swim Center in Redmond (see our Indoor Recreation chapter). However, the district also offers a selection of year-round activities and recreation programs, including youth and adult team sports, tennis and golf lessons, yoga, and recreation and play activities for tots, along with an extensive swimming program. Pick up one of the quarterly recreation program schedules at the above address for the latest information. Ball fields are available for $50.00 per day plus $9.00 per hour for a supervisor; applications are available at the Rimrock Drive office. City parks are managed by the Redmond Public Works Department, 875 Southeast Sisters Avenue, Redmond, (541) 504–2000.

City Parks

Baker Park
Southwest 17th Street and Southwest Obsidian Avenue, Redmond
(541) 504–2000

This open-lawn neighborhood park has a covered picnic area, barbecue stand, play equipment, rest room, and benches for sitting back and relaxing.

Bowlby Park
Corner of Highland Avenue and Rimrock Drive, Redmond
(541) 504–2000

Bowlby Park is in the southern end of Dry Canyon, which runs through Redmond. The park has tennis courts and a softball field.

Dry Canyon Trail
West Redmond
(541) 504–2000

Dry Canyon, a natural area of rimrock, junipers, and native grasses that runs in a north-south direction through the west side of Redmond, is one of the city's unpolished gems. The city has been acquiring portions of the canyon little by little and has now developed a 3-mile paved trail in its northern portion. It's a wonderful hike that's also popular with bicyclists, in-line skaters, and families with kids in strollers. Access is near the Redmond Wastewater Treatment Plant off Northwest Pershall Way or at West Fir Street, where a stairway into the canyon has been constructed.

Hayden Park
Southwest Quartz Avenue and Southwest 35th Street, Redmond
(541) 504–2000

This park is in a newer neighborhood in the growing southwest corner of Redmond. A pleasant, three-acre park of hilly, mani-cured lawn, it offers a picnic table, barbecue stand, rest room, and playground.

High Desert Sports Complex
Off Northeast Negus Way, Redmond
(541) 504–2000

The High Desert Sports Complex has four softball fields and an "airport" for radio-controlled airplane enthusiasts.

Kalama Park
South 17th Street and West Kalama Avenue, Redmond
(541) 504–2000

With a flower garden, picnic tables, a barbecue stand, rest rooms, playground equipment, and a softball field, Kalama Park offers a little something for just about everybody.

Quince Park
Northwest Quince Avenue and Northwest 10th Street, Redmond
(541) 504–2000

In a developing part of Redmond, on the north end of town, Quince Park has a playground area and paved walking paths within a pleasant open-lawn environment.

Ray Johnson Park
Fifth Street and Highland Avenue, Redmond
(541) 504–2000

A quiet retreat next to busy U.S. Highway 97, Ray Johnson Park has rolling terrain, green grass, stands of trees, and some natural areas, along with horseshoe pits and picnic tables.

Sam Johnson Park
South 15th Street, Redmond
(541) 504–2000

Sam Johnson Park is in Dry Canyon. It offers shade trees, a covered shelter, rest rooms, and a playground in a pleasant, older Redmond neighborhood.

Umatilla Sports Center
Umatilla Avenue, Redmond
(541) 504–2000

The Umatilla Sports Center offers baseball and soccer fields, along with a large parking lot, designed to meet the needs of the residents of this growing corner of Redmond.

State Parks

Cline Falls State Park
Off U.S. Highway 20, 4 miles west of Redmond
(800) 551–6949

A thoroughly lovely park along the tree-lined Deschutes River makes this day-use area a great place for a relaxing picnic and some time spent listening to the river rolling by. Respectable trout fishing can be had here as well, except in midsummer when the water level in the river gets a tad on the low side. The site has rest rooms and complete picnic facilities.

Peter Skene Ogden Wayside
Off U.S. Highway 97, 9 miles northeast of Redmond
(800) 551–6949

A wayside rest area for car travelers, this small park also offers a spectacular view into the Crooked River Gorge and the Crooked River below. Stay away from the edge! The park also has rest rooms and is wheelchair-accessible.

Smith Rock State Park
Off U.S. Highway 97, 9 miles northeast of Redmond
(541) 548–7501

Sheer cliffs rise up to 400 feet above the Crooked River, which winds its way through the gorge known as Smith Rock State Park. This park is considered one of the crown jewels of Oregon's state park system. Rock climbers come from all over the world to test their skills on its cliffs and crags, which they share with the hawks and eagles that live and nest here. Ten miles of moderately strenuous trails will take you throughout the park, from the tree-lined riverbank to the tops of the sagebrush-covered ridges. It's a steep half-mile walk into the canyon from the parking lot. For the less hardy, the views of the cliffs and canyon are spectacular right from the parking and picnic areas. A wildfire burned about one-third of the 641-acre park in August 1996, but an extensive recovery effort, including planting native trees and grass and fencing off burned areas while they regrow, has brought the park's flora and fauna to recovery, although you can still see signs of that conflagration throughout the area.

The park is a full-service day-use area with picnic tables, barbecue stands, heated rest rooms, and solar-powered showers. There is no RV camping. However, there is a bivouac area for tent camping, which is

Rock climbers challenge themselves on the steep cliffs of Smith Rock State Park near Terrebonne.

PHOTO: JIM YUSKAVITCH

used primarily by rock climbers. There is a day-use fee of $3.00 per car per day. Overnight tent camping is $4.00 per person, which also includes the day-use fee.

Sunriver/La Pine Area

Because Sunriver is a private community and La Pine is an unincorporated city, there are no organized public parks and recreation departments in southern Deschutes County. However, the community of La Pine has volunteer parks commissioners who have worked to establish and maintain several parks in the area. Sunriver also has one park that is open to the public.

City Parks

Finley Butte Road Park
Finley Butte Road and Walling Lane, La Pine
(541) 536–2223
In downtown La Pine, Finley Butte Road Park is an open-space park with two baseball fields and a third under construction. The ball fields are open to anyone, and no advance reservations are required.

Fort Rock Park
East Cascade Road, between Circles 4 and 11, Sunriver
(541) 593–2411
Although in the private community of Sunriver, Fort Rock Park is open to the general public free of charge. The park features picnic tables and barbecue facilities, basketball and tennis courts, a horseshoe pit, a children's playground, and a small covered pavilion. Families and nonprofit organizations can rent the park for $35 per day. For corporate functions, the cost is $125 to $225 per day, depending on group size. A $100 refundable deposit is required when you make your reservations.

Leona Park
end of Riverland Road, La Pine
(541) 536–2223
Donated by a former local resident in memory of his late wife, Leona Park is a forested two-acre plot along the Little Deschutes River. Currently open space, future plans call for its development as a neighborhood park, including a wheelchair-accessible fishing facility.

Rosland Park
Burgess Road, 1 mile west of U.S. Highway 97, La Pine
(541) 536–2223
Rosland Park is a beautiful 40-acre patch of pine forest along the Little Deschutes River. It has a 20-acre camping area, with 11 large sites capable of accommodating four or five RVs or other vehicles. There are, however, no RV hookups, and camping here is strictly primitive. Nevertheless, its location is well-worth the lack of amenities. The park has 20 acres of frontage along the Little Deschutes River. Camping fees are $7.00 per vehicle per night. Day use fees are $1.00 for La Pine residents and $3.00 for nonresidents.

White School Park
Corner of First Street and Harrington Road, La Pine
(541) 536–2223
White School Park was named after the schoolhouse, formerly on this site, which collapsed under the weight of an unrelenting buildup of snow during the winter of 1992–93. City officials used the insurance money to construct a large warehouse-style building, which they hope to eventually turn into a community center complete with a gymnasium, stage, and meeting room. There is also a small playground here.

State Parks

LaPine State Park
Off U.S. Highway 97, 10 miles northwest of La Pine
(541) 536–2071
LaPine State Park is one of the gems of Central Oregon. It sits astride the Deschutes River, not too many miles from its headwaters in the Cascade Mountains. Visitors relax in the shade of big pines or don their waders for a little first-rate trout fishing (see our Fishing chapter). Hiking along forest trails, mountain biking, and wildlife watching are just some of the activities that lure

people here year after year. Picnic facilities are available for day use, as is a meeting hall, which is free for the use of groups who have reserved five or more campsites. Otherwise it costs $25 per day to rent. The park boasts 95 RV camping sites with full hookups and 50 sites with electricity as well as five cabins and three yurts. Camping rates are in the $13 to $15 range per night. Cabins cost $35 per night while yurts are available for $27. Rest rooms and showers are also available. Park staff gives nature talks during the summer season. The park is open year-round and is popular with snowshoers, cross-country skiers, and snowmobilers during the winter months. For additional information on LaPine State Park, see our Camping chapter. To make campsite reservations, call (800) 452-5687.

Prineville Area

Crook County Parks & Recreation
398 Northeast Fairview Street, Prineville
(541) 447-1209

Crook County Parks & Recreation offers a variety of recreational activities for young people and adults and also manages the parks. Softball, bowling, karate, bicycle safety, art lessons, pottery classes, and dog-obedience classes are just a small sampling of the offerings. The department also operates an outdoor pool facility during the summer months. Pool-related activities include swimming lessons, swimnastics, and programs to introduce toddlers to water and swimming. Nonprofit groups may reserve parks for day events. Costs, depending on the number of people and type of event, range from free for groups of 40 or less up to around $40.

City Parks

There is no charge for using the ball fields in Prineville. Organized groups who use city fields pay for electricity to light night games and make arrangements to volunteer to do maintenance and park clean-ups.

Crooked River Park
Oregon Highway 27, 1 mile south of downtown Prineville
(541) 447-1209

Prineville's prime location for sports fans, Crooked River Park has softball and soccer fields along with picnic facilities (including a covered area that can be reserved), rest rooms, two playground areas, an amphitheater, and a volleyball court. All of this is along the scenic Crooked River.

Davidson Park
South Main Street and Southeast Third Street, Prineville
(541) 447-1209

Davidson Park has one hardball field, which the local high school baseball team uses, and three youth fields that double as softball fields for adults. The full-size ball field also has bleachers.

Harwood Park/Kilowatt Field
North Harwood Avenue and West Eighth Street, Prineville
(541) 447-1209

This open, grassy park along Ochoco Creek, which runs through Prineville, has picnic tables and a swing set for the kids. Kilowatt Field, across the street, is where local softball players head.

Mountain View Park
On Mountain View Drive off Coombs Flat Road, Prineville
(541) 447-1209

This tiny park on Ochoco Creek features a small gazebo and is primarily used as a pleasant picnic location by local neighborhood residents. The Juniper Art Guild building, where Crook County Parks & Recreation offers many of its programs, is also located here.

Ochoco Creek Park/Stryker Field
Northeast Fourth Street, between North Elm Street and Fairview Street, Prineville
(541) 447-1209

Along Ochoco Creek, this park offers open space, big cottonwood trees, picnic tables, horseshoe pits, and a small outdoor amphitheater. The city's public swimming pool is here. This is also the site of the Wildland Firefighters Monument, a bronze statue erected by the parents of nine members of the Prineville Hotshot crew who died while fighting a forest fire on Colorado's Storm King Mountain in July 1994. Dedicated in June 1996, the monument honors all wildland firefighters.

Pioneer Park
East Third Street, between South Court Street and South Elm Street, Prineville
(541) 447-1209

A small, downtown bit of green, Pioneer Park has benches for relaxing under its shade trees, a small stage for events and performances, and playground equipment. Also of interest is a small, original pioneer cabin complete with original 1800s furnishings that has been relocated to the park from its former home in the nearby desert. You aren't allowed to go inside, but you can look through the windows and wonder how those pioneers managed. The Prineville City Hall and Crook County Courthouse are also within the park area, making it a great people-watching location.

County Parks

Ochoco Lake Park
Off U.S. Highway 26 along Ochoco Reservoir, 7 miles east of Prineville
(541) 447-1209

This pleasant park is nestled on a tree-filled hillside along popular Ochoco Reservoir. It serves primarily as a camping area for visitors who come to fish, swim, and boat in this High Desert lake. There are 18 campsites. Each site has picnic tables and fire pits, but no hookups or running water are available. The park is generally open from early April through October, depending on the weather. Campsites are $14 per night.

State Parks

Ochoco State Wayside
Off U.S. Highway 126, 1 mile west of Prineville
(800) 551-6949

This state wayside offers great views of the surrounding countryside, including the Crooked River, the city of Prineville, surrounding ranch and farmlands, and the not-too-distant Ochoco Mountains. Fireworks are set off here for Prineville's Fourth of July celebration (see our Annual Events chapter).

Prineville Reservoir State Park
Off U.S. Highway 26, 17 miles southeast of Prineville
(541) 447-4363

Fishing, swimming, boating, and rock hounding are what bring most visitors to Prineville Reservoir State Park at the base of the Ochoco Mountains. Spend your visit in your boat on the lake (which is formed by Bowman Dam on the Crooked River) fishing for trout and bass (see our Fishing chapter) or use the park as a base of operations for rock-hounding or hiking trips to nearby lands managed by the U.S. Forest Service and Bureau of Land Management. You'll find 22 RV campsites with full hookups and 48 tent campsites. There are also two picnic sites within the park, including one with electricity. Rest rooms with hot showers are available. Boat rentals, food, and fishing supplies may be obtained at the park concession at Jasper Point, 3 miles east of the park. The swimming area is marked, and a boat launch is available. Campsite rates run from $13 to $20 per night. You can also rent a cabin for $55 to $45. (See our Camping chapter for more information.) The park is open year-round.

Madras Area

Madras does not have a city parks and recreation department. Its local parks are managed by the city's public works department. If you have specific questions about local parks, you may contact the City of Madras, 216 Northwest B Street, Madras, (541) 475-2622.

City Parks

Bean Park
East end of town on B Street, Madras
(541) 475-2622

This one-acre park features a volleyball court, horseshoe pits, picnic tables, playground, rest rooms, and a large parking area.

Friendship Park
Corner of Fourth and E Streets, Madras
(541) 475-2622

Less than an acre in size, Friendship Park is primarily intended as a pleasant rest and lunch stop for travelers along U.S. Highway 97. It offers picnic tables and shade trees. Because of its location next to the open grassy area of Westside Elementary School, the park "feels" larger than it really is. Madras' annual Collage of Culture is held here (see our Annual Events chapter).

Sahalee Park
Seventh and B Streets, Madras
(541) 475-2622

This downtown park occupies an entire city block and offers basketball courts, a playground, picnic shelter, rest rooms, and lots of large elm trees for shade.

Seventh Street Park
Seventh and A Streets, Madras
(541) 475-2622

A couple of picnic tables mark this small park on the westernmost edge of a mile-long bike path that runs along Willow Creek. The bike path is paved and lighted for the convenience and safety of late-evening hikers, joggers, and bikers.

County Parks

Juniper Hills Park
B Street, about .75 mile east of Fifth Street, Madras
(541) 475-4459

Juniper Hills Park has baseball diamonds and a paved bike path that runs around the park perimeter.

State Parks

The Cove Palisades State Park
Off U.S. Highway 97, 15 miles southwest of Madras
(541) 546-3412

Lake Billy Chinook, named after an Indian scout who accompanied explorer John C. Frémont into Central Oregon in 1843 (see our History chapter), was formed by the construction of Round Butte Dam in 1963 at the confluence of the Deschutes, Crooked, and Metolius Rivers. Covering 6 square miles and with 72 miles of shoreline, it's a hugely popular place during Central Oregon's warm, sunny summer months. Water-skiers, Jet-Skiers, and boaters find a cool paradise in the flooded canyon. Anglers love the reservoir for its kokanee salmon, brown trout, and rainbow trout. Of special interest is the trophy bull trout fishery—with fair odds of hauling in a 20-plus pound specimen (see our Fishing chapter). You'll find two marinas, a restaurant, a fish-cleaning station, and a store stocked with food, beverages, propane, and fishing supplies. There are several campgrounds along the lake featuring RV spaces with full hookups as well as tent camping. Full hookup RV sites run from $16 to $20 per night. Tent camping sites are $16. See our Camping chapter for more information. Rest rooms and showers are available in the park. The day-use fee is $3.00.

You may rent personal watercraft at Cove Marina, (541) 546-3521, on the lake's Crooked River arm, for $195 per day. Four-passenger, 14-foot fishing boats with motors are available for $55 per day. Eight-person ski boats are $255 per day. Houseboats may be rented for anywhere from just under $2,000 to nearly $2,200 for a week, depending on the number of people it sleeps. Boats may also be rented at Three Rivers Marina (no phone) on the Metolius River arm. You may rent a cabin on the lake for $65 per night depending on the time of year. Contact the park office for more information on cabin rentals.

The Cove Palisades State Park is also the site of two annual events of interest—Eagle Watch in February and Lake Billy Chinook Day in September (see our Annual Events chapter).

PGE Parks

Portland General Electric operates the Pelton-Round Butte hydroelectric dams on the Deschutes River. The Round Butte Dam has created Lake Billy Chinook, while the reservoir which has formed behind Pelton Dam, just downstream of Lake Billy Chinook, is known as Lake Simtustus. PGE runs two parks in the area as well as another half dozen or so in other areas of the state where it operates.

Pelton Park
East shore of Lake Simtustus, just north of Lake Billy Chinook
(503) 464-8515

Pelton Park, owned and operated by Portland General Electric, is on the shores of quiet, narrow Lake Simtustus deep in the Deschutes River canyon. It offers 70 campsites, a picnic area, a boat launch site and moorage, showers, and rest rooms. A small park store provides ice, cold drinks, groceries, and fishing tackle. Although there is a small area on the lake where waterskiing is allowed, the boating speed limit for most of the lake is 10 miles per hour, making it an ideal place for paddling your canoe or kayak through the quiet of a desert canyon. Just north of the park is the Pelton Wildlife Overlook, where a series of short trails lead to viewing platforms that

Insiders' Tip

Pilot Butte Partners is a volunteer group concerned with the care and maintenance of Pilot Butte State Park in Bend. If you'd like to become involved, contact the local state parks office at (541) 388-6211 for more information.

allow you to scan the waters below for great blue herons, ducks, geese, and a variety of other water-loving birds. Park campsites may be reserved beginning April 3 by calling (541) 475-0517. Basic campsites cost $14.50 per night. Campsites with electrical hookups are $20. The group campsite is $65. The park is open from late April through October.

Round Butte Overview Park
Off Belmont Lane, about 12 miles southwest of Madras
(503) 464-8515

PGE has created a nifty wildlife viewing area complete with interpretive displays of the Round Butte Hydroelectric Project and Deschutes River fisheries. Great views of Lake Billy Chinook and Round Butte Dam, 400 feet below in the canyon bottom, can be had from here as well. The park is open to the public free of charge. A picnic area accommodates up to 200 people. PGE is also involved in Eagle Watch, an annual February event (see our Annual Events chapter). Some of the Eagle Watch activities are held at this location.

Forests, High Desert, and Volcanoes

To read that Central Oregon has 24 golf courses is easily conceivable. It's not too surprising that our widely varied, gorgeous landscape has proved very popular for course architects and gung-ho golfers.

But what would you think if we told you that within a one-hour radius of the city of Bend there are more than 2 million acres of beautiful public lands just waiting for you to explore? This chapter provides you with an overview of the diverse range of natural wonders in the area surrounding Bend. Detailed information on camping, lodging, and recreational opportunities is provided in various other chapters in our guide.

Summer, winter, spring, or fall—regardless of the time of year, it's the incredible forests, mountains, and High Desert that attract people from far and wide to Central Oregon. You can choose warm or cold weather, snow or desert sands, tall pine forests or sparse junipers with great mountain views, placid lakes or singing rivers. Bend is completely surrounded with a year-round smorgasbord of recreational opportunities.

Imagine the city of Bend as the center of a clock. Bend is cradled from 4 to 11 o'clock by the Deschutes National Forest. Sunriver Resort and the town of La Pine are islands of private land in this vast sea of natural beauty. Just west of the national forest are the Mount Washington and Three Sisters wildernesses, and past the town of Sisters at about 11 o'clock is the Mount Jefferson Wilderness. Sweeping from noon to 4 o'clock on our Bend-area clock face are Bureau of Land Management (BLM) lands encompassing striking rock formations, fossil beds, and miles of juniper and sagebrush. Tucked beyond the BLM lands is the Ochoco National Forest, a cool oasis of pine trees and modest, 7,000-foot mountains rising out of the desert plateau.

Our Fiery Past

Central Oregon is a huge, living museum of volcanic activity that continues to evolve to this day. The exhibits are almost everywhere you look—rough, black lava flows among the pine trees; charcoal-colored cinder buttes shaped like inverted cones; the layered basalt cliffs along the lower Deschutes River and to the east. It's no wonder our towns are studded with rock shops, the most conspicuous one being the House of Rocks on U.S. Highway 20 west of Bend (see Kidstuff), where you can see a 6-foot lava rock perched atop an automobile.

About 200 million years ago, much of Oregon was covered by the Pacific Ocean. Early volcanic eruptions in the Wallowa, Klamath, and the now-eroded Western Cascade mountains added layers and layers of molten lava to southern and eastern Oregon. This pushed the coastline north and west and trapped part of the ocean until it became an inland sea. During this time, about 35 million years ago, the warm and moist air currents from the ocean still swept across Oregon, and our climate was subtropical. Imagine palm trees, avocados, and fig trees growing in Bend! You can see evidence of these warm climate plants at the John Day Fossil Beds National Monument (see our Daytrips chapter).

Central Oregon Natural Area Contact Numbers

Deschutes and Ochoco National Forests

www.fs.fed.us/r6/centraloregon

Bend/Fort Rock Ranger Districts
1230 Northeast Third Street (U.S. Highway 97 at Greenwood Avenue,
upstairs in Red Oaks Square), Bend, OR 97701
(541) 383–4000

Sisters Ranger District
U.S. Highway 20 at Pine Street, P.O. Box 249, Sisters, OR 97759
(541) 549–7700

Forest Supervisor-Deschutes National Forest
1645 East U.S. Highway 20, Bend, OR 97701
(541) 383–5300

Ochoco National Forest Headquarters/Prineville Ranger District
3160 Northeast Third Street (U.S. Highway 26 on the east end of town),
Prineville, OR 97754
(541) 416–6500

Big Summit Ranger District
33700 Northeast Ochoco Ranger Station Road (Oregon Highway 23),
Prineville, OR 97754
(541) 416–6645

Crooked River National Grassland
813 Southwest U.S. Highway 97, Madras, OR 97741
(541) 475–9272

Bureau of Land Management

Prineville District Office
3050 Northeast Third Street (U.S. Highway 26 on the east end of town, adjacent to the Ochoco National Forest offices), P.O. Box 550, Prineville, OR 97754
(541) 416–6700
www.or.blm.gov/Prineville

State of Oregon

Oregon Department of Motor Vehicles (Sno-Park permits)
1000 Southwest Emkay Drive, Bend, OR 97701
(541) 388–6322
www.odot.state.or.us

High Desert Management Unit/Oregon Department of Parks and Recreation
(state park information)
62976 O. B. Riley Road, Bend, OR 97701
(541) 388–6055
www.prd.state.or.us

Volcanic activity increased between 17 and 12 million years ago. The Cascade Mountains, as we know them, were created by thousands of volcanic eruptions along the area where two tectonic plates collided. Subsequently, this new mountain range blocked off the warm air currents from the ocean and caught the rain clouds in its peaks. Central Oregon became cooler and drier. Lava flows raised the northern areas of Central Oregon so that we no longer had an inland sea, and the Cascades blocked the westward drainage of water. Today the Cascade Mountain range, a series of volcanoes that stretches from Lassen Peak in California up to Mount Baker in Washington, is the most notable feature of our landscape.

A River Runs through It

The Deschutes River had to change its course many times as the ground shifted and lava flows interrupted its flow. Today the headwaters of the Deschutes River spring from the ground at the Lava Lakes. The river travels south, seeking a route to the ocean, before turning east and finally heading north until it reaches the Columbia River. The curving southern section of the river in the Cascade Lakes and Lava Butte region is referred to as the upper Deschutes. The northern section above Bend where the water flows north is called the lower Deschutes.

Along the upper Deschutes is a series of waterfalls (Pringle, Benham, and Dillon are the major ones) that were created by relatively recent lava flows (about 6,000 years ago) crossing the riverbed. These can be observed by hiking along the Deschutes River at the many access points between the Lava Lands Visitor Center and the Cascade Lakes Highway. The lower Deschutes cuts through some of the older lava flows that have been smoothed by glaciers, creating cliffs and canyons of layered basalt as the river passes Redmond and Madras. East of Redmond and Madras in the BLM lands and the Ochoco National Forest is evidence of glacial erosion exposing lava tubes and basaltic layers.

The rough, black lava that you see in the Deschutes National Forest is called "aa aa," a Hawaiian term. "Ah! Ah!" is what you might say if you ever tried to walk across this rough stuff barefoot! One excellent place to see aa aa lava is along the McKenzie Pass. Taking Oregon Highway 242 west of Sisters, you'll encounter a 19-mile-long zone of volcanic vents that spewed lava from 3,000 to 1,500 years ago. Stop at the Dee Wright Memorial Observatory at the top of the pass and walk along the interpretive trail through lava fields. Another good place to experience aa aa lava is at the Lava Lands Visitor Center, south of Bend.

One of the youngest lava flows in Oregon occurred 1,300 years ago and took the form of obsidian. This glistening black flow can be seen at the Newberry Crater. See the Deschutes National Forest section of this chapter for more on these attractions.

Minutes from downtown Bend is Pilot Butte, a 500-foot cinder cone. A road leads you to the top, via car or on foot, for fine views of nine mountain peaks or a nighttime view of city lights.

The Three Sisters are among the state's highest mountains and are visible from most places in Central Oregon. PHOTO: JIM YUSKAVITCH

Digging in the Dirt

The dirt you walk on in Central Oregon was not created the way most dirt is made, with the slow disintegration of stone from wind, water, and lichens. No, we did things the fast way here. Our many volcanic eruptions spewed miles of dust onto our lands, then glaciers ground up our hardened lava. Much of our dirt arrived about 7,700 years ago when Mount Mazama erupted, creating Crater Lake to our south (beyond the geographic scope of this book). Lava Butte, a cinder cone just south of Bend, added its share of dust and debris 7,000 years ago, and more was added as recently as 1,300 years ago when the Newberry Volcano last erupted.

You may notice that our dirt has a light, dusty quality and is rarely muddy. That's because it is mostly pumice, a fine volcanic sand that filters water rapidly. Our soft, sandy soils make hiking and horseback riding possible all year. The soil also loses its supply of water quickly, adding to the arid nature of our landscape.

One issue you may come across is that Newberry Caldera (formed by the Newberry Volcano in the Newberry National Volcanic Monument) and Crater Lake (formed by Mount Mazama 110 miles south of Bend) are both actually calderas, not craters. A caldera is formed when magma flows out of a volcano, leaving an empty chamber that collapses. A crater, on the other hand, is created when a volcano blows its top off. Calderas are craterlike in shape. For a long time Newberry Caldera was called Newberry Crater. Crater Lake is still Crater Lake.

There is no such thing as an extinct volcano. Our snow-topped peaks, lava-strewn meadows, and black and red cinder buttes are part of an ongoing process of geological activity. Mount St. Helens' explosion is one example of this. The McKenzie Pass lava flow is predicted to show some activity in the next few hundred years, and the South Sister mountain might wake up in the next 1,000 years. Our last earthquake was in 1995, but it registered only a 2.0 on the Richter scale, a

Insiders' Tip

Before you head out, please read this chapter's Close-up, "Permits and User Fees." These are used extensively in our public lands. If you know about them ahead of time and come prepared, the impact on your enjoyment will be minimal.

baby by most standards. Although we know that Oregon will once again experience significant seismic activity, geologists seem to feel it's further in the future than what they expect for California. Still, you often hear about area bridges being refurbished to be more earthquake-resistant and building codes being upgraded.

Deschutes National Forest

There are two keys to understanding the big picture when you explore the 1.6-million-acre Deschutes National Forest. Both are conveniently located just south of Bend on U.S. Highway 97.

Nationally recognized, The High Desert Museum, (541) 382-4754, www.highdesert.org, is truly exceptional for its outstanding wildlife and early American exhibits, and we highly recommend it. Allow at least half a day to tour the exhibits and observe the naturalists give presentations on birds of prey, otters, and porcupines with live animal demonstrations. Special-event weekends occur once or twice a month during warm weather, which families might want to make a whole day out of. Call ahead for details. Although The High Desert Museum,

located 8 miles south of Bend, is at the edge of the national forest, it is a private entity and collects its own entrance fees. (Read more in our Attractions chapter.)

Equally exceptional is the natural experience offered at the Lava Lands Visitor Center, (541) 593-2421, headquarters of Newberry National Volcanic Monument, which is managed by the Deschutes National Forest. There are exhibits on the ancient and recent volcanic history of this area as well as natural history, fantastic interpretive trails through lava fields where the Apollo astronauts trained to walk on the moon, and a bus ride to the top of Lava Butte, a cinder cone with great views. Lava Lands, open May through October, lies in the center of the Lava Butte Geological Area. (See our Attractions chapter for more information.)

A great side trip from the Lava Lands Visitor Center is Benham Falls. You'll see the sign as you enter the visitors center parking lot. The road ends 4 miles later at a shaded picnic area. From here it's a short scenic hike, suitable for families, along the Deschutes River to the falls, where the water tumbles down a cascade of lava rocks.

Newberry National Volcanic Monument

While you are in the area, visit the southeastern half of the Newberry National Volcanic Monument by heading 16 miles south on U.S. 97 and taking the Oregon Highway 21 turnoff to Newberry Caldera. Newberry Caldera stars the shield-shaped Newberry Volcano, which erupted over a period of time from 7,700 years ago up to 1,300 years ago and covers 500 square miles. Paulina Peak, elevation 7,985 feet, is the highest point of Newberry Mountain remaining after the volcano collapsed into itself, creating a caldera almost 5 miles wide. The caldera contains two snow-fed lakes—Paulina Lake (Paulina rhymes with "Dinah") and East Lake—along with the fascinating Big Obsidian Flow with its easy, mile-long interpretive trail through a mountain of black glass. Indians used the obsidian to make arrowheads and cutting tools, then traded their obsidian products with tribes as far away as California and western Canada. Newberry Volcano offers students of geology the opportunity to see almost every type of volcanic feature known to man—from cinder cones, spatter cones, tuff cones, ash flows, lava casts, and tubes to gaseous vents and hot springs.

During summer, cars without trailers can drive up a narrow, twisting, and sometimes hair-raising road to the top of Paulina Peak for incredible 360-degree views that encompass Washington to California, the Oregon Cascade Mountains, and the Basin and Range region of eastern Oregon. Just west of the caldera is a parking lot with a sign for Paulina Falls. The short hike to the falls is worth the view of the 80-foot-high north and south falls. The peak, falls, and lake were named after Chief Paulina, a Paiute who successfully raided white settlers for years before being shot down by Howard Maupin in 1867 (see our History chapter).

Besides its wealth of natural beauty and geological complexity, the Newberry Caldera area has great summer lakeside RV and tent camping, fishing, two rustic resorts with marinas and cabins, plus hiking, Nordic skiing, and snowmobile trails. Newberry Crater is over 6,300 feet in elevation, so you can expect the temperatures to be on the cool side.

Newberry Caldera lies in the middle of Deschutes National Forest's Fort Rock Ranger District, an area filled with volcanic wonders, including the Lava Cast Forest and Lava River Cave State Park.

The Lava Cast Forest can be reached from U.S. 97 via Forest Service Road 9720, opposite the turnoff to Sunriver. Travel 9 miles southeast, and you will come to the site where lava flows surrounded a forest of trees about 6,000 years ago. The trees burned as the lava cooled, leaving hollow places in the lava in the shapes of tree trunks.

The Lava River Cave State Park is open from mid-May to mid-October. There is an entrance fee of $2.50 for adults and $2.00 for teens ages 13 to 17; children ages 12 and younger enter free. Wear warm clothing and sneakers, and either bring flashlights or rent lanterns at the cave. Two lanterns work better than one for lighting up the lavacicles, soda straws, a tube within a tube, sand spires, and pinnacles. The dead-end trail is 2.4 miles long round-trip. During winter the cave is closed so no one will disturb hibernating bats.

With the exception of Newberry Caldera, much of the Fort Rock District area is dry High Desert and is usually accessible by car for year-round exploration. Fall and spring are ideal times to explore the desert when temperatures are moderate.

If you haven't purchased an official Deschutes National Forest map at one of the Forest Service district offices, The High Desert Museum and the Lava Lands Visitor Center sell them as well. If you plan to do any camping, hiking, Nordic skiing, or fishing in the forest, we recommend that you take a map along. By the way, the Newberry National Volcanic Monument won't be marked on the national forest map because the monument was not created until 1991, three years after the map was published. An excellent publication from the Deschutes National Forest is *Volcanic Vistas, Guide to the Deschutes National Forest,* an annual tabloid that features a myriad of interesting facts and short articles about the forest and the monument. It's free. On June 16, 2000, the decision was made to combine the Deschutes and Ochoco National Forests under the leadership of one forest supervisor, so you will find maps and other materials for both forests in each ranger station.

Insiders' Tip

Where's there's water, there will be mosquitoes in the summer. Bring repellent. If you camp in the desert, chances are that mosquitoes will be rare.

Permits and User Fees

These are the days of user fees, and there are a bunch of them in place for the lands managed by the U.S. Forest Service (which also manages our national monument), Bureau of Land Management, and State of Oregon. It helps to remember that the national forests, national monument, and BLM lands are federal, while state parks are handled, obviously, by the state of Oregon. The BLM is completely separate from the other two national agencies (you'd think they were in separate countries), but the Deschutes National Forest administers the Newberry National Volcanic Monument, so they cooperate on some fees. When it comes to user fees, you have to be sure to pay the right agency. They don't share funds!

The Deschutes National Forest and the other national forests in Oregon and Washington charge visitors to park at trailheads. This is an "experimental" fee, part of the Recreation Fee Pilot Program. All Northwest forests began participating in this pilot program in January 1999. You may purchase a regional (good throughout Oregon and Washington) Trail Park Pass for $5.00 per day or $30.00 for the season. Trail Park Passes may be purchased at forest service district offices, the Central Oregon Welcome Center, the Sisters Chamber of Commerce and some sporting goods stores and resorts. These fees are to be used to improve our local forests.

Many of the lakes and rivers in the Deschutes National Forest do not require Trail Park Passes to park and fish or go boating, but if there is a trailhead nearby (within a quarter-mile) you'll need one. You will need a Trail Park Pass to park at Elk Lake, Sparks Lake, Tumalo Falls, the Fall River campground and the Dee Wright Memorial Observatory, to name some of the most popular sites. If you are camping at one of these spots, your camping fee receipt qualifies as a Trail Park Pass for the days that you are camping. On the forest map, trailheads are marked with a red "T"; the Ochoco National Forest map has them indicated with a red "TH." If you are a frequent forest user or plan to be here for a week or so, it might be easiest to buy the season pass so you don't have to worry about parking at or near a trailhead. Trail Park fees do not apply to BLM or state lands.

This fee program has been very controversial and the object of intense protest. You may see leaflets in stores or pizza parlors urging forest users not to buy the passes. Some people think it burdens users with too much bureaucracy or penalizes visitors who are just sightseeing (such as at the Dee Wright Memorial Observatory); others don't believe the monies will actually be returned to the area where they were collected. Signs at trailheads indicating where passes are required have been vandalized and stolen, and demonstrations have been held to protest the passes. Currently, if forest service personnel find your car parked without a pass, they will leave you an envelope so you can pay the fee when you return.

The Oregon Parks and Recreation Department charges day-use fees at certain state parks including Tumalo, Smith Rock, and The Cove Palisades. The fees are $3.00 per vehicle per day or $25.00 per calendar year and can be purchased at state offices and G.I. Joes in Bend. Day passes can be purchased at the park offices, and via envelopes and drop boxes in the park parking lots. Park rangers may or may not have seasonal passes on hand for sale. (See our Parks chapter for more information.)

Camping fees are charged for most developed campsites no matter where you set up. Most of them involve putting your money into an envelope and dropping it in a box. You can avoid paying a camping fee by camping in an undeveloped area. If you pay to camp at a state park or national forest campground, again, your camping fee receipt can be used as a day-use pass or Trail Park Pass (see our Camping chapter).

While we are on the topic of recreational paperwork, you will need a free wilderness permit to hike or backpack in any of our wildernesses. These are available at the trailheads. Only two locations in the wildernesses have a quota limit (allowing only a certain number of people in during a given time), and both are accessed through and managed by the Willamette National Forest offices. The areas are Obsidian in the Three Sisters Wilderness (McKenzie District) and Pamelia Lake in the Mount Jefferson Wilderness (Detroit Lakes District).

The Sno-Park permit is a user fee that is charged by the Oregon Department of Transportation (ODOT) to cover the costs for plowing parking areas in the national forests. It is administered by the Department of Motor Vehicles. Sno-Park permits cost $4.00 per day, $12.00 for three days or $16.00 per season and are available for purchase at DMV offices and the Central Oregon Welcome Center. Sno-Parks in the Deschutes and Ochoco national forests are marked on forest service maps with a red or blue snowflake. If you wish to do any kind of snowplay in the national forests (other than at Mt. Bachelor Ski Area) that involves parking your car, you'll need a Sno-Park permit.

LaPine State Park

On the west side of U.S. 97, a mile north of Oregon 21, is the signed turnoff for the LaPine State Park (surrounded by the national forest; managed by the State of Oregon) on State Rec Road. A boatable section of the Deschutes National Wild and Scenic River winds through the park. Tent and RV camping, swimming, hiking, snowshoeing, and Nordic skiing are also popular in this state park, which is open all year.

Nearby (back in the Deschutes National Forest) is Fall River, a famous fly-fishing-only spring creek, and the Fall River Hatchery, a good destination for a family outing. Kids can buy fish food for a quarter and feed the trout from 7:00 A.M. until dark, or until 8:00 P.M. during summer. To get to the hatchery from the LaPine State Park, head east on State Rec Road, take a left onto Huntington Road, then another left onto South Century Drive (Forest Service Road 42). The hatchery is about 5 miles west on South Century.

Before you get to the hatchery, about 4 miles west of the Huntington/South Century intersection, is an unmarked turnoff to the south on Forest Service Road 4360 that will take you to Fall River Falls, then on to Pringle Falls on the Deschutes River.

If you get hungry while visiting The High Desert Museum or exploring Newberry National Volcanic Monument or LaPine State Park, you can grab a bite to eat at the museum's Rimrock Cafe or stop in at Sunriver, which is just west of U.S. 97 about halfway between Lava Lands Visitor Center and the Newberry Caldera turnoff. Six miles south of Oregon 21, the town of La Pine also has restaurants, grocery stores, and other amenities.

Cascade Lakes Highway

Southwest of Bend is a very popular scenic loop that offers an excellent way to experience the heavily wooded national forest. The backbone of this loop is the Cascade Lakes Highway, which starts as Century Drive west of Bend, then becomes Forest Service Road 46 as the road enters the National Forest.

If you are just passing through Central Oregon, the 66-mile loop (some of which ventures outside our coverage area) makes for a pleasant day's drive, with a choice of side roads that can get you back to U.S. 97 so you can shorten the length of your trip. The highway's elevation runs between 4,400 and 6,500 feet as it cuts through forests of ponderosa and lodgepole pine

A Central Oregon visitor buckles up for a snowshoe adventure. PHOTO: WANDERLUST TOURS

and mountain hemlock. The stretch of highway west of Mount Bachelor to the Deschutes Bridge is closed during snowy winter, but the parts of the road that are lower in elevation—east of Mt. Bachelor Ski Area and south of Deschutes Bridge—are open all year. Sno-Parks along Century Drive, at Deschutes Bridge, as well as the Edison Sno-Park on Forest Service Road 45, offer various opportunities for winter recreation, as you will discover in our Snowplay chapter. Sunriver and the town of La Pine provide the closest year-round amenities.

Mount Bachelor Ski Area, the largest ski area in the Northwest, is generally open from Thanksgiving through June. This fabulous 9,065-foot mountain offers beginner to expert slopes for skiers and snowboarders, as well as 56 kilometers of groomed Nordic ski trails (see Snowplay). During summer the ski area offers mountain bike riding and a spectacular chairlift ride to the top of the mountain. The closest lodging is about 15 miles east on Century Drive.

Along the Cascade Lakes Highway are at least 10 trout-filled lakes, some linked by the upper Deschutes River, plus numer-ous campgrounds and a few rustic resorts with cabins and RV camping. If you stay in one of the 300-plus campsites (described in our Camping chapter), you will find plenty of open spaces to get away from it all.

The northernmost lake, Todd Lake, is a glacial depression that was filled with runoff water. Sparks, Davis, Elk, and Lava Lakes were created when lava flows dammed what is now the Deschutes River. Hosmer Lake, at the southern end of Elk, is a picturesque lake restricted to fly-fishing and people- or electric-powered water-craft. The two largest lakes, Wickiup and Crane Prairie, are actually reservoirs that irrigate ranch lands in Bend, Redmond, and Madras via the river. In dry years their levels can drop very low in late summer, especially on Wickiup. Connecting the two reservoirs are the Twin Lakes, which were formed by small craters created by rising lava.

The reflections of towering Mount Bachelor and its northern neighbors, the 9,775-foot Broken Top and the cone-shaped, 7,775-foot Tumalo Mountain, can be seen in all of these lakes. All the lakes offer fishing, boating, and camping.

Above the lakes, osprey, bald eagles, and bats hunt for food. Black bear and deer roam the forests, and campsites are alive with ground squirrels and chipmunks, which you should resist feeding. Bear occasionally get into the campgrounds too, so take precautions about hiding your food.

Numerous trailheads along Cascade Lakes Highway lead into the Three Sisters Wilderness, named for its three sleeping volcanoes. Tallest of the three, the white-capped South Sister stands proudly by herself at 10,350 feet. Middle Sister and North Sister, both glacier-shrouded at 10,047 and 10,085 feet, respectively, stand shoulder to shoulder. Surrounding these alpine peaks are miles of trails through green meadows and cool conifers, and hundreds of lakes and streams. Wilderness permits are required for day hikes and overnight stays and may be obtained for free at the trailheads. Parking at the trailheads, however, is not free—please see our Close-up on Permits and User Fees. Bicycles and motorized vehicles are prohibited from wilderness areas.

Other Deschutes National Forest Access Points

A handy access point to the Deschutes National Forest close to Bend is at Tumalo Falls. From downtown, head west on Franklin Avenue skirting Drake Park, turn right onto Galveston and keep going west for 11 miles on Skyliners Road. The road turns to gravel when it becomes Forest Service Road 4603, and after 3.5 miles on this gravel road you arrive at the falls. Along the road to the falls, you will see an area damaged by a forest fire in 1979.

A viewpoint for the falls is wheelchair-accessible. The falls can be seen from the parking area, or you may get closer to the falls via an easy trail. Trails also lead west into the Three Sisters Wilderness. The sections of the trail between the falls and the wilderness area that are still in the national forest zoom with mountain bikers. During winter the main road is plowed to where the pavement ends at Skyliner Sno-Park, 3.5 miles east of the

falls, providing opportunities for Nordic skiing and snowmobiling. In summer you will need a Northwest Trail Pass, and in winter a Sno-Park permit, to park here.

Heading north from Bend, the next Deschutes National Forest access point is via the picturesque town of Sisters. From U.S. Highway 20 in downtown Sisters, turn south onto Elm Street toward Three Creek Lake on Forest Service Road 16. This beautiful, mostly paved road starts at an elevation of 3,184 feet and climbs for 12 miles through a sunny ponderosa forest to 5,700 feet. Along the way are forest service campgrounds and two Sno-Parks. Horse camping enthusiasts, mountain bikers, and off-road vehicle fans especially love this area's rugged beauty and dirt roads. In summer you can follow dirt roads all the way south to the Cascade Lakes Highway. In winter, Forest Service Road 16 is busy with snowmobilers and Nordic skiers.

On the west side of Sisters, Oregon Highway 242 heads over the McKenzie Pass (elevation 5,324 feet), which provides outstanding views of six peaks from the windswept Dee Wright Memorial Observatory. The observatory was built in the 1930s by the Civilian Conservation Corps and offers a fascinating interpretive walk

Insiders' Tip

The BLM publishes two excellent maps: Central Oregon Public Lands ($7.00) and the BLM Oregon Recreation Guide, which is free. We suggest picking up a copy of each before starting your adventures. They are available at the BLM office in Prineville and in Bend at Bend Mapping & Blueprint.

A pee-wee skier makes a friend at Mt. Bachelor Ski Area. PHOTO: BERT SAGARA/MT. BACHELOR SKI RESORT

through lava fields. It was severely damaged by lightning in 1989, but was recently renovated. You can still see the tracks of an old wagon trail that was built over the lava in 1872. Oregon Highway 242 is open only during summer and is not recommended for trailers.

Oregon 242 separates two wilderness areas: Mount Washington to the north and Three Sisters to the south. Trailheads (including those for the Pacific Trail) and primitive Forest Service campgrounds (some above the treeline) fringe the road. You will need a Northwest Trail Pass to park even briefly at the observatory and at some campgrounds, if you are not camping there.

Heading northwest from Sisters on U.S. 20 will take you past Black Butte, a cinder cone 6,466 feet in elevation—make the hike to the top for great views. Southwest of the cinder cone is a deluxe resort, Black Butte Ranch, which offers fine dining, condo rentals, and world-class golf. A

few miles west of Black Butte Ranch is the turnoff for Camp Sherman, a rustic village with rental cabins, vacation homes, small resorts, nine Forest Service campgrounds, a village store, and a top-notch restaurant—all located in the Metolius River Recreation Area.

At Camp Sherman, the upper Metolius River, famous among fly-flingers, emerges out of nowhere in the form of a huge spring and runs north through the village. There is a trail that follows the river from the headwaters to the Camp Sherman store. Fishing enthusiasts of both the fly and spin variety pack the campgrounds every summer weekend. North of Camp Sherman, the lower Metolius National Wild and Scenic River offers great whitewater rafting and kayaking. The ponderosa forest around Camp Sherman is laced with gravel roads, making this a wonderful spot for family mountain biking. Some cabins can be rented in the winter by snowmobilers, Nordic skiers, or anyone wanting to experience a true winter wonderland. Watch for deer on the road.

Some of the gravel roads heading west from Camp Sherman end at the Mount Jefferson Wilderness, another popular hiking and backpacking destination. Wilderness permits are required for day hikes and overnight stays, and, as always in wildernesses, bikes and motor vehicles are not allowed. (Again, see our Close-up on Permits and User Fees.)

Continuing west, on the south side of U.S. 20, is the year-round resort area of Suttle Lake and Blue Lake, where you will find camping, RV hookups, a marina, waterskiing, and, in the winter, snowmobiling and Nordic skiing. It's a great place for family vacations. Scout Lake, a tiny lake with its own campground tucked south of Suttle Lake, is very shallow, so its water warms up enough for swimming. Gravel and dirt roads heading south from Suttle Lake lead backpackers to trailheads for the Mount Washington Wilderness.

One stop farther along U.S. 20 is the Santiam Pass, at an elevation of 4,817 feet. On the north side of the highway is the Santiam Sno-Park, one of the best sledding spots in Central Oregon, and a trailhead for the Pacific Trail is nearby. Opposite the Sno-Park is Hoodoo Ski Bowl, which is open during heavier snow periods and is very popular with families (see our Snowplay chapter). Down the road from Hoodoo is the Ray Benson Sno-Park, which offers excellent Nordic skiing, and south of that is Big Lake, with camping and good hiking. Permits for winter parking in the Sno-Park areas (including Hoodoo) and for summer in general are required (see our Close-up on Permits and User Fees).

Ochoco National Forest

For a major change of pace, we'll move east of Prineville to touch on the western edge of the Ochoco National Forest, which includes the Crooked River National Grassland.

The Ochoco National Forest offers a nice contrast to the Deschutes National Forest. The Ochoco Mountains are older, smaller, and more moderate in temperature than the Cascades. They get about 30 inches of precipitation per year at the highest elevations—enough to supply the ponderosa pines, firs, and western larch. Though its peaks sometimes have as much as 6 feet of snow on them, the Ochoco National Forest lacks the tremendous snowpack the Deschutes National Forest has. That means fewer rivers and lakes and little or no snowplay. Since water is a primary attraction to the Deschutes area, it comes as no surprise that the drier Ochoco forest doesn't have the crowds you'll find in the Deschutes forest. It definitely has a more relaxed air about it.

The Ochoco National Forest is oddly pieced together in three separate sections that reach almost out to Burns (132 miles east of Bend), plus a section for the Crooked River National Grassland. The western portion of the forest's largest section (the Prineville Ranger District and part of the Big Summit Ranger District), the southernmost section (also in the Prineville Ranger District), and the grassland all fall within the coverage area of our book.

Walton Lake is one of the Ochoco National Forest's few recreational lakes, and it is man-made. It was created when the Isaac Walton League of Prineville dammed a spring in the headwaters of Ochoco Creek. To get to Walton Lake take U.S. 26 and then Oregon Highway 23 east out of Prineville for 25 miles until you get to the Ochoco Ranger Station, then head 7 miles northeast on Forest Service Road

22. People- or electric-powered boating is permitted on the lake, which is stocked with trout. There is a beach for swimming and picnicking and a campground, which fills up during peak summer periods. Hiking opportunities starting at the lake campground are excellent.

Wildlife and Wildflowers

A herd of feral horses lives along Forest Service Road 42 in the Big Summit Ranger District. The horses are shy but will tolerate closer viewing distances than deer or elk. Be sure to keep your distance if foals are present, as the herd's behavior could become aggressive. When the herd population exceeds 60, some of its members are made available for adoption by the Bureau of Land Management.

Wildlife viewing is a big attraction in the Ochoco National Forest, as is hunting. Elk and deer are commonly seen, as well as antelope. For great wildlife viewing, continue east on Forest Service Road 42 until you reach Big Summit Prairie. Unfortu-nately, the public is locked out of this privately owned area, but the road around the 10,000-acre prairie is public, and wildlife can be viewed from the road with binoculars. Antelope can be seen from Forest Service Road 42, and there is another herd that can be seen near the end of Forest Service Road 30-050. At the intersection of Dudley Creek and Forest Service Road 42 is a beaver colony. Elk can be seen all over the prairie but most often along Forest Service Road 22 and Forest Service Road 4210. The north fork of the wild and scenic Crooked River travels along the southern edge of the prairie. Cattle graze the prairie in summer.

The Big Summit Prairie is actually even more famous for its wildflowers. The blooms reach their peak in May and June. Wild peonies, Missouri iris, mountain ladyslippers, as well as the rare Peck's mariposa lily found only in the Ochocos can be identified with a brochure called *Wildflowers of Big Summit Prairie*, published by the Ochoco National Forest, the BLM, the Native Plant Society of Oregon, and the Crook County Chamber of Commerce. It is available free at Ochoco forest and BLM offices. If you'd like to spend a few days at the prairie in comfort, the Ochoco National Forest has a cabin for rent on the eastern edge of the area (see our Camping chapter).

Another interesting attraction of this forest is Steins Pillar, named (with a misspelling) after Maj. Enoch Steen. This is a volcanic monolith, 350 feet high and 120 feet wide, that was formed 44 million years ago. Erosion removed the dirt from around this welded tuff of lava, leaving an outstanding landmark. At its base are Mill Creek and pastoral ranches. From Prineville, head east 6 miles on U.S. 26, pass the Ochoco Reservoir, and turn north on scenic Mill Creek Road. Follow the signs to Steins Pillar, where you will find a viewing turnout and a parking area for the trail.

Other Ochoco National Forest Highlights

There are three wilderness areas within the Ochoco National Forest—Mill Creek Wilderness to the west, Bridge Creek Wilderness in the center, and Black Canyon Wilderness to the east. The Mill Creek Wilderness has interesting geological formations similar to Steins Pillar. Wilderness permits for day hiking or backpacking can be obtained at the trailheads for free.

Between Prineville and Madras is the 106,000-acre Crooked River National Grassland, administered by the Ochoco National Forest. This is land that was once homesteaded (somewhat unsuccessfully) but was repurchased by the federal government in the late 1930s to make into a wildlife preserve. In the center of the grassland is the Rimrock Springs Wildlife Management Area. This wetland environment of springs and ponds creates an oasis in an otherwise arid landscape. It is adjacent to U.S. Highway 26, 17 miles north of Prineville. Bring your binoculars to view song birds, waterfowl, aquatic mammals, and raptors. There is a 1.5-mile, barrier-free trail that leads to an observation deck and continues on to a viewpoint for the Cascade Mountains. Antelope, deer, and coyote can also be seen in the grassland. There are two campgrounds and one horse camp.

The Ochoco National Forest's Big Summit and Prineville Ranger Districts have about 160 developed campsites spread between 14 campgrounds. The largest of these, at Walton Lake, has 30 sites and potable water. Many others are small and somewhat remote, and you'll need to bring your own water. The Ochoco forest also has some nice dispersed campsites along Forest Service Road 22 and Forest Service Road 42. These would almost pass as developed, but they don't have tables or toilets, and they're isolated from other campsites. There is no charge for dispersed camping here or anywhere. For additional information, contact the Ochoco National Forest at (541) 416–6500. The Forest Service requires Northwest Trail Passes.

The town of Prineville has all amenities, including some good restaurants (see our Restaurants chapter). A couple of convenience stores can be found along U.S. 26 near the Ochoco Reservoir.

BLM—The High Desert

The High Desert is too dry to support the big conifers you see on the western side of Central Oregon. Instead you will find areas of twisted juniper trees, meadows of native grasses, great expanses of sagebrush, and beautiful rock formations and canyons left by lava flows and carved by glaciers and water. Much of the High Desert between Bend, Madras, and Prineville is public land managed by the Bureau of Land Management (BLM). These arid lands were once used primarily by ranchers and miners, rock hounds, and folks with four-wheel-drive vehicles. Nowadays, however, many people have come to cherish this rugged landscape for its natural beauty, geological treasures, and recreational opportunities.

Temperatures are generally 10 to 20 degrees warmer in the High Desert than in the national forests, with the mercury often reaching 100 degrees in summer. Winter night temperatures plunge below freezing, but the area gets very little snow, so it is generally accessible all year. There are only a handful of marginally developed BLM campgrounds (bring your own water to most of them), but the adventurous will find unlimited numbers of dirt roads with turnouts where they can pull off to the side for car or truck camping under the stars.

Just west of the town of Redmond is a major trout fishery, the Deschutes River, a nationally designated wild and scenic river, that flows north through ranch lands interspersed with BLM lands. Access is easy at Cline Falls State Park on U.S. Highway 126 west of Redmond, and from Northwest Lower Bridge Way off U.S. 97, which is west of the ranching community of Terrebonne at the north end of Redmond.

East of Terrebonne is Smith Rock State Park, a day-use park with awesome rock cliffs that are famous among rock climbers. The cliffs feature more than 1,000 climbing routes, including two of the most difficult in the nation (see our Parks and Other Outdoor Recreation chapters). Non-climbers can enjoy hiking the 10 miles of trails, fishing, or just watching the climbers from the picnic area at the bottom of these beautiful walls alongside the Crooked River. Terrebonne has a couple of restaurants, small grocery stores, and gas stations.

South of Prineville at mile marker 12, Oregon Highway 27 becomes the Lower Crooked River National Back Country Byway. Here it winds through open ranch lands and shallow canyons as it hugs the east bank of the Crooked River, a nationally designated wild and scenic river. This beautiful 8-mile section of river and road contains 14 developed BLM sites for camping, picnicking, hiking, fishing, and bird-watching.

Oregon 27 turns from pavement to gravel as it passes the Prineville Reservoir, where it leaves the Crooked River behind and continues 24 dusty miles south through juniper forests and sagebrush to U.S. Highway 20 near Millican. Prineville Reservoir is held by the Bowman Dam, an 800-foot-long, rolled-earth, and rock-filled dam. The reservoir covers 310 acres and is popular for year-round boating and fishing.

At the intersection of Oregon 27 and U.S. 20 is the BLM's Millican Valley Off-Highway Vehicle (OHV) Recreation Area, where off-road enthusiasts can let it all hang out—with caution! No passes or permits are required to enjoy BLM lands.

Our Outdoor Adventure Comes Full Circle

For folks who enjoy looking up at the stars, the Pine Mountain Observatory is open to the public on summer weekend nights. Follow the signs from U.S. 20 at the Millican gas station and head south toward 6,300-foot Pine Mountain. The road crosses BLM land and ends up back on Deschutes National Forest soil at the observatory.

Pine Mountain Observatory is operated by the University of Oregon, and it contains three large telescopes, including a 32-inch model that is the largest in the

Northwest. When we were there we saw Saturn's rings! This is a gathering point for stargazers, many of whom stay at the Forest Service campground, set up their own telescopes, and share their discoveries via excited whispers in the darkness. While you are waiting for night to arrive, you can hike to the top of Pine Mountain for a view of the setting sun. (See our Attractions and Daytrips chapters for much more on Pine Mountain Observatory.)

We have now come full circle, leaving you off 30 miles southeast of Bend on lonely U.S. 20. Limiting our discussion to an area within a one-hour radius was tough—the public lands don't end here. In fact, this is just the beginning. If you give yourself two or three hours, there are many other great places to explore! (See our Daytrips chapter for great destinations that are farther afield.)

Pick an experience—cool forests, snowy slopes, wide open High Desert, a journey through the past or present involving water or land or both—then start making your plans for a memorable vacation or weekend getaway.

Snowplay

Ask most anyone in the Northwest what they think of when someone mentions Bend, and they will probably say, "Snow!" However, as famous and wonderful as our snow is to all of us in our neck of the woods, it is still a well-kept secret on a national scale.

Maybe that's because snowplay in Central Oregon is all about performance, not the paparazzi or celebrities. You probably won't see any movie stars, the president, or the Kennedys. But you might see the U.S. Ski Team working out at Mt. Bachelor Ski Area, taking advantage of one of the longest ski seasons in the United States, or maybe some big-name professional riders attracted by one of the best snowboard camps in the world at High Cascade.

Skiing in Central Oregon is affordably priced, and our ski areas are often less crowded than other major Western resorts. There are literally thousands of acres and hundreds of miles of trails for great Nordic skiing, and hundreds more miles for snowmobiling. Another great thing about winter in Central Oregon is that (other than the time around Christmas and New Year's, when demand peaks for a week and rates top out at their holiday highs) it's our second busiest season. That means lodging is usually easy to come by, and if you look around you'll find plenty of ski package deals. Restaurants are busy but not so booked that you have to call way ahead for reservations.

A Western Winter Wonderland

To understand snowplay in Central Oregon, one must first get a picture of winter in Central Oregon. First of all, don't worry if you drive into Bend and you don't see any snow. Remember, we are on the dry side of the Cascade Mountains, which means you usually have to go to a higher elevation to get precipitation. Bend can have no snow at an elevation of 4,000 feet, while the Mt. Bachelor Ski Area parking lot, at about 6,000 feet, might have 6 feet of snow.

Seven years out of ten, the towns along U.S. Highway 97 will get only a foot of snow for the year, though in heavy snow years the city of Bend has received up to 100 inches of the white stuff. Moderate winter temperatures—ranging from about 40 degrees during the day to about 15 degrees at night—are pretty typical for Bend and Redmond, with occasional colder and warmer spells. Sisters, Sunriver, and La Pine might be 5 degrees colder, and Prineville and Madras are usually 5 to 10 degrees warmer than Bend. Of all the towns in Central Oregon, Sisters and Sunriver are the snowiest. In those towns, you will probably be able to walk out your front door, step into your Nordic skis or snowshoes, and head out for a great day in the snow.

There's one other little logistical detail you should know about. Although it's easy to find snow to play in here in Central Oregon, parking your cruiser takes a little planning. When there is snow on the ground, you must park in one of our Sno-Parks—plowed, off-road areas maintained by the State of Oregon. Sno-Park permits are required from November 15 to April 30. You don't need one to park at Mt. Bachelor Ski Area (because it is privately maintained), but you do at Hoodoo Ski Bowl, as it is on leased Forest Service land and is plowed by the state. You will also need a permit to park in all of the Sno-Park areas along the Cascade Lakes Highway, U.S. Highway 20 west of Sisters, and in the Ochoco Mountains along U.S. Highway 26.

Sno-Park permits cost $3.00 for a day, $7.00 for three days, or $15 for the season, and can be purchased at any Oregon Department of Motor Vehicles office, the Central Oregon Welcome Center, area resorts, and ski and sporting-goods stores. Because these are state-issued permits, you may not be able to buy them at Forest Service ranger stations, though there is usually a sign in the window telling you the nearest place to get one. If you live and play in Central Oregon or visit several times a season, the $15 season pass is not too much money to drop for a winter's worth of convenience.

Getting Your Bearings

The most popular snowplay areas are concentrated in the Deschutes National Forest, including the area around the Newberry National Volcanic Monument. Bend, Sisters, Sunriver, and La Pine are the key access towns. Most of the Ochoco National Forest gets too little snow for good snowplay. Still, in the heaviest snow years there is some snowplay at the Ochoco Divide and Marks Creek Sno-Parks, and at the Bandit Spring rest area, about 30 miles east of Prineville on U.S. Highway 26.

This chapter is organized by type of snowplay sport, then by geographical area. Outlying areas are grouped with their most-used access points. For example, the Cascade Lakes Highway is covered in the Bend section. We cover alpine skiing and snowboarding, Nordic skiing and snowshoeing, snowmobiling, ice-skating, and tubing/sledding. Snow camping is not covered specifically, as it is allowed anywhere in the national forests where you can leave your car at a Sno-Park. At the end of this chapter are listings of outfits that offer guided snow trips and shops with gear rentals.

Please refer to our Forests, High Desert, and Volcanoes chapter to read more about the Deschutes National Forest and for a list

of ranger stations. Check out our Getting Here, Getting Around chapter to learn the best winter routes in and out of Central Oregon. Our various accommodations chapters and the Restaurants and Nightlife chapters cover the range of local amenities in each area.

Alpine Skiing and Snowboarding

Snow reports are the hot topic of conversation in Central Oregon starting around Halloween. Everyone—from business owners wearing Dockers and oxford button-downs to kids in baggy pants and Vans—waits impatiently for the ski areas to open. Eyes are cast up to the mountains to see if the peaks look whiter than they did the last time they were checked.

Finally, the good news comes. Restaurants, easily accessed and comfortably patronized mostly by locals since Labor Day, start to fill. The sidewalks get busier, and people who normally work Monday through Friday can't always be reached during business hours. It's the ski season!

We have two great downhill ski areas, each with its own personality. Mt. Bachelor Ski Area, just outside of Bend, is the biggest, with world-class runs and events and a long snow season. Located west of Sisters, Hoodoo Ski Bowl is more family-oriented, smaller, and less expensive than Mt. Bachelor, but when the snow is good, Hoodoo still offers a great day of skiing.

Bend

Mt. Bachelor Ski Area
Cascade Lakes Highway, 22 miles west of Bend
(541) 382–2442, corporate offices,
(541) 382–7888, recorded ski or summer report,
(800) 829–2442, information and reservations
www.mtbachelor.com

Mt. Bachelor first opened in 1958 with one Pomalift, two rope tows, and a small day lodge. Today it's the Northwest's largest ski area with 70 runs, 12 lifts (including seven super-express quads), and a 3,365-foot vertical drop. At an elevation of 9,065 feet, the average annual snow base is 250 to 300 inches. Twenty-five percent of the alpine terrain is rated expert, with four double-black-diamond runs. Advanced runs make up 35 percent of the terrain and intermediate runs 25 percent, leaving 15 percent for novice skiers. Mt. Bachelor's lift system has been voted best in the nation for the last several years in a row because of its speed, and reduced waiting time in lines.

Mt. Bachelor has also been on the cutting edge of snowboarding. It was one of the first ski areas to offer boarders world-class events and complete access to runs. In late 2001 the Super Pipe was opened, built to Olympic specs with 17-foot walls and 400-foot runs. Also in 2001, the new Terrain Park was introduced for free-style skiing and boarding. More than 1 mile in length, the park features rails, spines, hips, and jumps.

In 2001, Mt. Bachelor added the Family Tubing Park, another cutting-edge attraction where participants rent special snow tubes that have been designed to work with a tow-lift system, making the uphill part a snap. This is definitely a cut above the old inner-tube hills you may remember as a kid. Five different downhill lanes offer a variety of excitement levels.

The traditional Daily Lift Ticket costs $42 for adults, or $45 for holiday periods; for teens ages 13 to 18 and seniors ages 65 to 69, lift tickets are $35 ($37 holidays); $24 ($26 holidays) for children ages 6 to 12. Kids age 5 or younger and seniors 70 and over ski free. The electronic SkiData ticketing system allows for personalized lift tickets with discounts for multiple days, for families, or for use on a point system.

A basic Rossignol ski package can be rented from Bachelor Ski and Sport Shop Alpine Rental for $23 for adults and teens and $15 for kids ages 6 to 12. Snowboarding-gear packages rent for $28 for adults and $22 for kids. This 22,000-square-foot retail building offers a complete line of skis and snowboards for purchase, demo rentals, outerwear, and accessories. The Sunrise Ski Shop at the Sunrise Lodge offers a smaller selection of equipment and outerwear in a boutique-type atmosphere, while the Pine Marten Accessories Shop at the Pine Marten Lodge has those little items like sunglasses that help make life on the slopes more enjoyable.

Mt. Bachelor promotes an active calendar of events (see our Annual Events chapter). In 2002, the final qualifier Chevy U.S. Snowboard Grand Prix competitions that determined who made the U.S. snowboard team for the 2002 Olympics was held here.

With nine levels of ski clinics in a ski instruction program called Perfect Turn, it's no wonder Mt. Bachelor produces top-notch skiers. Clinics for levels one through five take place at the Learning Center, where you can pick up your lift ticket, rent equipment (with instruction for beginners), and meet up with your ski pro. More advanced clinics meet on the slopes. Call the reservations number listed above to set up a clinic date, and ask about free beginners lessons on certain Sundays. NASTAR-format race clinics are also available, and Mt. Bachelor even has a race department to help the Mt. Bachelor Ski Education Foundation coordinate its City League racing teams. Call the main office for more information.

There are five day lodges at Mt. Bachelor, with 13 food-service operations ranging from pizza, juice, and espresso bars, to upscale contemporary dining with a view. Parking is free, and valet parking is available. There is no overnight lodging at the ski area; the nearest lodging is 20 minutes east on Century Drive heading toward Bend, and at Sunriver, which is about 18 miles south and east. Self-contained RVs may park free for up to five consecutive nights in a special section of the Mt. Bachelor parking lot. Contact the security office for a parking permit. A medical facility is available for walk-in and emergency treatment.

The Mt. Bachelor Daycare Centers were voted number one in America by *Snow Country* magazine. The two centers, one at West Village Lodge and one at Sunrise Lodge, take children from six weeks of age on up. The Snowplay/Daycare program is a pre-ski lesson for kids starting at age 3, and it costs $40 to $45. A combination day care and half-day ski lesson called Mountain Masters, for kids ages 4 and older, runs $85. The day-care centers fill up early on busy weekends, so reservations are strongly recommended. For holiday weekends, call at least six weeks in advance.

Challenge Oregon Adaptive Ski Program, a Bend-based nonprofit organization that is run largely by volunteers through donations, helps provide opportunities for disabled kids to experience the thrill of skiing. Mt. Bachelor participates by providing discounted lift tickets. If you would like to know more about COASP, call the main number at Mt. Bachelor—they will direct you to the right person.

The award-winning Mt. Bachelor Super Shuttle bus runs from a modern transit center/parking lot at the corner of Colorado and Simpson Avenues on Bend's west side. The cost for the 22-mile trip is $3.00 each way, or pick up a season pass for $75.00. The Mt. Bachelor Ski Area parking lot can fill up by late morning on winter weekends when the snow is prime, so we recommend using the shuttle instead of driving to the mountain.

Check out the subsequent listing in the Nordic Skiing and Snowshoeing section for details on Mt. Bachelor's cross-country offerings, and see our Guided Trips section for information on dogsledding.

Sisters/Camp Sherman Area

Hoodoo Ski Bowl
Santiam Pass, 22 miles west of Sisters
(541) 822-3799; (541) 822-3337, snow phone
www.hoodoo.com

Established in 1938, Hoodoo has earned a reputation for being our most family-oriented ski area. The rates are the lowest in Central Oregon, and the runs are divided between easy, moderate, and difficult. The ski area offers 4 lifts and 24 alpine runs with a maximum 1,035-foot vertical rise. Snowboards are allowed on the alpine runs. The beautiful 60,000-square-foor lodge, completed in 2002, has a huge dining and seating area with a giant fireplace, equipment rentals, and a stage for live music. The closest overnight lodging is in Sisters and Camp Sherman. (See our Nordic Skiing and Snoeshoeing section for information on Hoodoo's Nordic trails.)

A full Saturday or Sunday lift ticket costs $26.00 for adults and teens, and $19.50 for juniors ages 6 to 12. Kids younger than age 6 ski free. Alpine ski gear can be rented at $16 per day for adults or $12 for kids. Hoodoo also rents snowboard packages for $30. Kids and adult private ski lessons are available for both alpine skiing and snowboarding. The Friday Night City League teams race for points starting in January.

Hoodoo's summit is at only 5,703 feet. That means snow conditions are sometimes less than perfect, and there is no snow-making equipment. They offer an hour's worth of free skiing, so you can test the conditions.

You will need a Sno-Park permit (see our Close-up on Permits and User Fees in our Forest, High Desert, and Volcanoes chapter) to park in the Hoodoo Ski Bowl parking lot. You should also get a report on road conditions before making the trip, as this area gets frequent snow squalls. Hoodoo's Web site has a live link from one of ODOT's cameras aimed at Santiam Pass, or call ODOT at (800) 977-6368 for recorded road conditions.

The Hoodoo ski season usually runs from the beginning of December through March, with some April weekend skiing, snow permitting. The area closes on Wednesday except during the month of December, when it's open daily except for Christmas. See our Annual Events chapter for information on Hoodoo's Winter Carnival in February.

Nordic Skiing and Snowshoeing

Nordic skiers and snowshoers have several outstanding places to get away from the crowds and gas engines—out where you can almost hear the sound of falling snowflakes along with your own steady breathing and your feet moving across the snow. The Deschutes National Forest offers the best season-long Nordic enjoyment, but cross-country skiing and snowshoeing can be done on any public land where you can find a legal place to park your car. Right after a good snowfall you can ski in city parks in Bend, Sisters, and Sunriver.

Most people head for the areas of the Deschutes National Forest west of Bend, and west and south of Sisters, for reliably good Nordic conditions. The Cascade Lakes Highway, U.S. Highway 20, and Forest Service Road 16 are dotted with Sno-

Parks—parking areas maintained by the state of Oregon. Trail maps are available at the Sno-Park trailheads.

The Blue Diamond trails are for nonmotorized use only. Trail etiquette states that people on foot keep to the right when using Orange Diamond trails, which are snowmobile trails. The Blue Diamond trails are built and maintained by volunteers from the Oregon Nordic Club as well as other supporters. If you would like to volunteer, call the district volunteer coordinator at (541) 383-4794. Where applicable, we have listed the milepost numbers with each Sno-Park. However, you can't always see mileposts in winter when the snowbanks are 6 to 8 feet high; sometimes you'll have to check your odometer.

The Sno-Parks along the Cascade Lakes Highway are popular training grounds for Nordic competitors, and several Central Oregon residents have competed in the Olympics.

Bend Area

Shevlin Park
Shevlin Park Road, Bend
(541) 389–PARK (7275) ext. 118 (Bend Bend Metro Park & Recreation District)

This is one of the largest and prettiest city parks, though any city park will do when Bend catches its occasional significant snowfalls. Shevlin has groomed Nordic ski trails. From downtown Bend take Newport Avenue to Shevlin Park Road. You will not need a Sno-Park permit. For information on Shevlin Park and other local parks, call the Bend Metro Park and Recreation District at the listed number.

Skyline Park
Mount Washington Road, Bend
(541) 389–PARK (7275) ext. 118 (Bend Bend Metro Park & Recreation District)

Another city park for handy Nordic skiing is Skyline, the only place where there are lights for night skiing. Snowshoers and Nordic skiers will find public parking here without needing a permit; it's perfect for short, family-size jaunts. Skyline is on Mount Washington Road next to Broken Top Resort.

For the fitness-minded, Nordic skiing is a great way to spend a sunny winter day. PHOTO: WARREN MORGAN/MT. BACHELOR SKI RESORT

Skyliner Sno-Park and Tumalo Falls Sno-Park

Due west of Bend is the Skyliner Sno-Park area, where there are 6 miles of easy to more difficult Nordic trails and two warming shelters. Watch out for the risk-taking folks sledding down Suicide Hill, where sledders get seriously injured every year. From downtown Bend, head west on Franklin Avenue skirting Drake Park, turn right onto Galveston, and keep going straight west 11 miles on Skyliners Road until the road ends where the plowing has stopped.

Cascade Lakes Highway and Forest Service Road 45 Sno-Parks

Due to its 6,000- to 7,500-foot elevation, this part of the Deschutes National Forest usually has excellent snow from November through June and offers many snowplay opportunities. From downtown Bend head west on Franklin Avenue past Drake Park, turn right onto Galveston, then left onto Century Park Drive, which will turn into the Cascade Lakes Highway.

The north side of the Cascade Lakes Highway offers superb Nordic skiing with a 64-mile network of trails that links all four of its Sno-Parks. We recommend this area to snowshoers, too. There are so many beautiful acres of snow here, you could spend all of your time just skiing in this area if you wanted to. Be careful about leaving the trails—people get lost every year in this vast territory. Overnight parking is allowed in the Sno-Parks for hardy types who want to snow camp, but do not camp in the warming shelters; they're for day-use only. Firewood is usually provided in the shelters. Bring matches and paper for starting a fire.

Meissner Sno-Park
Cascade Lakes Highway, Milepost 14

Nine of the 14 miles of easy to moderately difficult trails at Meissner are groomed by volunteers. This area has five warming shelters and is off-limits to snowmobiles and mushers.

Swampy Lakes Sno-Park
Cascade Lakes Highway, Milepost 16

This section of the trail system contains about 25 miles of easy to very difficult trails, along with six warming shelters.

Vista Butte Sno-Park
Cascade Lakes Highway, Milepost 18

You have your choice of 6 miles of more difficult to most difficult trails starting from this trailhead. (Note that Vista Butte Sno-Park is not on the official Deschutes National Forest map.)

Mt. Bachelor Ski Area
Cascade Lakes Highway, 22 miles west of Bend
(541) 382–2442, corporate offices,
(541) 382–7888, snow report,
(800) 829–2442, information and reservations
www.mtbachelor.com

Mt. Bachelor Ski Area is almost at the end of the plowed section of the Cascade Lakes Highway. Nordic skiers will enjoy the 56 kilometers of mostly intermediate-level groomed trails. The cozy log building housing the Nordic center contains ski rentals and sales, a small cafe counter (with what some folks say is the best food at Mt. Bachelor), a waxing area, and a shop. Best of all, there's a wonderful woodstove in the center surrounded by benches, soggy hats and gloves, and red-cheeked skiers sipping hot drinks. Full-day trail passes cost $12.00 for adults and $5.25 for kids ages 6 to 12, seniors are $7.50, or free if they're over 70. Nordic ski lessons are $23, and advanced clinics are available. Adults can rent Nordic ski packages for $16 per day, telemark packages for $25, and snowshoes for $12.

The Deschutes National Forest gives free presentations, snowshoe nature walks, and Nordic ski tours with a naturalist. For more information on these programs, contact the Bend/Fort Rock Ranger Station at (541) 388–5664.

Insiders' Tip

For ski area weather conditions, check out our two ski area Web sites: www.mtbachelor.com or www.hoodoo.com. For road conditions, including live camcorder shots of the mountain passes, go to ODOT's Web site at www.tripcheck.com or call (800) 977-6368 for ODOT's recorded information.

For winter recreation enthusiasts, Central Oregon offers unlimited options. PHOTO: WANDERLUST TOURS

For more information on Mt. Bachelor Ski Area amenities, check the previous listing in this chapter's Alpine Skiing and Snowboarding section.

Edison Sno-Park
Forest Service Road 45

Just east of Mt. Bachelor Ski Area is a turnoff to the south for Forest Service Road 45 that leads to Edison Sno-Park, where there are 24 miles of easy to most difficult Nordic ski trails. Continue the drive south on Forest Service 45, then east on Forest Service Road 40, and you'll end up at Sunriver, where you will find food, fuel, and lodging. (If you have the official Deschutes National Forest map, please note that Forest Service Road 45 does go all the way north to connect with Forest Service Road 46 near Vista Butte Sno-Park, which is not on the map.)

Dutchman Flat Sno-Park
Cascade Lakes Highway, Milepost 22

This is as far as you can drive on the Cascade Lakes Highway in winter. Dutchman is shared by all users. For Nordic skiers it has 19 miles of easy to most difficult trails. This is also the starting point for the intrepid folks who cross-country ski 12 miles along the unplowed highway to Elk Lake Resort (see our Resorts, Ranches, and Vacation Rentals chapter). There is no overnight parking at this very popular, usually crowded Sno-Park.

Sisters/Camp Sherman Area

Sisters and the village of Camp Sherman are surrounded by miles of ponderosa forest that's split up between the Deschutes National Forest and two wilderness areas: Mount Jefferson and Mount Washington.

From Sisters, you can head south to Three Creek Lake, west on Oregon Highway 242, or west on U.S. 20 to find snowplay. Camp Sherman is right in the middle of public lands. All you have to do there is find a public parking spot along the main roads and trek or ski to your heart's content. In Camp Sherman there is a small market with food and fuel. A number of year-round resorts along the Metolius River offer a whole winter's worth of snow at your doorstep. The town of Sisters has year-round lodging and all the expected amenities.

Three Creek Lake
Forest Service Road 16

The Three Creek Lake area is accessed from downtown Sisters by heading south on Elm Street, which turns into Forest Service Road 16. The road leads uphill to two Sno-Parks—Lower and Upper Three Creek Lake. The views from the road are worth a quick scenic car ride, even if you aren't going to play in the snow. From Upper Three Creek Lake Sno-Park you can access a 12-mile network of Nordic trails ranging from very easy to most difficult.

Oregon Highway 242

Here's a nice place where you can park without a Sno-Park permit. Oregon Highway 242, also known as the McKenzie Pass Highway, is plowed 7 miles west of Sisters. A half-mile west of the 86 mile marker is a small plowed parking area, and there is another one a mile farther, where the road stops at Little Butte. North and south of the parking areas, you'll find Forest Service land shaded by ponderosa pine trees; the snow lingers, and it's good for a backcountry jaunt. Athletes in good condition can ski or trek west on Oregon 242 up to Belknap Crater at McKenzie Pass, about a 1,000-foot gain in elevation, for some awesome views. Oregon 242 is a shared corridor with snowmobiles.

Corbet Sno-Park
U.S. Highway 20

Approximately 13 miles west of Sisters, Corbet Sno-Park is right in the middle of a network of dirt roads that run north and south of the highway. South of the highway are Blue and Suttle Lakes. There are Nordic-only trails around the two lakes that are networked with the Ray Benson Sno-Park trails at Santiam Pass (see next listing).

Santiam Pass
U.S. Highway 20

Twenty-eight miles west of Sisters on U.S. 20 is Santiam Pass, with two Sno-Parks

and the Hoodoo Ski Bowl. Next to the ski area, the Ray Benson Sno-Park has a network of Nordic ski trails. On the north side of U.S. 20 at the Santiam Sno-Park, you'll see folks tubing, and some snowshoeing can be done. Santiam Pass is at an elevation of 4,750 feet, where the forests are thinner and sunny days can provide awesome views. The sun can be shining in Bend while the snow is being driven sideways at Santiam Pass, so get a road report before you head out by calling ODOT at (800) 977–6368, or check out local conditions at Hoodoo Ski Bowl's site, www.hoodoo.com.

Hoodoo Ski Bowl
Santiam Pass, 22 miles west of Sisters
(541) 822–3799; (541) 822–3337, snow phone
www.hoodoo.com

Hoodoo offers a total of 15.8 kilometers of groomed Nordic trails. About 7 kilometers are groomed daily; the rest are only groomed on weekends. A trail pass costs $5.00 for adults and teens, $4.00 for juniors ages 6 to 12. Ski packages can be rented at $11.00 for adults and teens or $9.00 for juniors. A $20 Nordic First Time Skier Package includes gear, 90 minutes of instruction, and a trail pass. See the listing for Hoodoo in our Alpine Skiing and Snowboarding section for more information on this family-oriented ski area.

Sunriver/La Pine Area

Newberry National Volcanic Monument
Oregon Highway 21
www.fs.fed.us/r6/centraloregon/index

This is a beautiful area to snowshoe, ski, and snow camp around the lakes. From U.S. 97 about halfway between Sunriver and La Pine, take the Oregon Highway 21 turnoff east to Newberry Caldera. For Nordic skiers there are about 12 miles of trails. The elevations here run between 4,700 feet and 7,800 feet. Stay off the ice at Paulina Lake and East Lake because the water underneath is heated by hot springs, and the ice will be soft.

When you arrive at Six-Mile Sno-Park or Ten-Mile Sno-Park, you might want to check the trail signs to find out where the snowmobile trails are so that you can avoid them. There are cabins, a small market, a restaurant with seasonal hours, fuel, and first aid available at the Paulina Lake Resort Lodge, (541) 536-2240. Public telephone service is available at Paulina Lake Lodge and East Lake Lodge (which is closed in winter), both of which must be reached on foot. The nearby towns of Sunriver and La Pine offer all amenities including lodging. A trail map is available from the Bend/Fort Rock District Ranger Station in Bend.

Snowmobiling

The Deschutes National Forest has hundreds of miles of Orange Diamond snowmobile trails, created and maintained by volunteers of the Moon Country, La Pine Lodgepole Dodgers, and Sisters Sno-Go-Fers clubs. These trails are often shared by Nordic skiers, snowshoers, and mushers. Keep to the left when passing pedestrian traffic and slow down when passing dog teams. The clubs publish excellent snowmobile trail maps printed on newsprint that can be found at the ranger stations.

Bend Area

Wanoga Snowmobile Sno-Park
Cascade Lakes Highway, Milepost 15

On the south side of the Cascade Lakes Highway is the Wanoga Snowmobile Sno-Park, which features access to 150 miles of groomed snowmobile trails. It has four warming shelters and overnight camping is allowed in the Sno-Park.

Dutchman Flat Sno-Park
Cascade Lakes Highway, Milepost 22

The Cascade Lakes Highway is closed west of Mt. Bachelor at Dutchman Flat Sno-Park. At the Sno-Park the highway turns into a popular snowmobile route. You can access the 150-mile network of snowmobile trails from this point. There is no overnight parking here due to this Sno-Park's popularity and crowds. Dutchman is usually full on weekends.

Edison Sno-Park
Forest Service Road 45

Just east of the Mt. Bachelor Ski Area is a turnoff to the south for Forest Service Road 45. From there, it's about 3 miles to Edison Sno-Park, where you can access the 150 miles of groomed snowmobile trails.

Sisters/Camp Sherman Area
Three Creek Lake
Forest Service Road 16

Access the Three Creek Lake area from downtown Sisters by heading south on Elm Street, which turns into Forest Service Road 16. The road leads uphill to two Sno-Parks: Lower and Upper Three Creek Lake. Snowmobile trails tap into the Sisters/Mt. Bachelor trail system from both Sno-Parks. Not only is there virtually unlimited snowmobiling from this trailhead, but the views are also awesome.

Oregon Highway 242

Also known as the McKenzie Pass Highway, Oregon 242 is plowed 7 miles west of Sisters. A half-mile west of the 86 mile marker is a small plowed parking area, and there is another one a mile farther, where the road stops at Little Butte. North and south of the parking areas are Forest Service roads for some pleasant snowmobiling. You will not need a Sno-Park permit for these two parking areas.

Snowmobilers can continue west up the hill on Oregon 242 for the awesome views from the McKenzie Pass. Here you must stay on the road, as motorized vehicles are not allowed in the wilderness areas on either side.

Corbet Sno-Park
U.S. Highway 20

Approximately 13 miles west of Sisters on U.S. 20 is the Corbet Sno-Park, which taps you into the vast, groomed, Sisters/Mt. Bachelor snowmobile trail network.

Ray Benson Sno-Park
U.S. Highway 20

Twenty-eight miles west of Sisters on U.S. 20, turn south toward Hoodoo Ski Bowl, and on your left will be the Ray Benson Sno-Park. This area offers excellent snow-mobile trails that connect with Three Creek Lake. Santiam Pass is at an elevation of 4,750 feet—the forests are thinner, so sunny days will provide some gorgeous views. However, being closer to the crest of the Cascades, the Santiam Pass gets more than our usual amount of bad weather, so get a road report before making this trip.

Sunriver/La Pine Area

Newberry National Volcanic Monument
Oregon Highway 21

From U.S. 97, take the Oregon Highway 21 turnoff toward Newberry Caldera to the Six-Mile or Ten-Mile Sno-Parks. Here you will find more than 100 miles of groomed snowmobile trails. The elevations run between 4,700 and 7,800 feet. Do not drive on the ice at Paulina Lake and East Lake—the water underneath is heated by hot springs, and the ice will be soft.

There are cabins, a small market, fuel, and first aid available at the Paulina Lake Resort Lodge, (541) 536-2240, and tele-phone service is available at both Paulina Lake Lodge and East Lake Lodge (closed in winter). Both lodges must be reached by snowmobile. The nearby communities of Sunriver and La Pine offer all amenities, including lodging.

Ice-Skating

Bend

Shevlin Park
Shevlin Park Road
(541) 389-7275 (PARK) ext. 118
(Bend Metro Park and Recreation District)

This convenient, family-oriented park offers ice-skating when it's cold enough

Insiders' Tip

Deer are common on the road in the winter. Keep an eye out.

for the pond to freeze, as well as skate rentals for $2.00 or $3.00. Top off your afternoon with a 50-cent hot chocolate. From downtown Bend take Newport Avenue to Shevlin Park Road. You will not need a Sno-Park permit.

Inn of the Seventh Mountain
18575 Southwest Century Drive
(541) 382-8711, (888) 466-7686 ext. 600
www.7thmtn.com

On the road to Mt. Bachelor, the Inn of the Seventh Mountain has an open-air ice-skating rink that is open to the public dur-ing scheduled times. Call for specific hours. The $5.00 charge includes skate rental. Private skating lessons are available.

Sunriver/La Pine Area

Sunriver Village Mall Courtyard
(541) 593-5948

The covered ice-skating rink at Sunriver Mall Courtyard is open to the public. The cost to skate is $5.00 for adults and $4.00 for kids. Skate rental is $1.00.

Tubing and Sledding

You might hear of other areas besides the three we mention below, but these are gen-erally considered the safest places to go tubing or sledding. There is no charge to use these Deschutes National Forest lands, but you will need a Sno-Park permit to park at Edison and Santiam Sno-parks. Mt. Bachelor added a Family Tubing park to its roster of attractions, where you will have to buy a lift ticket.

Bend Area

Edison Sno-Park
Forest Service Road 45

On the Cascade Lakes Highway just east of the Mt. Bachelor Ski Area is a turnoff to the south for Forest Service Road 45. Follow this road about 3 miles to Edison Sno-Park. Families will find hills and slopes for a fun afternoon of snowplay.

Mt. Bachelor Ski Area
Cascade Lakes Highway, 22 miles west of Bend
(541) 382–2442, corporate offices,
(541) 382–7888, snow report,
(800) 829–2442, information and reservations
www.mtbachelor.com

Nonskiers and skiers alike will have fun in Mt. Bachelor's Family Tubing Park, definitely a cut above the old inner-tube hills you may remember as a kid. Special snow tubes designed to be used with the two tow lifts make the uphill part a snap, and five different downhill lanes offer a variety of excitement levels.

Sisters/Camp Sherman Area

Santiam Sno-Park
U.S. Highway 20

Santiam Sno-Park, 28 miles west of Sisters on the north side of U.S. 20, is probably the biggest snow-sledding hill that is safe enough to be recommended by the National Forest Service.

Guided Trips and Rides

Oregon Trail of Dreams
Sunrise Lodge, Mt. Bachelor Ski Area,
Cascade Lakes Highway,
22 miles west of Bend
(541) 382–2442, (800) 829–2442

Insiders' Tip

If you live at or near sea level, be prepared for some breathless days on the slopes. Our snowy elevations range between 5,000 and 9,000 feet, so plan on taking it easy the first couple of days you are here.

Inspirational, exhilarating, and thrilling are words used to describe the sled-dog rides offered by this concessionaire at Mt. Bachelor. Rides can be as short as the 10-minute kiddie rides, which costs $10 per child less than 80 pounds. Or, on a weekday you can pack up to 350 pounds of adults and gear on a sled for $375 and head out on the 26-mile round-trip ride to Elk Lake and back. The more standard ride is a one-hour trip in the vicinity of the ski area; it's $60 per person, and you can choose to help with the care and feeding of the pooches. Reserve through the main Mt. Bachelor reservations number, listed above.

Quest of the West
20540 Mary Way, Bend
(541) 389–0323
www.questofthewest.com

Quest promises scenic and exhilarating excursions around the Three Sisters, Mckenzie Pass, and Mt. Washington. On a clear day the views are awesome. Although winter time can be excellent, March through May is actually prime snowmobiling time. The nice weather and good snow set-up provides for a great experience. You'll zoom across the slopes aboard 2001-model Ski-Doos with paddle tracks. A two-hour excursion is $74 for a single or $99 for a double (two persons on one snowmobile). A four-hour excursion goes for $110, or $140 for a double. Call Quest ahead of time if you are interested in including lunch, for an extra charge, and they also offer lodging packages in Bend and Sisters. Quest of the West has an exclusive snowmobile guide permit for the Sisters District in the Deschutes National Forest, and also for the McKenzie National Forest.

River Ridge Stables
Inn of the Seventh Mountain,
18575 Southwest Century Drive, Bend
(541) 389–9458

Jingle bell your way through the Deschutes National Forest around and about the Inn of the Seventh Mountain Resort in a sleigh pulled by dapple-gray percherons. Halfway through the 45-minute ride is a stop for a cup of hot chocolate or hot apple cider. The sleighs are big—holding as many as 12 or 16 guests. Although River Ridge operates out of the resort, sleigh rides are open to the public as well as resort guests. The fare for adults is $15.00, kids ages 5 to 12 cost $8.00, and younger children are free.

Saddleback Stables
22777 Crestview Lane, Bend
(541) 593–6995

Over the meadow and through the woods and along the Deschutes River is where your sleigh will take you for a frosty day of snowplay. Saddleback Stables operates out of its stable facility at Sunriver Resort next to the marina. Here you may enjoy a 30-minute ride in a handcrafted Amish sleigh pulled by one or more of their fine steeds wearing a beautiful Amish harness and bells—maybe Katy the Shire, or one of the beautiful Belgian draft horses. Sleighs fit up to six people for $59 per ride. Hot chocolate awaits upon your return. Call for reservations.

Wanderlust Tours
143 Southwest Cleveland Avenue, Bend
(541) 389–8359, (800) 962–2862
www.wanderlusttours.com

Wanderlust makes it easy to have a snow adventure. If something short and sweet is in order, they offer a 3½-hour snowshoe hike complete with guide/interpreter, snowshoes, and hot chocolate for $32 per person. When the winter moon is full, Wanderlust offers special moonlight tours for $40. For the truly winter-ready, there's an overnight snow-camping trip that includes snowshoes, a tent, and three hearty meals for $225 per person, where you will snowshoe out to the campsite. A 45-minute sled-dog ride to the campsite adds a lot of excitement, and a little more luxury, and puts the cost for the camping trip at $345 per person. Just in case you don't travel with your whole garage full of gear, other camping gear is available for rent from Wanderlust. Wanderlust promises that you will have a low-impact experience respectful of delicate ecosystems. Call in advance for reservations—well in advance for the sled-dog tour.

Snow Gear Shops

If a region's enthusiasm for certain sports can be judged by the number of gear shops it has in town, then Central Oregon must be crazy about snow. Bend and Sunriver in particular have a lot of shops. All of our ski shops offer rentals and are listed below along with snowmobile rental places. Rental rates are subject to change. Snowblades, miniature skis for skating across the snow, are a new product that many shops will be adding to their list of rental equipment.

Ski packages include skis with bindings, boots, and poles. Snowboard packages come with board, bindings, and boots. Snowshoes are usually rented by themselves, but if you like to use poles, everyone we talked with said they'd throw them in. Juniors' packages, usually for ages 6 to 12, are typically discounted. Most skis and snowboards are not reservable, except at Summit Sports in Sunriver. Snowmobiles should always be reserved a day or more ahead of time.

Seven days a week, including holidays, you can expect the alpine ski shops to open an hour before Mt. Bachelor's lifts get started. All the shops listed sell Oregon Sno-Park permits except for Smoked Monkeys in Bend, and Summit Sports and Sunriver Snowboards in Sunriver. Shops throughout Central Oregon are listed in alphabetical order. All the stores accept Visa and MasterCard, but don't count on the other brands of plastic.

Bend Ski & Board Sport
1009 Northwest Galveston, Bend
(541) 389–4667
www.bendskiandboard.com

Located right on the road to Mt. Bachelor, Bend Ski & Board rents—you guessed it—just about every kind of board made, from snowboards ($25), Nordic skis ($12), shaped skis ($16/adults, $14/juniors), and snowblades ($15) to skateboards and wakeboards. You will also find snowshoes ($12) and jacket/pant combos ($16) for rent. Bend Ski & Board also sells a full line of hard goods, outerwear, and accessories, and the shop offers overnight ski and

Hiking and cross-country skiing opportunities abound in the Three Sisters Wilderness. PHOTO: JIM YUSKAVITCH

snowboard tuning. It's open every day, starting one hour before the lifts open.

Chrome Pony Bike & Ski
One West Mall, Sunriver
(541) 593–2728
You'll find the Chrome Pony across from Sunriver Village next to Baja Norte. Besides ski and apparel sales, it offers rentals of Volkl alpine ski packages at $15 a day for adults, $12 for juniors. Chrome Pony also has Nordic ski packages available for $12 ($10 for children) and Burton snowboard packages for $25. Snowshoes can be rented for $10. The shop is open every day.

Eurosports
182 East Hood Avenue, Sisters
(541) 549–2471, (800) 382–2471
Sisters is not a ski town per se, but Eurosports does offer rental equipment, plus outerwear and hardware for purchase. An alpine ski package goes for $14, shaped for $20, Nordic for $12, and snowboards for $25. Junior ski packages are a few dollars less, and all packages include boots. For those folk who like to look at

the scenery as they snowplay, Eurosports also rents snowshoes for $12. Eurosports is open daily.

4 Seasons Recreational Outfitters and Lucky Chucky's Snowboard Shop
2 Country Mall, Sunriver
(541) 593–2255
Next to Sunriver's medical building across from the village, 4 Seasons offers a full line of ski gear, apparel, accessories, and service. Alpine packages start at $15 per day or $34 for 3 days ($10/day or $22/3 days for juniors) and go up to $25/$40 for packages with demo skis. Nordic packages rent for $20 for adults or $15 for juniors. 4 Seasons also has snowshoes for $10. Next door is 4 Seasons' snowboard shop, Lucky Chucky's, which offers snowboard packages for $20, plus $15 for each extra day. 4 Seasons and Lucky Chucky's are open every day, all year.

Mountain Supply of Oregon
834 Colorado Avenue, Bend
(541) 388–0688, (800) 794–0688
Formerly on Northwest Division Street, Mountain Supply's nice new facility is on

Colorado Avenue, not far from the Mt. Bachelor park-and-ride lot. This is a traditional, backpacking-type store. Mountain Supply outfits folks for nonmotorized sports like Nordic skiing, skijoring (being pulled on skis by a horse), and snowshoeing. It also provides snowboards but not alpine skis. Nordic touring packages rent for $10 a day, backcountry ski packages for $14, and telemark ski packages for $25. Snowshoes are $8.00. The store is open seven days a week.

Pine Mountain Sports
133 Southwest Century Drive, Bend
(541) 385–8080

Pine Mountain Sports specializes mostly in backcountry snow sports, including cross-country and telemark skiing, and snowshoeing. Their rental packages consist of hardware (no clothing) in adult sizes. Nordic ski packages rent for $10 per day, and a telemark ski package goes for $25. For a good aerobic workout, or for those who like to spend more time looking at the scenery than putting miles behind them, try renting a pair of snowshoes for $10. If you are the adventurous type and like to head out where the snow is deep and the slopes are steep, they can outfit your party with transceivers and probes for $10 a day per person. Stop by any day on the way to Mt. Bachelor or Tumalo Falls.

Powder House
311 Southwest Century Drive, Bend
(541) 389–6234

This place has a huge selection of skis, apparel, and accessories. A basic alpine package rents for $14 for adults and only $10 for juniors. A high-performance ski package with shaped skis goes for $19 a day. Nordic ski packages are available for $10, snowboards for $24, and snowshoes rent for $9.00. If you didn't bring any snowplay outerwear, you can rent a jacket and bib pants for $9.00 each. Powder House is open every day.

Skjersaa's Ski and Snowboard Shop
130 Southwest Century Drive, Bend
(541) 382–2154

Located on the route to Mt. Bachelor, this ski and board shop sells a full line of apparel and gear, with name-brands such as Burton, Airwalk, K2, and Salomon. Alpine packages go for $15 for adults, $10 for juniors. Snowboard packages rent for $25, and snowshoes are $10 (poles optional). In business since 1958, Skjersaa (pronounced "sheershaw"), Bend's oldest ski shop, is open daily.

Stone's Ski & Sports
345 Southwest Century Drive, Bend
(541) 389–0890, September through May,
(541) 593–8369, in summer
www.sunriversports.com

Owned by the same folks who own Sunriver Sports, Stone's offers a full line of apparel, gear, and accessories. Alpine ski packages here start at $16 for basic gear, $25 for performance-level gear, and $35 to demo the new stuff. Junior alpine packages go for $10. Nordic ski packages rent for $12 and junior-sized Nordic packages for $10; Nordic skating packages are $18. Snowshoes rent for $12; poles are optional. This high-end downhill ski shop is open daily from September through late May.

Insiders' Tip

When an Oregon Department of Transportation (ODOT) highway sign reads TRACTION DEVICES REQUIRED, chains must be used on two-wheel-drive vehicles. If you have a four-wheel-drive vehicle with mud-and-snow tires, you do not need chains when you see this sign. However, when you see an ODOT CHAINS REQUIRED sign, all vehicles must have chains.

Summit Sports
7 Ponderosa Road, Sunriver
(541) 593–5252, (800) 871–8004
www.summitsportsonline.com

Across from The Country Store in the village, this rental-only shop offers a full range of snowplay gear from skis to ski sleds. Alpine ski packages rent for $15 a day and $10 for each additional day for adults ($20 for performance skis) or $10 plus $5.00 for junior sizes. Nordic ski packages go for $10.00 for adults, $8.00 for juniors. Snowboard packages are $20 and snowshoes rent for $15 a day. Skis and snowshoe rentals are discounted on additional days. Snowmobiles with trailers are available to rent for $140 per day. The shop takes rental reservations, which most places don't do, and they also can handle on-line reservations. Although they do not sell Sno-Park permits, the Country Store market across the street does sell Sno-Park permits.

Sunnyside Sports
930 Northwest Newport Avenue, Bend
(541) 382–8018
www.sunnysidesports.com

This shop specializes in sales and rentals of racing and touring Nordic skis. It also carries a complete line of apparel and accessories. A basic touring package rents for $10.00 for adults, $8.00 for kids. Nordic skating packages go for $20 a day, and snowshoes are available for $10. If you'd like to take Baby along, you can rent a sled for $10 a day. Sunnyside is open every day, and you may call for daily wax conditions.

Sunriver Snowboards
Sunriver Village Mall, Building 15, Sunriver
(541) 593–6989

This way-cool, full-service board shop rents packages for $25 a day, or for an extra six bucks you can demo a hot new board package. While you're there check out shades by Oakley, Smith, and Dragon, apparel by Burton, K2, and LibTech, and new, high-performance snowboards, all available for purchase. The shop is open daily. Sunriver Snowboards does not sell Sno-Park permits, but the Country Store market in Sunriver does.

Sunriver Sports
Sunriver Village Mall, Building 16, Sunriver
(541) 593–8369

In keeping with the upscale nature of Sunriver Resort, Sunriver Sports is a tony ski shop with classy high-performance duds from Bogner and Fila, Patagonia and Marmot. Alpine ski packages here start at $16 for basic gear, $25 for performance-level gear, and $35 to demo the hottest new stuff. Junior alpine packages go for $10. Nordic ski packages rent for $12, Nordic skating packages for $18, and junior-size Nordic packages for $9.00. For $20 you can rent a snowboard package, and it's an extra $6.00 to demo the latest boards. Finally, for us 3-mph types, Sunriver Sports rents snowshoes for $12; poles are optional. Drop by seven days a week.

Village Bike Shop
Sunriver Village Mall, Building 21, Sunriver
(541) 593–2453

"Bike" may be the name, but in winter, skis are the game here. Pick up a set of adult alpine gear for $18 per day, or $14 for juniors. Nordic packages go for $14 for adults and $12 for juniors. Snowboard packages (with Clicker bindings) can be rented for $20 to $25, and snowshoes rent for $10. They offer discounted rates for multiple-day rentals. The Village Bike Shop is the only place we know that rents sleds and tubes, each for $8.00 a day. It's open every day except Christmas, and while you are there you can purchase apparel and accessories to complete your outfit.

Golf

More Options Than You
Have Clubs

About Our Course Listings

Golf Shops

Welcome to the golf Mecca of the Northwest—
Central Oregon. We've got 24 golf courses that test
players of all skill levels, along with abundant sunshine, sparkling air and outstanding
views.

Black Butte Ranch, Eagle Crest Resort, and Sunriver Resort are three resorts that
offer two or three courses on-site—a very efficient setup for the golfer who likes to have
some variety while staying in one spot. Sunriver guests can add a nearby course, Quail
Run in La Pine, to make it four to choose from. Bend, Sisters, and Redmond have a 14-
course smorgasbord, all within a 30-minute radius. Prineville's Meadow Lakes Golf
Course, Crooked River Ranch Golf Course, Madras' Nine Peaks Golf Course, and Kah-
Nee-Ta Resort are all on Central Oregon's outskirts to the north and east, but these
warm climate, desert courses have their own attractions.

More Options Than You Have Clubs

If a challenging game is your goal, we have
some of the most demanding courses in
America. The River's Edge Golf Course,
right in Bend, is perhaps the most challenging course in all of Oregon. Central
Oregon's world-class facilities play host to
many national and regional tournaments
including *Golf Digest*'s Pacific Amateur
Golf Classic, which takes place at Awbrey
Glen, Black Butte Ranch, Eagle Crest,
Sunriver, and Widgi Creek.

Our wide range of elevations and
topographies offers our golfing guests a
choice of climate and year-round play. Our
warmest winter course is Kah-Nee-Ta
Resort, northwest of Madras at a sunny,
1,500-foot elevation; winter daytime tem-
peratures are usually in the 50s and 60s.
Other relatively warm spots include Nine
Peaks Golf Course in Madras, Meadow
Lakes Golf Course in Prineville, Crooked
River Ranch in Crooked River, Redmond's
Juniper Golf Club, and The Greens at
Redmond.

For a refreshingly cool summer game
in Bend, try Widgi Creek, where the fairways are surrounded by pine forest at a
4,000-foot elevation. Here, summer temperatures usually hover around 75 or so.
Three other cool, forested courses are out-

side of Sisters—including Aspen Lakes
and Black Butte Ranch's Big Meadow and
Glaze Meadow. Starting in November,
you can expect snow to close down all of
Sisters' fairways, as well as the courses to
the west and south of Bend. In town,
Bend and Redmond's courses are open
through the winter, weather-permitting;
they'll be closed when snowy or muddy.

Second only to the scenery are visitor
comments about how fast our area greens
are. Local experts say it has something to
do with the combination of quickly drain-
ing sandy soil and the short, bentgrass
greens that are standard here. Your first
drive will probably look good, but you'll
have to concentrate on accurate putting
to make the hole a successful one.

About Our Course Listings

In this chapter you will find listings on all
the courses in Central Oregon that allow
public play. (We omitted four beautiful
but members-only country clubs, Broken
Top Club, the Bend Golf and Country
Club, Awbrey Glen, and the Prineville
Country Club.) Widgi Creek may eventually become members-only, but until all
available memberships are sold, public
play is allowed. Sunriver Resort's championship golf course, Crosswater, is considered a resort course, which means it's

Central Oregon has 24 spectacular golf courses. PHOTO: THE RIVERHOUSE

open to guests of Sunriver Resort but not to the public. Since Sunriver Resort is on our list of recommended places to stay, we have included Crosswater.

In some cases the golf courses are outside the town limits of our core communities, so we have enlarged each town to be an "area." Many of our courses are part of resorts; please see our Resorts, Ranches, and Vacation Rentals chapter for more extensive information on resort amenities. If you fall in love with one of our resorts and want to own a piece of the dirt, many have homes or homesites available. The pro shop or the lodging phone number can put you in touch with a listing realtor.

On all area courses, tank tops, tube tops, and swimsuits are not appreciated; on many they are definitely not allowed, and men's shirts should have collars. Metal spikes are not allowed. Whether you are playing at a cool, high elevation or low

in a hot desert canyon, the summer sun is a significant hazard. Use sunscreen, wear a hat, and drink plenty of nonalcoholic beverages to prevent heat or altitude sickness.

Yardages mentioned are for the men's white tees. Greens fees and cart rentals are quoted for 18 holes on 18-hole courses. If a course has only nine holes, the fees stated are for nine holes. Cart rental rates are always separate from the greens fees, as some places charge by the number of riders and others have a flat rental rate per cart for a round of golf. Prices quoted are for the high summer season. Junior rates are for the nonvoting segment of the population, ages 17 and younger. All of our golf courses accept MasterCard and Visa. Only the places that accept additional cards have credit cards noted in their listings. At the end of this chapter is a list of stores that sell golf equipment.

Bend Area

Lost Tracks Golf Club
60205 Sunset View Drive, Bend
(541) 385-1818

In southeast Bend next to the Deschutes National Forest, Lost Tracks is a classic-style, par 72 golf course with mature trees, glistening lakes, lava rock outcroppings, and mountain views. The compact, 6,245-yard course is easily walked, and the three sets of tees are designed for all skill levels. You will understand the course name when you see the railroad car that makes a bridge to signature hole No. 16, a par 3 with an island green.

Owner/builder Brian Whitcomb and Steve Breuning, director of golf, are the PGA pros on hand, and assistant PGA pro Kit Grove offers lessons at $40 per hour. The public can play for $58, or $25 for juniors, and it is an extra $14 for a cart. The pro shop offers rental clubs for $20, and there's a snack bar. Lost Tracks is open all year, weather-permitting.

Mountain High Golf Course
60650 China Hat Road, Bend
(541) 382-1111

Beautifully landscaped with natural-looking ponds, brooks, and tall ponderosa pines, Mountain High offers four sets of tees on 18 holes that will challenge all skill levels. This par 72, 6,058-yard course is a popular site for tournaments and vacationers. Signature hole No. 5 has an island green.

There is no pro shop, but Mountain High accommodates guests with club rentals for $10, and there is a snack bar. Greens fees run $40, and there are discounts for spring and fall play. The toughest decision you'll have to make is whether to walk this lovely course or use one of the complimentary carts. Reservations for summer weekend tee times are recommended. Mountain High is usually open from April 1 through October 31.

Orion Greens Golf Course
61525 Fargo Lane, Bend
(541) 388-3999

This compact, nine-hole course is more challenging than it looks, with four par 4 and five par 3 holes. Players say you will use all your clubs on this brilliant executive course. You'll need good karma for signature hole No. 9: An island hole with two bunkers and four trees, it's a 129-yard par 3.

Although the white tees are a very walkable 2,900 yards, for $10 you might enjoy renting one of the Rolls-Royce carts, complete with the Rolls-Royce figurine on the hood. Even if you like to walk, a game will only take you 90 minutes or so. We suggest reserving a set of three tee times up to a month or so ahead at this popular little course. There is a pro shop that rents clubs for $6.00, and a nice restaurant, The Coho Grill. Greens fees are $15 ($12 in winter), or only $12 after 4:00 P.M.

River's Edge Golf Course
400 Northwest Pro Shop Drive, Bend
(541) 389-2828

River's Edge was featured in *Golf Digest*'s Best Places to Play for 1997. Said to be the most difficult 18-hole course in Oregon, River's Edge invites you to bring your "A" game. It is owned by the adjacent River-house resort motel, which offers golf packages (see our Hotels and Motels chapter). With its convenient, close-in location, this par 72 course designed by Robert Muir Graves is very popular with business travelers and convention-goers, as well as vacationers and locals.

The white tees play 6,130 yards. The hillside setting is walkable (but then, so's Mount Hood). You'll get a good workout, especially hoofing it uphill between Nos. 8 and 9. The first eight holes are fairly flat but narrow. After No. 8, the course gets very hilly, but it opens up to scenic views of the Cascades, including Mount Jefferson and Mount Hood. There's a nice view overlooking the Deschutes River from the 8th hole. The signature hole, No. 6, is a par 4, 360-yard uphill adventure with a pond on each side. The good news is that you are rewarded with the sight of a pretty waterfall near the hole.

PGA pro Linden Blackwell is director of golf, and Mark Payne, also a PGA member, is the teaching pro. Lessons run about $40 for 30 minutes, and River's Edge offers junior clinics for ages 8 to 17 throughout the summer. The pro shop rents clubs for

Insiders' Tip

If you are coming to Central Oregon from an area that's near sea level, you might want to consider renting a cart. Our 3,000- to 4,000-foot elevations can leave you breathless if you are not accustomed to golfing at higher altitudes.

as some beautifully framed views of white-topped peaks. The signature hole, No. 11, is a 216-yard par 3 that demands a tee shot over a lake onto an undulating green. No. 15, a par 3, has a grand view overlooking the Deschutes River. The course can be walked, but you may want to ride if you aren't used to the 4,000-foot elevation. The elevation also makes this one of our cooler spots, with heavy snows during the winter. Another, more pleasant consequence of the elevation is that your ball will travel a bit farther than it will at sea level. This fairly new, par 72, 5,911-yard course is already home to a number of tournaments every year—something to keep in mind as you make your plans.

Todd Carver heads up an impressive staff of two PGA pros, offering lessons for $45 per half hour. The pro shop rents clubs for $25 per round, and a cart rents for $14 per rider. Greens fees run $85 on weekends; on weekdays they drop to $59. Juniors play for $15.

Sisters/Camp Sherman Area

Aspen Lakes Golf Course
17204 Oregon Highway 126, Sisters
(541) 549–4653

The most recent addition to Central Oregon's course offerings, its first nine holes, named Faith, was completed in 1997. The next nine, called Hope, was completed in 1999. The owners haven't set a completion date for the final nine, which will be called Charity (each named after early names for the Three Sisters mountains). Now that Hope has arrived, the 18 holes play as a par 72 course.

For now, it is immediately apparent that the 3,012-yard first nine holes are unique. Red sand bunkers made from Central Oregon crushed volcanic cinders dot the deep green turf rimmed by dense stands of pine and juniper trees. Aspen Lakes was the first course in Oregon to enroll in the Audubon Signature Cooperative Sanctuary Program, which emphasizes environmentally sensitive designs using local materials. *Northwest Travel* magazine included No. 5, a long par 4, in its Top 18 Holes for 1998. Golfers of all

$7.50. Bogey's serves casual food. Greens fees are $48, but drop to $25 after 4:00 P.M. Juniors play for half-price. At least 65 percent of guests rent carts, which cost $13 per rider. The course is open all year, unless there's snow. You can reserve a tee time up to 30 days in advance or when you make a room reservation.

Widgi Creek Golf Club
18707 Century Drive, Bend
(541) 382–4449, pro shop
(541) 317–5000, lodging

Tucked into the Deschutes National Forest along the Deschutes River, Widgi Creek is one of our most scenic courses. It's tough to say which is the real reason people come here—the awesome setting, or the fairly difficult, 18-hole championship course designed by Robert Muir Graves in 1990. Regardless, Widgi Creek is becoming one of Bend's newest destination resorts. (In a previous lifetime it was known as Pine Meadows Country Club, but since it was restored to first-class status you would never know it had a history at all.) Townhome rentals were added as amenities in 1998, bringing Widgi Creek closer to becoming a full-service resort (see the listing for Elkai Woods at Widgi Creek in our Resorts, Ranches, and Vacation Rentals chapter).

Fairways have been cut into the forest, making for some challenging shots as well

skill levels utilize the five tee positions. The course is fairly level but long and narrow, so some folks may want to rent a cart—it's $16 for 9 holes; $28 for 18. Lessons are by appointment and cost $45.

Aspen Lakes is conveniently located five minutes east of Sisters on Oregon Highway 126. From the highway, head north a quarter-mile to the pro shop entrance on Camp Polk Road. The pro shop rents clubs for $10 for 9 holes, $20 for 18. Greens fees are $29 for 9 holes, $55 for 18. Juniors play for half-price after 2:00 P.M. on weekends and after noon on weekdays. American Express and Discover are accepted as well as Visa and MasterCard. Being set at a 3,100-foot elevation, Aspen Lakes is open seasonally—generally from March into November.

Black Butte Ranch
U.S. Highway 20, Black Butte Ranch
(541) 595–1500, (800) 399–2322, golf;
(541) 595–6211, main switchboard;
(800) 452–7455, lodging

It can safely be said that in our land of incredible scenery, this has to be one of the most drop-dead gorgeous settings in all of Central Oregon. Black Butte Ranch is a full-service, upscale resort 8 miles west of Sisters with two 18-hole championship golf courses. The awe-inspiring white peaks of the North and Middle Sister, Mount Washington, Three Finger Jack, and Mount Jefferson loom in the distance, framed by dark ponderosa pines that stand at what seems to be just an arm's length away.

"Something for everyone" and "two of the Northwest's finest" pretty well wrap it up as far as the golf options at Black Butte. Both of these outstanding courses feature classic, par 72 layouts designed in the late 1970s and early 1980s. Of the two, the hilly Glaze Meadow course offers more variety, but it also requires a bit more accuracy and is popular with target golfers. Big Meadow is loved for its outstanding general layout, clever bunkering, and green design. Detailed discussions of each course follow.

Director of golf and PGA pro J. D. Mowlbs oversees an impressive staff of PGA professionals. Private lessons with the pros run $30 to $40 per half hour. The Black Butte Ranch Golf School teaches golfers of all ages and skill levels. A typical four-day class costs about $500.

Both courses have snack bars. Tee times can be reserved up to one week in advance for the general public, or two weeks ahead of time for resort guests and residents. Greens fees range from $35 to $65 depending on the day of the week and time of day. Both pro shops rent clubs for $25 per set. Carts may be rented at each course for $30 per round.

Nongolfing companions will also enjoy a vacation at the resort, where they can get physical through horseback riding, bike riding, swimming, and tennis. At an elevation of 3,300 feet, Black Butte gets plenty of snow in the winter, so the golf courses usually close at Thanksgiving and reopen in March. During winter the greens are carefully covered. The resort accepts American Express, Discover, and Diner's Club along with MasterCard and Visa. (For more information on lodging options and amenities at Black Butte Ranch, see our Resorts, Ranches, and Vacation Rentals chapter.)

Big Meadow Golf Course
(541) 595–1545

The par 4 No. 14 at Big Meadow probably qualifies as the signature hole for all of Black Butte Ranch. There is an incredible view of the jagged, white-capped digits of Three Finger Jack. *Golf Digest* lists the 6,456-yard, par 72 course, designed by Robert Muir Graves in 1976, as one of its top courses in Oregon. Greg Hanway is the head PGA pro for Big Meadow.

Glaze Meadow Golf Course
(541) 595–1270

Ranked among the Top 100 Golf Courses by *Links* magazine, 6,273-yard Glaze Meadow offers five par 5s, lots of doglegs, and tight, tree-lined fairways. Designed by Gene "Bunny" Mason in 1981, Glaze Meadow features spring-fed water hazards on the front nine where the course covers flat mountain meadows. The back nine gets quite hilly. Kelvin Lattenmeyer is the

Practicing beneath a mountain backdrop—a beautiful way to improve your game. PHOTO: BOB POOL

head PGA pro for this course. *Golf Digest* awarded this course its silver medal for being in the top 50 courses in America.

Redmond Area

Crooked River Ranch Golf Course
5195 Club House Road, Crooked River
(541) 923–6343

As Gary Popp, Crooked River's head PGA pro, says, "When you lose a ball on hole 5, it's toast!" He's referring to the Ranch's par 4 signature hole, where the second half of the dogleg approach actually spans the 300-foot-deep Crooked River Canyon. The other 17 holes aren't cliffhangers, but all have equally stunning desert scenery.

This par 71, 5,355-yard course designed by Gene "Bunny" Mason and Jim Ramey offers a moderately difficult game. During summer the challenge is met by resort guests, tourists, and local residents. Its warm, canyon climate enables Crooked River to stay open all year, catering in the off-season to small business conventions that stay at the resort as well as retirees.

PGA golf pro Tim Layton joins Popp to offer a combined 25 years of experience to students for $25 per half hour or so. The pro shop rents clubs for $8.00 to $12.00, and there's a snack bar on the course, plus two restaurants in the center of the community (see our Other Communities chapter). Weekday greens fees are $25 for adults and $17 for juniors—$30 on weekends. A cart may be rented for $25, though the course is very walkable. Summers in the Crooked River Canyon area are often hot and always dry, so if you take to the course you'll want to drink plenty of water or nonalcoholic beverages.

Eagle Crest Resort
1522 Cline Falls Road, Redmond
(541) 923–2453, front desk; (877) 818–0286, golf shop

Eagle Crest is a High Desert resort with a wide range of amenities, but its key delights are three 18-hole, par 72 championship golf courses. The lure of emerald green fairways and sparkling ponds nestled among hills of sagebrush, juniper trees, and rugged rock outcroppings is so compelling that a nongolfer might long to pick up a club just to enjoy the scenery.

Both courses are open year-round, thanks to the dry desert climate. A common reaction among first-timers here is that the fast greens require accurate putting. Head PGA pro Terry Anderson, considered one of Oregon's top golfers, heads up a staff of six professionals; lessons cost between $40 and $60 per half hour. The Resort Course and the newer Ridge Course each have a pro shop (clubs rent for $10 per nine holes) and a snack bar. Individual course descriptions follow. Greens fees range from $22.50 to $65.00 and the resort offers golf packages. Carts rent for $25 per round. Call up to two weeks ahead for a tee time.

For family-oriented recreation or some quality practice time, try the fun but challenging 18-hole putting course at the Ridge Course. It's $8.00 for adults and $4.00 for kids ages 17 and younger, equipment included. Eagle Crest Resort accepts American Express and Discover in addition to MasterCard and Visa.

Resort Course
(541) 923–4653

Designed by popular Northwest golf architect Gene "Bunny" Mason, this 6,260-yard, par 72 course's signature hole is No. 2, a par 5 dogleg through a canyon fairway some 80 feet below. Some folks might prefer to rent a cart for this long course built in 1987. The fairways are wide open but still challenging to the low handicapper.

Ridge Course
(541) 923–5002

Beautiful wildflowers and stunning views make this 5,616-yard par 72 course, designed by John Thronson in 1993, a

> **Insiders' Tip**
> Bring your camera on the course; you'll want to take some of our magnificent scenery home with you.

popular one. The view of Smith Rock from the par 3 No. 12 is awesome.

Mid Iron Course
(541) 923–5002

Completed in 2000, the Mid Iron Course is a 4,160-yard par 63 course also designed by John Thronson.

The Greens at Redmond
2575 Southwest Greens Boulevard, Redmond
(541) 923–0694

This nine-hole, par 29 executive course at the corner of Yew Avenue and Canal Boulevard (1 block west of U.S. Highway 97) will test your skills. There are three sets of tees; the whites have a yardage of 1,505. The signature hole on this course, designed by the renowned Robert Muir Graves, is No. 6, a par 4 over water.

PGA golf pro Dick Mason offers lessons at $30 per hour. The snack bar serves beer and wine. You may rent clubs from the pro shop for $3.00, and a cart goes for $9.00, but the course is easy to walk. Greens fees are a very reasonable $15 for nine holes. The low fees and lesson rates are especially appreciated by novice golfers. This is a popular year-round course, but you don't usually need tee times.

Juniper Golf Club
139 Southeast Sisters Avenue, Redmond
(541) 548–3121

Affordable prices, a convenient location near the airport, and 18 well-maintained holes make the Juniper Golf Club a popular course for families and value-oriented duffers. This par 72, 6,241-yard course is easily walkable through a High Desert setting with lava rock outcroppings. Signature hole No. 2 is noted for its photo-op Cascade views from Mount Hood (near Portland!) in the north all the way south to Mount Bachelor.

Greens fees are $35.00 for adults, $17.50 for juniors. If you prefer to ride, carts rent for $25 per 18 holes. Staff PGA pro Bruce Wattenburger teaches adults at a rate of $25 per 30 minutes and $40 per hour; it's $15 for 30 minutes for juniors. Clubs may be rented from the pro shop for $12, and there's a snack bar. This munici-pal course is open all year, and you can reserve tee times up to a month in advance.

Sunriver/La Pine Area

Quail Run Golf Course
16725 Northridge Drive, La Pine
(541) 536–1303, (800) 895–4653

Eight miles south of Sunriver, Quail Run is a relaxed, family-oriented nine-hole regulation course. Most guests walk this well-maintained course, enjoying wide, tree-lined fairways and views of Mount Bachelor, Broken Top, the Three Sisters, and Mount Paulina. The yardage from the white tees is 3,185.

What this par 36 course lacks in size it makes up for in quality. The only championship nine-hole course in Central Oregon to have two PGA golf pros onboard (Gary Brannies and owner Bill Martin), Quail Run offers an excellent practice facility as well as lessons at $35 for 45 minutes. It also features cart rentals at $7.00 per rider for nine holes ($12.00 for 18 holes), a snack bar, and a pro shop where a set of clubs rents for $5.00 for nine holes and $8.00 for 18 holes. The greens fees make family play affordable ($22 for 9 holes and $38 for 18; juniors play at half-price after 2:00 P.M.), and a relaxed pace attracts many visitors from Sunriver Resort. There is also a $22 twilight rate for 18 holes with exact hours varying depending on the season

Reservations for tee times—available as far in advance as you choose—are recommended during the summer months. The course is open from about March 15 through November 1, depending on the severity of the winter.

Sunriver Resort
One Centre Drive, Sunriver
(541) 593–1000; (541) 593–7849, Ron Seals; (800) 386–2243

Sunriver is a major, full-service resort with three championship courses boasting 54 flags. The Woodlands and the completely renovated Meadows are moderately priced and open to the public. Crosswater, a higher-priced tournament course, is open to members and guests of Sunriver Resort, which operates the Sunriver Lodge and rents out hundreds of vacation homes (see our Resorts, Ranches, and Vacation Rentals chapter). On all three courses the pace of play is monitored to prevent bottlenecks, and snack and beverage carts are available. A more detailed look at each course follows.

Crosswater usually co-hosts the Pacific Amateur Golf Classic in October. The three courses also host numerous regional tournaments that can bring in extra crowds and tie up the golf pros. Check on the tournament schedule before you set your vacation dates.

Sunriver Resort Golf Schools offer one- to three-day customized schools for four persons or more, as well as scheduled classes starting at one hour in duration. Managed by golf pro Ron Seals, who currently competes in state and regional PGA tournaments, group instruction runs from $20 per person for the one-hour classes up to about $400 for the three-day classes. Private lessons with Seals start at $80 per hour. Private lessons with other instructors start at $60 per hour; rates vary for multiple students. Private lessons use videos as a learning tool.

The resort courses accept American Express, Discover, and Diner's Club in addition to MasterCard and Visa. Golf packages are available. Sunriver does get snow in the winter, so courses are open three seasons only.

Crosswater
17600 Canoe Camp Drive, Sunriver
(541) 593–6196; (541) 593–4402, reservations

When they named Sunriver's new golf course Crosswater, they meant exactly that. Depending on where you tee off, you can cross water, including the Deschutes River and Little Deschutes River, at least seven times. This par 72, 6,185-yard course (from the white tees) designed by Bob Cupp and John Fought appeals to intermediate to advanced golfers who like a game where they can use every club in their bag.

In 1995 Crosswater won *Golf Digest*'s award as America's Best New Golf Course and has been in *Golf Magazine*'s Top 100 Courses ever since then. In fact, in 1998 the publication rated it No. 15 in America.

There are five sets of tees on this traditional, heathland-style course. All 18 holes are considered signature holes, but the best photo-op is at No. 9, where you can see Mount Bachelor across the Deschutes River. No. 12, a 687-yard par 5 from the gold tees, is the longest hole in the Northwest.

The second-longest course in America at a whopping 7,683 yards from the championship tees, it's no wonder they include the cart rental in the greens fees, which range from $120 to $160 during the high season. A set of Titleist DCI clubs with graphite shafts may be rented for $35. Food and alcoholic beverages are offered at The Grille and Lounge; The Tern restaurant serves casual food like burgers. In order to play at Crosswater, you must either be a club member or a guest at the Sunriver Lodge, or you must rent a vacation home from Sunriver Resort (not one of the other property-management companies at Sunriver). Reserve tee times when you reserve your room.

Meadows
One Center Drive, Sunriver
(541) 593–7858; (541) 593–4402, reservations

Referred to as Sunriver's original golf course, the Meadows is no longer its original self. In fact, the course underwent a complete renovation and reopened in 1999.

The John Fought design is fairly tough, with pine tree–strewn meadows reminiscent of a classic Southeastern style. In fact, the new par 71 Meadows is comparable to some of the best courses in North Carolina,

> **Insiders' Tip**
> A hat is always a good idea in this High Desert country. The sun can be pretty hot during a Central Oregon summer, and shady spots on the course can be few and far between.

with lots of water features and a new bunkering strategy—and the view of Mount Bachelor from No. 16 is "enormous."

The course has four sets of tees, including the 6,033-yard whites, and is walkable. On the lower level of the Sunriver Lodge, which overlooks the course, is the Merchant Trader Cafe. Greens fees range from $85 to $125 (summer rates) and include a cart. Club rentals are $35.

Woodlands
West Core Road, Sunriver
(541) 593–3703; (541) 593–4402, reservations

If a quality experience in moderation is more your style, you might choose Woodlands over Crosswater. The course length is shorter (only 6,088 from the white tees), and the public greens fees are less expensive. Greens fees range from $85 to $125 (summer rates) and include a cart. Rates are lower in spring and fall.

Moderation does not mean a lesser experience. This Robert Trent Jones Jr. course is a highly-rated championship course that will challenge any level of player. Accuracy is required from all four sets of tees to avoid the lava rock outcroppings and abundant water hazards, and you will need every club in your bag. No. 18 is a challenge, with a dogleg across a lake. Although every fairway surrounded by pine and lodgepole forest is scenic, the best photo-op is at what many consider to be Woodlands' signature hole, No. 7, where you can see Mount Bachelor at the end of a sloping fairway.

McDivot's Cafe serves casual foods. You can rent clubs at the pro shop for $35.

Prineville Area

Meadow Lakes Golf Course
300 Meadow Lakes Drive, Prineville
(541) 447–7113, (800) 577–2797

After traveling through miles of sagebrush, the lush green fairways that spread over the valley floor captivate the eye as you descend the steep grade down Oregon Highway 126 into the town of Prineville. Through this green carpet snakes the Crooked River, flanked by sparkling lakes. As you enter town, turn south on Meadow Lakes Drive, and you've arrived at Prineville's 18-hole championship golf course.

This oasis in the desert would not have been possible without the novel idea of using treated effluent water to irrigate the 160 acres of manicured turf. When it was built in 1993, Meadow Lakes was the first-ever recipient of the *Golf Digest* National Environmental Leaders Award.

Meadow Lakes is a very walkable 5,849 yards. The abundance of water seems almost incongruous with its setting, and the course's design really seems to flaunt its aquatic elements. No. 14, considered Meadow Lakes' signature hole, takes you through water on two sides, and No. 16 has a hidden pond just waiting to swallow your Maxfli. Greens fees run $32 on the weekend or $22 on weekdays. It's $14 for juniors, who can avail themselves of the junior program on Monday and Tuesday evenings. Carts are available for $12 per rider, and the pro shop rents clubs for $12. Guests can take advantage of the snack shop and a good restaurant. Reservations for weekend tee times are suggested.

Madras Area

Kah-Nee-Ta Resort Golf Course
12 miles north of U.S. Highway 26, Warm Springs
(541) 553–1112 ext. 3371, (800) 554–4786

Imagine a sunny resort with warm winter days, comfortably hot summers, an 18-hole championship golf course, an Olympic-size swimming pool fed by hot mineral springs, and a masseuse on staff. Throw in a casino for entertainment when darkness falls. What could be better?

The beautifully maintained par 72 course is laid out at the bottom of a canyon amid rugged desert scenery with the meandering Warm Springs River cutting through the fairways. The par 5 signature hole, No. 17, crosses the river. For those looking to improve their game, PGA golf pros include director of golf Joe Rauschenburg and his assistant, Cooper Chitty. They will give you some expert advice for $38 per hour, or $18 per hour for juniors.

Vacationing families and business convention-goers make up a large part of the resort's regular clientele. And you can golf guilt-free while traveling with non-golfing companions at Kah-Nee-Ta. The list of other recreational activities includes rafting, horseback riding, swimming, tennis, and miniature golf.

Like most everything else at Kah-Nee-Ta, the greens fees are reasonably priced: It's $38 all the time for adults and $22 for juniors. The 5,828-yard course is easy to walk, but for those who prefer to ride, carts are available for $25 a round. The course has a snack bar and a pro shop, where clubs may be rented for $10. Golf packages are available. The public can reserve tee times two weeks in advance; resort guests can reserve any time when they make room reservations. And by the way, a nice half-hour Swedish massage at Kah-Nee-Ta's Spa Wanapine is only $40, or you can splurge with the half-hour deep muscle massage for only $50.

To get to Kah-Nee-Ta from Madras, travel 15 miles toward Portland on U.S. Highway 26 until you reach the Confederated Tribes of Warm Springs reservation town of Warm Springs. Turn north at the sign, and continue 12 miles until the road ends at the resort. To find out more about the resort, see our Resorts, Ranches, and Vacation Rentals chapter. For more information on the reservation, see our Other Communities chapter.

Nine Peaks Golf Course
1152 Northwest Golf Course Drive, Madras
(541) 475-3511

The name says it all. The views from all 18 holes here are pretty gorgeous, but No. 16

Insiders' Tip
Your drives are likely to travel farther at higher elevations.

puts you in sight of all nine peaks from Mount Bachelor north to Mount Hood. One of the reasons this course can claim such views is its wide open fairways. Since the pace is pretty relaxed here, you have time to take it all in. Summers are hot and dry, and winters have plenty of sunny days in the 50s and 60s when you can grab your clubs on a moment's notice.

This is definitely one of our more mellow golf courses. Most of the time, walk-ins are welcome. Greens fees are an easy $22, and it's another $20 for a cart; most folks walk the fairly level 6,280 yards. The course has a snack shop and pro shop (clubs rent for $5.00), but there is no staff pro and no lessons. Who needs 'em when you've got such a nice place to relax and play as you are? Nine Peaks takes Discover as well as MasterCard and Visa.

Golf Shops

All our golf courses except Mountain High in Bend have pro shops where you can purchase equipment and related golf items. If you want to rent equipment, you may do so at all 21 public golf courses. There are three Central Oregon golf shops that sell equipment as well as apparel and accessories.

Bend

High Desert Golf
20420 Robal Lane
(541) 389-3919, (800) 659-3919

Located behind Mountain View Mall, High Desert Golf features one of the top 100 driving ranges in the United States, with two levels and 64 hitting stations. Its golf shop has an on-site, full-service workshop. They can build custom equipment and will repair or refinish your old clubs in a jiffy. It's also well stocked with equipment and apparel for men, women, and juniors. High Desert Golf is open seven days a week from 9:00 A.M. to 7:00 P.M., and accepts MasterCard, Visa, American Express, Discover, and Diner's Club.

Las Vegas Discount Golf & Tennis
1180 South U.S. Highway 97
(541) 383-2944

Located next to the Outback Steak House, this store offers a complete line of equipment, a ladies boutique, and an indoor driving range. They can also do re-gripping and re-shafting. Open seven days a week, Las Vegas accepts MasterCard, Visa, American Express, and Discover.

Redmond

The Missing Link Discount Golf Shop
1935 U.S. Highway 97, Redmond
(541) 923-3426, (800) 310-3426

At The Missing Link's new location just south of the Safeway in Redmond, you can buy a full line of new equipment. They also take trade-ins, sell used equipment, and have a shop where they can customize clubs and perform repairs. In summer, The Missing Link is open seven days a week; in the off-season, they're open Monday through Saturday. MasterCard and Visa are accepted.

Fishing

In Central Oregon, anglers are as ubiquitous to our rivers and lakes as fish. No fair-weather fishers, you'll see them out pounding the water winter, spring, summer, and fall, rain or shine. And there is plenty of water to pound. Our forest lakes and desert lakes are full of trout. Some have salmon and bass as well. The region is criss-crossed with crystal-clear streams, both large and small, with the Deschutes River the centerpiece of it all. And the gorgeous scenery that seems to surround just about all our streams and lakes makes fishing here all the more pleasant.

It's pretty easy to get started fishing in these parts. If you need gear, a jaunt to a local fishing shop will take care of that. And, although fishing equipment may be a bit expensive these days, the advice you'll get from shop staff isn't—and it's worth its weight in fish. Most employees of local fishing shops are well-versed in the ways of the wily trout that inhabit Central Oregon waters. Ask lots of questions, especially if you are new in town. They can help you decide where to go, when to go, and what kind of gear, flies, lures, and bait you'll need.

And since many fishing shops run guide services as well, they can also take you fishing. There are quite a few fishing guides in Central Oregon, as you might expect, who run trips to many area lakes, reservoirs, and rivers. Some are fly-fishing only, some specialize in lure fishing, others do it all. Hiring a guide is not only ideal for beginning anglers looking to maximize their enjoyment of a day on the river and fishing success, but can also be a great way for experienced anglers new to the area to familiarize themselves with local waters before striking out on their own.

We've put together an overview of Central Oregon's favorite fishing hot spots as well as a list of local guides and outfitters to help you make the most of your fishing expeditions, whether you plan to go it alone or hire an expert. Either way, if you're not hooked on Central Oregon fishing, it's only because you haven't tried it yet.

Central Oregon Sport Fish

Although there are a variety of game fish here, Central Oregon is trout country. Rainbow trout are the primary native trout species, often referred to locally as "redsides" or "redbands." Over the past century, non-native brook, lake, and brown trout, raised in hatcheries, have been introduced into streams, lakes, and rivers throughout the state, including Central Oregon. Other species of fish that are stocked in area waters include land-locked Atlantic salmon, a native to the East Coast and northern Europe, and kokanee salmon. Kokanee are landlocked sockeye salmon and are native to the Pacific Northwest.

Probably the most prized, and most difficult to catch, Central Oregon fish is the steelhead. Steelhead are a form of rainbow trout that live their adult lives in the ocean, returning to the stream where they were born to spawn. These spawning runs of steelhead enter the Deschutes River from July through October, with the best fishing usually in September. Because of the high-protein food available to these fish while they are in the ocean, steelhead grow considerably larger than their freshwater-bound cousins. Steelhead in the 20-pound range are caught on the lower Deschutes River, however the average is more like five to eight pounds.

One of the more interesting game fish here is the bull trout. This fish is related to brook trout and for many years was deliberately eliminated from Pacific Northwest streams and lakes because they preyed on other trout and salmon species that were regarded as more valuable to anglers. But attitudes changed over the years, and today there is a highly prized trophy bull trout fishery at Lake Billy Chinook, where these fish may grow to more than 20 pounds (see the Lake Billy Chinook listing). Unfortunately, bull trout were recently designated under the Endangered Species Act as under threat of possible extinction due to the destruction of their habitat throughout much of their range.

There is also a small number of warmwater game fish in a few area ponds and reservoirs, including largemouth and smallmouth bass, bullhead, and crappie, with their own cadre of sportsmen and women dedicated to catching them at every opportunity.

Fishing Regulations

Angling regulations in Oregon tend to be a bit complex, so before you put your worm on the hook you'll need to take a careful look at the rules in force for the place you intend to fish. In Central Oregon, there is quite a mix of regulations for our various streams and rivers, including different fishing seasons for different stretches of river and different species of fish. Many Central Oregon streams are now open year-round. Some streams allow fishing with bait while others are restricted to flies or lures with barbless hooks. Bag limits vary too, of course, although many anglers today practice catch-and-release whether or not it is required on the stream they are fishing. Many rivers and streams where year-round fishing is permitted have catch-and-release, fly, or lure fishing-only rules during the winter months.

In order to protect self-sustaining wild populations of trout, steelhead, and salmon, many Central Oregon streams have regulations that allow you to take home only fish stocked from hatcheries. All wild fish must be released unharmed. To help anglers tell the difference, hatchery fish have their adipose fin, which is a small fin on the back, just forward of the tail fin, clipped before they are stocked. So when you catch a trout, salmon, or steelhead with a complete, unclipped adipose fin, you've got a wild one on your hands.

In addition to the current issue of the *Oregon Sport Fishing Regulations,* you'll also need a fishing license and a salmon-steelhead tag if you intend to fish for those species. Resident annual fishing licenses are $19.75. To be considered a resident you must have lived in Oregon for at least six months. Licenses for kids ages 14 to 17 are $6.75. Younger children don't need a fishing license. Nonresident annual licenses are $48.50. If your fishing plans are short-term, you can also buy one-day and seven-day licenses for $8.00 and $34.75, respectively. If you aspire to catch a lower Deschutes steelhead, a salmon-steelhead tag is $16.50, in addition to your regular license. You can get licenses, tags, and regulation booklets at any fishing shop or sporting-goods shop (see the listing of guides and outfitters at the end of the chapter). For certain Central Oregon waters that are on or border the Warm Springs Indian Reservation, a tribal fishing permit is required. For more information see the descriptions for Lake Billy Chinook, Lake Simtustus, and the lower Deschutes River within this chapter. Specific questions about state fishing regulations, and some advice on where to fish as well, can be had from the staff at the local Oregon Department of Fish and Wildlife office. Their address is listed below in the "Fishing Events" section.

Lakes and Reservoirs

Bend Area

Cascade Lakes

Although many anglers make a beeline to Central Oregon's crystal-clear trout streams and rivers, the Cascade Lakes offer some of the best fishing opportunities in the area, particularly for non–fly fishers. There are more than a dozen lakes, both large and small, easily accessible from the Cascade Lakes Highway, southwest of Bend, or west of La Pine. A number of the larger ones have resorts where you may buy fishing gear and licenses and rent boats. Cabins and campgrounds are also available at many of these areas. While a couple of these high-country lakes are fly-fishing only, most allow anglers to use a variety of baits and lures. Make sure you check the state fishing regulations before you go.

Some of the largest and most popular fishing lakes in the central Cascades may also be reached from the La Pine area via County Roads 42 and 43. Because the northern portion of the Cascade Lakes Highway is generally closed by snow until Memorial Day, these roads also provide anglers with early-season access to the southernmost Cascade lakes.

For additional information on the lakes listed below, see our Daytrips and Resorts, Ranches, and Vacation Rentals chapters. You can also find more information about the High Cascade Lakes in the Other Outdoor Recreation and Camping chapters.

Cultus Lake

This lake, up to 200 feet deep, is off the Cascade Lakes Highway around 50 miles from Bend. While there are medium-size rainbow trout here in the 8- to 12-inch range, Cultus Lake anglers often come here specifically for the lake trout, which grow up to eight pounds and more. To catch these big guys, you'll need to troll deep with lures. There are brook trout here as well. You can rent a boat at Cultus Lake Resort.

Crane Prairie Reservoir

Crane Prairie Reservoir covers some 5 square miles and was created by the damming of the upper Deschutes River. It is extremely popular with anglers, who find a variety of sport fish, including rainbow trout, brook trout, and kokanee salmon. And the fish here get big. Although rainbow trout average around a foot long, a five-pound fish isn't a big deal. And they have been known to approach 20 pounds. Brook trout in the six-pound range have been caught. Anglers hook these fish on

just about anything from worms and lures to flies. Largemouth bass were illegally introduced into the lake in the late 1970s, providing warm-water anglers with sport as well, although there are concerns about the long-term effects of these fish on the local trophy trout population, as bass are known to feed on young trout and salmon. You'll want a boat to make the most of a Crane Prairie Reservoir fishing trip. You can rent one at Crane Prairie Resort.

Davis Lake

The southernmost lake along the Cascade Lakes Highway, Davis Lake is fly-fishing-only, with rainbow trout the primary quarry, although there are some largemouth bass here as well. This rather shallow lake is located in a beautiful forest setting with great views of the Cascade Mountains to the west. It is possible to wade portions of the lake, although you'll be better off with a float tube or canoe.

Devils Lake

You'll find Devils Lake right along the Cascade Lakes Highway about 29 miles from Bend. It's a small, shallow lake with rainbow and brook trout and a perfect place to take kids for an afternoon of fishing.

Elk Lake

Elk Lake is more popular with sailors and sailboarders than with anglers, but it does have kokanee salmon and brook trout up to 14 inches long. The lake is off the Cascade Lakes Highway about 32 miles from Bend. You can rent boats at Elk Lake Resort.

Hosmer Lake

This dumbbell-shaped lake nestled beneath Mount Bachelor is a favorite destination for fly fishers who pursue the landlocked Atlantic salmon stocked here by the state. There are also brook trout here that may reach up to four pounds, although they are wary and more difficult to catch than the salmon. You'll need a boat or float tube to be successful, as bank access can be difficult due to the dense vegetation. This lake is limited to fly-fishing-only with barbless hooks, and all salmon must be released unharmed. This lake is also a favorite of canoeists (see our Daytrips and Other Outdoor Recreation chapters).

Lava Lake

This lake is one of the best rainbow trout fisheries in Central Oregon. The rainbows here may approach 20 inches in length. Brook trout are also present. As with most of the High Cascade Lakes, you're better off with a boat, which can be rented at Lava Lake Lodge. However, anglers fishing from shore with bait and lures also do just fine. You'll find Lava Lake 38 miles from Bend off the Cascade Lakes Highway.

Little Lava Lake

Located about a quarter-mile southeast of Lava Lake, this lake is the source of the Deschutes River. You'll do best fishing here for brook and rainbow trout—which reach up to 15 inches in length—if you have a boat. You can rent boats at nearby Lava Lake Lodge at Lava Lake.

North Twin Lake

North Twin Lake is 44 miles from Bend off the Cascade Lakes Highway and has rainbow trout that average around 10 inches. Fishing here tends to be pretty good, although South Twin Lake is a bit more popular because of the amenities available at Twin Lakes Resort (see the listing for South Twin Lake below and in the Resorts, Ranches, and Vacation Rentals chapter).

South Twin Lake

Odds of having a successful day of rainbow trout fishing are consistently pretty good at South Twin Lake. Anglers catch them on just about anything, including lures and flies, although bait seems to be the favorite method. The trout here aren't especially big, averaging around only 10 inches, but they're great fun to catch on those days when they're really biting. South Twin Lake is about 40 miles from Bend, off the Cascade Lakes Highway. There is a full-service resort at the lake where you may rent a boat.

Sparks Lake

Located 28 miles from Bend along the Cascade Lakes Highway, Sparks Lake is a fly-fishing-only body of water in a gorgeous mountain setting. Because it's rather shallow, it offers a particular challenge to anglers, who must make careful and delicate fly presentations to avoid scaring their quarry away. You'll find rainbow and brook trout plying the waters of Sparks Lake. Fishing from a boat or canoe is best.

Todd Lake

The Todd Lake turnoff is off the Cascade Lakes Highway about 23 miles from Bend. A 100-yard trail leads to this 45-acre lake. Fishing here is for brook trout up to 15 inches in length. There is also limited walk-in camping.

Wickiup Reservoir

This reservoir, as with Crane Prairie Reservoir, was formed by damming the upper Deschutes River. When it is full, it is about 10,000 acres in size, making it the largest lake in the area. It's also well-known for its trophy brown trout fishery. Anglers have caught brown trout here in the 10-pound range, although the average fish is more like 2 or 3 pounds. You'll also find rainbow trout and kokanee salmon—a favorite quarry of anglers here. Fishing from the banks is workable; if you want a chance at the big ones, you really need a boat. You can rent one from Twin Lakes Resort and from there access Wickiup Reservoir via the reservoir's Deschutes River arm.

Sisters/Camp Sherman Area

Suttle Lake

This easily accessible gem is located right off U.S. Highway 20 about 14 miles west of Sisters. Brown and rainbow trout ply its waters along with kokanee salmon. A warm summer afternoon will find whole families settled in along the shore with lawn chairs, lunches, and lines in the water, watching their bobbers for a fish to bite. Offshore, the serious kokanee fishermen troll lures back and forth across the lake all day long.

Three Creek Lake

You'll find this lake at the 6,600-foot level in the high country 17 miles south of Sisters off Three Creek Road. Rainbow and brook trout here grow to an average of 8 to 15 inches. Nestled in a bowl beneath the spectacular Tam McArthur Rim on the edge of the Three Sisters Wilderness, this 78-acre lake can be very busy during the summer months. You can fish from the bank or rent a small boat at the Three Creek Lake resort. There are also two campgrounds here. The lake is in the Deschutes National Forest.

Sunriver/La Pine Area

East Lake

Located in the Newberry National Volcanic Monument about 25 miles south of Bend off U.S. Highway 97, East Lake has been a longtime local fishing hot spot. At 1,044 acres in size and 180 feet deep, it holds a prolific fishery of rainbow trout, Atlantic salmon, kokanee salmon, and brown trout. Anglers here use bait, lures, and flies and sometimes catch a monster-size brown trout. The current record is a 22½-pounder. Boats may be rented at East Lake Resort.

Paulina Lake

Paulina Lake is 250 feet deep and sprawls over 1,531 acres on Newberry National Volcanic Monument. It has rainbow and brown trout along with kokanee salmon.

The rainbow trout here average 9 to 14 inches, although there are some 5-pounders swimming about the lake's depths as well. You can rent boats at Paulina Lake Resort. Paulina Lake is 25 miles south of Bend off U.S. 97.

Prineville Area

Antelope Flat Reservoir

The fast-growing rainbow trout at Antelope Flat Reservoir average about a foot long, although the odds aren't too bad for catching 18-inchers. A smallish body of water of about 170 acres, this is a popular spot for locals who fish with bait from the bank. In recent years, fly fishermen using float tubes have been visiting here as well. Antelope Flat Reservoir is about 30 miles southeast of Prineville in the Maury Mountains section of the Ochoco National Forest. It is located off Forest Service Road 17.

Ochoco Reservoir

Just 5 miles east of Prineville, this reservoir offers very good rainbow trout fishing, especially in the spring and fall. Anglers here use flies, bait, and lures from both the bank and boats with good success. It is also a fairly popular ice-fishing spot, and one of the few in Central Oregon, since most lakes here are buried by snow during the winter months. Ochoco Reservoir is located adjacent to U.S. Highway 26.

Prineville Reservoir

Known for its largemouth and small-mouth bass fishing, Prineville Reservoir was formed by damming the Crooked River. When it is full, it covers about 5 square miles. Rainbow trout are also stocked here. Worms are the bait of choice of anglers, who fish from the bank and from boats. Prineville Reservoir is about 12 miles southeast of Prineville. The most popular access point is at Prineville Reservoir State Park via Juniper Canyon Road (see our Parks chapter).

Walton Lake

Hidden away in the Ochoco National Forest about 25 miles northeast of Prineville, this lake is stocked with rainbow trout that average 8 to 10 inches long, although you may sometimes catch a nice 16-incher. Anglers here use flies, bait, and lures, and the lake is small enough to easily fish from the bank. There are two Forest Service campgrounds, which can be quite busy during summer weekends. Boats with gas-powered motors are not allowed. You can reach Walton Lake by driving east from Prineville on U.S. 26 to County Road 23, then following Forest Service Road 22 to the campgrounds.

Madras Area

Haystack Reservoir

Haystack Reservoir, 8 miles south of Madras and a couple of miles east of U.S. 97 in the Crooked River National Grassland, contains largemouth bass, kokanee salmon, rainbow trout, bullhead, and crappie. Because of its open banks, Haystack Reservoir is easily fished from shore.

Lake Billy Chinook

This heavily visited reservoir is located in The Cove Palisades State Park 15 miles southwest of Madras off U.S. 97. It has brown and rainbow trout as well as smallmouth and largemouth bass. However, kokanee salmon and bull trout are the most-sought-after fish species here. Fishermen troll lures throughout the lake in search of kokanee and gather in hordes on the lake's Metolius arm in September, when these landlocked salmon begin to congregate for their annual spawning run up the Metolius River. At this time of year, anglers may catch 15 or 20 in a single day with little trouble. Bull trout are usually caught by trolling large lures that imitate minnows in deep water. Bull trout in the lake average 10 to 15 pounds but can grow up to 23 pounds. You'll need a boat to fish here, which can be rented at the park's two marinas. For more information on Lake Billy Chinook and The Cove Palisades State Park, see the Parks chapter. Because the Metolius arm of the reservoir borders the Warm Springs Indian Reservation, you must have a tribal fishing permit, in additional to your state fishing license, to fish this section. Per-

mits are $6.25 and may be purchased at most Central Oregon sporting-goods stores and fly shops (see the list of guides and outfitters later in the chapter). You can obtain more information by calling the Confederated Tribes of Warm Springs at (541) 553–3233.

Lake Simtustus

Adjoining Lake Billy Chinook immediately to the north (see the Lake Billy Chinook description), Lake Simtustus is a long, narrow reservoir containing rainbow trout and kokanee salmon. Because Lake Simtustus is within the Warm Springs Indian Reservation, the extra permitting is the same as with Lake Billy Chinook, listed above. You should also see our Parks chapter for more information.

Rivers and Streams

Bend Area

Middle Deschutes River

With so many places to fish in Central Oregon, visitors, as well as locals, often forget they're in a town where a river runs through it. While the stretch of the Deschutes River that flows through Bend isn't on anybody's list of the area's hottest fishing spots, it nevertheless offers some surprisingly decent angling opportunities. And the beauty of it is, it's just a few blocks away from just about anyplace in the city. You can spend a quiet evening wetting a fly just a few minutes' drive (or walk) from your home or hotel and maybe even get in a few casts before breakfast. Since many Bend-area parks have been established along the Deschutes River, there are quite a few places with public access. Rainbow trout are the fish most commonly associated with the Deschutes River; however, the Bend stretch is reputed to harbor a good population of brown trout as well.

There are several parks in the area where you can begin your urban fishing experience, including Drake Park, in the downtown area, and at Harmon Park directly across the river from Drake Park. The river along Pioneer Park on Northwest

Hall and Portland Avenue also has possibilities. Sawyer Park on O. B. Riley Road, in the north part of town, is a good bet as well. The Deschutes River Trail passes through this park, providing the urban angler with additional access to the river. You can ride your bike along the trail, allowing you to fish more water in a shorter period of time (see the Mountain Biking section of the Other Outdoor Recreation chapter for more information on the Deschutes River Trail). The fast water just downstream from the bridge at Colorado Avenue is also worth a cast or two.

Moving west, just outside the city limits, is Tumalo State Park off U.S. 20, with great access to the Deschutes River. You'll run into private property more quickly if you fish downriver, so your best bet is to head upstream.

Sisters/Camp Sherman Area

Metolius River

Originating from springs in the Three Sisters Wilderness, the Metolius River flows fully formed from the ground near Camp Sherman, a dozen miles west of Sisters. It is surely the most beautiful stream in Central Oregon, crystal-clear and cold, as it snakes its way through old-growth ponderosa pine forest interspersed with cedars, its bank lined with dense vegetation. Because it is spring-fed and maintains a temperature in the 39 to 40 degree range, it is not as productive a fishery as some of the other trout streams in Central Oregon, and it takes some practice to learn how to fish it well. But the many anglers who fish here year-round are testimony to the outstanding fishing experience the river can provide to those who take the time to know it.

Most of the angling on the Metolius River takes place between Camp Sherman and Bridge 99, 7 miles downstream. This stretch is fly-fishing-only, and all trout must be released unharmed. Rainbow trout are the primary quarry, although there are bull trout present as well. Downstream from Bridge 99 you are allowed to fish with lures as well as flies. The Metolius River is located in the Deschutes National Forest and has numerous campgrounds along the stretch between Camp Sherman and Bridge 99. To get there go

During late summer and fall, anglers flock to the middle and lower Deschutes River to fish for steelhead, king of sportfish. PHOTO: JIM YUSKAVITCH

west on U.S. 20 for about 8 miles, then turn right onto Forest Service Road 14 at the Camp Sherman turnoff and follow it for about 6 miles to the river.

Redmond Area

Middle Deschutes River

The most commonly fished stretch of the Deschutes River in the Redmond area is at Lower Bridge. To get there drive north from Redmond on U.S. 97 for about 5 miles, then turn left onto Northwest Lower Bridge Way, immediately north of Terrebonne. Head down this road for about 6 miles to the river crossing and a parking area on the left. Years ago this was a secret spot for locals. It's a bit more popular today, although by no means overcrowded.

Because a considerable amount of water is pumped from the river during the summer to irrigate nearby farmers' crops, the best time to go is in the early spring, especially on the occasional warm, sunny day in March. No need to get up early either; the fish here don't start biting until midmorning, after the sun has been up for a few hours. The riverbanks are heavily vegetated with willows and other shrubs, making the water a bit of a tussle to get to.

Once you're there, wade along the bank and cast your fly close to the river's edge, where brown trout like to lie in wait. There are some nice trout, in the 14- to 16-inch range, to be taken here. Current fishing regulations allow you to use only flies and lures on this portion of the river. You'll catch more fish with flies. The Lower Bridge area is open to fishing year-round.

Sunriver/La Pine Area

Upper Deschutes River

The upper Deschutes River near its headwaters provides a fine small-stream fishing experience. The most popular section is the reach between Crane Prairie Reservoir and the campground at Deschutes Bridge, at the junction of the Cascade Lakes Highway and Forest Road 4270 in the Deschutes National Forest. There are lots of small brook trout here as well as wild, native rainbow trout, which must be released unharmed.

Fall River

Fall River is a pretty little spring-fed trout stream that rises in the Deschutes National Forest north of Wickiup Reservoir. It is restricted to fly-fishing only with barbless hooks, and all wild rainbow trout must be released unharmed (hatchery trout have clipped fins to aid in their identification). There are also brook trout and brown trout present. Fall River is about 16 miles south of Bend along Forest Road 42. The lower 4 miles of the river flow through private lands. A small section of the river passes through LaPine State Park (see our Parks chapter).

Prineville Area

Crooked River

Bowman Dam on the Crooked River, which holds the body of water southeast of Prineville known as Prineville Reservoir, has also resulted in some pretty good fishing in the river below by creating what is known as a tailwater fishery. This occurs because cold water from the reservoir is released into the river below, helping to keep water temperatures at an optimum level. The result is that you will find fine rainbow-trout fishing on this

Insiders' Tip

Polarizing sunglasses are an important item in any angler's kit. They not only protect your eyes from the glaring High Desert sun, but they also allow you to better see beneath the surface of the water as you search for fish.

stretch of river, with lots of pools and riffles. Bowman Dam is about 19 miles south of Prineville on Oregon Highway 27. The 6 or 7 miles below the dam is generally the best fishing segment, with public lands along the banks and numerous campgrounds and picnic areas as well. The Crooked River is open to fishing year-round. It is restricted to fly-fishing and catch-and-release only during the winter, although most anglers here practice those techniques all the time.

Madras Area

Lower Deschutes River

The lower Deschutes is Central Oregon's blue-ribbon trout and steelhead stream. Deschutes River rainbow trout, genetically distinctive to this river and often referred to as "redsides," are among the most beautiful rainbow trout you'll ever catch, and they typically run in the 10- to 15-inch range. While rainbow trout are available to anglers all year, steelhead move into the river from July through October. The Deschutes was once a first-class chinook salmon fishery as well, but populations of these fish have declined significantly in recent years, primarily due to human-caused factors. The river is sometimes opened to angling for these Pacific Northwest icons when population levels permit.

The most-fished part of the river is the reach between Warm Springs and Trout Creek, about 17 miles downriver, because there is quite a bit of bank access and very good trout-fishing water. The area upstream and downstream from Maupin, about 43 river miles downstream from Warm Springs, is also a popular stretch to fish as there is public bank access and a gravel road running along the river. But floating by raft or drift boat is by far the best way to fish the Deschutes since it allows you to reach some of its best fishing spots that are inaccessible to bank anglers and waders. Because it is illegal to fish from a boat on the Deschutes, the typical method is to float the river, stopping to fish at various likely spots for a while, then moving on. This allows anglers to fish good spots around gravel bars in the middle of the river that nonboaters can't get to.

Because there are many rapids on the lower Deschutes, you'll want to have some white-water experience before running it on your own. Many local fishing guides offer float trips on the lower Deschutes (see the listings later in this chapter). If you're unfamiliar with the river, you may want to hire one for a daytrip, or longer. Because of the lower Deschutes' combination of rapids and striking desert canyon scenery, many outfitters also offer white-water rafting trips here as well (see the listings in the Other Outdoor Recreation chapter).

Most of the lower Deschutes is limited to fly-fishing or lures. Most anglers on the river are fly fishers, although many switch to lures during the steelhead season. Because the river borders the Warm Springs Indian Reservation for 31 miles, there are some special regulations in effect. Nonmembers of the tribe are restricted to fishing on the eastern half of the river that borders the reservation only, except for a 6-mile segment between Dry Creek and Trout Creek. Here, anglers are permitted to fish both sides of the river, including along the banks of the reservation. But you must have a tribal fishing permit, in addition to your state fishing license. Permits are $6.25 and may be purchased at most Central Oregon sporting-goods stores and fly shops (see the list of guides and outfitters later in this chapter). You can obtain more information by calling the Confederated Tribes of Warm Springs at (541) 553–3233.

Fishing Events

Free Fishing Weekend
Oregon Department of Fish and Wildlife,
61374 Parrell Road, Bend
(541) 388–6363

Held on the second Saturday in June, Free Fishing Weekend is an opportunity for residents and visitors alike to get out and fish without needing a license, although all other state angling regulations still apply. A number of related activities, especially for kids, are held at various locations throughout Central Oregon (and at about 70 locations statewide) that may include fishing, games, environmental education programs, and fish- and nature-related art activities. For the adults, fishing clinics and classes are often held during this day as well, making it a good opportunity for beginning fishermen to learn basic techniques and for more experienced anglers to learn new skills.

Central Oregon events typically are held at Prineville Reservoir State Park, Sun-river Marina, and Wizard Falls Hatchery; however, exact locations may vary from year to year, so you'll need to double-check for the latest schedule of event locations. Free camping is often offered at area state parks and National Forest campgrounds in conjunction with Free Fishing Weekend.

Kids Fishing Day
Crook County Parks and Recreation, Northeast 398 Fairview Street, Prineville
(541) 447–1209

This event is sponsored by Crook County Parks and Recreation and local members of Trout Unlimited, a national fish conservation organization. It's a day of family fishing for rainbow trout in Ochoco Creek at Prineville's Ochoco Park, with prizes for all the kids no matter how big or small their catches are. Ochoco Park is on Northeast Fourth Street between North Elm Street and Fairview Street North (see also the Parks chapter). Kids Fishing Day is generally held on a day during the second week of June.

Guides and Outfitters

Bastian's Rising Trout Fly Fishing Guides
21811 Hideaway Hills, Bend
(541) 382–7852

This outfit specializes in the fine art of dry-fly-fishing for rainbow trout and steelhead on the lower Deschutes River between Warm Springs and its mouth. All-day float trips are $375 per person. Overnight trips are $300 per person, with a three-person minimum. They supply all food and can set you up with gear as well, if you don't own your own.

Camp Sherman Store & Fly Shop
Camp Sherman
(541) 595–6711

In addition to a complete selection of fly-fishing gear, this shop can set you up with fully-guided fishing trips on the Deschutes, Santiam, Crooked, and McKenzie Rivers, along with area lakes. One-day river fishing trips are $275 per person. Lake excursions are $300 for two people for a full day and

$200 for two for a half day. Guided trips include all equipment. For experienced fly fishers with their own gear, a "river taxi" is available, consisting of a boat, shuttle, and bare-bones guide service on the Deschutes River for $185 for up to three people.

Carbone's Fly-Fishing Guides and Outfitters
1946 Northwest Awbrey Road, Bend
(541) 389-7599

Local fishing guide Rodger Carbone offers one- and three-day fly-fishing drift boat trips down the lower Deschutes, from Warm Springs to Trout Creek or Maupin, depending on how long you want to stay on the river. Daytrips are $180 per person with a minimum of two people. Three-day trips cost $795 per person with a minimum of four people. He can also arrange for equipment rental for clients without their own fishing gear.

Cascade Guides & Outfitters/The Hook Fly Shop
Sunriver Village Mall, Building 21, Sunriver
(541) 593-2358

Based out of The Hook Fly Shop, Cascade Guides and Outfitters' most popular guided fishing trip is a float down the lower Deschutes for rainbow trout. A full-day trip for two people is $350. For three people it's $450. An overnight excursion is $550 per person. They also offer longer trips at $275 per day per person, with a three day, three-person minimum. Steelhead trips on the lower Deschutes are $375 for two people. They also guide on Davis, Hosmer, and East Lakes as well as Crane Prairie Reservoir. An all-day guided lake fishing trip (which includes a boat) is $325 for one to two people and $425 for three people. Half-day trips are $225 for up to two people and $325 for three. Walk-in guided trips on the Crooked, Fall, and upper Deschutes Rivers are $325 for a full day for a minimum of two people. Half-day walk-in trips are $150 per person and $50 for each additional angler. They also offer a fly-fishing school for $200 per person. The Hook Fly Shop also has a full complement of fly-fishing gear for sale.

Crane Prairie Resort/Mickey Finn Guides
Off Cascade Highway, 46 miles southwest of Bend
(541) 383-3939

With 30 years experience helping clients catch fish in the Cascade lakes, Mickey Finn Guides will take you in pursuit of lunker trout and fightin' bass for $295 per day for the first two people and another $75 per person for each additional angler. They guide on all the Cascade Lakes Highway–area lakes, although they specialize in fishing Crane Prairie Reservoir.

Deschutes River Outfitters
61115 South U.S. Highway 97, Bend
(541) 388-8191

Deschutes River Outfitters has 15 guides available to take anglers on guided float fly-fishing trips on the lower Deschutes, walk-in trips to the upper Deschutes, Fall, and Crooked Rivers, as well as excursions to such Cascade Lakes Highway hot spots as Hosmer Lake, East Lake, Davis Lake, and Crane Prairie and Wickiup Reservoirs. Lower Deschutes River float trips are $300 for one angler, $350 for two, and $450 for three. Three-day trips run from $2,000 for two people up to $5,400 for six. Four-day trips range from $2,600 for two people to $7,200 for six. A full-day walk-in guided river trip is $300 for one or two anglers. Half-day trips cost $200 for two. Cascade Lakes trips are $325 per day for one to two people. A half-day of lake fishing costs $225 for one or two anglers. Deschutes River Outfitters also has a full complement of fly-fishing gear for sale, including many hand-tied flies.

Fin N Feather Fly Shop
785 West Third Street, Prineville
(541) 447-8691

For $275 for one or two persons, guides from the Fin N Feather Fly Shop will not only take you on a walk-in, daylong fishing trip to the nearby Crooked River, but will also instruct you on identifying aquatic insects and tying the flies that imitate them, right along the banks of the river. A half-day outing is $175. Fin N Feather Fly Shop also sells a full complement of fly-fishing gear.

Fishing on the Fly
P.O. Box 242, Bend
(541) 389–3252

In May, June, and July, guide Tim Dority will take you down the lower Deschutes River by drift boat in quest of rainbow trout; from August through October, the action switches to steelhead fishing by jet-boat. Fishing on the Fly has equipment available for rent, will cook your lunch right along the river, and guarantees you 10 hours of actual fishing time over the course of the day. The cost for a day trip is $175 per person.

Fly & Field Outfitters
143A Southwest Century Drive, Bend
(541) 318–1661

The High Cascade lakes, the Crooked and Deschutes Rivers, and some select private lakes are on the guided fly-fishing menu at Fly & Field Outfitters. An all-day lake fishing trip is $300 for one or two people. A half-day outing is $200 for one or two anglers. You can also do a one-day, two-lake trip for $350 for up to two anglers. Walk-in river trips are $300 per day for one to two anglers and $100 for each additional angler up to four. Half-day walk-ins are $175 for up to two people and $50 for each additional person. Lower Deschutes trips run $350 for up to two anglers and $450 for three. Multiday trips are $275 per day per person, with a three-day minimum. They also teach still-water and river fly-fishing classes, which include equipment, instruction, lunch, and one half-day of fishing for $200 per person. Fly-casting lessons are $40 an hour for private lessons and $25 for group lessons. In addition, Fly & Field Outfitters offers a full selection of fly-fishing and upland game bird and waterfowl hunting equipment.

The Fly Box
1293 Northeast Third Street, Bend
(541) 388–3330

You can book a variety of guided fishing excursions at this Bend fly shop, including one-day and multiday float trips on the lower Deschutes for trout and steelhead, walk-in trips on the Crooked and Deschutes Rivers, as well as excursions to some private trout lakes. One-day Deschutes River trip rates are $290 for one person, $360 for two people, and $425 for three people. Overnight trips are $475 per person, with a two-person minimum. Three- to five-day trips are $275 per person per day. A full-day walk-in trip on the Deschutes is $190 for one person and $275 for two. An all-day walk-in on the Crooked River is also $190 per person. Fishing on private trout lakes costs $150 per person per day. The Fly Box also offers private fly-fishing lessons for $195 for one person, $275 for two, and $350 for three. They supply all equipment needed for the class. The Fly Box also has a full complement of fly-fishing gear for sale.

The Fly Fisher's Place
151 West Main Street, Sisters
(541) 549–3474

The Fly Fisher's Place owner, Jeff Perin, will set you up with guided daylong drift-boat trips down the Deschutes River from Warm Springs to Trout Creek for $330 per day for two people. McKenzie River float fishing trips cost $275 per day for two people. For $250, two anglers can get a guided walk-in fishing trip on the Crooked River. Lunches are provided on daytrips, along with some equipment. The Fly Fisher's Place also sells a full complement of fly-fishing gear.

Garrison's Guide Service
P.O. Box 4113, Sunriver
(541) 593–8394

With seven guides available, this outfit covers virtually all the fishable lakes, streams, and rivers in the Deschutes National Forest. They specialize in spin-fishing from pontoon boats but will take clients on fly-fishing adventures as well. Spin-fishing rates are $150 per day for the first person and $75 each for additional anglers. Guided fly-fishing costs $200 per day for the first angler and $40 each for additional people.

Catch-and-Release Tips

Catch-and-release fishing is becoming increasingly popular in Central Oregon, as in the rest of the country. And in some streams, it is mandatory. To release a fish unharmed, make sure you wet your hands before touching the fish lest you rub off its protective, slimy coating. And don't stick your fingers in its gills. After carefully removing the hook, gently lower the fish back into the water, cradling it in the palm of your hand (or hands if it's a big one!). Let the fish rest for a moment, and it will swim off. If it is exhausted from the fight and lethargic, or even motionless, you can still probably revive it. Cradle the fish in the water with its mouth facing upstream. This allows water, from which the fish derives oxygen, to flow through its gills. If you are in a lake or reservoir, with no current, move the fish forward and backward in the water to manually force water through its gills. This will usually revive a fish that has not been somehow fatally injured during the process of being caught.

John Judy Flyfishing
P.O. Box 122, Camp Sherman
(541) 595–2073

John Judy Flyfishing will take you on one-day guided fishing trips down the lower Deschutes River for trout until mid-August, then for the elusive steelhead thereafter. Daylong guided floats are $375 for two people. Multiday guided float trips are $275 per day per person. John Judy also guides the guests at the House on the Metolius, a lodge at Camp Sherman (541–595–6620) along private riverside property. This is the only commercial-fishing guide service available on the Metolius River. However, you must be staying at the lodge to take advantage of it.

Oregon Llama Adventures
61702 Teal Road, Bend
(541) 382–5028, (888) 722–5262
www.packllama.com

For something a little bit different, try a fully-guided fly-fishing trip into the Three Sisters or Mount Jefferson Wilderness Areas with the assistance of llamas to carry your gear and food. Trips to spectacular alpine lake country are $200 per person per day, with a two-person minimum. They also offer fishing trips to the Blitzen River and Mann Lake in the remote desert country of southeast Oregon. All fishing gear, including float tubes, and lunch are included. Fishing les-sons are also available for about $50 per person, depending on the size of the group. See the Other Outdoor Recreation chapter for more outdoor excursions offered by Oregon Llama Adventures.

The Patient Angler
55 Northwest Wall Street, Bend
(541) 389–6208

This local fly-fishing store also arranges one- and three-day guided fishing trips on the lower Deschutes River for $180 per person for two or more people. Longer trips can also be arranged upon request. They also offer fishing trips to a few area private trout fishing lakes. Costs to visit these locations are $180 for one to two people and $250 per day for four to five people on weekdays. The rate is $300 per person on weekends, with a two night minimum. The Patient Angler also sells a full complement of fly-fishing gear.

Quest of the West
20640 Mary Way, Bend
(541) 389–0323

Quest of the West offers fishing trips for trout and steelhead on the lower Deschutes and McKenzie Rivers; for bass and steelhead on the John Day River, just east of the Central Oregon area; and for trout, bass, steelhead, and salmon on the Umpqua River west of Crater Lake National Park. Float trips cost $200 per

Gone Fly-Fishin'

One of the great things about visiting Central Oregon is that there are lots of easy-to-get-to places to fish close to hotels and resorts," says Jeff Perin, fly-fishing guide and owner of The Fly Fisher's Place fly shop in Sisters. And because there are so many nearby rivers to fish, you can easily get in a little time on the water during your visit. Here is some of Jeff's advice to help get your Central Oregon fly-fishing adventure off on the right foot.

Equipment

"Bring your favorite rod with you," advises Perin. "But make sure it balances with the kind of fishing we have here." Central Oregon guides usually recommend fly rods from 7½ to 9 feet long and a 2- to 6-weight line. Nine-foot-long leaders generally work well for all but the wariest of fish. You'll want chest waders, too. Many traveling anglers leave their waders behind to avoid the trouble of packing and lugging them. Perin counsels against that. "In many Central Oregon rivers, you'll need to wade out into the water to get to the fish," he says. When it comes to the contents of your fishing vest, all you need is a couple of fly boxes—one for dry flies and one for nymphs—plus clippers, forceps (for removing the hook from the fish's mouth), fly floatant, and extra leaders. Then stop in at an area fly shop and pick up a selection of the most effective local flies.

Best Bets for Anglers on a (Time) Budget

If you're like most people who visit Central Oregon, you probably have a list of things to do and see as long as your fly rod. So if you want to squeeze a little fly-fishing into your busy vacation schedule, you'll have to be efficient.

The first thing to figure out is where to go. Well, that's a fairly easy one. Most fly anglers in search of trout around these parts head to one of four rivers—the Deschutes, Crooked, Metolius, or Fall. But once you get there, then what? Read on for what you need to know to make the most of your precious time on each of these rivers. Also, check the listings in this chapter for additional river information.

Deschutes River

A true Western blue-ribbon trout stream, some stretches of this river harbor up to 4,000 trout per mile. You'll find area anglers talking about the Deschutes River as three separate segments—the upper Deschutes, from Bend upstream to its headwaters at Little Lava Lake; the middle Deschutes, from Bend to Warm Springs; and the lower Deschutes, from Warm Springs to its mouth on the Columbia River. Each stretch has its own character that dictates how to fish it.

The upper Deschutes changes from a small stream in the mountains to a good-size river by the time it reaches Bend. The best areas to fish here are around Wickiup and Crane Prairie Reservoirs and Little Lava Lake. "It's also known as a real nice brook trout fishery that some people really like," says Perin.

For visitors based in Bend or Redmond, the middle Deschutes may be your best bet. There is good access around Terrebonne and Crooked River Ranch, and it has a healthy population of brown and rainbow trout in the 12- to 14-inch range. Fishing is best here from Valentine's Day until mid-July. After that, the water becomes a bit too low for good angling.

Wading into the river and casting into the riffles and along the cattail-lined banks or directly at rising trout is the way to go here. If you're coming from out of town, call a local fly shop to see what kinds of insects will be hatching on the river during your visit. March Browns, Elk Hair Caddis, and Blue Winged Olives are typical flies that work well here. Fishing deep with nymphs is also an effective technique here, with Flash Back Pheasant Tails, Beadhead Princes, and Hare's Ears being good choices. Local guides suggest fishing weighted nymphs in the riffles on a floating line with a strike indicator. The area around Lower Bridge near Terrebonne can provide particularly nice dry-fly-fishing during February and March, especially during the warmer parts of the day between 11:00 A.M. and 3:00 P.M.

The lower Deschutes around Warm Springs and South Junction has good access for folks in cars or on foot. With about 4,000 rainbow trout (locally called Deschutes red-sides) per mile averaging around 16 inches in length, this is a prime place to wet a fly.

For dry-fly fisher-folk, the two weeks after Memorial Day are special on the Deschutes River because that's when the salmon flies—a large mayfly—hatch and begin crawling along the grassy banks and overhanging trees. The ones that fall into the water are gobbled up by voracious rainbow trout. Anglers join in the action by casting salmon fly imitations, including Clark's Stones and Sofa Pillows, along the banks. You'll want a good, stout rod of 9 or 9½ feet and 5- or 6-weight line to fish here.

The lower Deschutes is a difficult place to just show up and fish effectively if you've never been here before. If you've got a little extra time, it's well worth hiring a guide, who can show you the ins and outs of fishing one of the West's best trout rivers.

Crooked River

Anglers visiting the Crooked River for the first time are often put off by its milky, muddy appearance. But don't let that fool you. It's almost always "off-color," as we call it, and it doesn't affect fly-fishing one bit. Although the Crooked River fishes well year-round, it's best from September through March, making this a favorite destination for anglers looking for some fall or winter fly-fishing action.

The 6- or 7-mile stretch below Bowman Dam, with a respectable 3,000 or so rainbow trout per mile, is the place to go. It's important to wade while fishing the Crooked River, as the fish tend to be concentrated along the banks or around weed beds—you'll want to be out in the middle of the river so that you can cast into those areas. The river is relatively shallow, but you need to wade slowly and carefully, as it is difficult to see the rocks on the bottom of the stream through the milky water.

An effective fly to use on the Crooked is a nymph known as a scud, which is an imitation of a freshwater shrimp. Other nymphs used here include Serendipities and Pheasant Tails. Blue Winged Olives, Comparaduns, and Adams are good dry flies to try. The trout you'll catch in the Crooked River average in the 8- to 10-inch range.

Metolius River

The Metolius has a reputation for being a difficult river on which to catch fish. The saying around The Fly Fisher's Place is that "it's the most beautiful river you'll ever get skunked on." But, according to Perin, it is simply one of those rivers where it's important to know what kinds of insects hatch there and when, so you can select the proper fly to use.

"One of the real draws of the Metolius is the green drake hatch," Perin explains. "It's a very big, juicy mayfly that hatches in late spring, early summer, and again in early fall. These hatches bring the big fish up to the surface." The golden stone hatch here runs from about the Fourth of July until mid-October, making the Metolius unique in this regard—this hatch generally only lasts a few weeks in most Western rivers.

Good flies to use on the Metolius include Green Drakes, Golden Stones, and Pale Evening Duns. Flies that resemble crippled or drowning insects such as Captive Duns, Knock Down Duns, and Sparkle Duns also work well. Because the Metolius is so clear and the rainbow trout so wary, you'll want to use a 15-foot-long leader when fishing this river.

Fall River

"The Fall River has developed into one of Central Oregon's newest fishing hot spots," says Perin. This is partly because the Oregon Department of Fish and Wildlife and local fly-fishing clubs have teamed up to improve fish habitat along the stream, and partly because the state stocks a lot of rainbow trout here. Perin explains that while many fly fishers today prefer to fish for wild trout, when they look into the clear, spring-fed waters of Fall River and see large numbers of fish swimming about, they tend to overlook the fact that many of them have come from a hatchery.

This is one of the area's smaller rivers, so lighter tackle is appropriate. You'll do fine with a 7½-foot rod and a 2- to 3-weight line. Dry flies, nymphs, and streamers take fish here throughout the season. Pale Morning Duns and Blue Winged Olives are two dry flies effective on the Fall River throughout the summer months.

An angler gently cradles a Deschutes River redsides. PHOTO: THE FLY FISHER'S PLACE

person per day. For overnight trips, add another $30 per person per day. They also run guided hunting trips on both these rivers and white-water floats on the lower Deschutes and John Day Rivers. For more information see their listing in the Hunting section of the Other Outdoor Recreation chapter.

Sunriver Fly Shop
1 Venture Lane, Sunriver Business Park, Sunriver
(541) 593–8814

A fully-stocked fly shop, this enterprise also offers guided one-day fly-fishing jaunts to the Crooked River for $200 for the first angler and $40 for each additional. They also offer full-day trips to private Buckhorn Lake, near Terrebonne, for $225 per day for one to two anglers.

Sunriver Guides & Outfitters Ltd.
P.O. Box 3012, Sunriver
(541) 593–8247
www.sunriverguides.com

This outfit guides on the upper and lower Deschutes River, Crooked River, Fall River, Little Deschutes River, and the Cascade lakes. One-day drift-boat float trips on the lower Deschutes run $275 for one person, $325 for two, and $375 for three people. River walk-in guided trips are $130 per person for a half-day and $175 per person for a

full day. Walk-in trips on the Crooked River are $75 per person. Fishing trips on the Cascade lakes and upper Deschutes are $225 per day for one person and $175 per half-day. Sunriver Guides & Outfitters also offers a full-day sight-seeing trip down the lower Deschutes River, including a gourmet lunch, for $150 per person and three-hour floats on the Little Deschutes and upper Deschutes for $110.

> ## Insiders' Tip
> Sometime the action is slow, and the fish just don't seem to be biting. A good approach to take at times like these is to sit along the riverbank and watch the water. You'll be surprised how often you will eventually spot fish rising to feed on insects, thus revealing their location to you.

Fly-fishing on Central Oregon rivers is becoming almost as popular as golf. PHOTO: THE FLY FISHER'S PLACE

Other Outdoor Recreation

What's your idea of outdoor fun? What do you seek from the wilderness, the rivers, the mountains? Heart-pounding rides down wild rivers, spray in your face and the threat of being ejected from your raft at any moment? A quiet walk in the woods, a glimpse of a deer in a clearing and gray jays following through the trees, hoping for a handout? Perhaps a serious workout, careening full-tilt on your mountain bike down a forest trail, the trees a blur and the jays left in the dust? Or perhaps you'd rather pitch your tent along an alpine lake, then kick back and watch the mountains turn magenta at sunset? No matter which of these kinds of experiences appeals to you, you'll find it—and more—here. Central Oregon and outdoor recreation are synonymous.

Hiking and Backpacking

With two national forests totalling more than 1.7 million acres, six wilderness areas, a national grassland, and miles of wide-open rangelands, Central Oregon offers nearly unlimited opportunities for hitting the trail. Whether you're looking for a quiet day hike through pine woodlands or a weeklong backpacking trip into mountain high country, there's an excursion out there that's just what you are looking for. Because there are so many trails available in Central Oregon, we've just mentioned a few of our favorites to give you an idea of what's out there. Serious hikers will want to pick up a copy of one of the many trail guidebooks available at local bookstores. You can also get trail information and maps from local Forest Service offices.

If you intend to hike or camp in Central Oregon wilderness areas, you'll need to get a free wilderness permit. Self-service permits are available from boxes at wilderness trailheads. It just takes a few minutes to fill out the form, which asks for your name, address, the number of people in your party, your destination, and how long you will be visiting the wilderness area. This information helps the Forest Service keep track of use levels in these areas and aids in managing them for their pristine and wild qualities.

If you intend to hike on trails in the national forests, not only in Central Oregon but throughout the state, you'll need a Northwest Forest Pass. These cost $30.00 for an annual pass and $5.00 for a day pass and are available at all Forest Service offices as well as many outdoor equipment stores.

Bend Area

Cascade Lakes Highway

Numerous trails off the Cascade Lakes Highway, southwest of Bend, provide the gateway to the forests, lakes, mountains, and wilderness areas of the surrounding Deschutes National Forest. Signs marking trailheads are posted all along the highway, making most of the trails easy to find.

To reach the area from Bend, drive out Century Drive, following the signs to Mount Bachelor and the Cascade Lakes Highway, where you will soon begin climbing into the mountains. At about the 16 mile mark, you will come to the Swampy Lakes Trailhead on the north

Planning Your Trip

No matter what kind of outdoor adventure you have in mind, it will go much more smoothly with some advance planning and up-to-date information. You can obtain maps, advice, and current information about Central Oregon's recreational opportunities from the following organizations.

Bend Mapping & Blueprint Inc.
922 Northwest Bond Street, Bend
(541) 389–7440
This company in downtown Bend has an excellent selection of maps of Central Oregon and beyond.

Bend Metro Park & Recreation District
200 Northwest Pacific Park Lane, Bend
(541) 389–7275
If you are looking for outdoor recreation opportunities beyond what is offered by local commercial outfitters, give the Bend Metro Park & Recreation District a look. It offers a variety of outdoor classes and trips year-round.

Bureau of Land Management
3160 Northeast Third Street, Prineville
(541) 416–6700
The Bureau of Land Management oversees public rangelands throughout Central Oregon. If you plan to explore lands under its jurisdiction, BLM can provide you with maps and advice.

Oregon Department of Fish and Wildlife
61374 Parrell Road, Bend
(541) 388–6363
For hunting and fishing regulations and information on where to go, give the staff at the Oregon Department of Fish and Wildlife a call. They'll be glad to help.

Prineville Chamber of Commerce
390 North Fairview Street, Prineville
(541) 447–6304
The Prineville Chamber of Commerce can help direct rock hounds to area hot spots.

U.S. Forest Service-Deschutes National Forest
1645 U.S. Highway 20 East, Bend
(541) 383–5300

Bend-Fort Rock Ranger District-Deschutes National Forest
1230 Northeast Third Street, Bend
(541) 383–4000

Sisters Ranger District-Deschutes National Forest
Corner of Pine Street and U.S. Highway 20, Sisters
(541) 549–7700
Deschutes National Forest has numerous recreational opportunities to satisfy a wide variety of recreational interests. These offices have maps, brochures, and other information that can help you plan your trip.

U.S. Forest Service-Ochoco National Forest
3160 Northeast Third Street, Prineville
(541) 416–6500

Lookout Mountain Ranger District-Ochoco National Forest
3160 Northeast Third Street, Prineville
(541) 416–6500

Paulina Ranger District-Ochoco National Forest
171500 Beaver Creek Road, Paulina
(541) 477–6900
Before heading into the Ochoco Mountains, stop at the forest headquarters in Prineville or at one of the ranger district offices to pick up maps and any other information you may need.

side of the road. A popular and easy 4-mile round-trip hike, this trail will take you through pleasant pine forest and meadowlands. Although you won't find any spectacular mountain views here, it's a perfect place to take a short afternoon excursion since it's relatively close to town. This trail is also popular with mountain bikers and cross-country skiers.

If it's views you're after, continue driving another 5 miles past Swampy Lakes to the Tumalo Mountain Trail. There is a sign marking the trailhead on the north side of the road. The 1.5-mile hike up 7,775-foot Tumalo Mountain is a bit of a workout, but your reward will be gorgeous views of Mount Bachelor, Broken Top, and the Three Sisters.

For a pleasant lake hike on mostly level terrain, try the 2-mile Todd Lake Trail. The turnoff to Todd Lake is at about the 23-mile mark. About 6 miles beyond the Todd Lake junction is Devils Lake, right along the highway. It's crystal clear, with a half-mile trail leading along the southern shoreline. This is a great place to stretch your legs and have a picnic. Another nice hike is the trail to Lucky Lake, which you will find on the west side of the road about 5 miles south of Elk Lake. It is about a 1.5-mile hike up a gentle slope, which steepens a bit as you near this lovely mountain lake.

Three Sisters Wilderness

If it's a wild experience you crave, an excursion into the Three Sisters Wilderness is sure to satisfy. Managed by the Deschutes National Forest, this sprawling 283,402-acre area has deep forests, mountain lakes, and four of Central Oregon's major peaks—10,094-foot North Sister, 10,053-foot Middle Sister, 10,358-foot South Sister, and 9,175-foot Broken Top. Primary access points into the area from the Cascade Lakes Highway begin at Sparks Lake, Devils Lake, Elk Lake, and Cultus Lake. Most hikers and backpackers head for the Green Lakes area and the surrounding alpine meadows, which can become quite crowded during summer weekends. But there are enough trails here to provide solitude for hikers and backpackers who are willing to get off the

beaten path. Free wilderness permits are required for each party entering the wilderness, whether for a daytrip or longer. Permits can be picked up at boxes located at each trailhead.

Sisters/Camp Sherman Area

This area offers a number of nice hikes ranging from easy to rather difficult. A favorite is the Metolius River Trail, which offers a 6.5-mile loop along the spring-fed Metolius River from the Wizard Falls Fish Hatchery downstream to Bridge 99, crossing the river, then following the opposite bank back to the hatchery. It's a delightful walk through a ponderosa pine forest on easy ground. To reach the hatchery, drive 8 miles west on U.S. Highway 20 from Sisters, then go right onto Forest Service Road 14 at the Camp Sherman turnoff. From there, follow the signs to the hatchery.

Another nearby leisurely hike can be found by continuing on U.S. 20 past the Camp Sherman turnoff for another 4 miles and turning left onto Forest Service Road 2070 at Suttle Lake. Go another 3 miles to the Suttle Lake Picnic Area, starting point for the 3.2-mile trail that circumnavigates this large lake nestled in a forest of firs and pines. There is a resort at Suttle Lake.

For something a bit more challenging try the Black Butte or Black Crater Trails. The Black Butte Trail is 4 miles long round-trip and takes you to the summit of 6,440-foot Black Butte and wonderful views of the surrounding forest and mountains. This trail is steep—with an altitude gain of more than 1,600 feet from the trailhead to the summit—so pace yourself. To get there drive west from Sisters on U.S. 20 for 6 miles, then turn north onto Forest Service Road 11. Drive for another 4 miles, then turn left onto Forest Service Road 1110. From there it is 4 miles to the trailhead.

The Black Crater Trail is off Oregon Highway 242 (the McKenzie Highway), about 11 miles west of Sisters. The trailhead is on the south side of the road. The Black Crater Trail is 7.6 miles round-trip

A backcountry explorer heads back home after a jaunt in the Three Sisters Wilderness. PHOTO: JIM YUSKAVITCH

and gains more than 2,300 feet in elevation from the parking lot to the crater's 7,251-foot summit. Because this trail takes you into the Three Sisters Wilderness, you will need a wilderness permit, which can be obtained at the trailhead.

Three Sisters Wilderness

You can also access the Three Sisters Wilderness Area, which lies partly in the Willamette National Forest west of the Cascade crest, from Oregon 242. Popular departure points here include Pole Creek, Dee Wright Observatory, and Frog Camp.

Mount Washington Wilderness

This 52,516-acre wild area lies between Oregon 242 and U.S. 20, straddling the crest of the Cascade Mountains. Its easternmost third is in the Deschutes National Forest, and its western portion is in the Willamette National Forest. Deep forest, extensive lava flows, and 7,802-foot Mount Washington are its main highlights. Trail access into this wilderness area is along the summit of McKenzie Pass off Oregon 242 and from the Big Lake area off U.S. 20 on the Santiam Pass. Wilderness permits are required to hike and camp here. Trails in this wilderness area range from a couple of miles to just over 12 miles.

Mount Jefferson Wilderness

The two main peaks found in this huge 117,354-acre wilderness on the Cascade crest just north of U.S. 20 are 10,495-foot Mount Jefferson and 7,848-foot Three Fingered Jack. The easiest access to the Mount Jefferson Wilderness is via the Pacific Crest Trail trailhead, on the north side of U.S. 20 on the summit of Santiam Pass. From this trailhead, it is just 2.5 miles up a gentle grade to Square Lake. This is a popular afternoon hike for those who want to get a taste of the wilderness without venturing too far.

For the hardy, the Pacific Crest Trail leads deep into the mountains, with many feeder trails branching off to other locations within the Wilderness Area. Access to the eastern portion of the wilderness can be had by following logging roads from the Metolius River Area, but you should obtain a national forest map before attempting to find your way to these trails. As with the other Central Oregon Wilderness Areas, permits are required here as well.

Redmond Area

Smith Rock State Park
U.S. Highway 97, 9 miles northeast of Redmond
(541) 548-7501

Smith Rock State Park has about 10 miles of hiking trails through a spectacular canyon cut by the Crooked River. A trail runs along the length of the river through the park, and if you're up to it, you can climb to the top of Misery Ridge for grand views of the Cascade Mountains to the west and surrounding rangelands. For more information on Smith Rock State Park, see our Parks chapter.

Sunriver/La Pine Area

Newberry National Volcanic Monument
58201 South U.S. Highway 97, Bend
(541) 593-2421

Newberry National Volcanic Monument is the focus of hiking activity in this part of Central Oregon. There are more than 100 miles of trails throughout the monument, but you'll find the most interesting ones around Paulina and East Lakes. A nice introductory walk is the 1-mile loop trail from County Road 21, on the south side of Paulina Lake to Big Obsidian Flow, one of the largest flows of obsidian in North America. Another short, easy hike is the half-mile loop trail to the base of Paulina Falls on the west end of Paulina Lake.

If you are in the mood for a bit longer walk, try the Little Crater Loop. It starts at Little Crater Campground on the east side of Paulina Lake and loops through forests of hemlock along the side of Pumice Cone. You'll have good views of Paulina Peak, Big Obsidian Flow, and surrounding lakes. This trail is 3 miles long.

For the more ambitious, the 7.5-mile Paulina Lakeshore Loop takes you around

A Walk in the Woods

Sooner or later, even Central Oregon's nonoutdoor types—whether visitor or resident—succumb to the area's natural beauty and venture up a mountain trail for a look-see. A little advance planning and thought will make even a short hike into the Central Oregon wilderness more enjoyable and safer.

When contemplating an outdoor excursion, the first thing you'll want to determine is what type of experience you are after and what kinds of natural wonders you'd like to see. Central Oregon has deep forests of big trees, glacier-cloaked mountains, rushing streams, ice-cold lakes, mountain meadows, and desert canyons, to name just a few. If you crave broad mountain vistas then a hike into the high country on a blue-sky day is what you need. If you hope to catch a glimpse of an elusive herd of elk, skulking about a forest meadow in the wee dawn hours will be your better bet.

Since most of the recreational lands in Central Oregon are managed by the federal government, the best way to get started planning a trip is to head down to a local U.S. Forest Service or Bureau of Land Management office (see the "Planning Your Trip" Close-up in this chapter). They have lots of maps, brochures, and guides that are available for free or for a small charge. Staff members are also very familiar with the lands they manage and are always happy to give advice and suggestions on good places to go and current trail conditions. Don't forget that on National Forest lands you will need a trail park pass to park at trailheads. That program is explained in greater detail in our Forests, High Desert, and Volcanoes chapter.

Aesthetics aside, the practical aspects of picking a day-hike destination largely involves the difficulty of a hike and your overall physical condition. For experienced hikers in good shape, a 10-mile day hike may be no big deal, while for others a trip of just a few miles, with lots of breaks to rest and sightsee, will be just the ticket. The overall condition of a trail and total elevation gain also affects a hike's difficulty rating as well as the amount of time it will take you to complete it. An average walking pace on level terrain is about 3 miles per hour. On more rugged terrain, though, most people slow down considerably. When you visit the Forest Service or Bureau of Land Management office, ask a staff member about the difficulty level and time needed for hikes that interest you.

The next consideration is what to take along with you. Even for a day hike in good weather, you'll find it's wise to have a few specific items along for safety and comfort, and if you have room in your backpack, perhaps a couple of additional things to enhance your overall enjoyment.

First of all, you'll need a small backpack or daypack to put your gear in. Inside you should have the basics, which includes trail snacks and lunch, water (in an unbreakable Nalgene bottle), and a waterproof or water-resistant coat or jacket just in case the weather turns unexpectedly bad. You'll also want a small first-aid kit, map and compass, sunscreen, sunglasses, flashlight, matches in a waterproof container, and pocketknife.

How you dress for your hike depends largely on the prevailing weather and season. Shorts are perfectly appropriate for hiking on hot summer days while long pants are better for cooler weather. Some hikers walk in shorts, but bring along light pants or wind pants just in case it gets cool and breezy over the course of the day. If you expect cooler weather, rain, or are hiking during early spring or late fall, you might want to consider adding some extra clothing to your pack, including gloves and a wool or fleece hat. If it's warm and sunny, you'll still want a hat—preferably a broad-brimmed one—to keep the sun off your head.

Day hikers don't need the rigid, heavy-duty boots that backpackers, who carry heavy loads over long distances, need. The trend in day-hiking boots in recent years has been toward lighter nylon and Gore-Tex construction, ideal for short trips on established trails. Tennis shoes and lightweight sneakers aren't recommended, though, as they do not give adequate ankle support for backcountry hiking.

If you have room and don't mind hefting a little extra weight, a camera, binoculars, and field guides to birds and wildflowers will add an additional dimension of enjoyment to your trip.

Most Central Oregon trails are well marked, including at trailheads and along the trails, so you don't really need to be an expert pathfinder to reach your destination. Still, it's a good idea to check your map now and then to help keep you oriented and track your progress. While hiking, walk at a comfortable pace. If you can talk to your companions while hiking without becoming out of breath, that's just

A hiker crosses a stream in the Three Sisters Wilderness. PHOTO: JIM YUSKAVITCH

about right. And if you start feeling pooped, why, that's a perfect time to stop for a few minutes to admire the scenery or take a closer look at those trailside wildflowers. Just make sure that your pace is fast enough to reach your destination and be back at the trailhead before dark.

A final suggestion: Before you leave the house, make sure you tell a friend or family member where you will be hiking and when you expect to return. Now have a good trip, and don't forget the Golden Rule of all wilderness wanderers—take only pictures and leave only footprints.

the entire lake. Better give yourself all day for this one. And for the truly hard-core, there is the Crater Rim Loop. This 20-mile trek circumnavigates the entire rim of the crater that holds Paulina and East Lakes. It's a true high-country adventure.

There are many more hikes available in this area as well as in the rest of the monument. Staff at the monument can tell you about other trails and give you suggestions. For additional information on Newberry National Volcanic Monument, see our Daytrips chapter.

Prineville Area

The Ochoco National Forest, 14 miles east of Prineville, is often neglected by outdoor enthusiasts. But those willing to make the drive to this corner of Central Oregon will find some excellent hiking opportunities. You can get a good feel for the special beauty of this forest on the 1.4-mile Ponderosa Loop. The trailhead is easily accessed at the Bandit Springs Rest Area, 22 miles east of Prineville on U.S. Highway 26. The trail passes through old-growth ponderosa pines, wildflower meadows, and rolling terrain. Another nice hike is the Stein's Pillar Trail. It is 5 miles round-trip and takes you through old-growth ponderosa pines, meadows, and craggy ridges, offering great views of the valley below. The last mile or so is a bit steep. To get there go 9 miles east of Prineville on U.S. 26, then turn left onto Mill Creek Road. After driving about 6.5 miles, go right onto Forest Road 3300-500, which will take you to the trailhead.

The more difficult Lookout Mountain Trail begins at the Ochoco Ranger Station, at the junction of County Road 23 and Forest Roads 22 and 42. This trail goes up the northeast side of Lookout Mountain, with wonderful views of the Cascades from the summit. The Ochoco National Forest has three delightful wilderness areas—Mill Creek Wilderness, Bridge Creek Wilderness, and Black Canyon Wilderness. Although these are smaller than the wilderness areas of the Deschutes National Forest and lack big mountains, you'll often find that you have them all to yourself. If solitude is what you seek, you'll want to make the effort to check them out. You can get a list of Ochoco National Forest hiking trails at the Ochoco National Forest Headquarters, 3160 Northeast Third Street, Prineville, (541) 416-6500.

Hiking and Backpacking Guides and Outfitters

Oregon Llama Adventures
61702 Teal Road, Bend
(541) 382–5028, (888) 722–5262,
(541) 595–2088
www.packllama.com

Oregon Llama Adventures is the only Central Oregon outfitter licensed to offer guided llama packing trips into the wilds of the Deschutes National Forest. They offer guided, fully catered, llama pack trips into the Mount Jefferson and Three Sisters Wilderness Areas as well as to other scenic forest locations for $150 per person per day. Custom trips from a gourmet lunch trip on up to seven days duration are also available. These gentle and friendly animals will carry all your food and gear, leaving you free from the encumbrances of a heavy pack. For prices starting at $270 they will also do a drop-camp, where they will pack in all your gear to a predetermined campsite—and back out again as well. They also offer guided fishing trips (see our Fishing chapter).

Wanderlust Tours
143 Southwest Cleveland Avenue, Bend
(541) 389–8359
www.wanderlusttours.com

Trips that explore the subtle beauties of nature are the hallmark of this outfitter, which offers a variety of outdoor excursions throughout Central Oregon. They also offer guided trips to all the locations listed in our Daytrips chapter. Their professional naturalist guides will not only lead you to Central Oregon's best places but will also give you the lowdown on the critters, plants, geology, and history of these areas to boot.

They offer full-day hikes for $32 per person, $30 for kids under age 12, as well as half-day hikes for $60 for adults and $50 for kids. Included in each trip are the services of a naturalist guide, a deli lunch, and transportation.

Wanderlust Tours also offers canoe, snowshoe, and cross-country skiing trips. Check out the Rafting, Kayaking, and Canoeing section in this chapter, as well as the Snowplay chapter.

Mountain Biking

Mountain biking has really taken off in Central Oregon as riders have discovered the thrill of careening down a steep forest track. Although there are quite a few designated mountain-bike trails in Central Oregon, most hiking trails in the area are open to bikers as well. But there are some exceptions. Mountain bikes are not allowed on trails in wilderness areas. And some trails outside of wilderness areas are reserved for hikers and equestrians only. Signs posted at trailheads will tell you if there are any restrictions.

The trails described below are only a short sampling of what's available. There are a couple of good mountain-biking guides to Central Oregon available at local bookstores. You can also pick up trail brochures at the Ochoco and Deschutes National Forests offices (see the "Planning Your Trip" Close-up in this chapter). Deschutes County also publishes a biking guide brochure. You can get a free copy at the Deschutes County Public Works Department, 61150 Southeast 27th Street, Bend, (541) 388–6581.

Bend Area

As with hiking, mountain-bike trips into the Cascades near Bend usually begin from the Cascade Lakes Highway. Swede Ridge Loop is a 9-mile trail that begins at the Swampy Lakes trailhead, 16 miles from Bend, and takes you through a forest environment, around Swampy Lakes, to the Swede Ridge Shelter—a shelter for cross-country skiers. Another good ride to be had off of the Cascade Lakes Highway is the Todd Lake/Three Creek Lake Road. It begins at the Todd Lake junction and follows Forest Road 370 for 12 miles to Forest Road 16. It takes you into the high country and along the Three Sisters Wilderness with terrific views of Broken Top. It's a bit of a climb to the summit, but the ride down is well worth the effort. To make a one-way trip on this trail, park a second car at the junction of Forest Roads 370 and 16.

For a grand tour, take the 31-mile Sparks Lake, Lava Lake, Edison Butte Trail system around Mount Bachelor. You can start at Sparks Lake off the Cascade Lakes Highway, 26 miles from Bend, or at Lava Lake, 39 miles from Bend. Get a map before you go. You can find good maps of this area at the Deschutes National Forest headquarters or at Bend Mapping & Blueprint (see this chapter's Close-up, "Planning Your Trip").

Closer to Bend, you'll find the Deschutes River Trail to be a pleasant ride. It's about 10 miles long one-way and follows a mix of single-track, dirt, and gravel roads along the Deschutes River. To get there, take the Cascade Lakes Highway 7.5

A mountain biker pauses to take in the view along the Metolius River. PHOTO: JIM YUSKAVITCH

miles west of Bend to Forest Road 41. Go left, following the signs to Lava Island Falls. Lots of hikers and equestrians use this trail as well, so be careful. For some easy, relaxed riding, try the paved and dirt roads in Shevlin Park, west of Bend off Northwest Shevlin Road (see our Parks chapter).

Sisters/Camp Sherman Area

You can start your mountain-bike excursion right from Village Green Park in downtown Sisters (see our Parks chapter). Hop on your bike and head south on Forest Road 16 (Three Creek Lake Road), then turn left onto the trail after crossing Squaw Creek. There are two loops to choose from: 6-mile Eagle Rock Loop and 16-mile Peterson Ridge Loop.

If you'd like to get a little higher up in the mountains, drive west from Sisters on U.S. 20 for 17 miles to the Corbet Sno-Park and ride up the steep cinder roads to the top of Cache Mountain. From the 5,579-foot summit, you'll have fabulous views of

the Three Sisters and Mount Washington. The ride back down is beyond exhilarating. It's a 17-mile round-trip.

There is also an upper and lower mountain-bike loop on Black Butte, 10 miles west of Sisters. The scenic McKenzie Highway (Oregon 242) between Dee Wright Observatory and the snow gate, 9 miles from Sisters, is a favorite bike ride for locals. This highway is closed by snow during the winter (actually, it's usually closed from mid-November to early July). The trick is to time your ride in the spring or early summer when most of the snow has melted from the road but before it is reopened to motor vehicle traffic. It's a steep 8-mile climb to the top, but you have an entire highway to yourself on the way back down. There are 105 miles of trails in the Sisters/Camp Sherman area along with more than 1,000 miles of forest roads suitable for mountain biking. Pick up a Deschutes National Forest map at the national forest offices in Bend (see our "Planning Your Trip" Close-up) or at the local Sisters Ranger District office at the corner of Pine Street and U.S. 20, (541) 549-7700.

Sunriver/La Pine Area

Newberry National Volcanic Monument offers some spectacular, though challenging, mountain-bike trails. The Newberry Rim Trail, which circles the crater that contains Paulina and East Lakes, is open to biking. The trail is 21 miles long, although there are numerous side trails and roads allowing you to vary the distance of your ride. The views are unparalleled, but you'll need to be in pretty good shape to enjoy them, as this route involves some pretty steep climbs and descents.

Another ride in the monument is the Peter Skene Ogden Trail. The trail begins at the Ogden Group Campsite, off U.S. Highway 97, 25 miles south of Bend. It climbs uphill for 8.3 miles along Paulina Creek. To reduce conflicts with hikers, bikers are not allowed to travel downhill on this trail. However, you may return to the trailhead via a dirt road that follows power lines on the south side of the creek. For more information on Newberry National Volcanic Monument, see the Sunriver/La Pine Hiking section in this chapter and our Daytrips chapter.

Prineville Area

The Ochoco National Forest and Crooked River National Grassland have 92 miles of trails and 600 miles of roads closed to motor vehicles, making for abundant mountain-bike routes. A good "build your own" bike route can be had at McKay Saddle in the Ochoco National Forest. Start your ride at the junction of Forest Roads 27 and 2720. From there, the sky's the limit. The many primitive roads in the area enable you to pick a variety of loops, lengths, and difficulty levels, but you'll need a forest map to do your planning; pick up an Ochoco National Forest map at the Ochoco National Forest office in Prineville (see address below). Independent Mine #808 Trail is an 8-mile loop that takes you through mountain meadows with grand vistas of the surrounding countryside in a near-wilderness environment. Start at the Round Mountain Trailhead 7 miles from the Ochoco Ranger

Station on Forest Service Road 42. Follow this trail to Trail #808.

Lookout Mountain, described in the Prineville Area "Hiking" section, is also an excellent mountain-bike route, as are many of the other hiking trails in the forest. The Crooked River National Grassland, between Redmond and Madras and managed by the Bureau of Land Management, is another overlooked recreation area. Miles of primitive roads across open rangelands and rolling hills provide outstanding opportunities for mountain biking, particularly during the winter when other parts of Central Oregon are snowed in. You can obtain information on the Crooked River National Grassland from the Bureau of Land Management, 3050 Northeast Third Street, Prineville, (541) 416-6700. Maps for the Ochoco National Forest may be obtained from that agency's office, at 3160 Northeast Third Street, Prineville, (541) 416-6500.

Mountain Bike Guides and Outfitters

High Cascade Descent Mountain Bike Tours
P.O. Box 8782, Bend
(541) 389-0562, (800) 296-0562
www.paulinaplunge.com

The Paulina Plunge is the trademark, and most popular, mountain-bike ride offered by this outfitter. This trail, in the Newberry National Volcanic Monument, drops 2,500 feet over the course of 6 miles, passing six waterfalls along the way. Some 2,000 people take the plunge each summer. The trip costs $50. Bikes and helmets are included in the cost of the trip. For another $5.00 you'll get lunch.

> ## Insiders' Tip
> When mountain biking on area trails, remember that equestrians and hikers have the right-of-way.

Summit Sports
7 Ponderosa Road, Sunriver
(541) 593–5252
Pacific Crest Mountain Bike Tours offers two-hour guided rides in the Sunriver area for $35, five-hour rides from Tumalo Falls to Shevlin Park for $45, and an eight-hour trip between Todd Lake, on the High Cascade Lakes Highway, to Shevlin Park for $55. Bikes and helmets are included. Summit Sports also runs guided two-day trips in the High Cascades area and in the Mount Hood area, farther north. Call for the latest rates.

Horseback Riding

You don't have to be in Central Oregon very long to figure out that this is horse country. More than a few people have moved here specifically so they can buy enough land to own a horse or two and spend sunny summer days riding the range. As with hiking, there are so many miles of trails, primitive roads, and thousands of acres of open country to explore that the possibilities for equestrians are nearly limitless. You can ride through a sagebrush-dotted landscape on a canyon rim overlooking a raging river or plod gingerly along narrow trails deep into forest wilderness.

Some of the more popular trails in the Deschutes National Forest include the 17.3-mile Metolius-Windigo Trail, 5.7-mile Windy Lakes Trail, 10.9-mile Summit Lake Trail, and 4.7-mile Fawn Lake Trail. Surrounding lands managed by the Bureau of Land Management offer great High Desert cross-country rides beneath the Big Sky.

In addition to trails, there are also established horse camps in the Deschutes and Ochoco National Forests with facilities including corrals, tie stalls, box stalls, and loading chutes, along with picnic tables, rest rooms, potable water, and other amenities for both human and beast. Many of these campsites have fees ranging from $5.00 to $16.00 per night, and some require reservations. Many of these camps are run by concessionaires. So if you've just rolled into town with your horse trailer in tow, call the Forest Service for current information. They can also help you with trail information based on your riding interests and skill level. A Forest Service contact phone number is provided with each horse camp listed below. But greenhorns need not be left out of the fun. If the closest you've ever been to a horse is watching the lost episodes of *Bonanza,* never fear. There are a number of local outfitters who can set you astraddle a gentle steed for a trail ride through country you won't soon forget. But you'll have to supply your own cowboy hat.

Horse Camps

Cultus Corral
Forest Service Road 4630 off the Cascade Lakes Highway, 4 miles south of Deschutes Bridge
(541) 383–4000
This camp is 40 miles from Bend in the High Cascade Lakes area (see our Daytrips chapter and other listings in this chapter). It can accommodate up to 200 people and 30 horses. There are 11 sites with a four-horse corral, shelters, fire rings, and toilets. You need to come supplied with drinking water. There is a fee of $5.00, but reservations are not required.

Deschutes National Forest
Chief Paulina Horse Camp
Off County Road 21, 22 miles south of Bend
(541) 383–4000
This camp has 14 campsites, a rest room, water for horses, and corrals. The daily fee is $12, but reservations are not necessary. It's 22 miles south of Bend off U.S. 97 and is a staging area for rides into Newberry National Volcanic Monument (see our Daytrips chapter).

Graham Corral Horse Camp
Forest Service Road 340, 6 miles northwest of Sisters
(541) 549–7700
In the forest northwest of Sisters, this camp was used as a sheep and cattle counting and gathering area in the late 1800s and early 1900s. It has a large corral, reconstructed to resemble the original, with a loading chute, 13 two-family campsites, tables, a toilet, and potable water.

The popular Metolius-Windigo Trail passes through this site. There is a fee of $12, but reservations are not required.

Quinn Meadow Horse Camp
Off the Cascade Lakes Highway, 29 miles
west of Bend
(541) 383-4000
A large number of trails can be accessed from this horse camp between Sparks and Elk Lakes off the Cascade Lakes Highway. It has 24 campsites along with corrals, tie stalls, rest rooms, and a community shelter. The fee is $12 per night for the two-horse corrals and $16 per night for the four-horse corrals. There are also additional vehicle fees. Call for the latest rates. Reservations can be made by calling (877) 444-6777.

Sheep Springs Horse Camp
Forest Service Road 12, 11 miles north of
Sisters
(541) 549-7700
There are 40 box stalls and 10 tent/trailer campsites at this camp, along with toilets, picnic tables, and fireplaces. Water is available. You can access the Metolius-Windigo and Bear Valley horse trails from this camp. There is a fee of $12, and reservations are required; call (877) 444-6777.

Sisters Cow Camp
Off Pole Creek Road #15, 2.5 miles south of
Sisters
(541) 549-7700
Another historic site, used by ranchers prior to 1920 to gather and ship their stock, Sisters Cow Camp is just south of Sisters. It features a corral and loading chutes, tables, and fireplaces. Spring water is available for the horses but is not recommended for people. There are no fees, and reservations are not required.

Three Creek Meadow Horse Camp
Three Creek Lake Road, 18 miles south of
Sisters
(541) 549-7700
You'll find this high-country camp south of Sisters along a lovely mountain meadow near Three Creek Lake. Because this meadow is fragile, campers should

not camp, ride horses, or drive vehicles across it. You can access many trails from this site, including the Metolius-Windigo Trail. It has 9 tent/trailer campsites, 36 box stalls, fireplaces, toilets, and 11 picnic tables. There is a $10 fee, but no reservations are necessary.

Whispering Pines
Off Forest Service Road 800, 11 miles
southwest of Sisters
(541) 549-7700
Nine campsites with tables and fireplaces, a toilet, and 36 box stalls are the features available at this camp. No potable water is available; however, a nearby stream will water your horses. There is a fee of $8.00, but no reservations are needed.

Ochoco National Forest
Allen Creek Horse Camp
Forest Service Road 550, 50 miles east of
Prineville
(541) 416-6500
On Big Summit Prairie, this horse camp has five campsites, tables, fire pits, toilets, and 16 box stalls. Creek water is available for the horses. There is no fee, and reservations are not required.

Cyrus Horse Camp
Off Forest Service Road 5750, 12 miles south
of Madras
(541) 475-9272
This small camp, on the Crooked River National Grassland off U.S. Highway 26 between Prineville and Madras, has five campsites with picnic tables and fire rings. Facilities for horses consist of 18

Insiders' Tip

Never go on an outdoor excursion without telling someone at home where you are going and when you plan to return.

stalls and water for stock only—depending on the season. Call ahead to find out if stock water will be available for the time you plan to visit. No toilets are available, and you'll need to bring drinking water. There is no fee, and reservations are not required.

Dry Creek Horse Camp
Off Forest Service Road 3370-200, 15 miles east of Prineville
(541) 416–6500

Five campsites, 18 horse stalls, toilets, spring water, and fire rings are the amenities at this camp. No fee or reservations are required.

Mud Springs
Off Forest Service Road 5740, 55 miles east of Prineville
(541) 477–6900

Mud Springs, adjacent to the Black Canyon Wilderness in the northeast corner of the Ochoco National Forest, has six campsites, four corrals, and water for horses. No fee or reservations are required.

Salter's Cabin
Off Forest Service Road 42,
8 miles northeast of Paulina
(541) 477–6900

This small cabin site, visible from the road, also serves as a horse camp. It has two picnic tables, a fire ring, an outhouse, two horse corrals (one wood and one wire), and water for your stock. There is no fee to camp here.

Horseback Riding Guides and Outfitters

Black Butte Stables
Black Butte Ranch, 13892 Hawksbeard Road, Black Butte
(541) 595–2061
Black Butte Stables at Indian Ford
70895 Indian Ford Road, Sisters
(541) 549–1948

From June through Labor Day, Black Butte Stables offers daily horseback rides into the nearby Deschutes National For-

est. Daily rides range from one-half to two hours in length and cost $20 to $50 per person. You can also book a group ride for $80 per person, or an all-day trip into the Three Sisters Wilderness or Mount Jefferson Wilderness for $125 per person. For the truly adventurous, Black Butte's wranglers will take you on a multiday pack trip deep into the Cascade Mountains backcountry. Costs for these trips vary greatly, depending on the length of the trip and services desired.

Eagle Crest Equestrian Center
Eagle Crest Resort, 1522 Cline Falls Road, Redmond
(541) 923–2072

The program at the Eagle Crest Equestrian Center is affiliated with Black Butte Stables and offers the same types of rides in the surrounding rangelands as well as prices. Half-hour trips are $20 per person, one-hour trips are $30, one-and-one-half-hour rides are $40, and a full two hours on the range will cost you $50.00.

River Ridge Stables
Inn of the Seventh Mountain,
18575 Southwest Century Drive, Bend
(541) 389–9458

Horseback rides along the wild Deschutes River are offered daily from April through September by the wranglers at River Ridge Stables, based at the Inn of the Seventh Mountain, one of Central Oregon's popular resorts. River Ridge has one-hour rides for $26, one-and-a-half-hour rides for $29, and two- and three-hour rides for $35 and $50, respectively. A half-day jaunt through the forest costs $60 per person. For an additional $20, you can hit the trail for the entire day; the price includes lunch. Kids age 12 and younger ride for $2.00 less than the above-mentioned prices.

Hunting

Hunting is a long-standing tradition here, and many Central Oregonians continue to pursue this ancient endeavor that, for a brief time each year, allows human beings in this high-tech era to become participants in the endless cycle of life and death that has fueled nature since the beginning.

Central Oregon is big-game country, and proof of that can be found in the hoards of hunters who roll into its High Desert and mountain country each fall, pulling trailers behind them, en route to a deer or elk camp that their family may have trekked to for generations. Mule deer and Rocky Mountain elk are found throughout the region. The Ochoco Mountains are particularly well-known as a prime elk-hunting area. Duck hunters flock to the High Cascade lakes on opening day, particularly Crane Prairie and Wickiup Reservoirs. Valley quail hunters roam the open country of the Crooked River National Grassland, near Madras, or on surrounding private farmlands, if they can get permission from landowners. The hardy breed of hunter who pursues chukars, a type of partridge that inhabits rugged High Desert rimrock country, generally heads to the canyonlands of the lower Deschutes River.

Before planning a hunting trip in Central Oregon, you'll want to check with the local Oregon Department of Fish and Wildlife office, where you can pick up the latest regulations booklet and determine what types of licenses, tags, stamps, and other permits you will need to hunt various species of Oregon game animals. For hunters unfamiliar with the area, department staff members are happy to give suggestions on places to hunt. The Oregon Department of Fish and Wildlife can be reached at 61374 Parrell Road in Bend, (541) 388–6363.

Hunting Guides and Outfitters

Quest of the West
20640 Mary Way, Bend
(541) 389–0323

Float the Deschutes River in search of the elusive chukars that inhabit this rugged canyon country, or venture down the remote John Day River, farther east, for chukars and ducks. Both the Deschutes and John Day hunting float trips run $200 per person per day. If you want to make it a multiday trip, add $30 per person per day. Quest of the West also offers guided trout and steelhead fishing trips on the lower Deschutes River and steelhead and bass fishing excursions on the John Day River. The rates are the same as for hunting expeditions. For $74 per day, they'll also take you on a white-water rafting adventure on the lower Deschutes. For overnight trips, you'll need to add $30 per day to cover food and other equipment. Rafts are available for rent to experienced river runners for $90 to $110 per day.

Off-Highway Vehicle Riding

Thousands of miles of primitive roads throughout National Forest and Bureau of Land Management lands provide a multitude of opportunities for off-highway vehicle enthusiasts. There are several officially designated off-highway vehicle riding areas in Central Oregon. These include the Millican Valley, 25 miles east of Bend off U.S. Highway 20; the East Fork Rock area, 20 miles east of Bend off U.S. 20; and Christmas Valley, 70 miles southeast of Bend off Oregon Highway 31. These areas are managed by the Forest Service and

Insiders' Tip
Central Oregon has such a wide variety of outdoor recreational opportunities that quite a few specialty guidebooks have been published on the area, including hiking, biking, fishing, and climbing guides. Many outdoor enthusiasts use FalconGuides. Look for them in local and national bookstores.

Bureau of Land Management. Off-highway aficionados should contact these agencies for maps and current regulations when planning excursions (see the "Planning Your Trip" Close-up in this chapter).

Off-Highway Vehicle Rentals

Quest of the West
20640 Mary Way, Bend
(541) 389–0323

If you'd like to get a taste of off-highway vehicle riding but don't own one, Quest of the West will set you up with a four-wheeler for $135 per day, along with a $600 refundable deposit. During the winter, they will also take you on two-, four-, and six-hour guided snowmobile excursions to the McKenzie Pass area. Two-hour trips are $74 for the driver and $25 for a passenger; four-hour trips are $110 for the driver and $30 for the passenger; the six-hour excursion is $155 and $35, respectively.

Rafting, Kayaking, and Canoeing

While Central Oregon is blessed with numerous free-flowing streams, around these parts river-running and white-water thrills usually mean the Deschutes River. The most popular section of the Deschutes, by far, is the lower river, from Warm Springs as far as its confluence with the Columbia River, 95 miles downstream. This part of the Deschutes flows through a spectacular desert canyon with first-class trout fishing (see our Fishing chapter), some two dozen major rapids, numerous smaller and unnamed ones, and an impassable waterfall. The other stretch of the Deschutes favored by rafters and kayakers is the portion between Aspen Camp and Lava Island Falls, some 5 or so miles southwest of Bend. Big Eddy Rapid, site of the Big Eddy River Festival held each September, is on this part of the river. Parts of the Metolius and Crooked Rivers are also run by white-water enthusiasts, but these require considerable expertise. Another white-water river that is popular with locals, although not really a Central Oregon stream, is the upper McKenzie River. The McKenzie River flows through the Douglas fir forest of the wet, west side of the Cascades, directly west of Central Oregon. And although we're partial to the High Desert, we have to admit that the McKenzie River country is not too shabby. A float down that river is a first-rate experience, and it's close enough to Central Oregon that many local commercial river guides offer half- and full-day trips down it. Another west-side river, just south of the McKenzie, that is also gaining popularity with Central Oregon river outfitters is the North Umpqua—a delightful river trip as well.

For those in search of a quiet flat-water canoe float, the Deschutes River at Mirror Pond, along Drake Park in downtown Bend, is an excellent place for a pleasant close-to-home experience. For flat-water canoeing in a more wild setting, just about any of the High Cascade lakes that are accessible from the road will suffice, although local canoeists are particularly fond of Hosmer Lake for its intimacy and scenic setting. Cultus and Sparks Lakes are also favorite canoeing destinations. For more information on the High Cascade lakes, see our chapters on Daytrips and Resorts, Ranches, and Vacation Rentals.

It is possible to rent kayaks and rafts from local outfitters for do-it-yourself white-water trips. However, unless you know what you are doing and are familiar with our rivers, we strongly recommend that you sign on with a professional river guide service. You'll find a list of area white-water rafting guides below. Outfitters here typically have a schedule of daily river trips, lasting anywhere from a couple of hours to all day. The usual procedure is to meet your guide at a predetermined location along the river you are going to run, although some services will pick you up at local resorts or the airport in Redmond. The outfitter will supply you with life vests and any other equipment needed for your trip. Lunches are generally included with all-day trips, but not necessarily with shorter ones. Once your trip is over, the guide service will give you a ride

If white-water thrills aren't your cup of tea, there are plenty of opportunities for a quiet float on placid waters. PHOTO: JIM YUSKAVITCH

back to your starting point. Most local guide services offer multiday trips on the Deschutes. Some also offer trips on other out-of-the-area Oregon white-water rivers as well as rivers in other states.

The Bend Metro Park & Recreation District often offers a variety of kayak, canoe, and other water-related classes and trips during the summer months (see the Planning Your Trip Close-up in this chapter and our Parks chapter).

White-water Rafting Guides

All Star Rafting & Kayaking
405 Deschutes Avenue, Maupin
(541) 395–2201, (800) 909–7238

Based in the heart of the Deschutes River's prime rafting stretch, All Star Rafting & Kayaking runs river trips ranging from one day to seven days. Half-day Deschutes River trips cost $40 to $55 per person, overnight excursions are $100, and three-day trips are $325. All Star also runs white-water trips on the McKenzie, North Santiam, and Owyhee Rivers in

Oregon and the Wind River in Washington State. And if you're interested in kayaking, All Star offers guided inflatable kayak excursions.

Bend Outdoor Center
1244½ Northeast Second Street, Bend
(541) 389–7191

Daylong guided white-water rafting trips on the lower Deschutes River are $85 per person. A one-half day flat-water float on the lower Deschutes River is $55. All-day white-water trips on the McKenzie and North Umpqua Rivers are $75 and $95, respectively. The Bend Outdoor Center also offers canoe and kayak lessons and is a full outdoor retail shop.

Blazing Paddles
63528 Saint Cloud Court, Bend
(541) 388–0145

Founded by former employees of a large white-water rafting company who found the trips too "canned" and impersonal, Blazing Paddles specializes in small groups and runs a 17-mile stretch of the lower Deschutes River just below Maupin.

Wild, Wild Weddings

When love is in the air in Central Oregon, it can often end up in the wilderness. At least if Madeleine Landis of Wilderness Weddings is involved, that is.

"I got married in 1990," relates Madeleine, "and I had a hard time finding someone who could do a wilderness wedding." She and her groom, Tom, finally found someone from California to perform the ceremony among the trees and mountains they both love. It was at that point that Madeleine had what she calls an "aha!" experience. She loved romance and nature, so why not do wilderness weddings herself for other like-minded couples?

So in 1991, after being ordained a minister with the non-denominational Universal Life Church, Wilderness Weddings was born, making its home in Camp Sherman, a Central Oregon outback community along the banks of the lovely Metolius River.

"There are a lot of people who want something in between a formal wedding and a little quicky at the county courthouse," says Madeleine. There has, in fact, turned out to be so many people looking for that "in between" marriage ceremony experience in the Central Oregon wilds that husband Tom finally became an ordained minister as well to help with the workload.

Couples poised for wedded bliss seek Madeleine out for a variety of reasons. Some have fond memories of childhood summer vacations in Central Oregon and want to be married here. Others may have a cabin in the area and think it a grand idea to combine their nuptials and a country getaway. Some make it into a big splash, coming from as far away as the East Coast to rent a place at Black Butte Ranch, Eagle Crest Resort, Sunriver Resort, or some other ritzy digs, get hitched against a magnificent mountain backdrop, then throw a bash for all their friends.

More typically though, a wilderness wedding is likely to be a small, quiet affair—and not always held far out in the wilderness. Madeleine has done her share of trekking miles into the backcountry to perform ceremonies. She also does lots of weddings involving horses and has climbed to the summits of Hoodoo Butte and Mount Bachelor to hitch mountain climber types. Her husband once married a couple as they floated down a wild river—he in a raft and the bride and groom drifting alongside in kayaks. They divvy up weddings according to skills and interests; he does the downhill-skiing weddings, she does the cross-country-skiing ones.

Couples often just pick a nice, pleasant spot along a stream or in a mountain meadow not too far from a road so that their less outdoorsy guests won't be excluded. A favorite location is in the ponderosa pines along the banks of the Metolius River or in the surrounding forest.

In addition to picking the perfect location, Madeleine likes to give the couple the opportunity to personalize the wedding ceremony. She gives the groom- and bride-to-be several different ceremonies and vows to choose from.

"I encourage them to write their own versions," she says. "Most people change a few words here and there or add a poem or a story." Madeleine will also do what she calls "children's vows," for couples with children from previous marriages, welcoming them as part of the new relationship between the adults in their lives.

Then there are the couples who have something quite different from a quiet wedding in the wilderness in mind. Perhaps Madeleine's most notable experience in that vein was the time she married a skydiving couple, performing the ceremony as the airplane took off from the Redmond Airport. At the conclusion of the ceremony, bride and groom leapt out the plane's door and into the wild blue yonder. "I didn't have to jump," she recalls, "but I had to wear a parachute in case I fell out." She's done a wedding in a hot-air balloon and another with a medieval theme, with the happy couple, guests, and minister all in costumes right out of the days of yore.

Ultimately, though, it's all about the marriage. "The important thing isn't the gimmicks," says Madeleine, "but the feelings behind it. And when all outdoors is your wedding chapel, those feelings can blossom like wildflowers in the spring.

Wilderness Weddings start at $150. Madeleine can be reached at (541) 595–2089.

A couple recite their vows under towering pines along the Metolius River as Madeleine Landis looks on.
PHOTO: JIM YUSKAVITCH

For $90 per person you get a shuttle pick up and return transportation, along with a continental breakfast and an awesome teriyaki barbecue lunch.

Destination Wilderness
161 North Elm Street, Sisters
(541) 549-1336

You can become one with the water when you run the McKenzie or North Umpqua Rivers in paddle rafts, inflatable kayaks, or solo catarafts with the guides from Destination Wilderness.

Half-day trips on the McKenzie are $55 for adults and $40 for kids younger than age 16. Full-day trips cost $85 for adults and $65 for kids. Full-day trips on the North Umpqua River are $105 for adults and $90 for kids. A special trip offered by this outfitter is the Raft, Draft, and Cast, featuring two or three days on the McKenzie River, including white-water rafting, hiking, fishing, soaking in riverside hot springs, and a special delivery of Oregon microbrews delivered right to your campsite. This trip costs $260 to $275.

New for this outfitter is the Adventure River Center on the McKenzie River, offering a variety of excursions and outings, including fly-fishing, mountaineering, hiking, mountain biking, and rafting. Both trips and instruction are available with prices beginning at about $75 per person for a day activity.

Imperial River Company
304 Bakeoven Road, Maupin
(541) 395-2404

The proprietors of this 11-room lodge on the banks of the lower Deschutes River will take you on a daylong white-water float trip for $79 for adults and $69 for kids younger than age 12. Trips include shuttle and lunch. Multiday trips start at $230 per person. Rooms at the lodge run from $70 to $110 per night for two people.

Inn of the Seventh Mountain
18575 Southwest Century Drive, Bend
(541) 382-8711

Take a two-hour white-water rafting trip down the upper Deschutes River just upstream from Bend. Trips are offered daily from mid-June to Labor Day. The cost is $33 for adults and $27 for kids ages 8 to 12. (Younger children are not allowed on the trips for safety reasons.) You can book your trip up to 10 days in advance.

Ouzel Outfitters
P.O. Box 827, Bend
(541) 385-5947, (800) 788-7238
www.oregonrafting.com

Ouzel Outfitters will take you on one-, two-, and three-day white-water float trips on the lower Deschutes, McKenzie, and North Umpqua Rivers. Day floats on the Deschutes are $90 for adults, $75 for kids. A two-day trip is $250 for adults and $225 for kids. A three-day trip runs $365 and $325. A daytrip on the McKenzie River is $85 for adults, $70 for children. A half-day trip is $55. One-day trips on the North Umpqua are $100 for adults and $85 for children. A two-day trip goes for $250 for adults and $225 for kids. Ouzel Outfitters also offers multiday white-water trips on Oregon's Rogue and Owyhee Rivers and the Salmon River in Idaho.

Quest of the West
20640 Mary Way, Bend
(541) 389-0323

This outfitter offers float excursions on the lower Deschutes and John Day Rivers as well as guided hunting and fishing trips. White-water trips are $74 per person per day. For more information, see the listing in the Hunting section of this chapter.

Rapid River Rafters
P.O. Box 8231, Bend
(541) 382-1514

With Rapid River Rafters, you can run the lower Deschutes or upper McKenzie Rivers and get an all-you-can-eat hot chicken lunch to boot. Deschutes daytrips cost $75 for adults and $70 for kids. Add another $5.00 for weekend trips. Upper McKenzie River trips go for $75.00—$5.00 less for children. You can also take two- and three-day floats on the lower Deschutes for $215 and $325, respectively.

Summit Sports
7 Ponderosa Road, Sunriver
(541) 593–5252

White-knuckle runs through roaring rapids are great for some rafters, but others prefer the more subtle and serene aspects of the river environment. Summit Sports will set you up with a canoe or kayak and shuttle service for a do-it-yourself flat-water float on the upper Deschutes River—or provide you with a guide. A two-hour float from Wickiup Reservoir to Pringle Falls is $35. An all-day trip from the falls down to Sunriver is $45.

Sun Country Tours
531 Southwest 13th Street, Bend
(541) 382–6277
Building O, Sunriver Village Mall, Sunriver
(541) 593–2161

Sun Country Tours offers a family-oriented river experience with three-hour and all-day white-water floats on the upper and lower Deschutes River. They also have two- and three-day trips as well. The short trip costs $35 for adults and $30 for kids younger than age 12. A day float is $80 for adults and $70 for kids. Add an additional $5.00 for weekend trips.

Wanderlust Tours
143 Southwest Cleveland Avenue, Bend
(541) 389–8359
www.wanderlusttours.com

If paddling a canoe on a Cascade Mountains lake sounds like the perfect way to pass some time, Wanderlust Tours can satisfy. They offer half-day guided canoe trips on a variety of Central Oregon high-country lakes, running from 9:00 A.M. to 1:00 P.M., and 1:00 P.M. to 5:00 P.M. The cost is $35 per adult and $30 for children under age 12. Don't forget your bathing suit!

For something a bit more daring (and beautiful) come along on one of their moonlight canoe trips. These happen during the four nights bracketing each month's full moon. After paddling silently across a moonshine-dappled lake, you'll celebrate back on shore with hot apple cider. The cost is $40 per person, and kids must be age 8 or older.

Rock Climbing and Mountaineering

Any place with mountains is sure to attract mountain climbers. And Central Oregon has plenty of both. The High Cascade peaks, shimmering on the horizon, beckon mountaineers to ascend their lofty heights year-round, while the jagged crags and vertical terrain of Smith Rock State Park challenge rock climbers from all over the world. If the freedom of the hills calls and you're an experienced climber, Central Oregon is your oyster. If not, check out the professional climbing guides listed in this section.

Cascade Mountains

Mount Jefferson (10,497 feet); Three Fingered Jack (7,848 feet); Mount Washington (7,794 feet); North (10,094 feet); Middle (10,053 feet), and South Sister (10,358 feet); and Broken Top (9,175 feet) are the Central Oregon peaks that draw climbers. Although they may appear glorious and benign from a distance, looks can be deceiving. All of them are in wilderness areas, where you may have to hike a half-dozen miles or more before you can even begin your ascent. And dangers abound, both obvious and subtle, including remoteness, loose rock, glaciers, avalanches, and the ever-present possibility of a sudden, and deadly, storm. If you're going to climb mountains safely in Central Oregon, you'll need training in climbing techniques, the proper equipment, and companions with similar credentials.

> ## Insiders' Tip
> While most developed trails in Central Oregon are well-marked, always bring a map and compass along on your outings.

Smith Rock State Park
U.S. Highway 97, 9 miles northeast of Redmond
(541) 548–7501

During the past 20 years, Smith Rock State Park has risen from a rather obscure local rock-climbing area to one of international fame. It's the most popular rock-climbing area in the United States. There are about 1,000 climbing routes here, including two of the most difficult rock climbs in the country. Two climbing outfits in Central Oregon offer guided climbs and classes at the park (see the listings in this section). For additional information on Smith Rock State Park, see our Parks chapter.

Climbing Guides

First Ascent Climbing Services Inc.
1136 Southwest Deschutes Avenue, Redmond
(541) 548–5137, (800) 325–5462
www.goclimbing.com

This guide service offers one-on-one and group climbs at Smith Rock State Park. It also teaches a variety of rock-climbing classes suitable for climbers of all skill levels. Private, guided climbs cost $190 per day for one person, $110 each for two, $100 each for three, $90 each for four, and $80 each for five or more people. Half-day guided climbs are $60 per person. First Ascent Climbing Services Inc. also offers guided climbs on some special routes at Smith Rock, ranging from $200 for one person to $110 per person for three people. They also offer rock-climbing instruction. Prices depend on the course length and complexity of instruction.

INCLIMB
550 Southwest Industrial Way, Studio 39, Bend
(541) 388–6764

INCLIMB guides will take you on a half-day climb at Smith Rock State Park for $72.50 per person or $145 for the whole day. For two or more people, it's $65 per person for a half day and $90 per person for a full day. INCLIMB also offers Camp Rock, two- and three-day rock-climbing

camps for kids ages 10 to 18. It costs $250 and $350 per kid, respectively. All climbing equipment is included.

Rock Hounding

Rock hounds come from far and wide to Central Oregon, and Crook County in particular, to search for thundereggs, agates, jasper, obsidian, petrified wood, and limb casts—formed when ancient lava flows encased tree limbs—to add to their collections. The tools of rock hounds (also known as "pebble puppies") are basic. A pickax, rock hammer, and shovel are all you need to begin collecting the earth's geologic bounty. And Crook County is a favorite destination for people who dig rocks in all their colors, textures, shapes, and sizes.

There are quite a few areas on public lands open to rock hounds. Information on Central Oregon rock hound mines may be obtained from the Prineville Chamber of Commerce, 390 North Fairview Street, Prineville, (541) 447-6304; Ochoco National Forest, 3160 Northeast Third Street, Prineville, (541) 416-6500; and the Bureau of Land Management, 3050 Northeast Third Street, Prineville, (541) 416-6700. Experienced rock hunters can get maps and directions to well-established and productive Prineville-area digs, some of which are listed below. If you've never done any rock collecting before but are curious to give it a try, check out the commercial rock-hounding operation listed under Commercial Digs. That way you can see what it's all about before venturing out on your own.

Public Mining Areas

Eagle Rock
Off Oregon Highway 380 (Post-Paulina Highway), 15 miles southeast of Prineville
(541) 447-6304

Although this site has a reputation for difficult digging because of the rough terrain, rock hounds who search the base of the rimrock area may be rewarded with fine specimens of dendrites and agates.

Green Jasper
Off U.S. Highway 26, 30 miles northeast of Prineville
(541) 447–6304

As its name implies, green jasper is what you'll find here, but they're scarce. You'll have to work for your prizes.

Limb Cast Area
Off Oregon Highway 380 (Post-Paulina Highway), 65 miles southeast of Prineville
(541) 447–6304

Limb casts tinged in white, green, and pink draw rock hounds to this area, which includes a total of seven different mining sites.

Maury Mountain
Off Oregon Highway 380 (Post-Paulina Highway), 40 miles southeast of Prineville
(541) 416–6500

There are four separate public mining claims in this area, which is known for its yellow, green, and moss agates.

Obsidian
Off Oregon Highway 27, 38 miles south of Prineville
(541) 447–6304

The obsidian to be found at this mining area almost rivals the rainbow in its colors and hues. You'll find shades of silver, gold, black, cinnamon, mahogany, and more. But be sure to keep your vehicle on the road—sharp shards of obsidian are capable of slicing tires.

Vistaite
Off Forest Service Road 22, 48 miles northeast of Prineville
(541) 416–6500

The diggings here yield green and buckskin-colored agatized picture jasper.

White Fir Springs
Off U.S. Highway 26, 46 miles northeast of Prineville
(541) 447–6304

Jasper thundereggs are the attraction at this mine. Your best bet is to search in areas with signs of past digging.

White Rock Springs
Off U.S. Highway 26, 50 miles northeast of Prineville
(541) 447–6304

Especially beautiful jasper thundereggs are also the attraction here, though they are difficult to find in this area.

Commercial Digs

Richardson's Recreational Ranch
Old U.S. Highway 97, Madras
(541) 475–2680

If you think you might dig rock hounding but aren't quite ready to scour the desert for a claim of your own, Richardson's Recreational Ranch offers neophytes an opportunity to try out this popular Central Oregon pastime. Thundereggs—agate-filled nodules—are the specialty here, and you can rent a pick and have a go at finding a few for your collection, along with jaspers and a variety of agates, on the property 14 miles north of Madras. You'll pay 50 cents per pound to take your finds home with you. There is no entry fee, and Richardson's is open from 7:00 A.M. to 5:00 P.M., with digging going on from May to November. There is a rock shop on the premises where you can purchase a variety of collectible rocks, and there is a free campground but no hookups. (For more information on Richardson's Recreational Ranch, see our Attractions chapter.)

Watersports

Lake Billy Chinook, at Cove Palisades State Park 15 miles southwest of Madras, is Central Oregon's watersports central. This 6-square-mile reservoir formed by the damming of the Deschutes, Crooked, and Metolius Rivers attracts many thousands of water lovers who come to swim, water-ski, and ride personal watercraft (which may be rented at Cove Marina). Prineville Reservoir State Park is also a popular swimming and waterskiing area. For more information on both parks, see our Parks chapter.

You can rent personal watercraft at the Cove Palisades Marina for $195 per day, $125 for four hours, and $75 for two hours. Waterskiing enthusiasts who don't own boats can rent a 20-footer with a 225-horsepower motor for $255 per day (plus a refundable $300 deposit). These boats will accommodate eight people, and the rental price includes skis, vests, and tubes. Fourteen-foot boats with motors are $55 for a day rental, and $30 for three hours. If you are in the mood for an extended stay on Lake Billy Chinook, houseboats are also available for rent as well. A 10-sleeper is $1,995 per week, while a 12-sleeper will set you back $2,195 per week. There is a deli at the marina where you can stock up on sandwiches before weighing anchor and heading out.

Quest of the West
20640 Mary Way, Bend
(541) 389–0323
Quest of the West rents personal watercraft for $140 per day, along with a $600 refundable deposit. White-water-grade rafts are available for rent for $90 per day or $110 per day for overnight trips (because rafts for multiday excursions must be rigged differently). Again, a $600 deposit is required. Quest of the West also rents four-wheel-drive off-highway vehicles (see this chapter's section on Off-Highway Vehicle Riding). In addition to gear rentals, this outfitter offers guided hunting and white-water rafting trips; for more information, check the "White-water Rafting Guides" and "Hunting Guides and Outfitters" sections of this chapter.

In the Cascade Lakes area, Elk Lake draws sailors and board sailors. Nearby Cultus Lake has pleasant sandy beaches to relax on. Swimming, sailing, and waterskiing are popular activities here. See our Daytrips chapter for more information on the Cascade Lakes area.

Boat and Personal Watercraft Rental

Cove Palisades Marina
Crooked River Arm, The Cove Palisades State Park, Culver
(541) 546–3521

Indoor Recreation

Bend

Sisters/Camp
 Sherman Area

Redmond

Sunriver/La Pine
 Area

Prineville Area

Madras Area

In an area known for its abundant outdoor recreation offerings, it will come as no surprise that most of our indoor options for fun are definitely not of the couch-potato variety. In fact, a brisk hike in the woods may be downright relaxing compared to a 20-lap swim at a local indoor pool or an evening of heaving a 17-pound bowling ball.

We have health clubs galore to keep you in shape when you don't have time to get out and climb those mountains that shimmer on the horizon. Some of our indoor recreation is even designed to help you prepare for outdoor adventures. You can practice your bow-hunting technique at an indoor archery range or hone your rock-climbing skills on an artificial indoor climbing wall. And if you really are an unrepentant sofa spud, don't despair—we do have movie theaters.

Central Oregon parks and recreation departments also offer a variety of classes and other indoor recreational opportunities. You'll find these listed in our Parks chapter. We've organized this chapter by geographical region, with recreational categories then arranged alphabetically.

Bend

Archery

Del's Archery Den
61510 American Lane
(541) 382-8396

Test your skills in the ancient art of bowmanship against a computerized shooting system that flashes images of big-game animals on a computer screen. The staff at Del's will fit your arrows with special tips that blunt their force when they hit your target. For the traditionalist, there are also 10 regular, lighted, 20-yard indoor shooting lanes. It costs $24.00 per hour for the electronic system and $3.00 an hour for traditional shooting, and you need to supply your own bow and arrows. Del's is open Monday through Friday from 11:00 A.M. to 9:00 P.M., and 10:00 A.M. to 6:00 P.M. on Saturday. It is also a retail store carrying a full range of archery equipment.

Bowling

Lava Lanes
1555 Northeast Forbes Road
(541) 318-5656

Bend's newest bowling alley features 24 lanes of tenpin action, a full-service pro shop, and 3,000 square feet filled with video arcade games. Bleachers Bar and Grill is on the premises and serves wine, beer, and liquor. There are pool tables in the bar along with eight television sets, all tuned to your favorite sporting events. On Friday and Saturday nights, the folks at Lava Lanes turn on the black lights, music, and fog machine for "cosmic bowling." Adults pay $2.95 per game. For seniors and children, it's $2.50. Shoe rental is $1.50 for adults, but shoes are provided free for bowlers age 18 and younger. Lava Lanes is open every day from 9:00 A.M. to midnight.

Sun Mountain Fun Center
300 Northeast River Mall Avenue
(541) 382–6161

This family-friendly, nonsmoking bowling alley and amusement center provides lightweight balls for kids and puts out bumpers to keep them from rolling into the gutter. With 24 lanes of tenpin bowling, a video arcade, pool tables, and a snack bar, there are plenty of activities to keep the whole family busy. It costs $2.75 per game and $1.25 for shoe rental. Sun Mountain offers pizza and birthday parties for children. Outside you'll find an 18-hole minigolf course and a go-cart track.

There are always open lanes, even during league bowling hours. Sun Mountain is open from 11:00 A.M. to 11:00 P.M. Monday through Thursday, 11:00 A.M. to 1:00 A.M. on Friday and Saturday, and 11:00 A.M. to 11:00 P.M. on Sunday. On Friday and Saturday nights from 9:00 P.M. to closing, they crank up the music and turn on the strobe lights for "Neon Bowling."

Health and Fitness Clubs

Acrovision Sports Center
63255 Jamison Street
(541) 388–5555

Adults are welcome, but this facility is primarily for kids from preschool on up. The main activities are gymnastics, tae kwon do, and rock climbing on an indoor artificial climbing wall. Kids can start tae kwon do at age 4 and rock climbing at age 7. Gymnastics are open to all ages. Acrovision Sports Center offers lifetime memberships for a one-time fee of $29 to $43.50, plus monthly dues.

Athletic Club of Bend
61615 Mt. Bachelor Drive
(541) 385–3062

With 80,000 square feet and a full-time staff of 50, the Bend Athletic Club is by far the largest health and fitness club in Central Oregon. The club offers a full range of free weights and cardiovascular equipment, two indoor and two outdoor pools, tennis and racquetball courts, a gymnasium, a rock-climbing wall, and a steam room and sauna. You won't find another club in the area with so much to offer under one roof.

The club also offers physical therapy, massage, personal trainers, child care, youth activity programming, and social dining at Scanlon's restaurant, which is on the premises. Initiation fees run from $450 to $975, and monthly dues range from $77 to $131, including tennis and nontennis rates as well as rates for singles, couples, and families. The club tends to draw its membership from Bend's more upscale crowd.

Bend Fitness
1569 Northeast Second Street
(541) 389–2009

This is a family-oriented club offering weightlifting, aerobics, a 15-meter indoor pool, swimming lessons, private racquetball instruction, a Jacuzzi, a sauna, and day-care service. There are three trainers on staff. Monthly dues depend on how much you put down for the initiation fee. For $219 down, you will pay $19 per month. If you put nothing down, you'll pay $45 per month. Drop-in visitors pay $5.00 for a daily pass.

The Body Shop
61470 South U.S. Highway 97
(541) 388–1685

Two lines of Nautilus machines and a wide variety of free weights, aerobics classes (including a bicycle "spinning" program), and personal trainers are available at The Body Shop. A hot tub, sauna, and child-care services are also offered, along with a variety of memberships, depending on the kinds of programs you are interested in and number of people included in the membership. For example, one person is $94 for the first month and $25 per month thereafter. Drop-ins are $9.00 per person.

Gold's Gym and Aerobics Center
2410 Northeast Twin Knolls Drive
(541) 389-4653

A worldwide franchise, Gold's Gym is popular with locals who travel frequently, because a membership will get you into any of their facilities. Gold's in Bend has a full schedule of aerobics classes along with a complete line of cardiovascular machines and free weights. They offer personal trainers, a tanning booth, massage, and day care, along with classes in tae kwon do and yoga. They have a variety of rates, plans, and special offers on a month-to-month basis.

Juniper Swim and Fitness Center
800 Northeast Sixth Street
(541) 389-7665

Operated by the Bend Metro Park & Recreation District, you'll find a full description of this facility in the Bend "Swimming" listings.

World Gym West
805 Southwest Industrial Way, Suite 6,
(541) 388-5639
World Gym North
104 Northeast River Mall,
(541) 382-9433

These two gyms feature Hammer Strength equipment designed to isolate muscles and eliminate stress on the joints. They also have a complete complement of cardio equipment and offer aerobics classes including step, sculpted, step and sculpted, abdominal, and pilates, as well as tae kwon do, yoga, and kick boxing. Personal trainers are available. The west gym is open Monday through Thursday 5:00 A.M. to midnight, Friday 5:00 A.M. to 9:00 P.M., Saturday 8:00 A.M. to 4:00 P.M. and Sunday from 10:00 A.M. to 6:00 P.M. The north gym is open Monday through Friday 5:00 A.M. to 4:00 P.M. and from 10:00 A.M. to 6:00 P.M. on weekends. They have a variety of membership plans available.

Movie Theaters

Mountain View 4
Mountain View Mall, off U.S. Highways 97 and 20 on the west end of town
(541) 382-6347

Located inside on the mall's north end, Mountain View 4 has four auditoriums. Admission is $3.00 for adults, seniors, and children at all times.

Old Mill 10
Old Mill District, 680 Powerhouse Drive
(541) 382-6347

Featuring 10 auditoriums, this theater is Bend's largest and newest and features the on-premises Gourmet Cafe. Admission before 6:00 P.M. for adults is $5.00 and $4.50 for children and seniors. After 6:00 P.M., adults are $7.00, while children younger than age 11 and seniors age 62 and older are $4.50.

Pilot Butte 6
2717 Northeast U.S. Highway 20
(541) 382-6347

In addition to the usual Hollywood fare, Pilot Butte 6 also offers regular showings of independent films. Admission is $6.50 for adults for all shows beginning after 6:00 P.M. and $4.50 for shows starting before 6:00 P.M. Children younger than age 11 and seniors age 62 and older are $4.50 at all times.

Rock Climbing

Acrovision Sports Center
63255 Jamison Street
(541) 388-5555

Acrovision Sports Center has a 12-by-24-foot indoor rock-climbing wall. However, this facility focuses primarily on programs for children. For more information, see the listing in the Bend "Health and Fitness Clubs" section of this chapter.

Athletic Club of Bend
61615 Mt. Bachelor Drive
(541) 385–3062

Central Oregon's largest full-feature health club has a rock-climbing wall. For more information, see the listing in the Bend "Health and Fitness Clubs" section of this chapter.

INCLIMB Rock Gym
550 Southwest Industrial Way, Studio 39
(541) 388–6764

Need to warm up for that big rock-climbing trip to Smith Rock State Park, or just looking for a different kind of workout? INCLIMB Rock Gym has 7,500 square feet of climbing surface that will challenge climbers of all ability levels. Both top rope and lead climbing are available, and about half of the climbing terrain is suitable for bouldering. The rotating climbing wall, called the "rock and roll," is a bit like a gerbil wheel, allowing you to climb an infinite amount of vertical feet without a rope. And with 80 to 100 climbing routes open at all times, you won't have to wait in line the way you do at some popular outdoor climbing areas. They also have a high ropes and team course.

The rock gym is open Monday through Friday from noon to 9:00 P.M., noon to 8:00 P.M. on Saturday, and noon to 5:00 P.M. on Sunday. A day pass is $10. A monthly bouldering pass is $35, while the complete package pass is $40 per month. For an additional $7.00, they'll provide all the gear you need for your climbs. INCLIMB offers rock-climbing instruction, a youth program, and guided rock-climbing trips to local hot spots.

Roller Skating

Midtown Rock, Rink and Roll
51 Northwest Greenwood Avenue
(541) 388–1106

A family-oriented roller-skating rink with video arcade games, this center is a favorite location for throwing birthday parties for kids. A variety of party packages are available, including balloons, ice cream, and pizza. Private parties are available by special arrangement. The fee aver-

ages about $5.00 per person to use the skating rink, and that includes skate rental. They also offer special skating rates for groups. The center is open Thursday from 7:15 to 9:00 P.M., Friday from 7:00 to 11:00 P.M., Saturday from 1:00 to 5:00 P.M. and 7:00 to 11:00 P.M., and Sunday from 1:00 to 4:00 P.M.

Swimming

Juniper Swim and Fitness Center
800 Northeast Sixth Street
(541) 389–7665

Actually a full fitness center administered and operated by the Bend Metro Park and Recreation District, the Juniper Swim and Fitness Center features two indoor swimming pools (one 25-meter, six-lane pool and one kiddie pool) and one 40-yard, eight-lane outdoor pool, which is covered for use during winter. The center also has a weight room, group exercise studio, hot tub and sauna, and offers child-care service. Daily fees are $3.00 for adults, $2.50 for seniors age 60 and older, and $1.00 to $2.25 for youths depending on their ages. A monthly membership plan is also available. The center is open Monday through Friday from 5:30 A.M. to 10:00 P.M., Saturday from 8:30 A.M. to 6:30 P.M. and Sunday from 10:30 A.M. to 6:30 P.M.

Sisters/Camp Sherman Area

Health and Fitness Clubs

Cascade Fitness
172 East Main Street, Sisters
(541) 549–1729

Serving a broad range of community members, Cascade Fitness has cardio exercise machines, free weights, a tanning booth, and day-care service. They offer classes in aerobics and martial arts. Personal trainers and a masseuse are also available. The membership initiation fee is $50. Monthly dues are $30, and the minimum age for membership is 14. There is a $6.00 drop-in fee for nonmembers.

Sisters Athletic Club
413 West Hood Street, Sisters
(541) 549-6878

One of Central Oregon's newer clubs, the Sisters Athletic Club offers a full complement of cardio and weight-lifting equipment. Programs and classes include spinning, yoga, pilates, and relaxation meditation. Massages are available, as are personal trainers. The club also offers day care.

Membership fees for singles are $200 for initiation, plus $42 per month. There are also family and student plans available. Drop-ins are $10.

The Sisters Athletic Club is open Monday through Friday from 5:00 A.M. to 8:00 P.M., Saturday from 8:00 A.M. to 1:00 P.M., and Sunday from 9:00 A.M. to 2:00 P.M.

Redmond

Bowling

Premier Bowl
132 North Sixth Street
(541) 548-3314

Eight lanes of tenpin bowling, a video arcade, video poker, and keno are the attractions at Premier Bowl. There is also a snack bar that serves wine and beer. It's $2.50 per game and $1.00 to rent shoes. Premier is open daily from 10:00 A.M. to 10:00 P.M.

Health and Fitness Clubs

Body Smart Fitness
2392 South U.S. Highway 97
(541) 923-1625

A mix of local people work out at Body Smart Fitness, availing themselves of circuit machines, free weights, treadmills, bicycles, stair climbers, and other equipment. A one-year contract is $20 per month for the first person with a declining payment scale for additional people. Or you can join on a month-to-month basis at a cost of $30 per month for the first person. Corporate memberships are $15 per month. Body Smart Fitness is open from 5:00 A.M. to 8:00 P.M. Monday through Friday and 9:00 A.M. to 5:00 P.M. on Saturday.

Cascade Nautilus
2441 Southwest Canal Boulevard
(541) 923-0827

You'll find a full line of Nautilus strength-training equipment here along with a cardio room filled with the usual accoutrements, including rowing machines, bicycles, skiing machines, and stair climbers. They also offer racquetball and volleyball and personal trainers. There is also tanning, a salon, and physical therapy available. Mostly a family-oriented workout center, a good percentage of its members come from the ranks of seniors.

Cascade Nautilus is open Monday through Friday from 5:00 A.M. to 8:00 P.M. and Saturday from 8:00 A.M. to noon. Membership is on a month-to-month basis, with a basic individual membership running $30 per month. There are also student and family plans available.

Downtown Athletic Club
430 Southwest Sixth Street
(541) 548-6530

Treadmills, stair climbers, and Nautilus machines are just part of the arsenal fitness seekers have at their disposal at the Downtown Athletic Club located—yes, downtown—and therefore within easy access for local business people. The club also features 21 different classes and programs ranging from aerobics to tae kwon do. Massage therapy is offered along with the services of their on-staff personal trainers.

There is a $25 initiation fee, with monthly fees ranging from $20 to $25. Drop-ins are $5.00. The Downtown Athletic Club is open from 5:00 A.M. to 8:00 P.M. Monday through Friday, from 7:00 A.M. to noon on Saturday, and from noon to 4:00 P.M. on Sunday.

Movie Theaters

Redmond Cinemas
Wagner Square, off U.S. Highway 97 on the south end of town
(541) 548–8777

This five-auditorium theater is in Wagner Square, on the west side of U.S. Highway 97. General admission for adults is $6.00 for shows beginning after 6:00 P.M. and $4.00 for earlier shows. Tickets for children and seniors are $3.50.

Swimming

Cascade Swim Center
465 Southwest Rimrock Drive
(541) 548–6066

Operated by the Central Oregon Park and Recreation District, the Cascade Swim Center has a 25-meter indoor pool, providing recreational swimming from 7:05 to 8:20 P.M. Monday through Friday and 2:00 to 3:50 P.M. on Saturday. For the more serious swimmer, lap swimming is available, though times vary—call ahead to find out the most recent schedule. The pool is open to everyone—you need not be a local resident to use it. Admission is $2.50 for adults and $1.25 for children.

Sunriver/La Pine Area

Bowling

La Pine Bowling Center
52510 U.S. Highway 97, La Pine
(541) 536–3121

La Pine Bowling Center offers 10 lanes of tenpin bowling in a nonsmoking environment. They have a snack bar, five video games, video poker, pool tables, and air hockey. The center serves wine and beer. It costs $2.50 per game to bowl and $1.00 for shoe rental. It is open seven days per week from 5:00 P.M. until the bowlers go home!

Prineville Area

Bowling

Crooked River Lanes
260 Northwest Second Street, Prineville
(541) 447–6200

Crooked River Lanes is open daily from 10:00 A.M. to 10:00 P.M. and offers 12 lanes of tenpin bowling. On Fridays between 9:30 and 11:00 P.M., you can bowl to a sound and light show. It costs $2.00 per game and $1.00 to rent shoes. A snack bar on the premises serves wine and beer.

Health and Fitness Clubs

Norm's Xtreme Fitness Center
120 West Third Street, Prineville
(541) 416–0455

Circuit trainers will appreciate this gym's Icarian and Body Solid strength-training machines as well as its extensive free-weight section. Appealing to both residents and visitors, the center also offers aerobics, tanning, sauna, and salon. They also carry an extensive line of supplements and workout clothing.

The center is open 24 hours a day, Monday through Friday, 8:00 A.M. to 4:00 P.M. on Saturday and noon to 5:00 P.M. on Sunday. There are no initiation fees, and a typical monthly membership fee runs

$21.95. Corporate rates are available and drop-ins are $4.00.

Prineville Athletic Club
211 North Main Street, Prineville
(541) 447–4878
Friendliness and cleanliness are the hallmarks of this 6,000-square-foot, family-oriented gym. They have 21 aerobic machines and 3,000 pounds of free weights, along with aerobics, yoga, and martial arts classes, personal trainers, a nutrition program, and day care for the kids. Quite a few local corporations maintain memberships here for their employees. In business since 1988, it caters to people who aren't quite comfortable with the "powerlifter" set that frequents many other clubs. There are no initiation fees. Monthly dues run from $23 to $61. The club also has a punch-card program, offering 10 visits for $37 and 20 visits for $65. Drop-ins are $5.00.

Roller Skating

Crook County Parks and Recreation Department
Crooked River Primary School, 641 East First Street, Prineville
(541) 447–1209
The Crook County Parks and Recreation Department offers roller skating in the Crooked River Primary School gymnasium from September to June. Adults are welcome, but it's primarily for youngsters. The cost is $3.00 per person, and you must supply your own skates. You'll need to call the Parks and Recreation Department office for exact dates and times.

Madras Area

Bowling

Madras Bowl
66 Northeast A Street, Madras
(541) 475–3353
This 12-lane bowling alley has video poker, arcade games, and a snack bar that serves pizza, beer, and wine. It's open Monday through Saturday from 9:00 A.M. to 11:00 P.M. After 9:00 P.M. on Friday and 7:00 P.M. on Saturday, it's "Glow in the Dark," when a light show accompanied by music livens things up considerably. Bowling is $2.75 per game, $3.75 for "Glow in the Dark." Bumper bowling is also available. Shoe rental is $2.00.

Health and Fitness Clubs

New Energy Fitness Center
123 Southwest J Street, Madras
(541) 475–9369
A full-feature health club, New Energy Fitness Center has a broad selection of Nautilus machines and free weights along with two tanning beds and a steam sauna, hair salon, snack bar, and locker room with showers. New Energy also offers a full aerobics program, massage therapist, martial arts training, and a tumbling class for kids. Day care is available. Memberships are on a monthly basis and run from $15 to $25, depending on your membership category. For a $25 deposit, club members can have 24-hour, 7-days-a-week access to the fitness center. Nonmembers may work out for $4.00 per day.

Women Only Gym
242 Southwest Fourth Street, Madras
(541) 475–9375
As its name implies, this small gym caters to women only. It has about 85 members, most of whom are older than 50. The gym has more than 20 exercise machines, including treadmills, bikes, rollers, and stair-steppers. It also offers small aerobics classes. Members are given a key to the gym and may come for their workout anytime, 24 hours a day, seven days a week. A variety of plans are available.

Insiders' Tip
Don't forget that etiquette dictates that you don't bowl at the same time the player in the lane next to you is taking a turn.

Spectator Sports

Bicycle Races
Ski Races
Sled Dog Races
Rodeos and Horse
Events

Central Oregon is the sort of place where people are more likely to participate than to watch when it comes to competitive games. But for those who enjoy seeing athletes give their all, there are some spectator sports around these parts—many of them are just not of the traditional variety.

The Cascade Cycling Classic is a hot bicycle road race that briefly turns downtown Bend into a rush of color and speed; spectators can really get up close and personal. As you might expect, Mt. Bachelor Ski Area hosts a full slate of ski races. And this is still cowboy country, of course, so we have our share of rodeos and horse shows that provide great entertainment in the tradition of the Old West.

We've listed the primary spectator sports to be found in the Central Oregon area. Also check our Annual Events chapter for additional competitive events that tend to draw spectators, including the U.S. Bank Pole Pedal Paddle marathon in May and the Black Butte Classic Sheep Dog Trials in October.

Bicycle Races

Cascade Chainbreaker Mountain Bike Race
Race Around the Bend
1135 Northwest Galveston Avenue, Bend
(541) 389–4224

Take a bunch of mountain biking aficionados and the Central Oregon backcountry, put them together, and what do you get? Two exciting mountain bike races with courses set up for riders of just about every ability level, along with great action for those who like to watch, that's what. The courses range anywhere from 11 to 36 miles and cover a variety of terrain from steep uphill to flat-out, full-speed-ahead level track. The Cascade Chainbreaker Mountain Bike Race is held every year in late April, while the Race Around the Bend takes place on the Sunday of Memorial Day Weekend. Sanctioned by the Oregon Bicycle Racing Association, these events attract racers from around the Pacific Northwest as well as a smattering of bikers from other parts of the country. Most spectators stick to the start/finish areas while others head off into the woods to stake out a spot somewhere along the race route.

The exact course locations often change from year to year, so you will need to call ahead for details or pick up a map at the start/finish sites, which remain constant. The staging area for the Cascade Chainbreaker Mountain Bike Race is located on private forest lands just past Shevlin Park, while the start/finish location for the Race Around the Bend is located off Skyliner Road, 3 miles from the Deschutes River. Both areas are well signed during race days.

Cascade Cycling Classic
1293 Northwest Wall Street, No. 1336, Bend
(541) 382–5962

The Cascade Cycling Classic was started in 1980, making it one of the longest-running road-bike stage races in North America. A series of five or six races is held over the course of the five-day event. The Classic is held each year in mid-July. The complete course is more than 100 miles long, and the racers work in teams, applying strategy as they cover ground. For example, a team may ride together at a pace fast enough for competing teams to keep up with, but also fast enough to discourage passing—that way one of their number can break away and attempt to take the lead. Each day the leader of the race is given the leader jersey, which that racer's team will defend during the next day's stage.

Each year this event attracts well over 100 competitors from all over the world. In 1998 four-time Tour de France winner Lance Armstrong competed in the Cascade Cycling Classic. Because the stage races cover so many miles over a four-hour period on courses in the Mount Bachelor and Tumalo State Park areas, they do not offer particularly good spectator opportunities. However, two criteriums (lap races held on a one-half to 1-mile circuit) are also held as part of the overall race schedule and offer cycling aficionados the chance to see road-bike racing up close. The racers typically do about 50 laps. The criteriums are generally held in the downtown Bend area on city streets. The exact location varies from year to year, so you'll need to watch for announcements in the local media or call the race office. You can watch the Cascade Cycling Classic for free.

Pickett's Charge!
930 Northwest Newport Avenue, Bend
(541) 382-8018

Named after Tom Pickett, a pioneer in mountain-bike racing in Central Oregon, this race is held each year during the second Sunday in June. Mountain-bike racers come from throughout the Pacific Northwest and northern California to race in its three categories—beginner, sport, and pro expert.

Insiders' Tip
Many of Central Oregon's spectator events are open to anybody. If you find yourself wishing that you were participating in a race instead of just watching, the odds are that you can.

Held in the forested terrain off the Cascade Lakes Highway, the starting line is at Wanoga Sno-Park, while the finish line is at the Virginia Meissner Sno-Park. Because the racers spread out through the woods at this event, it is best watched at the start or finish lines.

Ski Races

Mt. Bachelor Ski Education Foundation
1004 Southwest Emkay Drive, Suite 400, Bend
(541) 388-0002

A variety of alpine and Nordic ski races, along with snowboard races, are held at Mt. Bachelor Ski Area (on the Cascade Lakes Highway, 22 miles west of Bend) throughout the ski season. These events are sponsored by the Mt. Bachelor Ski Education Foundation, a nonprofit group that develops and supports alpine and Nordic ski and snowboard race training and competition in Central Oregon.

The racing season generally kicks off in mid-December and runs through early April. The Sun Cup has been held here since 1964 and is part of the Northwest Cup Series and a qualifying event for the Junior Olympics. Race schedules and events vary from year to year, so you'll need to call ahead for the latest information.

Sled Dog Races

Chemult Annual Sled Dog Races
Dawson House Lodge, U.S. Highway 97, Chemult
(541) 365-2232

Held since 1994 in Chemult, 35 miles south of La Pine, the Chemult Annual Sled Dog Races are a tad out of the area covered in this book, but the event is so much fun to watch we had to include it. Part of a national sled dog racing circuit, as many as 70 or more dog teams and their drivers vie for a purse of several thousand dollars at this event, held on the last weekend in January at the Walt Haring Sno-Park Area off U.S. Highway 97 on the north end of town.

Individual races include a 24-mile race from Chemult to Miller Lake and back; an eight-dog, 8-mile race; a six-dog, 6-mile race; a four-dog, 4-mile race; a 4-mile novice race; and a 2.5-mile race for junior mushers. There's also a 2.5-mile skijoring race, where dogs pull their ski-clad humans down the track.

One of the great things about watching sled-dog races is that you can get right into the staging area, where the mushers are harnessing up their dogs, who are howling in excitement and anticipation of hitting the trail. You'll be surprised to see the range of dog breeds used in these races. The huskies and malamutes are expected, but there are German shepherds, hound dogs, and quite a collection of mutts as well. Mushers are looking for strength, speed, and stamina in their dogs. Good looks alone will get you nowhere at a sled-dog race.

Most spectators gather at the starting line to watch the dogs and mushers take off. The teams will disappear into the forest for anywhere from 15 or 20 minutes to a few hours, depending on the length of the particular race, before reappearing on the homestretch, giving you plenty of time to meet them at the finish line. Admission is free.

Rodeos and Horse Events

Crooked River Roundup
Crook County Fairgrounds, 590 Southeast Lynn Boulevard, Prineville
(541) 447–4479
Professional rodeo cowboys have been showing up at the Crooked River Roundup for the past 60 years to ride broncs, rope calves, and generally put on a great show for their Central Oregon fans. It's held each year on the last weekend of June with shows on Friday and Saturday evenings and Sunday afternoon. General admission is $12 for adults and $10 for kids younger than age 12. For more information on the Crooked River Roundup, see the listing in our Annual Events chapter.

Oregon High Desert Classics Horse Show
J Bar J Boys Ranch, 62895 Hamby Road (2 miles east of Bend off U.S. Highway 20)
(541) 389–1409
www.jbarj.org

A saddle bronc does its best to buck off a courageous cowboy. PHOTO: DESCHUTES COUNTY RODEO

This hunter and jumper competition is one of the Pacific Northwest's largest horse shows. Some 500 thoroughbred horses, many worth hundreds of thousands of dollars, are judged on style, skill, and timing as they negotiate a course of high and low jumps. Many horses entered in this event are in training for future Olympic competitions. The Oregon High Desert Classics Horse Show is held at the J Bar J Boys Ranch just outside of Bend during the last two weeks of July. It's free to the public and is enormously popular with Central Oregon's large contingent of horse enthusiasts. For more information about this horse show, see our chapter on Annual Events.

Sisters Rodeo
Sisters Rodeo Grounds, 4 miles east of
Sisters off U.S. Highway 20
(541) 549–0121
About 20,000 spectators show up for the Sisters Rodeo, which is held on the second weekend of June at the rodeo grounds just east of Sisters. Performances start at 7:00 P.M. on Friday, 1:00 and 7:00 P.M. on Saturday, and 1:00 P.M. on Sunday. Other rodeo-related activities during the course of the weekend include a parade through downtown Sisters and a cowboy dance at the Sisters Middle School. Rodeo

tickets run from $8.00 to $12.00; kids younger than age 12 get in free for the Friday evening show. For more about the Sisters Rodeo, see the listing in our Annual Events chapter.

Other Horse-related Events

Crook County Fairgrounds, 1280 South Main Street, Prineville
(541) 447–6575
Deschutes County Fairgrounds,
3800 Southwest Airport Way, Redmond
(541) 548–2711
Jefferson County Fairgrounds,
430 Southwest Fairgrounds Road, Madras
(541) 475–4460
With Central Oregon's ranching and cowboy tradition still largely intact, you'll find quite a few horse-related spectator events happening at our three county fairgrounds throughout the year. These include barrel racing, roping championships, high school and peewee rodeos, and cutting and paint horse shows to name a few. Since these are not necessarily regularly held events, you'll need to call the various county fairground offices for the most up-to-date schedule.

Daytrips

As you thumb through the various chapters in this book to familiarize yourself with Central Oregon, we're sure you'll agree that there is plenty to do. But just in case you need a bit of a jump start to get you going, we've put together a few short trips within the general area that should go a long ways toward giving you a good overview of what we have to offer. And just to make things a little more interesting, we've thrown in a couple of trips that will take you a bit out of the area but are nevertheless worth the extra travel time, perfect for a day or weekend when you're in the mood for something a bit different. See you on the road.

Cascade Lakes Scenic Byway
Century Drive and Cascade Lakes Highway

Oregon has a dozen scenic byways, designated by the state in recognition of the unparalleled beauty and interesting attractions to be found along their routes. Two of those byways are Central Oregon's own (see also the McKenzie Pass—Santiam Pass Scenic Byway listed below).

The Cascade Lakes Scenic Byway is a must-see for any visitor to Central Oregon. This 66-mile drive takes you from Bend to Oregon Highway 58, south of La Pine. In between is prime Oregon mountain country, a string of crystal-clear lakes, wilderness trails, and campgrounds. Allow at least three or four hours to begin to take it all in.

Start your journey in Bend on Century Drive, following the signs to Mount Bachelor and the Cascade Lakes Highway. You'll begin a long, steady climb through the open pine woodlands of the Deschutes National Forest with fantastic views of the desert country to the east. At about 20 miles from Bend, you'll come to 9,060-foot-high Mt. Bachelor Ski Area, one of the largest and most popular ski areas in the Pacific Northwest. Mount Bachelor is on the west side of the road. Directly across is Tumalo Mountain, a favorite winter destination for local backcountry skiers. The Cascade Lakes Highway is closed at this point during the winter months.

A point of interest here, on the east side of the road, is a flat treeless area called Dutchman Flat. Known as a "pumice desert" in reference to the volcanic material that covers it, the area has not accumulated enough soil to allow much in the way of plant growth, rendering it a curious open area surrounded by a sea of trees.

Round a curve or two beyond Mount Bachelor and be prepared for a heart-stopping view of South and Middle Sister—10,350 and 10,047 feet high, respectively—and so close you think you can reach out and touch them. Now you're in high lakes country. There are more than a dozen lakes along this route, in fact, each with its own special attributes and character. Devils Lake is a small, clear body of water and perfect for lazy picnicking and mountain watching. Elk Lake attracts gobs of High Desert sailors—both the traditional and windsurfer variety—each summer. There is also a lodge here that operates for most of the year and offers camping, overnight accommodations, a grocery store, and boat rentals.

For those looking for a bit of close-to-the-road wilderness, Hosmer Lake fills the bill nicely. Canoeists like to paddle this quiet reed-lined lake in the shadow of Mount Bachelor while watching the ospreys soar overhead. It's also one of the few places in Oregon that is stocked with Atlantic salmon, making it a special place for fly fishers. Other lakes along the route include Lava and Little Lava Lakes and Cultus Lake, one of the few here with sandy beaches. North and South Twin Lakes are water-filled volcanic craters known as maars. They're both about 60 feet deep and have no inlets or outlets. President Herbert Hoover took a fishing vacation on South Twin Lake in 1940. And Crane Prairie Reservoir, at nearly 5 square miles in size, is the home of lunker trout, as is the even larger Wickiup Reservoir. Both lakes were created by damming the Deschutes River to provide irrigation water for farmers in the arid lands below.

Cultus and South Twin Lakes and Crane Prairie and Wickiup reservoirs all have resort facilities variously featuring camping, groceries, gas, and rentals of boats, canoes, and kayaks, as well as trail access to the surrounding forest. Any one of them makes a great place to stop, stretch your legs, and take in some fresh mountain air.

A particular point of interest at Crane Prairie Reservoir is the Osprey Observation Point, off the highway about a half-mile south of Quinn River Campground. A short walk from the parking area takes you to an observation station where you may see these beautiful birds of prey dropping out of the sky and diving into the lake as they hunt for fish.

The final lake you'll pass before coming to Oregon 58 is Davis Lake, formed when an ancient lava flow blocked its outlet. It's an excellent spot to watch wildlife, especially waterfowl. There are Forest Service campgrounds here. At Oregon 58, turn southeast to U.S. Highway 97 and drive north 53 miles back to Bend. For more information on the Cascade Lakes Highway and surrounding environment, see our chapters on Resorts, Ranches, and Vacation Rentals; Forests, High Desert, and Volcanoes; Snowplay; Fishing; and Other Outdoor Recreation.

Crater Lake National Park
Off Oregon Highway 138, about 90 miles south of Bend, Crater Lake
(541) 594-2211

There once stood, in the southern Oregon Cascades, a majestic snow-covered mountain looming perhaps 12,000 feet high above the surrounding countryside. Geologists today call it Mount Mazama. But the mountain was a volcano, and one day, some 7,700 years ago, it sprung to life, erupting in a massive explosion that shattered its summit, pulverizing hundreds of square miles of surrounding land, snapping trees like match sticks, and sending ash and pumice many miles into the air,

You've got to see Crater Lake for yourself to believe it. PHOTO: JIM YUSKAVITCH

Visitors relax on the back deck of Crater Lodge in Crater Lake National Park. PHOTO: JIM YUSKAVITCH

darkening the sky for days. The ash sent forth by the explosion covered 5,000 square miles 6 inches deep. When the dust and smoke cleared and the sun shown once again, all that was left of the great peak was a caldera that eventually filled with water from rain and snowmelt, forming what we know today as Crater Lake. At 1,932-feet deep, it's the deepest lake in North America, the second-deepest in the Western Hemisphere, and the seventh-deepest lake in the world. It's 6 miles across at its widest point.

Native Americans knew about the place, considered it sacred, and avoided it, never even mentioning the lake's existence to early white explorers. In fact, Crater Lake wasn't discovered until 1853 when wandering prospectors accidentally stumbled onto it. It was designated a national park in 1902.

Crater Lake National Park is a straight 90-mile shot from Bend, down U.S. Highway 97 and Oregon Highway 138. Although, with an early start, you can do it in a day and be home in time for a late dinner, it's such a beautiful place that we strongly recommend you don't rush your trip.

From Bend you'll come into the park at its north entrance, which is closed during the winter (the park averages 44 feet of snow annually). A long, gradual climb will take you through deep forest and out into an open pumice desert, where little vegetation grows, before reaching Rim Drive at North Junction. This 33-mile drive is the park's tour de force, taking you completely around the caldera rim with numerous turnouts to park and view the lake. On a bright, sunny day the water is so blue it's hard to believe it's real. Near the lake's western shore is Wizard Island, a small volcanic peak that grew inside the caldera soon after the big blast. The elevation along Rim Drive averages around 8,000 feet to a little over 8,100 feet. The road is narrow and winding, and there are steep drop-offs in some places, so drive carefully.

As difficult as it may be to tear yourself away from the lake's beauty, include a stop at Rim Village on the south end of the rim. There are additional overlooks and a walking path along the caldera's rim here, as well as a cafeteria, gift shop, and visitor information center. Have a look at the historic Crater Lake Lodge, located a short walk east of the village. Built between 1909 and 1924, it eventually fell into disrepair and was closed in 1989. However, after an extensive refurbishing effort, the lodge reopened to the public in 1995. Open from May 20 through October 20, it boasts 71 guest rooms and a restaurant presented in 1930s decor. There's nothing quite like relaxing in rustic-style chairs on the lodge's back deck overlooking the lake on a fine, sunny day in August. Rooms run from $115 to $225 per night. And if you're interested in staying here, we recommend reservations as far in advance as you can manage (541-830-8700). For the more hardy, there are two campgrounds in the park that accommodate both tent campers and RVers. There are many picnic areas within the park as well.

While the action centers around the lake, this 183,000-acre park is sewn in by a delightful and lovely old-growth Pacific Northwest forest, transversed by babbling brooks and populated by a host of wildlife, from the Clark's nutcrackers that swoop down out of the trees to beg a meal (don't feed them) to seldom-seen black bears and elk that live deep in the backcountry. There are a number of short trails of a mile or less that will get you off the beaten path in short order and to park sites that many car-bound visitors never see.

If you want to write park officials in advance of your visit, do so at P.O. Box 7, Crater Lake, OR 97604.

Fort Rock and Christmas Valley, off Oregon Highway 31, about 35 miles southeast of La Pine
Oregon State Parks, 20300 Empire Avenue, Suite B1, Bend
(541) 388-6211
Deschutes National Forest, 1645 U.S. Highway 20, Bend
(541) 388-2715
Bureau of Land Management, P.O. Box 151, Lakeview
(541) 947-2177

Fort Rock State Park is the focal point of this trip, featuring a bit of history, a little nature, and a whole bunch of desert landscape oddities—all conveniently located in the same area.

A defunct volcano, Fort Rock was worn away by the waves of a great lake that once covered this area during the most recent Ice Age. From a distance it resembles a battlement. Up close it's a ring of stone 200 to 325 feet high. It was also near here, in a small cave, that anthropologist L.S. Cressman discovered a mother lode of 9,000-year-old sandals in 1938—the most ancient evidence of human occupation in Oregon (see our History chapter). A haven for hawks, owls, and eagles that love to soar and hunt among its crags and surrounding open country, the Fort Rock and Christmas Valley areas also harbor some rather unusual features worthy of exploration.

Fort Rock is reached by driving about 27 miles southeast of La Pine on Oregon Highway 31, then turning left at the sign for Fort Rock. It's about 7 miles off Oregon 31. Fort Rock State Park has rest rooms and picnicking and you may hike around the rock or carefully clamber along its walls. It's a good place to watch for birds of prey soaring overhead or perched on a cliffside ledge.

Also located in the area are three lava tube caves, Derrick Cave and South Ice Cave, along with Fort Rock Cave, where the famous sandals were discovered, of course. There is also Crack-in-the-Ground, a 2-mile-long fracture in the earth, with some sections reaching 50 feet deep. It can be found about 8 miles north of the town of Christmas Valley. To the east of Christmas Valley is the Lost Forest, a small patch of remnant ponderosa pines that have managed to persist in the desert. Nearby are sand dunes that will make you think you're at the beach and Fossil Lake, where the fossil remains of Ice Age animals are uncovered from time to time by the relentless desert wind. A rugged lava field, known as the Devil's Garden, is located northeast of Fort Rock, while to the northwest is Hole-in-the-Ground, created by a volcanic explosion 13,000 to 18,000 years ago.

A thoroughly fascinating area to visit, it's also remote, and some of these features are a little difficult to find, although well worth the effort. Before going you should contact the U.S. Forest Service office in Bend and the Bureau of Land Management office in Lakeview for maps, directions, and current information on road conditions.

John Day Fossil Beds National Monument
Off U.S. Highway 26, 60 miles northeast of Prineville
(541) 987–2333

Just an hour or so outside Central Oregon lies one of the richest fossil beds in North America, holding the ancient remains of long-extinct amynodonts, brontotheres, hyaenadonts, and other critters who looked as strange as their names.

A slice of this remarkable 54-million-year-old record-in-the-rocks, where scientists from throughout the world come to study, may be found at the John Day Fossil Beds National Monument. The monument is administered by the National Park Service and divided into three units, all within about 30 minutes of each other by car.

Start your explorations into the past at the visitors center on County Road 19, just off Oregon Highway 26 about 5 miles west of Dayville. Here on the Sheep Rock Unit of the monument, you'll find a nice interpretive center in an old, converted ranch house, plus a fossil museum and a gift shop that's well-stocked with books on paleontology and geology.

Take the time to watch the 17-minute orientation video produced in 1993 by high school students from nearby Dayville. Called "Impressions of the Past," it features clay animation, simulated volcanic erup-

tions, and carefully constructed miniature sets of the jungle environment that once covered this desert landscape. It's great fun to watch, and informative too. The staff will show it on request, and you may purchase a copy of the video for $16.95. Before you move on, walk about the grounds a bit and take in the landscape. The John Day River flows by the center and wildly colorful cliffs and bluffs rise above. The grounds are well-manicured, with big shade trees and a number of picnic tables.

Other points of interest at the Sheep Rock Unit include views of the colorful Sheep Rock formation, a half-mile trail through a bed of fossils at Blue Basin, and access to the John Day River at several places along the road. All trails, viewpoints, and other places of interest are well-marked throughout the monument.

The other two areas that make up this fascinating place are the Clarno and Painted Hills Units. The Clarno Unit, on Oregon Highway 218 about 40 miles northeast of Madras, offers two quarter-mile trails along eerie rock formations and spires called the Palisades. These impressive crags were formed by successive flows of ash and mud—the result of the volcanic activity that marks much of this whole region's past. Amenities at this unit are limited to a parking area, rest rooms, some interpretive signs, and water.

The Painted Hills Unit consists of strikingly colored hills and mounds formed by volcanic ash. Three trails, ranging from a quarter-mile to 1.5 miles, will lead you through this strange landscape of bronzes, pinks, reds, blacks, and tans. A particularly large number of leaf fossils have been found by scientists at this location. The Painted Hills Unit is off U.S. 26, about 45 miles northeast of Prineville. Facilities here include parking, rest rooms, and picnic tables.

The national monument is open year-round. The visitors center is open seven days a week from 9:00 A.M. to 6:00 P.M. from Memorial Day through Labor Day. After Labor Day to Thanksgiving, the center is open daily from 9:00 A.M. to 5:00 P.M. From Thanksgiving through February, the center closes on holidays and weekends.

A trip to John Day Fossil Beds National Monument invites visitors to travel back in time—geologically speaking. PHOTO: JIM YUSKAVITCH

Malheur National Wildlife Refuge
Off Oregon Highway 205, 30 miles southeast
of Burns, Princeton
(541) 493–2612

If you're a lover of birds or wide-open western spaces, we've got a trip for you. Malheur National Wildlife Refuge, in the heart of real cowboy country, is known as one of the country's best locations for birding and an all-round haven for wildlife and gorgeous desert scenery.

It's about a three-and-a-half-hour drive from Bend. We've done it in a day, but we strongly recommend that you spend at least one night so you can prowl the refuge first thing in the morning when things are hopping.

To get there, pack your field clothes, binoculars, camera, and bird guide and head east from Bend on U.S. Highway 20 to Burns. Burns is about 130 miles across what some folks regard as the "stinking desert." But we find it to be a landscape steeped in Western history, and a good portion of this road traces the route of Meek's Lost Wagon Train (see our History chapter). If you get into Burns late, we rec-

ommend the Sage Country Inn, a delightful bed-and-breakfast at 351½ West Monroe, (541) 573–7243. It's a fine old, refurbished Georgian-Colonial home built in 1907 and run by three local ranch ladies who serve up a first-class breakfast. The rooms are classy, comfortable, and reasonable ($65 to $85), and the proprietors will feed you cold beers or iced tea while you sit on the front porch and observe life in a genuine cow town.

From Burns head south on Oregon Highway 205 for about 25 miles, then turn left on a well-signed gravel road to the refuge headquarters. Here you can do a little bird-watching on the grounds or at the waterfowl observation pond, pick up some maps and brochures, or browse through the small natural-history museum.

The best way to see wildlife here is by driving the auto-tour route, which runs down the center of this 185,000-acre refuge along the Blitzen River. Give yourself at least three hours to do the tour. Most people start at the southern end of the refuge near the town of Frenchglen. Overnight accommodations here include a Bureau of

the highest peak in Eastern Oregon. A rather rough 66-mile loop road, which begins near the Page Springs Campground entrance, will take you across its high-elevation plateau, along several very spectacular glacier-carved canyons, and to within a quarter-mile of the summit. The road is closed during the winter months. There are bighorn sheep and mule deer up here as well as large stands of aspen trees that turn a blazing gold color each October. And the views of the eastern desert from the rim are indescribable. But be forewarned. A trip to this country has turned the heads of more than a few unsuspecting travelers and transformed them into lifelong "desert rats."

McKenzie Pass—Santiam Pass Scenic Byway
Oregon Highways 242 and 126 and U.S. Highway 20

The McKenzie Pass—Santiam Pass Scenic Byway is a popular route for visitors traveling to Central Oregon from population centers west of the Cascades, who often make a day of it—even though it's only a couple of hours drive as the crow flies—stopping at scenic viewpoints, picnicking at campgrounds, or wandering on forest trails. This route is particularly spectacular in the fall, between late September and mid-October, when autumn colors are at their best. This 82-mile loop drive begins and ends in Sisters. Depending on how often you stop and get out of your car, it should take you anywhere from three to five hours.

Land Management campground called Page Springs and Camper Corral, a private RV campground just south of the refuge boundary. If you'd rather sleep indoors there is the historic Frenchglen Hotel with eight rooms that run $53 per night (541-493-2825). Another option is Hotel Diamond, located about 13 miles east of the refuge in the ranching community of Diamond. Rooms run from $60 to $90 per night (541-493-1898).

About 300 species of birds have been observed at Malheur National Wildlife Refuge at one time or another. And since much of the refuge is a wetland, many of those are waterfowl and shorebirds. Hot spots along the auto-tour route include the P Ranch (home of eastern Oregon cattle baron Peter French, who was gunned down in an argument with a neighbor in 1897). The original ranch house has burned down, but there are still some old structures remaining. This is a good spot to see roosting turkey vultures in the evenings. Knox Pond often has flocks of elegant sandhill cranes while a variety of ducks, geese, and other waterfowl can usually be spotted at Benson Pond and Buena Vista Ponds. Spring and fall are the best times to visit.

While you are here, you may want to drive the Steens Mountain Loop Road, immediately to the southeast of the refuge. Steens Mountain is 30 miles long and 9,773 feet at the summit, making it

Start your trip on the western edge of town where Oregon 242 and U.S. 20 converge, bearing left onto Oregon 242. Then, before you've barely gone a mile, pull over to your left along the Patterson Ranch to see dozens of llamas grazing on a lush, green pasture with the peaks of the Three Sisters looming on the horizon. Some consider this to be most spectacular view in the state, and we can't disagree with them. A few years back the ranch obtained a herd of elk, which can often be seen in the distance. If you don't spot them in the open pasture, scan the wooded area at the west end of the ranch, where these magnificent animals often bed down during the midday heat.

From here you'll begin a gradual climb through the ponderosa pines of the Deschutes National Forest on your way to the 5,325-foot-high McKenzie Pass, following the route of the old pioneer McKenzie wagon road (see our History chapter). The road becomes narrow and winding, so drive carefully. Windy Point is at about milepost 10 and has a small turnout where you can stop and view the huge lava fields that covers much of the pass. In another 3 miles, you'll break out onto the summit, a wide-open wonderland of lava flows and unobstructed views of the Three Sisters, Mount Washington, Three Fingered Jack, and Mount Jefferson. There are two parking lots and rest rooms. Here you'll also find the Dee Wright Observatory, a stone building accessible by a short flight of stairs with windows framing the various Cascade peaks. If you feel like stretching your legs, there's a quarter-mile paved interpretive trail on the north side of the road leading through the lava fields. Some of these lava fields poured forth from the depths of the earth as recently as 400 years ago.

Now the road heads down the west slope of the Cascade's moist forests of Douglas firs, vine maples (which turn a vibrant red in the fall), and ferns typical of this side of the mountains. There are a number of small lakes along this stretch, including Scott Lake, accessible by driving north about a mile or so up Forest Service Road 1532—a great place to stop and explore. There is also a Forest Service campground here.

About 10 miles west of the summit of McKenzie Pass, at the bottom of the dizzying, winding section of road called Deadhorse Grade, you'll come to Proxy Falls, one of the most popular stops on this route. There is parking here, along with rest rooms and picnic tables. An easy 2.5-mile trail beginning at the parking area on the south side of the highway will take you to the falls. About 8 miles beyond Proxy Falls, you'll come to the junction of Oregon 126. Turn right.

This 20-mile stretch of road takes you through the Willamette National Forest past a variety of campgrounds and along the scenic upper McKenzie River. You can access the McKenzie River trail via a number of places along the route including Trail Bridge and Ice Cap Creek campgrounds. Sahalie Falls is another must-see along the highway. There's a parking area with rest rooms on the west side of the road about a mile north of Ice Cap Creek Campground. The trail leads 25 yards or so to a viewpoint. A couple miles up the road from the falls is Clear Lake, a popular destination for anglers and campers.

At the junction with U.S. 20, turn right for the final leg of your tour. This road takes you over 4,817-foot Santiam Pass, the location of Hoodoo Ski Bowl and numerous trails heading off into the Mount Washington and Mount Jefferson Wilderness areas (see our Other Outdoor Recreation chapter) before dropping down onto the east slope of the Cascades and back into Central Oregon. Between the 20-mile segment from the summit to Sisters, you'll pass Suttle Lake and Suttle Lake Resort (a fine place to fish or boat), the turnoff to the Metolius River Recreation Area (see our Fishing and Other Outdoor Recreation chapters), and the exclusive Black Butte Ranch community and resort (see the Neighborhoods and Real Estate chapter).

McKenzie Pass is closed during the winter months. It's typically open from June to early November, but opening and closing dates vary from year to year depending on snow conditions, so you should check with the Forest Service at (541) 549-2111 for current conditions. In addition, due to the narrow roads on McKenzie Pass, Oregon 242 is closed to

Insiders' Tip

When traveling Oregon's back roads it's always a good idea to inquire locally about current road conditions before venturing into out-of-the-way areas.

vehicles longer than 35 feet, and cars pulling trailers are not advised.

Newberry National Volcanic Monument
58201 South U.S. Highway 97, Bend
(541) 593–2421

The 56,000-acre Newberry National Volcanic Monument, which is managed by the U.S. Forest Service, was created in 1990. Virtually in Bend's backyard, a daytrip here is nearly mandatory for anyone visiting Central Oregon. The area has been a popular attraction for years, drawing campers and anglers to 1,500-acre Paulina Lake, named after the Paiute chief who led a war against white settlers in Central Oregon in the 1860s (see our History chapter) and 1,000-acre East Lake. You'll also find more than 150 miles of hiking trails here. But the real attraction of the monument is its geology, which includes massive lava flows, volcanic craters, caves, and an eerie forest of trees cast in lava. The best place to begin exploring this living laboratory of Central Oregon's volcanic history is at the Lava Lands Visitor Center, just 13 miles south of the city, off U.S. 97. Here you can see a variety of interpretive exhibits, hike nearby trails, and pick up information to help you plan your day of exploring.

Start your field excursions with a trip by shuttle bus up 500-foot Lava Butte, near the visitors center. The butte was formed by a volcanic eruption more than 6,000 years ago and is encircled by a 9-square-mile lava flow. On the summit, you can look into the shallow crater that once bubbled with molten rock and drink in panoramic views of the Cascade Mountains and High Desert. Once you've gotten your first taste of this landscape frozen in time, your next stop should be Lava River Cave, 1 mile south of the visitors center off U.S. 97. Here you can rent a lantern and wander through this cave, which was created when the outer portion of a lava flow hardened and the inner still-gooey stuff oozed out, leaving a hollow tube behind. Dress warmly because the inside of a lava tube cave maintains a year-round temperature of 32 to 45 degrees Fahrenheit due to the insulating properties of the basalt from which it was formed. There are two segments to Lava River Cave, a 5,400-foot downhill section and a 1,560-foot uphill section. Numerous other lava tube caves are scattered throughout the monument.

From there, hop in your car and head south on U.S. 97 for about 3 miles; then turn east on Forest Service Road 9720 to the Lava Cast Forest, where a molten lava flow swallowed up a patch of pines 7,000 years ago, leaving nothing but hollow lava tree casts behind. It's about a 6-mile drive on a gravel road to the forest. A 1-mile paved trail from the parking lot takes you on a loop through this volcanic curiosity.

Your next stop should be Paulina and East Lakes, reached via County Road 21 off U.S. 97 about 12 miles south of the visitors center. Both lakes are in the bottom of the caldera of Newberry Crater, a 500-square-mile volcano that makes up the primary landscape of the monument's southern reach. Just west of Paulina Lake, right off the county road, is Paulina Falls. Stop at the parking area and walk the short path to take a gander at this rushing sheet of water that plunges 80 feet over volcanic cliffs to the canyon below.

With depths up to 250 feet, Paulina Lake is one of the deepest in Oregon. East Lake is up to 180 feet deep. There is excellent fishing for brown trout, brook trout, rainbow trout, and kokanee salmon, and locals have been fishing here long before it became a national monument (see our Fishing chapter).

Within the Paulina and East Lake areas you'll find a visitors center, 10 campgrounds, and seven picnic areas. There are also four trailheads varying in difficulty and ranging in length from a half-mile to the 21-mile hike around the crater's rim.

Two other sights you should check out before you pack up the picnic basket and head home are Paulina Peak and Big Obsidian Flow. Big Obsidian is a massive lava flow that formed 1,300 years ago when a vent on the side of Newberry Volcano spewed 170 million cubic yards of pumice and obsidian. A 1-mile trail leads through a corner of this flow. Native Americans, who lived in the area dating back 10,000 years, mined the obsidian for tools and traded it with surrounding tribes. Paulina Peak is also well-worth exploring. A winding road, beginning at the visitors center, takes you to outstanding views from the peak's 7,985-foot summit.

A one-day entrance fee to the monument is $5.00 per car. You may also purchase a season pass for $30. Campground fees run from $7.00 to $12.00 per night. For more information on camping in the monument, see our Camping chapter.

Pine Mountain Observatory
Off U.S. Highway 20, 35 miles northeast of Bend
(541) 382-8331

Technically speaking, this is more of a night trip than a daytrip. But it should definitely be on your list of things to do and places to go. Pine Mountain Observatory was built in Central Oregon in 1967, where the clear air and lack of bright city lights make it a perfect location for viewing the heavens. The observatory is operated by the University of Oregon as a research and educational facility. They have 15-, 24-, and 32-inch telescopes, each housed in a separate observatory building. The 32-incher is one of the biggest scopes in use in the Pacific Northwest.

And the best thing about Pine Mountain Observatory is that, rather than a bunch of stuffy old scientists who want to be left alone, the staff here actually likes visitors to show up. They have a full public education program that includes a tour of the facility, an introduction to basic astronomy, and a chance to see how modern astronomy works (like telescopes that

produce images of sky objects on computer screens). And, yes, they let you look through their big telescopes, where you can search the sky for heavenly sights ranging from relatively nearby planets to galaxies formed long ago and far away. The moon, nebulas, and star clusters are on the menu as well.

You'll want to make an evening of it at the very least. And many people turn it into an all-nighter. The observatory is open to the public on Friday and Saturday evenings between Memorial Day and Labor Day. The staff greatly appreciates it if you call ahead before coming. This not only helps them determine how many visitors they can expect but also allows you the opportunity to check current weather conditions on the mountain, which at 6,300 feet in elevation can be considerably different than the weather in Bend at any given time. For this reason, always bring a warm coat, hat, and gloves. Snacks and hot drinks are good ideas as well. You should also bring a small flashlight with you, but cover it with a red filter (which can be just a piece of plastic report or notebook cover from an office supply store, cut to fit and fastened on with tape) to protect your and other visitors' night vision. Binoculars are useful, and if you have your own telescope, that's even better—although if you do bring one, be forewarned that observatory staff will put you to work helping them find heavenly bodies for the crowd. The staff also has a pair of big eye binoculars from a naval destroyer that are helpful for observing planets and globular clusters (groups of stars within the Milky Way Galaxy), which they pass around for visitors to try out.

If you want to spend the night, there is a U.S. Forest Service campground on the mountain with room for about 75 tent campers along with four RV spots, although hookups aren't available. You'll need to bring your own water, too, as none is available at the campground.

The best times to visit the observatory are the week before or after the new moon, when the sky is at its darkest and more astronomical objects are visible. Viewing during the week before and after the full moon is not quite as good because of the increased brightness of the night sky. However, you can still observe the planets and the moon.

To reach Pine Mountain Observatory, drive east from Bend on U.S. Highway 20 for about 26 miles. Just beyond the town of Millican, turn south on the graded road and drive 8 miles to Pine Mountain. Make sure you dim your headlights as you approach the parking area as a courtesy to stargazers who have arrived before you. Groups of eight or more should call to make reservations for a visit. There is a suggested donation of $2.00 per person.

Neighborhoods and Real Estate

Bend

Sisters/Camp Sherman Area

Redmond

Sunriver/La Pine Area

Prineville Area

Madras Area

Ask just about anybody around these parts why they moved to Central Oregon, and they are likely to say it was for the lifestyle. If you're thinking of resettling here, that's probably your reason as well. "It's amazing how many people come here to visit and fall in love with the place," says Sisters Realtor Dick "Rhino" Reinertson. And sooner or later, many of those folks end up in his or another area Realtor's office. In fact, you can usually tell the Central Oregon visitors from the locals, because the visitors are the ones walking around with real estate brochures clutched in their hands.

Local agents and brokers tell us that they're pretty busy right now, but like all real estate markets, Central Oregon has had its ups and downs. The area experienced a bit of a boom in the early 1970s, when a number of ranches and other large parcels of land were carved up into subdivisions and resorts, then marketed primarily as vacation homes and recreational properties. At that time Central Oregon's largely rural agriculture and timber economies simply didn't have the employment base to sustain very many new full-time residents.

Things slowed down again during the recession of 1981–1982, when interest rates went up to 18 and 20 percent. But then the local market took off like a rocket. Central Oregon's sunny weather, gorgeous landscape, and laid-back country living were discovered by weary urbanites longing for a home far from the madding crowds. Among the most prominent group of newcomers were retirees from Southern California, who were able to cash in on years of home equity in the then-booming California real estate market. That allowed many to buy nice homes in Central Oregon with plenty of cash left over. During the decade of the 1980s, the population of Deschutes County grew by 20 percent.

And even when the national economy staggered a bit in the late 1980s and early 1990s, the Central Oregon real estate market soared, largely because prices were relatively low. Redmond Realtor Rob Trout, who has lived here most of his life, relates, "People would come to me and say 'I would love to live here if I could only make a living.'" That is more possible now than ever before.

To their credit, local civic and business leaders have been determined not to allow Central Oregon to become a place where only the wealthy can afford to live—a fate that has befallen many Western resort areas. They have successfully worked to attract new businesses that offer family-wage jobs. These companies, which include manufacturing and high technology firms, complement Central Oregon's traditional natural resource–based economy. Add in the fact that a surprising number of Central Oregon residents are free agents, making a living out of their homes by engaging in everything from writing and photography to international marketing consulting and freelance computer programming.

This influx of working people has sparked a demand for affordable housing, which local developers and builders are meeting with the construction of numerous new subdivisions. Today the median price of a home in Bend is $136,00. In Redmond it's about $110,500. An average home in Madras and Prineville hovers at around $84,900. In Sisters the average is about $205,000. The cost of living in Central Oregon is reasonable, too. In Bend it's just slightly above the national average.

Central Oregon real estate values have skyrocketed in recent years, generally doubling in value since 1990, with about 20 percent of that increase happening during the last two years of that decade. Real property values are expected to double once more by 2007.

Many of the people moving to Central Oregon are looking for "dream ranches." Ranches can be found throughout Central Oregon, but when you get into agricultural real estate you get into a whole new can of worms, so to speak. Says Barbara Nicholson of Tumalo Real Estate, "Specialization is a key to professional representation. There are so many factors involved in acreage property purchases. Land use and zoning regulations, irrigation water rights and public lands access, wells and septic, just to name a few." Many realty agencies have farm/ranch specialists. Use one.

We've talked with nearly 50 Realtors to bring you the lowdown on Central Oregon's real estate scene, what's available and what you can expect to pay. We have arranged our information using the six geographical regions that make up our coverage area. If you want more specifics, drop in to see a local Realtor—many agencies here are open seven days a week. And if you're in the area in May or July, check out the Central Oregon Home and Garden Show or the Central Oregon Tour of Homes, two annual home- and real estate–oriented events that are very informative (see our Annual Events chapter).

Happy house hunting!

Bend

The City of Bend has just over 53,000 residents, making it the largest Oregon city east of the Cascades. As such it has attracted many new businesses to fuel a real estate boom that started in the mid-1980s and continues to this day. Despite its rapid growth, Bend offers plentiful and varied housing options. New homes and new subdivisions are started monthly, and there is a strong "move-up" market (with folks moving to more expensive addresses) in existing homes as well. The different areas of Bend can best be described by dividing the town into quadrants, roughly using U.S. Highway 97 and U.S. Highway 20 as our axes. We'll start with close-in neighborhoods— those nearest to downtown.

Northwest is the oldest section of town. West of the Deschutes River is an area of small, Craftsman-style mill houses built around 1910 to 1940. They were called "lunchbox" houses because they were made of scraps of wood (jokingly described as so small the workers smuggled them home in their lunch boxes). A 900-square-foot home in this very popular area would cost about $110,000 to $120,000; larger homes go up to $160,000. Near Drake Park, east of the river and very close to downtown Bend, are larger houses of the same period that start at about $300,000 and go up to more than $1 million.

Northeast also has charming older homes, with slightly larger lots, in the $115,000-and-up price range. This neighborhood has walking access to several small parks as well as the shopping along U.S. 97; it's just a few minutes from St. Charles Medical Center.

The smaller houses in close-in Northwest and Northeast would be considered starter homes. They may or may not have a single-car garage, and most have had some degree of renovation by now.

Just a bit farther out in Northeast is an area of newer subdivisions such as Tamarack and Wishing Well. These neighborhoods have single family ranch and split-level homes that are mostly under $160,000. Jump south of this area, and you find a similar situation with 20-year-old subdivisions such as Desertwoods and Nottingham (with the Robin Hood street names), also in starter-home price ranges. Boonesborough, with 2- to 20-year-old homes on two-and-a-half-acre lots in Northeast Bend, will run you anywhere from $160,000 to $420,000, and construction quality varies. This subdivision allows horses and is adjacent to public land for riding.

In 1991 the city extended the sewer systems to include the area around 27th

Street (funded in part by local developers), and that opened up a huge area for development. Costco, Safeway, and other retailers quickly snapped up space at the intersection of 27th Street and U.S. 20. One of the subdivisions built in the early-to-mid-1990s is called Providence, and it offers houses in the $120,000 to $150,000 range. The trees are still small in this area, but houses are comfortable—most single- and two-storied, some with attached two-car garages.

Retirees and move-up buyers can find areas dotted around Bend that offer great values for homes in the 1,500- to 2,000-square-foot range, priced from $120,000 to $200,000. East of 27th Street and south of U.S. 20 is a 15- to 20-year-old development called Kingsforest. Lots are roomy, trees are mature, and you can buy into this neighborhood for $145,000 to $205,000. Nearby is the pretty (and newer) Ponderosa Estates, offering houses with gray clapboards that go for $180,000 to $240,000. Developers left some ponderosa pine trees standing to retain the mature landscaping look.

In the Northwest area, development spread to the hills, where there are more deluxe, higher-priced subdivisions. In the areas closer to Bend but farther from the golf courses are West Bend Village, Newport Hills, and Rockaway Estates, where homes go for about $145,000 to $300,000. Houses in Awbrey Butte cost more—they're in the $280,000 to $650,000 range.

Premium homes in the Bend area are usually around golf courses. These are often very spacious (3,500 to 5,000 square feet) new homes with mountain or city views. New homes with great views at Awbrey Glen in Northwest Bend go for $280,000 to $650,000. Homesites next to the River's Edge Golf Course, also in Northwest Bend behind the Riverhouse Resort, start at $670,000. Here, wildlife and the Deschutes River are at your door, and it's an easy 1.5-mile walk along the river to downtown Bend.

There are a number of golf course communities south of Bend. All of the golf course developments have beautiful landscaping, curving paved roads with cul-de-sacs, mature ponderosa pine trees,

custom outdoor lighting, and heavy-duty "covenants, conditions, and restrictions," (known from here on out as CC&Rs) that result in lookalike houses. Realty offices frequently have agents specializing in golf communities.

In Southwest Bend, prestigious Broken Top is a beautiful, gated golf community featuring upscale townhomes and large houses built since 1992. A few half-acre homesites are still available from $100,000 on up to $500,000 depending on proximity to the fairways and views (and some sites are larger). Townhome resales range from $335,000 to $435,000, and houses start at $500,000 and go up to $1 million.

East of U.S. 97 off China Hat Road are Mountain High and Lost Tracks, subdivisions that have all been started within the last 12 years. Houses in Mountain High are in the $200,000 to $400,000 range. Three-quarter-acre lots are going for $125,000 to $250,00. Houses on one-acre to one-and-a-half-acre lots in Lost Tracks sell for $150,000 to $400,000.

Deschutes River Woods is an affordable area on the rise. It's also southwest of Bend—from U.S. 97, take Baker Road west. This area, with pine trees and river or canal frontage, has a range of home types and sizes. One- and two-acre lots can be purchased for $40,000 to $50,000; homes start at $80,000 and top out at about $300,000 for a nice place on the Deschutes River. Some houses are served by the private Avion Water Company; some have wells.

Slightly more expensive ($200,000 to $600,000) are the Southeast Bend homes at Woodside Ranch and Sundance, off of Knott Road. This is a beautiful area of juniper trees and sagebrush, and homes should be built with fire-resistant roofs and landscaping. Some homes have outstanding views spanning from Mount Bachelor to Mount Hood.

Many hunter and jumper horse ranches are found in Southeast Bend along Tekampe Road. East of Tekampe, along Rickard and Billadeau Roads, are English and dressage ranches. Nice 10- to 20-acre ranches in these areas go for around $300,000-plus, while the big fancy places— the kind with 160 acres and 4,000-square-foot homes—can bring $500,000 to more than $1 million. Note that many of the small-acreage developments allow horses, but if this is important to you, you should double-check zoning restrictions. Some do not allow any livestock. And check the CC&Rs for rules on home businesses.

Tumalo

Tumalo, just north of Bend, is an older community of 5- to 80-acre ranches. This area has become extremely popular in the last 10 years. Properties move so quickly that buyers interested in Tumalo should work with a Realtor who specializes in this region. (For much more on Tumalo, see our chapter on Other Communities.)

Real Estate Companies

Bend Real Estate Inc.
145 Northeast Revere Avenue, Suite E
(541) 389–2222, (800) 856–2226

Just because this agency is on the small side (eight agents total), doesn't mean it's short on service. Did you ever have a Realtor who offered to go with you to your bank and help you get financing? The office's agents can help with financial qualifications and credit issues or by showing clients how to acquire a loan in the future if they don't qualify now. Bend Real Estate has a commercial and investment specialist. Office hours are Monday through Saturday. Sundays are available by appointment.

Coldwell Banker Morris Real Estate
486 Southwest Bluff Drive
(541) 382–4123

One of the highest sales volume offices in Central Oregon, Morris Real Estate has been around since 1969. The 35 full-time sales associates and associate brokers handle residential and commercial listings in Bend, Tumalo, Powell Butte, and Alfalfa. There is also a ranch property specialist with 22 years of experience. *Options* is a free monthly buyers' guide published by this office. Drop by Monday through Saturday, or call for a Sunday appointment.

Cushman & Co. Preferred Properties
61999 Broken Top Drive
(541) 383–7600, (800) 382–7690

In June 1998 exclusive sales of homesites offered by the developer, Broken Top, at the gated Broken Top community were taken over by this satellite office of Cushman & Co. Preferred Properties. The office, with a staff of five, is run by broker Cate Cushman. The office is open daily.

Everett C. Turner Realtors GMAC Real Estate
822 Southeast Third Street
(541) 388–4444

Everett C. Turner has been in the Central Oregon real estate business since the mid-1960s and has seen more than a few changes in that time. He and his staff of 10 sell all types of properties throughout the Central Oregon region including residential, commercial, bare land, and farms and ranches. "I have a ranch specialist on staff and he's a real cowboy," says Turner. They are open Monday through Friday.

Investwest Commercial Real Estate
142 Northwest Hawthorne Avenue
(541) 382–1313

Investwest concentrates exclusively on commercial properties including leasing, business sales, and valuations, as well as farms and ranches. The office is open Monday through Friday.

Professional Realty Group
300 Southeast Reed Market Road
(541) 382–5657, (800) 700–5657

Founded in 1990, this agency has since grown to employ 47 sales agents, including three brokers. The company specializes in marketing small residential subdivisions, golf communities, and other resorts all over Central Oregon. It also handles some commercial properties. The company produces its own bimonthly publication, *Professional Realty Buyers' Guide*. They are open Monday through Saturday, and Sunday by appointment.

RE/MAX Manzanita Properties
230 Southeast Third Street
(541) 389–0200; (541) 389–0703, commercial office; (800) 285–4454, message phone

Owner/broker Harold Marken says his firm offers experienced agents and one of the best support staffs in town. Of his 30 agents, about half hold advanced licenses; the overall average experience is about 10 years, with one senior broker with 27 years experience. The office handles primarily residential listings; acreages and ranches are handled by an in-house ranch specialist agent. The office is open Monday through Saturday.

John L. Scott Real Estate-Bend
1195 #2 Northwest Wall Street
(541) 317–0123

This agency has 13 agents who specialize in residential homes in urban and rural Bend. The office is open daily.

Steve Scott & Company Realtors
685 Southeast Third Street
(541) 388–8989

After being born and raised in Bend and working in the industry for 21 years, Steve Scott started his own agency in 1994. He achieved his goal, which was to provide competent sales expertise with a "100 percent office," meaning everyone at the agency works full-time and is essentially an independent agent working under one umbrella. Each agent handles the market-ing for his or her listings, giving customers a soup-to-nuts personal touch. Twenty-five agents have an average of 11 years of experience with residential, commercial/industrial, and investment real estate sales.

The office specializes in residential subdivisions and has in a number of cases sold a large piece of land to a developer, helped with the permit process, and then handled sales of the new homes. Potential buyers should call the office, and they will be matched up with the agent best suited to serve their needs. The office is open Monday through Saturday.

Tumalo Real Estate
64619 West U.S. Highway 20
(541) 382–0288

Conveniently located between Bend and Sisters, Tumalo Real Estate serves all the real estate needs of its customers. Four licensed agents service listings in Bend, Tumalo, Sisters, and Redmond. In addition to residential and commercial properties, Tumalo Real Estate has two specialists on board. Owner/broker Barbara Nicholson, with more than 20 years of real estate sales experience, specializes in acreage properties. A horse enthusiast herself, she is familiar with the needs and considerations of country home buyers and sellers. Tumalo Real Estate is open Monday through Saturday, and Sunday by appointment.

Sisters/Camp Sherman Area

During the past 60 years, Sisters has evolved from a small outback community dominated by timber industry workers into one of the most desirable places to live in Central Oregon. Nestled against the east slope of the Cascade Range, blessed with breathtaking views of the Three Sisters mountains, and surrounded by a forest of ponderosa pines, Sisters is a picture-perfect Western mountain town. Although only about 900 folks live within the city limits, some 6,000 people make their homes in the immediate area year-round.

New housing is going up throughout Central Oregon as more people move to the area. PHOTO: JIM YUSKAVITCH

That figure is reported to triple during the summer months, when many people settle into second homes and cabins to spend the sunny season.

Today, Sisters has largely staked its claim on the tourist industry, although it does have a growing light-industrial base. In the 1980s city planners established a strict development code requiring all buildings to be constructed with an 1880s motif, giving the town a clean, Western atmosphere. During the summer months, the primary tourist season, visitors flock here to browse in the downtown shops and enjoy the many outdoor recreation opportunities in the surrounding forest.

Back in the 1940s, the modest homes in Sisters' core downtown area were used primarily by loggers and their families, who lived there while trees were being cut in the nearby Deschutes National Forest. The timber they cut was shipped by a long-gone railroad line that ran from Green Ridge in the forest to the Brooks-Scanlon mill in Bend. There, the timber would be processed into lumber. The workers would stay in Sisters for six or eight months until their employer's logging contract with the U.S. Forest Service

was completed, then they would move on, only to be replaced by other loggers when a new timber-cutting operation began.

After many years of effort by community leaders to obtain funding, Sisters is in the process of having a sewer system installed. Previously, all city businesses and homes were on septic systems.

Downtown Sisters neighborhoods are a mix of mobile homes and stick houses (the local term for homes made of wood) that run anywhere from $80,000 to $200,000. Much of the real estate activity here in recent years has been concentrated on commercial lots for retail and office space and high-density residential areas suitable for apartments.

Although people from Oregon's urban locales had been building small vacation homes in the area for decades, it was in the mid-1960s to early 1970s that local developers began to promote this corner of the Cascade Mountains as a recreational getaway. "The original concept was that this was a great place to have a second home," says Dave Goodwin, longtime Sisters-area real estate broker of Sam Goodwin & Associates in Sisters. "People from the Willamette Valley and Portland would have a second home here as a place to get away and go horseback riding and fishing."

This push to promote Sisters as a second-home and recreation area has resulted in the development of subdivisions in the outlying forest—today that's where the majority of the area's year-round residents live. The first was Black Butte Ranch, started in 1970, 8 miles west of Sisters on the site of a former working cattle ranch. Black Butte Ranch is a rather exclusive, gated 1,850-acre resort community with 1,253 homesites. Properties go for anywhere from $200,000 for a basic lot to more than $1 million for a home. Amenities include a lodge, restaurant, two 18-hole golf courses, 19 tennis courts, and miles of biking and running trails. In addition to the ranch's full-time residents, it is also a popular place for visitors to stay (see our Resorts, Ranches, and Vacation Rentals chapter).

Another exclusive development is Cascade Meadow Ranch, located on 360 acres surrounded by National Forest lands a few miles west of Sisters off U.S. Highway 20. Developed in the early 1980s, it has 24 two-acre homesites and equestrian facilities. Homesites will set you back $250,000 to $300,000; home prices begin at $1 million. Tollgate, a forest subdivision with more than 400 homesites, is across the highway from Cascade Meadow Ranch. It was started in 1973 as another second-home development, although today most Tollgate homeowners are full-time residents. Lots sell for about $70,000 to $80,000, while homes range anywhere from $145,000 up to around $300,000.

Immediately north of Sisters is Indian Ford Ranch, a 1,700-acre subdivision divided into a half-dozen sub-developments. Lots cost about $100,000 to $220,000 and homes are generally in the $150,000 to $600,000 range (although some sell for more than $800,000). One- to two-and-a-half-acre lots at Squaw Creek Canyon Estates, northeast of Indian Ford Ranch, run anywhere from $70,000 to $100,000 (depending on the size of the lot and whether it offers a view on the rim of the canyon) with homes going for $140,000 to $350,000. Lots at Crossroads, just off the scenic McKenzie Highway, sell for around $70,000 or $80,000. Homes here, including mobile and stick built, are $100,000 to $300,000.

Among the more recent developments are Buck Run, just within the southern limits of Sisters (lots are going for $65,000 to $130,000, homes for $250,000 to $370,000). Next to Buck Run is a new development called Coyote Springs. Lots here are $70,000 to $120,000. Another new offering in the Sisters area is Timber Creek, with homes in the $175,000 to $235,000 range.

Aspen Lakes is a 560-acre development 3 miles east of town, which, when completed in 2002 or 2003, will boast 115 homesites on one-acre lots, plus an 18-hole golf course (eventually to be expanded to 27 holes; see our Golf chapter). Homesites are selling for anywhere from $145,000 to $299,000. A major new development is in the works on Sisters' western city limits. Pine Meadow Ranch will be a mixed-use development incorporating single- and multifamily housing, a motel, convention center, and retail shops. Lots here are selling for $69,000 to $135,000. Just down the road to the west is the new gated manufactured home development, The Pines. Homes here start at $140,000, with a typical three-bedroom, two bath place in the low $170,000s.

If you're interested in going to the farthest reaches of civilization as we know it here in Central Oregon, you only have to drive a dozen miles west of Sisters to the tiny burg of Camp Sherman along the gorgeous Metolius River. A popular spot for campers and anglers, Camp Sherman has a number of small resorts, bed-and-breakfasts, and private summer cabins built on lands leased from the U.S. Forest Service. There

Insiders' Tip
Cable television is limited to urban areas. Homes outside the urban boundaries rely on satellite-dish reception.

is typically not much real estate for sale at any given point in time, but when there is, homes run around $235,000 to $350,000. Lots sell for $100,000 to $110,000. You can pick up a small cabin for about $150,000 to $250,000.

Real Estate Companies

Aspen Lakes Sales Office
16900 Aspen Lakes Drive, Sisters
(541) 549–4588, (800) 866–3981
The Aspen Lakes sales office sells property at Aspen Lakes, a 560-acre, 115 homesite golf course development 3 miles west of Sisters. Now in the third phase of a total of four, one-acre homesites in the development (scheduled for completion by 2002 or 2003) are priced from $145,000 to $299,000.

Coldwell Banker Reed Bros. Realty
291 West Cascade Street, Sisters
(541) 549–6000
Black Butte Ranch Lodge, Black Butte Ranch
(541) 595–6000
"We're the oldest and largest real estate company in Sisters," says Bill Reed, who, along with his brother Mike, has been helping people find homes and property in the Sisters area since 1972. This is one of the two oldest businesses in town. Open seven days a week, Reed Bros. Realty is a full-service agency with a staff of 20. It is also the exclusive on-site brokerage office for Black Butte Ranch.

Ponderosa Properties
221 South Ash Street, Sisters
(541) 549–2002
The Dyer family consists of Camp Sherman natives who have been in the real estate business since 1974. They started Ponderosa Properties in 1991 and handle residential and commercial properties, bare land sales, and ranches, and they manage vacation rental property around Sisters, Black Butte Ranch, and Camp Sherman. Ponderosa has a staff of 16, including three brokers and a variety of agents, property managers, and support personnel.

R.A. (Dick) Howells Company
220 Southwest Ash Street, Sisters
(541) 549–5555
Dick Howells came to Sisters in 1973 to manage Black Butte Ranch. Now he sells property and builds homes exclusively at the ranch through his company, which he started in 1981. They also do property management.

Rhino Ranch and Realty
503 East U.S. Highway 20, Suite B, Sisters
(541) 549–0551
More than a decade ago, Dick "Rhino" Reinertson and his wife were up from California's Bay Area visiting friends, fell in love with Sisters, and moved here. Now he and his two agents help urban refugees find their own Sisters paradise. Says Reinertson, "Why listen to the jets fly overhead when you can hear the geese fly over instead?" Rhino Ranch and Realty concentrates on residential properties.

Sam Goodwin & Associates
440 East Cedar Street, Sisters
(541) 549–4606
"We cover all of Central Oregon, but we seem to keep pretty busy here in Sisters and Black Butte," says Sam Goodwin of the real estate office he opened in February 1995. He has one agent and three associate brokers who deal in all types of property. Goodwin & Associates focus on the Sisters area, the Black Butte Ranch, and Camp Sherman.

Redmond

"People come to Central Oregon for the clean air, quality of life, and sunny days," says Redmond real estate broker Rob Trout of Trout Realty. "When they come to Redmond, they often have a specific way of life in mind that they are searching for. These people are usually looking for homes on small acreage, making those properties the most difficult to find in Central Oregon."

During the past 10 or 15 years, Redmond has seen quite a bit of expansion as people have moved here, particularly from Southern California, in search of a home in the wide-open spaces of Central Oregon. The city of Redmond alone has grown from around 7,000 people to nearly 13,000 residents in that span of time and many more people now live in the surrounding area.

The Redmond area is characterized by rolling juniper and sagebrush lands, buttes, and canyons, the most notable of which is the canyon cut by the Deschutes River, Central Oregon's major waterway. It is this landscape that has been drawing newcomers here since the mid-1980s in search of a piece of rangeland to call their own. Trout credits much of this growth and the good economic times that have come with it to the Redmond Economic Development Assistance Partnership, which was formed by community leaders in the late 1980s to boost Redmond's economy. At that time, Central Oregon was coming out of a deep depression that hit especially hard in Redmond and similar areas that were largely dependent on the timber industry and had little economic diversification.

The efforts of the partnership, along with the fact that real estate prices were still low at that time, helped bring new industrial development and jobs to the area. And since Redmond's industrial zone is concentrated on the east side of the city, industry is developing away from residential areas, minimizing its impact on the area's quality of life.

Because of Redmond's history as a rural, working-class city, there is not much in the way of classic old homes available. Many older homes were originally "laborer's cottages" that have been through numerous owners and remodeling ventures through the years. But the area has seen a boom in new subdivisions to meet the housing needs of people moving to the area to take jobs or retire. The cost of a three-bedroom, two-bath home in a mid-priced subdivision is about $110,000, although you can still find affordable homes in the area for less.

Many of the properties available in the Redmond area, especially those with acreage, were developed before Oregon's strict land-use planning laws were passed

in 1973. These regulations limit development of forest and farmlands. Depending on who you talk to, these laws are either hailed as being instrumental in slowing urban sprawl or are considered an unfair infringement on property rights.

Crooked River Ranch near Terrebonne is a good example of a development that preceded the land-use legislation. Built along the Crooked and Deschutes Rivers in the early 1970s as recreational property where you could park your camper and enjoy the outdoor amenities, it made the transition to a residential community 10 years later. With 2,600 home sites, it is the largest subdivision in Oregon. The one- to five-acre lots start at $29,000 and go up to $70,000 for parcels with river views. Homes are priced at $60,000 to $150,000 for manufactured homes and $100,000 to $400,000 for stick-built homes depending on the size of the property and its view. (See our Other Communities chapter for much more on Crooked River Ranch and Terrebonne.)

Tetherow Crossing, along the Deschutes River west of town, is another pre-land-use-law development, as is La Casa Mia, which was intended to be a Spanish-style development but now has mostly contemporary ranch-style houses. Chaparral Estates and Whispering Pines are typical Redmond subdivisions with homes priced anywhere from $100,000 to $300,000. Newer build-to-order subdivisions in Redmond include Red-Hawk, where home prices start at $125,000, and West Canyon Estates, with prices ranging from $142,000 to $170,000.

Other new, affordable Redmond-area subdivisions are The Greens at Redmond and Cascade View estates, where homesites start at just under $50,000 and custom homes are priced at $149,000 and up.

A return to the traditional community concept is also beginning to take hold in Redmond, as developers begin to plan subdivisions as small communities. Fair Haven, off Antler Avenue in Redmond, takes this approach with a master plan that includes single- and multifamily housing, ponds, bike paths, parks, a community church, a small commercial center, and a market.

For those with more upscale tastes, Eagle Crest Resort, located on Cline Falls

Highway between Redmond and Sisters, has two 18-hole golf courses, an equestrian center, a hotel and conference center, two sports centers, and more than a mile of frontage along the Deschutes River. Lots here go for $69,000 to $150,000 while homes are in the $200,000 to $450,000 range. (See our Resorts, Ranches, and Vacation Rentals chapter for more on Eagle Crest.)

But many people who move to Redmond look first at residential acreage on which to build a home. These are typically two-, five-, or 10-acre parcels that were once part of a 40-acre or larger property that has been subdivided. Water is an important consideration when purchasing acreage, since these parcels are typically not on city water service. Some parcels include water rights for irrigation; others have wells. If you plan to have horses or livestock, you may want irrigation rights. A well will do nicely for home water needs. These larger parcels can sell for anywhere from $175,000 to $3 million, with water rights and quality of the property's pastures and timber resources playing a big role in pricing.

Real Estate Companies

Canyon Real Estate Inc.
14465 Ranch House Road, Crooked River Ranch
(541) 548-4514

Specializing in residential properties at Crooked River Ranch, Canyon Real Estate opened its office with a staff of four in February 1997 and has been doing a brisk business ever since. Owner/broker Jillian Darnielle has five agents who sell residential and commercial properties in the Redmond, Terrebonne, and Culver areas.

Century 21 Gold Country Realty
2421 South U.S. Highway 97
(541) 548-2131

With one broker and 26 agents, this real estate company offers specialists in a variety of property types, including commercial properties and farms and ranches. In business since the late 1970s, it serves most of Deschutes County. If you're mov-

ing to Central Oregon, ask about Gold Country's relocation and referral services—they can help pinpoint special services you may require in your new home and coordinate your move with your former hometown real estate agent.

Coldwell Banker Mayfield Realty
809 Southwest Canyon Drive
(541) 548-1250

Owner Bob Mayfield tells us that his firm, established in 1959, is the oldest continuously operating real estate company in Redmond. It's a general agency working with residential and commercial properties, farms and ranches, and bare land. It's also out in front of the high-tech curve, offering multimedia presentations of listings that prospective clients may view at the agency office or in their own homes via the laptop computers that all the agents carry with them. With its 13 agents, Mayfield Realty serves the entire Central Oregon area, from Madras to La Pine.

Crooked River Realty
5135 Clubhouse Road, Crooked River Ranch
(541) 923-2000
8222 North U.S. Highway 97, No. 104, Terrebonne
(541) 504-8000
14510 Ranch House Road, Crooked River Ranch
(541) 923-1000

Nancy Popp's Crooked River Realty deals in residential, commercial, resort, and farm property, as well as bare land throughout greater Central Oregon, including Crooked River Ranch. There are 14 agents working between the three offices for this agency, which has been in business since 1972.

Dunn & Dunn Realty
1515 West Antler Avenue
(541) 923-6612

"Most of my customers end up being friends of mine," says Judy Dunn, who's been in the business since the mid-1980s. She concentrates on small acreage and residential and business properties in Redmond and Crooked River Ranch, the areas she knows best.

Eagle Crest
68397 Cline Falls Road
(541) 923–9625

The Eagle Crest sales office sells vacation ownerships, fractional ownerships, lots, and homes at 700-acre Eagle Crest Resort, which overlooks the Deschutes River between Redmond and Sisters. (See our rundown on the Redmond real estate scene for more on Eagle Crest.)

ERA Bill Jordan Company Realtors
210 South Fifth Street
(541) 548–5036

"We're primarily a residential and commercial brokerage," says owner and broker Bill Jordan, "but we're getting into ranches as well." In business since 1984, Bill Jordan Company Realtors serves Bend, Redmond, Sisters, Madras, Prineville, and east to John Day, about 100 miles away. In addition to a broker, there are four associate brokers and five agents.

Golden Eagle Realty
738 Southwest Highland Avenue
(541) 923–1942

Golden Eagle Realty's staff of two deals in all types of properties in Redmond, Culver, Bend, and Prineville.

Highland Realty
P.O. Box 1635
(541) 923–2311

In business for 10 years, Highland Realty's one broker and five agents specialize in residential property and bare land throughout Central Oregon.

Coldwell Banker Commercial Kerr, Oliver & Brock
755 Southwest Sixth Street
(541) 548–2772

Coldwell Banker Kerr, Oliver & Brock specialize in commercial and industrial real estate and business opportunities such as restaurants, RV parks, and rural and ranch properties throughout Central Oregon.

Redmond Real Estate & Associates
1550 West Highland Avenue
(541) 548–6111

"We do it all," says owner and broker Rick Hinman who, along with six agents, covers the real estate scene from Madras to La Pine as well as eastern Oregon out to John Day. In addition to residential and commercial properties, timeshares, working farms, and ranches, Hinman and his crew would be happy to help settle you into your own High Desert hobby ranch.

RE/MAX Land & Homes Real Estate
1730 Southwest Parkway Drive
(541) 923–0855

Owner and broker Tom Lewis has been selling real estate for just about forever, but his RE/MAX office opened in March 1998. Lewis' staff deals in residential properties with acreage, commercial properties, farms and ranches, bare land, and investment properties, including international investment properties. The staff of 10 covers all of Central Oregon.

Trout Realty
1241 Southwest Highland Avenue
(541) 548–8158

Founded in 1972 by George Trout, Trout Realty is the oldest independently owned real estate company in Redmond. "In this day of mega-franchises, we feel that we provide capable and trustworthy services," says George's son, Rob. Specializing in Redmond-area properties, the primary focus is on residential projects, but Trout also has commercial and property management divisions.

> ## Insiders' Tip
> The *Bulletin* publishes a real estate section in its Saturday edition that includes extensive property listings as well as stories about the local real estate scene and interesting area properties.

Windermere/Central Oregon Real Estate
1502 Southwest Odem Medo Road
(541) 923-4663

This agency works all of Central Oregon from Madras south to La Pine. Its bread and butter is residential real estate, but Windermere also deals in a wide variety of other properties, including eastern Oregon ranches and resorts. It also has builders' resource division that markets subdivisions. Windermere is the sixth-largest real estate company in the nation, with offices throughout the Pacific Northwest. This office has one broker and 17 agents on staff.

Sunriver/La Pine Area

Sunriver and La Pine encompass a large area to the south of Bend comprised mainly of vacation home properties and public lands managed by the U.S. Forest Service and the Bureau of Land Management. The region can best be described by dividing the private lands into three separate areas: Sunriver, which includes Sunriver Resort; South Bend, which is the area immediately south of Sunriver Resort that is often incorrectly lumped together with Sunriver; and the small community of La Pine, which includes Wickiup Junction.

Sunriver is a beautiful, planned resort community centered around three golf courses, 29 tennis courts, a shopping village, and many other amenities. It is 15 miles south of Bend and is nestled against the Deschutes River bordering the Deschutes National Forest. There are approximately 4,700 homes within the 3,300-acre resort.

Sunriver's outstanding recreational opportunities make it a very popular location for vacation homes and homes for active retirees. Visitors and residents enjoy the 33 miles of paved walking and bike paths, along with cross-country skiing and snowshoeing, ice skating, fishing and canoeing, pools, and golf privileges. Sunriver is 20 minutes from alpine skiing at Mt. Bachelor Ski Area (see our chapters on Snowplay and Resorts, Ranches, and Vacation Rentals).

Lots were first made available in 1968 and average a quarter-acre in size. The first condominiums were built in 1972. There are still some lots available, ranging in price from about $120,000 up to $250,000 for a lot on a golf green or next to the Deschutes River. Condos range in price from $40,000 to $200,000, depending on proximity to a golf course, the views offered, and the age of the unit. Homes vary from a low $120,000 for a small cabin up to over $1 million. About 75 percent of home purchases in Sunriver are made by second-home purchasers, mostly from the Willamette Valley.

There are very strict CC&Rs within the community. House colors are limited to nine shades of gray and beige, remodeling affecting the outside of homes must be approved by the architectural committee, and landscaping has its own set of guidelines. Roofs were originally required to be shake, but new fire considerations require that replacement roofs be made of composite shingles, metal, or tile. Sunriver has its own sewer and water systems, a fire department with emergency medical technicians, and a clinic with doctors on call 24 hours a day. The resort is also popular because of its low crime rate.

Vacation rentals are plentiful, as many homes are bought for investment purposes and are not occupied by the owners on a full-time basis. "Values are too high these days for owners of investment properties to make a profit on renting out their condos or houses, but the rental income does defray the monthly maintenance costs until the owners are ready to retire and move into their Sunriver home," according to Beverly Sherrer of Coldwell Banker First Resort Realty. Potential investors should consult their accountants to see if there are potential tax advantages for them in renting out their properties. Typical summer rental prices range from $189 per night for a small condo that sleeps four to six, up to $799 a night for a large, executive home that sleeps up to a dozen. The highest rates are for June through August, and again at Christmas. Discounted rates are available for spring and fall. Rentals are handled by property-management companies; see our listings in the Resorts, Ranches, and Vacation Rentals chapter.

The opportunity to experience small-town life attracts many new residents to Central Oregon.
PHOTO: JIM YUSKAVITCH

Another upscale neighborhood, just south of Sunriver, is Three Rivers, which includes both small acreages and some riverfront sites. Homesites here are selling for $15,000 to $180,000. Homes range anywhere from $290,000 to $5 million.

South Bend encompasses the area immediately west of Sunriver and as far south as State Rec Road. South Bend was originally developed by a tourist from Encino who fell in love with the area when he visited in 1962. He purchased hundreds of acres of land and divided it up into half-acre lots, which were marketed on television as Oregon Water Wonderland. House styles and values vary quite a bit, but $150,000 is average, and most are owned by full-time residents.

This area is typified by a high water table that makes 30- to 60-foot deep wells possible. Some neighborhoods have community water and sewer systems (because the water table is too high there for septic systems), but in most areas each home has a well and private septic system. It is required by state law to have the well and septic system checked when buying a home. Undeveloped land purchasers should make their offers contingent upon approval of a septic feasibility test.

La Pine

The area south of State Rec Road is considered to be La Pine, a community of 15,000 full- and part-time residents. The original town of Rosland was settled around 1900, but when U.S. Highway 97 came through just east of town, some of the town's buildings were relocated to be next to the highway, and the town was renamed LaPine. In recent years the postal service decided LaPine should be spelled as two words, La Pine, and this is now the official spelling. Huntington Road, the old stagecoach highway, still has some of the town's municipal buildings, including the library, post office, and the La Pine elementary and high schools.

Despite some disagreement about spelling, La Pine residents are unified when it comes to appreciation of their location. Bordered on all sides by national forest or BLM public lands, the town tends to attract fisher-folk, hunters, and other people who just plain don't want to be in the heart of civilization. The area is heavily forested with jack pine and ponderosa pine, though in recent years much of the jack pine has had to be logged off to stop the progress of a beetle infestation. There are said to be more than 100 lakes and streams within 30 minutes of town, as well as lots of elk, deer, and coyotes.

At one time logging was strong here, but now La Pine is more of a retirement community. Up until the 1950s, when the first subdivision was created, La Pine's population was about 150. The biggest influx of residents happened in the 1960s, and the area is once again on the upswing, driven by new retirees who want affordable housing. The town boasts three medical offices, a senior center, a couple of social clubs, and two markets with drugstores. However, La Pine is still a small town with a small-town feel to it. When you ask for a phone number, you're likely to get just the last four digits.

Most of the residential development is west of U.S. 97, and it's a mixed bag of older single-wide mobile homes, newer double-wide manufactured homes, and old and new wood houses. One area broker says she's seen land prices go from $3,000 to $30,000 per acre in the two decades she's spent selling real estate in La Pine. Home prices currently range from $90,000 to $120,000. La Pine doesn't really have new subdivisions going up the way Bend has. The more typical scenario is houses built in older subdivisions that have been slow to fill up until recently. The Day Road area in northeast La Pine is a good example, where a new three-bedroom, two-bath home on a one-acre lot in an older subdivision will go for $120,000 to $140,000. One-acre lots in the La Pine area cost about $21,000 to $25,000. Larger parcels of 5 to 20 acres are becoming increasingly scarce in south Deschutes County, but typically run from $50,000 to $70,000. Most homes have private wells (20- to 90-feet deep) and septic systems, but the downtown area has a city sewer system. There is very little irrigation water available, but some smaller horse properties irrigate with well water or feed hay.

Real Estate Companies

Coldwell Banker-First Resort Realty
Sunriver Village, Building No. 9, Sunriver
(541) 593–1234, (800) 452–6870

First Resort Realty was first opened in 1973 to handle resales of Sunriver residential properties, and it is Sunriver's second-oldest realty company. In 1986 it became affiliated with Coldwell Banker. Today First Resort covers Sunriver, South Bend, and La Pine from this office. Because the office includes a property-management division that services late-arriving renters, hours run from 8:00 A.M. to 10:00 P.M. on weekdays and until 11:00 P.M. on Friday and Saturday during the summer months. (First Resort closes slightly earlier in the off-season months.)

Dennis Haniford's Cascade Realty
51477 U.S. Highway 97
(541) 536–1731, (800) 522–1731

Dennis Haniford is the broker/owner of this nine-agent office. It specializes in La Pine properties only, including residential, commercial, industrial, and investment properties. Office hours are extensive—8:00 A.M. to 6:00 P.M. Monday through Saturday and 10:00 A.M. to 4:00 P.M. on Sunday.

John L. Scott Real Estate-La Pine
16430 Third Street, La Pine
(541) 536–1188, (800) 677–1314

In 1994, Carol Raebel, owner/broker, took over this agency, which was established in the 1970s; in 1995 it became affiliated with John L. Scott. There are currently six sales agents (plus a broker) covering primarily residential homes, plus some acreages and commercial properties, in the large area of Lake County, Deschutes County, and northern Klamath County. The office is open seven days a week.

John L. Scott Real Estate-Sunriver
Sunriver Village, Building No. 11, Sunriver
(541) 593–1211, (800) 547–1016

This office has one broker and six sales agents. It was established in 1972, and today specializes in golf properties throughout Central Oregon. They publish the free, monthly *Homes* magazine and are open seven days a week.

LaPine Realty
51415 U.S. Highway 97, La Pine
(541) 536–1711, (800) 829–1711

Established in 1971, LaPine Realty has one full broker, owner John Thomas, and six sales associate brokers. The office specializes in the La Pine area, covering residential, commercial, and recreational property sales. It also manages several rental properties. LaPine Realty does not have a national affiliation because John says he wants his company to be a home-town real estate office. LaPine is open most of the year from Monday through Saturday, and staff members will gladly make an appointment for Sunday. In summers, the office is open daily.

RE/MAX Sunset Realty
Sunriver Village, Building No. 2, Sunriver
(541) 593–2122, (800) 458–0424

A Century 21 office since 1996, Sunset Realty operated as an independent agency for six years prior to affiliating with the national organization Century 21, then switching to RE/MAX in 2000. Although they serve all of Central Oregon now, Sunset's 15 sales agents and one broker specialize in Sunriver, South Bend, and La Pine properties. Open daily, Sunset focuses on residential real estate.

Sunriver Realty
Sunriver Village, Building No. 5, Sunriver
(541) 593–7000, (800) 547–3920

This was the original realty office for Sunriver when the resort opened to sell lots in 1968. Twenty-five agents now cover residential properties throughout Central Oregon. The office, next to the post office in Sunriver Village, is open 363 days a year (all except for Christmas and Thanksgiving).

Village Properties
Two Country Mall, Sunriver
(541) 593–7368, (800) 786–7483

This four-agent office is headed up by owner/broker Mark Halvorsen. Established in 1983, Village Properties special-

izes in Sunriver and the surrounding area. The office is open daily.

Prineville Area

Believe it or not, people are moving to Prineville to get away from the hubbub and traffic of Bend. "But it's still close enough to commute to your job and not so far away that you feel isolated," says Kathy Overall of The Associates Real Estate in Prineville. Retirees from western Oregon and surrounding states are also coming to the Prineville area, along with a different breed of newcomer—telecommuters and others who harness the modern technology of computers, fax machines, and the Internet to earn their salaries and can live anywhere they choose.

Prineville is a small ranching and logging community on the western edge of the Ochoco Mountains. It's perfectly situated for those who seek a quiet, rural lifestyle away from the tourists and traffic that are becoming more common in other parts of Central Oregon. With a population of only 7,255, it's easy to settle in and get to know everyone. And there is more of a selection of real estate to choose from way out here than you might think.

Insiders' Tip
Throughout Central Oregon, you should check into the domestic water supply when buying property. Urban areas will have city water, but it may not be obvious where the boundaries are. You may be getting into piped or hauled private company water, wells, or ditch water ("pasturized") systems.

Typical of the small towns in Central Oregon, there's not much available in the core downtown area of Prineville. With few places to build within the city limits, most of the new housing and building lots are springing up on the city's edges. Affordable three-bedroom, two-bath homes in a relatively new subdivision, like the North Ridge project going on the north end of town, run from $82,900 to the high $90,000s. South of Northridge is the new subdivision of Stone Ridge. Its Craftsman-style homes are in the $119,000 to $130,000 range. Stone Ridge West will offer basic ranch houses for about $100,000. Two-acre lots with all utilities can be had for $56,000 at High Desert Estates, 3 miles south of town, which includes preparation for building.

Other subdivisions in the area include West Ridge on the lower Crooked River and Mountain View Estates near Powell Butte, which offers great views of the Cascades. There are some small subdivisions by the Prineville Golf and Country Club (see our Golf chapter) with two- to three-acre lots and irrigated 40- and 60-acre parcels. Three- and four-bedroom homes on several irrigated acres go for around $200,000 to $250,000. As for lot prices, five-acre parcels without irrigation run from $39,000 to $79,000; small lots with irrigation water are priced in the $49,000 to $75,000 range.

Forty-acre Prineville-area ranchettes will set you back $350,000 to $500,000, while you will be hard-pressed to find real, working 250- to 4,200-acre ranches for less than $1 million. Some top out close to $4 million. Many people who shop the Prineville real estate market end up purchasing a lot or small bit of acreage and building a house to their own specifications, rather than buying into an already developed subdivision.

Real Estate Companies

The Associates Real Estate
715 Northwest Third Street, Prineville
(541) 447-3940
In business since 1983, the 14 Realtors at The Associates work mostly within Crook County but venture into adjacent Deschutes, Wheeler, Grant, and Wasco Counties as well. They have expertise in commercial, industrial, and residential properties, as well as with ranches, farms, and bare land.

Coldwell Banker Sun Country Realty
750 Northwest Third Street, Prineville
(541) 447-4433
In business since 1993, Sun Country Realty handles all types of properties, primarily in Crook County. The office has one broker, one associate broker, and 12 agents.

Hill & Associates
553 Northwest Third Street, Prineville
(541) 447-3951
Doing business in Central Oregon since the late 1960s, Hill & Associates serves Crook, Wheeler, Jefferson, and Grant Counties and specializes in residential and commercial properties as well as bare land and multifamily housing. There is one broker, one associate broker, and four agents on staff.

Insiders' Tip

Homes in Central Oregon that are outside city limits usually have septic systems rather that sewer hookups. When buying property with a septic system, make sure you find out how old the system is and get an assessment of its current condition. Septic systems generally have a lifespan of about 20 years.

Simmons Realty, Inc.
238 North Main Street, Prineville
(541) 447–5638

Elsie Simmons, whose husband started the business in 1950, has seen plenty of changes in Prineville. "I've watched people move here by the hundreds," she says. There are two brokers on staff. They work mostly with residential property, though they deal with some commercial and bare land throughout Crook County and a bit of Wheeler County.

Madras Area

You won't find any hobby farmers on small ranchettes in the Madras area. This is serious agriculture country, where farmers grow commercial crops such as mint, flower seeds, garlic, sugar beets, carrots, radishes, potatoes, bluegrass, and wheat. Located in Jefferson County, on the northern edge of our Central Oregon coverage area, Madras is a blue-collar town of slightly more than 5,000 people—far from the bustle of activity found farther south.

Speculative home building has only come to this area in the past ten years or so. Typical real estate activity in the Madras area has traditionally centered around local residents who rented or owned small homes in the downtown area, saved their money, then bought a small parcel in the outlying rural area and built their dream house. That pattern still exists today, though there are also recreational properties available as well as a number of newer subdivisions in the area.

Madras' real estate properties fall into three basic categories: existing homes on 6,500-square-foot city lots, one- and two-acre parcels, and working farms and ranches of 80 or more acres. A basic 1,000- to 1,500-square-foot, two- to four-bedroom home in Madras and the nearby communities of Culver and Metolius runs anywhere from $65,000 to $100,000. City lots to build on, if you can find them, run $20,000 to $35,000.

A subdivision in these parts is any development with at least four lots. There are a number of these in the area, including Morning Crest, Juniper Estates, Juniper Acres, Sunnyside Estates, Silverado, and Cascade Estates, most of which are springing up to the southeast and northeast of town. Most subdivision home prices average between $95,000 and $130,000. Homes in Sunnyside Estates, for example, start at $117,500.

Vacant rural, two-acre lots go for $30,000 and up; it's more like $100,000 and up for parcels with homes. There are very few homesites available that are larger than two acres since much of the Madras area is zoned exclusively for farm use. Large working farms of 80 acres or more—many of which have been in the hands of local families for generations—sell for anywhere from $350,000 to more than $2 million.

Recreational properties also are available, primarily at Three Rivers on the Metolius River arm of Lake Billy Chinook, a popular watersports area at The Cove Palisades State Park. However, these five-acre lots have no city services or hookups for water, no telephone, and no other utilities for that matter. If you want those amenities, you have to provide them yourself. These lots go for $30,000 and up. Developed lots in the area, with homes incorporating elaborate propane and solar energy systems, sell for as much as $200,000.

Real Estate Companies

Coldwell Banker
Dick Dodson Realty
83 Southwest K Street, Madras
(541) 475–6137

Dick Dodson serves all of Jefferson County. He and his associate broker specialize in residential properties, but they handle commercial properties, farm and ranch lands, and bare lands as well.

F & G Properties
1113 Southwest Kenwood Drive, Madras
(541) 475–1089

F & G Properties was established in 1992 and deals in residential property throughout Central Oregon. It has one broker and three agents. F & G also sells homes at Juniper Crest, a subdivision it has developed.

Home Town Realty
210B Southwest Culver Highway, Madras
(541) 475-7986

Home Town Realty is a locally owned company with one broker and four agents. It's been in business since 1995. While they work quite a bit in residential sales, they also handle recreational properties around Lake Billy Chinook and have an agent on staff who specializes in farms and ranches.

Jim Waldorf Real Estate
2565 Southwest Bear Drive, Madras
(541) 475-3992

Jim Waldorf Real Estate does a lot of work with commercial property sales, but it is basically an all-purpose real estate office. Owner/broker Jim Waldorf and his three agents sell properties throughout Oregon.

Midland Realty GMAC Real Estate
715 Southeast Adams Drive, Madras
(541) 475-6161

Specializing in Jefferson County real estate and handling everything from recreational properties to production farms, Century 21 Midland Realty has been serving the Madras area since the early 1980s.

Insiders' Tip

The Visitors Information Center (63085 North Highway 97, Bend) has tons of real estate brochures and magazines, as well as other valuable information for people looking into moving here.

Retirement

Senior Centers

Volunteer
   Opportunities

Educational
   Opportunities

Recreational
   Opportunities

Senior Services

Independent Living

Central Oregon has long been a magnet for retirees attracted by the beautiful scenery, golf courses, great fishing, wide-open spaces, clean air, beautiful forests, and sunny weather, to name just a few of a hundred reasons. A Central Oregon retiree typically has an above-average income and often has retired early. In recent years many retirees have come here from Southern California after selling homes in the booming real estate market of the late 1980s and walking away with enough cash to buy nice, large homes in Central Oregon with tidy sums left over. While those days may be over, Central Oregon continues to draw retirees from throughout the country, especially to the La Pine area, where real estate tends to be less expensive (see our Neighborhoods and Real Estate chapter).

Because many Central Oregon retirees tend to be active and younger, with more upscale tastes and hobbies, the activities described in other chapters—from golf and fishing to annual events and the arts—will also be of interest. However, everyone isn't out on the golf course or in the trout stream. We also have a vibrant and active retired population that socializes at senior centers, volunteers within the community, and brings the experiences and wisdom of their many years to everything they do and everyone they touch. And of course, there are also many social services available for those seniors who, due to their health or income, need a little help to get by.

Senior Centers

A ubiquitous part of the senior scene, senior centers are among any community's most valuable resources. They provide a place for seniors to meet and stay active. They also serve as home bases for a variety of services designed to help keep seniors healthy, independent, and connected with the community at-large. And they are there to give aid if you should find yourself in need of help. Get acquainted with your local senior center, and see what they have to offer. You'll be glad you did.

Bend Senior Center
1600 Southeast Reed Market Road, Bend
(541) 388-1133

Owned by the United Seniors of Bend, the local senior citizens' organization, the Bend Senior Center is the place to be for area retirees with an itch to scratch. There is pool all week long, cribbage in the evenings, bingo on Wednesdays, a live band and dancing every Tuesday and Thursday, and line dancing and pinochle on Fridays. The "Singing Seniors" and "Serenaders" perform each week as well. Hot lunches are served weekdays at noon through the Senior Meal Site program. The suggested donation is $2.50. Senior volunteers also deliver meals to homebound seniors as part of the Meals-on-Wheels program.

The center sponsors a variety of health-related programs including blood pressure exams and foot-care clinics. An in-home care program will send an outreach worker to help with just about anything, from housecleaning to after-surgery assistance. The center will also help seniors make contact with the variety of social-service programs available in the Central Oregon area.

In addition to its recreation facilities, the center has a thrift store and gift shop. United Seniors of Bend has about 200 members age 55 and older. A one-year membership is $1.00. Lifetime membership is $12.

Bend Metro Park & Recreation District's Fit & Over Fifty program provides plenty of activities for area seniors. PHOTO: BEND METRO PARK & RECREATION DISTRICT

Redmond Senior Center
325 Northwest Dogwood Avenue, Redmond
(541) 548–6325

Plenty of activities greet patrons of the Redmond Senior Center. You'll find live music and dancing every Wednesday. Hot lunches are served at noon (with a suggested donation of $2.50 for those age 60 or older and $4.50 for those under age 60), followed by bingo, cribbage, whist, or some other enticing game. Culture isn't ignored either: Art classes and Spanish lessons are regular offerings. Health seminars, taught by local healthcare professionals, are held on a variety of subjects, and regular blood-pressure and foot-care clinics are available as well. The Meals-on-Wheels program delivers hot food to homebound seniors, and caseworkers are available to provide outreach services.

La Pine Senior Center
16629 Burgess Road, La Pine
(541) 536–6237

Because many retirees to Central Oregon settle in the La Pine area, the La Pine Senior Center is probably the busiest in the region. Most programs here are provided by the Central Oregon Council on Aging (see the listing under Senior Services).

A "wellness team" provides educational talks and materials, and the center sponsors a health talk, presented by a local healthcare provider, once a week. They also sponsor a regular Social Services Resource Forum, where local social-service agencies provide information on services and assistance available to Central Oregon seniors. The center provides outreach work to assist homebound seniors and helps arrange for any services they may need. The center serves hot meals at noon on Tuesday, Wednesday, and Thursday for a suggested donation of $2.50. They also deliver hot meals to homebound seniors.

Soroptimist Senior Center
180 Belknap Street, Prineville
(541) 447–6844

There's a television set in the lobby of the Soroptimist Senior Center, but there are usually so many things happening here it hardly ever gets turned on. The center offers pool tables, board and card games, line dancing, exercise classes, and live bands and dancing on Fridays. The "55 Alive" class is a two-day safe-driving course for seniors. Graduates are eligible for a 10 percent discount on car insurance.

Two minivans operating out of the center provide daily transportation for seniors and the disabled who live within a 5-mile radius of downtown Prineville. A bus also takes seniors to nearby Redmond for shopping once each week. On weekdays at noon, nutritious, hot meals are served as part of the Senior Meal Site program. The suggested donation for meals is $2.00 for people age 60 or older and $4.00 for those younger than age 60. Home-delivered meals are available.

At tax time volunteers are available to assist seniors in filling out tax forms. The center is owned by Soroptimist International of Prineville.

Madras Senior Center
860 Southwest Madison Street, Madras
(541) 475–6494
Musical entertainment accompanies the Meals-on-Wheels program offered at the Madras Senior Center on Tuesday, Wednesday, and Friday. The suggested donation is $2.50. Meals-on-Wheels also delivers to the homebound. The center features a variety of other programs and services for seniors including legal aid, health talks, and monthly blood-pressure readings, as well as pool tables and board games. Constructed in 1993, the center building is one of the nicest facilities in Jefferson County and is available for groups to rent for meetings, wedding receptions, and other events and functions. For rental information, call (541) 475–4811.

Volunteer Opportunities

Retirees often find that volunteer work provides the perfect way to keep busy, put their professional skills or hobbies to good use, and contribute to the community. There are a variety of volunteer opportunities in Central Oregon for retirees—and younger people as well. The listings that follow give some starting points.

Retired & Senior Volunteer Program
2500 Northeast Neff Road, Bend
(541) 388–7746
Part of a nationwide program that connects retired and semi-retired people with volunteer positions in their communities, the Central Oregon office of the Retired & Senior Volunteer Program opened in fall 1996. Its mission is twofold. First and foremost, it helps community organizations and agencies better accomplish their goals by providing them with talented, skilled, committed, and caring people to help them with day-to-day tasks. Secondly, research and experience have shown that seniors lead happier and healthier lives when they remain occupied in constructive endeavors.

RSVP provides the perfect vehicle for seniors with a lifetime of knowledge and experience to join with community organizations who need that knowledge. Prospective volunteers meet with RSVP staff, who help match their skills and interests with available volunteer positions. The program is open to anyone, retired or semi-retired, age 55 and older.

The High Desert Museum
59800 South U.S. Highway 97, Bend
(541) 382–4754
If you have a bent for education and enjoy meeting and talking to lots of people, the volunteer opportunities available at The High Desert Museum may be right up your alley. You could find yourself giving interpretive talks to museum visitors about anything from eagles to lizards, or presenting educational programs to school children on field trips or in their classrooms. Other opportunities include working at the gift shop, helping with special museum events, and staffing the admissions desk.

If you're more of a behind-the-scenes person, you can work with the museum's collections and artifacts, assist in the resource library, do some light typing and filing in the office, or roll up your sleeves and help landscape and maintain the grounds. And you don't have to be an expert to volunteer. Museum staff will train you before you go to work; because of the effort and time the museum's training

At the Bend Metro Park & Recreation District, volunteer opportunities abound for seniors who want to lend their skills and wisdom to area youth. You can help the recreation staff work with kids (as well as adults) with special needs, teach a youngster to swim, coach a sports team, or assist with district-sponsored community events, to name just a few options. If you're blessed with a green thumb, you can sign on to help maintain one of the city's many beautiful parks. For more information on the Bend Metro Park & Recreation District, see the listing in our Parks chapter.

program involves, they ask that volunteers be willing to make a long-term commitment.

U.S. Forest Service Deschutes/Ochoco National Forest
1645 U.S. Highway 20, Bend
(541) 383–5300
Oregon Department of Fish and Wildlife
61374 Parrell Road, Bend
(541) 388–6363
Bureau of Land Management
3050 Northeast Third Street, Prineville
(541) 416–6700

Because Central Oregon is blessed with such a rich legacy of natural resources, there are many opportunities to help with a variety of outdoor conservation projects—particularly in the areas of wilderness, recreation, fish, and wildlife. The best approach is to call some of the local natural resource management agencies, let them know your interests and skills, and ask what kinds of upcoming projects they have planned that may require volunteer help. They'd love to hear from you.

One weekend project, for example, had more than 100 volunteers helping fishery biologists survey a trout stream in the Ochoco National Forest. But it wasn't all work. The group was rewarded for its day of labor with a barbecue dinner accompanied by live musical entertainment.

Bend Metro Park & Recreation District
200 Northwest Pacific Park Lane, Bend
(541) 389–7275

Educational Opportunities

Retirement is no time to stop learning. Central Oregon has many resources to allow you to continue a lifelong course of self-improvement—whether it's a long-sought-after college degree that you finally have time to earn or just a desire to take some fun classes to meet new people.

Central Oregon Community College
2600 Northwest College Way, Bend
(541) 383–7700

Central Oregon Community College is a fully accredited two-year college that offers associate of arts, science, and general studies degrees as well as one-year certificates and two-year associate of applied science degrees in more than 30 technical and career fields. They have a wide selection of classes that may be taken with or without college credit. For more information see the listing in the "Colleges and Universities" section of the Education and Child Care chapter.

Central Oregon University Center
2600 Northwest College Way, Bend
(541) 383–7256

The University Center, based at Central Oregon Community College, offers about 23 baccalaureate and masters degree programs from 10 private and public Oregon universities and colleges, enabling Central Oregon residents to earn undergraduate and graduate degrees without having to travel out of the area. Retirement may be the perfect opportunity to get that new college degree! For more information see the listing under "Community and Continuing Education" in the Education and Child Care chapter.

Central Oregon Community College
Community Education Bend Center,
2600 Northwest College Way, Boyle
Education Center, Bend
(541) 383–7270
Sisters Center, 160 South Oak Street, Sisters
(541) 549–7331
Redmond Center, 255 Southeast Salmon
Drive, Redmond
(541) 504–2900
La Pine/Sunriver Center, Aspen Alley #8,
La Pine
(541) 536–2020
Prineville Center, 413 West Third Street,
Prineville
(541) 447–4418
Madras Center, 281 Southwest Third Street,
Madras
(541) 475–2136
Warm Springs Center, 1110 Wasco Street,
Warm Springs
(541) 553–1428

Another program of Central Oregon Community College, community centers throughout Central Oregon offer a wide variety of classes, talks, workshops, and seminars—some fun, some serious—on a year-round basis. Classes run anywhere from one or two days or evenings to several months depending on the subject matter and the depth to which it is being taught. Most classes cost less than $40, and a senior discount is available. For more information see the listing in the "Community and Continuing Education" section of the Education and Child Care chapter.

Recreational Opportunities

Bend Metro Park & Recreation District
200 Northwest Pacific Park Lane, Bend
(541) 389–7275

With the great outdoors beckoning everywhere you look, you can't spend all your time on the golf course. Through its Fit & Over Fifty Outdoor Programs, the Bend Metro Park & Recreation District can take you on a mountain or desert hiking trip, or biking on quiet country roads and along forest trails. If you don't mind getting wet, they'll put you in a canoe or kayak for a pleasant day's paddle down a local river or across a glassy, smooth lake. There's no need to be stuck indoors during winter, either, when you can don a pair of snowshoes or skis and venture into the winter wilderness beneath a sunny Central Oregon sky.

The district also offers a variety of senior-oriented programs at the Juniper Swim and Fitness Center. These include water exercises, arthritis aquatic exercise, recreational swimming, aerobics, and weight training. For more information on the Bend Metro Park & Recreation District and the Juniper Swim and Fitness Center, see the chapters on Parks and Indoor Recreation, respectively.

Senior Services

There are lots of social services available in Central Oregon for seniors and other people in need of a little help. The programs listed below are good starting points to get answers for any questions you may have or to find services you may be looking for. Senior centers, listed previously, are also excellent resources for tracking

Insiders' Tip

It's easy for retirees to stay fit and active in Central Oregon with the many options available, from outdoor excursions offered by the parks and recreation department to daily workouts at a local gym.

Retirees are drawn to Central Oregon's wide-open spaces, clean air, and sunny weather. PHOTO: JIM YUSKAVITCH

down services. In fact, you may find the help you are seeking is available from your local center. If not, they can almost certainly refer you to the program or agency that can help.

Central Oregon Council on Aging
1036 Northeast Fifth Street, Bend
(541) 382–3008
Oak and West Main Streets, Sisters
(541) 549–4112
325 Northwest Dogwood Avenue, Redmond
(541) 548–6325
16629 Burgess Road, La Pine
(541) 536–3207
180 North Belknap Street, Prineville
(541) 447–6844
860 Southwest Madison Street, Madras
(541) 475–6494

A private, nonprofit organization, the Central Oregon Council on Aging is dedicated to providing assistance to senior citizens throughout Central Oregon. With caseworkers at all area senior centers, COCOA offers many important services for seniors, including health screenings, health and wellness education, nutrition programs, and case management that helps seniors

make important decisions about their healthcare and other living needs.

One program run by COCOA, and unique to Oregon, is Oregon Project Independence (OPI). Based on a sliding-fee scale, OPI provides in-home care for seniors including housekeeping, shopping, meal preparation, personal care, and laundry services. Many of the programs provided at area senior centers are run by COCOA.

Dial-A-Ride
Bend, (541) 389–7433
Sisters, (541) 549–4112
Redmond, (541) 548–0466
La Pine, (541) 536–3207
Prineville, (541) 447–6429
Madras, (541) 475–6494

A nifty service for car-less seniors in Central Oregon is the Dial-A-Ride program. If you need to get around town for doctor appointments, shopping, or errands, just call the Dial-A-Ride dispatcher closest to your location to schedule a ride. A bus will pick you up at home, take you where you need to go, then return you to your home.

The suggested donation is $1.00 for in-town service and $3.00 for out-of-town rides for those over age 60. Younger folks pay $2.00 and $6.00, respectively. Due to the program's popularity, you'll need to schedule your ride anywhere from one day to one week in advance, depending on how busy your local Dial-A-Ride program is.

Senior and Disabled Services Division
1001 Southwest Emkay Street, Suite C, Bend
(541) 388–6240

A state program under the auspices of the Oregon Department of Human Resources, the Senior and Disabled Services Division offers a variety of programs for seniors and disabled people. Some of the programs the division runs or can put you in contact with include health and nutrition services, access to counseling, long-term and respite care, adult day-care services, in-home services, help in finding employment, and the opportunity to become involved in senior and disabled advocacy.

Independent Living

Central Oregon has a few independent-living facilities for seniors who do not particularly need ongoing medical care or other types of assistance or supervision. These facilities typically cater to those who are seeking a simpler lifestyle (free of some of life's more difficult and time-consuming chores), like-minded neighbors of the same age, and an on-site staff who can respond to emergencies, just in case.

Aspen Ridge
1010 Northeast Purcell Boulevard, Bend
(541) 385–8500

Aspen Ridge offers independent-minded seniors 70 apartments, including studios and one- and two-bedrooms. Residents are provided three meals a day along with housekeeping and linen service. A staff activity director plans a variety of daily social and entertainment events as well as outings. Transportation for shopping, doctor's appointments, and other errands is also available for residents without their own vehicle. Other amenities here include a library, computer room, beauty salon, ice-cream parlor, putting green, billiard room, and fitness center. Staff is on hand 24 hours per day, ready to help with whatever might come up.

Bend Villa Court
1801 Northeast Lotus Drive, Bend
(541) 389–0046

This independent-living complex for seniors has a total of 123 units (35 are residential-care units) including studio, one-bedroom, and two-bedroom apartments. Each apartment has three emergency buttons in various rooms that will summon staff members 24 hours a day in the event of an emergency.

Bend Villa Court serves three meals a day to residents in its restaurant-style dining room, and it provides housekeeping and linen services, laundry facilities, and a full recreation and social program. Bus transportation throughout the area is also available to residents.

Harmony Healthcare
95 Northeast Xerxes Avenue, Bend
(541) 382–0479

Harmony Healthcare has 35 apartments available for independent living, including both one- and two-bedroom units. Three meals a day are provided for residents along with housekeeping and linen services and a recreation and social program. Parking is available for residents with cars, but about-town transportation is not provided. They will, however, help you arrange a ride through the local Dial-A-Ride program (see the Dial-A-Ride listing in this chapter). Staff members are on hand to help out 24 hours a day.

Insiders' Tip
On the first Sunday of the month, the local daily paper, the *Bulletin*, publishes an extensive list of organizations seeking volunteers.

Stone Lodge
1460 Northeast 27th Street, Bend
(541) 318–0450

Stone Lodge's 112 apartments are a mix of studio and one- and two-bedrooms. Three meals a day are provided along with complete housekeeping services. There are lots of activities in progress on a daily basis including games, cards, and bingo. A bus is available to take residents to shopping areas, to doctor's appointments, and to other outings. Staff members are on hand around the clock every day.

The Summit
127 Southeast Wilson Avenue, Bend
(541) 317–3544

Studio, one-, and two-bedroom apartments are offered at The Summit, along with individually air-conditioned rooms. Residents receive three meals a day in a restaurant-style dinning room. Housekeeping and linen services are available, as well as a complete program of recreational and social activities. Parking is provided for residents with cars. Staff, who are available 24 hours a day, will help residents arrange for local transportation through the Dial-A-Ride program. Affiliated retirement and assisted-living centers also include The Heights in Redmond, (541) 923–5452, and Ochoco Village in Prineville, (541) 416–3600.

Insiders' Tip
Volunteering is a great way for retirees to keep busy and pass on the benefits of a lifetime of knowledge, experience, and skills to others in the community.

Prairie House
51485 Morson Street, La Pine
(541) 536–8559

This mixed independent and assisted-living residence has a total of 54 studio or one-bedroom apartments. All meals are provided for residents, along with housekeeping services. In addition to an exercise room and lots of on-site activities, residents here go on a variety of outings, from shopping excursions to fishing trips. Each apartment has an emergency call system and staff is available 24 hours per day, year-round.

Healthcare

Hospitals
Immediate Care
Alternative Healthcare
Veterinary Services

We Central Oregonians count our high-quality healthcare system among our blessings. The largest and most extensive regional medical facilities are in Bend. But Redmond, Prineville, and Madras all have their own community hospitals as well. Sunriver has one of the only 24-hour immediate-care facilities outside of a hospital in Central Oregon. More than half the patients seen by our doctors come from a 25,000-square-mile area of Central and Eastern Oregon. In fact, the population of Central Oregon's extended patient community is approaching 200,000.

Our clean air, gorgeous scenery, recreational opportunities, and relaxed lifestyle are responsible for attracting some of the best doctors and medical staff in the West. Between all four of our area hospitals, we have some 250 affiliated doctors covering just about every specialty—from allergies to vascular surgery.

Our area hospitals and doctors belong to an organization called CONet (Central Oregon Network), a cooperative effort to improve healthcare in Central Oregon. One of the programs that is in use and under continuing development is a database system whereby patients' X rays and lab results can be made available to doctors in CONet. That way, lab tests do not have to be duplicated for the convenience of different specialists, and doctors from different areas can consult on one case.

All of our hospitals have trauma centers, with St. Charles Medical Center's Level II trauma center being the most advanced. (The nearest Level I is in Portland.) A Level II trauma center can handle everything except the most acute brain injuries. In all of our cities, we dial 911 for emergency services.

While Central Oregon is very up-to-date in terms of healthcare, it lags behind the rest of the country in two areas. First, while we have plenty of traditional healthcare insurance providers, HMOs (health maintenance organizations) have been slow to get a foothold here, though in the past year they have made progress and several are now available. If you are planning on moving here, you may need to change your health insurance provider, so give yourself plenty of time to work it out. Consult with local insurance agents, who will know what is available here.

Secondly, alternative medicine, although represented locally by qualified practitioners, has not made as much headway into the established medical community as it has in other parts of the country. But our communities are growing by leaps and bounds, and we can look forward to these areas growing as well.

Pets, horses, and livestock form a very important part of Central Oregon's population. The section in the Yellow Pages for veterinarians is almost half as large as the main physician section. We have vets who treat everything from gerbils to buffalo. There are clinics with cozy in-town offices for small pets, livestock vets with mobile vans, and clinics with big stalls and slings for large animals. We even have a major new equine hospital, one of only two in Oregon.

Hospitals

Central Oregon Community Hospital
1253 North Canal Boulevard, Redmond
(541) 548-8131
Central Oregon Community Hospital is a 48-bed full-service facility offering inpatient and outpatient services. The hospital opened its doors in 1952 as an acute-care center serving the community of Redmond and the surrounding area. The hospital's medical staff includes family physicians, obstetricians/gynecologists, internists, surgeons, orthopedists, and urologists.

The hospital offers 24-hour emergency services. It is a Level III trauma center and has access to Air Life of Oregon air medical transport. Central Oregon Community Hospital has in-house CT scanning and round-the-clock laboratory and anesthesiology services.

The Birth and Family Center offers a variety of birthing services such as Jacuzzi tubs located in its homelike birthing suites, and breast-feeding support services provided by certified lactation specialists. Central Oregon Community Hospital also offers an FDA-certified mammography service.

COCH also offers community public education and disease prevention programs for children and adults. Together with Bend's St. Charles Medical Center, Central Oregon Community Hospital co-sponsors the Best Care Treatment Center for drug and alcohol rehabilitation.

Central Oregon Community Hospital is owned and operated by Cascade Health Services, which also owns St. Charles Medical Center.

Mountain View Hospital & Nursing Home
470 Northeast A Street, Madras
(541) 475-3882

This combination hospital and nursing home has 36 beds for acute care and 68 beds for long-term care. It serves Jefferson County, one of the fastest-growing counties in the state and one of the most ethnically diverse—25 percent of the county's population is Native American and 15 percent is Hispanic. Mountain View offers extensive inpatient and outpatient services, including a birthing center with six private family birthing suites, each with a bathroom with Jacuzzi tub. Other features and programs include a new physical therapy wing with state-of-the art facilities, home health/hospice care, community education, a pharmacy, 24-hour laboratory, and emergency services, including a Level IV trauma center and Air Life services.

Pioneer Memorial Hospital
1201 North Elm Street, Prineville
(541) 447-6254

Built in 1950, the Pioneer Memorial Hospital is a community-owned, not-for-profit hospital serving more than 20,000 residents in Crook and Wheeler Counties.

Managed by Banner Health Systems, the hospital is licensed for 35 beds and has a staff of more than 170 employees. The hospital's medical staff includes 10 independent, 14 specialty, and 9 consulting physicians. The newly expanded Emergency Department has been rated a Level III trauma center. PMH offers a five-bed intensive-care unit and a CT scanner. The hospital also has a new Family Birthing Center with three suites, and home health/hospice services. Its Community Outreach program offers the community a variety of preventative, rehabilitative, and wellness seminars throughout the year.

St. Charles Medical Center
2500 Northeast Neff Road, Bend
(541) 382-4321

St. Charles Medical Center has received international acclaim for its unique healing environment and has been identified as a national leader in preventive care and early detection of disease, heart services, obstetrics, endometriosis treatment, rehabilitation, orthopedics, cancer care, end of life care, and overall patient satisfaction.

Founded in 1918, St. Charles has more than 200 physicians on its medical staff representing over 40 specialties. As the regional referral center for nearly 200,000 people in a 31,000-square-mile area of Central and Eastern Oregon, St. Charles offers comprehensive medical, surgical, and trauma care. The medical center is Oregon's only Level II trauma center east of the Cascade Mountains. It also has the region's only Level III Neonatal Intensive Care Unit. More than 70 percent of the babies born in Central Oregon are born at St. Charles (over 1,300 per year on average).

St. Charles offers leading-edge technologies, including Oregon's only electron beam tomography scanner for detecting coronary disease, state-of-the-art digital cardiac catheterization facilities, CAT scanners, magnetic resonance imaging, and other advanced technologies.

Other St. Charles–affiliated facilities and services include the St. Charles outpatient SurgiCenter, the Central Oregon Regional Laboratory, the Central Oregon Cancer Treatment Center, Cascade Home Care, Therapeutic Associates, the High Desert Sleep Center, the Best Care Treatment Center for drug and alcohol rehabilitation, and the St. Charles Rehabilitation Center. Air Life of Oregon, an air medical service with helicopter and airplane transport, is based here. There is also a Ronald McDonald House on the St. Charles campus to house families of young people seeking care at the hospital and surrounding clinics. St. Charles will soon complete its innovative Center for Health and Learning.

Unique approaches, such as 24-hour room service for patients, volunteer musicians and therapeutic music programs, a free recreational vehicle park for patient families, and a fishing pond for rehabilitation therapy, have drawn national praise. With 1,500 employees, St. Charles is the largest employer in Central Oregon. *Oregon Business Magazine* has consistently named St. Charles as one of the 100 best places to work in Oregon. St. Charles is owned and operated by Cascade Health Services, which also owns Central Oregon Community Hospital in Redmond.

Air Ambulance

Air Life of Oregon Inc.
St. Charles Medical Center, 2500 Northeast Neff Road, Bend
(541) 385–6305; (800) 522–2828, general information; 911 for emergencies

Air Life of Oregon is a private helicopter and aircraft ambulance service that works with all four community hospitals. The Air Life membership fee of $45 per year per family protects against out-of-pocket expenses ($3,500 to $8,000 per flight) should your health insurance not cover

St. Charles Medical Center is a national leader in modern healthcare. PHOTO: JIM YUSKAVITCH

Be careful out there! But if you do take a tumble, rest assured that our regional medical facilities will put you on the road to recovery in no time. PHOTO: MT. BACHELOR SKI RESORT

air ambulance services. Some insurance policies do cover air ambulance charges, so check your policy before joining. If you are already covered and live in a rural area, you should contact Air Life and arrange to give them descriptive information on your specific location. Even if a resident lives in town, he or she may benefit by Air Life membership in case emergency transportation from a local hospital to St. Charles Medical Center is needed. Air Life's helicopters operate within a 150-mile radius of St. Charles Medical Center in Bend, where they are based. They also operate two fixed-wing aircraft.

Drug/Alcohol Treatment

Visions of Hope Recovery Center
676 Negus Way, Redmond
(541) 504–9577

This center, less than a half-mile from the Central Oregon Community Hospital, consists of a large ranch house that was converted in 1997 to a residential drug and alcohol treatment facility. The center has 4 detox beds and 12 resident beds. A converted barn houses the conference facilities, where the outpatient program is held. Care is provided by Bridgeway Inc., which staffs the center around the clock, and treatment usually lasts four to five weeks. Patients pay on a sliding scale according to ability to pay, and the state pays for any expenses not covered by the patient or insurance.

Immediate Care

Immediate-care facilities treat non-life-threatening emergencies on a walk-in basis. More severe and life-threatening conditions should go directly to the emergency room of the nearest hospital. You can always dial 911 for an ambulance.

Bend Memorial Clinic
1501 Northeast Medical Center Drive, Bend
(541) 382–2811

BMC is the largest multi-specialty medical group in Central Oregon with nearly 50 board-certified physicians and 150 allied health professionals. It has a full-service laboratory, radiology department, optical department, and pharmacy. Although there are satellite offices in Sisters, Redmond, and La Pine, the main Bend office is the only one to offer immediate care.

Immediate-care hours are 8:00 A.M. to 8:00 P.M. Monday through Friday, 8:00 A.M. to 4:00 P.M. Saturday, and 1:00 to 4:00 P.M. on Sunday, every day of the year. Doctors are available by phone around the clock to discuss urgent but not critical health problems; call the main number to be put in touch with a physician. BMC is across the street from St. Charles Medical Center.

High Desert Family Medicine
57057 Beaver Drive, Sunriver
(541) 593–5400

Sunriver and La Pine lack a full-fledged hospital, but they do have a 24-hour immediate-care and family-medicine facility. X-rays, lab work, and plaster casting are all done on-site. A physician is available around the clock, and the facility has a small supply of pharmaceuticals for emergency patients. It also serves as a family-practice clinic. Their hours are 8:00 A.M. to 5:00 P.M. Monday through Friday.

High Lakes Health Care
76 Northeast 12th Street, Madras
(541) 475–3874; (541) 475–6100, after hours

This clinic, one of four in the High Lakes group, is a small, three-physician office

Insiders' Tip
Many Central Oregon medical centers and health clinics offer "wellness classes" to help people manage existing medical conditions, or to learn how to lead a healthier lifestyle. Ask your physician for recommendations.

that offers a full range of services, including prenatal care, obstetrics, pediatrics, and family and geriatric care. Staff doctors are on call for the emergency room at the Mountain View Hospital, and sometimes non-life-threatening cases that come to the ER are sent to High Lakes offices for treatment. Walk-ins are accepted during office hours, 8:00 A.M. to 5:00 P.M. Monday through Friday and 9:00 A.M. to 4:00 P.M. on Saturday. During other hours, patients should go to the Mountain View Hospital.

Mountain Medical Group
1302 Northeast Third Street, Bend
(541) 388-7799
Since 1986, Mountain Medical Group has offered urgent care 365 days a year. The clinic provides courteous, professional service for most illnesses and minor injuries. Hours are 8:00 A.M. to 8:00 P.M. Monday through Saturday and 10:00 A.M. to 6:00 P.M. on Sunday.

Alternative Healthcare

Central Oregon, and more specifically Bend, has a small but growing number of alternative healthcare providers including naturopaths, acupuncturists, and massage and aroma therapists. The existing medical and resident communities have been slow to accept alternative methods of care.

Health-food stores, listed below, are very good sources for up-to-date information on local practitioners of alternative healthcare. The Curiosity Shoppe, at 1314 Northwest Galveston Avenue in Bend, (541) 382-3408, has promoted alternative medicinal practices for 18 years and sells aromatherapy supplies. The shop has a bulletin board with business cards from care providers and information about classes. Two free local newspapers that can usually be found at healthfood stores and some restaurants, the *Green Pages* and the *Source*, carry advertisements for providers. The Yellow Pages is another good source. When using the Yellow Pages, look up naturopaths (N.D. instead of M.D.) under the Physicians—Naturopaths heading. Acupuncturists, Aroma Therapy, and Massage—Therapeutic each have their

own headings. And when evaluating non-physician care providers, ask about the person's licensing, training, and years of experience, and ask for references.

Health-food Stores and Organic Foods

Cornucopia Natural Foods
1721 Southwest Odem Medo Road, Redmond
(541) 548-5911
What customers like most about this store is the knowledgeable staff. Sharing information is a big part of the services here, and local physicians even refer patients to Cornucopia. Inside the store is a good selection of vitamins, packaged health foods, books, and health and beauty aids, as well as bulk grains and herbs. In the back, you'll find about 20 feet filled with refrigerated organic items like beverages and soy products. The shop connects with The Daily Bread (see Restaurants), which makes it nice for customers who are waiting for a sandwich order to come next door and browse the health supplies. Cornucopia is open from 9:00 A.M. to 6:00 P.M. Monday through Friday, and from 10:00 A.M. to 6:00 P.M. on Saturday.

Country Store Health Foods
228 Northeast Greenwood Avenue, Bend
(541) 382-5200
On Fridays, local nutritionist and radio celebrity Betty Kreger (she airs on radio station KBND) spends the whole day at Country Store, talking with customers. The store features a lot of vitamins, minerals, and herbs, plus a small amount of groceries, store-packaged bulk foods, soy products, dried fruits, and nuts. The store is behind the Wilson's Mattress Shop next to the Wild Bird Center on the side of the building. It's open Monday through Saturday from 9:30 A.M. to 6:00 P.M.

Devore's Good Food Store & Wine Shop
1124 Northwest Newport Avenue, Bend
(541) 389-6588
Just walking into this old building with its dark wood and creaky floors, artfully arranged organic produce, and wonderful smells is a satisfying experience. The small

grocery selection features ethnic products such as jars of Indian seasonings, as well as bulk grains. A new and expanding area is homemade prepared foods. Customers can pick up a container of fresh soup, Devore's will microwave it, and then folks can sit on the porch with their soup and munch packaged fresh salads or wrapped sandwiches. Hours are 8:00 A.M. to 7:00 P.M. Monday through Saturday and 10:30 A.M. to 6:00 P.M. on Sunday.

General Nutrition Center
Mountain View Mall, 63455 North U.S. Highway 97, Bend
(541) 388–4718

This GNC chain outlet offers a large selection of vitamins, supplements, herbs, protein sports drinks, and natural beauty products. Hours are 10:00 A.M. to 9:00 P.M. Monday through Friday, 10:00 A.M. to 7:00 P.M. Saturday, and 11:00 A.M. to 6:00 P.M. Sunday.

Great Harvest Bread Company
835 Northwest Bond Street, Bend
(541) 389–2888

This bakery in downtown Bend specializes in breads and pastries made (as much as possible) with organic flours, unrefined sugar, and no preservatives. As you enter, the first thing you'll notice is the overwhelmingly wonderful smell, and then the sample tray that's right in front of the entry. Folks in the know drop by around noon and taste their way through lunch. Favorites include the nutty-tasting white bread, a sweet whole-wheat bread, and big cinnamon rolls, but the daily specials can be more exotic. Drop in Monday through Friday from 7:00 A.M. to 6:00 P.M. and Saturday from 7:00 A.M. to 5:00 P.M.

Nature's Bounty
320 North Court Street, Prineville
(541) 447–2247

This store has something for everyone, starting off with fresh cinnamon rolls and muffins from Great Harvest Bread Company in Bend. Vitamins for every need, nutritional supplements, tincture of dandelion, sports supplements, fresh dairy and nondairy products and eggs, and

bulk rice, beans, and flours are available. If they don't have it, they'll get it for you. Stop by Monday through Friday from 9:00 A.M. to 5:30 P.M.

Nature's General Store
1950 Northeast Third Street, North Wagner Mall, Bend
(541) 382–6732

A juice bar and vegan lunch counter are just two of the things that set this health-food store apart from the rest. A selection of organic wines is another. There is a large selection of vitamins, minerals and supplements, fresh organic produce, bulk grains, and wheatless breads. The staff can answer your questions Monday through Friday from 9:00 A.M. to 9:00 P.M., and Saturday and Sunday from 9:00 A.M. to 8:00 P.M.

Wild Oats Market
2610 Northeast U.S. Highway 20, Bend
(541) 389–0151

Located kitty-corner to COSTCO in the Forum Center, Wild Oats Market is one of 114 affiliated stores flung from coast to coast that specialize in natural foods and other goods. The Bend store opened in 2000.

The atmosphere is a combination of back-to-earth foods and neighborhood markets patronized by Central Oregon's neo-hippies and young professionals alike. If you are an aficionado of natural foods and other products, you're likely to find just about anything you need from bulk foods and soy products to vitamins and nutritional supplements. Meatless hot dogs and burgers, organic strained baby food, natural skin moisturizers, and nondairy desserts and drinks are just a sampling of their offerings. The less discriminating will find plenty of good food as well, including a fully stocked meat and seafood counter and a great selection of cheeses and wines.

Of special note, four food counters— The Wild Kitchen, Asian Table, Tortilla Luna, and Tuscan Grille—offer up pizzas, sandwiches, wraps, empanadas, and Asian noodle dishes (to name but a few). You can take out one of these delicious dishes or eat it right there at one of the tables in a corner of the store, complete with a gas fireplace for added ambiance.

The store also offers regular speakers who talk on a variety of subjects. Recent offerings have included "life restructuring" and the scientific basis of "gut feelings." Market staff brings in regular musical guests as well, such as Central Oregon pianist and singer Kelly Almond, folk singer and songwriter Dan Chavers, and guitarist Doyle Lodor. Pick up a monthly schedule of events on your next shopping trip.

Wild Oats Market is open daily from 8:00 A.M. to 10:00 P.M.

Veterinary Services

Veterinarians are plentiful in Central Oregon. In fact, it seems there's at least one in every neighborhood. They tend to specialize in three areas: small animals (dogs, cats, and sometimes novelty pets such as hamsters or ferrets); small animals plus livestock, which requires special handling equipment and experience; and equine care, which is a specialty unto itself. Horses make up a very large segment of the animal population here, especially in Deschutes County, and it's one that requires lots of veterinary services.

For dogs and cats we suggest that you visit a few clinics ahead of time. Ask to see the kennel areas and note the degree of cleanliness. Small details, like an open bag of dog biscuits sitting on the counter in the kennel room, are important. Hours of operation and location may be the deciding factor for people who work. Be wary of advertised specials for spaying and neutering, as they may not include hidden costs such as anesthetic, anesthesia pre-testing, or boarding.

Livestock and equine care is best obtained through neighborhood referrals. Approach neighbors with the same kind of stock that you have and get the names of their vets. Although the ads in the Yellow Pages infer that many clinics are good with all animals, you can discover hidden specialties among care providers (such as small ruminants or llamas or miniatures) only by approaching other owners of like animals. If you have an exotic breed, you may need to contact a few feed stores to see if anyone knows someone with your breed, or a breed association.

Since initial care often involves a farm-call, it's helpful to use a vet who is familiar with your neighborhood and to learn about your neighbors' experiences with this professional. Ask your neighbors about specific problems their animals had and how much the vet charged to treat them. Office visit and farm-call fees vary greatly, so it's wise to research two or three vets. Even if you are new to the area, identifying yourself as a livestock owner will usually open up a floodgate of advice and camaraderie; having problems with the health of a stock animal, or even a dog or cat, is actually a good way to get to know the neighborhood.

Perhaps the most noteworthy development in Central Oregon's veterinary scene was the opening of the Bend Equine Medical Center in 1998. This major, state-of-the-art facility is only the second of its kind in Oregon, the first being in Corvallis at Oregon State University. It is expected that the center's presence will have a significant impact on increasing the number and caliber of horse breeders and trainers in Central Oregon.

Bend Equine Medical Center
19121 Couch Market Road, Bend
(541) 388–4006

Dan Harrison, DVM, and Wayne B. Schmotzer, DVM, Dipl. ACVS, opened this state-of-the-art surgical and medical hospital for horses in September 1998. Located at the corner of U.S. Highway 20 in the community of Tumalo about 8 miles west of Bend, this 7,000-square-foot facility serves every equine need. The surgery wing has an elaborate overhead rail system to transport anesthetized horses, a hydraulic operating table, anesthesia and ventilating equipment for adult horses and foals, and a radiology unit. Two intensive-care stalls with observation room and seven regular patient stalls enable the hospital to provide the 24-hour care necessary for surgery patients. A laboratory and pharmacy are also available.

Reproduction services are one of the center's specialties, including semen testing and freezing, artificial insemination, and seminars on equine reproduction. Dental care is another specialty of Drs. Harrison and Smotzer. On the grounds of the center are a fully equipped breeding shed, corrals, lameness exercise area, and trailer parking.

Education and Child Care

Education

For a region considered by many to be out in the boondocks, Central Oregon has a surprising variety of educational opportunities and services for everyone from toddlers to adults. We have excellent public schools with state-of-the-art technology and award-winning teachers, Christian and secular private schools, Oregon's oldest community college, and a respectable amount of child care. You can even earn a bachelor's or master's degree from nearly a dozen Oregon universities without ever leaving town.

The most exiting recent development here in education is the new Oregon State University branch campus, which opened for business in the fall of 2001. After a keen and lengthy competition between Corvallis-based OSU and the University of Oregon, located in Eugene, OSU was given the nod, largely because its technical and natural resources curriculum was regarded as more appropriate for Central Oregon and the kinds of jobs and industries expected in the future.

With a four-year university in the area, many Central Oregon high school graduates will be able to move into higher education without leaving town, while students from other areas of the state and country will likely find the Central Oregon branch of Oregon State University a fine place to attend as well. In addition, the presence of the university will bring more research to the area, along with the additional cultural and educational opportunities and resources—not just for students but for all area citizens—that institutions of higher learning bring to their communities.

Public Schools

Bend/La Pine School District
520 Northwest Wall Street, Bend
(541) 383–6004
This is the largest school district in Central Oregon, serving more than 13,000 students in the communities of Bend, Sunriver, and La Pine. Bend is the most populous community within the district and has 12 elementary schools, 4 middle schools, and 4 high schools with a total student enrollment of about 11,500. La Pine, 30 miles south of Bend, has one elementary school, one middle school, and one high school with a total student population of about 900. The school in Sunriver, which also serves the nearby areas of Spring River and Fall River, has about 270 students attending kindergarten through 5th grade. After completing 5th grade, students here transfer to schools in either Bend or La Pine.

District elementary schools serve grades kindergarten through 3, 4, or 5, depending on the location. Middle schools serve grades 6 through 8, except for La Pine Middle School, which serves grades 5 through 8. The high schools serve grades 9 through 12.

For students currently enrolled in a district school, registration for the upcoming school year is conducted in the spring. Registration for students transferring from another school district is conducted at their assigned school after August 1. School assignments are based on where students and their parents or legal guardian reside. To attend kindergarten, children must be 5 years old by September 1 of the year of enrollment.

Parents and teachers listen as kids read in their classroom on "Read Across America Day."

PHOTO: PEGGY HUMPHREYS/BEND-LA PINE SCHOOL DISTRICT

The core elementary school curriculum in the Bend/La Pine School District focuses on building basic skills in reading, spelling, handwriting, math, social studies, computer education, library skills, art, music, and physical education. Some of the larger schools offer a "neighborhood" concept, which breaks up the school into smaller groups of students in grades K–5. Most of the district's elementary schools also permit students to enroll in classrooms with single-age or multiage students.

The middle school curriculum continues to build on a student's mastery of subjects begun at the elementary level, while offering opportunities for students to take a variety of elective and exploratory programs.

At the high school level, students continue to pursue traditional core areas of study as well as a variety of elective subjects. To graduate from high school, students must earn 25 credits.

Co-curricular activities and clubs at district high schools include such areas as drama, speech, and music. Opportunities for boys to participate in athletic programs include football, baseball, basketball, cross-country, track, wrestling, tennis, golf,

skiing, swimming, and diving. For girls there are soccer, basketball, softball, volleyball, track, tennis, golf, swimming, diving, and skiing.

More than 40 percent of Bend/La Pine School District high school seniors take the Scholastic Achievement Test (SAT), and they consistently score above the national average. The latest available district SAT scores show students scoring 11 points higher than the national average in verbal proficiency and 29 points higher in mathematics.

The school district also offers a work-study program in cooperation with local businesses called the School-to-Work Alliance, a Talented and Gifted program and a variety of services and assistance for students and families with special needs.

Sisters School District
440 East Cascade Street, Sisters
(541) 549–8951

With one elementary school, one middle school, and one high school, the Sisters School District serves a total of about 1,170 students.

The Sisters Elementary School contains grades K–5 and has about 430 students. The courses of study here include math, science, social studies, health, language arts, music, and physical education, with the rigorousness of instruction increasing with each grade level. A number of other programs, intended to enrich and expand on the core curriculum, are offered, including blended classrooms, literature-based whole-language learning, computer lab, and field trips. Co-curricular activities for elementary students include volleyball, basketball, flag football, and gymnastics through the local community organization SOAR (Sisters Organization for Activities and Recreation).

The middle school has about 300 students in grades 6 through 8. Sixth-grade students stay in their homerooms all day; 7th grade students receive instruction in science, math, the humanities, physical education, and health. A program called Cruise, which incorporates exploratory classes in art, technology, computers, and living skills, is also integrated into the 7th grade curriculum. In addition, students take one elective class and have an opportunity to receive instruction in Spanish in addition to their regular curriculum.

Eighth graders pursue studies in social studies, science, math, English, physical education, and health along with three elective courses. During the winter months, after-school classes in downhill skiing are available for middle school students and 5th graders from the elementary school. Other middle school co-curricular activities include basketball, football, volleyball, cross-country, track, wrestling, music, yearbook, and student government programs.

About 450 students attend Sisters High School. They must earn 26 credits through the course of their high school career to receive a diploma. In addition, they must also show proficiency in speaking and in working with computers. Sisters High School students have a wide selection of co-curricular programs and activities available to them, including drama and musical productions, applied technology projects, science projects and competitions, participation in student government, involvement with school yearbooks, work experience opportunities, and help-

ing with community volunteer projects. High school sports include football, volleyball, basketball, soccer, baseball, wrestling, golf, track, swimming, skiing, girls softball, cheerleading, and dance team. The high school is on block scheduling, which is set up for students to take their courses over a two-day period, attending 95-minute classes every other day.

Sisters School District students currently test above the state average in all grade levels tested, with the exception of mathematics, which tested around the state average. Their writing scores are among the highest in Oregon. In 1997, 67 percent of Sisters high school seniors took the SAT, scoring 24 points above the corresponding national average.

The Sisters School District also provides services to students with special needs at all of its schools along with a program for at-risk students who are 16 years or older. Honors English, trigonometry, pre-calculus, and physics programs are offered at the high school level.

Black Butte School District
Camp Sherman
(541) 595–6203

In operation since 1881, the Black Butte School District consists of one schoolhouse with about 30 students and two teachers. It serves grades kindergarten through 12, although all students have the option of transferring to another school when they reach the junior high and high school levels. One unique aspect of this tiny school district is the tremendous amount of parental involvement, particularly their willingness to volunteer for many tasks for which the district would otherwise have to pay.

The close teacher-parent-student relationship fostered at Black Butte School pays off in increased student-teacher contact time—about a month more than other school districts in the area. Because the students are able to do five days worth of work in four days, they are treated to a ski outing every Friday during the winter months. And every three years, the students take a field trip to Washington, D.C., as part of their civics studies.

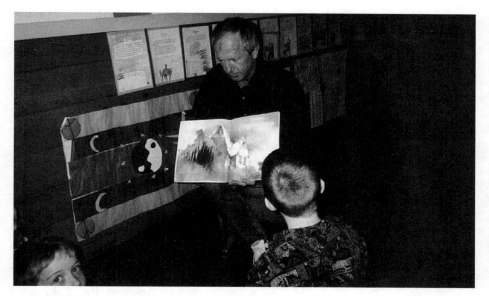

Central Oregon has excellent schools and teaching staffs. PHOTO: MARY BETH PEARL/BEND-LA PINE SCHOOL DISTRICT

Redmond School District
145 Southeast Salmon Drive, Redmond
(541) 923-5437

The Redmond School District sprawls across 550 square miles of High Desert country. Its six elementary schools, two middle schools, one high school, and one alternative high school serve about 5,100 students. In 1985, Obsidian Middle School was recognized as one of the best schools in the country by the Oregon and U.S. departments of education. In the past 15 years, three teachers from the district have been selected as Oregon Teacher of the Year, making the Redmond School District the most recognized school district in Oregon for its teaching excellence.

In addition to its core curriculum—similar to other area districts at all grade levels—the Redmond District has a number of community-based programs, including the Start Making A Reader Today program, or SMART; the Special Friends program, where adults volunteer to work on a one-on-one basis with at-risk youth; and a cooperative business/education partnership program. The district also requires students to be passing all their classes before being allowed to participate in co-curricular programs and activities—

of which the district offers a wide spectrum. A technology wing recently constructed and outfitted at Redmond High School exemplifies the district's commitment to teaching students skills for the next century. The high school also has child-care and teen-parent programs.

In 2000 the Redmond School District spent about $5,650 per student. Students within the district typically score above the average in national and state testing.

Crook County School District
1390 Southeast Second Street, Prineville
(541) 447-5664

With passage of a school bond by voters in 1993, the Crook County School District has been able to build new school facilities and repair aging ones. A modern high school with a computer lab, auditorium, and several gymnasiums was constructed in 1996.

With a current enrollment of about 3,000 students, the district operates three elementary schools serving students from kindergarten through the 5th grade, one elementary school serving grades K through 6, a recently remodeled middle school serving grades 6 through 8, and one high school. Paulina School, 53 miles southeast of Prineville, serves grades K through 8.

Although very much a rural school district (the Powell Butte Elementary School has been recognized as the best rural school in the region because of its students' high test scores), Crook County is not letting technology leave their students behind. All schools within the district have computers connected to a district-wide network. Currently, there are 500 computers hooked up to this network, along with an additional 200 self-contained computers available for use by students and staff.

Co-curricular activities offered by the district include Future Farmers of America, Crooked River Ecosystem Education Council, Fishing Club, Rodeo Club, Honor Society, drama, cheerleading, school newspaper, band, choir, and Foreign Language Club. Sports for boys include football, baseball, basketball, soccer, tennis, golf, wrestling, cross-country, and track. Girls can participate in volleyball, soccer, basketball, cross-country, softball, golf, tennis, and track.

A special-education program is offered by the district for students with disabilities. Children up to age 5 with special needs may attend the Larson Learning Center preschool, which is operated under contract with the school district and is at Crooked River Elementary School.

Jefferson County School District
445 Southeast Buff Street, Madras
(541) 475-6192

With an overall enrollment of a little more than 3,000 students, the Jefferson County School District operates four elementary schools in Madras and surrounding communities including Madras Elementary, Warm Springs Elementary, Metolius Elementary, and Westside Elementary. It also runs one middle school in Madras for grades 5 through 8 and a senior high school, also in Madras, that serves grades 9 through 12.

The overall core curriculum at Jefferson County schools is similar to other schools in the region, including programs in agriculture and forestry at the high school level. But because the district serves students from a variety of cultural backgrounds—including many Hispanic and Native American kids (the district includes the Warm Springs Indian Reservation, and 36 percent of its students are Native Americans, while some 23 percent are Hispanic)—it offers a number of special programs such as Native American studies and English as a Second Language.

Other special programs include the Buff Learning Center for at-risk kids. Located at the senior high school, the center includes a program where students rebuild used computers. A full range of co-curricular activities including Future Business Leaders of America, Future Farmers of America, Honor Society, Spanish Club, Art and Photo Club, track, basketball, soccer, softball, golf, and wrestling are also offered. In 1997 the district began an all-day kindergarten program at Warm Springs, which has since been expanded to Westside and Madras Elementary Schools.

The district is also up to speed in the technology department. Its new middle school, built in 1995, has computers in every classroom and is in the process of being connected to the Internet. The senior high school has a full lineup of computers as well. The Jefferson County School District has a total of 425 employees, including 200 certified teaching staff.

Private Schools

Although Central Oregon has excellent and innovative public schools, there are also a number of private schools for parents who prefer other options for their children. These include both denominational and nondenominational religious schools with strong, Bible-based courses of study, as well as secular institutions that offer small class sizes, specialized curricula, and college-preparatory programs.

Bend

Bend Community School
6133 South Highway 97
(541) 317–0854

Self-directed learning supported by state-of-the art technology is the cornerstone of Bend Community School. Students are provided the opportunity to focus on their individual uniqueness along with that of their fellow students and the local and global community as they pursue their interests and passions. The school's philosophy is that a child, given a positive and enriched learning environment combined with the support and encouragement of engaged adults, will have the tools necessary to become an independent learner and master of the technologies of the future. The school serves grades 5 through 8. Three teachers are on staff, and enrollment is about 45 students.

Morning Star Christian School
19741 Baker Road
(541) 382–5091
www.morningstarchristianschool.org

A Christian school featuring the ABEKA curriculum, Morning Star Christian School is strong on the basics—reading, writing, math, and phonics—and promotes a Bible-based learning environment for its 220 students. The teaching methods are traditional, and the Bible-study approach is from a conservative interdenominational viewpoint. Morning Star Christian School was founded in 1982. It serves students from preschool through the 11th grade. The school has 19 teachers on staff.

Sunriver Preparatory School
19888 Rocking Horse Road
(541) 318–9020
www.sunriverprep.org

A college-preparatory school founded in 1983, Sunriver Preparatory School serves students from pre-kindergarten through the 12th grade. A rigorous college-preparatory program is emphasized, especially in the Upper School, which includes art, music, drama, foreign language, and computers as well as a traditional core academic program. Every spring, students participate in Traveling School, venturing to such locales as Washington, D.C. and Mexico as part of their studies. Students become involved in local community-service projects and are eligible to participate in any public school program that is not offered by Sunriver Preparatory School. Currently there is a staff of 23 teachers serving an enrollment of 160 students. All graduates have been accepted into four-year colleges.

Three Sisters Seventh-day Adventist School
21155 Tumalo Road
(541) 389–2091

A fully accredited denominational Christian school with five teachers and an enrollment of about 60 students in grades K through 10, Three Sisters Seventh-day Adventist School is primarily for Seventh-day Adventist families, though they are open to anyone seeking a structured

Insiders' Tip
Most Central Oregon school districts have information packets and fact sheets about their schools, including facilities, curriculums, extracurricular activities, and special programs.

Christian-based education for their children. The aim here is to provide a Christ-centered learning environment that challenges and nourishes students spiritually, socially, intellectually, and physically. In addition to core academic subjects, the school offers sports and outdoor educational activities along with essential living skills to prepare students for eventually living on their own.

St. Francis of Assisi School
2450 Northeast 27th Street
(541) 382-4701

This Catholic school was founded in 1936 and serves students from preschool through the 8th grade. It has 25 teachers and a student enrollment of 300. A varied curriculum of study, enhanced by the example of Jesus and grounded in high academic standards, allows St. Francis of Assisi School to offer its students a quality Catholic education. In addition to core subjects, the school offers classes in music, band, Spanish, art, computers, and library skills. The school has a parent involvement policy that requires parents with children in preschool and kindergarten to donate 25 hours per year for fund-raising events, school projects, and social functions. Parents with children in grades 1 through 8 must donate 50 hours.

Seven Peaks Elementary School
2150 Northeast Studio Road
(541) 382-7755

An independent, nonprofit school serving students from preschool through the 5th grade, Seven Peaks Elementary School features the innovative Core Knowledge curriculum including phonics through the Signatures program and Mathlands, where teachers develop in their students a deeper understanding of mathematical problems by encouraging them to think, investigate, and make connections in their studies. Students further develop math skills through computations and practice drills. Students also participate in music and art classes and receive instruction in foreign language. In addition to classrooms, the school also has a library and recently-completed indoor activity room. Seven Peaks Elementary School has about 140 students.

Trinity Lutheran School
2550 Northeast Butler Market Road
(541) 382-1850

Founded in 1959, Trinity Lutheran School enrolls about 280 students in preschool through the 8th grade. It is a denominational Christian school with a curriculum that emphasizes such core academic subjects as spelling, phonics, reading, math, handwriting, literature, science, health, social studies, physical education, art, music, and foreign language in a Christ-centered environment. Trinity Lutheran School is accredited with the National Lutheran Schools Association. The school has 17 teachers and moved into new facilities in 1994.

Redmond
Central Christian Schools
2234 Southeast Sixth Street
(541) 548-7803

An interdenominational Christian school founded in 1992, Central Christian Schools offers kindergarten through grade 12 at its campus. With about 120 students and 13 teachers, the school's mission is to teach and exemplify Christ, commitment, and character and to serve their students, parents, community, and world. Utilizing the ABEKA and Bob Jones curricula, Central Christian Schools views itself as an extension of the home

Insiders' Tip
If you have a skill or special knowledge and are interested in teaching, call one of Central Oregon Community College's community-education centers and propose that you teach a class.

and strives to help parents meet their responsibilities to teach their children. The Bible-based course of study includes art, music, drama, foreign language, and computers along with a strong core curriculum in reading, math, writing, and other basic skills. Students also participate in retreats, field trips, community-service projects, sports, and other activities. Central Christian Schools is in the process of building a new campus that they hope to move into by 2003 or 2004.

Prineville Area

Crook County Christian School
835 South Main Street, Prineville
(541) 416-0114

Opened in 1994, Crook County Christian School provides a nondenominational Bible-centered learning environment for its 175 students in preschool through 12th grade. The ABEKA curriculum is used by the school's staff. Music, art, and a big drama program are offered in addition to the core program that particularly emphasizes phonics, reading, handwriting, math, and Bible study. The high school curriculum is accredited.

Homeschooling

Crook-Deschutes Education Service District
145 Southeast Salmon Avenue, Suite A,
Redmond
(541) 923-8900
Jefferson County Education Service District
445 Southeast Buff Street, Madras
(541) 475-6192

Another education option that some families choose is homeschooling. Homeschooling was originally made popular by those whose religious beliefs sometimes clashed with public school curricula. Today parents may decide to teach their children at home for a variety of reasons, ranging from the fear of school violence to an attempt to help a child who is having learning or behavioral problems.

About 1,200 families in Deschutes and Crook Counties are currently involved in homeschooling. There is no set curriculum for teaching kids at home; parents are on their own to develop their coursework,

though some schools will provide suggestions to help parents get started. The state does require that parents who choose this option notify their Education Service District in writing that they plan to teach their kids at home. Children who learn at home must also be tested in grades 3, 5, 8, and 10. Parents must hire a home tester for this task. Occasionally, a state tester is available to conduct these assessments.

Once homeschooled children reach high school age, they may begin taking state-accredited courses or elect to take their GED exam. The local education service district will provide parents with a list of accredited courses. Accredited homeschooling curricula may be purchased from a number of private, mostly religious, organizations. Central Oregon has two education service districts, listed above, that can answer questions about homeschooling and help you get off on the right foot.

Colleges and Universities

Central Oregon Community College
2600 Northwest College Way, Bend
(541) 383-7700

Nestled on a 193-acre pine-cloaked hillside on the west side of Bend, Central Oregon Community College was founded in 1949, making it the oldest community college in Oregon. Fully accredited by the Northwest Association of Schools and

Colleges, COCC offers associate of arts, science, and general-studies degrees as well as one-year certificates and two-year associate of applied science degrees in more than 30 technical and career fields. COCC also has transfer programs for students intending to continue on to a four-year university. About 3,700 students enroll each term, with around one-third of those typically registering as full-time students. The college has on-campus student housing available, making it unique among the state's community colleges. Scholarships, financial-aid programs, and college loans are available to students

In addition to its basic academic programs, COCC offers a variety of other educational opportunities for area residents, such as community education, the chance to earn a four-year or master's degree (see the following section on Community and Continuing Education), many programs and seminars aimed at assisting local businesses, and adult basic education, which includes high school completion courses, preparation for taking the General Equivalency Diploma test, and English as a Second Language.

Community and Continuing Education

Central Oregon State University
20365 Empire Avenue, Bend
(541) 312–8361

An exciting new development in higher education is the opening of an Oregon State University campus in Bend, allowing Oregon residents to attend a four-year educational institution without leaving town. Classes began during fall 2001. Initially, courses are being held in classrooms on the Central Oregon Community College campus. Funding has been secured to construct a separate higher education building to house the University's programs on the community college campus across from the library.

A total of 24 bachelor's degrees are being offered, including computer science, environmental studies, humanities, information technology, liberal studies, natural resources, nursing, and international busi-

ness. In addition, 11 master's degree programs will also be offered, such as civil engineering, public administration, business administration, and teacher education.

Central Oregon University Center
2600 Northwest College Way, Bend
(541) 383–7256

Based at Central Oregon Community College, the University Center offers about 28 baccalaureate and master's degree programs from 10 private and public Oregon universities and colleges, permitting Central Oregon residents to earn undergraduate and graduate degrees without having to travel out of the area. Utilizing COCC faculty and facilities, visiting faculty from other colleges and universities, and television and Internet communications, the University Center's degree and certificate programs include business, education, liberal arts and sciences, manufacturing, publishing, and social work. The University Center has proven to be a particularly valuable resource for those who have previously attended college, left before completing their degree, and now wish to go back and finish their studies.

Central Oregon Community College
Community Education
Bend Center, Boyle Education Center,
2600 Northwest College Way, Bend
(541) 383–7270
Sisters Center, 160 South Oak Street, Sisters
(541) 549–7331
Redmond Center, 255 Southeast Salmon
Drive, Redmond
(541) 504–2900
La Pine/Sunriver Center, 51456 U.S. Highway
97, Aspen Alley #8, La Pine
(541) 536–2020
Prineville Center, 413 West Third Street,
Prineville
(541) 447–4418
Madras Center, 281 Southwest Third Street,
Madras
(541) 475–2136
Warm Springs Center, 1110 Wasco Street,
Warm Springs
(541) 553–1428

Another program of Central Oregon Community College, community centers throughout Central Oregon offer a wide variety of classes, talks, workshops, and seminars—some fun, some serious—on a year-round basis. Foreign languages, painting, sculpture, outdoor sports, gardening, photography, nature study, computers, dancing, cooking, and fields trips to interesting parts of Oregon and the world are just a small sampling of the kinds of classes you'll find at local community education centers.

Classes run anywhere from one or two days or evenings to a period of several months depending on the subject matter and the depth to which it is being taught. Most classes cost less than $40, and a senior discount is available.

The High Desert Museum Education Program
The High Desert Museum, 59800 South U.S.
Highway 97, Bend
(541) 382-4754
The High Desert Museum offers a year-round program of workshops, classes, and field trips for all ages, focusing on subjects ranging from natural history to arts and crafts. You can learn how to track wildlife, make a Northwest Indian basket, or head off on a field trip with museum naturalists to watch birds and wildlife in some secret corner of the Great Basin Desert. Classes are modestly priced, ranging from free for a short lecture to a couple of hundred bucks for a multiday nature excursion. See our chapters on Annual Events and Attractions for more on The High Desert Museum.

Child Care

With about 450 providers, Central Oregon has a pretty good selection of child-care options. Still, your personal situation will dictate how easy or difficult it will be to obtain the type of care you are after. Parents with regular nine-to-five work schedules have an easier time finding child care than those who work odd hours and weekends. If you live far out in a rural area, you will also find it more difficult than those who live in or near population centers. There is a shortage of infant-care providers in the area.

Insiders' Tip
Your best bet for finding good child care in Central Oregon is to start your search as early as possible.

There are three basic kinds of child-care providers in Oregon—family child care, group home child care, and child-care centers. Family child care typically involves one person, registered with the state, who provides child care in his or her home. State registration requires that the prospective provider attend a child-care class and submit to a criminal background check. State officials then come to the child-care provider's home and inspect it for safety and sanitation and sometimes for fire hazards. By law, family child-care providers may have no more than 10 children under their care.

Group home child-care providers also operate out of private homes and are registered and inspected by the state. However, they may have up to 12 children in their care because they are allowed to hire employees. Child-care centers are inspected and certified by the state, operate out of commercial business facilities, and employ a number of child-care workers.

When seeking child care, parents should look closely at every provider they consider. Ask questions. What's their background? How long have they been in operation? What kind of training have they had? Do they have a criminal record? Are they registered with the state? Is the house safe? Are gates locked? Are ladders put away? Are household poisons out of reach? What's the ratio of children to provider(s)? Asking these questions—and having them answered to your satisfaction—will go a long way toward finding the child-care provider who is just right and making that first morning when you drop your child off go a little easier.

In Central Oregon, you'll pay $2.00 to $2.50 per hour for infant care and around

$1.85 to $2.50 per hour for child care for preschoolers and school-age kids up to 12 years old. Professional baby-sitters run from $5.00 to $8.00 per hour.

Child Care and Baby-sitting Referral Services

Child Care Resources-COCAAN
2303 Southwest First Street, Redmond
(541) 548-2380

This nonprofit organization is part of the National Association of Child Care Resource and Referral Agencies, working under the umbrella of the Central Oregon Community Action Agency Network, and exists to help parents find safe, high-quality child care.

Child Care Resources staff will answer questions about child-care options in Central Oregon, educate parents on how to go about choosing a child-care provider, and even supply a computer printout of close-to-home child-care providers for parents to inspect. For short-term child care, they can also put you in touch with baby-sitters who will come to your home or hotel, fully prepared with toys, games, and goodies. English and Spanish are spoken at Child Care Resources.

Special Education and Needs

Central Oregon has many agencies, programs, and support groups for parents and children with special needs as well as programs intended to assist in the health and development of all children. The following is a sample of just some of the Central Oregon programs available. If none of these provide exactly what you are looking for, staff members at any one can steer you in the right direction.

Head Start
520 Northwest Wall Street, Bend
(541) 388-2486

Operating under the umbrella of Central Oregon Community College, Head Start is part of a national preschool program for 3- and 4-year-olds from low-income families or families with special needs. Locally, Head Start serves about 215 families in Deschutes and Crook Counties through its 11 classrooms in Sisters, Terrebonne, Redmond, Prineville, Bend, La Pine, and the Sunriver area. The program also offers an extensive parental education and training program that will assist parents with just about everything—from help with child-raising skills to entering the workforce.

Deschutes County Early Intervention and Infant and Toddler Programs
1406 Northwest Juniper Street, Bend
(541) 389-5437

Staff at the Deschutes County Early Intervention and Infant and Toddler Programs provide support and therapy for children from birth through age 2 who have developmental delays or diagnosed disabilities ranging from cerebral palsy to Down syndrome. They have counselors, nurses, and a variety of therapists who work with the kids. Parent groups are also organized to keep families fully involved in their child's progress. This program is provided free of charge.

Early Childhood Special Education
520 Northwest Wall Street, Bend
(541) 383-6353

This program works in partnership with Deschutes County Early Intervention and Infant and Toddler Programs to provide specialized preschool and therapy for children ages 3 to 5 who have developmental delays and diagnosed disabilities.

Insiders' Tip

If your child or your family needs any kind of special assistance, call your local school district. They can refer you to the most appropriate program to meet your needs.

Ready, Set, Go
1029 Northwest 14th Street, Bend
(541) 317–3133

Another Central Oregon Community College–managed program, Ready, Set, Go gives support and assistance to anyone who has recently had a baby. They do this through home visits, providing new parents with information on raising their baby, and referrals to any special programs the family may be in need of.

Family Resource Center
1010 Northwest 14th Street, Bend
(541) 389–1724

A nonprofit United Way agency, Family Resource Center staff can direct people to the right program or agency for just about any problem imaginable through their FamilyTrax program—from respite care to finding emergency food, clothing, or shelter. Especially useful is their publication *The Parent and Family Resource Book*, full of valuable information for families in need. They also provide family forums and parenting classes along with a variety of other services.

Twentieth Century Initiative
205 Northeast Fourth Street, Prineville
(541) 416–0924

A federally funded project of the Department of Education, the Twentieth Century Initiative offers a safe place for kids to be between 6:00 A.M. and 6:00 P.M. utilizing public school facilities. The program offers a variety of educational and recreational activities for children from preschool through middle school ages. Fees are on a sliding scale depending upon the financial resources of the parents. For example, full care from 3:00 to 6:00 P.M. runs from $10 to $54. Drop-in day care starts at $2.00 per hour.

Media

Newspapers
Magazines
Television
Radio
Movie, Television, and
Advertising Productions

It wasn't so many years ago that the Central Oregon media scene consisted mostly of the local newspapers that had been publishing in area communities since those towns were founded back in our pioneer period. Today, there is a great variety of print and electronic media reflecting the diverse interests and backgrounds of the people who have been moving to Central Oregon in recent decades. We have four local television stations that produce their own programming as well as 14 radio stations representing seven formats.

But what really indicates the growth and diversity of Central Oregon's media is the increase in the number of local print publications—many of which have been founded within the past few years. These small publications are typically weekly or monthly special-interest newspapers, focusing on a particular subject or targeting specific segments of the community. The fact that there are a variety of demographic groups within Central Oregon—be it retirees, outdoor enthusiasts, ranchers and farmers, or business people—is testimony to our area's recent growth and diversification.

Business, tourism, and rural-oriented publications have been around for some time, but we now have newspapers and magazines that promote everything from organic farming to families. We even have an alternative weekly paper, fresh off the drawing board in 1997, that barely 10 years ago would have been regarded as completely inappropriate (if not plain weird) for this area. While some of these newer, smaller publications have staffs and offices, many are one-person operations, being generated in homes by a publisher-editor-advertising director all wrapped up in one and laboring under the same pressures and deadlines as the big papers.

We've put together a comprehensive list to help you find the sources of news, information, and entertainment you're looking for in all the formats and media available in Central Oregon.

Newspapers

Dailies

The *Bulletin*
1777 Southwest Chandler Avenue, Bend
(541) 382–1811
www.bendbulletin.com

Long an influential force in Central Oregon, the *Bulletin* was founded in 1903 in a log cabin in what is now Drake Park in downtown Bend. It expanded to become a daily newspaper in 1916. Robert W. Chandler purchased the paper in 1953. Chandler believed a newspaper should play an active role in the community, and under his editorship the *Bulletin* was a strong advocate for schools, libraries, and other local measures that improved Central Oregon's quality of life. In the same spirit of contributing to the community, the *Bulletin* sponsors the regional finals for the Scripps-Howard National Spelling Bee (the popular national finals are in Washington, D.C.); the Literate Bee, a local spelling bee to benefit literacy programs at Central Oregon Community College; Project SMART (Start Making a Reader Today); and the annual Fourth of July fireworks at Pilot Butte in Bend.

After Chandler's death in 1996, John Costa, former executive editor of the *Idaho Statesman*, was hired as editor-in-chief of all the newspapers owned by the *Bulletin*'s parent company, Western Communications. Western Communications owns nine newspapers in Oregon and California, including the *Bulletin* and the *Redmond Spokesman*.

Beginning in May 1998, the *Bulletin* added a Saturday edition, making it a seven-day-a-week paper. The *Bulletin* is delivered in the morning.

In 2000, the paper moved into its brand-new 87,000-square-foot building on 10 acres overlooking the Deschutes River in Bend's Old Mill District. The paper employs 175 people. It has a circulation of 35,000. Home delivery in Deschutes County is $10.50 per month.

The *Oregonian*
1320 Southwest Broadway, Portland
(503) 221–8327

The *Oregonian* is the state's largest daily morning newspaper. Highly regarded, it covers national and world events and news, Portland metro news and happenings, and issues throughout the state. The *Oregonian* has a correspondent who covers Deschutes, Crook, and Jefferson Counties, and the paper often runs stories about Central Oregon. Many area residents buy the *Oregonian*, along with their local paper, to get the broadest range of news possible. Rates for home delivery varies depending on where in Central Oregon you are, but typically runs between $15 to $17 per month. The *Oregonian* is also available at news boxes and markets throughout the area. A copy of a daily edition is 35 cents; a Sunday edition is $1.50. Established in 1850, the *Oregonian* has a circulation of more than 350,000.

Statesman Journal
280 Church Street Northeast, Salem
(503) 399–6611

A daily paper serving the mid–Willamette Valley in Western Oregon, the *Statesman Journal* covers national, statewide, and local Willamette Valley news. However, because it reports from Salem, the state capital, it's a good source for political news. The *Statesman Journal* is available by mail subscription for about $290 per year. You can pick it up at news boxes and markets throughout Central Oregon. A daily

issue is 50 cents, and a Sunday issue is $1.50. The *Statesman Journal* has a daily circulation of about 60,000.

Weeklies and Biweeklies

Central Oregonian
558 North Main Street, Prineville
(541) 447–6205

If you're a high school sports fan in Prineville, you're in luck. The *Central Oregonian* gives its readers extensive coverage of local sports. You'll also find news about this community of 8,205, as well as items about Crook County at large, profiles of local personalities, and classified ads selling everything from pigs to tractors. The *Central Oregonian* was founded in 1881 and is published every Tuesday and Thursday. A subscription in their core distribution area of Prineville and Powell Butte is $30 per year. A subscription by mail throughout Crook County is $38 per year. Subscriptions mailed to Deschutes, Jefferson, and Wheeler Counties cost $46 per year. A subscription mailed to any other location is $52 per year. The paper's circulation is 4,600.

Spilyay Tymoo
1100 Wasco Street, Warm Springs
(541) 553–1644

The reporters from *Spilyay Tymoo*, which means "Coyote News," cover the Indian Country beat, writing about issues of importance to the 2,700 subscribers, most of whom live on the Warm Springs Indian Reservation. Executive Editor Mike Van Meter runs local news stories on education, fishing rights, cultural heritage, economic

> ## Insiders' Tip
> Many Central Oregon newspapers now have Web pages, so you can peruse their contents from the comfort of your computer screen.

development, sports, and tribal council issues and pulls national stories relating to Native Americans off the Associated Press newswire. Published twice a week and distributed free to tribal members, *Spilyay Tymoo* was established in 1976. A mail subscription is $15 per year.

The *Madras Pioneer*
241 Southeast Sixth Street, Madras
(541) 475–2275

Founded in 1904, the *Madras Pioneer* keeps its 3,900 subscribers up-to-date on all the happenings throughout rural Jefferson County, from the latest high school sports scores to the most recent issues faced by the Madras City Council. Published every Wednesday, an in-county subscription is $21 per year. Subscriptions mailed to addresses outside Jefferson County cost $28.

The Pioneer also publishes the full-color *Sageland Magazine*, celebrating life in Jefferson County. There are fall/winter and spring/summer editions, which are distributed free of charge.

The *Nugget*
442 East Main Street, Sisters
(541) 549–9941
www.nuggetnews.com

Many readers of the 6,000-circulation 32-page weekly, the *Nugget*, live outside Central Oregon. They subscribe because they are thinking of moving here, but want to get a feel for what small-town life is like around these parts before taking the plunge. They would be hard-pressed to find a better paper for that task. Though it may be small-town, the *Nugget* gives thorough coverage to all the news that matters to residents of its western Deschutes County beat. Whether it's a heated city council debate about a new development proposal or a high school concert, locals look forward to reading about it on Wednesday when the *Nugget* comes out.

Published since 1976, current editors and publishers Kiki and Eric Dolson took over in 1982, modernizing the paper's operations and expanding its staff and content. Says Kiki: "Many small-town papers are having a rough go of it these

days, but we've got good support within the community. People really enjoy reading the *Nugget*."

The paper is distributed locally for free. A year's subscription delivered by third-class mail is $25; it's $70 to receive it by first-class mail.

The *Redmond Spokesman*
226 Northwest Sixth Street, Redmond
(541) 548–2184

About 90 percent of the news in the *Redmond Spokesman* is local and 85 percent of that is specific to the immediate Redmond area. Published weekly on Wednesdays, the paper follows the news, activities, and lifestyles of the people who live, work, and play in Deschutes County from Terrebonne to Tumalo. Owned by Western Communications, which also owns the *Bulletin* in Bend, the *Redmond Spokesman* has a circulation of around 5,000. It began publishing in 1909. A one-year, in-state subscription is $18. An out-of-state subscription is $30. A single copy costs 35 cents.

The *Source*
704 Northwest Georgia Avenue, Bend
(541) 383–0800
www.sourceweekly.com

Started in July 1997 by Paul Butler and Aaron Switzer in the tradition of alternative weeklies, the *Source* covers local issues, news, art, entertainment, and opinion in the Bend, Redmond, Sisters, and Sunriver areas. "We don't follow the traditional approach of objective journalism," explains publisher and editor Switzer. "We try to evaluate stories and get to the truth of the matter."

Inside the *Source's* pages you'll find stories on everything from local politicians and politics to how to find the perfect mate, along with in-depth news pieces on such issues of local concern as hiking trail fees and increasing traffic congestion. Culture coverage includes reviews of music, dining, art, and cinema. The paper has the most complete local entertainment listings in the area. Distributed free and published every Wednesday, the *Source* has a circulation of 10,000.

Monthlies and Bimonthlies

Cascade Arts and Entertainment
330 Northeast Marshall Avenue, Bend
(541) 388–5665
www.cascadeae.com

"I started *Cascade Arts and Entertainment* because I love the arts and I wanted to let the Central Oregon community know about all the wonderful treasures and talented people we have here," says editor and publisher Pamela Hulse Andrews, who also publishes *Cascade Business News*. Established in 1995 and with a circulation of 12,000, *Cascade Arts and Entertainment* does a particularly thorough job of covering Central Oregon's performing and fine-arts and museum scenes. It has expanded to include fashion and area dining as well. Of particular value is its monthly roundup of local art exhibitions, festivals, events, literature, poetry, museum, music, dance, theater, and workshop happenings in the Central Oregon area. *Cascade Arts and Entertainment* is distributed free, but you can receive it by mail for $20 per year.

Cascade Business News
330 Northeast Marshall Avenue, Bend
(541) 388–5665
www.cascadebusnews.com

Within a month after Pamela Hulse Andrews started *Cascade Business News* in 1994, her closest competitor (and former employer) was defunct, leaving her top-dog of the local business news scene and at the helm of the only paper in Central Oregon completely devoted to business. Published during the first and third weeks of the month, *Cascade Business News* is packed with stories about local business and the issues—local, statewide, and national—that affect it.

Highly popular with Central Oregon entrepreneurs, it's widely regarded as an important tool for local business development. *Cascade Business News* is distributed free, but it is also available by mail subscription for $29 per year. A mail subscription includes a comprehensive directory of Central Oregon businesses. The paper has a circulation of 10,000.

Central Oregon Family News
P.O. Box 826, Bend
(541) 385–1849

Central Oregon Family News was started in 1997 as a vehicle to help connect parents and kids with family-oriented events throughout Central Oregon. Published monthly, this 16-page newspaper combines feature stories of interest to parents alongside comprehensive listings of events, activities, and classes that range from the latest offerings of local parks departments to parenting classes and support groups. *Central Oregon Family News* is distributed free.

Sunriver Scene
57455 Abbott Drive, Sunriver
(541) 593–6068

Born in the late 1970s as a small newsletter for the residents of the resort community of Sunriver, the *Sunriver Scene* has blossomed into a full-fledged, 36-page newspaper over the past half-dozen years. It's a very community oriented newspaper. Stories in the *Sunriver Scene* vary from light features to business news to covering issues affecting the Sunriver community. The *Sunriver Scene* has a circulation of about 9,000, including distribution to the approximately 4,200 residents of Sunriver. The paper is free, but a mail subscription is $18 per year.

The *Sagebrush News*
1395 Southwest Lynn Boulevard, Prineville
(541) 416–2082
www.sagebrushnews.com

This 32-page tabloid has been hitting the streets every two weeks since 1993. In May 2000, founders Betty and Gene Moe sold the *Sagebrush News* to current publisher Tim Satterfield. He has kept the paper's original focus, covering all the unusual and fascinating people and other aspects of the sprawling High Desert country. He also publishes occasional special issues, which have included horses, dogs, and other subjects of interest to the paper's rural readership.

Local histories, tales of journeys to ghost towns, and the works of cowboy poets are just a few of the paper's offerings, which its 15,000 loyal readers devour cover to cover. Satterfield's beat is the High Desert of the West, from the east slope of the Cascade Mountains east to Boise, and from Winnemucca, Nevada, north to Walla Walla, Washington. The *Sagebrush News* is distributed free locally; a mail subscription is $22 per year

Magazines

Cascades East
716 Northeast Fourth Street, Bend
(541) 382–0127

This four-color, 64-page quarterly magazine has been published since 1976. Each issue of *Cascades East* shares with its readers the many things to do and see in Central Oregon while providing glimpses into the lifestyles of those who are lucky enough to live here. Feature stories include such subjects as outdoor recreational activities, the arts, business, area events, and real estate, to name just a few. *Cascades East* has a circulation of about 10,000 and has subscribers in more than 40 states. It is also placed in more than 4,500 motel and resort rooms throughout the area—you're likely to see it if you are staying in Central Oregon. A two-year subscription is $16.

Conscious Living
557 Northeast Quimby Avenue, Bend
(541) 388–9040

Formerly the *Central Oregon Green Pages*, *Conscious Living* focuses on the principles of holistic living, sustainable lifestyles, and the connection between the human spirit and the environment. Published bimonthly, *Conscious Living* also has lots of ads from local "green" businesses. It has a circulation of about 15,000. Subscription rates are $24 for one year and $40 for two years.

Small Farmers Journal
192 West Barclay Drive, Sisters
(541) 549–2064

This tabloid-size quarterly magazine focuses on sustainable farming, organic gardening, and the traditional use of animals for farm power. It's absolutely packed with information that any farmer using old-time methods to work the land needs to know. A typical 130-page issue contains stories on working horse breeds, preparing farm-raised animals for the table, technical overviews of horse-drawn farm machinery, and lots of practical advice on soils, gardening, and building various structures useful to the small organic farmer. There is also an extensive and lively letters-to-the-editor section. *Small Farmers Journal* has about 20,000 subscribers all over the world. A one-year subscription in the United States is $30. A subscription outside the country is $45 ($40 for Canada). A single issue costs $8.50. The company also publishes a series of how-to books on subjects related to organic farming.

Television

A full range of television viewing is available throughout most of Central Oregon. Depending on where you live, over-the-airwaves network affiliates that can be picked up by antenna include affiliates of ABC (KATU and KEZI), CBS (KOIN), NBC (KGW, KTVZ), Fox (KPDX), UPN (KPTV), and Oregon Public Broadcasting (KOAB). All are broadcast out of Portland except KEZI and KTVZ.

However, Central Oregon's mountainous terrain blocks television signals to many parts of the area. And frequent mountain storms can play havoc with transmitting and relay equipment and, in turn, with TV signals. Most people around here opt for cable, which allows reliable signal transmission as well as a greater selection of programming (see the listing of cable television companies in this chapter). However, homes outside our local town areas are not serviced by cable and have to rely on antenna or satellite reception. Central Oregon does have a few local television stations, which are listed below.

KTVZ-TV
62990 O. B. Riley Road, Bend
(541) 383–2121

This local television station is an NBC affiliate and offers a full lineup of programming from the NBC network. It also produces its own local newscasts, which air Monday through Friday at 6:30 A.M. and 5:00, 6:00, and 11:00 P.M., as well as at 6:00 P.M. on Saturday and Sunday.

KFXO-TV
63140 Britta Street, Bend
(541) 382–7220

Fox network affiliate KFXO-TV opened its Bend studio in 1996. In addition to offering programming provided by the Fox network, it also airs locally produced programs.

COTV-Bend Cable Channel 11
63090 Sherman Road, Bend
(541) 382–9460

Owned by Bend Cable Communications (see subsequent listing), COTV is what is known in the cable industry as a "local origination channel." That means that a significant number of the programs it airs are produced locally at the station's studios. About half of this station's programming is produced in-house, including high school sports coverage and airing of Bend City Council and Bend/La Pine School District meetings. Cable Channel 11 also broadcasts the Resort Sports Network, infomercials, and Christian rock videos *Praise TV*. COTV will also broadcast shows proposed by outside freelance producers if they can come up with advertising sponsors.

Channel 48 TV
P.O. Box 1, Powell Butte
(541) 923–4848

Channel 48 TV is a low-powered television station that has been broadcasting since 1988. It airs country/western music videos, local events, and school sports. It broadcasts over the air, but subscribers to Crestview Cable TV (see cable television listings) can also pick it up. Channel 48's signal reaches north to Warm Springs, south to Bend, east to Prineville, and west to Sisters and Black Butte Ranch.

Cable TV Companies

Bend Cable Communications
63090 Sherman Road, Bend
(541) 382–5551

Serving the communities of Bend, Redmond, Sisters, Black Butte Ranch, and parts of Tumalo, Bend Cable Communications offers 43 channels with its basic service, which costs $31.95 per month. It also offers a variety of packages, which include such premium channels as Starz, Home Box Office, The Disney Channel, Showtime, and The Movie Channel. Rates for these packages range from $39.95 to $71.95

Chambers Cable of Sunriver
2 Venture Lane, Sunriver
(541) 593–1296

If you live in or near Sunriver, Chambers Cable of Sunriver will be the cable company you'll need to call to get connected.

Insiders' Tip

The *Bulletin*, Bend's local daily newspaper, publishes a comprehensive television guide for Central Oregon every Saturday.

Insiders' Tip

Satellite dishes are becoming more popular as a way to pull television signals into the home, especially in the more remote areas of Central Oregon where cable is not currently available.

The basic service is $33 per month and includes 48 channels. Premium channels, which include two Home Box Office channels, two Showtime channels, and Robert Redford's Sundance Channel (which airs independent films) are available. Premium channel subscriptions range from $9.95 to $16.94. Also available are five pay-per-view channels.

Crestview Cable Communications
350 Northeast Dunham Street, Prineville
(541) 447–4342
For $15.40 to $28.65 per month, residents of Prineville, Crooked River Ranch, Madras, Metolius, Culver, and La Pine can sign up for 13- to 47-channel (depending on which community you live in) basic service. Basic service includes The Disney Channel. Crestview Cable also offers Cinemax and Home Box Office. These premium channels cost $10 per month for one, $18 per month for both.

WANT-TV
20332 Empire Avenue, Suite F7, Bend
(541) 382–4031
WANT-TV works a bit differently from other television providers. They'll come out and set up an antenna at your home to receive television signals from overhead satellites via a receiver on Grizzly Mountain near Prineville. This allows those people living in areas where there are no cable television lines to still receive cable

television. WANT-TV serves the Madras, Culver, Prineville, Powell Butte, Sisters, Redmond, and Bend areas.

The only catch is that you need to have a good "line-of-sight" signal to Grizzly Mountain. WANT-TV technicians will come out and determine how strong and constant your signal is before installing an antenna. The 27-channel basic service is $22.95 per month. Premium channels are $7.00 to $11.00 per month.

Radio

While the number of radio stations broadcasting in Central Oregon can't compare with what's available in the big cities, we still have a reasonable variety of programming formats to chose from. Country-Western music, as you might expect, dominates the lineup. Reception is generally pretty good throughout the area, but if you go driving along some of our mountain roads you'll encounter places where it's impossible to tune anything in. We've included a listing of area radio stations along with their call letters and town of origin to help you find the tunes you enjoy most.

Adult Contemporary
KMGX 100.7 FM (Bend)
KLRR 101.7 FM (Bend)

Christian Pop/Rock
KNLR 97.5 FM (Bend)

Country-Western
KMTK 99.7 FM (Bend)
KSJJ 102.9 FM (Bend)
KRCO 95.1 FM (Prineville)
KRCO 690 AM (Prineville)

News, Talk, Sports
KICE 940 AM (Bend)
KBND 1110 AM (Bend)

Nostalgia/Oldies
KQAK 105.7 FM (Bend)

Public Radio
KOAB 91.3 FM (Bend)

Rock

KXIX 94.1 FM (Bend)
KWPK 96.5 FM (Bend)
KTWS 98.3 FM (Bend)

Movie, Television, and Advertising Productions

With such scenic grandeur at nearly every turn, it should come as no surprise that the film and television industry has often utilized Central Oregon as a location for their productions. No fewer than 24 feature-length movies and television series have been filmed in the Central Oregon area since 1946.

Some notable Hollywood films made here include *Golden Earrings* with Ray Milland and Marlene Dietrich in 1946 ("A good deal of torso work goes on which I can't help feeling they're a bit too old for," said one critic of the time); *The Way West,* a 1967 effort starring Kirk Douglas, Robert Mitchum, Richard Widmark, and Sally Field; and 1974's *The Apple Dumpling Gang,* with Don Knotts, Tim Conway, and Slim Pickens. *Rooster Cogburn,* starring John Wayne and Katherine Hepburn, was also made in Bend in 1974. *Even Cowgirls Get the Blues,* based on the Tom Robbins novel of the same name and starring Uma Thurman, was filmed in Central Oregon in 1992.

Television series filmed in the area include the legendary *Have Gun—Will Travel,* starring Richard Boone. It was shot in Bend from 1958 to 1961. The short-lived series *McKenna,* with Chad Everett, was filmed in Bend in 1994. One of the more unusual Central Oregon television productions was *From Oregon with Love,* a Japanese TV series about a young girl who came to Oregon from Japan to live on a ranch. The series was shot in Central Oregon from 1984 to 1992. Apparently wildly popular with Japanese audiences, thousands came to Central Oregon as tourists to see the place where their favorite TV show was made.

Central Oregon business development leaders don't actually go out and promote the area to the film industry. Instead, what generally happens is that a movie or television producer who thinks Oregon might have the right "look" for their production contacts the Oregon Film Office in Portland and lets them know what kind of setting and scenery they are after. If the film office staff think that Central Oregon might have the look the producer is searching for, they'll contact area chambers of commerce.

Jackie French, director of the Bend Chamber Visitors and Convention Bureau, keeps a file of more than 700 photographs on hand that shows the various looks of the Central Oregon area. If she hears of movie or television producers searching for a look she feels Central Oregon has, she'll make contact with them and try to sell the area as a location for at least a portion of the filming.

But there's more to attracting Hollywood's business than just pretty scenery. "Film producers are looking to see if the area has the facilities that a production crew needs," says French. "That means lodging, restaurants, stores to buy supplies, and things for the crew do when they're not working. They also want to know if the community wants the business and if they'll make the film a top priority. And Central Oregon most definitely does."

One of the most exciting movie productions filmed here in recent years was when producer, director, and star Kevin Costner came here in 1997 to shoot part of his post-apocalyptic extravaganza *The Postman.* Shot during April and early May of that year, *The Postman* used locations throughout the area, including the spectacular scenery around Smith Rock State Park north of Redmond. About 250 extras were hired to appear in the movie and another 200 local workers were hired for everything from set construction to secretarial work.

The production dropped a total of about $6.5 million into the local economy during the 42 days of filming. And of course, Kevin Costner sightings were rampant throughout Deschutes County during this time. One quick-thinking bartender at Bronco Billy's Ranch Grill and Saloon in Sisters, with a camera close at hand, even managed to bag a photo of herself arm-in-arm with the Hollywood heartthrob when he dropped by unexpectedly one evening.

More low-key, but more common than feature films and TV series, are the numerous commercials that are shot in the area every year. These range from car commercials to fashion shoots for mail-order catalogs. In fact, the fall 1997 L. L. Bean catalog featured nattily clad models cavorting at Smith Rock State Park—a favorite location for television and photo shoots.

Insiders' Tip

When you are out exploring Central Oregon, make sure you pick up copies of local newspapers and other publications in the communities you visit. They are full of local news, events, and other happenings that you may want to check out during your visit.

Worship

Worship has always been an important part of the fabric of Central Oregon—from the nature-based religions of the region's Native Americans to the Christianity that dominates religion here today. Religion, in fact, played a significant and even pivotal role in the settling by whites of not only Central Oregon, but also the entire state.

Between 1824 and 1836, an evangelical movement led by "born-again" Christians was sweeping the eastern United States—a movement whose adherents believed strongly in missionary work. A rumor that a group of Nez Perce Indians had traveled to St. Louis in 1831 desiring to learn about Christianity sparked interest among members of this evangelical community who wanted to send missionaries to the Oregon country on a venture to save the souls of the "savage" races who lived there.

In 1834, Methodist Jason Lee was recruited for Oregon missionary work, setting up shop near Salem on the west side of the Cascade Mountains. In 1836, Henry and Eliza Spalding and Dr. Marcus and Narcissa Whitman, who were sponsored by the Presbyterian, Congregational, and Dutch Reformed churches, settled in the area of present-day Walla Walla, Washington, to live and teach among the Walla Walla and Cayuse Indians. But their efforts to convert the Indians to Christianity met with little success. The Indians were a hard sell and saw few benefits to themselves in converting to the white man's religion.

And the missionaries never really warmed up to the natives. Indeed, the writings of the Whitmans in their journals and letters reveal little sympathy or empathy for their spiritual charges. Relations between the missionaries and the natives deteriorated. A smallpox epidemic, almost certainly (although inadvertently) introduced by whites, swept the local Indian population. Convinced the Whitmans and Spaldings were responsible, and perhaps weary of their presence and suspicious of their motives, a band of Cayuse Indians killed them, along with a dozen of their missionary associates, on a bleak November day in 1847.

While the efforts of missionaries to the Northwest were not particularly successful in converting Native Americans to Christianity, they were wildly successful in fanning the flames of the great western migration beginning in the 1840s. The missionaries established outposts of civilization, breaking the trail for those who came later, and sent word to friends back home describing the opportunities that awaited anyone with the gumption to make the journey to Oregon and a new life.

Early pioneer groups headed to Oregon were made up mostly of families and were mainly Protestant. When they finally began to settle in Central Oregon in the late 1800s, pioneer families often commandeered schoolhouses or other community buildings for use as places of worship. Services were sometimes conducted in the private homes of congregation members. But as these settlements in the wilderness grew, the desire for churches dedicated to the pioneers' spiritual needs became a priority. By the early 1900s, churches reflecting the religious denominations of the first settlers to this region began to spring up across the High Desert.

Methodists, Episcopalians, and Presbyterians

The Methodist faith was probably the first Christian denomination introduced into Oregon with the arrival of missionary Jason Lee in western Oregon in the early 1830s. The first Methodist church in Central Oregon was most likely built in Prineville in 1889. The first Methodist sermons in Bend were organized by a Rev. McDonald, who preached to his flock beginning in 1900. The schoolhouse in which he preached was on what is now Drake Park in downtown Bend.

By 1906, the Bend Methodist Episcopal (the two denominations shared the worship facility) was formed. There was no regular minister. One of the church's 20 or so members would teach Sunday school, while sermons were preached by visiting ministers from Prineville or by traveling evangelists.

Methodists in Madras built their first church, the United Methodist Church, in 1907. Central Oregon now counts seven Methodist churches within its boundaries. The Trinity Episcopal Church in Bend sprung from the efforts of seven devout Episcopalian women, who opened their homes for worship beginning in 1904 with a pastor from The Dalles presiding. During this time period, there were not very many Episcopal priests in Oregon. The few who were available often had to make long, difficult journeys to see their far-flung parishioners.

In 1908, four years after these women began their efforts, they formed the Episcopal Ladies Guild with the goal of eventually establishing an Episcopal church in Bend. In 1909, a local resident donated land on which to build the Trinity Episcopal Church, although the church was not built until after the arrival of the parish's first full-time priest, the Reverend Mr. Tebeau, in 1923.

Episcopalians had been active in Madras and Jefferson Counties since the turn of the 20th century, with Episcopal priests holding services in ranch homes throughout the area. St. Mark's, in Madras, was built in 1950. Today, eight Episcopal churches can be found in Central Oregon.

Bend heard its first Presbyterian sermon in 1900, when Prineville's Rev. B. F. Harper began coming to town on a regular basis. In 1902 he organized a nondenominational Sunday school. A cooperative endeavor between local Presbyterians, Methodists, and Baptists, the Sunday school met in a log cabin in downtown Bend on land that would eventually become Drake Park. Although these three denominations went off to form their own congregations soon after, the Sunday school remained a joint effort into the early 1920s.

Bend's First Presbyterian Church was officially formed in 1903, when the Rev. W. H. Hall came down from Portland, organized the election of a board of trustees, and formed articles of incorporation. The cornerstone to the first church was laid in 1912. They used the building from 1914 to 1962, when they moved into a new building on Ninth Street, which is still in use today. The first Presbyterian church in Prineville was built in 1904. There are now four Presbyterian churches in Central Oregon.

Roman Catholicism: An Early Option in Oregon

Catholics came to Oregon with the first wave of missionaries when Frs. Blanchet and Demers arrived in western Oregon in 1839 to do ideological battle with the

Insiders' Tip

For the latest religious news and a calendar of upcoming happenings, check the religion section of the *Bulletin*. It appears in each Saturday edition.

already-ensconced Methodists. The first Catholic priest in Central Oregon was probably the Rev. Toussaint Mesplie, who arrived in the area in 1847. Based out of The Dalles on the Columbia River, he ministered to the residents of the Warm Springs Indian Reservation (although the federal government had decreed Presbyterianism as the reservation's "semi-official" religion).

Catholicism didn't come to Central Oregon in a big way until 1910, when two Capuchin priests were assigned to posts in Bend. For their church they utilized an old schoolhouse, which was purchased for $75 by a local parishioner and donated to the Catholic community. It became the St. Francis Parish. As Bend's population grew—particularly during the timber boom years from about 1916 to the mid-1920s, when new residents streamed into town to work at the bustling lumber mills—a larger church eventually became a necessity. A new brick church was built in 1920 with its dedication held on November 7 of that year. Today, the St. Francis of Assisi parish has a congregation of about 1,700 families.

The Capuchin fathers worked to establish missions in Prineville and Madras that would finally become parishes in their own right. In 1915, St. Joseph's Catholic Church was built in Prineville and became an official parish in 1943. Early masses in Madras were held at the Sixth Street home of Emily Morrow. In 1911 an unused schoolhouse was purchased to become that community's first Catholic church. In Redmond, the St. Thomas Parish was established in 1941. There are currently 10 Catholic churches in Central Oregon.

Arrival of the Baptists

The first church built in the city of Bend after its incorporation in May 1904 was a Baptist church, constructed on the corner of Irving and Oregon Streets in the downtown area. Built in the fall of 1904, the church served not only as a place of worship, but also as a sort of community facility where plays, concerts, and a variety of other social activities were held. It also had

a large bell inside its 55-foot-high tower, which beckoned the congregation to worship on Sundays and served as the new community's fire-alarm bell for a few years. The First Baptist Church burned in 1920 and was rebuilt to a serviceable condition in 1923. It was later torn down, and a new church building was constructed on the site in 1969.

The Baptists arrived in Prineville considerably earlier, with the first Baptist Church organized there in 1873. Between 1894 and 1898, Baptist records for Crook County show there were 250 conversions, 611 sermons preached, 15 marriages performed, and four churches founded in surrounding areas. Pastor Charles P. Bailey, who presided over these accomplishments, traveled 7,000 miles by horseback during that four-year period, earning a total salary of $2,500.

In Madras, the First Baptist Church started out as a Sunday school held in local homes beginning in 1905. Services were later relocated to a local schoolhouse, then moved into the congregation's first church-owned church building in 1944.

Today, there are 26 Baptist churches in Central Oregon, including Baptist, Conservative Baptist, Independent Baptist, Missionary Baptist, and Southern Baptist denominations.

A Host of Other Faiths

The Christian churches established early in Central Oregon's settlement period reflected the religious beliefs first brought to Oregon in the hearts and souls of the

The Lord's Carpenters

Everybody should have a decent place to live. And that simple statement defines the core purpose of Habitat for Humanity, a Christian housing ministry founded in 1976 by millionaire Arkansas businessman Millard Fuller and his wife, Linda. Today, Habitat for Humanity, based in Americus, Georgia, operates in 54 countries with more than 1,400 affiliates in the United States. To date, they have built 50,000 houses worldwide for people who otherwise might never have had a decent place to live.

There are five Habitat for Humanity affiliates in Central Oregon—in Bend, Sisters, Madras, Redmond, and the La Pine-Sunriver area. Their mission is simple: Help low-income folks build modest, decent homes for themselves and their families and help integrate them into the community at large.

And how do they do that? They raise money locally to buy land and building materials. A network of dedicated volunteers from all walks of life provide construction labor. The result is that Habitat for Humanity is able to build solid homes for a fraction of what it would normally cost. In fact, they can build a three-bedroom home in Bend for about $56,000 in a market where comparable homes may go for twice that amount. And, of course, they then find a family to live in it.

"Bend Area Habitat builds about five homes a year," says Chuck Tucker, executive director of Habitat for Humanity's largest Central Oregon affiliate. "Habitat is run by various volunteer committees. And one of those committees selects families for housing."

When a local Habitat for Humanity affiliate is ready to begin construction of a new home, they begin a search for an eligible family, and a call is put out through churches, social service agencies, and other avenues inviting families in search of a

Habitat for Humanity volunteers help build a house in Bend. PHOTO: BEND HABITAT FOR HUMANITY

home to apply. There are three primary criteria Habitat uses in selecting a family. First and foremost is the family's need for appropriate housing in comparison to their current situation (which has included whole families living in one small room or in a car under a railroad bridge).

Second, the family must have the ability to pay for the house. Habitat for Humanity isn't in the handout business; they help people help themselves. Families selected for a home pay for it through a 20-year, no-interest mortgage that Habitat for Humanity carries, although they are only paying for the cost of housing materials, since construction labor is all volunteer.

The third criteria to qualify for a home is the family's willingness to become partners with Habitat throughout the course of the project. Families waiting for a home are required to put in 500 hours of sweat equity, which might include anything from helping to build their home to working on fund-raising campaigns.

The willingness and ability of a family to become partners with Habitat is a crucial part of the process. "What's most important," says Tucker, "is getting the families to communicate with the volunteers, to form contacts and to become involved in the community." Because many of these families have "slipped through the cracks" and have sometimes become alienated and isolated from society at large, Habitat For Humanity feels that integrating families as active members of the community is vital to their long-term stability.

Since the Bend Area Habitat for Humanity was established in 1989, it has built 34 homes for a total of 172 people, including 120 children. Even though it is a Christian-based organization, it is nondenominational, and you do not need to be a member of a church to be eligible for housing. Each Habitat for Humanity affiliate is also required by the national headquarters to donate 10 percent of its fund-raising earnings to the organization's international program. To date, money donated by Bend Habitat has helped build 54 houses overseas.

"Habitat is really unique," says Tucker. "I'm not really sure who benefits from the program the most, the families who get housing or the volunteers. You see the results of what you do and the accomplishments of the organization. It's fulfilling in so many ways."

If you would like to find out more about Habitat for Humanity in the Central Oregon area, contact Bend Area Habitat for Humanity, 1860 Northeast Fourth Street, Bend, (541) 385–5387.

westering pioneers who crossed the American continent between 1840 and 1860 in search of a new and better life. But as more people came to Central Oregon in the first decades of the 20th century, a growing variety of religious beliefs and denominations found their way here as well.

Seventh-Day Adventists made their first inroads into Central Oregon at the turn of the 20th century, when horseback-riding Adventist Bible salesmen came through on their regular Prineville-to-The Dalles circuit. In the 1920s, tent meetings were held in the area, and in 1941 a Seventh-Day Adventist pastor and his wife came to Prineville to begin work on establishing a church, which was built in the fall of that year. Today, there are five Seventh-Day Adventist churches in Central Oregon.

On May 3, 1917, 25 Christians meeting in the Evangelical Lutheran Church in Bend voted unanimously to start a church to be called the First Church of Christ. They had their first baptism 27 days later. Lots for a church site were purchased in the downtown Bend area later that year

There are about 40 different faiths in Central Oregon and more than 130 individual churches or ministries. PHOTO: JIM YUSKAVITCH

Christ, Church of God, Church of God of Prophecy, Echos of Calvary, First Church of God, and Foursquare Church were added to the list.

Today there are nearly 40 different religions or denominations represented in Central Oregon, with a total of about 150 individual churches or ministries including, in addition to those already mentioned, Anglican, Apostolic, Baha'i, Eckankar, Evangelical, Friends, Jewish, Open Bible Standard, Pentecostal, Religious Science, Unitarian, and nondenominational.

for $400. They built the church in 1918.

The seeds of Prineville's Lutheran church were planted in 1940 when a group of local ladies expressed a desire to begin having Lutheran services in their town. With the help of the president of the Pacific District of the Norwegian Lutheran Church of America, a pastor (who would also conduct services in Prineville) was brought to Bend. Services were held in local homes and businesses until the mid-1940s, when church members were able to raise enough money to finance the construction of a church in Prineville.

And just a year before the Lutheran ladies began their quest, one E. E. Taylor showed up in Prineville, hosted a tent revival meeting, and stayed around for five weeks—just long enough to help start the Prineville Church of the Nazarene. Some additional assistance from three local residents came in the form of $900 for the purchase of a small downtown building to be used as the church. Within four years attendance grew to 60 people.

The Prineville ward of the Church of Jesus Christ of Latter-day Saints was formed in 1940. The Bend stake was established in 1968. Christian Scientists were meeting in Prineville by the 1930s.

By the late 1940s, when Oregon experienced another wave of immigrants as GIs returned home from World War II and set out to make new lives for themselves, Central Oregon could count a growing roster of churches, including Assembly of God, Full Gospel, Christian Science, Latter-day Saints, Nazarene, and Jehovah's Witness. By the mid-1970s, the Church of

The Religious Community Keeps Growing

Current religious activity in Central Oregon ranges from traditional services to a wide range of activities sponsored by various churches. On any given week you may find opportunities to attend religious education and discussion groups, attend a concert by a Christian music group, receive instruction in meditation, or listen to the sermons of local pastors on a variety of spiritual matters.

Along with spiritual growth, Bend-area churches are experiencing physical growth as well. Due to the yearly 6 percent growth rate of its congregation during the past 10 years, the First Presbyterian Church in Bend has broken ground on a 19,000-acre, $2 million expansion that will include a new sanctuary, administrative wing, music center, and increased parking. St. Francis of Assisi Catholic Church has broken ground on a major expansion as well, encompassing a 3-phase, 10-year construction project that includes a 57,000-square-foot school and parish center, a new church, and a wing containing a cafeteria, gymnasium, and facilities for the church's various programs. Also on the drawing board is a 400-space parking lot, all on a 17-acre lot. The price tag is expected to run about $6 million.

Two Jehovah's Witness kingdom halls have been built in Bend during the past couple of years. Grace Community Presbyterian Church and Southside Assembly of God Church have also recently constructed new churches to facilitate increasing attendance. And the Church of Jesus Christ of Latter-day Saints hopes to build a major new church and stake center in Bend as well.

From a few families meeting quietly in pioneer ranch homes to express their faith in God to multimillion-dollar church centers bursting at the seams with worshippers, religion, like everything else in Central Oregon, has grown and prospered. If the next 100 years are anything like the last century, that trend is only likely to continue.

> **Insiders' Tip**
> The Habitat for Humanity thrift shop in Sisters has a reputation for having among the best used goods for sale of all the shops in Central Oregon because of the high-quality items donated by local upper-income residents.

Other Communities

Drive just five minutes north or east of Bend and you leave behind the bustling cosmopolitan world of big retail stores, four-lane thoroughfares, high-tech business parks, and bookstores that sell the *New York Times*.

You are now entering the quiet world of our roots—our ranch lands, farmlands, and rangelands. Green pastures stretch out before you, tiny white plumes of water arc from a distant wheel line, and beyond that, expanses of brown, sagebrush-dotted hills roll on as far as the eye can see. In one pasture cattle graze, in the next a half-dozen horses trot and kick their heels. In a field lined with fancy white fencing, llamas perk their inquisitive ears at you, their frolicking babies oblivious to your passing.

In other chapters of this book we have focused on the six area towns that contain most of our restaurants and museums, motels, and movie houses. We have talked about places to play in the snow, in the lakes or in our streams. We have jumped back millions of years to the time when Central Oregon would have been a tropical, beachside resort had we all been around then—the era before the formation of the Cascades.

Let's now look to the evidence of our recent past that lives on today—the stuff dreams and movies are made of . . . cowboys and Indians, tepees and farmhouses, ranch dogs and big pickup trucks. This chapter covers in alphabetical order some of the small ranching communities that you drive through when traveling between our cities. You may see these town names in the real estate section of the classifieds and wonder where they are. Here, the ranching communities are described from a ranching and real estate perspective, and we include information on agriculture, irrigation, and growing seasons, along with some interesting historical tidbits.

This chapter also covers the Warm Springs Indian Reservation, a 1,000-square-mile chunk of Central Oregon. Warm Springs is populated by fewer than 4,000 Native Americans, who are slowly but surely becoming an economic force in Central Oregon—even as they continue to provide cultural enrichment.

Alfalfa

This small ranching community of roughly 400 families lies 12 miles due east of Bend. Two-lane country roads that are popular with cyclists wind through green pastures large and small. The land is rolling, occasionally rimmed with low, eroded bluffs. Alfalfa is considered to be part of Bend, and it has a Bend telephone prefix. But when you are here, you are a world away from any city.

From Bend, drive east on Neff Road. (An alternate route is to go east on U.S. Highway 20, in which case you'd turn north on the Powell Butte Highway where the signs say TO BEND AIRPORT, and then turn east on Neff Road.) Neff turns into Walker Road, and then you'll turn left onto Alfalfa Market Road. When you get to the Alfalfa Store, (541) 382–0761, you'll know you've arrived at the heart of the community.

Open seven days a week, this wonderful little country store sells a little of everything, from milk to fishing tackle, ice to video rentals and gas. Pre-made sandwiches and cans of soda can be purchased and enjoyed at a small picnic table outside. It's a nice spot to watch the world slowly pass by. The store opens at 7:00 in the morning. From Sunday through Thursday, it closes at 7:00 P.M.; on Friday and Saturday, they stay open late—8:00 P.M.!

Alfalfa has an 80-day growing season similar to Bend, so ranchers are limited to growing grass and alfalfa. Two cuttings of alfalfa are typical, though warmer weather may allow three cuttings. Since the yields on hay are usually low, Alfalfa's grass is generally considered to be somewhat more suitable for grazing livestock than for haying. Cattle are the most common livestock here, and there are some purebred bull-producing operations. You will also see small flocks of sheep and horse ranches. The land has fairly good soil and is relatively free of rocks.

Some of the ranch houses date from the early 1900s, which is when the irrigation system was formed. The Central Oregon Canal goes right through Alfalfa and is currently managed by the Central Oregon Irrigation District, (541) 548-6047, which is headquartered in Redmond. Water rights are valued at about $1,500 per acre. Well depths run in the area of 600 feet.

Parcels in Alfalfa are typically in the 40- to 200-acre range. A recent listing for 10 irrigated acres in Alfalfa was for $145,000. A 40-acre parcel with a nice house, shop, and barn and 36 acres of irrigation will sell for $400,000 and above. A 40-acre piece of bare land with no irrigation goes for around $125,000. Alfalfa is in the Redmond School District. Coldwell Banker Mayfield Realty in Redmond, (541) 548-1250, is one company that does a lot of business in the Alfalfa area.

Crooked River Ranch and Terrebonne

We'll just touch on Crooked River Ranch and Terrebonne in this chapter because they already have some coverage in the Neighborhoods and Real Estate, Hotels and Motels, Camping, and Golf chapters as part of the Redmond area.

Terrebonne is a small ranching community that serves as the gateway to Crooked River Ranch, and it offers the ranch's residents a convenient place to get groceries, hardware, and farm tractor supplies. The ranch, a residential subdivision formed in the early 1980s, is more of a bedroom/retirement community. Terrebonne and Crooked River Ranch share a zip code and tend to complement each other.

Terrebonne is almost a suburb of Redmond, which is just five minutes to the south. U.S. Highway 97 forms the main street through town. Here you will find La Siesta Cafe, (541) 548-4848, a longtime fixture in this small community. It serves some of the best Mexican food around in simple style. About 4 miles to the east is Smith Rock State Park, preserving a spectacular canyon along the Crooked River.

The two small grocery stores right on the main highway are the Terrebonne Thriftway, (541) 548-2603, and the Terrebonne Mini Market & BP/Ferguson's, (541) 923-0729. The Terrebonne True Value Hardware Store, (541) 548-8707, sits back from the highway near the Thriftway.

In the center of Terrebonne is its oldest neighborhood, with small houses and very small, 25-by-100-foot lots or groups of lots. These small properties have outdated sewage systems that need to be replaced, but current zoning restrictions have strict requirements regarding the size of the property needed (the ratio of house

Insiders' Tip

Pull the map out of your glove box and plan a day of exploring Central Oregon's back roads and byways for a close-up look at genuine rural America.

You'll see as many llamas as cows on Central Oregon ranches—or at least it seems that way.

PHOTO: BEND CHAMBER OF COMMERCE

square-footage to acreage) to put in a new septic system. A small place in town may cost less than $100,000, but adding on or upgrading the property may be prohibited by the septic feasibility question. There is talk about putting in a public sewer system, but nothing definite is planned. If buying one of these starter homes is of interest to you, you should definitely check into this issue.

Due to the septic problems in town, much of the new growth is occurring in the outlying areas, where you'll find a preponderance of mini-ranches in the two- to five-acre size range. Views are lovely, with green pastures and an occasional mature, broadleaf shade tree. A Cascade peak or two can be seen from some spots. A home dating from the 1960s or 1970s on five acres will sell in the $150,000 to $200,000 range. Some places have Central Oregon Irrigation District water rights (the COID headquarters is in Redmond at 541–548–6047). A 22.5-acre farm in Terrebonne with 22 irrigated acres, house, two barns, and an apartment recently listed for $335,000.

With close to 4,000 residents, Crooked River Ranch is a town unto itself. The *Bulletin* newspaper, based in Bend, even has a special category for Crooked River in its Neighbors section on Saturday. The ranch can be reached from the north end of Terrebonne by turning west on Northwest Lower Bridge Way. Follow the big signs 7 miles to the center of the subdivision. The eastern boundary of the ranch is defined by the Crooked River. Although it is only about 15 minutes from Redmond, the ranch actually straddles two counties, Deschutes and Jefferson, and is served by the Redmond and Culver school districts.

Crooked River Ranch is a 10-mile-long piece of property comprised of 12,000 acres, 11,000 of which have been divided into one- to five-acre parcels. The remaining 1,000 acres consists of common property housing an 18-hole golf course (see our Golf chapter), swimming pool, motel (see our Hotels and Motels chapter), a mini-market/gas station called The Trading Post, (541) 923–5451, three restaurants, a chapel, a realty office, RV parks (see our Camping chapter), and other public and recreational areas. A semiwild flock of an unusual breed of hair sheep (they look like goats) wanders through the common areas, nibbling on weeds and grass.

Residents enjoy hiking and bird- and wildlife watching in the adjacent 8,000 acres of public lands. These public lands are an important feature to residents who own pleasure horses. There is no irrigation water available at Crooked River Ranch. Domestic water is supplied by a private water company, the Crooked River Ranch Water Company, and some of the larger, outlying parcels have wells that range from 150 feet deep in the southern portion of the ranch to 800 feet in the northern areas.

These small acreages and the communal amenities appeal to retirees (which make up about 50 percent of the residents), as well as to families who commute to area cities. Much of this arid land is in the Crooked River Canyon, so many properties have views of sagebrush and juniper trees but no mountains. Tidy yards feature lawn figures (elves, Bambi, etc.), and small lawns or xeriscape landscaping are fairly common. Some of the small acreages have grandiose or tongue-in-cheek names posted on signs at the end of driveways—D & D Snake Ranch, Reschke's Roost, Wally's Folly.

Lots here sell for $29,000 to $70,000, while homes range from $60,000 for a mobile home on a smaller lot to $400,000 for a large house on a five-acre lot. The area is serviced by Canyon Real Estate, (541) 548-4514, and Crooked River Realty in Crooked River Ranch, (541) 923-2000. Crooked River Realty also has a branch office in Terrebonne, (541) 504-8000.

Culver and Metolius

The sign at the edge of town says CULVER IS OREGON! This is a high-spirited agricultural town, where reverence for family, patriotism, and honest work is especially evident during the annual Great America Day Celebration, which takes place the weekend following the Fourth of July weekend. They consider this to be a big Culver family reunion, with barbecues, a parade, a volleyball tournament, and many other fun activities. Residents of the smaller, neighboring town of Metolius are included in the festivities.

Culver and Metolius are 8 miles and 4 miles, respectively, southwest of Madras near the Lake Billy Chinook Reservoir. Culver, which is incorporated, has an in-town population of 802, but it claims a total of more than 1,500 souls including outlying regions. Metolius modestly sticks to 635 townies.

Many of this valley's settlers came from Idaho in 1946 when the North Unit Irrigation system opened, and large pieces of irrigated land were offered for sale for the first time. Up until that time a few ranchers ran large herds of cattle and flocks of sheep across the dry rangelands (see our History chapter). Much of the land is fairly flat, and many places have an unobstructed view of the Cascades.

A noticeable and important difference between this area and the rest of Central Oregon is that early water rights in Deschutes County were given out at the rate of 80 acres per person. Later in the century, when Culver and Metolius were being developed, water rights were given out at the rate of 160 acres per person, or 320 acres per couple. Hence, parcel sizes in the Madras area are larger and more commercially viable than in Bend. In this region, "farms" are considered irrigated acreage with crops; whereas "ranches" are those 1,000-plus-acre expanses of dry rangeland to the east and north of Madras. If you

> **Insiders' Tip**
> If you are looking for a dream mini-ranch where you can raise a few head of something, check on local zoning ordinances for rules on having livestock on the property. Different counties and zones have different rules.

In spite of the region's growth, rural scenes are still common in Central Oregon. PHOTO: JIM YUSKAVITCH

were to walk into a real estate office in Madras and tell them you were interested in a 20-acre ranch, the agents would do their best to refrain from laughing.

Agriculture in the Culver/Metolius area is also quite different from the rest of Central Oregon. Here there is a 110-day growing season, compared with Bend's 80-day season, or the 90-day season in Redmond and Prineville. Bend, Redmond, and Prineville have ranching; Culver and Metolius have mostly farming with a little ranching. An extra month makes a very big difference in determining what will successfully grow in a region. Eighty days produces grass to feed livestock or to produce two or three cuttings of hay; 110 days produces row crops to feed people, or three or four cuttings of hay.

Winter temperatures in Culver are usually in the mid-40s during the day and in the 30s, or sometimes 20s, at night. Spring comes earlier in this valley of the Deschutes and Crooked Rivers than anywhere in Central Oregon. Tulips will be in full bloom at the low, 2,633-foot elevation, while the tips of the leaves are just starting

to peek out of the soil in Bend at 4,000 feet. Summer days are hot—90 to 100 degrees—and the nights are cool.

Culver and Metolius have found a niche market in seed crops—carrots, garlic, onions, bluegrass, and flowers raised for their seeds. Cool nights produce hardy seeds that earn more per acre than raising the actual vegetables or harvesting hay would earn. A lot of acreage is still committed to such conventional crops as alfalfa, wheat, and sugar beets. Peppermint was a big cash crop here until soil fungus diseases forced most farmers to switch to seed crops.

Soils are relatively deep and of a better quality than the southern areas of Central Oregon. This region's lava formations are much older than Bend's, and the soil has had more time to mature and develop from pumice sand (like you'll find in Bend) to a more diversified and arable material.

Still, due to our arid climate, even Central Oregon's best soils lack organic matter and do not retain moisture, so constant irrigation is necessary. The first water rights were claimed in 1913, but these were rights to water that could not be delivered until the construction of Wickiup Reservoir in the mid-1940s and completion of the North Unit Main Canal. Madras' North Unit Irrigation District, (541) 475-3625, now manages about 60,000 acres of irrigated lands.

This region depends on Mexican workers, who regularly work for the same farmers every spring, summer, and fall, then return home to Mexico for the winter. This Hispanic community is very tightly knit. Family and friends provide new sources of labor. If you drive around Culver and Metolius during summer, you will see workers in almost every field maintaining irrigation ditches, moving wheel lines, repairing pivots, and helping with the harvesting. The Great America Day Celebration now includes Hispanic food booths in an effort to embrace this important sector of the community.

Domestic water is provided by a huge municipal water system, the Deschutes Valley Water District, made necessary by the depth of the wells (800 feet and deeper) and the fact that some ground water has been lightly contaminated with nitrates. The municipal water originates from springs at Opal Springs, south and west of Culver. This excellent water is then pumped through hundreds of miles of pipes throughout the Culver/Metolius area. Some of it is bottled and sold by Earth H2O and Opal Springs Water Company, both located in Culver.

Irrigated farmland costs between $1,500 and $2,000 per acre, plus the value of the buildings. A 360-acre piece with an older house and a couple of barns will sell for close to $600,000. Lots in Culver's newest subdivision, East Valley Estates, are going for $25,500 to $28,500. Midland Realty GMAC Real Estate in Madras, (541) 475-6161, does a fair amount of farm sales. A rancher and Culver resident since 1983, Everett Decker handles many Culver and Metolius farm sales as an agent at John L. Scott Realty in Redmond, (541) 548-1712.

The city of Culver has a rather interesting history of relocating. It first started up as a stage stop near Haystack Reservoir and was named after its first postmaster, O. G. Collver. True to Oregon tradition, the name was misspelled when the town moved to its current location around 1910, where its buildings lined up facing the new railroad tracks. When the Old Culver Highway was put in east of the buildings, the structures had to be turned around to face the road. By the time U.S. Highway 97 came through in 1946, bypassing the town by 2 miles, Culver had had enough of moving and stayed put.

In downtown Culver the biggest store is called The Store, a bright blue building on the corner of First Avenue (the Old Culver Highway) and E Street. The Store, (541) 546-8641, is a good-size market with a broad selection of fresh and preserved foods, a deli, espresso, basic necessities, and general-store-type items like fishing tackle. The Store is open daily from 7:30 A.M. to 9:00 P.M. The Culver Market, (541) 546-6032, is 1 block north on First Avenue. This convenience store is open daily, 6:30 A.M. to 10:00 P.M., and it has the usual items (including video rentals). It also serves as a tourist information center with a rack of brochures.

Pug's Mug is a cute espresso and sandwich shop on First Avenue (see our Restaurants chapter). Just a bit north of Pug's is Beetle Bailey Burgers, a nonsmoking fast-food joint with good burgers that's open for lunch and dinner daily. (On summer weekends, burger-starved folks can pick up a juicy one starting at 8:00 A.M.) The smoking-allowed Round Butte Inn Restaurant & Lounge, (541) 546-8551, in the center of town, daily serves American food for lunch plus pizza for dinner. The lounge is open late. The Gateway Inn Restaurant/Lounge, on First Avenue at C Street, (541) 546-2405, also offers daily family dining for breakfast, lunch, and dinner. The Gateway Inn has one nonsmoking table in a smoking-allowed dining room.

There is a small amount of industry in Culver, including Round Butte Seed Growers, Earth H2O, and the Opal Springs Water Company, plus Seaswirl Boats. Culver has three schools covering kindergarten through 12th grade. Finally, there's a free RV dump behind the fire station at First Avenue and A Street.

Metolius has much in common agriculturally with Culver, though its location closer to Lake Billy Chinook attracts some residents solely for the recreational opportunities. In town you'll find a couple of small convenience stores and a tortilleria (taco place). Many of Metolius' in-town residents are agricultural workers. The Desert Inn, on Jefferson Avenue (Old Culver Highway), (541) 546-2872, is a smoking-allowed restaurant and bar that's open daily from lunch through late night. It serves American food. Metolius children take buses to schools in Madras.

prominent livestock, with a few high-performance, purebred ranches that breed Angus and exotic bulls. Driving around you will also see some flocks of sheep and horse ranches.

In town, a horse grazes across the road from The Country Store, (541) 548-4328, a convenience store that's open daily from 7:00 A.M. to 9:00 P.M. in the summer on weekdays and Saturday (8:00 P.M. the rest of the year), and 8:00 A.M. to 8:00 P.M. on Sunday. Open since the 1920s, the store sells a small selection of groceries and gas and rents videos.

Along the store's front porch wall a wide range of properties for sale are posted by two real estate companies: Coldwell Banker Mayfield Realty in Redmond, (541) 548-1250, and The Associates Real Estate, (541) 447-3940, in Prineville. Generally speaking, ranch properties fall in the 80-acre size range. Some recent acreage listed in the Powell Butte area included a 78-acre septic approved parcel for $237,500 and a 38-acre property for $145,000.

Homes with acreage are also sought-after in this area. Some typical offerings include a three-bedroom, two-bath home on two acres for $124,000, a three-bedroom,

Powell Butte

White-topped Cascade peaks, distant blue hills, green pastures with grazing cattle, and quiet roads lined with mature poplars describe the Powell Butte landscape. This community is in Crook County on Oregon Highway 126, about halfway between Redmond and Prineville. As you enter the community, the road sign reads POWELL BUTTE—HOME OF GOOD STOCK, GOOD CROPS AND GOOD NEIGHBORS. Just west of the town is the intersection of the Powell Butte Highway, which cuts diagonally southwest toward the Bend Airport. This makes Powell Butte almost as convenient for commuting to Bend as it is to Redmond and Prineville.

The short, 90-day growing season and shallow, rocky soil limits the crops to grass for pasture, perhaps three cuttings of hay, and some seed potatoes. There are also a few dairies in Powell Butte. Cattle are the

Insiders' Tip

The political climate in Oregon is currently opposed to turning rural farmlands into residential properties. When you purchase bare farm or ranch property zoned Exclusive Farm Use (EFU), you will need to get a Conditional Use Permit (CUP) in order to build a new home, and these can be difficult to get.

two-bath home and barn on five acres for $178,000, and a three-bedroom, 2.5-bath house on 40 acres for $285,000. Powell Butte area subdivisions are increasingly serving as bedroom communities for Prineville, Redmond, and Bend. Powell Butte also has a grade school that serves grades kindergarten through 6. Upper grades are bused to Prineville.

Tumalo

Tumalo is a small community immediately north of Bend that extends northeast and southwest of U.S. 20. It was a small town around the turn of the 20th century, but in the 1980s the post office closed, and Tumalo was absorbed into Bend. It now has a Bend mailing address, shares the main Bend zip code, and has Bend telephone prefixes. It still, however, retains a separate identity.

What were once 80- to 200-acre cattle ranches have been broken down and gentrified into small, high-end hobby farms of 5 to 80 acres along with some entrepreneurial enterprises. Horses and llamas are prevalent. Smaller herds of beef cattle, fine Angus bull operations, dairy cows, sheep, goats, small pens of pigs, ostrich, fowl, and victory gardens are also common. A small commercial greenhouse operation on Cline Falls Road raises natural herbs for Northwest markets and restaurants, as well as medicinal sprouts.

Breeders of fancy horses, including endurance racers, are increasing in number, especially since the June 1998 opening of the Bend Equine Medical Center, (541) 388-4006, at Couch Market Road and U.S. Highway 20; it's the only surgical center for horses between Corvallis, Oregon, and California. At his shop on Cline Falls Road, nationally recognized saddler Steve Ray makes custom endurance saddles that sell for $2,000 and up.

Tumalo has a short, 80-day growing season. Northeast of U.S. 20 is open range country with 360-degree views. Winters are cold, windy, and dry, and summers have warm days and cool nights. Eastern Tumalo is more suited to larger grazing operations and some grass and alfalfa hay production.

Southwest of U.S. 20, Tumalo gets closer to the skirts of the Cascades, where there are more conifers, more snow in the winter, and rockier soils. This part of Tumalo is slightly more expensive and upscale, perhaps due to the picturesque pine forests framing the white peaks of the Three Sisters mountains. The Deschutes River cuts through a canyon on the southern and eastern boundary of Tumalo. Surrounding this region to the north, east, and west are BLM public lands—a big attraction for horse owners. The Tumalo Irrigation District in downtown Tumalo, (541) 382-3053, gets its water from the Deschutes River and Crescent Lake and has served this area since the turn of the 20th century.

Property values are generally high in Tumalo, due to this area's proximity to Bend, great views, and attractive pastoral landscape. Wells are expensive because they are deep—anywhere from 500 to 700 feet. Irrigation water rights are also very expensive at $3,500 per acre. Ten acres with irrigation and a barn but no house can fetch as much as $175,000. With a new, 2,200-square-foot home and a well, the same property would be $500,000. Twenty dry, undeveloped acres with great views typically list for $125,000 to $200,000. A 100-acre irrigated property with a 4,000-square-foot house would cost close to $1 million. Tumalo Real Estate, in the yellow farmhouse on U.S. 20 at Bailey Road, (541) 382-0288, is owned by Tumalo resident Barbara Nicholson and specializes in rural Tumalo properties (see our Neighborhoods and Real Estate chapter).

In the center of town, northeast of the intersection of Cook Avenue (which turns into Cline Falls Road) and U.S. 20, is the Tumalo Store, (541) 389-1021, a convenience store that is open daily until 10:00 P.M. It sells the usual convenience store stuff such as groceries, hot dogs, and sodas, and they rent videos and pump gas. Behind the store is a recycling center. If you want to meet someone in Tumalo, the Tumalo Store is the key landmark. Next to it is the Tumbleweed Cafe, (541) 385-8413, a very tidy fast-food restaurant that does burgers for lunch and dinner. They are open from 11:00 A.M. to 5:00 P.M.

Across the street is a wonderful little fresh-produce store called Farmer John's. It specializes in local produce when possible (California produce the rest of the year), plus breads and pastries, good coffee, garden plants, and holiday goods. Next to the highway is the Tumalo branch office of Windermere/Central Oregon Real Estate, (541) 383-3525 (see our Neighborhoods and Real Estate chapter).

Across the highway is the Tumalo Feed Company, a superb steak dinner house (see our Restaurants chapter). Tumalo has an excellent elementary school; students in higher grades take the bus into Redmond.

Warm Springs Indian Reservation

Sprawling over more than 1,000 square miles of Central Oregon real estate in Jefferson and Wasco Counties, the Warm Springs Indian Reservation is populated by members of The Confederated Tribes of Warm Springs. It is one of Central Oregon's most interesting, and in many ways, least known, communities. Most Central Oregonians are well aware of the reservation, but few have spent much time there

or know any of its residents. In fact, most of the reservation is off-limits to nontribal members. But in spite of the fact that the tribes generally keep a low profile, their contribution to the cultural and economic diversity of Central Oregon is undeniable.

About 3,500 people, mostly of Wasco, Warm Springs, and Paiute background, live on the reservation. Its story starts in 1855, when Native Americans of the Wasco and Warm Springs tribes negotiated a treaty with the federal government that created the Warm Springs Indian Reservation. Under the deal, these tribes gave up about 10 million acres of their traditional territory. In return, the reservation was established for their exclusive use. The tribes also retained their traditional rights to hunt, fish, and gather other foods on lands off the reservation.

Although this arrangement resulted in a significant loss of the tribes' historic territories, it was in fact a victory of sorts, since the treaty gave them a guaranteed homeland at a period in history when large numbers of white settlers were beginning to move into Central and Eastern Oregon. Without a treaty, the Native Americans may have eventually lost it all. In 1879, Paiutes began moving onto the reservation, forced there by the federal government in the aftermath of local Indian wars in which they had been participants (see our History chapter).

Every June, the tribes hold a powwow, open to the public, to celebrate the signing of this treaty. It's attended by Native Americans from all over the West as well as local Warm Springs Reservation residents, who dress in their finest regalia of buckskin and beadwork and perform traditional dances and ceremonies (see our Annual Events chapter).

Although the people of the reservation strive to maintain their traditions and cultural identity, they're by no means living in the past. They have governed themselves since 1938 through an 11-member Tribal Council, which includes three traditional chiefs who serve for life along with eight elected members who serve three-year terms. A chief executive officer handles the tribes' administrative operations. As part and parcel of this self-governing system,

Every June The Confederated Tribes of Warm Springs hold a powwow that is open to the public.

they have their own professional staff of foresters, planners, biologists, soil scientists, and other specialists to help manage the tribes' vast natural resource base.

They are also engaged in a number of successful enterprises. These provide jobs for tribal and nontribal members as well as investment income for reservation infrastructure development and community programs and services such as healthcare, fire protection, education, and utilities. In fact, The Confederated Tribes of Warm Springs is one of Central Oregon's top-10 employers, providing about 1,300 jobs.

Since more than half the reservation is forest, it was only natural that the tribes began their sojourn into economic enterprise in the forest-products arena. The first major logging operation on reservation lands was begun in 1942, resulting in the removal of 500 million board feet of timber during a 20-year period, with the income providing dividends to tribal members. Between 1967 and 1968, the tribes purchased a lumber mill in Madras and another, non-Indian-owned mill on the reservation, and Warm Springs Forest

Products was born. This tribally owned company mills timber cut on reservation lands into commercial lumber products.

Probably the best-known tribal enterprise is Kah-Nee-Ta Resort, located in the heart of the reservation, surrounded by canyons and rangeland. Since opening its doors in 1964, it has offered luxury accommodations and recreational activities including swimming, fishing, horseback riding, mountain biking, and golf (see our Resorts, Ranches, and Vacation Rentals chapter). In 1996 the tribes added the Indian Head Gaming Center to the resort with slot machines, keno, blackjack, and poker, posting their first profits—$2.2 million—in 1998.

Another impressive tribal enterprise is The Museum at Warm Springs, a $7.6 million, 25,000-square-foot museum dedicated to educating visitors about tribal culture and history. Opened in 1993, it houses one of the nation's largest collections of Native American artifacts (see our Attractions chapter).

Other businesses that are helping the tribes reach self-sufficiency include The

Plaza at Warm Springs, located on U.S. Highway 26 across from The Museum at Warm Springs. This center includes a hair salon, restaurant, and several stores featuring Native American crafts. You'll also find Warm Springs Composite Products, part of a joint venture with an outside corporation to develop fireproof products from diatomaceous earth for manufacturing fireproof doors and insulated furnace parts used by heavy industries. Yet another source of income for the tribes is the revenue derived from electricity produced by three hydroelectric dams on the Deschutes River, which runs along the reservation's eastern border.

Holding onto ancient traditions while making their way in the modern world.... It's a delicate balancing act for members of The Confederated Tribes of Warm Springs. But as they strive to build their financial base and seek an expanding role in shaping Central Oregon, the people of Warm Springs will finally control their destinies across the economic landscape as surely as their ancestors once ruled the forests and plains.

Index